THE ILLUSTRATED ENCY(

BATTLESHIPS
& CRUISERS

THE ILLUSTRATED ENCYCLOPEDIA OF
BATTLESHIPS & CRUISERS

A COMPLETE VISUAL HISTORY OF INTERNATIONAL NAVAL WARSHIPS FROM
1860 TO THE PRESENT DAY, SHOWN IN OVER 1200 ARCHIVE PHOTOGRAPHS

INCLUDES COMPREHENSIVE CHRONOLOGICAL DIRECTORIES OF BATTLESHIPS
AND CRUISERS, FEATURING OVER 400 WARSHIPS AND THEIR SPECIFICATIONS

PETER HORE AND BERNARD IRELAND

southwater

This edition is published by Southwater, an imprint of Anness Publishing Ltd, Blaby Road, Wigston, Leicestershire LE18 4SE; info@anness.com

www.southwaterbooks.com; www.annesspublishing.com

Anness Publishing has a new picture agency outlet for images for publishing, promotions or advertising. Please visit our website www.practicalpictures.com for more information.

Publisher: Joanna Lorenz
Senior Editor: Felicity Forster
Project Editor: Daniel Hurst
Copy Editor: Tim Ellerby
Cover Designer: Nigel Partridge
Production Controller: Mai-Ling Collyer

Previously published in two separate volumes, *The World Encyclopedia of Battleships* and *The Illustrated Guide to Cruisers*.

PUBLISHER'S NOTE
Although the information in this book is believed to be accurate and true at the time of going to press, neither the authors nor the publisher can accept any legal responsibility or liability for any errors or omissions that may have been made.

PAGE 1: **USS** *Long Beach.*
PAGE 2: *Nelson.*
PAGE 3: *Mikuma.*

Contents

Introduction

This comprehensive volume looks closely at the scientific and mechanical progress of battleship and cruiser design through the centuries and offers readers a fascinating historical and global insight into the intriguing world of naval warships. It is split into two clearly defined parts: the first looking at the history and development of battleships, and the second exploring the fascinating lineage of cruisers. Each part includes a detailed history of the most important developments in warship design and manufacture, and a comprehensive directory, giving an extensive global and chronological view of individual warships. Finally, there is a thorough glossary detailing the correct meanings of commonly used technical terms.

Battleships

The first half of this book charts the fascinating history of the battleship, from the first broadside ironclads of the mid-19th century through the development of the Dreadnoughts and on to the last battleships built during World War II. It also chronicles the main battles and naval operations mounted by the world's foremost naval powers, notably Britain, the United States, Germany, France, Italy and Japan.

This style of sailing ship, capable of taking its place in the line of battle, or a "line-of-battle ship", dominated warfare at sea from the 16th to the 19th century. Then, just as the British navy delivered the victory in 1805 at the Battle of Trafalgar, new technology became available, revolutionizing battleship design.

TOP: USS *Merrimac* engages USS *Monitor*. ABOVE: HMS *Warrior* was so strongly built that she has survived until today. She has been beautifully restored and can be seen in Portsmouth, England.

This revolution encompassed the use of steam engines at sea, breech-loading guns, the rotating turret, armour and above all the increase in size of ships. There were developmental dead ends as well. The paddle ship with its exposed wheels was useless as a vehicle of war; the paddlewheels and boxes were too vulnerable to damage and restricted the size of broadside armament that could be mounted.

Other lines of development took unexpected turns. The monitor was designed for coastal defence and for war in the estuaries and rivers, and was highly successful in the American Civil War. However when given a little more sea-keeping capability, the monitors became a powerful weapon of offence, mounting some of the largest guns, which were taken from their "big sister" battleships. In two world wars monitors

were used in operations from the Arctic to Africa, and indeed at the end of their lives the shore-bombardment role of some battleships could be compared to that of an over-large monitor. In this sense the monitor stands in line with the development of the cruise and ballistic missiles launched from submarines.

The battleship itself, broadly defined here as a capital ship mounting guns of 255mm/10in calibre or more, took on many different shapes for the first 20 years of its life as a distinct species. Many early designs had large, heavy barbettes which meant a low freeboard and loss of sea-keeping – the alternative was a high-sided ship with a consequent loss of stability. This period was marked by some exceedingly odd and ugly ships.

By the end of the 19th century the design of the battleship had more or less settled on a ship of about 10,160 tonnes/10,000 tons carrying two twin barbettes or turrets, one forward and one aft, sometimes with side-by-side funnels, and a speed of 18 knots was considered fast. Then, a British admiral, Jacky Fisher, changed everything with his concept of a battleship which would "dread nought". It was not his idea alone. The Italian naval engineer Vittorio Cuniberti's proposals for an all-big-gun ship were widely published and there were simultaneous developments in the same direction in several other countries. However, it was Fisher's energy, enthusiasm and drive which brought the first ship, HMS *Dreadnought* into being, and halted warship-building

TOP: **Battleships were still fought in the line of battle which maximized the number of guns that could be brought to bear on a target. The smoke from burning coal advertised their position.** ABOVE: **Big-gun ships still needed to be protected against smaller craft.** ABOVE LEFT: **Each shell was the size of a man.**

worldwide while friends and rivals considered what had been achieved. Although the design was not perfect, the ship was revolutionary in nearly every respect and thereafter battleships had to be classified by reference to this one ship: battleships had become pre-Dreadnoughts, Dreadnoughts or super-Dreadnoughts.

There were only two large-scale fleet actions in which they were involved: the Battle of Tsushima in 1905 between pre-Dreadnoughts and the Battle of Jutland in 1916 between Dreadnoughts. There were also actions in World War II, but battleships were soon relegated to auxiliary roles such as forming an anti-aircraft screen to defend aircraft carriers and for shore bombardment. By the end of World War II the type was obsolete, although in the US Navy (USN) the battleship lingered on, seeing action in the Vietnam War and the 1990–1 Gulf War.

Following this history, there are detailed chronological directories that describe the most famous of these ships in three sections: pre-Dreadnoughts, battleships of World War I and battleships of World War II. The first half of this book is thus the story, told through the careers of individual ships, of the development, deployment and demise of the battleship, which dominated naval strategy for 150 years.

9

Cruisers

The second half of this volume explores the development of cruisers. Of the main categories of warship, the cruiser has enjoyed by far the least attention from historians and researchers. The reason is probably one of definition. Battleships and aircraft carriers, destroyers and submarines all have clearly defined identities and duties; the dates of their introduction and/or demise being likewise apparent. In contrast, the cruiser was a category that emerged, rather than being conceived for some specific purpose.

Until the mid-19th century, the term "cruiser" was applied to a "cruising ship", one that was not tied to the battle line. "Seventy-fours" and smaller, down to frigates, might be given independent commissions, joining corvettes, sloops, cutters and lesser craft in the general discomfiture of the enemy and his trade. The freedom of such commands yielded experience (and prize money) that founded many an illustrious naval dynasty.

During the long period that followed the fall of Napoleon, the duties of the cruiser were again best defined by its label in that they revolved around maintaining the peace and "showing the flag" throughout the far reaches of an often restive empire. Categorized as "colonial sloops" or "corvettes", these small ships, their machinery still very much auxiliary to sail, were the "cruising ships" of the time.

By virtue of sheer weight, the introduction of the ironclad resulted in the demise of the multiple gundecks of the all-wooden era. The armoured single-decker (strictly speaking, a frigate) became the new line-of-battle ship. Continuous and rapid improvement in artillery, in protection and in machinery began to give designers broader options in specification but

TOP: **Typical of the screw corvettes that policed the world's empires, the German *Augusta* dries sails at anchor. As her gundeck is not covered, the gun-ports are clearly visible.** ABOVE: **All ocean raiders face the common problem of eventually requiring skilled dockyard assistance. The Confederate cruiser *Alabama* was thus apprehended outside Cherbourg in June 1864.**

due to weight, forced compromises on them. There began a clear divergence between vessels bearing heavy armament and protection, and others that favoured speed, with their gun battery and armour reduced accordingly. Here lay the origins of the Victorian battleship and the great armoured cruisers which could eclipse them in both cost and size.

Cost, in this protracted period of peace, became an ever more dominant factor. Smaller cruisers were required, a process facilitated by two further innovations: the essentially Italian concept of the protective deck and the availability of heat-treated, "cemented" steel armour with greatly improved resistance to penetration. For the same degree of protection, armour plate could now be thinner and lighter.

A choice of cruiser types was now possible: First Class armoured ships to act as a fast wing of the fleet and to under-take opposed reconnaissance; Second Class, usually protected, cruisers for general fleet duties and trade protection; small

Third Class vessels, lightly protected, for colonial policing, and a new category of Scout Cruiser, from which emerged the Destroyer Leader.

World War I and successive inter-war treaties resulted in the new classifications of "heavy" and "light" cruisers. The former type was used by the Japanese with particular imagination and effectiveness, almost as latter-day Second Class battleships.

To their still-relevant roles of reconnaissance, tracking and reporting, cruisers found further roles during World War II. Widespread amphibious operations showed them indispensable in fire support. Convoys to Malta and North Russia, and American fleet activities in the Pacific resulted in the continuing development of the new style of anti-aircraft cruiser.

Kamikazes and German stand-off guided bombs brought about the requirement for guided anti-aircraft missiles. American construction programmes had produced scores of identical gun-armed cruisers, but it proved uneconomical to convert them to guided-missile ships.

From a multiplicity of guided-missile systems emerged the essentially anti-aircraft "destroyer" and anti-submarine "frigate". Combine their systems and function and one arrives at the current definition of the cruiser, highly expensive, highly complex and multi-purpose.

The directories in this volume are divided into three sections covering pre-World War I, World War I and 1918 to the present day. Each offers a country-by-country view of history's most important cruisers, with full technical specifications for each.

Taken together, the composite parts of this comprehensive volume provide the historian or military enthusiast with a truly fascinating overview of some of the world's most impressive warships and the part they have played in shaping history.

ABOVE LEFT: **One of the nine Eclipse-class protected cruisers, HMS *Minerva* dated from 1895. Note the auxiliary spotting top to assist the ship in her defence of the Suez Canal.** TOP: ***Scharnhorst* coaling at Valparaiso shortly after von Spee's victory at Coronel in 1914. Note the mix of 21cm/8.3in and 15cm/5.9in guns.** ABOVE: **The beauty of a cruiser at speed is caught well in this image of the Italian heavy cruiser *Fiume* of 1930. One of four Zara-class ships, she exceeded 35 knots on trials. Together with two sisters, she was sunk at Matapan in 1941.**

ABOVE: **As can be appreciated from this 1960s photograph of the USS *Chicago*, hopes that early missile systems could be fitted easily into war-built cruiser hulls were misplaced.**

BATTLESHIPS

IMAGE: **The gun turret of the battleship *Missouri*.**

The History of Battleships

The term battleship derives from "line-of-battle ship", meaning a ship strong enough to fight in the line of battle – but there was confusion of nomenclature. *Warrior,* laid down in 1859, was certainly the strongest ship of her time yet she was never officially a battleship, only a frigate (because of her single gun deck), though later she was rated an armoured cruiser. The French called all the new battleships that developed in the later 19th century and 20th century *cuirassé*, and the Spanish called them *acorazado*, but these terms concentrated on the protective nature of armour. When the Germans came to build their navy they were more precise, using the terms *linienschiff, panzerschiff, schlachtschiff* and *schlachtkreuzer* to indicate different waypoints in the development of the battleship. The British navy began to re-introduce the term battleship around 1880 to mean a recognizable type of ship that was heavily armed and armoured. As technology advanced with the advent of steam, with propellers, breech-loading guns, turret mountings, turbines, armour plating, gun propellant and explosive power, so the modern battleship evolved.

LEFT: **A view taken onboard a USA battleship of the New Mexico class during the capture of Saipan in 1944. A sister ship follows next astern and the USS *Pennsylvania* completes the line ahead.**

LEFT: **The Crimean War was in fact a campaign and part of a larger war, more accurately known as the Russian War 1854–6, which raged on a global scale, and depended heavily upon sea power as this crowded anchorage in the Crimea shows.** BELOW: **For an attack upon Kinburn, the French navy devised some armoured box-like ships, just visible through the smoke, with which they could approach the low-lying Russian fortifications. These craft, which were little more than rafts, are generally considered the genesis of the modern battleship.**

The Russian War

By the time of the Russian War of 1854–6, all the ingredients for a revolution in battleship design and construction were in place. Steam propulsion had been successfully applied at sea to a large number of paddle ships and shortly thereafter many wooden walls had been converted to screw-steam propulsion. British shipyards were proficient in building iron hulls, armour was beginning to be applied to warships and guns were increasing in killing-power.

The actual impetus for the development of the battleship grew out of the campaign in the Black Sea, which is sometimes erroneously known as the Crimean War. The combined British and French fleets, which arrived in the Black Sea in March 1854, were massively superior to any force that the Russians could put to sea. The problem faced by the allies was therefore how to take the war to their opponents.

In November 1853 a Russian fleet had destroyed a squadron of Turkish frigates using shell fire. Louis Napoleon III, who considered himself an artillery expert, proposed a shellproof battery for dealing with the threat and for attacking the coast.

Technology was just about to produce 100mm/4in armour plate and this was tested independently in Britain and France to construct a number of batteries, with their armour fitted together with tongue-and-groove joints and bolted to the hull. The resulting vessels were scarcely manoeuvrable under their own steam power and were unwieldy under sail, which meant that they had to be towed for most of their passage.

In 1855 three French batteries saw action at Kinburn in the Crimea, where, in flattery to the Emperor, they were credited with destroying Russian shore positions. A more realistic assessment is that the low-lying Russian earthworks were flattened by mortar and bomb fire and blasted at close range by the accompanying battleships. Nevertheless, Kinburn saw the first use of armoured steam warships in battle.

The British took this basic idea a step further and built an immense fleet of gunboats and mortar vessels with which to attack St Petersburg – the news alone was sufficient to bring the Tsar to the negotiating table. On St George's Day 1856, the Royal Navy organized a review of their fleet to remind the Russians and the rest of the world of its power. The war was no sooner over than France began to think up ways of designing a ship that could challenge the Royal Navy, resulting in Dupuy de Lôme designing the first seagoing ironclad, *Gloire*.

Swedish influences in the United States Navy

The lessons of the Russian War and developments in warship design were noted in the USA where three Swedes, Ericsson, Fox and Dahlgren, strongly influenced the early United States Navy (USN).

John Ericsson had been an engineer in the Swedish Army when he moved to Britain in 1826 to sell his ideas, not all of them successful, for steam engines, screw propellers, large guns and even engines driven by hot air instead of steam. Ericsson was recruited to work in the USA and, with Robert Stockton, designed the heavily armed screw-driven USS *Princeton*. However, after an explosion in one of *Princeton*'s guns, for which Ericsson's design was blamed, he took up a career in civil engineering until the outbreak of the American Civil War. Ericsson designed and built a revolutionary armoured ship, *Monitor*, carrying her guns in a rotating turret, which like many of his designs was novel but not entirely successful. Active until his death at age 83, Ericsson continued to produce ideas for submarines, self-propelled torpedoes and heavy ordnance.

John Dahlgren was the son of the Swedish consul in Philadelphia, who after some years in the USN started work in the Washington Navy Yard, helping to found the USN's ordnance department. He designed the Dahlgren gun, a smoothbore cannon made in a variety of sizes, which became the standard weapon of the Union navy during the American Civil War. In 1863 he commanded the South Atlantic Blockading Squadron and saw his guns in action at Charleston.

Gustavus Vasa Fox retired after nearly 20 years in the USN. In the American Civil War, after volunteering to command an expedition to relieve the garrison at Fort Sumter, Fox was appointed chief clerk of the Department of the Navy and then Assistant Secretary of the Navy, where his honesty and efficiency were much needed. Fox effectively became the chief of naval operations. He kept in touch personally with senior officers and planned many of the navy's campaigns against the Confederacy. Fox was also a keen advocate of new technology including Ericsson's *Monitor*.

In mid-1866 Fox crossed the Atlantic in the monitor *Miantonomoh*, demonstrating the sea-worthiness of a low-freeboard, armoured turret ship. Fox visited northern Europe, including Russia, and the officers of his squadron used the opportunity to collect naval intelligence. However, Fox soon resigned from office to enter business. The USN went into a decline that lasted for the next few decades and the early promise of an oceanic navy went unfulfilled.

BELOW: **The USN continued to build low-freeboard monitors and to make trans-Atlantic crossings until the 20th century: here a US monitor passes a high-sided broadside French ship, herself a survivor from an earlier age.**
RIGHT: **One of the first acts of the newly pacified USA was to send a naval mission to Europe led by the Secretary of the Navy Gustavus Fox, in the un-seaworthy-looking monitor *Miantonomoh*.**

Captain and the end of sail

Captain Cowper Phipps Coles was first inspired to design turntable mountings for heavy guns following the use of ordnance mounted on rafts during the Crimean War.

Coles was well aware of the disadvantage of a broadside battery in a steamship being that only half the armament could be brought to bear, and then only on one side or other of the ship's heading, thus restricting ships to fight broadside-on as they had always done under sail. He advocated turrets for warships and had invented a working mounting so that the guns could be brought to bear at more or less any bearing. Furthermore it was recognized that the weight of Coles's mountings required them to be mounted on the centreline of warships, unlike swivel guns which had long been mounted along the sides.

Even before the clash between *Monitor* and *Merrimac*, the British Admiralty had tried Coles's revolving turrets in *Trusty* in 1861, and in 1862 had ordered a coast defence ship *Prince Albert* and converted *Royal Sovereign*, a 120-gun three-decker, for coastal defence, each with no less than four turrets. The success of these ships and news from the USA led to the design of *Monarch*, the first ocean-going turret ship, armed with four 305mm/12in guns in two turrets. Inefficient engines with high coal consumption meant that ships like *Monarch* still required sails for long passages. However, the forest of masts and rigging which a sailing ship needed was incompatible with centreline turrets which required clear arcs of fire to be effective. Coles proposed the use of tripod masts to help solve this problem.

Coles was critical of the design of *Monarch*: she was a high-freeboard ship and he was convinced that a low-freeboard design, such as that of *Monitor*, would give additional protection. After he had won the backing of Parliament, the public and *The Times* newspaper, the Admiralty reluctantly ordered a ship from Lairds at Birkenhead to be built to Coles's specification.

Whilst *Captain* was being built between 1867 and 1870 there was insufficient attention to weight control and consequentially she was 813 tonnes/800 tons heavier than planned. Edward Reed, the Admiralty's Chief Constructor, was already concerned about the stability of Coles's design which would have a freeboard of just 2.44m/8ft; however the additional weight reduced this to just 2m/6ft 6in. The metacentric height was very small so that she rolled slowly; at 14 degrees of heel her gunwales were in the water, and at 21 degrees she was unsafe.

Captain was the first ship of her size to have twin screws, another of Coles's ideas, but she was also given a large sail plan of some 3,715sq m/40,000sq ft.

Two revolving centre-line turrets, with twin 305mm/12in, 25.5-tonne/25-ton, muzzle-loading rifled guns firing 270kg/600lb shells, were mounted on the main deck. The stern, midships and forecastles were linked by a flying deck, and restricted the angles of fire or "A" arcs of the guns. The three strongly built masts with tripod supports instead of traditional standing rigging were fitted. On trials *Captain* appeared to confound her critics; she manoeuvred well under

LEFT: Despite *Captain*'s high sides and continuous upper deck, the men in white uniforms show how low in the ship the guns were mounted. It is evident from the photograph that *Captain* was a low freeboard barbette ship with a dangerously heavy top hamper, which would eventually prove fatal.
ABOVE: A close-up of one of *Captain*'s massive turrets shows that the deck above is only a flying bridge. This arrangement kept the rigging clear of the arcs of fire.

power and was a steady gun platform. However, the results of heeling experiments, in the summer of 1870, were not made known to the Admiralty or to the ship before she sailed to join the Channel Squadron. In her was Coles, as an observer, and among the midshipmen was the son of Sir Hugh Childers, First Lord of the Admiralty, who had backed Coles against the advice of his own Board of Admiralty.

West of Cape Finisterre Admiral Sir Alexander Milne, Commander-in-Chief of the Mediterranean fleet, had witnessed gunnery practice onboard *Captain*, and as the wind freshened he returned to his flagship, *Lord Warden*. Shortly after midnight on September 7, a strong gust of wind blew out many sails throughout the fleet. *Captain,* however, was knocked over and capsized, sinking quickly, with the loss of 481 of her 499 crew. Ironically, had she been a less strongly built ship the masts might have broken away and saved her.

In the inquiry which followed, blame was shared between the Admiralty, Coles himself and the builder. However, following the disaster no more broadside or central battery ships were laid down, and shortly afterwards the Royal Navy began to reduce the rig of its capital ships, the loss of *Captain* marking the beginning of the end of sail in the Royal Navy.

ABOVE: **A view of *Captain* under construction when her designers and builders lost control of her weight. The photograph shows just how little freeboard she had.** BELOW: ***Captain*'s first voyage was a success and, although this fanciful picture shows her in a storm, with water spilled across her decks, she caused no concern for her stability. She was so strongly built that instead of her sails blowing out or her masts going overboard, the freshening wind caused her to capsize.**

The Battle of Lissa

The Battle of Lissa in the Adriatic in 1866 was the first fleet engagement involving ironclad ships. Even a tactical victory for the Austrians could not save the war for them, but when the gunnery of the day proved ineffective against armour, other navies drew the wrong lessons and ramming was given a bogus tactical status for the rest of the century.

Italy was allied with Prussia, which was fighting Austria for dominance of the German states in the Austro-Prussian or Seven Weeks War. After Prussia had defeated Austria on land, Italy, wanting to gain Italian-speaking provinces from Austria, attempted to use its navy to make territorial gains, and bombarded the island of Lissa or Vis in the eastern Adriatic. The Italian fleet commanded by Admiral Carlo Persano including the broadside ironclads, *Regina Maria, Pia San Martino, Castelfidardo, Ancona, Re d'Italia, Re di Portogallo, Principe di Carignano, Terribile,* and *Formidabile,* the turret ram *Affondatore,* and the coast defence ships *Palestro* and *Varese,* then commenced an assault on the island of Lissa.

The Austrian Admiral Wilhelm von Tegetthoff guarded the Adriatic cities of Pola and Trieste until he became convinced that the island of Lissa was the Italians' main effort and he immediately set sail for the island. His fleet consisted of the 90-gun ship of the line *Kaiser,* and the broadside ironclads *Erzherzog Ferdinand Max, Habsburg, Kaiser Max, Prinz Eugen, Juan de Austria, Drache* and *Salamander.*

As Persano prepared to land on July 20, after two days of bombardment, Tegetthoff appeared out of the fog from the north-west, his fleet formed into a wedge with *Erzherzog*

TOP: **During the Battle of Lissa, the Italian ship *Re d'Italia* was damaged astern and rammed while lying stopped in the water. Her loss gave false authority to the concept of the ram.** ABOVE: **The wooden wall *Kaiser* after leading Tegetthoff's second wedge, consisting of wooden frigates, into battle. It was damaged in the ramming of *Re d'Italia* and had to be repaired in Malta. Nevertheless, the Battle of Lissa seemed to prove that even a traditional wooden wall could be successfully used as a ram – a false deduction which still deluded naval architects and naval officers for much of the rest of the century.**

Ferdinand Max in the centre of an arrowhead formation of seven ironclads, followed by a second wedge of wooden warships, led by the elderly *Kaiser,* and a convoy of troops.

Though some of Persano's ironclads were absent, he was still numerically superior but his forces were divided and unprepared. Furthermore, he was caught in the middle of landing troops and with boats in the water. Persano divided his strength by distributing his ironclads into mixed squadrons, with older wooden and sailing ships, and decided, apparently at a late moment, to command his fleet from the *Affondatore.* Forming a hurried line of battle, he is alleged to have said disparagingly of the Austrians, "Here come the fishermen".

Battle commenced at 10.30, when Tegetthoff, still in wedge formation, increased speed and broke the Italian line, rather like Nelson at Trafalgar, ordering his ironclads to turn to port and to sink the enemy centre with their rams. The leading Austrian ironclads then turned to port to attack the Italian centre. In the fierce close-quarters mêlée which ensued, wreathed in smoke from the guns and funnels, Tegetthoff was able to concentrate his seven ironclads against four Italian ironclads. There were several attempts at ramming in which *Ferdinand Max* and *Palestro* succeeded in ramming each other, and Persano in *Affondatore* twice missed hitting *Kaiser*. Then, when *Re d'Italia*'s stern was damaged and she lay stopped in the water, Tegetthoff rammed her at about 11 knots and she sank in a few minutes. Even *Kaiser* somehow managed to damage her bows and had to be sent to the Royal Navy base at Malta for repairs.

Following two hours of manoeuvring, shortly after noon, the Austrian ships were north of Lissa and the Italians to the west; Lissa had been saved. Gunfire continued until mid-afternoon, and at about 14.30 Palestro exploded following a fire which had been started during the morning's action. The Italians, now short of coal, retired to Ancona.

The deciding factor in this battle was that the Austrians were better led and better trained, overcoming the Italians' superiority in numbers and quality of ships; however, this was to be overlooked by commentators at the time. Despite the fury of the fight, few ships suffered significant damage and most attempts at ramming had been unsuccessful. However the Battle of Lissa influenced ship design for the rest of the century, leading to some ships being specifically designed for ramming, even after improvements in gunnery and the development of the torpedo made such tactics suicidal.

The ram has enjoyed a modern reincarnation as the streamlined bulbous bow of merchant ships and in "chin sonars" for frigates, but there is no evidence that it aided ship performance in the 19th century, although architects may have unconsciously discovered how to streamline their designs.

ABOVE: **The Italian coast defence ship** *Palestro* **and the German battleship** *Erzherzog Ferdinand Max* **rammed each other during the course of the Battle of Lissa in 1866.** BELOW: **Austria's toehold on the Adriatic included the ancient city-port of Venice and this made her a sea power: the Austrian admiral Wilhelm von Tegetthoff fought in the North Sea as well as at the Battle of Lissa. The Austro-Hungarian navy had global aspirations which included deployments beyond the Mediterranean to the West Indies during the Spanish American War and to China.** BOTTOM: **Late in the deployment and immediately before the battle the Italian Admiral Carlo Persano transferred his flag to** *Affondatore* **and lost control of his fleet.**

The Battle of Tsushima

The imperial rivalry between Russia and Japan over control of Manchuria and Korea brought about one of the most decisive battles of naval history. Japan had defeated China in a war in 1894–5, but had been denied her conquests, particularly of Port Arthur on the Liaotung Peninsula, by the international community. In 1896 Russia made a treaty with China which included the right to extend the Trans-Siberian railway across Manchuria to the Russian port of Vladivostok, and two years later gained a lease over Port Arthur. Japan rapidly expanded its army, whilst the railway, which was completed in 1904, enabled Russia to begin a slow build-up of its forces in the Far East. However, when Russia reneged on an agreement to withdraw troops from Manchuria, Japan launched a surprise attack and bombarded Port Arthur and the Russian ships there. The Japanese army overran Korea and the Russian army fell back; Port Arthur was besieged and surrendered on January 2, 1905.

Meanwhile the Russian Baltic Fleet, renamed the Second Pacific Squadron, was despatched from Europe under the command of Admiral Rozhdestvenski. This might have been a fine demonstration of the use of sea power, but the logistic difficulties facing Rozhdestvenski were enormous. Britain, allied with Japan, would not sell coal or grant harbour facilities to the Russians. France, however, granted access to its colonial ports and Germany chartered-out a fleet of 60 colliers of the Hamburg-Amerika Line. Nevertheless, the Russian ships were not designed for a 29,000km/18,000-mile voyage nor for tropical conditions, and Russian morale, as well as equipment, seem to have broken down. A Third Pacific Squadron, composed of weak and elderly ships, transited the Suez Canal to join Rozhdestvenski at Madagascar, where he was delayed while fresh contracts were being drawn up for the supply of

TOP: **The Battle of the Yalu River on August 10, 1904, preceding the Battle of Tsushima. Here the Japanese ships in traditional line-ahead fire the opening shots of the engagement.** ABOVE: **The Japanese fleet under manoeuvre. Every calibre of weapon was fitted in the pre-Dreadnoughts, including machine-guns for anti-torpedo boat defence. These pictures show once more how coal-burning gave away the position of pre-Dreadnought and Dreadnought era battleships. Coal also limited the endurance, measured in speed and range, of coal-powered steamships.**

coal. Kamranh Bay in French Indo-China was the last port before the motley Russian fleet crossed the South China Sea; British-owned Singapore and Hong Kong were, of course, denied to Rozhdestvenski.

There were two routes from Kamranh to Vladivostok. East about the Japanese home islands would require Rozhdestvenski to coal at sea while exposed and open to Japanese attack. The direct route lay west of Japan and led via Tsushima Strait into the Sea of Japan. Steaming slowly to conserve fuel and keep his fleet together, he entered the strait on the night of May 26/27, where the Japanese fleet, commanded by Admiral Togo, was waiting.

Togo was one of several Japanese officers who had been trained by the Royal Navy and he had studied in England from 1871–8. As captain of the cruiser *Naniwa* he had sunk a Chinese troopship en route for Korea, thus precipitating the Sino-Japanese war. His Nelson-like order before the Battle of Tsushima was "The fate of the Empire rests upon this one battle; let every man do his utmost."

Togo's cruisers spotted the Russians heading north-east and reported this by radio. By mid-morning Rozhdestvenski was being followed by two Japanese divisions and Togo while the main battle fleet was approaching from the north. Rozhdestvenski attempted to form a line of battle as ships appeared from the mist and vanished again, but missed signals and poor seamanship threw his ships into confusion.

When the mist cleared in the early afternoon, Togo's concentrated, disciplined and faster fleet was north-east of Rozhdestvenski and on an opposite course. Using his speed, Togo crossed the Russian fleet, which was now in two columns, led his fleet in a 180-degree turn and steadied on a parallel course on the Russians' port side. Later he again crossed the Russians' line of advance, though by now they were in disarray.

The Russians fought bravely but the battle was soon decided. Rozhdestvenski's flagship was one of four Russian battleships destroyed by the concentrated fire of Togo's ships, and with the loss of any kind of central command the battle

TOP: **The Russian** *Osliabia*, **a Peresviet class battleship, sunk at the Battle of Tsushima in May 1905. Togo's victory over Rozhdestvenski's fleet gave Japan victory in the war.** ABOVE LEFT: **The Russian battleship** *Tsessarevitch* **photographed in Port Arthur in 1904 where she was blockaded. Her funnels show damage received during the Battle of the Yalu River. The Russians fought bravely in all their engagements, but they were overwhelmed by numbers or by superior logistics.** ABOVE: **A Japanese print showing the destruction of the Russian flagship. Victory marked the ascendancy of the Imperial Japanese Navy and Togo was hailed as the new Nelson.**

became a mêlée and then a massacre. Of the Russian fleet of 45 ships, only two destroyers and the light cruiser *Almaz* reached Vladivostok, and six others reached neutral ports. The rest were sunk, beached, or surrendered.

The battle gave victory to the Japanese in the war, and the annihilation of the Russian fleet altered the balance of power in Europe. Royal Navy officers witnessed the battle from Japanese ships and noted the effectiveness of heavy guns at long range.

The Great White Fleet

The voyage of the Great White Fleet in 1907–9, despatched round the world by the American President Theodore Roosevelt, marked the coming of age of the United States Navy (USN) following a period of revival. The voyage also marked the beginning of the "American" century, presaging the leading role which the USN would take in the 20th century. However despite newspaper acclaim and public pride in the USA, the fleet was obsolescent and to naval planners the voyage revealed strategic weaknesses.

Roosevelt was a navalist who been influenced by and then in turn influenced the American naval strategist Alfred Mahan. As a young man Roosevelt had written *The Naval War of 1812*, which praised the performance of the USN in that war somewhat uncritically, and he had also contributed to Laird Clowes's seven-volume history of the Royal Navy. When Roosevelt became president of the USA, after a period of naval expansion which he himself had helped to stimulate, Japan was beginning to be seen as more of a threat than Britain.

In the summer of 1907 Roosevelt approved a proposal that the American battle fleet should make a demonstration by deploying from the Atlantic to the Pacific coast of the USA. The USN had been considering sending a fleet on a deployment into the Pacific for some time, though quite when Roosevelt agreed that this should become a circumnavigation is not clear. Roosevelt probably only came gradually upon the idea that

such a move would act as a deterrent to the Japanese, impress the American taxpayer, and garner support for more battleships. The long deployment round South America and through the Magellan Straits would also help show the need for the Panama Canal.

ABOVE: **American battleships at Port Said, Egypt. The voyage of the Great White Fleet relied upon a fleet of hired British colliers and upon British-controlled facilities like the Suez Canal.** BELOW: *Connecticut* **leads battleships of the US Atlantic Fleet in 1907. The paint scheme was responsible for the name "white fleet", the supply of coal restricted its operations and smoke gave away its position.**

ABOVE: **Life onboard – a scene which must have been familiar throughout all fleets over many years; peeling vegetables. By the age of steam, however, scurvy was almost unknown.** ABOVE RIGHT: **Rear Admiral C. M. Thomas, USN, onboard** *Minnesota*, **1907. The admiral's use of a handheld signal book is another scene which would have been familiar in the age of sail.** RIGHT: **Fourth of July festivities onboard the battleship** *Connecticut* **in 1908 during the Great White Fleet's historic circumnavigation.**

The battleships were accompanied by several auxiliary ships and on the first part of their voyage by a flotilla of early destroyers. The 14-month-long voyage by 14,000 sailors covered some 22,500km/43,000 miles and made 20 landfalls on six continents. They were led initially by Rear Admiral "Fighting Bob" Evans who had made his career in the Spanish-American War.

Significantly the fleet's first visit was to the British island of Trinidad in the West Indies for coal, and then, on the first leg of its voyage, to Rio de Janeiro, Chile, Peru, Mexico, and on to San Francisco, where *Alabama* and *Maine* were replaced by *Nebraska* and *Wisconsin*. The fleet then visited Hawaii, Auckland, Sydney and Melbourne. The celebrations when the Great White Fleet arrived in Australia in 1908 were only surpassed by those which had been held for the federation of Australia. Over 80,000 people stood on South Head to watch the fleet enter Sydney Harbour and crowds, parties, speeches and parades greeted the Americans. This did not stop American officers using the opportunity to draw up plans to invade or capture these ports in the event of war with the British Empire.

The fleet then steamed on to Yokohama, Manila, Colombo and Suez, where it arrived on January 3, 1909. The voyage had become something of a race to be home before Roosevelt's successor was sworn in as the new president, and not even an earthquake in Sicily could delay the fleet very much; they were back in Hampton Roads, Virginia, on February 22, 1909.

The voyage of the Great White Fleet may have served its purpose politically, but before they had even set out, every ship had been rendered obsolescent by the launch of the British all-big-gun battleship *Dreadnought*. Just as significantly, the fleet had found there were few American bases to support it and instead the ships had had to rely upon another fleet, of some 50 chartered colliers. Good Welsh or Appalachian coal was unobtainable and the colliers often turned up late with very inferior coal. Worse, the colliers were nearly all British. The lesson was clear; impressive as the Great White Fleet was, the USN would have to – and did – develop its own logistical train.

Within only a few months of returning to the USA the battleships of the Great White Fleet were painted grey and their pole masts were replaced by lattice masts.

The 18 new battleships of the Great White Fleet

Alabama	Kearsarge	Missouri	Vermont
Connecticut	Kentucky	Nebraska	Virginia
Georgia	Louisiana	New Jersey	Wisconsin
Illinois	Maine	Ohio	
Kansas	Minnesota	Rhode Island	

Cuniberti, Scott and Sims

In addition to Fisher, three men stand out as having strongly influenced the development of the big gun and the design of the *Dreadnought*. The Italian naval architect and engineer Vittorio Cuniberti was descended from a successive line of innovative Italian naval architects such as Brin and Micheli. At the beginning of the 20th century Cuniberti had drawn up plans for a ship with a single calibre of big guns, but the project was regarded as too ambitious for the Italian navy, and in 1902 he was given permission to publish an article in *Jane's Fighting Ships*, then a newly established publication. The article was entitled: "An Ideal Battleship for the British Fleet" and his ideas were for "a moderate-sized, very swift vessel with the greatest possible unified armament". An article that was published three years earlier in German in the *Marine Rundschau*, "Ein neuer Schlachtschifftypus" had attracted little attention, but by 1904 navies around the world were about to analyse the Battle of Tsushima and its implications for warship design.

At this time guns were laid by eye, so the direction officer needed to see the fall of shot in order to estimate the range adjustment. Cuniberti and others appreciated that as guns of all calibre improved and could be fired to the limits of visual observation it was increasingly difficult to distinguish the fall of

ABOVE: Cuniberti's ideas were taken up in several countries, where some smaller navies did not slavishly copy Fisher's Dreadnought but designed all-big-gun ships from first principles, like the small but purposeful and elegant *España*, seen here.

one shot and thus make the appropriate corrections. Cuniberti actually lampooned the American practice of fitting up to four different calibres, writing, "Looking to America, one realizes that chaos reigns in the designing department of the United States Navy, and hardly a month seems to pass without a new type being brought out, more and more loaded with guns." Whether Cuniberti's ideas actually influenced any British decision or the ideas arose spontaneously and simultaneously in different navies is not known but Fisher was the first to implement them.

Meanwhile in the Royal Navy, Percy Scott was improving the accuracy of gun laying. Scott is best known for his efforts during the Boer War in 1899 when as captain of the cruiser *Terrible* he designed makeshift gun carriages for the ship's guns so they could be taken up-country by a naval brigade to help the army at the siege of Ladysmith. He was training commander at the gunnery school, HMS *Excellent*, in

Portsmouth, 1890–3, a member of the Ordnance Committee, 1893–6, captain of HMS *Excellent* in 1904, and Inspector of Target Practice in 1908, and in 1916 he was called from retirement to create the Anti-Aircraft Corps for the defence of London against air attack. Scott was a prolific inventor who devised a loading tray to teach faster loading, a "dotter" designed to help his gun layers record accurate bearings, and introduced director firing from a centralized position in the ship. The gunnery technology of the day was capable of firing a shell ten miles, and Scott helped the Royal Navy to hit targets at these ranges more accurately. After the war he argued that the advent of submarines and aeroplanes meant that the day of the battleship, which his inventions had helped to perfect, was over.

William Sims, a Canadian by birth, joined the USN and between regular appointments was a naval attaché in Europe. Sims reported on new ship designs and improvements in gunnery and wrote directly to President Theodore Roosevelt criticizing the efficiency of the USN. He supported Roosevelt in arguing for the USN adopting an all-big-gun Dreadnought fleet against others, including the now elderly Mahan who advocated a mixed calibre and a "balanced fleet". Roosevelt made Sims his protégé and he went on to introduce the continuous aim method developed by Scott to the USN. He commanded the battleships *Minnesota*, 1909–11 and *Nevada*, 1916–17. Sims was briefly president of the US Naval War College but in March 1917 he was made the USN's representative in London. When the USA entered World War I he took command of all American destroyers operating from British bases, helping to establish convoys to overcome the strangulating effect of German U-boats. Like Scott he became an apostate regarding battleships and in retirement was an advocate of naval aviation. Despite the contributions these men made, the modern battleship is indelibly linked with Fisher and his *Dreadnought*.

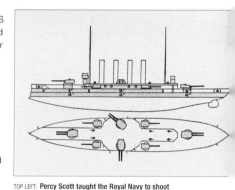

TOP LEFT: **Percy Scott taught the Royal Navy to shoot and he was a prolific inventor. He later argued against the retention of the battleship because it was rendered obsolescent by new weapons.**

TOP RIGHT: **As a junior officer William Sims supported Theodore Roosevelt by advocating an ocean-going fleet.** ABOVE: **A line drawing of Cuniberti's proposed all-big-gun battleship: even Cuniberti retained some smaller guns, essential for anti-torpedo defence. His proposals, however, did not go as far as having the guns on the centreline so that they could all be brought to bear on one target.**

Goeben and battleships in the Black Sea

The bombardments by the German Admiral Wilhelm Souchon of the French ports in North Africa at Bône and Philippeville on August 3, 1914, were the first shots of the war at sea in World War I. His subsequent escape through the Mediterranean was a disgrace to the all-powerful Royal Navy and the arrival of his modern battlecruiser at Constantinople later that month brought Turkey into the war on the side of the Central Powers. Souchon's bombardment of Odessa on October 29 opened the war between Turkey and Russia, but, when he met a squadron of Russian pre-Dreadnoughts in the Black Sea, Souchon failed to use his speed and firepower to destroy his foe.

At the outbreak of war Souchon commanded the only German ships in the Mediterranean, the modern battlecruiser *Goeben* and the light cruiser *Breslau*. His orders were to cooperate with the Austro-Hungarian and Italian fleets and interdict the passage of French troops across the Mediterranean. When Austria declared war against Serbia on July 28, *Goeben* and *Breslau* were at Pola and by August 1, when Germany declared war on Russia, Souchon's ships had moved to Brindisi, where, fearing internment after Italy had declared its neutrality, he sailed west in the direction where the Royal Navy thought he might make for the Atlantic. Though Britain had yet to join the war, the battlecruisers *Indomitable*

ABOVE: The German *Goeben*, having altered the balance of power in the Dardanelles and Black Sea, hoisted the Turkish flag and was briefly captured at Novorossiysk before being handed back to the Turks in November 1918.

and *Indefatigable* looked for Souchon, and met him on August 4 returning eastwards. Both sides were at action stations but their guns were trained fore and aft, and as the British turned to follow, Souchon increased speed and gradually lost sight of the British battlecruisers.

Souchon coaled at Messina, feinted towards the Adriatic and headed for the Dardanelles: he was found again by the Royal Navy which acted timidly and he escaped to Constantinople. Meanwhile on August 2, two Turkish battleships completing in British yards, *Resadiye* and *Sultan Osman I* (formerly the Brazilian *Rio de Janeiro*), were confiscated by the Royal Navy and commissioned as *Erin* and *Agincourt*.

On August 16 Germany announced the sale of Souchon's squadron to Turkey as *Sultan Yavuz Selim* and *Middilli*, Souchon became commander-in-chief of the Turkish battlefleet and his German crew continued to man their ships.

On November 18, 1914, *Goeben* intercepted the Russian battlefleet consisting of the pre-Dreadnoughts *Estavii, Ioann Zlatoust* (both 1903), the 1905 *Pantelimon*, the 1895 *Rostislav*,

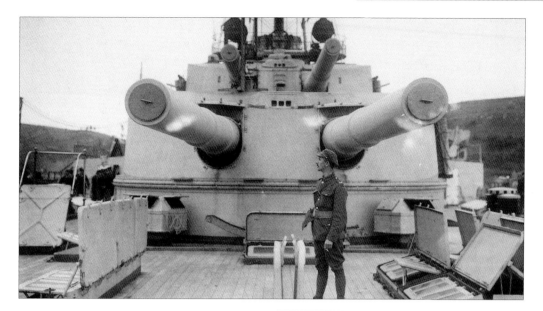

and the 1891 turret ship *Tri Sviatitelia* returning from bombarding Turkish positions. Souchon was eager for a fight and expected to find the Russians easy prey, but he was unpleasantly surprised by the weight and accuracy of the Russian fire.

Poor visibility eliminated *Goeben*'s guns' range advantage, and the Russians, who had learned some lessons from their defeat at Tsushima, were practised as a centralized firing unit. This meant that the centre ship in a three-ship group would pass ranges and bearings to coordinate the fire of the other ships. The older *Rostislav* and *Tri Sviatitelia* were not part of the firing unit and were free to fire on *Breslau*.

In the quarter hour's engagement which ensued, at ranges of 5–8km/3–5 miles, *Breslau* took shelter on *Goeben*'s disengaged side from the hail of fire and *Goeben* was hit 14 times, mainly by *Evstafii*. *Evstafii* was hit four times before *Goeben* veered off into the mist and did not attempt to renew the engagement.

Thereafter there was stalemate in the Black Sea, and *Goeben* did not challenge the Russian pre-Dreadnought Black Sea Fleet. While the Russians operated as a squadron they were relatively free to bombard Turkish ports and positions until even *Goeben* was affected by coal shortages.

After many other actions, *Goeben* and *Breslau* sortied from the Dardanelles to raid Salonika on January 20, 1918, where they sank the British 355mm/14in gun monitor *Raglan* and the smaller 235mm/9.2in gun *M28*. *Breslau* was mined and sunk and *Goeben* was beached after hitting three mines herself. She was repaired in time for the surrender of the mutinous Black Sea Fleet on May 2, 1918.

Rebuilt in 1927–30, and again in 1938 and 1941, she was renamed *Yavuz Selim*. The ex-*Goeben* was offered back to

TOP: A close-up of *Goeben* after turrets while under military guard. Presumably no officer is watching this man smoke. ABOVE: *Goeben*, the ever-elusive German battleship, at last in British hands. From her escape from the Royal Navy in the Mediterranean in 1914 until the Armistice in 1918, *Goeben*, whether she was German or Turkish, had a major impact on the strategic balance in the Black Sea and altered great power politics.

Germany in 1963 but the offer was refused and so after a period as a museum ship she was scrapped in 1976. Souchon's own career ended in ignominy when in late October 1918 he was removed from his command at Kiel by mutineers.

Jacky Fisher

Jacky Fisher, or Admiral of the Fleet Lord Fisher of Kilverstone, was the father of the Dreadnought revolution, a revolution which changed naval warfare and the balance of power between nations. Fisher linked the old sailing navy with the new, having been nominated by the last of Nelson's captains. As a young officer he served in the Crimea and in China at the battle of Fatshan Creek. Specializing in gunnery, he served on *Warrior* when she was new, and was responsible for a number of innovations including the introduction of electrical firing circuits in the guns of *Ocean* in 1869, and helped to found the Royal Navy's experimental school in HMS *Vernon*. Later he commanded the battleship *Inflexible* at the bombardment of Alexandria in 1882 and took command of the Naval Brigades when they landed.

As Director of Naval Ordnance Fisher introduced a range of modern weapons to the Royal Navy and as an admiral he was responsible, as Third Sea Lord, for delivering the ships ordered under the Naval Defence Act of 1889. Whilst serving as Commander-in-Chief, Mediterranean, he concentrated on firing at long ranges, taught the fleet to manoeuvre in tight formations at maximum speed, and studied the tactics that this implied. Then as Second Sea Lord he reformed the officer and rating structure and training which he implemented whilst Commander-in-Chief, Portsmouth.

From the 1880s onwards Fisher increasingly turned to politics to promote the Royal Navy and his ideas, using his friendship with the journalist W T Stead. He also made influential friends in royal circles and amongst politicians, particularly Winston Churchill.

Fisher brought this powerful suite of technical, strategic and political skills, together with his forceful character, to the office of First Sea Lord in 1904. He advocated the use of submarines and ensured that at the outbreak of World War I the Royal Navy had one of the largest fleets of submarines. Whilst in the Mediterranean he had conceived the idea of the large armoured cruiser, which became the battlecruiser, and though he could not solve the problem of ships having to fight in line-of-battle, he proposed the creation of mixed "fleet units". In response to the danger posed by the rise of the German fleet, Fisher concentrated the Royal Navy in home waters, and needing the manpower for new, larger warships, he controversially paid off many older ships on overseas stations as they were too weak and too slow. Above all, however, Fisher pressed for speed and hitting power in warships.

LEFT: **A famous picture of Fisher's protégé, John Jellicoe, mounting a ladder onboard the battleship *Iron Duke*. Jellicoe was a man consumed by self-doubt, despite the impression of dynamism given by this picture.** BELOW: **An unusual picture of Fisher relaxing with visitors onboard the battleship *Renown*.**

The concept of the all-big-gun battleship was not new. The Italian designer Vittorio Cuniberti had written about it and been published in Germany and Britain, and similar ideas were being developed in the USA. Fisher's critics said that by building the all-big-gun battleship he made every other battleship obsolete including all the Royal Navy's, but it seems that it was an idea whose hour had come, and for once the Royal Navy was first. *Dreadnought* was Fisher's brainchild and it was his fanatic drive and energy which made the development time so short: within months he had decided upon the 305mm/12in gun armament and opted for every innovation available, Professor Barr's 2.74m/9ft optical rangefinder accurate to 6,400m/7,000yd, steam turbines rather than reciprocating engines, and enhanced underwater protection. By robbing the Lord Nelson class of their guns Fisher was able to claim that he had built *Dreadnought* in twelve months and she was officially completed on Trafalgar Day 1906. However, Fisher also made personal enemies, and was forced to retire in 1910, continuing to give advice from retirement in France. He became mentor to Winston Churchill when he was First Lord of the Admiralty, and it was under his tutelage that Churchill persuaded the British government to take a stake in the Anglo-Iranian Oil Company (which grew into British Petroleum) in order to ensure oil supplies for the Royal Navy. Then, after Prince Battenberg was forced to resign as First Sea Lord in 1914 on grounds of his German background Fisher was recalled. As First Sea Lord he was responsible for sending battlecruisers to the South Atlantic in response to the German victory at Coronel, but subsequently fell out with Churchill over his interference in operational matters during the Dardanelles campaign, and resigned.

Fisher was also responsible for advancing the career of John Jellicoe. Jellicoe was not an inspirational leader like Fisher and failed to make best use of his ships when Fisher's mighty fleet of Dreadnoughts was tested at the Battle of Jutland in 1916.

ABOVE: **Jacky Fisher, as he was universally known, seized upon good ideas and turned them into his own but he also had the energy and force of character to make them happen.** BELOW: **Fisher had many ideas, including the concept of a fleet unit and the battlecruiser, and he was an advocate of the submarine. But his greatest brainchild, for which he is best known, was** *Dreadnought*, **a new type of warship that made all preceding battleships obsolescent, and from which the type took its name.**

The Anglo-German naval race

In the early 20th century the Royal Navy was at the height of its power, was superior by a ratio of two to one to any other navy, and had been at peace for the best part of 100 years – there had been no general war since 1815. The French navy had not really been a threat for many years, and the Russian navy had suffered a crushing defeat at Tsushima in 1905 by the Japanese navy which was under British tutelage. However, the German navy was beginning to grow and establish overseas bases, and the United States Navy (USN) had shown its potential by the cruise of the Great White Fleet in 1907–9.

Royal Navy relations with the USN were cordial and Sims, for example, had been one of the first foreign visitors to inspect *Dreadnought*. On a personal level many British and German officers knew and liked each other, but relations with the German state deteriorated. Kaiser Wilhelm II and naval chief Admiral von Tirpitz wanted a modern navy for personal and prestigious reasons as much as for securing an overseas empire, and they wanted a large navy even if this meant challenging the Royal Navy. The Kaiser's brother, Prince Henry of Prussia, who was also an honorary Admiral in the Royal

ABOVE: **As well as Dreadnought-type battleships, the German navy also employed airships to carry out reconnaissance for the High Seas Fleet.** BELOW LEFT: **Grand Admiral Alfred von Tirpitz who encouraged the German Kaiser to challenge the Royal Navy by building up a "Riskflotte", which helped bring about World War I.**

Navy, made the German navy a respectable profession for ambitious young Germans, while the Kaiser ordered the works of the American naval strategist, Captain Mahan, to be translated and placed in the wardrooms of all his ships. Wilhelm II had absorbed the lesson from his reading of Mahan that a large navy and great power status were synonymous. Perhaps also his cousins on the British throne with their command of the Royal Navy gave him an inferiority complex. The Kaiser was ably assisted by Tirpitz, who had joined the Prussian navy in 1865 and then the navy of the new German Empire when it formed in 1871. Tirpitz, who had commanded the East Asiatic Squadron in 1896–7 when a treaty was concluded with China, returned to Berlin to commence his challenge to the Royal Navy by building up the German navy.

Up until the 1890s the German navy had been a coastal defence force. However, harnessing German industrial power, new German Navy Laws in 1898, 1900, 1908 and 1912 envisaged a balanced fleet which by 1920 would include 38 battleships. Tirpitz's concept was of a *riskflotte* or risk fleet: he reasoned that Britain would not go to war with Germany if Germany possessed a significant fleet, because, although the Royal Navy would win any campaign at sea, it would be so weakened that the two-power standard would be broken and Britain exposed to defeat at sea by France, Russia or even the USA.

RIGHT: **This photograph dated November 28, 1918, shows the German fleet at Scapa Flow after the British Grand Fleet had escorted it into internment.** BELOW: **King Edward VII of Great Britain and his nephew Kaiser Wilhelm II of Germany – it was partly Wilhelm's jealousy of his uncle which drove him to build up the German navy. Books have been written about the extent to which Anglo-German rivalry was a personal affair between the British and German royal families, and a political inevitability of German reunifications in the late 19th century.** BELOW RIGHT: **The German navy at Kiel before World War I, making its challenge to the Royal Navy.** BOTTOM: **This photograph is entitled "the last [large calibre] firing of the German fleet" and shows the effect of firing a broadside – and the resulting smoke. The extent of the German challenge to Britannia's rule of the waves was taken seriously by the Royal Navy.**

The result was somewhat different. Britain became concerned that German naval expansion would provoke French and Russian shipbuilding, and therefore concluded a treaty with Japan. The treaty allowed the Royal Navy to maintain only token forces in the East, and other steps were taken to reduce British imperial commitments: Jacky Fisher brought many ships home from their overseas stations, and paid off older warships to man the new. The larger countries of the British Empire were urged to help create an empire navy by establishing their own navies, like the Royal Australian Navy. Then in 1904 Britain unexpectedly joined in an *entente cordiale* with her long-time enemy, France, and, after the annihilation of the Russian navy at the Battle of Tsushima, Britain and Germany were left to face each other across the North Sea. The launch of *Dreadnought* in 1905 temporarily halted battleship building in Germany, while the German navy designed new ships, but once the naval arms race started afresh it became one of the catalysts of World War I. As war loomed, the French navy was persuaded to concentrate its forces in the Mediterranean, while the Royal Navy took on the defence of the North Sea and northern France.

Despite the efforts of Wilhelm II and Tirpitz, the German battleship building programme never came near to matching the Royal Navy and the challenge tailed off with the approach of war as the German army diverted resources from Wilhelm's navy. In the same period 1907–16, USA completed 14 battleships, Japan and France seven each, Italy and Austro-Hungary five each, Brazil and the Argentine two.

The Battle of the Falklands

The Battle of the Falklands in 1914 was regarded as a triumphant vindication of Jacky Fisher's much-criticized concept of the battlecruiser, a name given by the British Admiralty in 1911 to a new class of heavily armed cruisers.

The outbreak of World War I found Admiral von Spee, commanding the German East Asiatic Squadron, cut off in the western Pacific, with half the world and the Royal Navy between him and home. Without supplies of coal Spee's chances of reaching Germany were slim, and he headed for the west coast of South America, detaching one cruiser to make a diversion into the Indian Ocean. The British divided their forces, and a mixed squadron of elderly ships under Admiral Cradock entered the eastern Pacific. The German squadron contained two large vessels, *Scharnhorst* and *Gneisenau*, which were crack gunnery ships. When Cradock clashed with Spee's squadron off Coronel, the Germans were able to hold him at long range, and the British cruisers *Good Hope* and *Monmouth* were sunk on November 1, 1914.

This blow to British prestige unleashed all the latent energy and resource of the oldest and most powerful of the navies. All available cruisers were ordered to concentrate in the River Plate, and from Britain, two of the latest and fastest battle

ABOVE: The battlecruiser *Invincible* was flagship of the British squadron at the Battle of the Falklands in December 1914. Admiral Sturdee's rapid deployment to the South Atlantic, ordered pre-emptorily when more work was still needed in the dockyards at Devonport, was timely and he beat the German admiral to the Falklands by only a few hours.

cruisers, *Inflexible* and *Invincible*, were detached from the Grand Fleet and hurried south under the command of Admiral Sturdee – both battlecruisers still had some dockyard mateys working onboard. Sturdee's order gave him an almost free hand, and, as Commander-in-Chief South Atlantic and Pacific, the largest geographical command ever entrusted to a single admiral. The British force concentrated at the Abrolhos Islands and then steamed on southwards with the ships formed in a scouting line at 19km/12-mile intervals.

Sturdee's ships arrived at the Falklands on December 7, 1914, and as the British coaled their ships, the Germans arrived the following morning. As Spee turned away, his ships belching black smoke, Sturdee ordered his ships to sea and the chase began with the Germans already hull down on the Southern horizon. Spee ordered his light ships to make for South American ports whilst the *Scharnhorst* and *Gneisenau*

prepared to take on the British battlecruisers, who, each flying three ensigns, caught up and commenced firing shortly after 13.00. The Germans were in line abreast chased by the British in quarter line. The fall of shot threw up mountains of water, the peaks rising to over 90m/300ft above the water, but there were few hits at long range.

As *Scharnhorst* and *Gneisenau* turned to port, their firing was "beautiful to watch", with perfect ripple salvos all along their sides. A brown coloured puff with a centre of flames masked each gun as it fired, straddling the British ships, and causing splinter damage. In *Inflexible*, one officer noted, "We could hear the shells coming with a curious shrill whine which gradually got deeper and then pop, pop as they burst in the water". In the German ships the long-range plunging fire of 305mm/12in shells was devastating: one German survivor reported that he could feel his whole ship shake and the decks rippled like a caterpillar. At about 14.00 Spee altered course and drew out of range, but by 15.00 the British had closed the range again, and a fierce exchange began. At 15.40 Spee turned 180 degrees away, and Sturdee turned his ships together to port. Then at 16.20 the *Scharnhorst* suddenly turned over and sank.

TOP: When Spee's German squadron was spotted approaching the Falklands, the British cruiser *Kent* was at anchor and so the first ship to get under way. ABOVE LEFT: *Invincible* making an immense amount of smoke in order to work to her full speed of 22 knots, and flying a battle ensign (probably taken from the cruiser *Carnarvon*). ABOVE: The German battleships *Scharnhorst* (seen here when new in 1910) and *Gneisenau* formed the core of Admiral von Spee's squadron, whose route home was barred by the Royal Navy.

An hour later, after both British battlecruisers had concentrated their fire on *Gneisenau*, she too stopped, gradually turned over and sank. Over 2,000 men were killed in the blazing wrecks or drowned in the freezing waters. Only the German cruiser *Dresden* escaped from the Battle of the Falklands and she was to be hunted down later. Within months of the outbreak of war the German navy's attempts at commerce raiding using surface ships had been brought to an end.

The British battlecruisers had proved they could protect trade and pursue a fleeing enemy, but whether they could also provide a heavy scouting force to the main fleet or close support to the battlefleet would be proved at the Battle of Jutland in 1916.

New bottles for old wine

Even before their heyday at the Battle of Jutland in 1916, the construction of battleships was beginning to falter. In World War I Britain and Italy both had the same operational requirement to manoeuvre on the flanks of their armies and to bombard the enemy with heavy guns. Full-sized battleships, whether obsolete or not, were unsuitable to operate in shallow waters and so specialized ships were built. Although none of these ships bore any resemblance to the low-freeboard monitors of the previous century, the name "monitor" was applied to the resulting single-turret ships.

On the rivers and coasts of the northern Adriatic, the Italian navy converted barges captured from the Austrians into gun platforms, creating a class of monitor that was largely un-armoured. The largest of these were the *Alfredo Cappellini* and *Faa di Bruno,* which used the guns from the battleships *Francesco Morosini* and *Cristoforo Colombo*. The *Monte Santo* and *Monte Sabotino* had guns from the Caracciolo class of battleships, which had been cancelled in 1916.

In Britain, 355mm/14in guns intended for Greece were purchased from their American maker and fitted to the new monitors, which, presumably under Churchill's influence, were

ABOVE RIGHT: **In the line of evolution of the battleship,** *Glatton* **(1871) represents an obscure type designed both for coastal defence and bombardment of the enemy coastal targets.** BELOW: **The Royal Navy took the concept of the coast attack ship and built a large number of monitors during World War I. One of the last of these was** *Terror,* **sunk in the Mediterranean in 1941.**

given the names *Admiral Farragut, General Grant, Robert E. Lee* and *Stonewall Jackson*. However, following protests from the USA their names were changed to *Abercrombie, Havelock, Raglan* and *Roberts*.

During 1914 and 1915 the Majestic class of 1890s vintage pre-Dreadnoughts were laid up to provide their 305mm/12in guns for the Lord Clive class of monitors, this time all named after British generals. Three of these, *Lord Clive, Prince Eugene* and *General Wolfe,* were later fitted with a single 455mm/18in gun in a fixed mounting.

Strangely, the next two monitors were named after French generals, *Marshal Ney* and *Marshal Soult*. They were built with 305mm/12in turret guns taken from the battleship *Ramillies*, thus delaying her completion until 1917. Many smaller monitors were also built, including two coastal defence battleships bought from the Norwegians while under construction, *Gorgon* (ex *Nidaros*) and *Glatton* (ex *Bjorgvin*). Last, largest and most successful to be built were two 380mm/15in gun monitors, *Erebus* and *Terror*. *Erebus* survived torpedoing in 1917, but was sunk by a German dive-bomber off North Africa in 1941.

Characteristic of the new British monitors was their seaworthiness and they saw action in the Dardanelles, in the Adriatic and on the Belgian coast. At the end of the war some were sent to the White Sea and the Baltic to fight the Bolsheviks. Many of the new monitors also carried a single aeroplane for spotting the fall of shot, until they were replaced by shore-based aircraft of the newly formed Royal Naval Air Service. In World War I the Royal Navy led the world in naval aviation and two ships, the battlecruiser *Furious* and the battleship *Eagle* (formerly the Chilean *Almirante Cochrane*) were converted to aircraft carriers. *Furious*, designed as a light battlecruiser with two single 455mm/18in guns, underwent two conversions. In the first conversion she was given a flying-off deck by covering over her forecastle. The aircraft were then recovered from the water by crane after flying off.

In September 1917 she was taken in hand again, her remaining big gun removed and she was given a full length flightdeck. In June 1918 *Furious*'s Camel fighters drove off enemy aircraft and in July they successfully attacked Zeppelin sheds at Tondern in what must rate as the first carrier-borne aircraft strike. *Furious* also served in World War II.

In 1918 the partly completed *Almirante Cochrane* was also purchased for conversion to a through-deck aircraft carrier, although she was not completed until the 1920s. Amongst several other cancelled aircraft carrier projects, the first modern purpose-built aircraft carrier in the world was *Hermes*, laid down in 1918 and completed in 1924.

TOP: **While Germany concentrated on lighter-than-air machines, such as the Zeppelin, the Royal Navy developed the use of fixed-wing aircraft. At first each battleship and cruiser was fitted with one or two aircraft, but soon it was realized that a dedicated ship was needed. As the battleship approached its zenith, the Royal Navy began to build dedicated aircraft carriers. The light battlecruiser *Furious*, with her two single 455mm/18in guns, was converted in two stages.** ABOVE MIDDLE: **The after turret was removed to make a hybrid ship but this was unsuccessful.** ABOVE: **In 1917 she was fully converted before being completely rebuilt between the wars.**

In the USN a class of fast, heavy battlecruisers intended as a counter to the Japanese Kongo class and the British Hoods was cancelled. The two hulls were then taken in hand and built into aircraft carriers, the *Lexington* (CV2) and *Saratoga* (CV3). Likewise steel assembled for *Ranger* was used to build the USN's first purpose-built carrier. However the story of these ships belongs to another book. Aircraft carriers would replace battleships as the capital ships of the future.

North Sea actions 1914–15

The Battle of Heligoland Bight was the first major surface action at sea in World War I when, in late August 1914, Commodore Tyrwhitt, based at Harwich, conducted a sweep into the Heligoland Bight with cruisers and destroyers, while Beatty's First Battle Cruiser Squadron provided cover. On the morning of August 28 Tyrwhitt sank some torpedo boats but was soon outnumbered by the rapid reaction of German cruisers, and as Tyrwhitt fell back on the British battlecruisers, *New Zealand* and *Invincible* were damaged and the cruiser *Arethusa* had to be towed home. The German light cruisers *Mainz*, *Ariadne* and *Köln* were sunk and three other German cruisers were damaged, further enhancing Beatty and Tyrwhitt's reputations as fighting admirals.

Thereafter, the German tactics were to make raids into the North Sea with the hope of drawing individual British ships and formations into U-boat traps where the Royal Navy's numerical superiority could be whittled away until the German High Seas Fleet could meet the British Grand Fleet on more or less equal terms.

On December 16, 1914, the High Seas Fleet Scouting Group, as the German battlecruisers were known, bombarded the English east coast towns of Hartlepool, Whitby and Scarborough. Several hundred civilians were killed or wounded, though not without a coastal battery damaging some of the German ships including the armoured cruiser *Blücher*. Intelligence had given the Royal Navy warning of the raid and six battleships, four battlecruisers and several

TOP: **The German battle fleet during firing practice and manoeuvring for the photographer.** ABOVE: **The Dreadnought revolution coincided with the centenary of the Battle of Trafalgar in 1805, and the names of the new battleships reflect the Nelson age. This is the British battleship *Temeraire* painted by A. B. Cull.**

cruisers, under Admiral Warrender, were deployed. However, the German admiral, Hipper, and his battlecruisers *Seydlitz*, *Moltke*, *Von der Tann*, and *Derfflinger*, plus cruisers and destroyers, was covered by the High Seas Fleet under its Commander-in-Chief, Ingenohl.

Warrender saw Ingenohl's ships and closed, mistaking the High Seas Fleet for the smaller raiding force, while Ingenohl mistook the British force for Jellicoe's Grand Fleet of Battle. Ingenohl acted cautiously, ordering Hipper to proceed with his bombardment without apparently telling him of the British ships, while withdrawing the High Seas Fleet towards its bases. Warrender chased Ingenohl until he realized that the east coast ports to the north of his position were under attack, when he turned towards Hipper.

Meanwhile, eight pre-Dreadnoughts were sailed from Rosyth and the Grand Fleet from Scapa Flow, all three movements threatening to encircle Hipper: however, inept communications by the British allowed him to escape.

When the Germans attempted to repeat their successful raid on the east coast ports in January 1915 the British were pre-warned, again by intelligence, and better prepared. As a result Hipper's three battlecruisers were intercepted by Beatty's five battlecruisers at the Battle of Dogger Bank on January 24, the first direct clash between such ships.

Consequently the armoured cruiser *Blücher* was sunk and Hipper's flagship, the battlecruiser *Seydlitz*, was damaged, while on the British side Beatty's own flagship, *Lion*, was also badly damaged. Nevertheless Beatty transferred to *New Zealand* and continued his pursuit of the Germans until the threat of mines and U-boats caused him to break off the attack. Dogger Bank was a moral victory for the Royal Navy but not a decisive battle, although it made the German navy ever more cautious in its excursions into the North Sea.

One of the more memorable images of the war at sea is that of *Blücher* capsizing with her sides covered with men. *Blücher* was last in the German battle line formation, where she was repeatedly hit. At a range of 18,000m/20,000yds, a shell from *Princess Royal* penetrated her forward ammunition handling spaces causing a catastrophic fire. Beatty might have been able to do more damage to the other German ships but his fleet concentrated their fire on *Blücher* and allowed the other German vessels to escape, although *Seydlitz* was badly damaged and on fire. Like other German ships *Blücher* proved difficult to sink: a torpedo provided the *coup de grâce*.

TOP LEFT: **The Indefatigable class of battlecruisers, one of which was *Australia*, bore the brunt of the North Sea actions. Often by the time squadrons of the Grand Fleet could deploy from Scapa Flow, the Germans had returned to harbour.** TOP RIGHT: **Returning from the bombardment of English east coast towns in January 1915, the armoured cruiser *Blücher* was caught by British forces and sank.** ABOVE: ***Derfflinger* was one of the three battlecruisers under the command of the German admiral Hipper.**

The Battle of Jutland followed much the same theme, with a threatened raid intending to draw out the British fleet which would then be destroyed piecemeal. After Jutland the High Seas Fleet rarely left the Heligoland Bight, and there were few opportunities for the British Grand Fleet to come to grips with its enemy, while Beatty kept the Grand Fleet ready at Scapa Flow.

The Battle of Jutland

Jutland was the greatest battleship engagement of all time. On the outbreak of World War I most Royal Navy officers expected a decisive battle, *der Tag* (the day), between the battleships of the Grand Fleet, commanded by Admiral Jellicoe, and the German High Seas Fleet, commanded by Admiral von Pohl. However, German strategy was defensive, and on sweeps into the North Sea, the Germans avoided contact with the larger Grand Fleet. On the other hand, Beatty, in command of the British battlecruisers, adopted an aggressive strategy and at the Battles of the Heligoland Bight in December 1914 and of Dogger Bank in January 1915 the Germans were lucky to escape without serious losses.

However, when Admiral von Scheer replaced Pohl in command of the High Seas Fleet in January 1916, he prepared a strategy of attrition to counter the Royal Navy's distant blockade. He hoped to defeat the British by making hit-and-run raids on North Sea coastal towns that would bring the ships into battle piecemeal where they would be destroyed by minefields, submarines and local concentrations of superior numbers of German surface warships.

In May 1916 Scheer sent his battlecruisers out, under Admiral Hipper, hoping to draw Beatty's battlecruisers on to the High Seas Fleet. However, when British naval intelligence became aware of these plans, the Grand Fleet sailed from Scapa Flow as well as the battlecruisers from Rosyth.

TOP: **Close-up of the German battlecruiser *Seydlitz* on fire during the Battle of Jutland. Despite her after-turrets being burned out she reached Germany and was repaired.** ABOVE: **The British battleship *Warspite* flying three battle ensigns at about 18.00 during the "run to the north" on May 31, 1916. The German fleet is to the south-east.**

At 15.20 on May 31, 1916, the cruiser *Galatea* made the time-honoured signal "Enemy in sight" and Beatty turned his battlecruisers to the south-east to engage, opening fire at extreme range. As Beatty closed the range, *Indefatigable* and *Queen Mary* were hit and blew up and he uttered his infamous remark that there was "something wrong with our bloody ships today". Later it was thought that the British practice of achieving rapid fire by storing ready-use ammunition in exposed positions might have been the cause of losing these fine ships.

Beatty also lost contact with the supporting Fifth (Fast) Battle Squadron, and, after he had sighted the German High Seas Fleet, at 16.46 he turned towards Jellicoe, thus ending the first phase of the battle known as the run to the south.

At 17.33 Jellicoe and Beatty sighted each other's forces. Warned of the presence of the High Seas Fleet, Jellicoe now deployed the Grand Fleet into line of battle and crossed the head of the German line, but as he did so a third battlecruiser, *Invincible*, was hit and also blew up. At 18.33 Scheer ordered a simultaneous 16-point (180-degree) turn: to Jellicoe it seemed that the Germans had vanished in the haze. Twenty minutes later Scheer ordered another turn and again the head of his line came under fire, then at 19.18 he ordered a final 16-point turn.

Meanwhile Jellicoe, fearing a torpedo attack and unwilling to risk a night action, had made two alterations of course away from the Germans. Jellicoe was much criticized for this: had he taken greater risks at this stage of the battle, there is every possibility that he would have inflicted heavy casualties on the Germans.

As night fell the battlecruisers engaged each other, but during the night Scheer set course for Horns Reef while Jellicoe steered for the Ems River. There were plenty of skirmishes, but no one informed Jellicoe that Scheer was crossing behind him and by morning the seas were empty.

Jutland was a material and tactical victory for Scheer and the High Seas Fleet, and the Germans scored a propaganda victory too by the way they reported the battle. However, it was a strategic victory for the Grand Fleet. While the Germans inflicted losses on the numerically superior Grand Fleet in the ratio of three to one, they had failed to break the British blockade or to wrest control of the North Sea from the Royal Navy.

On the other hand, the Royal Navy had failed to achieve the expected new Trafalgar, and the Navy and its public were bitterly disappointed. The German navy did not come out again until a mutiny and the armistice in 1918. Churchill summed affairs up when he said that Jellicoe was the only person who could have lost the war in an afternoon. The controversy about whether he could have done more continues to the present.

RIGHT: **John Jellicoe was Commander-in-Chief of the British Grand Fleet at the Battle of Jutland, the only man, Churchill said, who could have lost World War I in an afternoon.** FAR RIGHT: **Admiral Scheer commanded the German High Seas Fleet in 1916. His ships sank more than the British and his superior tactical handling of the fleet outwitted Jellicoe.** BELOW: **A German picture of the destruction of the British battlecruiser** *Queen Mary* **during the Battle of Jutland or Skagerrakschlacht at 16.26 on May 31, 1916. Beatty, when he saw his ships blowing up, asked if there was something wrong with the British ships.**

BRITISH LOSSES	GERMAN LOSSES
Battlecruisers	**Battlecruisers**
Indefatigable	Lutzow
Queen Mary	**Pre-Dreadnoughts**
Invincible	*Pommern*
Pre-Dreadnoughts	**Armoured Cruisers**
None	None
Armoured Cruisers	**Light Cruisers**
Black Prince	*Elbing*
Defence	*Frauenlob*
Warrior	*Rostock*
Light Cruisers	*Wiesbaden*
None	**Destroyers**
Destroyers	*S35*
Ardent	*V4*
Fortune	*V27*
Nestor	*V29*
Nomad	*V48*
Shark	**Crew Killed**
Sparrowhawk	2551
Tipperary	
Turbulent	
Crew Killed	
6097	

The scuttling at Scapa Flow

According to the terms of the armistice which brought about a temporary halt to the hostilities of World War I in continental Europe, Germany was obliged to have all her U-boats and about 70 surface warships interned, whose fate would then be decided by the treaty negotiations at Versailles.

When the German fleet steamed for the Firth of Forth they were met at sea by Beatty's Grand Fleet which had formed two parallel columns, comprising nearly 400 warships including 13 squadrons of battleships, battlecruisers and cruisers and the USN Sixth Battle Squadron. The Allied ships were at action stations even though their guns were trained fore and aft.

The German fleet arrived at the Firth of Forth on the morning of November 21. Beatty had no intention of treating this as merely an internment of the German navy, but was determined by stage management to make this an abject surrender, equivalent to major defeat in battle. The German navy was in an incipient state of mutiny, which Beatty dealt with by telling the plenipotentiaries of the Sailors' and Workers' Soviet of the North Sea command to "go to hell", and ordered that "the German flag will be hauled down at sunset and will not be hoisted again without permission".

Over the next few days the German ships were moved in groups to Scapa Flow, where they were all assembled by November 27. By mid-December 1918 the 20,000 crew members who had sailed the ships to Scapa Flow were reduced to maintenance crews of less than 5,000 officers and men, and in June 1919 these were further reduced to skeleton crews of less than 2,000.

TOP: *Seydlitz* leads the German battlecruisers into Scapa Flow on November 21, 1918. ABOVE: A close-up of the *Seydlitz* such as the British had not seen during the war. For four years the British Grand Fleet and the German High Seas Fleet had occupied each other's thoughts and actions. When they finally met, the British fleet was ready for action, though guns were trained fore and aft.

The armistice was extended several times while the treaty negotiations continued, in which, as far as the Royal Navy was concerned, the British were just as anxious to destroy the naval power of Germany as they were to prevent an increase in naval power of any other nation by the acquisition of the German ships. Finally it was agreed that all the interned ships should be surrendered and under the terms of the Treaty of Versailles Germany would only be allowed to keep six of her oldest pre-Dreadnought battleships of the Deutschland or Braunschweig classes, six light cruisers, 12 destroyers and no submarines.

LEFT: German battleship *Kaiser* taken from the air on November 21, 1918. BELOW LEFT: David Beatty, Jellicoe's successor as the Commander-in-Chief of the British Grand Fleet, caught open-mouthed as he watches the German High Seas Fleet entering an internment which he was determined to turn into surrender. BELOW: The wreck of the proud *Seydlitz* after she had been scuttled on June 21, 1919. The salvage of the German fleet took many years: the ships were raised and towed, mostly keel-up, to Scotland where they were broken up in the inter-war years. Some of the work was contracted out, so that by the 1930s there were German tugs, flying the Nazi's Swastika flag, engaged in towing the hulks between Scapa Flow and the Firth of Forth.

However, rather than allow the Royal Navy to seize his ships, Reuter, the German admiral at Scapa Flow, was making preparations to scuttle them. After he had read the details of the Treaty of Versailles in *The Times* newspaper, his only source of reliable intelligence, Reuter sent the cryptic message "Paragraph eleven. Confirm" on June 21, 1919, which was his order to scuttle the fleet. Although the British First Battle Cruiser Squadron immediately returned from exercises it was too late to prevent the German action.

Over 406,420 tonnes/400,000 tons of warships were sunk, including ten battleships (*Kaiser, Prinzregent Luitpold, Kaiserin, König Albert, Friedrich der Grosse, König, Grosser Kurfürst, Kronprinz Wilhelm, Markgraf,* and *Bayern*), and five battle-cruisers (*Seydlitz, Moltke, Von der Tann, Derfflinger* and *Hindenburg*), and also five cruisers and 31 other ships. Twenty-four other ships, including the battleship *Baden*, were beached by the British to prevent them from sinking. Officially the British were outraged and attempted to blame the government in Berlin for ordering the scuttling, but in private senior officers of

the Royal Navy were relieved that the German navy, once second most powerful in the world, had been reduced to a minor status, and that the problem of what to do with the interned ships had been resolved. Perversely Admiral Scheer, the last commander-in-chief of the High Seas Fleet, took pride that the honour of the German navy had somehow been saved.

The remnants of the old Imperial German Navy became the Reichsmarine in April 1919 under the Weimar Republic and were given the task of defending the German Baltic coast against attacks by the Bolsheviks who were consolidating their grip on the Russian state. Salvage operations on the sunken ships at Scapa Flow lasted over the next two decades. It was an ignominious end to Germany's imperial and naval ambitions.

The naval treaties

There were a number of international treaties that attempted to limit naval armaments, including the size and number of battleships. At the end of World War I the most modern units of the German High Seas Fleet had been interned at Scapa Flow, where they were scuttled in 1919, and Britannia, or rather the Royal Navy, once more ruled the waves. However, Japan, which had been following a British naval tradition and an ally since the Anglo-Japanese Treaty of 1902, and the USA, which had sent a squadron of battleships to join the Grand Fleet at Scapa Flow, represented new challenges.

The 1916 US Naval Program had called for ten battleships and six battlecruisers, which would give the United States Navy (USN) a fleet of modern battleships. In contrast, all the Royal Navy's battleships, except *Hood*, which was still incomplete, were pre-war. The Japanese also had a battleship-building programme, as did France and Italy. Then in November 1921, US President Harding convened a naval disarmament conference in Washington.

To the surprise of the British, the USA offered to scrap much of the 1916 and later programmes, and proposed a ten-year holiday on new construction. Specifically, the USA proposed that a ratio should be agreed for the number of ships which should be scrapped, and that the number of battleships retained by each nation should be used to calculate the numbers of other warships each nation could keep. Battleships would only be replaced when they were 20 years old and then they could not exceed 35,560 tonnes/35,000 tons standard displacement (the displacement of a ship fully equipped for sea except for fuel).

TOP: **USN warships being scrapped at Philadelphia in the 1920s. On the right is the battleship *Maine* (down by the bows) and centre (with her cage masts still in place) is the battleship *Wisconsin*. The Washington Naval Treaty caused the world's fleets to be culled.** ABOVE: **The first of a series of interwar naval conferences was staged in Washington in this specially converted theatre, where the delegates knew that they had the opportunity to make history.**

After weeks of negotiation, a formula was agreed of British to American to Japanese battleships in the ratio of 5:5:3, and to limit battleship guns to 405m/16in. A separate Four Power Treaty, which included France, attempted to neutralize the Western Pacific and ended the period of Anglo-Japanese cooperation. France and Italy were given smaller ratios, but France obtained parity in submarine numbers with Britain and the USA. The tonnage and gun size of cruisers was also limited, but not the number, Britain insisting that she needed large numbers of cruisers for the protection of Empire trade. The size of aircraft carriers was set at a maximum of 27,500 tonnes/27,000 tons, and the total tonnage was agreed for Britain and the USA as 35,560 tonnes/35,000 tons each, Japan 82,300 tonnes/81,000 tons, and France and Italy as 61,000 tonnes/60,000 tons each.

The Washington Naval Treaty of 1922, which seemed to have curtailed Anglo-American rivalry while making it impossible for Japan to challenge the USA in the Pacific, was to be effective for 15 years. Several issues remained unresolved but a subsequent naval arms limitation conference at Geneva in 1927 was not successful and France and Italy refused to attend. The British wanted to revise the Washington Treaty to allow 30,500-tonne/30,000-ton battleships with 340mm/13.5in guns. Britain and the USA disagreed about the number of cruisers that should be allowed – the USA wanted parity at 254,000–305,000 tonnes/250,000–300,000 tons for all cruisers. However, the Royal Navy thought it needed over 406,500 tonnes/400,000 tons for the defence of the Empire, and Japan wanted a limit on heavy, 205mm/8in-gun cruisers. The British hoped to set a new limit on the tonnage of submarines. However, the conference formally broke up without agreement though desultory talks continued, while the USA endeavoured to build cruisers to match those of the Royal Navy.

The controversy about cruisers continued at the London Conference of 1930. The Royal Navy conceded a limit of 25,400 tonnes/25,000 tons standard displacement and 305mm/12in guns, and the life was extended to 26 years. This was not accepted, but the numbers of battleships were reduced to a ratio of 15:15:9. A second London Conference was convened in 1935 at which Britain and the USA refused to grant parity to Japan, as this would have given her local superiority in the Far East. Japan then gave notice that she would withdraw from the original Washington Treaty, and Italy followed suit. The main benefit of this conference was the agreement signed by Britain, France and the USA that provided for notice to be given of intended construction. Italy, Germany, Poland and the Soviet Union later assented to this.

TOP: **The Japanese delegation, which came to Washington in 1921, included Count Shidehara (second left) and Admiral Kato. They were disappointed not to achieve parity with Britain and the USA.** ABOVE: **The guns of scrapped warships photographed lying in Philadelphia Navy Yard in 1923.**

Battleship numbers in 1939

COUNTRY	IN SERVICE	UNDER CONSTRUCTION
Britain	15	5
France	7	4
Germany	5	4
Italy	4	4
Japan	10	4
USA	15	8
Total	56	29

In 1935, Britain also agreed to an Anglo-German Naval Agreement that allowed Germany 35 per cent of the British tonnage in all classes of warships.

The Indian Ocean

The World War II battleship campaign in the Indian Ocean is one of the least known and studied, but nevertheless features many key aspects of battleship warfare. Two German surface raiders visited the Indian Ocean: the pocket battleship *Graf Spee* in October 1939, where she claimed a small tanker of 717 tonnes/706 tons south-west of Madagascar and then escaped back into the South Atlantic before Anglo-French hunting groups could find her, and the pocket battleship *Admiral Scheer*, which reached as far as the Seychelles in spring 1941 and was lucky to evade the hunting British cruisers. The purpose of these raids was to cause British and allied warships to disperse and to make them introduce the convoy system, which the Germans regarded as inefficient. However these raids were so short-lived that they had little effect on the actual distribution and deployment of Allied warships.

Until 1942, however, the Indian Ocean remained a relatively safe theatre of operations for the Royal Navy. Admiral Sir James Somerville, who had successfully commanded the battleships and aircraft carriers of Force H based at Gibraltar, had been sent to command a new Eastern Fleet based in Ceylon (Sri Lanka). Somerville formed his fleet in two groups, a fast division consisting of the battleship *Warspite* and two carriers, *Indomitable* and *Formidable*, and a slow division composed of the four battleships *Resolution, Ramillies, Royal Sovereign* and *Revenge*, and the carrier *Hermes*. Both

ABOVE: *Warspite* formed part of the fast division of Admiral Somerville's Eastern Fleet as he manoeuvred to avoid succumbing to superior Japanese naval power. BELOW: The slow division of Somerville's fleet comprised four elderly battleships, including *Ramillies*, which would have been no match for Nagumo's carriers. Thousands of men were engaged, and put at risk, in this strategic deployment.

Colombo and Trincomalee were poorly defended and Somerville made a secret base at Addu Atoll in the Maldives.

In early April the Japanese navy struck into the Indian Ocean. A force of carriers and cruisers entered the Bay of Bengal and sank 23 ships of 113,800 tonnes/112,000 tons, while Japanese submarines attacked shipping on the west coast of India. Meanwhile a strong carrier group (the same ships as had attacked Pearl Harbor) escorted by four fast battleships reached for Ceylon. However, the Japanese admiral Nagumo lost the element of surprise when his force was sighted on April 4 south of Ceylon, and Somerville was able to clear his ships from their ports.

Between April 5 and 9 Japanese air attacks were frustrated, and only a British destroyer and an armed merchant cruiser were caught in harbour, and two heavy cruisers were discovered at sea and sunk. Somerville's aggressive spirit led him to attempt a counter-attack, and the elderly carrier *Hermes* and two of her escorts were sunk when returning to Colombo. The Japanese then left the Indian Ocean, and Somerville, uncertain of where his enemy was, retired, sending his slow group to East Africa and his fast group to Bombay. The Japanese had thus secured their perimeter and reached the high tide of their expansion for little cost in either material or ships.

The British were now concerned about further Japanese raids into the Indian Ocean and about the neutrality of Madagascar, held by the Vichy French. A large force including two carriers and the battleship *Ramillies* was assembled at Durban for Operation Ironclad, the occupation of Diego Suarez, a natural harbour at the northern end of Madagascar. There on May 30 the Japanese counter-attacked using midget submarines and *Ramillies* was severely damaged, needing to be towed back to Durban for temporary repairs.

Thereafter Somerville's Eastern Fleet was reduced to reinforce other theatres, and throughout August he carried out diversionary raids using the carrier *Illustrious* and the battleships *Warspite* and *Valiant*. From September to November 1942 the remainder of the island of Madagascar was occupied and the Indian Ocean was relatively quiet for the next year, during which Axis submarines scored some successes.

In January 1944 the British Eastern Fleet was strengthened by the arrival of *Queen Elizabeth, Valiant, Renown* and several

ABOVE: **The Japanese admiral Nagumo, who had planned and led the air strike on Pearl Harbor, hoped to catch the British in Trincomalee, but Somerville was warned and escaped to a secret anchorage.**

carriers. This was in preparation for a series of strikes against Japanese-held positions on Sumatra beginning on April 19, by which time the Eastern Fleet included the Free French battleship *Richelieu*. Thereafter the war in the Indian Ocean was increasingly prosecuted using carrier-based aircraft, and in August *Valiant* was badly damaged and never again fully repaired after the dry dock she was in collapsed.

In November 1944 the British Eastern Fleet was split into the British East Indies Fleet including the battleships *Queen Elizabeth* and *Renown*, and the British Pacific Fleet based in Australia including the battleships *Howe* and *King George V*. Aircraft carriers, however, predominated in both fleets as the battle moved out of the Indian Ocean. After World War II the Indian Ocean once more became a naval power vacuum, until the growth of the Indian navy in the late 20th century.

RIGHT: **Later in the war the British Eastern Fleet was strengthened by the deployment of fast battleships like *Valiant* and several aircraft carriers. The distances involved were huge and Trincomalee became an important staging post and centre for training for the fleet both in its attack on the Japanese-held East Indies, and in its deployment to the east of Australia, where the British Pacific Fleet would be based.**

LEFT: The 380mm/15in guns of the battleship *Valiant* firing a broadside; astern of her are *Barham* and *Warspite*. These three ships, based at Alexandria in Egypt, formed the backbone of Cunningham's fleet.
ABOVE: "ABC" or Admiral Sir Andrew Cunningham, Commander-in-Chief of the British Mediterranean Fleet, was the greatest British Admiral since Nelson.
BELOW: The battleship *Renown* and the aircraft carrier *Ark Royal* belonged to Force H, which held the western end of the Mediterranean and could be deployed into the Atlantic.

Cunningham and the battleship war in the Mediterranean

The actions between the British and Italian fleets in the Mediterranean in 1940–3 were some of the last involving battleship against battleship, with characteristics reminiscent of the North Sea battles of World War I and a foretaste of the carrier battles in the Pacific. The driving spirit of the British Mediterranean Fleet was "ABC" Cunningham, who in June 1939 became Commander-in-Chief, Mediterranean Fleet, and is widely regarded as the greatest admiral since Nelson.

After the fall of France, the Royal Navy's first objective was the neutralization of the French fleet. When the French turned down all British suggestions to neutralize their fleet at Mers-el-Kebir, Admiral Somerville, commanding Force H, reluctantly fired upon his former allies. The battleship *Bretagne* blew up, *Provence* and *Dunkerque* were badly damaged, but *Strasbourg* escaped to Toulon. *Dunkerque* was torpedoed a few days later by *Ark Royal*'s aircraft. At Alexandria Cunningham persuaded the French Admiral Godfrey to agree to demilitarize his flagship, *Lorraine*.

In July 1940 Cunningham sailed from Alexandria with *Warspite*, *Malaya* and *Royal Sovereign*, and the aircraft carrier *Eagle* to cover convoys in the central Mediterranean. Intelligence told Cunningham that two Italian battleships, *Giulio Cesare* and *Conte di Cavour*, were escorting a convoy to North Africa, and Cunningham changed course to cut them off. *Warspite* hit *Giulio Cesare* at extreme range and as the Italians retreated Cunningham pursued them to within sight of

Calabria, scoring a moral victory which would set the tone for the rest of this war. Off Cape Spartivento on November 27, Force H, led by Somerville in *Renown*, exchanged long-range shots with *Vittorio Veneto* and *Guilio Cesare*, but, handicapped by the slower *Ramillies*, Somerville could not close with his quarry. A few weeks later, on February 9, 1941, Somerville took *Renown*, *Malaya* and the aircraft carrier *Ark Royal* into the Gulf of Genoa to bombard and mine Genoa, Leghorn and La Spezia. This time it was the Italian fleet which was too late to catch the British.

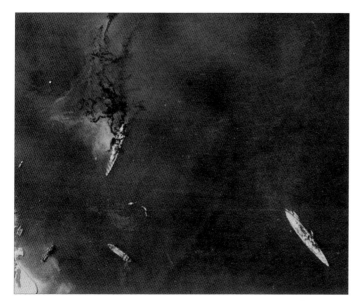

LEFT: **Aerial reconnaisance after the Fleet Air Arm attack on** *Taranto* **showed one Italian Cavour class battleship badly damaged, one beached with a heavy list to starboard and the other with her stern submerged and leaking oil.** ABOVE: **The Italian battleship** *Caio Duilio* **photographed on the morning after the attack, with the whole of her starboard side submerged.** BELOW: **The sad end for one of** *Illustrious*'s **Swordfish, recovered from the harbour after the attack on** *Taranto.* **Despite their frailty, the Swordfish could survive considerable damage.**

When Cunningham planned Operation Judgement in November 1941 – a complex passage of ships through the Mediterranean and an attack on the Italians in Taranto harbour – the Italians outnumbered Cunningham in every class of ship except carriers. *Malaya, Ramillies, Valiant* and *Warspite* formed the covering force, while torpedo-bombers from the carrier *Illustrious* sank or badly damaged *Vittorio Veneto, Caio Duilio* and *Conte di Cavour*. Japanese naval officers studied the results as they prepared for an attack on the US fleet at Pearl Harbor.

At the Battle of Cape Matapan in March 1941, the Italians sent the battleship *Vittorio Veneto* to interrupt British convoys south of Greece, and, again warned by intelligence, Cunningham sailed his ships. British cruisers retired eastwards towards Cunningham's battleships, hoping to draw the Italians into a trap, while the Italian Admiral Iachino hoped to catch them between his heavy cruisers and the *Vittorio Veneto*. However, aircraft from the carrier *Formidable* attacked the Italian battleship, and, without his own air cover, Iachino realized he must retreat westwards. *Vittorio Veneto* was hit once by torpedo, and the heavy cruiser *Pola* was stopped, also by a torpedo.

Iachino ordered ships to protect *Pola*, but shortly after ten o'clock that night, radar in the British battleships revealed their position. Immediately, *Barham, Valiant* and *Warspite* opened fire at close range sinking two Italian heavy cruisers, and in the night fighting which followed two Italian destroyers and *Pola* were sunk.

However, the end of the battleship age was marked in the Mediterranean by the dramatic sinking of the elderly *Barham*, which on November 25, 1941, with the battleships *Queen Elizabeth* and *Valiant* formed part of Force K hunting for Italian

convoys off North Africa. She was hit by three torpedoes from the German submarine *U-331*, quickly capsized and blew up with large loss of life.

Battleships played a supporting role in the Allied landings in North Africa and Sicily and in Italy. In November 1942 three US battleships covered the landings at Casablanca, whilst in the Mediterranean Force H covered the landings in Algeria. At Salerno in September 1943 the heavy guns of *Warspite* and *Valiant*, turned on targets ashore, played a major role in stopping a German counter-attack.

The surrender of the Italian fleet released the Royal Navy's capital ships for duties elsewhere and the war at sea in the Mediterranean was then mostly conducted by light ships. Nevertheless, during Operation Dragoon, the last major landings in the Mediterranean, in southern France, there were five battleships, one British, three American and a Frenchman, fighting for the liberty of France.

LEFT: **Pearl Harbor, December 7, 1941: a Japanese aerial picture that shows "battleship row" already under attack. A British officer who visited earlier and saw the Americans' lack of preparedness had noted "you can't miss".** ABOVE: **Admiral Isoroku Yamamoto, architect of the pre-emptive attack on Pearl Harbor, who realized that the only hope of defeating the USA was to wipe out its fleet. He might have succeeded but intelligence did not tell him that the USN carriers were not present.**

Nemesis at Pearl Harbor

When the British battleship *Warspite* visited Pearl Harbor in August 1941 one of her officers, a veteran of the Fleet Air Arm in the Mediterranean, saw battleship row and remarked, "Blimey, you can't miss!" The Imperial Japanese Navy (IJN) had followed events in the Mediterranean, particularly the attack on Taranto in which a handful of unsophisticated biplanes had crippled the Italian battle fleet.

The Washington Naval Treaty was aimed at preventing a naval arms race and forbade the building of naval bases closer to Japan than Singapore (UK) and the Philippines (USA). However, the Anglo-Japanese treaties were not renewed, and after the conquest of Manchuria in 1937, Japan invaded China. The USA aided China and imposed sanctions on Japan, eventually cutting off the supply of oil and raw materials. By 1940, Japan had aligned herself with Nazi Germany and was developing plans to occupy South-east Asia and seize the resources she needed. The Japanese army and navy were well versed in amphibious warfare and naval aviation, but the threat to Japanese plans was the US Navy (USN) fleet based at Pearl Harbor, Hawaii. Earlier in the century, the IJN had launched a pre-emptive strike on Port Arthur, and now Admiral Yamamoto devised a plan to annihilate the USN with a surprise attack.

The key element of Yamamoto's plan was the surprise use of aircraft carriers and naval aircraft on a scale never seen before. Training began in the spring of 1941, and the plan was approved in October. The carrier force commanded by Vice

Admiral Chuichi Nagumo consisted of six heavy aircraft carriers and their escorts, and a submarine force was deployed to sink any American warships that escaped from Pearl Harbor. Nagumo's fleet assembled in a remote anchorage in the Kurile Islands and crossed the northern Pacific unobserved. By dawn on Sunday December 7, 1941, the Nagumo fleet was some 320km/200 miles north of Hawaii.

At 06.00, the first wave of 181 planes composed of torpedo bombers, dive-bombers and fighters attacked the USN's Pacific Fleet at its anchorage and achieved complete surprise. There were more than 90 ships at anchor in Pearl Harbor, including eight battleships, seven in a row off Ford Island, and the *Pennsylvania* in dry dock close by. Within minutes of the first attack, all had been bombed and torpedoed. *West Virginia* sank quickly; *Oklahoma* turned turtle; a fire in *Arizona* ignited the forward magazine and she blew up; *California, Maryland, Tennessee, Pennsylvania,* and *Nevada* were also damaged.

Half an hour later, a second wave of 170 Japanese planes made a concentrated attack on *Nevada*, which despite damage got underway. However, *Nevada* had to be beached to keep the channel clear. The Japanese attack on Pearl Harbor ended shortly before 10.00 am, by which time 21 USN ships were sunk or damaged including, in addition to the battleships, three cruisers, four destroyers, a seaplane tender, the former battleship *Utah* (converted to a target), a repair ship, a minelayer, a tug and a floating dock. The Japanese had also

ABOVE: *Nevada* was the only USN battleship to get underway during the attack and is seen here moving away from other burning ships. Her ensign is still in the harbour position. RIGHT: The battleships *West Virginia* and *Tennessee* still upright but burning fiercely after the attack was over. Both ships were later repaired and fought in the Pacific theatre. BELOW RIGHT: *Arizona* was not to be so lucky. After a raging fire reached her forward magazine, she blew up. The US President called it "a day of infamy", and the effect of the attack was to shock and mobilize the American people and especially the USN. It was inevitable that the USA with its superior industrial might would eventually prevail over Japan.

struck at the airfields of Hawaii, where over 188 US aircraft were destroyed and 159 damaged, mostly on the ground.

Japanese losses were less than 10 per cent of the attacking aircraft, yet the attack on Pearl Harbor was not as successful as it might have been. By chance, there were no USN aircraft carriers in harbour. The carriers *Enterprise* and *Lexington* were at sea delivering aircraft reinforcements to other American Pacific bases and *Saratoga*, which might also have been present, was in refit on the West Coast. Damage to the harbour installations was slight, and these were quickly brought back into full use, and all but three ships sunk or damaged at Pearl Harbor were salvaged. Of the battleships, *Arizona* was too badly damaged to be raised, *Oklahoma* was raised but considered too old to be worth repair, and *Utah* was already considered obsolete.

President Roosevelt called the attack on Pearl Harbor "a day of infamy", while the blow to American prestige and anger at the sudden and unexpected strike precipitated the USA into World War II, with the USA declaring war on Germany as well as Japan.

Hunt for the *Bismarck*

Following the success of Operation Berlin in which the battleships *Scharnhorst* and *Gneisenau* had sunk 22 allied merchant ships during a two-month raid into the Atlantic, a new operation was planned. Operation Rheinübung would use Germany's newest and most powerful battleship, *Bismarck*. Originally, it was intended that *Scharnhorst* and *Gneisenau* would sail from Brest too, but neither was operational after being bombed. Consideration was also given to delaying the operation until *Tirpitz* was worked up, but the German leadership could not wait and the heavy cruiser *Prinz Eugen* was selected as *Bismarck*'s consort. The supporting force consisted of two supply ships, five tankers and two scouting ships despatched secretly into the Atlantic.

However, both warships were seen heading north off the Swedish coast and Fleet Air Arm reconnaissance confirmed that they had sailed from Bergen. *Bismarck* and the cruiser *Prinz Eugen* were next detected in the Denmark Strait late on May 23, by the watching British heavy cruisers *Suffolk* and *Norfolk*, who shadowed until the morning of May 24, 1940, when the battlecruiser *Hood* and the new battleship *Prince of Wales* came into action.

At 05.32, *Hood* opened fire on *Prinz Eugen* at 21km/13 miles range, and both German ships replied, firing at *Hood*. A fire started on *Hood*'s upper deck and at about 06.00 the Bismarck's fifth salvo hit and *Hood* blew up. The German fire now shifted to *Prince of Wales*, hitting several times and killing or wounding everyone on the bridge except the captain. However, *Bismarck* had been hit with two or three 355mm/14in shells before breaking off the action.

Although *Bismarck* was losing fuel and shipping water, the German admiral, Lütjens, decided to continue his North Atlantic sortie. With one boiler room out of action and speed reduced to 28 knots, he first feinted north while ordering *Prinz Eugen* to proceed independently, and then resumed a course towards western France.

TOP LEFT: **This stern view of the German battleship *Bismarck* gives some idea of the strength and size of the German monster. Nevertheless, though she sank the British *Hood*, her career was measured in months.** ABOVE: **Battle at sea between battleships took place at long range and often all either side saw of the enemy was distant smoke on the horizon.**

Around midnight Fleet Air Arm Swordfish torpedo bombers from the carrier *Victorious* found *Bismarck*, launched their torpedoes and hit her amidships on the armoured belt, with no apparent effect. Then during the night, *Bismarck* shook off *Norfolk* and *Suffolk*, which had been keeping contact by radar. Lütjens now had a chance to escape but, assuming that he was still being shadowed by radar, he thought that nothing would be lost by a long signal to Germany that gave away his position.

After 30 hours without a sighting, a Catalina flying-boat of the RAF, flown by a USN officer, Ensign Smith, spotted *Bismarck* on May 26. He held contact under fire while radioing *Bismarck*'s position and the cruiser *Sheffield* was able to resume shadowing.

LEFT: *Hood* at sea at speed painted by Edward Tufnell. *Hood* was an icon for the Royal Navy, regarded as one of the most handsome ships and, after her world cruise in the interwar years, certainly one of the best known. Her loss in May 1941 shocked the British nation and Royal Navy. BELOW: *Hood*'s consort was *Prince of Wales*, which was hit on the bridge, killing everyone there apart from her captain, but not before *Prince of Wales* had inflicted damage on the German. She broke off the engagement but remained in contact until she ran short of fuel.

ABOVE: In the final stage of the battle, *Rodney* closed to a few thousand metres/yards to pulverize *Bismarck* at the modern equivalent of point blank range while the battleship *King George V* stood off and hit *Bismarck* with plunging fire.

Meanwhile the Royal Navy was gathering in the Atlantic. On May 22, Admiral Tovey with the capital ships *King George V* and *Repulse* and the carrier *Victorious* had steamed west and south from Scapa Flow. *Rodney* and *Ramillies* had left their convoys and were steaming south-west and Captain Vian with the Fourth Destroyer Flotilla had left a troop convoy to sail east. *Bismarck*, although more than 600 miles from France, might yet reach safety before the Royal Navy could catch up.

However, Force H, consisting of the battlecruiser *Renown* and carrier *Ark Royal* were approaching from Gibraltar. A torpedo strike by Swordfish biplanes on the afternoon of May 26 found the shadowing *Sheffield* in error. As darkness fell, a second strike found its target but cloud offered little protection against *Bismarck*'s radar laid guns, and as the Swordfish converged from different bearings, *Bismarck* used her heavy

guns to raise walls of water against the frail aircraft. Many aircraft were damaged but none were lost and two torpedoes hit their target, jamming the rudders and dooming *Bismarck*. As engineers tried to free her steering, *Bismarck* steered north towards the British, while Captain Vian and his destroyers, including the Polish *Piorun*, made a series of torpedo attacks.

At 08.45 on May 27, Tovey's heavy ships caught up and opened fire. At first, *Bismarck*'s reply was accurate but she quickly became a wreck as *Rodney*'s 405mm/16in guns found the enemy range. *Rodney* closed to 3,650m/4,000 yards to fire at point blank range while *King George V*'s fire from 12,800m/14,000 yards plunged down on *Bismarck*, and, within 30 minutes, coordinated resistance had ceased. The fire-control positions were out of action, communications to the engine rooms and compartments below the armoured deck had been lost, and fires raged. A myth would grow up that *Bismarck*'s crew scuttled her, but between 10.15 and 10.35, the cruiser *Dorsetshire* torpedoed *Bismarck* from port and starboard, finally causing *Bismarck* to heel over and sink in five minutes. Only 115 men survived from a crew of more than 2,000.

Battleship versus battleship in the Pacific

LEFT: The modern *Washington* photographed off New York in August 1942. Her encounter with the elderly Japanese *Kirishima* in November was the last battleship-to-battleship engagement. BELOW: *Kirishima*, built as a battlecruiser, had been modernized with new guns and new armour in the interwar years and the Japanese navy rated her as a battleship. She is seen here in Sukumo Bay, 1937. The cut-away forecastle discloses her World War I origins and the upright funnels suggest a British provenance to her design.

The last great battle involving battleships would not be until the Battle of Leyte Gulf in October 1944, but by then battleships were ancillary to aircraft carriers and naval aircraft. However, the last battle in which battleship fought battleship in the Pacific was during the epic months-long struggle between the Japanese and the Americans over Guadalcanal in the Solomon Islands. The Japanese hoped to turn the Solomons into a base to cut off Australia, and in 1942 started to build airfields along the chain of islands. In turn, the Americans wanted to use Guadalcanal as their base of operations against the Japanese further north.

The first Battle of Savo took place on 12/13 November as the Japanese tried to reinforce their troops on the island and to bombard Henderson airfield: the Japanese force was centred on the battleships *Hiei* and *Kirishima*. The ensuing battle by night and in heavy rain was disorganized and both sides suffered as their formations passed through each other. The American cruisers and destroyers suffered more but the Japanese battleship *Hiei* sank next day.

Two nights later, on November 14/15, the Japanese *Kirishima*, the heavy cruisers *Atago* and *Takao*, the light cruisers *Nagara* and *Sendai*, and nine destroyers tried to bombard Henderson Field again.

Although *Kirishima* was constructed as a battlecruiser and completed in 1915, she had twice been modernized, in 1927–30 and 1935–6: her armour was improved, she was lengthened and had modern machinery installed. Armed with eight 355mm/14in guns, the Japanese rated her as a battleship.

She had received light damage during a night action off Guadalcanal on November 12/13, when she met the Americans again. Her opponents this time were the two new battleships *Washington* and *South Dakota*, both completed within the last few months and armed with nine 405mm/16in guns, and their escort of four destroyers.

The Americans were in line ahead, in the order: four destroyers, *Washington* and *South Dakota* as they made a sweep north between Russell and Guadalcanal, then east and south-east, passing north of Savo. At about midnight contacts were seen on radar to the east, and *Sendai* and a destroyer immediately came under heavy fire. A few minutes later *Nagara* and the Japanese destroyers engaged the American destroyers, sinking three and damaging the fourth.

However, *South Dakota* had been illuminated and came under particularly heavy gun and torpedo attack. None of the 30 torpedoes hit her but she was hit several times by shellfire and lost electrical supply to her radar. According to the American admiral's official report, "What appeared to be the South Dakota was seen at about 01.21 at a considerable distance to the south-eastward between this ship and Guadalcanal on a southerly course".

Meanwhile *Washington*, which had not been engaged by the Japanese, succeeded in closing the range. From 00.16 to 00.19 *Washington* fired 42 405mm//16in rounds and her gunnery was highly effective. Fire opened at 17,000m/ 18,500yd range and hits were obtained by the third salvo.

She opened fire again between 01.00 and 01.07 after the target had been tracked by radar. The range was 7,700m/8,400yd and a hit was probably obtained on the first salvo and certainly on the second. *Kirishima* was hit nine times and burst into flames. Her return fire ceased and she was seen on radar to perform a 500-degree turn and draw off to the north-east.

The last major Japanese naval thrust at Guadalcanal had been turned back. *Washington* had done what she had been designed for and defeated one of her kind. In fact, *Washington* was the only American battleship to defeat another battleship. All the other battleship duels between the USN and the Imperial Japanese Navy involved ship- or land-based aircraft.

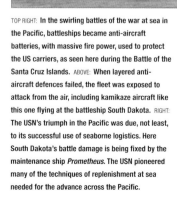

TOP RIGHT: **In the swirling battles of the war at sea in the Pacific, battleships became anti-aircraft batteries, with massive fire power, used to protect the US carriers, as seen here during the Battle of the Santa Cruz Islands.** ABOVE: **When layered anti-aircraft defences failed, the fleet was exposed to attack from the air, including kamikaze aircraft like this one flying at the battleship South Dakota.** RIGHT: **The USN's triumph in the Pacific was due, not least, to its successful use of seaborne logistics. Here South Dakota's battle damage is being fixed by the maintenance ship** *Prometheus.* **The USN pioneered many of the techniques of replenishment at sea needed for the advance across the Pacific.**

Battleship war in the Pacific

During World War II, the conflict in the east was primarily a naval war. After the Japanese attack on Pearl Harbor and the sinking of *Repulse* and *Prince of Wales* on December 10, 1941, the Japanese enjoyed an unbroken series of victories. Their aim was to occupy the American bases at Guam and Wake, capture the Philippines, seize Burma, Malaya, Singapore, and the Dutch East Indies, and then to fortify a ring of islands in the south and the central Pacific. The plan seemed to be successful and by early 1942 the Japanese had conquered an empire.

However, Japanese expansion reached its high-water mark in March 1942. The US Navy (USN) had been studying its strategy for a war in the Pacific for many years. The result was Plan Orange, which envisaged a campaign stretching across the Pacific Ocean and culminating in a decisive battle with the Imperial Japanese Navy (IJN). Accordingly, Admiral Nimitz began his counter-attack and in May 1942 the Japanese advance was stopped at the Battle of the Coral Sea. A month later, the Japanese suffered a major defeat at the Battle of Midway in the central Pacific. In August 1942, US Marines landed on Guadalcanal, beginning a month-long battle for possession. USN carrier-borne aircraft had supported the landings, but when the carriers withdrew the Japanese were able to counter-attack, and at the Battle of Savo Island, the Japanese navy sank four heavy cruisers, including the Australian *Canberra*, and one destroyer. Neither side could establish clear naval nor air superiority and the success of the campaign swung in the balance: Guadalcanal became a battle of attrition and in such a campaign the Americans were bound eventually to win.

The USN's strategy required resources and it required the development of the tactics and techniques of amphibious warfare and naval air power. Battleships were to play an

ABOVE: **Three ships from the South Dakota class were present at the Battle of Leyte Gulf:** *South Dakota*, *Massachusetts* and *Alabama*. **Here one of them fires a broadside from her main batteries.** LEFT: **Admiral Chester W Nimitz, the USN Commander-in-Chief Pacific during World War II, who led the US naval offensive, first from the Solomon Islands in 1942 to the north and west, and then, in 1944, to the coasts of the Japanese islands.**

ancillary role, bombarding enemy positions ashore and providing anti-aircraft defence for the fleet: as the war developed, USN battleships were massively rearmed with light guns. In November 1943, American industrial might was able to provide Nimitz with the strength he needed for an island-hopping campaign, and when US Marines met stubborn resistance and learned costly lessons, Nimitz opted to avoid strongly held islands and strike at the enemy's weakest points.

In 1944 and 1945 these hops developed into leaps as two amphibious offensives developed, American General MacArthur advancing via New Guinea into the Philippines and Nimitz reaching 3,200km/2,000 miles across the ocean from the Gilbert Islands to Okinawa. It was clear that while the Americans could replace their resources, the Japanese could not. At the Battle of the Philippine Sea in what USN pilots called "the great Marianas turkey shoot", Japanese naval air power was destroyed.

In October 1944, the Japanese navy planned to use their last carriers, including two hybrid conversions from battleships, *Ise* and *Hyuga*, to decoy American forces away from the beachheads of Leyte Gulf to enable their battleships to bombard them and to destroy the shipping offshore. The plan almost succeeded, with two battleship forces planned to converge on the invasion beaches. A southern force consisted of the battleships *Fuso* and *Yamashiro*, while a central force contained the five battleships *Yamato, Musashi, Nagato, Kongo* and *Haruna*. Opposing them were the six USN battleships *Iowa, New Jersey, Massachusetts, South Dakota,*

Washington, and *Alabama*: however, the USN fleet also contained 32 aircraft carriers and over 1,700 aircraft with experienced pilots, whereas the Japanese could only muster three carriers and fewer than 200 planes. The battle raged over several hundred miles of sea and although the Japanese reached the invasion beaches, they did not press home their attack. At the end of the Battle of Leyte Gulf, the Imperial Japanese Navy had effectively ceased to exist.

Japanese resistance did not end with the destruction of their fleet and in April 1945 off Okinawa, the Japanese launched large-scale suicide raids resulting in 26 Allied warships being sunk and many more damaged. A date had been set for the invasion of Japan when atomic bombs were dropped on Hiroshima and Nagasaki on August 6 and 9, 1945, and in Tokyo Bay on September 2, 1945, the battleship *Missouri* provided a theatrical background for the signing of the Japanese surrender. Also present were the American battleships *Colorado, Mississippi, Idaho, New Mexico, Iowa, South Dakota* and *West Virginia*, and the British battleships *King George V* and *Duke of York*.

The USA emerged from the war with global commitments and the largest navy the world had ever seen, but the age of the battleship was almost over.

ABOVE LEFT: **Many lonely beaches became battlegrounds, such as this beach in Leyte Gulf where Japanese shipping was bombed and strafed from the air by the advancing Allies' naval aircraft.** LEFT: **By 1945 nowhere was safe for Japanese battleships, not even their own home port of Kure, seen here under high level attack by the USAF.** ABOVE: **As Japanese air power waned, the Japanese resorted to kamikaze or suicide attacks, in which young inexperienced pilots tried to crash their aircraft into Allied ships. The damage caused – seen here in the Australian cruiser *Australia* – could be severe.**

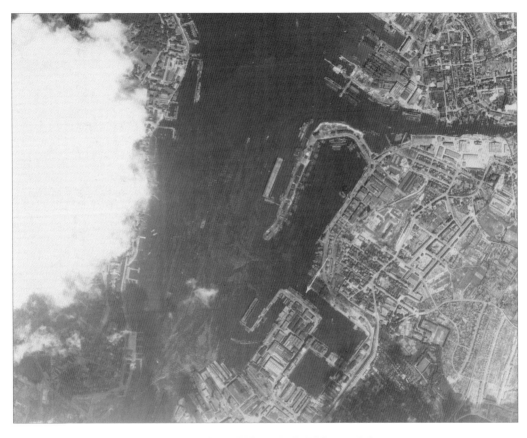

The German navy in World War II

In 1933–6 the revived German navy completed building the pocket battleships *Deutschland, Admiral Scheer* and *Admiral Graf Spee*. In 1935 the Anglo-German Naval Agreement was concluded, which allowed the Germans to build up to 35 per cent of the British warship tonnage. The Germans also drew up a secret "Plan Z" which by 1945 would give their navy six battleships, four pocket battleships and four battlecruisers in addition to the four battleships and three pocket battleships already in existence. However the outbreak of hostilities was to intervene well before this plan could be fulfilled.

In August 1939 two German pocket battleships, their supply ships and a force of U-boats were deployed into the Atlantic. On September 30, *Admiral Graf Spee* sank her first ship, and seven British and French hunting groups including three battleships were formed to hunt her down. After a brief sortie in November into the Indian Ocean, *Admiral Graf Spee* returned to the South Atlantic. On December 13 she met Force G, consisting of one heavy and two light cruisers, and was driven into Montevideo and scuttled.

ABOVE: **Through the cloud, aerial reconnaissance of Kiel, the German navy's base at the eastern or Baltic end of the Kiel canal, shows *Scharnhorst* alongside and vulnerable to attack.**

Meanwhile her sister ship *Deutschland* sank two ships in the North Atlantic and was ordered home where Hitler, fearing a loss of prestige should she be damaged or sunk under the name of the fatherland, had her renamed *Lützow*.

In early October *Gneisenau* sortied off Norway in a repeat of World War I tactics, to draw British ships within range of German U-boats and aircraft. *Hood, Nelson, Repulse, Rodney* and *Royal Oak* all sailed but did not make contact.

On November 23 *Scharnhorst* and *Gneisenau*, while attempting a breakout into the Atlantic, sank the armed merchant cruiser *Rawalpindi* but returned to Germany to avoid the searching British ships.

During the Norway Campaign in spring 1940 the battlecruisers *Scharnhorst* and *Gneisenau* covered the northern landings, and were briefly engaged by the British *Renown*, with

LEFT: *Scharnhorst* and *Gneisenau* were blockaded in western France for many months, but in February 1942 made a daring dash up the English Channel. Their escape was a tactical defeat for the Royal Navy but a strategic blunder for the Germans.

mutual, slight damage. The Germans escaped in a snowstorm and there were to be no other battleship-to-battleship engagements. However *Scharnhorst* was hit by a torpedo from the destroyer *Acasta* and again on June 13 by aircraft from *Ark Royal*. On June 20 *Gneisenau* was torpedoed by the submarine *Clyde*, blowing a huge hole in her bows. As a result both ships were out of action until the end of the year.

Between October 1940 and March 1941 *Admiral Scheer* raided in the Atlantic and Indian Oceans, sinking 16 ships of 100,650 tonnes/99,059 tons, including the armed merchant cruiser *Jervis Bay* and five ships of convoy HX84. The disruption to convoys across the Atlantic had a very serious effect on Britain, and diverted battleships to convoy protection. On February 8, 1941, *Scharnhorst* and *Gneisenau* found convoy HX106 escorted by *Ramillies* but declined to attack and *Ramillies* was too slow to catch them up. In March *Scharnhorst* and *Gneisenau* were sighted by aircraft from *Malaya* escorting convoy SL67 but again they escaped, finally taking refuge in Brest having sunk 22 merchant ships.

The hunt for the *Bismarck* is told separately, but her loss marked the end of independent raiding by German surface warships in the Atlantic, and when in June *Lützow* attempted a breakout she was torpedoed and forced to return to Germany.

The ships at Brest suffered repeated bomber attacks, and on February 11–13, 1942, they made a daring escape. The Channel Dash of *Scharnhorst, Gneisenau* and the cruiser *Prinz Eugen* was an embarrassment and a tactical defeat, but also a strategic gain for the Royal Navy. The Brest Squadron ceased to be a threat to convoys, the heavy ships were damaged by mines and two weeks later *Gneisenau* was so badly bombed at Kiel that she never went to sea again.

TOP RIGHT: **At the end of the Norway Campaign in the spring of 1940, during the invasion and counter-invasion of Norway by Germany and by Britain and her allies, the British carrier *Glorious* was caught and sunk by the German navy on June 8. Here the German warship *Scharnhorst* fires on the carrier.** RIGHT: **The German warships *Scharnhorst*, *Gneisenau* and *Hipper* at anchor in a Norwegain fjord in 1940.**

Thereafter the concentration of German ships in Norwegian waters dominated Royal Navy strategy in the north. The convoys had to be given strong escorts, including ships such as the battleships *Duke of York, Renown* and *King George V*, together with aircraft carriers.

Between March 6 and 9, 1942, *Tirpitz* was hunted by the British Home Fleet but when she was located, aircraft from the carrier *Victorious* failed to press home the attack. However *Tirpitz* never put to sea again. The story of convoy PQ17 and the Battles of the Barents Sea and of North Cape in 1942 and 1943 is also told separately.

Tirpitz was finally destroyed by RAF action in November 1944. In March 1945 *Gneisenau* was sunk as a block ship at Gdynia, in April *Admiral Scheer* was bombed and capsized, and shortly before Germany surrendered on 8 May, *Lützow*, the last of the German battleships, was scuttled.

Convoy PQ17 and the Battles of the Barents Sea and the North Cape

Hitler became obsessed with the idea that the British would invade Norway, and he wanted his heavy ships stationed there, where they were also a threat to the Arctic convoys which the Allies were pushing through to Russia. By July 1942 the threatening German ships consisted of *Tirpitz*, *Lützow*, *Admiral Scheer* and others. So when convoy PQ17 of 36 ships left Iceland on June 27 the escort consisted of American and British cruisers and destroyers, and the covering force contained the British *Duke of York* and carrier *Victorious*, and the USN battleship *Washington*. When on July 3 a false appreciation of intelligence led the Admiralty in London to withdraw the escort and concentrate the fleet against a reported movement by *Tirpitz*, there was a massacre of the convoy by U-boats and aircraft. Only 11 ships eventually reached Archangel over the next few days and weeks. In fact *Tirpitz*'s sortie was half-hearted, but the threat was sufficient to denude the convoy of its escort and halt Arctic convoys for the next three months.

In December 1942 convoy JW51B of 14 ships sailed from Scotland for Russia escorted by destroyers under the command of Captain Rupert Sherbrooke in *Onslow*, and covered by the cruisers *Jamaica* and *Sheffield*. Opposing the convoy were *Tirpitz* and *Lützow*, the cruisers *Admiral Hipper*, *Köln* and *Nürnberg*, and several destroyers. This long series of quickly changing and confused actions became known as the Battle of the Barents Sea.

As the convoy passed south of Bear Island in the darkness and snow, *Lützow*, *Hipper* and six destroyers put to sea to intercept it, and, on the morning of New Year's Eve, *Hipper* and three destroyers attacked the convoy from the north, driving it towards Lützow in the south. *Hipper* first fired on the destroyer *Obdurate*, but her approach to the convoy was thwarted by the destroyers *Onslow*, *Orwell* and *Obedient*, although Sherbrooke (who was subsequently awarded the VC) was badly wounded.

TOP: **Throughout World War II the German navy used the Norwegian fjords to try and outflank the Royal Navy and as bases for sorties into the Atlantic, or to attack Russian conveys. Here Admiral Hipper, Admiral Scheer and escorts leave for an operation.** ABOVE: **Threat of German capital ships to the Russian convoy caused the allies much anxiety, and in July 1942, after convoy PQ17 had been ordered to scatter, the route was abandoned until the days grew shorter.**

TOP LEFT: **A World War I picture of Admiral Franz von Hipper, who led the German battlecruisers at the Battle of Jutland in 1916.** ABOVE: **The Germans tried to hide their ships using camouflage and smokescreens when attacked.** LEFT: **The heavy cruiser** *Hipper,* **shown here at anchor in a Norwegian fjord, was part of the forces that threatened allied convoys.** BELOW: **Admiral Sir Bruce Fraser, photographed in January 1944 on the quarterdeck of** *Duke of York* **with his band of brothers, after the last-ever action between capital ships in home waters.**

Hipper sank a minesweeper and damaged the destroyer *Achates*, but when the British cruisers announced their arrival with accurate radar-laid gunfire *Hipper* was damaged and an escorting destroyer, *Friedrich Eckoldt*, was sunk. *Hipper* still tried to get into the convoy but the destroyers skilfully used smoke and the threat of torpedoes to keep her out.

Meanwhile *Lützow* approached from the south but was timidly managed and driven off by the remaining British destroyers: by noon of a very short midwinter's day both German ships were withdrawing, chased by their smaller opponents. The convoy reached Kola without loss whilst *Hipper* never saw action again, and *Lützow*'s intended breakout into the Atlantic was thwarted. When Hitler learned that the heavy German units had been driven off by light cruisers and destroyers, he raged, calling the heavy ships a waste of resources and ordering them to be paid off. The order was rescinded but Grand Admiral Raeder resigned.

Nearly one year later, on December 20, 1943, convoy JW55B consisting of 19 ships sailed for Russia covered by *Duke of York* and the cruiser *Jamaica*, while the return convoy RA55A sailed from Kola on December 23 protected by the cruisers *Belfast*, *Norfolk* and *Sheffield*. On Christmas Day *Scharnhorst* and five destroyers sailed to intercept. As convoy JW55B passed south of Bear Island in stormy weather, *Scharnhorst*'s approach was detected on radar and she was fired on and hit by the cruiser *Norfolk*. As *Scharnhorst* tried to

work to the north round the convoy, she was again engaged by the British cruisers and hit, although *Norfolk* was in turn badly damaged by 280mm/11in shells.

Scharnhorst then turned south away from the convoy but she was shadowed on radar, and her position reported to *Duke of York*, who was in an ideal position to the south-west to cut off her retreat. In a coordinated attack the cruisers fired starshells and attacked from one side of *Scharnhorst* while *Duke of York*, with the cruiser *Jamaica* close astern to confuse German radar, attacked from the other. The British battleship's 355mm/14in guns soon found their range and *Scharnhorst* was quickly silenced and finished off by some 10 or 11 torpedoes, sinking with huge loss of life.

The Battle of the North Cape was the last battleship-on-battleship action that took place between the Royal Navy and the German navy.

Where are they now?

Plenty of examples of battleships from all three phases of their development are still in existence today. Of the first phase, from what might be called the dead-end lines of development, a number of examples can be seen. The *Huascar*, a turret ship built in 1865 for the Peruvian navy, survives in Talcahuano, Chile. The 1868 French-built *Schorpioen* of the Netherlands navy, one of four ships of her class, can be seen at the Royal Netherlands Navy Museum at Den Helder. *Cerberus*, an 1870s British monitor, is a wreck off the coast of southern Australia, and the contemporary turret ram *Buffel* is in Rotterdam, the Netherlands. Two other monitors also survive – the coastal monitor *Solve*, with her fixed gun, is at Gothenburg, Sweden, and *M33,* a small bombardment monitor which saw much service in World War I, is at Portsmouth, England.

Warrior, the first broadside ironclad, is the only surviving example of the 45 iron hulls built by the Royal Navy between 1861 and 1877. She was obsolete within a decade of being built and placed in reserve. After her masts and guns were stripped she became a depot ship in Portsmouth, attached to the experimental and torpedo training school, to supply steam and electricity. She was sold in 1924 and became an oil fuel hulk at Pembroke Dock, Wales. Over the next 50 years some 5,000 ships refuelled alongside her. In 1979 *Warrior* was sold to a trust that had the vision of restoring her, which they did at Grays Shipyard in Hartlepool, and she is now on display as a museum ship in Portsmouth, England.

Mikasa, the 1902 pre-Dreadnought flagship of the Japanese navy at the Battle of Tsushima, is embedded in concrete in Yokosuka, Japan.

ABOVE: *Arizona*, sunk during the Japanese attack on Pearl Harbor, lies under the water where visitors can peer down but not visit her.
LEFT: Memorial services are frequently held over her wreck, which is an official war grave. Pearl Harbor is a major tourist destination for both Americans and Japanese.

The World War I USN battleship *Texas* is preserved at Houston, Texas, although she is displayed in the blue camouflage colour scheme and state of modernization which she was given in World War II. Other preserved USN battleships from World War II include *North Carolina* at Wilmington, *Massachusetts* at Fall River, *Alabama* at Mobile, *Iowa* at Suisun Bay, *New Jersey* at Camden, *Missouri* at Pearl Harbor, and *Wisconsin* at Norfolk.

The 1889 British pre-Dreadnought *Hood* lies upside down outside the breakwater at Portland, England, where she was sunk as a block ship in 1914. The wreck of the 1893 USS *Massachusetts* is an underwater archaeological preserve off Pensacola, Florida.

The short-lived 1911 British battleship *Audacious* lies where she settled in 1914 off Northern Ireland, and is not much visited.

ABOVE LEFT: **A piece of armour plate from the wreck of the Japanese** *Yamato*. ABOVE: **Two of her shells. The cars in the background give some idea of their size. The massive scale of the armour and armament were no proof against bombs and torpedoes from naval aircraft.** BELOW: **Attempts were being made to lift** *Utah*, **and she was still leaking oil as late as 1944. Eventually the decision was made to leave her as a war grave.**

From the epic battle in the North Sea in 1916, the 1908 German battleship *Thuringen* was used by the French navy as a target after World War I and large parts of her wreck can be seen from the shore at Plouhinec, France. *Ostfriesland*, also a veteran of Jutland, was ceded to the USA and expended as a target. Her wreck now lies 97km/60 miles off the Virginia Capes in deep water. *Lützow*, damaged and scuttled during the battle, lies 177km/110 miles from the Danish coast in 44m/144ft of water. One of her turrets lies besides the wreck, the other underneath the upturned hull, and 305mm/12in ammunition is scattered across the seabed. The remains of *Indefatigable*, the first capital ship to be sunk at Jutland, lie in the same general area, as does *Invincible,* broken in half by the explosion that ripped through her. *Queen Mary* was the second ship to blow up at Jutland, and her wreck was located in the 1990s, in a shattered condition.

Arizona and *Utah* in Pearl Harbor and *Royal Oak* at Scapa Flow are designated war graves, as are most of the other wrecks listed here.

The Japanese *Nagato*, laid down in 1917, was sunk at Bikini Atoll and lies upside down on the bottom of the lagoon at a depth of 55m/180ft in clear warm water, where she is reckoned to be the best battleship dive in the world.

The German pocket battleship *Graf Spee* was scuttled off Montevideo, Uruguay, where parts have been salvaged and there are proposals to lift the remains. *Repulse* and *Prince of Wales* were sunk by Japanese aircraft off the coast of Malaya, and both wrecks are regularly visited by the Royal Navy, who "fly" the White Ensign from their upturned hulls.

Finally, the mighty German battleship *Tirpitz* was broken up in the 1950s in the Norwegian fjord where she was eventually sunk, but large parts of the ship still litter the seabed.

Directory of Battleships

Pre-Dreadnoughts

The pre-Dreadnought battleships were a bewildering variety of vessels. Once the propeller had been married to steam propulsion, the choice for naval architects was between broadside and turreted guns. The first turrets were fitted on to small ships. Because of their weight, they could not be mounted in larger ships until steam engines became more reliable and the top hamper represented by masts and sails could be done away with. As armour temporarily outstripped the effectiveness of guns, the ram was thought to be the weapon of choice at sea and survived a remarkably long time until the torpedo and long range guns became available. Once all the elements of the modern battleship were present, the final problem to solve was that of hitting the target at long range. Before the use of radar, the only way of spotting the fall of shot was by eye and for accurate range-finding a single large calibre with all the guns slaved to a single fire control was necessary. Only when all these design problems had been resolved and the technology developed could the modern Dreadnought battleship come into being.

LEFT: *Implacable* sweeping majestically out of Malta, whose harbours were the proud base of the Royal Navy for more than a century and a half.

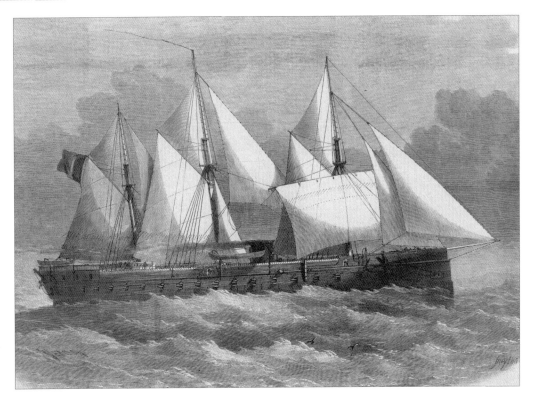

Gloire

In the Russian War 1854–6 Britain and France had formed an unlikely alliance against Russia, and during the war both navies had constructed armoured floating batteries, and used these to effect in the Black Sea against shore targets. Once the war was over France continued to develop the concept of an ironclad ship, primarily as a means of opposing her ancient enemy, Britain, and between 1858 and 1861 ordered no less than 16 broadside ironclads.

The first three, designed by Dupuy de Lôme, were Gloire and Invincible, laid down at Toulon in 1858, and, a few months later, Normandie at Cherbourg.

They were wooden-hulled and clad in wrought-iron armour. The hulls were 0.6m/2ft thick and covered by an armoured belt over 100mm/4in thick which extended from stem to stern and to 1.83m/6ft below the waterline, and there was a thinner layer of plating under the wooden upper deck. In the style of the screw ships that Gloire would replace, she was pierced for 38 guns on the main deck, although she never seems to have carried so many, an arrangement carried over from the days of sail. The armament differed throughout the class and with time. In Gloire, the original guns themselves were 160mm/6.4in rifled muzzle-loaders, although in an age when the technology of

ABOVE: **Despite having been recent allies in the Russian War, the French began building new ships in the late 1850s which would challenge the Royal Navy. The first of these was** *Gloire,* **a wooden-hulled ironclad ship incorporating the lessons which had been learned about the effect of modern guns. The use of wood limited the length of the hull.**

guns was also evolving rapidly, these were successively replaced by breech-loaders of different sizes. There were also four Paixhans shell guns on the upper deck.

Originally barquentine-rigged, the sail area was doubled to 2,500sq m/27,000sq ft when these ships were converted to ship-rig, but they were no more successful, despite French insistence upon building four of the class. Normandie and Invincible were built of poor timber that soon rotted and both were hulked up in 1871–2. Nevertheless, Normandie was the first armoured ship to cross the Atlantic, when she was sent to Mexico in 1862–3 in furtherance of Napoleon III's ambitions to found an empire there, but she returned with a centuries-old problem, an outbreak of yellow fever. Gloire lasted until 1879.

Ships of the Gloire class rolled badly and were not otherwise successful ships, nevertheless to France must go the honour of building the first armoured battleship.

When intelligence reached Britain of these new ships, there was an immediate response in the building of *Warrior*, a ship in every respect superior to *Gloire*. *Warrior* was not only larger by nearly 4,065 tonnes/4,000 tons, but faster and more heavily armed. Symbolically, the second of these ships was named *Black Prince*. It is surprising, therefore, that France, having introduced the first innovation, continued with her programme to build ships that were so much weaker than the British vessels.

Innovation nevertheless continued, and on the same day that *Gloire* was ordered, so was the iron-hulled *Couronne*. Though launched and completed after the *Warrior*, due to alteration to her plans during building, *Couronne* was another first for France: the world's first iron-hulled armoured battleship. Though similar in appearance to *Gloire*, her armour was unusual, consisting of a sandwich of teak, an iron lattice-work and more teak clad in iron plating. The upper deck armour was thicker, but did not cover the engine room spaces. There was no compartmentation, and in her last manifestation she was armed with eight 240mm/9.4in and four 190mm/7.6in guns on the main gundeck and two 120mm/4.7in and 12 1-pounder guns on the upper deck.

The French programme seemed unstoppable, and included two two-decker ironclads, also designed by Dupuy de Lôme and the only ships of their type ever built, *Magenta* and *Solferino*. They were also the first ships to have a spur ram, which projected 19.5m/64ft and was covered by a 14,225kg/14 ton steel cone, though their wide turning circle rendered them tactically unsuitable for ramming. The armament varied throughout their careers, and eventually the lower gundeck was removed. In another novelty, they carried two howitzers on the upper deck, capable of raining fire on an enemy ship.

Seemingly content with the *Gloire* design, a class of ten ships were all laid down in 1861, and all were wooden-hulled except the last, *Heroine*. Although the design had started a

TOP: **The British response to *Gloire* was immediate. *Warrior* was an iron-built, armoured ship, twice as big, twice as fast and twice as powerful as the French *Gloire* and her sisters.** ABOVE: **With the launch of *Warrior*, and *Black Prince* – a name surely chosen to send a message to the French – Britain and the Royal Navy announced their intention to maintain supremacy at sea.**

revolution and precipitated a naval arms race with Britain, many of these were still afloat in the 1890s when developments in gunnery made them obsolete, so strongly built were the hulls.

Gloire class

Class: *Gloire, Invincible, Normandie.*
Launched 1859–61
Dimensions: Length (at waterline) –
77.9m/255ft 6in
Beam – 17m/55ft 9in
Draught – 8.5m/27ft 10in
Displacement: 5,720 tonnes/5,630 tons
Armament: Main – 36 x 160mm/6.4in
RML guns
Machinery: 1-shaft HRCR, 8 oval boilers,
1,864kW/2,500ihp
Performance: 13 knots
Complement: 570 men

Warrior

By the mid-1850s, and the end of the Russian War, Britain was the world's foremost industrial nation and the Royal Navy had an overwhelming superiority in three-decker screw ships. It was policy to observe other nations' innovations and then use Britain's industrial and shipbuilding might to maintain the Royal Navy's supremacy. News from France of *Gloire* called this policy into action and in 1859 two ships were ordered, *Warrior* and *Black Prince*, designed by chief constructor Isaac Watts and engineer John Scott Russell. Unlike *Gloire* they were constructed of iron frames (in which the Victorian engineers excelled), which allowed a longer and stronger ship.

They were initially classed as frigates, because of their single main gundeck, and when completed they were the world's most powerful warships. Their strength lay not only in a broadside, on build, of ten 110-pounder, 26 68-pounder and four 70-pounder guns, but a complement of over 700 seamen and marines with field guns, muskets and cutlasses for warfare ashore.

Their high length-to-beam ratio (6.5:1) and fine lines forward and aft made them fast ships, though at slow speed they were not very handy. Ship-rigged, *Warrior* had a lifting screw and logged 13 knots under sail, while *Black Prince*, with a fixed screw, managed only 11 knots, but under combined sail and steam both ships could reach 17 knots. With taller funnels for increased draught to the boilers *Warrior* exceeded 14 knots under steam alone. The armour belt over the midships sections was 64.9m/213ft long and 6.7m/22ft deep and consisted of iron plates 4.6m/15ft by 0.9m/3ft and weighing 4,060kg/4 tons each which slotted together by tongue and groove. Other novel features included steam-driven capstans and watertight, armoured bulkheads fore and aft, and double bottoms that were compartmented. They were quite simply the biggest, the fastest and best armed and armoured ships in the world.

However, the British Admiralty was more concerned about the increased costs than the threat from France, so while continuing to build older-style wooden ships, the follow-on ships, *Defence* and *Resistance*, were smaller by about one third (6,100 tonnes/6,000 tons rather than 9,140 tonnes/9,000 tons). Then, when the French announced a programme to construct 30 seagoing ironclads, work on wooden line-of-battle ships halted. Instead two more ships of the Defence class, *Hector* and *Valiant,* were laid down, as were four *Warrior*-sized ships, the four-masted *Achilles*, and the magnificent five-

BELOW: *Warrior* was so strongly built that she has survived until today and can now be seen as a beautifully restored museum ship in Portsmouth, where, with her towering masts, she is one of the first and most memorable sights to greet the visitor to the several naval museums there.

masted 10,770 tonne/10,600 ton *Minotaur, Agincourt* and *Northumberland*. Also five (originally eight) 90-gun two-deckers, *Prince Consort, Caledonia, Ocean, Royal Oak* and *Royal Alfred*, were converted on the slips to wooden broadside ironclads and some purpose-built wooden broadside ironclads, including *Lord Clyde* and *Lord Warden*, were built to use up existing timber stocks. All of these ships were larger, faster and better armed than the Provence class, to a degree that ought to have deterred the French. By 1867, the Royal Navy had completed 19 broadside battery ships, easily outbuilding the French whose challenge collapsed for want of finance, industrial capacity and adequate designs.

The only area in which the British ironclads were possibly inferior was that they were armed with muzzle-loading guns. When *Warrior* was completed in 1861, Armstrong rifled breech-loaders were widely fitted throughout the fleet, but a series of accidents from flaws in the steel barrels and in the breech mechanisms caused these to be abandoned. For the next few years, the British Navy reverted to using a muzzle-loading rifled gun until by the 1880s the technology was sufficiently advanced, in other navies, for a reliable breech-loading gun to replace smooth bore guns.

These ships spanned an age of change. *Achilles* as completed in 1864 was the only British warship with four masts and had the largest sail area of any British warship. *Lord Warden* (1867) at 7,968 tonnes/7,842 tons was the heaviest wooden ship ever built and *Minotaur* the first ship to carry a searchlight. The *Hector* as a tender at the Royal Navy's experimental school, Vernon, was the first ship to be fitted with wireless, in 1900. Many of these ships also had exceptionally long lives: *Minotaur* and *Black Prince* were broken up in 1923, *Achilles* in 1925, *Northumberland* in 1927, *Defence* in 1935, *Valiant* in 1957, and *Agincourt* not until 1960. *Warrior* is still afloat and has been fully restored as a museum ship. She was restored internally and externally at Hartlepool before being towed to her present berth in Portsmouth.

Warrior

Class: *Warrior, Black Prince*.
Launched 1860–1
Dimensions: Length (at waterline) –
115.9m/380ft 2in
Beam – 18m/58ft 4in
Draught – 7.9m/26ft
Displacement: 9,284 tonnes/9,137 tons
Armament: Main – 4 x 205mm/8in MLR guns
Secondary – 28 x 180mm/7in MLR
and 4 x 20pdr BL guns
Machinery: 1-shaft, Penn HSET, 10 rectangular
boilers, 3,928kW/5,267ihp
Performance: 14 knots
Complement: 707 men

The first *Monitor*

*M*onitor was only one of 17 proposals considered by the Federal government of the USA in 1861, of which three were selected for construction: the conventional broadside-ironclad *New Ironsides*, the armoured ship *Galena*, and the wholly unconventional *Monitor,* which was designed by John Ericsson. Ericsson's ship was an armoured wooden raft, with a lower hull 38m/126ft long and 10.3m/34ft wide, overhung, turtle-fashion, by a platform 52.5m/172ft long and 12.5m/41ft wide: the overhang protected the sides, propeller and screw from ramming.

The USN had asked for a speed of 8 knots, but *Monitor*'s best speed was only 6 knots. Worse, the freeboard was only 35.5cm/14in, though the largely submerged hull, often awash, was less susceptible to rolling. The hatches, however, could only be opened in the calmest of weather and the hawse pipe in the hull was very near the waterline. The forced-air ventilators were 1.37m/4ft 6in high and the two square funnels were 1.83m/6ft high: even with forced ventilation temperatures inside *Monitor* were intolerable.

Ericsson's original sketch called for 150mm/6in armour on the side and 50mm/2in on the deck, made up of individual 25.4mm/1in plates bolted or riveted together. This, it was

TOP: *Merrimac* was rated by the USN as an auxiliary screw frigate when her burned hulk was captured alongside by the Confederate forces, who rebuilt her as an ironclad. ABOVE: John Ericsson, who was one of a group of Swedes who strongly influenced the USN in the mid-19th century. Ericsson was a prolific inventor who designed the first monitor.

calculated, would have sunk the *Monitor* and the side armour was reduced to 50mm/2in except around the turret where it was 200–230mm/8–9in. A pilothouse on the foredeck was built of 230mm/9in iron blocks.

So, Ericsson's heavily armoured, shallow-draft iron hull with its low profile had good protection against cannon shot and the unusual construction protected the vital parts from damage by

LEFT: **The launch of the first monitor. The name was chosen because, according to Gustavus Fox (another Swede), she was going to teach the Confederates – and the British – a lesson.**
BELOW: **In the battle between** *Monitor* **and** *Merrimac* **(now renamed** *Virginia***) neither ship could really damage the other and when** *Monitor* **retreated into shallow water,** *Virginia* **could not follow.** BOTTOM: **This diagram shows the saucer-like profile of** *Monitor***. Ericsson also devised a novel turret (not shown here) mounted on a spindle.**

ramming. The USN would have preferred a low-board ironclad with turrets on the Coles principle of a roller bearing, but Ericsson provided a single turret mounted on a central spindle with a bronze skirt resting on a ring of bronze. The turret was 6.1m/20ft in diameter and 2.74m/9ft high, and the roof was made of a grating of railway lines. The turret held two 280mm/11in Dahlgren smoothbore shell guns, and was powered by steam. The steam mechanism made training the guns jerky and imprecise.

Monitor was unlikely to teach the British Admiralty any lessons but she was well suited for coastal and riverine warfare during the American Civil War.

Built in a few months in the winter of 1861/2 at the Continental Iron Works in Greenpoint, Long Island, *Monitor* left New York after trials on March 6. She experienced heavy weather on her route south, and her exhausted crew reached Hampton Roads two days later. She fought her famous action against the *Merrimac*, the first between two armoured ships, on March 9, 1862. Neither ship could seriously harm the other and a further fight in April, after *Merrimac* had been improved by fitting more armour and now equipped with solid shot, was declined.

Monitor fought in the James River in support of the Army's Peninsular Campaign, before being sent to Washington for improvements that included a telescopic funnel, better ventilation, and davits. However, on December 31, 1862 *Monitor* was returning to operations in the South when she was caught in rough waters off Cape Hatteras and flooded by seawater that drowned her boilers. She foundered and 16 of her crew of 62 were lost.

The wreck of *Monitor* was rediscovered in 1974 and is on display at the Mariners' Museum, Norfolk, Virginia.

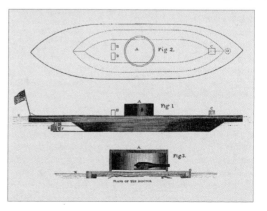

Virginia

After the Federal frigate *Merrimac* was captured alongside and partly burned in Gosport Navy Yard in Norfolk by advancing Confederate forces, she was successfully converted into an ironclad of unusual design. At the same time she was renamed *Virginia*.

Virginia was armed with a mix of guns behind an armoured casemate. This casemate was 51.8m/170ft long sloping inwards and upwards, and covered with layers of plates both horizontally and vertically. She had two significant disadvantages: her engines were not powerful enough for the additional weight of armour so she took a long time to manoeuvre, and she had the draught of a frigate, so that she was unsuited for warfare in estuaries and rivers.

However, on March 8, 1862 she attacked the blockading Federal fleet in Hampton Roads, sank the frigate *Congress* and the sloop *Cumberland*,

and could have turned the tide of the war. The next day when she renewed her attack she found *Monitor* had arrived. Neither ship could harm the other much and *Monitor* escaped into shallower water, where *Virginia* with her deeper draught could not follow.

As Union forces continued to advance, *Virginia* was destroyed by her crew in May 1862.

TOP: The retreating Federal forces burned *Merrimac* to the waterline, so it was a relatively simple matter to convert her to a turtleback ironclad. News of the conversion inspired the North to build *Monitor*.

ABOVE: This turtleback ironclad of unusual design was renamed *Virginia* after conversion. The sloping sides of the armour helped to protect her by letting shot glance off, and she was eventually destroyed by her own crew as the Union forces continued to advance.

Broadside ironclads

The building of broadside ironclads in the late 1850s and 1860s was stimulated by Anglo-French rivalry and the threat of war in northern and southern Europe.

In order to overmatch the French Gloire class, Britain, in addition to building iron-hulled broadside ships, converted a number of 90-gun wooden ships to ironclads in 1860–4, and other navies followed suit. Denmark, which was faced with the inevitability of war with Prussia over Schleswig-Holstein, converted *Dannebrog*, a 72-gun two-deck sailing ship, in 1863. Russia converted two frigates, *Sevastopol* and *Petropavlovsk*, to ironclads, and perhaps the oldest ship to be converted was the Dutch *De Ruyter*, first built as a 74-gun ship in 1831.

Interest in the Gloire class attracted customers to France, where broadside ironclads and central battery ships were built for foreign customers including Germany. The Italian navy, which was created in 1861 from the navies of Naples, Piedmont-Sardinia, Tuscany, the two Sicilies and the Papal States, bought purpose-built ships from yards abroad, including the French-built *Terrible* and *Formidable* and the Regina Maria Pia class, but the two kings, *Re d'Italia* and *Re di Portogallo*, were bought in the USA. As its industry developed, Italy began to design and build her own ships in yards in Genoa and Leghorn. Austria

responded by using her indigenous shipbuilding capacity at Trieste to build the Drache and Kaiser Max classes.

Spain bought one ironclad broadside from France, *Numancia*, and built another, *Tetuan*, at Ferrol, while the iron-hulled *Vitoria* and former wooden screw frigate *Arapiles* were built or converted on the Thames.

Turkey also ordered new-build ironclads from British yards, *Osmanieh, Mahmudieh, Abdul Aziz* and *Orkanieh*. This started the habit of the Royal Navy using foreign ships being built in British yards as a reserve of ships ready to be taken over in time of crisis.

The broadside ironclad was the end of the evolution of the ship of the line rather than a step in the development of the battleship. The new navies of Japan and Germany missed this phase altogether.

BELOW: **It was difficult to mount turrets in ocean-going ships and so broadside ironclads continued to be built for a number of years, including the 1864 French *Surveillante*.** BOTTOM LEFT: **Marking another stage in the evolution of the battleship, while retaining the broadside layout, *Deutschland*'s armament was almost all confined to an armoured central citadel.** BOTTOM: **While looking like a broadside ironclad, the 1865 Italian *Roma* combined several features including a ram and central battery.**

The monitors

Over 50 monitors were ordered during the American Civil War although many were not completed, and most were sold or broken up within ten years. When a new generation of monitors was built, Amphitrite class (1874), Monterey (1889) and Arkansas class (1899), they took the names of Civil War ships of which they were supposed to be "repairs".

In an attempt to make them seagoing, masts and super-structures were added, and the 3,455-tonne/3,400-ton *Miantonomoh* made a trans-Atlantic voyage, mostly under tow, with the Secretary of the Navy, Gustavus Vasa Fox, on board. Despite Fox's ambition that these monitors would teach the British a lesson, *Miantonomoh* had to use Royal Navy resources in Halifax, St John's, Queenstown, Portsmouth and Gibraltar to accomplish her remarkable journey. During a visit to France, Fox called on Napoleon III and his travels took him to Denmark in July 1866. He also visited St Petersburg in August for a month-long visit – although what the autocratic Tsar Alexander II thought of the representative of an upstart republic named after the king of one of his country's bitterest enemies is not known. Fox's aim was to study European naval

ABOVE: *Cerberus* was built in England to the order of the Australian state of Victoria. Her sides were built up and she was ship-rigged for her oceanic voyage of delivery. The remains of *Cerberus* can still be seen where she was sunk as a breakwater, though she is probably too far gone ever to be restored, and within a few years she will probably be lost forever.

technology, though naturally his ship excited much interest. *Miantonomoh* returned via Sweden, Germany, France, Portugal, Spain and Italy and in May 1867 crossed the Atlantic via a more southerly route and one last call, courtesy of the British, for more coal in the Bahamas, a journey of a staggering 28,587km/ 17,767 miles.

Used effectively in the waterways and rivers, the perceived success of the monitors resulted in them being copied by other nations, including Sweden, Norway and the Netherlands. The Swedes built American-style monitors also designed by Ericsson, who gifted guns built by Dahlgren, and the first ship in 1865 was called *John Ericsson*. Though initially armed with two 380mm/15in guns these were replaced in 1881 with 240mm/9.4in guns. *John Ericsson* had two sister ships, *Thordön*

ABOVE: **In addition to her twin 255mm/10in guns** *Cerberus* **carried a range of lesser guns. Here her crew are demonstrating how those guns would be manned.**
ABOVE RIGHT: **The Swedish monitor** *John Ericsson.* **Despite his work in the United States, Ericsson retained links with his country of birth and both he and fellow-Swede John Dahlgren represented designs and surplus equipment to the Swedish navy.** RIGHT: **Surprisingly the USN was still operating 19th-century-style monitors in World War I. Some even crossed the Atlantic and others were used as submarine depot ships, for which their low freeboard was especially suitable.**

(1866) and *Tirfing* (1867) and a slighter larger sister ship, *Loke* (1871). All had the low freeboards typical of their type and even in the slightest sea, the upper decks were awash.

Even the Royal Navy built some monitors, the oldest surviving being the *Cerberus*, built at Jarrow on the Tyne in 1867–8 and fitted out at Chatham. At Chatham the Admiralty refused to let her fly the White Ensign or even to provide naval victuals and the civil authorities refused to register her as a merchant ship, while her first Captain died of illness. Finally, an officer was sent from Melbourne to bring her to Victoria, Australia. Since her freeboard was only 0.91m/3ft, temporary bulwarks were fitted and she was rigged with masts and sail, which were useless for making headway but they steadied her when she ran into heavy weather. With bunkers for only 122 tonnes/120 tons of coal, she had to rely on frequent coalings, which gave plenty of opportunity for her crew to desert or mutiny, which they did in Portsmouth and Malta, preferring a spell in prison to the risks of the voyage, and the searing heat between decks. It did not help that another new-fangled ship, *Captain*, had capsized in heavy weather with large loss of life only a few weeks before.

However, *Cerberus* was the first steamship to combine a central superstructure with fore and aft gun turrets, and the first armoured warship built for Australia. In dispensing with sail power she preceded the Royal Navy's *Devastation* by three years, and she was the first steamship to pass through the newly completed Suez Canal. Once *Cerberus* reached Port Philip in 1871 she never left and, apart from an American plan to capture Melbourne prepared during the visit of the Great White Fleet, no one ever challenged the guardian of the hull's four 255mm/10in rifled muzzle-loading Armstrong guns. Her remains – she was scuttled as a breakwater off the Black Rock Yacht Club – are the oldest surviving warship to have served in the Royal Australian Navy.

Although the 20th century would witness a revival of the type, the low-freeboard monitor was a dead-end in battleship development. *Devastation*, with a similar layout but three times the size of *Cerberus*, did however set the pattern for future battleships. Amazingly some USN monitors continued to cross the Atlantic without being swamped and were used as submarine tenders in World War I where their low-freeboard was an advantage.

LEFT: **The French cruiser** *Dupuy de Lôme* **exhibits an extreme form of the ram. The French navy at the end of the 19th century was well known for its odd, even extreme, designs. Possibly naming this ship after one of the better naval architects was an attempt to legitimize the design.**

The rams

In the American Civil War, several ships were attacked by ramming, causing John Ericsson to design into *Monitor* elaborate features to protect her underwater form from ramming. The French were the first to construct a seagoing ram, the wooden-hulled armoured *Taureau* in 1863, which was built with a turtle deck, a large gun in a barbette and a long-spur ram, however she rarely left harbour.

The French were no more successful with the larger *Cerbere* class in 1865. However, the idea of ramming was boosted by the sinking of the *Re d'Italia* during the Battle of Lissa in 1866. Analysts failed to note that the *Re d'Italia* had already suffered rudder damage and was unable to manoeuvre out of the way.

In 1868, the Royal Navy responded with the ironclad ram *Hotspur*, an iron-hulled ship of 4,064 tonnes/4,000 tons whose ram projected 3.05m/10ft, but the low freeboard gave poor seakeeping qualities and she was only used for coastal defence. The much larger *Rupert* of 5,527 tonnes/5,440 tons was built in 1870 but was not much better, though both ships were modernized and survived into the 20th century.

Then in 1871, the British Admiralty's committee on Designs for Ships of War highlighted what it called the importance of ramming. Consequently, the British built the freakish torpedo ram *Polyphemus* in 1878, and the monstrous 6,096-tonne/6,000-ton turret rams *Conqueror* and *Hero* in 1879 and 1884, armed with 305mm/12in breech-loading guns. Naval officers and architects had just about overcome their nervousness when in 1893 *Camperdown* struck *Victoria*, though *Victoria*'s rapid sinking was due to poor inherent stability. Most pre-Dreadnought battleships were built with rams and Jacky Fisher even chose a design for *Dreadnought* that gave the appearance that she had a ram.

Nevertheless, it was a failed tactic: ramming could be effective only against ships that were unable to manoeuvre, and there was at least as much risk of damage to the ramming vessel as there was to the target in the approach under fire and in any collision. Rams may however have acted as bulbous bows and bestowed some streamlining on the pre-Dreadnoughts, and fear of ramming helped to improve damage control and promote the internal subdivision of ships.

BELOW: **A British battleship in dry dock showing her ram. Note also the open hatches of her forward-firing anti-torpedo-boat guns and booms for her anti-torpedo nets.**

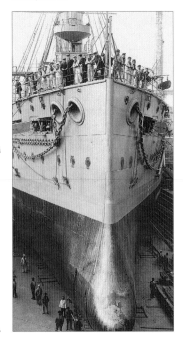

Barbettes

The first ironclad warships mounted guns in broadsides just like their sailing ship predecessors. At first during the battleship revolution ships' sides were protected by iron cladding and then individual guns were protected by shields. At the same time the early monitors and some small warships had turrets with roofs after designs by Coles and Ericsson. Smaller ironclad warships continued to be armed with guns in broadsides, but as the size of gun and the thickness of armour increased they were placed in armoured batteries known as casements.

As gun size increased again warships were generally fitted with fewer guns and these had to be sited on the centreline of low-freeboard ships and placed inside barbettes or fixed iron shields inside which the guns rotated on their mountings. The term barbette came to be applied to the open-topped, armoured enclosure used to protect guns on their turntable together with their crews. The guns fired over the top of their barbettes, but when roofs were added to mountings from the mid-1860s onwards, they became known as turrets again, and the name barbette was applied to the internal substructure which extended below deck. However, when it was introduced the barbette was considered an advance in naval

construction as it saved weight when compared to building a larger turret.

For example, the 9,144-tonne/9,000-ton *Devastation* and *Thunderer* of 1869 had muzzle-loading rifled 305mm/12in guns in twin turrets, fore and aft, but *Collingwood* of 1880 was 508 tonnes/500 tons larger and mounted her guns in barbettes. The barbettes in *Collingwood* were pear-shaped, 15.24m/50ft long and 13.72m/45ft wide, with an armoured trunk at the rear of the barbette for the ammunition hoist (compare with *Dreadnought* below), and the general layout proved to be the model for the majority of pre-Dreadnought battleships.

In 1868 the French were the first to build a barbette, to a British design, which penetrated the deck with an armoured trunk resting on the well-protected roller path. This enabled the French to build high-sided ships with their main guns well clear of the water but they proved to be vulnerable to gunfire and the ships of the Hoche class were held to be some of the worst French designs, despite many modifications while building. They were so heavy that most of the armour was underwater but they did have comfortable accommodation and were accordingly known as the grand hotels. The French also introduced splinter shields over the mountings to protect

their crews and by the 1890s this was the standard method of mounting heavy guns in battleships.

In Britain the *Royal Sovereign* of 1892 was one of the first designs in which the barbette was extended below deck to afford some protection to the magazine and ammunition hoists. In the *Majestic* of 1895 the barbette revolved with the gun, although the gun still had to return to a fixed angle of elevation and training for loading. The Italian *Re Umberto* of 1893 and British *Caesar* and *Illustrious* of 1895 were the first ships to have guns which could be loaded at any angle.

The design of the barbette required a very large diameter and one of the frequently overlooked but revolutionary aspects of the 1905 *Dreadnought* was her compact turrets with an internal diameter of just 8.23m/27ft.

The earliest ironclads still had wooden mountings with guns on trucks or slides whose recoil was controlled by ropes, but as the guns grew in size so pivoting iron slides and friction and later hydraulic means of restraining the recoil were introduced. The early guns' mountings in their barbettes were trained by hand although steam-powered, hydraulic and eventually electrical systems were later developed. Finally by about 1900 the barbette was no longer a feature of warship design.

LEFT: **The French *Tonnant* (1880) was intended as a coast defence ship to keep the British at bay. Note the barbettes are roofed over to protect the gun's crew from splinters.** ABOVE: **The French persisted in barbette mountings for their guns, as in *Magenta* (1890), though the larger hull enabled their designers to build more seaworthy ships.**

Turret ships

The French are credited with having introduced armoured floating batteries in the Crimea, during the Russian War of 1854–6, in order to attack Russian positions in support of the attack on Kinburn.

It was during the Russian War that British Captain Cowper Coles and the Swede, John Ericsson, made proposals for turret ships. Ericsson, after several years of attempting to interest the Royal Navy in his various inventions, had settled in the USA and there he successfully introduced a design that became known as a monitor. The USA became a prolific builder of monitors, and many other navies took up similar designs. In its simplest form the monitor remained a platform for bombarding the shore, though some of these grew to be quite large. Some subsequent designs such as the coast defence ship had many attributes of the true battleship.

However, real navies needed seagoing vessels capable of standing up to the heaviest ships in any other navy's order of battle. In the late 1850s, Cowper Coles made many proposals for ships fitted with guns mounted in cupolas including an 1859 plan for a ship with ten armoured cupolas. In response, the Royal Navy cautiously tried out an experimental turret in *Trusty* in 1861. The problem was to design a ship capable of crossing oceans, or in the British case the Channel, that could carry sufficient armour and armament to defeat any shallow-water monitor that might be waiting on the other side. Two of Cowper

Coles's designs were the Danish *Rolf Krake* (1863), and the Peruvian *Huascar* (1865), which did indeed cross open waters, but neither could be regarded as successful.

Rolf Krake, also described as an armoured battery ship, entered the Danish navy in 1863. Built by Napier & Sons in Glasgow she was the first Danish ship to be iron-built and carried four 205mm/8in guns in two double turrets mounted on

BELOW: **Showing how alternative designs co-existed, the *Dreadnought* (1875) had her funnels and other top hamper centralized amidships. Here she is cleared for action and her boats are being towed astern.** BOTTOM: **The British *Agamemnon* (1879) had turret mountings and, in an echo of the earlier, failed *Captain* design, these were mounted one deck lower with forecastle and aftercastle and flying bridge to carry the boats, searchlights and so on.**

the centre-line. The turrets rotated on a roller track which also supported their weight (unlike Ericsson's design for the first monitor in which the turret rested and rotated a central spindle). However, the fundamental principle that turrets should be mounted on the centre-line was soon lost as ships grew bigger, and was not rediscovered until the epoch-making *Dreadnought* was built in 1905. *Rolf Krake* took part in the War of Schleswig Holstein in 1864 and although not a decisive influence on the course of the war, she helped to persuade the Prussian ruler that his kingdom needed to build its own navy.

Huascar was also built in Britain according to a Coles design. She was twice tested in battle, against two unarmoured British cruisers in 1877, and against several Chilean sailing ships and two casemate ships in 1879. *Huascar* was captured by the Chileans and has been maintained as a trophy of war ever since.

The first British turret ship was the *Royal Sovereign*, formerly a three-deck line-of-battle ship, launched in 1849, which was cut down in 1862 and armed with 265mm/10.5in guns in a twin turret and three single turrets. She remained in service for a surprisingly long time as a coast defence ship. The first purpose-built design was the *Prince Albert* in 1866, whose 230mm/9in guns barely qualify her for a mention in this book but which, it is said, remained in commission until 1899 in deference to Queen Victoria's wishes.

The disadvantage with turrets was their weight, the main issue being that as the size of the gun increased, so too did the weight of armour and these large weights could not be carried high in the hull without risk of instability. The result was a number of low-freeboard ships with poor seakeeping qualities.

The problem is clearly demonstrated in the case of the seven battleships of the Royal Sovereign class of 1889–91 and the eighth ship ordered at the same time under the Naval Defence Act, *Hood*. All had similar 340mm/13.5in guns, but in

TOP: **The turret armour-clad *Devastation* at a naval review at Spithead (for the visit of the Shah of Persia) on June 23, 1873, painted by E. Wake Cooke and capturing the power and majesty of the new pre-Dreadnoughts.** ABOVE: **The German *Preussen*, photographed in Malta in 1890, is a turret ship; though even with her sailing rig reduced from the original she still displays many of the characteristics of a former generation of ships.**

the former, they were in barbettes. However, in order to carry the weight of a turret in *Hood*, the guns had to be fitted one deck lower.

The turret was the correct line for development rather than the barbette, but guns in turrets would not become standard until a smaller size of gun was established at 305mm/12in and the effectiveness of armour had also improved. This would allow the turret weight to be reduced, whilst the displacement of the battleship increased significantly.

LEFT: The French navy continued to build coast defence ships in the 1890s, and used many novel designs like the Bouvines class with a high forecastle and the heavy guns mounted aft, one deck lower. BELOW: The French seem temporarily to have lost their eye for good design and to have produced some exceptionally odd ships like the coast defence ship *Hoche*, laid down in 1881 but not completed until 1890.

Coast defence ships

The American Civil War was followed closely in Europe, and particularly in the Royal Navy, where a 121-gun ship of the line, *Royal Sovereign,* was turned into a coast defence battleship. The conversion in 1862 was not as extreme as that of the *Virginia*, because the *Royal Sovereign* was intended to be a seagoing ship, as was shown by her folding bulwarks. Her hull and deck were strengthened but not heavily armoured and she was fitted with a twin and three single 265mm/10.5in guns firing solid shot, later replaced by more effective 230mm/9in muzzle-loaders. Because of Cowper Coles's agitation, the Royal Navy also built the slightly smaller *Prince Albert* from scratch, with four 230mm/9in muzzle-loaders. Soon, however, the Royal Navy abandoned this line of development.

The Brazilian navy built a number of coast defence battleships, but only the low-freeboard, twin-turreted, French-built *Javary* and *Solimoes* had battleship-sized guns. The small Argentine navy possessed two low-freeboard monitors, *La Plata* and *Los Andes* (1874), with a narrow superstructure fore and aft that allowed end-on fire. *Almirante Brown* (1880) was built to an antiquated design with a central battery and single turrets fore and aft mounting eight 205mm/8in guns, which were replaced in 1897/8 with 265mm/10.5in guns.

In Sweden the coast defence ships *Svea, Göta* and *Thule* (1886–93) had 255mm/10in guns in a twin turret and *Thule* had a ram, while *Oden, Thor* and *Niord* (1897–9) had 255mm/10in guns in single turrets. Between 1900 and 1905, the Swedish navy built three more classes armed with 210mm/8.3in guns: *Dristigheten* (1900), four ships of the Äran class (1902–4) and *Oscar II* (1905).

Denmark competed with an unusual design, *Helgoland* (1878), a coast defence battleship with a single 305mm/12in gun and four 260mm/10.2in guns, and *Iver Hvitfeldt* (1886) with two 260mm//10.2in guns. Norway and the Netherlands also built several coast defence ships with guns under 255mm/10in. Austro-Hungary built *Monarch, Wien* and *Budapest* (1893), though these were too small to be effective battleships.

The coast defence ship in all its forms was, however, a byway in the development of the battleship.

BELOW: The German *Siegfried* photographed in 1889 mimicked the French design, but being larger also supported a forecastle mounting. The German Kaiser's navy began a period of rapid expansion, turning itself from a coast defence navy into a high seas fleet which would eventually challenge the Royal Navy.

Royal Sovereign class

Under the Naval Defence Act of 1889, £21 million was provided for the construction of ten battleships, 42 cruisers and other vessels over the next five years. The two-power standard whereby the Royal Navy would be maintained at strength equal to two other foreign powers was also endorsed: the enemies then were France and Russia.

The launch and completion of the seven ships of the Royal Sovereign class in just two years was itself an important message. Designed by Sir Samuel White, they were the most powerful battleships in the world, setting new benchmarks in firepower, armour and speed.

White's design was for an enlarged Admiral class barbette ship. The Royal Navy wanted better seakeeping than previous generations of low-freeboard ships. The armoured belt covered two-thirds of the ship's length and was up to 460mm/18in thick and the gun mountings were pear-shaped with 430mm/17in armour. The areas behind the main and

upper belts of armour were used as coalbunkers for additional protection. To save weight the 340mm/13.5in breech-loading guns remained in barbettes. The freeboard was raised to 5.5m/18ft by building another full-length deck, and the armour extended to cover the barbettes and a heavier secondary armament. On build, they were found to roll heavily but after bilge keels were fitted proved to be good sea-keepers capable of maintaining high speeds.

Such a large class meant that their effectiveness was increased by operating in squadrons. Few ships of this class, however, saw active service. The Royal Sovereigns were deployed in the Channel and Mediterranean Fleets, but after 1902 they served exclusively in home waters. From 1907 onwards, when superseded by the Dreadnoughts, the Royal Sovereigns were placed in reserve and most were scrapped by 1914. Only *Revenge* saw service in World War I, when she was deployed on the Belgian

ABOVE: **A coloured postcard of** *Empress of India* **(1891) dressed overall. The launch of seven ships of the same class in just two years was intended as a strong message to the world.**

coast to give fire-support to the army in 1914–15. Following this she was renamed *Redoubtable* and made a tender to HMS *Victory* until 1919.

Royal Sovereign class

Class: *Royal Sovereign, Empress of India, Ramillies, Repulse, Resolution, Royal Oak, Revenge.* Launched 1891–2

Dimensions: Length – 115.8m/380ft
Beam – 22.9m/75ft
Draught – 8.4m/27ft 6in

Displacement: 14,377 tonnes/14,150 tons

Armament: Main – 4 x 340mm/13.5in guns
Secondary – 10 x 150mm/6in, 16 x 6-pdr,
12 x 3-pdr guns and 7 x 455mm/18in torpedoes

Machinery: 2 shafts, 8 boilers, 6,711kW/9,000ihp

Performance: 18 knots

Complement: 712 men

Hood

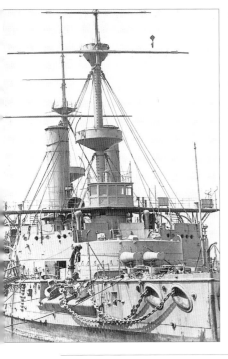

The debate about the design of the pre-Dreadnought battleship was not quite decided, and, under the Naval Defence Act of 1889, an eighth battleship was built, *Hood*. Although a sister ship to the Royal Sovereign battleships and sharing many features of their internal layout, she retained more of the characteristics of an earlier type, the turret ship.

Hood had similar machinery, armour and guns to the Royal Sovereign class, but instead of barbettes, she was fitted with turrets. The greater weight of the turrets meant that these had to be mounted one deck lower. In consequence *Hood* shipped water in even the slightest seaway and so could not maintain such high speeds as her half-sisters.

The design allowed direct comparison between the old and the new concepts, but was not a success. *Hood* saw service briefly in the Mediterranean but was soon withdrawn, used as a receiving ship and then for trials from 1911–14.

LEFT: *Hood* was the eighth battleship to be built under the Naval Defence Act of 1889. The weight of the turrets required them to be carried lower in the ship, and the value of a high freeboard for ships of an ocean-going navy like the Royal Navy was not as widely accepted as it should have been.

Hood became part of the Royal Navy's growing anti-submarine efforts and was the first ship to be fitted with bulges, intended to absorb the impact of a torpedo hit.

Hood

Class: *Hood.* Launched 1891
Dimensions: Length – 125.12m/410ft 6in
  Beam – 22.86m/75ft
  Draught – 8.38m/27ft 6in
Displacement: 14,377 tonnes/14,150 tons
Armament: Main – 4 x 340mm/13.5in guns
  Secondary – 10 x 150mm/6in, 10 x 6pdr,
  12 x 3pdr guns and 5 x 455mm/18in torpedoes
Machinery: 8 boilers, 2 shafts,
  9,000kW/16,000ihp
Performance: 16.7 knots
Complement: 690 men

Renown

Similar in armament to earlier Royal Sovereigns, *Renown* was 2,032 tonnes/2,000 tons heavier than *Centurion* and because she was beamier drew slightly less water. Her increased size was due to her heavier armour, a

Renown

Class: *Renown.* Launched 1895
Dimensions: Length – 124.34m/408ft
  Beam – 22m/72ft
  Draught – 8.15m/26ft 9in
Displacement: 12,548 tonnes/12,350 tons
Armament: Main – 4 x 255mm/10in guns
  Secondary – 10 x 150mm/6in, 12 x 12pdr,
  12 x 3pdr guns and 5 x 455mm/18in torpedoes
Machinery: 8 boilers, 2 shafts.
  6,711kW/9,000ihp
Performance: 17.5 knots
Complement: 674 men

trend which every successor ship followed until the battlecruisers were built. The outer edge of the protective armoured deck over the citadel was also sloped to deflect any shells which might penetrate the belt. She was flagship on the North America and West Indies station from 1897–9, and in the Mediterranean from 1899–1902. With her 150mm/6in guns removed, she carried the Duke and Duchess of Connaught and Prince and Princess of Wales on state visits to India. The role of royal (or presidential) yacht was frequently allotted to battleships.

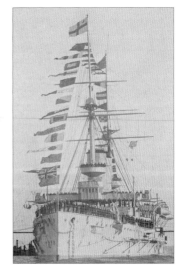

RIGHT: *Renown* was a handsome, comfortable ship much in demand by admirals as a flagship or as a royal yacht. She saw service in the Atlantic and Indian Oceans, the West Indies and Mediterranean.

Centurion and *Barfleur*

Centurion and *Barfleur* were the smallest of the British pre-Dreadnoughts and officially rated as second-class battleships. Their size enabled them to enter the major Chinese rivers. Although they could not stand up to other, larger Russian and Japanese ships, they could run down any armoured cruiser and as such, they might be regarded as the first battlecruisers.

A revolving armoured hood covered circular barbettes, marking an intermediate stage in the development of the turret. Both ships could reach 17 knots, and slightly higher speeds with forced draught. Both ships were reconstructed in 1901–4 when the 120mm/4.7in guns were replaced with the more usual 150mm/6in ordnance.

Both *Centurion*, which saw service on the China station between 1894 and 1905, and *Barfleur*, which served in the Mediterranean from 1895–8 and then on the China station until 1902, were recalled to home waters after Fisher's redeployment of the British fleet.

Centurion class

Class: *Centurion, Barfleur*. Launched 1892–4
Dimensions: Length – 109.73m/360ft
    Beam – 21.3m/70ft
    Draught – 7.8m/25ft 6in
Displacement: 10,668 tonnes/10,500 tons
Armament: Main – 4 x 255mm/10in guns
    Secondary – 10 x 120mm/4.7in, 8 x 6pdr,
    12 x 3pdr guns and 7 x 455mm/18in torpedoes
Machinery: 8 boilers, 2 shafts,
    6,710kW/9,000ihp
Performance: 18 knots
Complement: 620 men

LEFT AND BELOW: **The two small battleships of the *Centurion* class were specialized ships, intended for work overseas and able to enter China's rivers. *Barfleur* is seen here in Mediterranean paint scheme in dry dock (left) and at Malta (below). The twin side-by-side funnels were typical of the era.**

Majestic class

The Majestics were the largest single class of battleships ever built. Combining the successful features of the Royal Sovereigns with the improvements in layout adopted in *Renown*, like their predecessors they were good sea-going boats. The 305mm/12in guns became the British standard and proved superior to the previous 340mm/13.5in guns in everything except weight of shell. The extensive armoured belt was 230mm/9in thick and 305mm/12in to 355mm/14in at the bulkheads and barbettes, where, except for a small number of ready-use rounds, the guns had to be trained fore and aft for loading. The bridge, control tower and foremast were combined in the first six ships. By 1908, all carried some oil fuel in addition to coal, and *Caesar* and *Illustrious* had been fitted with new gun-mountings that enabled all-round loading.

All served in the Channel fleet, except *Victorious,* which served on the China station 1898–1900 and *Majestic*, flagship of the Mediterranean fleet 1895–1903. In World War I *Magnificent, Hannibal* and *Mars* were stripped of their guns, which then armed the Lord Clive class of monitors, and were employed as troopships. *Jupiter* escorted the Russian fleet down the English Channel on its way to defeat at the Battle of Tsushima, and after a period as a gunnery training ship was sent to Archangel as an icebreaker in February 1914, and served in the Far East and Middle East.

Illustrious became an ammunition ship. *Prince George*, which had a lucky escape when a torpedo that struck her off Cape Helles in 1915 failed to explode, and was hit by Turkish gunfire during a bombardment off the Dardanelles, survives as a reef off the Netherlands coast, where she foundered on the way to breakers in Germany in 1921. *Majestic* was sunk by a German U-boat. *Caesar* was one of the few pre-Dreadnoughts to see action after World War I, when she supported British operations in the Black Sea against the Bolsheviks.

LEFT: **Besides war fighting, battleships had a diplomatic purpose in peacetime, and this stern view of *Majestic* and the admiral's gallery hints at the luxury onboard, at least for one man.** ABOVE: **This Majestic class appears more warlike, painted all over in grey. The class survived World War I and individual ships were broken up in the 1920s.**

Majestic class

Class: *Magnificent, Jupiter, Majestic, Prince George, Victorious, Mars, Hannibal, Caesar, Illustrious.*
Launched 1894–6
Dimensions: Length – 128.3m/421ft
Beam – 22.9m/75ft
Draught – 8.2m/27ft
Displacement: 14,445 tonnes/14,890 tons
Armament: Main – 4 x 305mm/12in guns
Secondary – 12 x 150mm/6in, 16 x 12pdr,
12 x 2pdr guns and 5 x 455mm/18in torpedoes
Machinery: 8 boilers, 2 shafts,
8,950kW/12,000ihp
Performance: 17 knots
Complement: 672 men
All (except *Majestic*) were sold for breaking up in 1921–2.

LEFT: **British design, after a generation of change, was remarkably consistent during the pre-Dreadnought period. The Canopus class were only smaller versions of their predecessors. They saw service worldwide and also proved useful in World War I.** BELOW: **The Canopus class were the same length as the Majestics but had their funnels arranged in-line, and with their tall masts made handsome ships and good seagoing vessels.**

Canopus class

British battleship construction in this period showed a consistency in design, and the Canopus class were smaller and faster versions of the Majestics, designed for the Far East and intended to counter the growing naval power of Japan. New-style Krupp armour maintained protection while reducing the thickness and saving 2,032 tonnes/2,000 tons in weight. However, 25.4mm/1in and 50.8mm/2in deck armour was fitted when it was rumoured that the French were fitting howitzers in their ships.

The Canopus class had all-round loading, like *Caesar* and *Illustrious*, and the last of the class, *Vengeance*, was fitted with improved mountings that could also be loaded at any elevation. She had improved armour, giving her flat-sided mountings a "modern" appearance. All earlier British pre-Dreadnoughts had had side-by-side funnels but this was now abandoned in favour of a fore and aft arrangement. The Belleville water-tube boilers worked at 21.1kgcm/300psi, compared to the 11kgcm/155psi of cylindrical boilers, and on trials developed 10,100kW/13,500hp giving speeds of over 18 knots.

Typical of her class, *Glory* served on the China Station from 1900 until 1905 when the Anglo-Japanese alliance made her presence unnecessary. Refitted in 1907 with magazine cooling and fire control, she served in the Mediterranean fleet and then the reserve fleet. In 1914, she escorted Canadian troops across the Atlantic and was relegated to the North American and West Indies station as flagship. After briefly being guard-ship in Egypt, *Glory* was sent to Archangel to remain there until 1919 and was sold to breakers in 1920.

Ocean took part in operations in the Persian Gulf in October 1914 and was at the Dardanelles on March 18, 1915 when she was damaged by gunfire and then hit a floating mine. After an orderly abandonment, *Ocean* sank three hours later. In November 1914 *Goliath* took part in the operation against the *Königsberg*, a German commerce-raiding cruiser that had taken refuge far up in the Rufiji River in East Africa. She was hit twice by Turkish gunfire off Cape Helles in April and May 1915, and on May 13, she was torpedoed by the Turkish motor torpedo boat *Muavenet* and sank with the loss of 570 men.

Canopus class

Class: *Albion, Glory, Canopus, Goliath, Ocean, Vengeance.* Launched 1897–9
Dimensions: Length – 128.5m/421ft 6in
 Beam – 22.6m/74ft
 Draught – 8m/26ft 2in
Displacement: 13,360 tonnes/13,150 tons
Armament: Main – 4 x 305mm/12in guns
 Secondary – 12 x 150mm/6in, 10 x 12pdr,
 6 x 3pdr guns and 4 x 455mm/18in torpedoes
Machinery: 20 Belleville boilers, 2 shafts,
 10,100kW/13,500ihp
Performance: 18 knots
Complement: 682 men

LEFT: British naval architects were certainly able to design good-looking ships to a classic recipe: two double turrets, two funnels and two pole masts. ABOVE: The class continued the gradual evolution of the pre-Dreadnoughts. BELOW: Their usefulness continued into the Dreadnought era, although *Formidable* was sunk by a U-boat in the English Channel in 1915 and *Irresistible* by Turkish mines in 1916, and only *Implacable* survived World War I.

Formidable class

The three ships of this class continued the trend in development of the Majestic and Canopus designs, in which the use of lighter Krupp armour was used to give greater protection rather than to reduce size. Similar to Canopus, the armour belt was extended to the stern and bow. The armament was also similar to the earlier ships, but of larger calibre, and, like *Vengeance*, the 305mm/12in guns could be loaded on any bearing and elevation. To achieve this, a deep hoist opened into a working chamber beneath the guns, which also reduced the possibility of fire or blast spreading to the magazines.

They were fitted with inward-turning propellers resulting in improved speed (over 18 knots) and reduced fuel consumption, but at slow speeds they were difficult to manoeuvre.

All served in the Mediterranean from commissioning until 1908, when they were withdrawn to home waters, fitted with fire control and an array of wireless aerials. *Formidable* had been paid-off

into the reserve when World War I broke out, and she was sunk on January 1, 1915, while unescorted on passage in Lyme Bay west of Portland Bill. Struck by torpedoes from the German submarine *U-24,* she sank with heavy loss of life in the cold and darkness, and bad weather.

These pre-Dreadnoughts were not fit to fight in the main theatre of operations, the North Sea, and were relegated to secondary operations such as the landings at Gallipoli, where *Irresistible* was mined and sunk on March 18, 1915. The Turks had covertly laid an extra row of mines where the allies attempted to execute a plan to force their way through to Constantinople. The mines also trapped *Ocean* and the French battleship *Bouvet*: of 16 British and French battleships that took part in the attempt to rush the straits, three were badly damaged and three were sunk. *Ocean* and *Bouvet* sank in minutes, while

Irresistible took several hours to sink and was only saved from drifting on to the shore of Turkey by the strong stream emerging from the Bosporus.

Formidable class

Class: *Formidable, Irresistible, Implacable.*
Launched 1898–9
Dimensions: Length – 131.6m/431ft 9in
Beam – 22.86m/75ft
Draught – 7.9m/25ft 11in
Displacement: 14,733 tonnes/14,500 tons
Armament: Main – 4 x 305mm/12in guns
Secondary – 12 x 150mm/6in, 16 x 12pdr,
6 x 3pdr guns and 4 x 455mm/18in torpedoes
Machinery: 20 Belleville boilers, 2 shafts,
11,190kW/15,000ihp
Performance: 18 knots
Complement: 780 men
Implacable was broken up in 1921.

LEFT: *London* in camouflage and fitted as a minelayer. Her heavy guns were removed and she could carry an outfit of 240 mines. The dazzle patterns were meant to prevent U-boat commanders from achieving a torpedo-firing solution by accurate estimation of speed and course. BELOW: One of the newly completed London class entering Malta very early in the 20th century.

London class

The first three ships of the London class were constructed under the 1898–9 naval estimates and the last two under the 1900–1 estimates. They were largely repeats of the Formidable class with some changes to their armour, which included a longer armoured belt. All had Belleville boilers, except *Queen,* which was fitted with Babcock and Wilcox boilers. The designed displacement was 15,240 tonnes/15,000 tons although there was some variation across the class.

Venerable served in the Mediterranean and then in home waters.

Bulwark was an ill-fated ship. Intended as flagship of the Mediterranean Fleet, delays in her refit meant she joined the Home Fleet instead. In October 1907, she grounded needing repairs. While loading ammunition at Sheerness on November 26, 1914, she was destroyed by a massive internal explosion, with only a dozen survivors from her complement of over 700 officers and men. The cause was widely attributed to the unstable nature of the black powder in use, which destroyed several ships of this epoch.

London was flagship of the Channel Fleet in 1908 and of the Atlantic Fleet in 1910. In 1912, she was used in flying experiments, which included the first take-off from a ship underway, using a 7.3m/24ft ramp built out over a turret and used to launch a biplane. At the outbreak of war she was employed on Channel patrols until sent on the Dardanelles expedition. Transferred to the Adriatic in May 1915, she was based at Taranto until 1917. Her 305mm/12in guns were removed and the after-gun replaced with a 150mm/6in gun when she became a minelayer, carrying 240 mines.

Queen and *Prince of Wales* differed from the rest of the London class by having open 12pdr gun batteries amidships. Like *London*, both ships were engaged on Channel patrols before being sent to support the ANZAC landings at Gallipoli, and were then based in Taranto, partly to check the Austro-Hungarian fleet in the Adriatic. *Queen*'s 305mm/12in guns were removed in Italy and transferred to the Italian Navy in 1918. All were sold for breaking up in 1920.

London class

Class: *London, Bulwark, Venerable, Queen, Prince of Wales.* Launched 1899–1902
Dimensions: Length – 131.6m/431ft 9in
 Beam – 22.86m/75ft in
 Draught – 7.92m/26ft
Displacement: 14,733 tonnes/14,500 tons
Armament: Main – 4 x 305mm/12in guns
 Secondary – 12 x 150mm/6in, 16 x 12pdr, 6 x 3pdr guns and 4 x 455mm/18in torpedoes
Machinery: 20 boilers, 2 shafts, 11,190kW/15,000ihp
Performance: 18 knots
Complement: 714 men

LEFT: The battleship *Russell* in the 1900s. She has an extensive suite of radio aerials but no range-finding equipment to enable her to fire her heavy guns accurately at long range. BELOW: Though only a few years old, the Duncan class were made immediately obsolete by the Dreadnought revolution. *Albemarle,* seen here, was used as an icebreaker in World War I. BELOW LEFT: An evocative picture of the Duncans at sea and working as a homogenous squadron.

Duncan class

Four ships were ordered in 1898 in response to a perceived threat from France and Russia, and two more in 1899. Designed before the London class, and intended to catch fast Russian battleships, the Duncan class sacrificed armour for speed. The armour of the belts and around the barbettes was thinner than the Londons, and speed came from four extra boilers and a modified hull form. They were the first British battleships to exceed 19 knots. The Duncans operated in the Mediterranean until 1904–5 and then in home waters, with the exception of *Duncan, Exmouth* and *Russell,* which also served in the Mediterranean from 1908 until 1912.

Albemarle saw service in the Channel and Atlantic Fleets, and was flagship at Gibraltar until she became a gunnery tender in May 1913. At the outbreak of World War I she served on the Northern Patrol, the distant blockade of Germany where in November 1915 she was badly damaged by heavy weather while in the Pentland Firth. After repairs, she served as an icebreaker at Archangel, and after having her guns stripped out she became an accommodation ship at Devonport in 1917.

Cornwallis was the first ship to open fire in the Dardanelles, on February 18, 1915, and she took part in all the operations including the evacuation of troops from the peninsula. She was hit by three torpedoes from German U-boat *U-32* on January 9, 1917 and sank about 100km/60 miles south-east of Malta with the loss of 15 lives.

Exmouth and *Russell* bombarded Zeebrugge in November 1914 and again in May 1915, and both served in the Dardanelles. *Exmouth* returned to Britain and was paid-off in 1917, but *Russell* was mined, reputedly by the German U-boat *U-72,* on April 27, 1916, just off the coast of Malta with the loss of over 100 lives.

Montagu ran aground on Lundy on May 30, 1906, and was wrecked, although her guns were later salvaged.

The surviving ships were sold for scrap in 1920.

Duncan class
Class: *Duncan, Cornwallis, Exmouth, Montagu, Russell, Albemarle.* Launched 1901
Dimensions: Length – 131.7m/432ft Beam – 23m/75ft 6in Draught – 7.9m/25ft 9in
Displacement: 13,482 tonnes/13,270 tons
Armament: Main – 4 x 305mm/12in guns Secondary – 12 x 150mm/6in, 10 x 12pdr, 6 x 3pdr guns and 4 x 455mm/18in torpedoes
Machinery: 24 Belleville boilers, 2 shafts, 13,429kW/18,000ihp
Performance: 19 knots
Complement: 720 men

LEFT: **The King Edward VII class or "The Wobbly Eight" were so-called because, although very manoeuvrable ships, the design of their underwater form and balanced rudders caused lateral instability. Completed during and after the Dreadnought revolution, they were workhorses of the fleet.** ABOVE: **When modernized with torpedo bulges and improved fire-control (on tripod masts) they saw action throughout World War I.** BELOW: **Note the funnel bands painted so that one ship could be distinguished from another.**

King Edward VII class

Ordered in three batches between 1901 and 1903, the King Edward VII class marked a departure from the Majestic class derivatives. Their armament including four 235mm/9.2in guns mounted in single turrets on the upper deck and the 150mm/6in casement guns were moved up one deck to a central battery behind 180mm/7in armoured bulkheads. In consequence they were criticized because, not having a uniform secondary armament, it was almost impossible to distinguish between the fall of shot of various guns which prevented good fire control. Completed with fighting tops on pole masts, these were replaced by fire-control platforms on tripod masts.

In the battle of the boilers, the class was fitted with various steam plants. They were also the first British pre-Dreadnoughts to be fitted with balanced rudders, and though this gave them a small turning circle at speed, they had difficulty keeping a steady course and earned the name "The Wobbly Eight".

Most ships served prior to World War I in the Atlantic, Channel and Home Fleets and formed a single unit, the Third Battle Squadron, from May 1912 onwards. In August 1914, the Third Battle Squadron joined the Grand Fleet at Scapa Flow. Towards the end of the war, they were partially reconstructed, given anti-torpedo bulges and a tripod mast with director control platforms, and the 150mm/6in battery was replaced with four 150mm/6in guns placed one deck higher.

King Edward VII served briefly pre-war in the Mediterranean, but after she joined the Third Battle Squadron, was mined off Cape Wrath. Both engine rooms flooded and *King Edward VII* capsized and sank after 12 hours. *Commonwealth* distinguished herself by colliding with the battleship *Albemarle* in 1907 and in the same year by going aground.

The Royal Navy's interest in aviation was highlighted when in May 1912, *Hibernia* was fitted with a 30.5m/100ft-long runway over the forecastle and Commander Sampson made the first ever flight from a British ship, on May 4, 1912. All were culled after the Washington Naval Treaty, along with scores of other battleships in the world's navies, most of them of prewar design.

King Edward VII class

Class: *King Edward VII, Commonwealth, Dominion, Hindustan, New Zealand, Britannia, Hibernia, Africa.* Launched 1903–5

Dimensions: Length – 138.3m/453ft 9in
Beam – 23.8m/78ft
Draught – 7.8m/25ft 8in

Displacement: 15,835 tonnes/15,585 tons

Armament: Main – 4 x 305mm/12in and
4 x 235mm/9.2in guns
Secondary – 10 x 150mm/6in, 14 x 12pdr,
14 x 3pdr guns and 4 x 455mm/18in torpedoes

Machinery: 10, 12 or 16 boilers, 2 shafts,
13,420kW/18,000ihp

Speed: 18.5 knots

Complement: 777 men
New Zealand was renamed *Zealandia* in 1911.
King Edward VII was fitted with 10 Babcock and Wilcox boilers, *Dominion* and *Commonwealth* with 16 Babcock and Wilcox, *New Zealand* with 12 Niclausse; the others 12 Babcock and Wilcox.

LEFT: **The Royal Navy bought the two ships of the Swiftsure class, while under construction, from the Chilean navy in order to end an arms race in South America.** *Triumph* (formerly *Libertad*) **is seen at anchor at a fleet review.**

Swiftsure class

Class: *Swiftsure* (ex *Constitucion*),
Triumph (ex *Libertad*). Launched 1903
Dimensions: Length – 146.2m/479ft 9in
Beam – 21.6m/71ft
Draught – 7.7m/25ft 4in
Displacement: 11,990 tonnes/11,800 tons
Armament: Main – 4 x 255mm/10in and
14 x 190mm/7.5in guns
Secondary – 14 x 14pdr, 2 x 12pdr guns and
2 x 455mm/18in torpedoes
Machinery: 12 large-tube Yarrow boilers,
2 shafts, 10,490kW/12,500ihp
Speed: 19 knots
Complement: 800 men

Swiftsure class

Chile has long-standing connections with Britain, and it was in Chile's independence struggle that Lord Cochrane repeated and exceeded some of his exploits when he had fought the French and Spanish in the Great War of 1793–1815. Independence did not mean peace and Chile and its neighbours fought a series of wars and civil wars. During a war with Peru, the turret ship *Huascar* was captured in 1879, and so has been preserved. At a battle in 1891, during a revolution in which the Chilean forces supported the forces for change, the government torpedo gunboat *Almirante Lynch* sank the protected cruiser *Blanco Encalada*: this was the first successful use of a self-propelled torpedo against an armoured vessel.

In the 1890s Chile had ordered some ships from France, but when a border dispute threatened war with Argentina, Chile ordered two battleships from Britain: *Constitucion* and *Libertad*, designed by Sir Edward Reed. They were still building when the crisis in South America was settled, and the Royal Navy, which reckoned ships under construction for other governments formed a reserve, bought them both and they were re-named *Swiftsure* and *Triumph*. This also stopped the Russians from acquiring these ships for its war with Japan.

In comparison with other British ships, *Swiftsure* and *Triumph* were lightly armoured and lightly armed, and their beam and draught, limited by the size of Chilean docks, made them relatively long, thin and fast. Despite their powerful secondary armament, they were rated as second-class battleships. If they could not stand up to battleships, they could certainly run down and out-gun any cruiser or merchant ship and so, by 1913, *Swiftsure* became flagship of the East Indies station and *Triumph* had been sent to the China station. *Swiftsure* was scrapped in 1920, but *Triumph* was torpedoed by *U-21* off the Dardanelles on May 25, 1915.

LEFT: **These were small battleships by the Royal Navy's contemporary standards and were going to replace** *Centurion* **and** *Barfleur* **on the China station, but they were both recalled to the Dardanelles.**

Lord Nelson class

The Lord Nelsons were provided under the 1904/5 Estimates, and had a designed displacement of 16,765 tonnes/16,500 tons. The progress towards a heavier armament, first seen in *King Edward VII*, was taken a stage further in this design; all 150mm/6in guns were abandoned in favour of a complete secondary battery of 235mm/9.2in guns all mounted in turrets. This disposed of the unsatisfactory main deck batteries that, despite their limitations, had been repeated in every class since the Royal Sovereigns. The only other gun armament was 12pdr for torpedo boat defence, and these were mounted on a flying deck over an amidships structure reminiscent of Reed's turret ships. Owing to the limited space for shrouds, a tripod mainmast was adopted. The vessels were slightly heavier than the King Edward VIIs but docking restrictions required that their length be limited, so beam and draught were increased, and a squarer hull form amidships allowed some fining of the lines fore and aft to give a speed of 18 knots. They were good sea-boats and gun-platforms and had exceptional manoeuvrability. On trials, *Lord Nelson* made 18.7 knots with 13,008kW/17,445ihp and *Agamemnon* 18.5 knots with 12,878kW/17,270ihp.

In the long term, they were not successful ships because of the fire control problems with mixed-calibre armament. Their 305mm/12in guns were

new pattern 45-calibre weapons; the guns and mountings originally ordered for them were used in the *Dreadnought* and their completion was delayed while replacement guns were manufactured.

The waterline armour belt extended over the full length of the hull and was 305mm/12in amidships reducing to 230mm/9in and 150mm/6in forward and 100mm/4in aft. The upper belt extended from the stern to the after barbette only, and was 205mm/8in amidships reducing to 150mm/6in and 100mm/4in forward and closed by a 205mm/8in bulkhead at the after end. Between the upper belt

ABOVE: **It was the mixed armament of 305mm/12in and 235mm/9.2in guns, clearly seen here in *Lord Nelson*, photographed in 1917 at Malta, which made these ships pre-Dreadnoughts.** BELOW: *Agamemnon* **bringing up the rear of the British line of battle.**

and upper deck the bases of the 235mm/9.2in mountings were protected by a citadel of uniform 205mm/8in armour extending from forward to aft barbette.

Lord Nelson began her career as flagship of the Fifth Battle Squadron in the Channel Fleet, and in 1915 was sent to the Mediterranean. There she took part in the Dardanelles campaign, in which she hit and was hit by Turkish batteries, but sustained only light damage. She was kept in the eastern Mediterranean to bottle up the German *Goeben* and finally entered the Black Sea in November 1918. *Agamemnon* operated closely with *Lord Nelson*: together they destroyed Kavak Bridge in December 1915 and on October 30, 1918, the Turkish armistice was signed onboard *Agamemnon*, before both ships passed through the Dardanelles.

Lord Nelson class	

Class: *Lord Nelson, Agamemnon.* Launched 1906
Dimensions: Length – 135.2m/443ft 6in
 Beam – 24.2m/79ft 6in
 Draught – 7.9m/26ft
Displacement: 16,348 tonnes/16,090 tons
Armament: Main – 4 x 305mm/12in and
 10 x 235mm/9.2in guns
 Secondary – 24 x 12pdr, 2 x 3pdr guns
 and 5 x 455mm/18in torpedoes
Machinery: 15 boilers, 2 shafts,
 12,490kW/16,750ihp
Speed: 18 knots
Complement: 800 men

Maine

Class: *Maine*. Launched 1889
Dimensions: Length – 97.23m/319ft
Beam – 17.37m/57ft
Draught – 6.55m/21ft 6in
Displacement: 6,789 tonnes/6,682 tons
Armament: Main – 4 x 255mm/10in and
6 x 150mm/6in guns
Secondary – 7 x 6pdr, 8 x 1pdr guns and
4 x 355mm/14in torpedoes
Machinery: 4 boilers, 2 shafts, 6710kW/9,000ihp
Speed: 17 knots
Complement: 374 men

Maine

Authorized in 1886, *Maine* rated as a second-class battleship, forming part of the USN's North Atlantic Squadron when she was sent to Havana, Cuba, to protect American property and life during a revolutionary struggle against Spain.

On February 15, 1898, shortly before 22.00, an explosion tore *Maine* apart, shattering the forward part of the ship, sinking her and killing 260 officers and men. Although an official report concluded that Spain (then the colonial power in Cuba) could not definitely be blamed for the disaster, the USA was stirred into frenzy and two months later "Remember the *Maine*" became the war cry that started the Spanish-American War. *Maine* was raised and towed out to be sunk in the Gulf of Mexico in 1912. Her mainmast is in Arlington National Cemetery and her mizzenmast at the US Naval Academy, Annapolis.

Several ships of this era blew up suddenly, this usually being blamed on unstable ammunition, but in 1976 Admiral Hyman Rickover conducted a new investigation and decided that the cause was spontaneous combustion in *Maine*'s coalbunkers.

Texas

Part of the American flying squadron that blockaded Cienfuegos, Cuba, in May 1898, *Texas* later reconnoitred Guantanamo Bay. On June 16, she bombarded Cayo del Tore, destroying a fort there from 1,280m/1,400 yards' range in an hour and a quarter.

On May 19, a Spanish squadron under Admiral Pascual Cervera arrived in Santiago harbour on the southern coast of Cuba. While North American troops landed, a USN fleet blockaded the harbour. (These troops included the Rough Riders, a volunteer cavalry regiment led by Theodore Roosevelt who would subsequently do so much to advance the USN.) When the Spanish attempted to break out of Santiago, an unequal fight took place on July 3, 1898, known as the Battle of Santiago, between the Spanish squadron of cruisers and destroyers and the USN flying squadron that included the battleships *Texas, Indiana* and *Oregon*.

The Spanish fleet was annihilated, sealing the fate of the last Spanish colony in the Americas. *Texas* was expended as a target in 1911–12.

LEFT: These small (6,095 tonnes/6,000 tons) ships suggest that the USN was not yet thinking in oceanic terms, though when war broke out with Spain they proved useful in the Caribbean.

Texas

Class: *Texas*. Launched 1889
Dimensions: Length – 94.1m/308ft 10in
Beam – 19.4m/64ft
Draught – 6.9m/22ft 6in
Displacement: 5,728 tonnes/6,316 tons
Armament: Main – 2 x 305mm/12in and
6 x 100mm/4in guns
Secondary – 12 x 6pdr, 6 x 1pdr guns and
4 x 355mm/14in torpedoes
Machinery: 4 boilers, 2 shafts,
5,900kW/8,600ihp
Speed: 17 knots
Complement: 392/508 men

Indiana class

*I*ndiana was initially designated "BB1" but she and her sisters were later re-rated as coast battleships. Although larger than previous designs, they were over-armed and had only 3.35m/11ft freeboard. *Indiana* and *Massachusetts* were sunk as targets in the early 1920s while *Oregon* became a museum ship until 1942, an ammunition carrier in 1944, and was finally sold for breaking up in 1956.

During the Spanish-American War *Indiana* was deployed to intercept Cervera's Spanish squadron, which wild invasion rumours alleged was going to steam up the Potomac. *Indiana* did not join in the first phase of the Battle of Santiago, but when the Spanish destroyers *Pluton* and *Furor* emerged from harbour, she overwhelmed them.

Indiana made several training cruises carrying midshipmen of the US Naval Academy, which included a visit to Queenstown, Ireland, when she fired a 21-gun salute for the coronation of King George V. She served during World War I as a gunnery training ship, and afterwards served as a target for aerial bombs, was sunk in 1920 and sold for scrap in 1924. *Massachusetts* also blockaded Cuba,

although she missed the Battle of Santiago. However, she helped force the unarmoured cruiser *Reina Mercedes* ashore on July 6, 1898. Afterwards she served in the USN's North Atlantic Squadron and as a training ship. Scuttled off Pensacola Bar, she was declared Florida state property in 1956.

Oregon was slightly larger than her sisters. On her 22,530km/14,000-mile maiden voyage from San Francisco to Jupiter Point, Florida, to join the fleet assembling for the attack on Cuba, she demonstrated both the capability of the USN to deploy its ships, and the need for the Panama Canal. After the Battle of Santiago, *Oregon* was sent to the USN's Asiatic station. She cooperated with the US army in the Philippine insurrection, and was sent to Taku during the Boxer Rebellion in China. However, on June 28, 1900, she grounded on a rock in the

Straits of Pechili, and was nearly wrecked. In June 1925 she was loaned to the State of Oregon as a floating museum. At Guam in 1948 she broke her moorings during a typhoon and was found some days later 805km/500 miles away. She was finally scrapped in Japan.

Indiana class

Class: *Indiana, Massachusetts, Oregon.*
Launched 1893
Dimensions: Length – 106.95m/350ft 11in
Beam – 21.1m/69ft 3in
Draught – 7.3m/24ft
Displacement: 10,498 tonnes/10,288 tons
Armament: Main – 4 x 330mm/13in and
8 x 205mm/8in guns
Secondary – 20 x 6pdr, 6 x 1pdr guns and
6 x 455mm/18in torpedoes
Machinery: 6 boilers, 2 shafts, 6,710kW/9,000ihp
Speed: 15 knots
Complement: 473 men

BELOW: **The Indiana class (10,160 tonnes/10,000 tons) was able to deploy within the American hemisphere, from California to Florida, in time to influence the outcome of the war.** RIGHT: **Officially rated as BB-1, the size of *Indiana* is indicated by the sailors standing atop one of the 205mm/8in, side-mounted gun turrets in the 1890s.**

Iowa

The second ship of her name in the USN, *Iowa* served in the Atlantic Fleet. She fired the first shots in the Battle of Santiago on July 3, 1898, and overwhelmed the Spanish cruisers *Infanta Maria Teresa* and *Oquendo* in a one-sided 20-minute fight, setting both ships on fire and driving them ashore. *Iowa* rescued the survivors of these ships and of the cruisers and two other destroyers, including the Spanish commander, Admiral Cervera. The battle, which was the highlight of *Iowa*'s career, was not a true test of her design. After Cuba gained its independence, *Iowa* spent two and a half years in the Pacific, and in 1902 she became flagship of the USN South Atlantic Squadron.

Her subsequent career was typical of many of the USN pre-Dreadnoughts, few of which were seriously tested in battle. She was decommissioned in June 1903, recommissioned on December 23, 1903, and joined the North Atlantic Squadron to participate in the John Paul Jones Commemoration ceremonies in June 1905. *Iowa* was placed in reserve in July 1907, and decommissioned at Philadelphia in July 1908. She was rearmed in 1909 and, in additon to her military or pole foremast, was given a cage or lattice mainmast.

When recommissioned again in May 1910, *Iowa* served as a training ship in the Atlantic Reserve Fleet, making a number of training cruises to northern Europe, and she participated in the naval review at Philadelphia in October 1912. She saw limited service in World War I, first as a receiving ship, then as a training ship, and finally, when the USA had entered the war, as a guard ship in Chesapeake Bay. She was finally decommissioned on March 31, 1919.

TOP: *Iowa* in the white and buff paint scheme, similar to the Royal Navy's, which later gave the name to the "Great White Fleet". ABOVE: After World War I, *Iowa* was stripped of her guns and became a radio-controlled target ship used in bombing experiments. BELOW LEFT: Most large ships of the period carried complements of marines, and here US marines are seen at drill onboard *Iowa*.

Iowa

Class: *Iowa*. Launched 1896
Dimensions: Length – 110.5m/362ft 5in
  Beam – 22m/72ft 3in
  Draught – 7.3m/24ft
Displacement: 11,593 tonnes/11,410 tons
Armament: Main – 4 x 305mm/12in and
  8 x 205mm/8in guns
  Secondary – 6 x 100mm/4in, 20 x 6-pdr guns
  and 4 x 355mm/14in torpedoes
Machinery: 5 boilers, 2 shafts, 8,900kW/11,000ihp
Speed: 16 knots
Complement: 486/654 men

LEFT: Besides the Dreadnought revolution, there were other new weapons like the submarine. Here *Kearsarge* and an early USN submarine inspect each other, in about 1898. BELOW: *Kearsarge* was retrofitted with lattice or cage masts. The distribution of weight helped to reduce vibration in the spotting tops at the head of the masts and so improved the performance of optical rangefinders.

Kearsarge class

USN battleships were named after the states of the Union, except *Kearsarge*, which took her name from a steam sloop of the American Civil War that sank the Confederate raider *Alabama* off Cherbourg in 1864.

Kearsarge was flagship of the North Atlantic Station in 1903 and again in 1904. As flagship of the USN European Squadron, the German Kaiser visited her on June 26, 1903 at Kiel and the Prince of Wales on July 13 at Spithead. When the North Atlantic Battleship *Squadron* visited Lisbon, she entertained the King of Portugal on June 11, 1904, and on the Fourth of July in Phaleron, she hosted the King, Prince Andrew and Princess Alice of Greece. During target practice off Cape Cruz, Cuba on April 13, 1906, a powder charge ignited in a 330mm/13in gun killing two officers and eight men; four others were seriously injured.

Kearsarge was one of the Great White Fleet of battleships which President Theodore Roosevelt sent around the world in 1907. *Kearsarge* commenced a modernization programme in the Philadelphia Navy Yard in 1909, but she

had already been made obsolete by the Dreadnought revolution and was not commissioned again until 1915, when she took US marines to Vera Cruz, Mexico.

Kearsarge was used as a training ship for several years and then converted to a 10,160-tonne/10,000-ton crane ship. She retained her name until it was required for an aircraft carrier in 1941, then becoming a crane ship, and finally she was sold for scrap in 1955.

Fitted out in New York, *Kentucky* sailed via Gibraltar and the Suez Canal to become the flagship on the US Asiatic Station from 1901–4, visiting Hong Kong and the principal ports of China and Japan. She landed marines in Cuba in 1906 to protect American interests and property during an insurrection there and in 1907 was one of 16 battleships in the Great White Fleet.

During 1915 and 1916 *Kentucky* patrolled off Vera Cruz, watching American interests during the Mexican Revolution. Post-war she was used as a training ship, and scrapped in 1924 under the Washington Naval Treaty.

ABOVE: *Kearsarge* leading ships of the USN's European squadron in review past a line of British battleships (not shown) in 1903. She is followed by two cruisers, *Chicago* and *San Francisco*.

Kearsarge class

Class: *Kearsarge, Kentucky.* Launched 1898
Dimensions: Length – 114.4m/375ft 4in
   Beam – 22m/72ft 3in
   Draught – 7.16m/23ft 6in
Displacement: 11,725 tonnes/11,540 tons
Armament: Main – 4 x 330mm/13in and
   4 x 205mm/8in guns
   Secondary – 14 x 125mm/5in, 20 x 6pdr guns
   and 4 x 455mm/18in torpedoes
Machinery: 5 boilers, 2 shafts, 7,450kW/10,000ihp
Speed: 16 knots
Complement: 553 men
The 205mm/8in turrets were fitted atop the 330mm/13in turrets and trained together as one unit, an arrangement which did work well. Rearmed in 1909–11, both ships were fitted with cage masts fore and aft.

LEFT AND ABOVE: **Like** *Kearsarge*, **these two pictures show** *Wisconsin* **as built in the 1900s and** *Illinois* **(of the same class) after modernization immediately pre-war and in the grey paintwork which the USN adopted after the cruise of the "Great White Fleet".**
BELOW: **A rare picture of the period showing the hull shape of an American pre-Dreadnought –** *Illinois* **in dry dock in the New Orleans Navy Yard in 1902.**

Illinois class

When *Illinois* was flagship of the USN European Squadron, she ran aground off Christiania (now Oslo), Norway, and had to be docked in the Royal Navy dockyard at Chatham in 1902. Like many ships of her vintage she was used as a training ship in World War I. After the war she was laid up until being sold to the state of New York in 1921 for use by the Naval Militia. Demilitarized under the Washington Naval Treaty, *Illinois* was fitted out as a floating armoury in 1924 and became part of the New York Naval Reserve. She remained in New York until 1941, when she was renamed *Prairie State* so that her name could be given to a projected new battleship. In 1956 *Prairie State* was sold for scrap to the Bethlehem Steel Corporation.

From her commissioning in 1901, *Alabama* took part in fleet exercises and gunnery training in the Gulf of Mexico and the West Indies in the wintertime before returning north for repairs and operations off the New England coast during the summer and autumn. Exceptionally, in 1904, *Alabama*, in company with the battleships *Kearsarge, Maine* and *Iowa,* visited Portugal and the Mediterranean.

Although *Alabama* started out as part of the Great White Fleet, she was delayed for repairs in San Francisco, and did not visit Japan but, accompanied by the new battleship *Maine*, completed her circumnavigation of the globe via Honolulu and Guam, Manila, Singapore, Colombo, Aden and the Suez Canal.

On return to the USA she was placed in reserve, coming out only to be used for training. Eventually *Alabama* was sunk in Chesapeake Bay in bombing tests by planes of the US Army and her hulk sold for scrap in 1924.

Wisconsin was built on the West Coast and served her early years in the Pacific. In 1902 she hosted peace talks between Panama and Colombia which became known as the "The Peace of Wisconsin". From 1903–6 *Wisconsin* formed part of the USN Asiatic Fleet's Northern Squadron, steaming up the Yangtze River as far as Nanking. After her circumnavigation she remained on the East Coast and after an uneventful career was sold for scrap in 1922.

Illinois class

Class: *Illinois, Alabama, Wisconsin.* Launched 1898
Dimensions: Length – 117.6m/386ft
Beam – 22m/72ft 3in
Draught – 7.1m/23ft 5in
Displacement: 11,751 tonnes/11,565 tons
Armament: Main – 4 x 330mm/13in and
14 x 150mm/6in guns
Secondary – 16 x 6pdr, 6 x 1pdr guns and
4 x 455mm/18in torpedoes
Machinery: 6 boilers, 2 shafts,7,450kW//10,000ihp
Speed: 15 knots
Complement: 536 men
The dimensions given are for *Illinois*, but there were small differences between all three ships of this class. An unusual feature of the class was their side-by-side funnels. All three ships formed part of the Great White Fleet.

Maine class

The second *Maine* was laid down in Philadelphia a year to the day after the destruction of the first. She was launched in July 1901 and not commissioned until December 29, 1902. Like others of her vintage, she took part in the Great White Fleet, although in company with *Alabama* took a shorter route and arrived back on the Atlantic coast in October 1908 in advance of the rest of the fleet.

Used as a training ship in World War I, *Maine* took part in the review of the fleet at New York on December 26, 1918.

Maine operated with ships of the Atlantic Fleet until May 15, 1920, when she was decommissioned at Philadelphia Navy Yard.

The distinguishing feature of *Missouri*'s career, while serving in the USN Atlantic Fleet in April 1904, was a flashback from the left gun of her after turret that ignited powder charges in their ready stowage. There was no explosion but the subsequent rapid burning suffocated 36 of the gun's crew. Efficient damage-control measures prevented the spread of fire and by June *Missouri* was repaired and ready for service. An investigation into the cause of the fire led to improvements in the design of the turret and magazine, which were incorporated in the British monitor *Raglan*, which had American built turrets, and when *Raglan* suffered a turret explosion she sank without explosion.

All three ships differed in displacement and *Ohio*, built by the Union Iron Works at San Francisco on the west coast, was the smallest. *Ohio* was flagship of the USN's Asiatic Fleet, and at Manila in April 1905 embarked a party which comprised the Secretary of War William Howard Taft and Alice Roosevelt, the daughter of the president of the USA, for a tour of the Far East that included the Philippines, China and Japan.

Missouri and *Ohio* were also part of the Great White Fleet. All three ships were scrapped under the Washington Naval Treaty.

Maine class

Class: *Maine, Missouri, Ohio.* Launched 1901
Dimensions: Length – 120.1m/393ft 11in
  Beam – 22m/72ft 3in
  Draught – 7.4m/24ft 4in
Displacement: 13,052 tonnes/12,846 tons
Armament: Main – 4 x 305mm/12in and
  16 x 150mm/6in guns
  Secondary – 6 x 75mm/3in, 8 x 8pdrs guns and
  2 x 455mm/18in torpedoes
Machinery: 12 boilers, 2 shafts,
  11,930kW/16,000ihp
Speed: 18 knots
Complement: 561 men

LEFT: **After her loss in 1898, *Maine* was immediately replaced by a new pre-Dreadnought and sister ship to *Missouri* and *Ohio*.** BELOW LEFT: **A close-up of the forward 305mm/12in gun mounting in *Ohio*.**
BELOW: ***Missouri* was modernized pre-war with cage masts, fighting tops and turret-mounted rangefinders.**

LEFT: *Rhode Island* photographed off New York in 1909, clearly showing the superimposed turrets. Also the forward pole mast has been replaced by a lattice with searchlight platforms. ABOVE: *Nebraska*, before acceptance into the USN, making smoke and a bow wave while undergoing speed trials. BELOW: Sailors and marines in *Virginia* with something to cheer. Note the field gun in its component parts on the deck.

Virginia class

The largest single class of USN pre-Dreadnoughts was authorized in 1889 and 1900. They were larger again than their predecessors and, in spite of the unsatisfactory experience in *Kearsarge* and *Kentucky*, the superimposed turret arrangement was repeated. There were more than half a dozen different calibres of guns, with all the problems of ammunition supply and spotting fall of shot. When refitted in 1909–10, the 150mm/6in guns were removed, and the number of 75mm/3in guns reduced. At the same time the pole masts were replaced by cages. On trials, they were the first USN battleships to exceed 19 knots.

Virginia's career in Cuba, The Great White Fleet, in Europe and Mexico was unexceptional. However, coal supplies had been a problem during the fleet's circumnavigation and in 1910, *Virginia* experimented with equipment for coaling at sea. She was in refit at Boston when World War I broke out and her crew were employed boarding interned German merchant ships, *Virginia* made eight

trooping voyages, more than any other battleship, from France in 1918 and 1919. She was expended as a target. *Virginia* and *New Jersey* were bombed at anchor by the US Army. The trials were artificial, but gave a significant impetus to the development of aviation in the USN.

Georgia's career was punctuated by an explosion in her after 205mm/8in turret, when black powder ignited, killing ten officers and men and injuring 11, but no permanent or lasting damage to the ship was caused and within a few weeks she was back in service. A veteran of the Great White Fleet, she made five trooping voyages from France. *Georgia* finished her service in the Pacific Fleet.

The remaining three ships of this class had similar careers: they became veterans of the Great White Fleet and were used as troopships post-war. *Nebraska* replaced *Alabama* in the fleet when it arrived at San Francisco in May 1908, and *New Jersey* was expended as a target. *Rhode Island* and her remaining sisters were sold for breaking up in 1923.

Virginia class

Class: *Virginia, Nebraska, Georgia, New Jersey, Rhode Island.* Launched 1904
Dimensions: Length – 134.5m/441ft 3in
Beam – 23.2m/76ft
Draught – 7.2m/23ft 9in
Displacement: 15,188 tonnes/14,948 tons
Armament: Main – 4 x 305mm/12in, 8 x 205mm/8in and 12 x 150mm/6in guns
Secondary – 12 x 75mm/3in, 12 x 3pdr guns and 4 x 535mm/21in torpedoes
Machinery: 12 Babcock & Wilcox boilers, 2 shafts,18,980kW/19,000ihp
Speed: 19 knots
Complement: 812 men
On commissioning *Virginia* and *Georgia* had 24 Niclausse boilers, later replaced by 24 Babcock & Wilcox.

Connecticut class

Connecticut and Louisiana extended the fashion in the USN pre-Dreadnoughts for multiple calibres of guns, which was mocked by Cuniberti. With so many guns of similar calibre, it was impossible to spot the fall of shot and so to range the guns: in part, the *Dreadnought* was a reaction to this design trend. Both ships took part in the Great White Fleet's circumnavigation, *Connecticut* as flagship.

Connecticut was also flagship of the USN Atlantic Fleet between 1907 and 1912. In the pre-war years, she visited the Mediterranean and the Caribbean on various policing and ceremonial duties and in 1913 protected American citizens and interests during disturbances in Mexico and Haiti. Like *Louisiana*, she was fitted as a troopship, making four voyages in 1919 to bring US soldiers back from France. In the 1920s, *Connecticut* served on the west coast before being sold for scrap in 1923.

Soon after entering service *Louisiana* sailed for Havana in response to an appeal by the Cuban president for American help in suppressing an insurrection. The new battleship carried a peace commission led by the US Secretary of War, William H. Taft, who arranged for a provisional government of the island, and *Louisiana* stood by while this was set up. Next *Louisiana* became the presidential yacht, taking President Theodore Roosevelt to inspect work on the construction of the Panama Canal and on a brief visit to Cuba.

Louisiana made an extensive visit to Europe in 1910 and 1911 but was soon back in the Caribbean to protect American lives and property during revolutionary disturbances in Mexico in 1913, during tension between the USA and Mexico in 1914 and again in 1915.

During World War I *Louisiana* was used for gunnery and engineering training and in late 1918 and early 1919 she made four voyages as a troop transport from Brest with returning US soldiers. She was sold for scrap in 1923.

Connecticut class
Class: *Connecticut, Louisiana.* Launched 1904

Dimensions: Length – 139 m/456ft 4in
    Beam – 23.4m/76ft 10in
    Draught – 7.46m/24ft 6in

Displacement: 16,256 tonnes/16,000 tons

Armament: Main – 4 x 305mm/12in, 8 x 205mm/
    8in and 12 x 180mm/7in guns.
    Secondary – 12 x 3pdr guns and 4 x
    535mm/21in torpedoes

Machinery: 12 boilers, 2   shafts,15,300kW/16,500ihp
Speed: 18 knots
Complement: 827 men

ABOVE: *Connecticut* at anchor in the Hudson river on the occasion of the fleet review of 1911. The launch in the foreground is typical of those carried in battleships. LEFT: *Connecticut* steaming at high speed, photographed by Enrique Muller in 1907. BELOW: President Roosevelt addresses the ship's company of *Connecticut* on the quarterdeck on return from their circumnavigation.

LEFT: **A side-on view of one of the Vermont class. The mixed armament is distinctly pre-Dreadnought, while in Britain a revolution is taking place.**
BELOW: **A detail of the bow decoration of *New Hampshire* taken while in dry dock. The picture shows the eagle figurehead, but unfortunately not the shape of the hull.**

Vermont class

American industry was beginning to show its muscle and the Vermont class of ships were repeats of the preceding Connecticut class of ships. Uniformity of build in a successful design was something which only the USN and the Royal Navy could be relied upon to achieve. All six ships were, however, made obsolescent by the Dreadnought revolution. *Vermont* was another of the Great White Fleet, which after her return to the USA joined the Atlantic Fleet. Her service alternated between European cruises and Caribbean deployments until 1914, when she landed a naval brigade (or battalion in USN usage) of 12 officers and 308 seamen and marines at Vera Cruz. The other ships that the USN sent to Mexico included the battleships *Vermont, Arkansas, New Hampshire, South Carolina* and *New Jersey*. There was only one American fatality in the shore fighting which ensued.

Like other pre-Dreadnought battleships *Vermont* was equipped as a troopship in the winter of 1918–19 and made four voyages from France with some 5,000 troops. She was scrapped in 1923.

Apart from the Great White Fleet, *Kansas*'s service was distinguished by making five crossings from Brest as a

troopship. In 1920, she was visited by the Prince of Wales at Grassey Bay, Bermuda, and in November attended the inauguration of the new American governor of the German Samoa islands, ceded to the USA after World War I. Her name was struck from the Navy List on August 24, 1923, and she was sold for scrap in the same year.

Another member of the Great White Fleet, *Minnesota* led an unremarkable career until September 29, 1918, when she struck a mine, 32km/20 miles off Fenwick Island Shoal Lightship, which had apparently been laid by the German U-boat *U-117*. She was seriously damaged but suffered no loss of life. Repaired at Philadelphia, she was serviceable again by March 1919, when she brought 3,000 veterans from France. She was sold for scrap in 1924.

On her first deployment, *New Hampshire* carried a Marine Expeditionary Regiment to Colon, Panama, to protect and garrison Panama in 1908, and she attended the fleet review at New York that welcomed back the Great White Fleet. In 1916, *New*

Hampshire operated off Santo Domingo, where her captain had a hand in the newly installed government. In 1917 she was part of the convoy escort taking US troops to France, and in 1919 she made four voyages carrying them back again. *New Hampshire* was scrapped in 1923.

Vermont class

Class: *Vermont, Kansas, Minnesota, New Hampshire.* Launched 1905
Dimensions: Length – 139m/456ft 4in
Beam – 23.4m/76ft 10in
Draught – 7.6m/24ft 6in
Displacement: 16,256 tonnes/16,000 tons
Armament: Main – 4 x 305mm/12in,
8 x 205mm/8in and 12 x 180mm/7in guns
Secondary – 20 x 75mm/3in and
12 x 3pdrs guns
Machinery: 12 boilers, 2 shafts,
12,300kW/16,500ihp
Speed: 18 knots
Complement: 880 men
The four ships of the Vermont class were repeats of the Connecticut class, with only minor differences in the secondary armament and complement.

Mississippi class

Mississippi and *Idaho* were the last of the USN's pre-Dreadnoughts, and were laid down and completed when Fisher's Dreadnought revolution had already made them obsolescent. Like other USN pre-Dreadnoughts, they carried a main battery of heavy, medium and small calibre guns. In a reaction to the rising cost of battleships the US Congress had limited their size, so that *Mississippi* and *Idaho* were actually smaller, slower and shorter-ranged than their predecessors.

Originally, both ships carried a single pole mast forward (known as a military mast) but soon after commissioning they were fitted with a cage or lattice mast aft, and in 1910 the forward pole mast was replaced by a second lattice mast, which balanced the design.

Neither ship saw battle: apart from deployments to the East Coast of North America and to the Caribbean, both made cruises to Europe. However, in June 1912, *Mississippi* landed US marines in Cuba to protect US interests, and carried men and equipment to Pensacola, Florida, to build a naval air station. In April and May 1914, she transported seaplanes and crews to Vera Cruz, Mexico, when an American squadron landed a force of 800 marines and seamen during a period of political unrest. *Mississippi*'s use as a seaplane tender was probably the first overseas deployment of aircraft by the USN. In 1909 *Mississippi* and in 1911 *Idaho* entered the Mississippi River for a tour of central US states with no seaboard. In 1910, both ships visited France and Britain, where they must have looked old-fashioned.

In July 1914, *Mississippi* and *Idaho* were sold to Greece, becoming the only USN battleships ever to be transferred to a foreign power. They were renamed *Lemnos* and *Kilkis* respectively and served in the Greek navy until April 1941 when they were sunk by German dive-bombers at Salamis, thus becoming the first American-built battleships to be lost to air attack.

Mississippi class	
Class: *Mississippi, Idaho.* Launched 1905	
Dimensions: Length – 116.4m/382ft	
Beam – 23.5m/77ft	
Draught – 7.5m/24ft 8in	
Displacement: 13,210 tonnes/13,000 tons	
Armament: Main – 4 x 305mm/12in,	
8 x 205mm/8in and 8 x 180mm/7in guns	
Secondary – 12 x 75mm/3in guns and	
2 x 535mm/21in torpedoes	
Machinery: 8 boilers, 2 shafts,	
7,450kW/10,000ihp	
Speed: 17 knots	
Complement: 744 men	

BOTTOM: ***Mississippi*** at anchor off Philadelphia in 1908 for Founders' Week. The ship's name, ready for illumination, is picked out in lights on the after superstructure. BELOW: Possibly the USN's first carrier air group. A squadron of Curtiss flying boats and floatplanes embarked in *Mississippi* during the Mexican crisis in 1914.

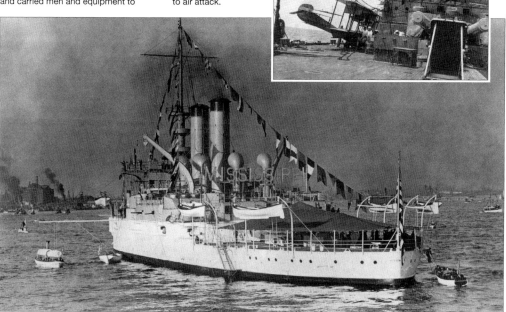

LEFT: *Yashima* and *Hatsuse* were built at the Armstrong Whitworth yard at Elswick. Here is *Hatsuse* at her launch on June 27, 1899. BELOW LEFT: *Fuji* and *Shikishima* were built at the Thames Iron Works on the Thames. Here is *Shikishima* at buoys in Malta, en route to Japan in 1900.

Fuji class

Class: *Fuji, Yashima.* Launched 1896
Dimensions: Length – 125.6m/412ft
 Beam – 22.5m/73ft 9in
 Draught – 8.1m/26ft 6in
Displacement: 12,518 tonnes/12,320 tons
Armament: Main – 4 x 305mm/12in,
 10 x 150mm/6in guns
 Secondary – 20 x 3pdr guns and
 5 x 455mm/18in torpedoes
Machinery: 14 boilers, 2 shafts.
 10,000kW/14,000ihp
Speed: 18 knots
Complement: 637 men

Fuji and Shikishima class

Building a navy was integral to Japan's rapid advance in the second half of the 19th century from feudal state to industrialized society. The first naval construction programme of home-built ships was influenced by the French *jeune école,* which advocated a fleet of cruisers and torpedo boats to counter battleships. However, the Sino-Japanese War of 1894–5 gave Japanese officers an appreciation of their navy's material and strategic necessities, and the Japanese, turning to Britain for battleships, came under the influence of the Royal Navy. Each ship of the 1896 expansion programme showed an improvement over the preceding one, although all six could be operated together.

The Imperial Japanese Navy began to build its strength in response to a perceived threat from the Chinese navy,

which had acquired a number of modern German-built ships. The Chinese ships were armoured turret ships but the six ships that Japan bought in Britain were the new generation of pre-Dreadnoughts.

Fuji and *Yashima* were improved Royal Sovereigns, with weight being saved by placing most of the secondary armament behind shields rather than in armoured casemates. *Yashima*'s keel was cut away towards the bow, giving her a smaller turning circle than *Fuji*. The ships were refitted in 1901 when 12pdrs replaced the 3pdrs. Both ships took part in the Russo-Japanese war. *Yashima* was mined off Port Arthur on May 15, 1904, was taken in tow but capsized. *Fuji* fired the last shot at the Battle of Tsushima to sink the *Borodino*. *Fuji* was refitted in 1910 and reclassified as a coast defence ship. Disarmed under the Washington

Treaty and used as a school ship, she capsized and was scrapped in 1945.

The two Shikishima class ships were improved British Majestics, and the armament was identical to the Fuji class. Both ships were at the bombardment of Port Arthur on February 9, 1904, and the subsequent blockade, where *Hatsuse* struck a mine on May 15, 1904. She was taken in tow by *Asahi* but struck a second mine whereupon her magazine exploded and she was lost. *Shikishima*, which was at the Battle of the Yellow Sea and the Battle of Tsushima, was classed as a coast defence ship in 1921, became a training ship in 1923 and was scrapped in 1947.

Shikishima class

Class: *Shikishima, Hatsuse.* Launched 1898–9
Dimensions: Length – 133.5m/438ft
 Beam – 23m/75ft 6in
 Draught – 8.4m/27ft 6in
Displacement: 15,088 tonnes/14,850 tons
Armament: Main – 4 x 305mm/12in and
 14 x 150mm/6in guns
 Secondary – 20 x 12pdr, 6/8 x 3pdr
 (6 x 1) guns and 5 x 455mm/18in torpedoes
Machinery: 25 Belleville boilers, 2 shafts.
 10,810kW/14,500ihp
Speed: 18 knots
Complement: 836 men (*Hatsuse* 741)

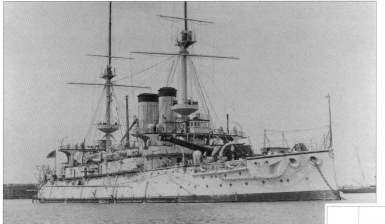

LEFT: *Asahi* at anchor in Portsmouth in 1900. Built by John Brown on the Clyde, she was one of the last Japanese ships to be built in Britain. BELOW LEFT: *Asahi*'s sister ship *Mikasa* underway. BELOW *Mikasa* still under construction in the Vickers yard at Barrow-in-Furness. The Japanese navy had a strong preference for having their ships built in Britain, and many Japanese naval officers and naval architects also studied in Britain at the end of the 19th century and admired what they found.

Mikasa and *Asahi*

*A*sahi was similar to the Shikishimas except she had two funnels instead of three. Mined on October 26, 1904, *Asahi* was repaired in time for the Battle of Tsushima. A gunnery training ship at the start of World War I, she was demilitarized after the Washington Naval Treaty, converted to a submarine salvage ship and torpedoed off Indo-China in 1942.

Mikasa was the last of six battleships ordered under the Japanese navy's ten-year programme of expansion. The 305mm/12in guns, which could be operated electrically or hydraulically and loaded at any angle of elevation or training, could fire at the rate of three shells every two minutes.

On February 8, 1904, *Mikasa* was Admiral Togo's flagship for a surprise attack on the Russian Far East Fleet at Port Arthur. When Admiral Vitgeft attempted a breakout to Vladivostok later in the year, he was defeated in the Battle of the Yellow Sea. Vitgeft was killed when the battleship *Tsessarevitch* was hit by a 305mm/12in shell and the Russian fleet took refuge in Port Arthur. *Tsessarevitch* escaped to Tsingtao, where the Germans interned her, and by January 1905, when the Japanese took Port Arthur from the landward, the Russians had lost no less than seven battleships. Admiral Togo was hailed as the new Nelson.

When Admiral Rozhestvensky arrived in the Korea Strait after a 29,000km/18,000-mile journey from the Baltic, Togo's fleet was inferior to the Russian, but the Japanese possessed speed, morale and a tactical scheme. Togo in *Mikasa* out-gunned and outmanoeuvred the Russians, who by the end of the day had suffered six battleships and four others sunk, four captured, and three ships interned. *Mikasa* was hit 32 times but no Japanese ships were lost.

A magazine explosion killed 114 of *Mikasa*'s crew in September 1906, but she was refloated in the same year, and is preserved as a memorial.

Mikasa and *Asahi*

Class: *Asahi, Mikasa*. Launched 1899–1900
Dimensions: Length – 130m/426ft 6in
  Beam – 22.9m/75ft 3in
  Draught – 8.3m/27ft 3in
Displacement: 15,444 tonnes/15,200 tons
Armament: Main – 4 x 305mm/12in and
  14 x 150mm/6in guns
  Secondary – 20 x 12pdr, 6 x 3pdr guns and
  4 x 455mm/18in torpedoes
Machinery: 25 boilers, 2 shafts.
  11,930kW/15,000ihp
Speed: 18 knots
Complement: 836 men
There were minor differences in size between the two ships.

LEFT: **After a number of evolutionary types of warships, the German Brandenburg class is the first recognizable pre-Dreadnought. This is** *Wörth,* **photographed in 1900.** BELOW LEFT: *Brandenburg.* **Lost in the hamper amidships is a third, twin turret, which had to be of lesser calibre than the other main turrets in order to train to port or starboard.**

Brandenburg class

After a number of classes of German-built central battery ironclads and a class of coast defence battleships, the Brandenburgs marked the beginning of a fateful, and fatal, era of German naval expansion. Disparagingly the Royal Navy nicknamed these ships the "whalers". They were unusual in having a midships turret, whose barrels had to be shorter than the fore and aft turrets in order that they could be trained through the centre line to port or starboard. This could have given the Germans a lead in a Dreadnought-type arrangement of all centre-line guns, but the midships mounting, sited aft of the after funnel, caused blast damage and the idea was abandoned. Nevertheless, in a

further manifestation of growing German ambition, ships of this class saw service in China during the Boxer rebellion.

They were modernized in 1902 and 1904 with new boilers and the top-hamper was cut down. One torpedo tube was suppressed and an extra 105mm/4.13in fitted, but their secondary armament was regarded as weak by the standards of the time. They were also the first German warships to be fitted with radio.

In 1910, two ships of this class were sold to Turkey for nine million marks each, *Kurfürst Friedrich Wilhelm* as *Heireddin Barbarossa* and *Weissenburg,* which became the *Turgut Reis.* On August 8, 1915, *Heireddin Barbarossa*

was torpedoed and sunk with the loss of 253 lives by the British submarine *E11,* commanded by Lieutenant Commander Martin Nasmith, in the Dardanelles. *Turgut Reis* became a training ship in 1924 and was broken up 1938.

Brandenburg served overseas in 1900–1 to further German imperial ambitions, but when general war broke out in 1914 she was obsolete, and was relegated to coast defence duties in 1915. She became an accommodation ship at Libau in 1916–18, and was broken up at Danzig in 1920.

Wörth was categorized as a coastal defence ship in 1915 and then used as an accommodation ship at Danzig where she was broken up in 1919.

Brandenburg class

Class: *Brandenburg, Kurfürst Friedrich Wilhelm, Weissenburg, Wörth.* Launched 1891–2
Dimensions: Length – 115.7 m/379ft 7in
    Beam – 19.5m/64ft
    Draught – 7.9m/26ft
Displacement: 10,668 tonnes/10,500 tons
Armament: Main – 6 x 280mm/11in and
    6 x 105mm/4.13in guns
    Secondary – 8 x 90mm/3.46in guns and
    6 x 450mm/17.7in torpedoes
Machinery: 12 boilers, 2-shaft TE,
    7,459kW/10,000ihp
Speed: 16 knots
Complement: 568 men

Kaiser class

Class *Kaiser Friedrich III, Kaiser Wilhelm II, Kaiser Wilhelm der Grosse, Kaiser Barbarossa,* Launched 1896–1900
Dimensions: Length – 125.3m/411ft
 Beam 20.4m/67ft,
 Draught 8.25m/27ft
Displacement: 11,920 tonnes/11,599 tons
Armament: Main – 4 x 240mm/9.4in, 18 x 150mm/6in guns
 Secondary – 12 x 88mm/3.46in guns and 6 x 450mm/17.7in torpedoes
Machinery: 12 boilers, 3 shafts.
 10,440kW/14,000ihp
Speed: 17 knots
Complement: 651

Kaiser class

Named after German emperors past and present, these four ships carried a smaller main gun (approximately 240mm/9.4in) but a heavier secondary armament. Some of the 150mm/6in guns were mounted in turrets rather than casemates, and the triple shafts were typical German arrangements. However in other respects the Kaiser class still compared unfavourably with British designs.

Partly in response to the Dreadnought revolution, the Kaisers were reconstructed in 1907–10, with taller funnels, reduced superstructure and some rearrangement of the secondary and tertiary guns. *Kaiser Wilhelm II*, with her complement increased by 63, was fleet flagship until 1906. All ships of this class were disarmed and used as hulks in the war years. *Kaiser Wilhelm der Grosse* became a torpedo training ship, *Kaiser Wilhelm II*

became an HQ ship for the commander-in-chief, and the others became floating prisons. All were broken up in 1920 and 1921. The bow ornament of *Kaiser Friedrich III* is in a museum in Dresden.

Wittelsbach class

The Wittelsbach class were improved Kaisers, although the improvements were not great: they carried a similar armament and somewhat extended armour. By World War I they were too slow and vulnerable to stand in the line of battle, and were used for training. By 1916 all ships of this class had been

disarmed, so when Germany signed away the High Sea Fleet in the Armistice of 1918, she was allowed to keep these obsolete ships. *Mecklenburg* became a floating prison, and was scrapped in 1921. Converted towards the end of World War I to depot ships for minesweeping motor launches,

Schwaben and *Wittelsbach* each carried 12 shallow-draught minesweepers, but they too were scrapped in 1921–2. *Zähringen* became a target ship in 1917, and in 1926 was converted so she could be radio-controlled. She was sunk by the British Royal Air Force bombing at Gotenhafen (Gdynia) in 1944.

Wittelsbach class

Class: *Wittelsbach, Wettin, Zähringen, Schwaben, Mecklenburg.* Launched 1900–1
Dimensions: Length – 126.8m/416ft
 Beam – 22.8m/74ft 9in
 Draught – 8m/26ft 4in
Displacement: 12,798 tonnes/12,596 tons
Armament: Main – 4 x 240mm/9.4in and 18 x 150mm/6in guns
 Secondary – 12 x 88mm/3.46in guns and 6 x 450mm/17.7in torpedoes
Machinery: 12 boilers, 3 shafts,
 11,180kW/15,000ihp
Speed: 17 knots
Complement: 683 men

Braunschweig class

The Braunschweigs marked a stepped improvement over the previous two classes of German pre-Dreadnoughts. The forward main gun was mounted on the forecastle instead of one deck above with a battery of lesser guns beneath. The guns were heavier (280mm/11in as opposed to 240mm/9.4in) and the armour was slightly thicker. Although 1,524 tonnes/1,500 tons larger, with extra boilers and three funnels, they produced a speed of 8 knots, which was one knot faster than the Wittelsbachs and Kaisers. However, the 280mm/11in guns were still lighter than the standard British 305mm/12in, and while they were being completed between 1904 and 1906, they were overtaken by the Dreadnought revolution. In the early part of World War I they were stationed in the Baltic, but between 1916 and 1918 they were disarmed.

Preussen and *Lothringen* were converted to depot ships for minesweeping motor boats in 1919 and broken up in 1931. One midships section of the hull of *Preussen* survived as a torpedo target and for explosive trials. Renamed *Vierkant* (meaning "even keel"), she was sunk by bombing in 1944 and not raised and broken up until 1954.

Braunschweig, *Elsass* and *Hessen* were rebuilt as coast defence ships in the 1920s, with much of their original armament, but were sold for breaking up between 1931 and 1935.

Hessen survived as a radio-controlled target ship and was then taken over by the Soviet Union in 1946 and given the name *Tsel*.

Braunschweig class

Class: Braunschweig, Elsass, Hessen, Preussen, Lothringen. Launched 1902–4
Dimensions: Length – 127.7m/419ft
Beam – 25.6m/84ft
Draught – 8.1m/26ft 7in
Displacement: 14,394 tonnes/14,167 tons
Armament: Main – 4 x 280mm/11in and 14 x 170mm/6.7in guns
Secondary – 18 x 88mm/3.46in guns, 4 x machine-guns and 6 x 450mm/17.7in torpedoes
Machinery: 14 boilers, 3-shaft TE, 12,677kW/17,000ihp
Speed: 18 knots
Complement: 743 men

LEFT: **Deutschland was the name of the last class of German pre-Dreadnoughts. Here one is seen passing eastbound along the Kiel Canal. Despite their obsolescence they took part in the Battle of Jutland.** BELOW: **A battleship of the Deutschland class firing a broadside to starboard.** BOTTOM: **Paint ship! A task familiar to sailors old and new in every navy. This essential work is not just for smartness but also keeps the hull well-maintained and rust-free.**

Deutschland class

The Deutschlands were the last pre-Dreadnoughts of the Imperial German Navy. They were similar to the Braunschweigs, but had slightly differently shaped funnels and thicker armour. The two twin turrets and the mixed secondary and tertiary armament marked the epitome of the pre-Dreadnoughts. Ordered and laid down amid rumours, and then hard news, of Fisher's Dreadnought revolution, all five ships of the class were completed at great expense while Germany considered its options of how to react to developments in Britain.

Although obsolescent, the Deutschlands took part in the Battle of Jutland in 1916, where concern for their vulnerability and slowness may have influenced Scheer's tactics. The weakness in the protection and magazine arrangements of the secondary armament was reckoned to have caused the loss of *Pommern* when a single torpedo, fired by a British destroyer, hit her and she blew up.

By 1917 all ships of the class had been removed from the line of battle. *Deutschland* was disarmed and broken up in 1920, but the three others survived into World War II. *Schlesien* and *Schleswig-Holstein* were refitted in the 1920s and rebuilt about 1930, when the fore-funnel was trunked into the midships one. Better anti-aircraft (AA) armament was fitted, and in World War II numerous 40mm/1.57in and other light AA guns were added as well.

After World War I, *Schleswig-Holstein* became an accommodation ship and then in 1926 flagship of the Kreigsmarine. Afterwards she became a training ship

for the newly resurgent Reichsmarine, but she was bombed and sunk in 1944.

Schlesien became an accommodation ship at the end of World War I, was refitted in the 1920s, and mined off Swinemunde in 1944.

Deutschland class

Class: *Deutschland, Hannover, Pommern, Schlesien, Schleswig-Holstein*. Launched 1904–6
Dimensions: Length – 127.6m/418ft 8in
Beam – 22.3m/73ft
Draught – 8.2m/27ft
Displacement: 14,218 tonnes/13,993 tons
Armament: Main – 4 x 280mm/11in and
14 x 170mm/6.7in guns
Secondary – 20 x 88mm/3.46in guns and
6 x 450mm/17.7in torpedoes
Machinery: 12 boilers, 3 shafts,
11,930kW/16,000ihp
Speed: 18 knots
Complement: 743 men

LEFT: **French designers produced several high-sided ships with massive superstructures during the 1890s, such as the *Brennus*.**

Brennus

Class: *Brennus.* Launched 1891
Dimensions: Length – 110.3m/361ft 10in
  Beam – 20.4m/66ft 11in
  Draught – 8.3m/27ft 2in
Displacement: 11,370 tonnes/11,190 tons
Armament: Main – 3 x 340mm/13.5in and
  10 x 160mm/6.4in guns
  Secondary – 4 x 9pdr and 14 x 3pdr guns
  4 x 455mm/18in torpedoes
Machinery: 32 Belleville boilers, 2 shafts,
  12,304kW/16,900ihp
Speed: 18 knots
Complement: 673 men

Brennus turret ship

The French built a number of turret ships of which *Brennus* was the last. Her designers tried to cram in too much and her masts and superstructure had to be reduced before she was considered safe. She was heavily armoured with a belt 255mm/10in to 455mm/18in thick, which extended upwards to cover her upper deck and the barbettes. She carried her three, long 340mm/13.4in guns in single and twin barbettes, and,

also unusual for her time, had no ram: this and her high freeboard qualified *Brennus* as the first true ocean-going battleship of the modern age.

In the previous ten years France had built ten mastless turret ships, but the centre-line armoured pivot turrets qualified *Brennus* as the first modern battleship. She was also protected with face-hardened armour made by the Harvey process invented in the USA.

Like many of her predecessors she was overweight and unstable. At just 5 degrees of heel her armoured belt was submerged and hydraulic power to the guns was interrupted, so both the superstructure and the military mainmast had to be reduced.

Charles Martel class

The French built five similar ships, sometimes considered as one class: *Charles Martel, Carnot, Jauréguiberry, Masséna* and *Bouvet. Charles Martel* had a high freeboard forward, a flying bridge between her funnels and was cut down aft. *Carnot* had a reduced superstructure, no flying deck or military mainmast, and her funnels were further apart. *Jauréguiberry* had a shorter hull which brought the guns close to the ends of the

ship, and, in the earlier days of water-tube boilers (needing numerous tight joints), she suffered a boiler explosion. *Masséna* was similar in appearance to *Charles Martel*, and *Bouvet*, generally regarded as the best of these ships, differed in the hull not being cut down and in having two short military masts.

The armament was generally similar: three 305mm/12in guns on the centre-line and two 275mm/10.8in guns

mounted midships on the tumblehome, and six 140mm/5.5in and numerous smaller quick-firing guns that varied throughout the class. These ships also had numerous small compartments, called the *tranche cellulaire*, which could be filled with coal or stores and were intended to limit the effects of damage.

LEFT: **The five ships of the Charles Martel class were meant to be one class, but as a result of being built in different yards by different designers, individual ships varied.**

Charles Martel class

Class: *Charles Martel, Carnot, Jauréguiberry, Masséna, Bouvet.* Launched 1893–6
Dimensions: Length – 115.5m/378ft 11in
  Beam – 21.6m/71ft
  Draught – 8.4m/27ft 6in
Displacement: 11,881 tonnes/11,693 tons
Armament: Main – 2 x 305mm/12in,
  2 x 275mm/10.8in and 6 x 140mm/5.5in guns
  Secondary – 4 x 9pdr, 12–18 x 3pdr guns and
  2 x 455mm/18in torpedoes
Machinery: 24 Lagrafel d'Allest boilers, 2 shafts,
  10,910kW/14,200 to 12,304kW/16,900ihp
Speed: 18 knots
Complement: 644 men

Charlemagne class

These were the first French battleships armed with two twin mountings, as was usual in other navies, and the first to have three shafts. Less beamy and lighter in displacement than the Charles Martel class, most observers reckoned they were too small.

It was recognized that early French designs were vulnerable to hull damage, so in the Charlemagne class the belt was extended from 1.5m/5ft below to 45.5cm/18in above the waterline, and in its midships portion it was 355mm/14in thick, tapering to 205mm/8in at the lower edge and 255mm/10in at the extremities. Inboard there was the usual French arrangement of a cofferdam and cellular compartments.

The main 305mm/12in guns were mounted in pivot turrets fore and aft, the 140mm/5.5in guns in a battery at the upper deck level (and two at forecastle deck level) and the tertiary 100mm/4in guns in the superstructure. All the Charlemagne class took part in World War I.

On March 18, 1915, *Gaulois* was engaged and hit by Turkish shore batteries and a single shell hit her port bow below the waterline, tearing off the hull plating. Flooding spread via the ventilation trunking and she had to be beached on Rabbit Island, north of Tenedos. After being refloated she went to Malta for repairs. However, on December 27, 1916, *Gaulois* was on passage from the French base at Corfu to Salonika when the German submarine *UB-47* eluded her escort and torpedoed her: she floated for 25 minutes, sufficient time for most of her crew to be rescued, before settling on an even keel.

Charlemagne was also in the bombardment groups but escaped serious damage, and survived the war to be stricken in 1920.

St Louis served seemingly without distinction or notoriety until she was scrapped in 1933.

TOP: **The French ships looked so big because they were compact. The Charlemagne class were smaller in displacement than their predecessors but more heavily armed.** ABOVE: **Like the British pre-Dreadnoughts, these French ships were relegated to secondary theatres of warfare.** *Gaulois* **was sunk off the Dardanelles, re-floated and sunk again.**

Charlemagne class

Class: *Charlemagne, St Louis, Gaulois.*
Launched 1896
Dimensions: Length – 114m/374ft in
Beam – 20.2m/66ft 5in
Draught – 8.4m/27ft 6in
Displacement: 11,278 tonnes/11,100 tons
Armament: Main – 4 x 305mm/12in,
10 x 140mm/5.5in, and 8 x 100mm/4in guns
Secondary – 20 x 3pdr guns and
2 x 455mm/18in torpedoes
Machinery: 20 Belleville boilers, 3-shafts VTE,
10,810kW/14,500iph
Speed: 18 knots
Complement: 694 men

léna class

In general design *léna* was an enlarged *Charlemagne* with a complete armoured belt extended above and below the waterline 325mm/12.8in thick amidships and tapering to 230mm/9in at the ends, and there was the usual, French, cellular layer below the armoured deck. The 305mm/12in guns were arranged with the 160mm/6.4in in casemates on the main deck, and the four amidships guns in sponsons over the pronounced tumblehome. Despite being fitted with bilge keels, *léna* was known to roll and pitch uncomfortably.

léna was one of a list of ships that suffered a spontaneous explosion. The magazine cooling gear had been removed while she was in dry-dock in Toulon, when decomposing nitrocellulose propellant ignited and set light to the after 305mm/12in magazine. The whole after part of the ship was wrecked and the midships section badly damaged, and she was afterwards used as a target.

Suffren, which took four years to complete, differed in that four of her 160mm/6.4in guns were placed in turrets on the upper deck and the rest in casemates. She was hit during the main attack on the Dardanelles on March 18, 1915, when three casemate guns were put out of action and an ammunition fire started. She was reputed to have been saved from explosion because the charges were in metal cases. However, on November 26, 1916, while on her way to refit at Lorient, *Suffren* was torpedoed and sunk by the German submarine *U-52* off the Portuguese coast. There were no survivors.

Henri IV was an experimental ship, not completed until 1903. She had only 1.22m/4ft freeboard over most of her length, except forward where it was built up to normal deck height, and there was the usual cellular layer inboard of the torpedo bulkhead. She had one of the first superfiring turrets, though the blast effects were said to be severe as the muzzle of the 140mm/5.5in gun barrel was too short even to clear the sighting hood of the 275mm/10.8in gun below it. *Henri IV* saw service at Gallipoli, survived World War I and was scrapped in 1921.

LEFT, BELOW LEFT AND BOTTOM: **The three ships seen here, *Suffren* (left) and *Henri IV* (below left) and *léna* (bottom), were singletons, built at a time of great change in French design. It was symptomatic that *Henri IV* spent over six years from being laid down to completion.**

léna class

Class: *Suffren.* Launched 1899
Dimensions: Length – 125.5m/411ft 9in
Beam – 21.4m/70ft 2in
Draught – 8.4m/27ft 6in
Displacement: 12,728 tonnes/12,527 tons
Armament: Main – 4 x 305mm/12in, 10 x
160mm/6.4in and 8 x 100mm/4in guns
Secondary – 22 x 3pdr guns and
2 x 455mm/18in torpedoes
Machinery: 24 Niclausse boilers, 3 shafts,
12,453kW/16,700ihp
Speed: 17.9 knots
Complement: 714 men

Class: *léna.* Launched 1898
Dimensions: Length – 122.2m/400ft 9in
Beam – 20.8m/68ft 3in
Draught – 8.4m/27ft 6in
Displacement: 12,050 tonnes/11,860 tons
Armament: Main – 4 x 305mm/12in,
8 x 160mm/6.4in and 8 x 100mm/4in guns
Secondary – 20 x 3pdr guns and
2 x 455mm/18in torpedoes
Machinery: 20 Belleville boilers, 3 shafts,
12,304kW/16,500ihp
Speed: 18 knots
Complement: 682 men

Class: *Henri IV.* Launched 1899
Dimensions: Length – 108m/354ft 4in
Beam – 22.2m/72ft 10in
Draught – 7m/22ft 11in
Displacement: 8,948 tonnes/8,807 tons
Armament: Main – 2 x 275mm/10.8in,
7 x 140mm/5.5in guns
Secondary – 12 x 3pdr guns and
2 x 455mm/18in torpedoes
Machinery: 12 Niclausse boilers, 3 shafts,
8,575kW/11,500ihp
Speed: 17 knots
Complement: 464 men

République class

Class: *République, Patrie*. Launched 1902–3
Dimensions: Length – 133.8m/439ft
    Beam – 24.3m/79ft 7in
    Draught – 8.4m/27ft 7in
Displacement: 14,839 tonnes/14,605 tons
Armament: Main – 4 x 305mm/12in and
    18 x 160mm/6.4in guns
    Secondary – 25 x 3pdr guns and
    2 x 455mm/18in torpedoes
Machinery: 24 Niclausse boilers, 3 shafts,
    13,423kW/18,000ihp
Speed: 19 knots
Complement: 766 men

République class

Previous French designs of pre-Dreadnought battleships had been poor compromises between armament and armour, but in *République* and her sister ships they were at last able to solve their design problem. However, this class took so long to build they were not completed until 1906 and 1908, when Fisher's revolution was well under way.

In appearance, they owed something to the experimental *Henri IV*, with a high forecastle that ran back to the mainmast. Their three funnels, two forward and one well separated aft, and a tall pole mainmast gave them a distinctive appearance. In addition to the armoured belt and decks the cellular construction that the French preferred consisted of a short cofferdam, a passageway and coal bunkers, before reaching a central passageway. The main guns were placed high in the ship and there were six twin-turreted 160mm/6.4in guns at the forecastle deck level. Both vessels saw out World War I in the Mediterranean, when *Patrie*'s casemate 160mm/6.4in guns were mounted ashore in Salonica. Both were stricken in the 1920s.

Liberté class

The *Liberté* was very similar to the *République*, the main difference being the secondary armament of ten 190mm/7.6in guns, arranged six in single turrets at forecastle deck level, and two in casemates forward at upper deck and aft at main deck levels.

The armour was similar to the *République*, but following the French practice of farming out construction to different yards all three ships differed slightly in their displacement and draught. The Liberté class also had improved anti-torpedo 9pdr and 3pdr guns, similar to those later fitted in *République*.

Liberté blew up in Toulon harbour in 1911, the cause again being spontaneous ignition of decomposing nitrocellulose propellant, this time in one of the forward 190mm/7.6in magazines. The flooding arrangements were found to be inadequate and the resulting fire and explosion affected all the fore part of the ship. She was a total loss, although the wreck was not raised and scrapped until 1925.

The other three ships stayed in the Mediterranean during World War I and were stricken in the early 1920s.

Liberté class

Class: *Democratie, Justice, Liberté, Verite*.
    Launched 1904–7
Dimensions: Length – 133.8m/439ft in
Beam – 24.3m/79ft 7in
Draught – 8.35m/27ft 5in
Displacement: 14,722 tonnes/14,489 tons
Armament: Main – 4 x 305mm/12in and
    10 x 190mm/7.6in guns
    Secondary – 13 x 9pdr, 10 x 3pdr guns and
    2 x 455mm/18in torpedoes
Machinery: 22 Belleville boilers, 3 shafts,
    13,795kW/18,500ihp.
    Justice had 24 Niclausse boilers.
Speed: 19 knots
Complement: 739 men

Danton class

After the 1904 Anglo-French Entente Cordiale, the French navy agreed to concentrate in the Mediterranean, and the Premier Armée Navale consisted of 21 battleships, including four newly commissioned Dreadnoughts and the six Danton class semi-Dreadnoughts. First, the French fleet escorted troop transports from North Africa and by the end of August 1914, 14 French battleships were based at Malta to forestall a breakout from the Adriatic by the Austro-Hungarian fleet. In September they bombarded Cattaro and Lissa, and two pre-Dreadnoughts joined the British squadron watching the Dardanelles to prevent the battlecruiser Goeben from breaking out.

Once Italy entered the war in May 1915, the French fleet moved to bases at Brindisi and Corfu. In the winter of 1915/6 the French evacuated the defeated Serbian army from Albania to Salonika, and in spring 1916 took an active part in the Dardanelles campaign. The pre-Dreadnoughts Gaulois, Bouvet, Charlemagne and Suffren were badly damaged when hidden Turkish guns came into action during the landings on March 18, 1915, and they ran into a minefield. Bouvet was sunk.

In December 1916, French warships forced the pro-German Greek government to support Allied policies, landing sailors in Athens, briefly bombarding the city and seizing Greek warships. Later in the war the French navy concentrated its efforts more on anti-submarine warfare and convoy protection, but in 1918 formed part of the Aegean Sea Squadron deployed to prevent a breakout from the Dardanelles by the Turks.

TOP: **By their date these ships are Dreadnoughts, but they incorporated many pre-Dreadnought features, such as a large calibre secondary armament mounted to port and starboard.** ABOVE: **The Dantons were impressive high-sided ships. Danton is seen here with her three portside twin 9-in guns trained out.**

The Danton class ships were the first large turbine-engine ships. Compared to République and Liberté class they were another 3,048 tonnes/3,000 tons bigger, the extra displacement being used for a heavier secondary armament rather than speed. Their large batteries of rapid-fire tertiary guns made them useful in the confined waters of the Mediterranean.

The ships fitted with Belleville boilers made slightly more than 20 knots on trials, while the others were a knot slower. During World War I all ships received additional 75mm/3in anti-aircraft guns, and Condorcet, Vergniaud and Voltaire had their

Danton class

Class: *Danton, Voltaire, Condorcet, Diderot, Mirabeau, Vergniaud.* Launched 1909–10

Dimensions: Length – 144.9m/475ft 5in
Beam – 25.8m/84ft 8in
Draught – 9.2m/30ft 2in

Displacement: 18,612 tonnes/18,318 tons

Armament: Main – 4 x 305mm/12in,
12 x 240mm/9.4in guns
Secondary – 16 x 75mm/2.95in,
10 x 45mm/1.77in guns and
2 x 455mm/18in torpedoes

Machinery: 26 Belleville boilers, 4 shafts (Parsons turbines), 16,778kW/22,500shp

Speed: 19.2 knots

Complement: 681 men

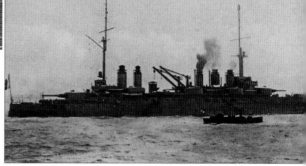

mainmasts shortened in 1918 so they could carry kite balloons. In 1918, the main guns had their range increased from 13,700m/14,983yd to 18,000m/19,690yd and the class were given a fire control system like other Dreadnoughts. All except *Danton* and *Diderot* were off to Athens in December 1916 when *Mirabeau* fired four rounds over the city as part of a pro-Allied demonstration, one of which landed near the Royal Palace.

Danton was zigzagging south-west of Sicily en route to the Allied blockade lines in the Straits of Otranto when, on March 19, 1917, the German submarine *U-64* torpedoed her. *Danton* was carrying drafts to the fleet greatly in excess of her own crew but fortunately she took some 45 minutes to sink and 296 men were saved. However, 806 men were lost, making this the worst disaster of the war at sea for the French navy.

Voltaire was also off Athens in December 1916 with four of her sisters, and in the Aegean in 1918. On the night of October 10/11, 1918, near Antikythira, she was twice torpedoed by the German *UB-48* but survived with little damage. On November 13, 1918, she was part of the Allied fleet which anchored off Constantinople.

Vergniaud and *Mirabeau* entered the Black Sea to operate off the Crimea against the Red Army. There *Mirabeau* ran aground in a snowstorm on February 13, 1919, and was salvaged in April 1919 only after the forward part of the ship including the main gun had been dismantled. She was used for trials and then stricken in 1921, though she and *Vergniaud* continued to be used for explosives experiments afterwards.

Condorcet, Diderot and *Voltaire* were modernized in the 1920s and fitted with improved underwater protection, but from 1927 onwards they served as training ships, and *Diderot* and *Voltaire* were stricken in the 1930s.

TOP: **This stern view shows how similar in size the main and secondary armaments were.** ABOVE: **The layout of the funnel made for easy recognition of the class.** BELOW: **Their appearance changed little during World War I.**

Condorcet became a depot ship at Toulon, where on November 27, 1942, an attempt to blow her up by loyal French officers was botched and she was taken over by the German navy as a barrack ship. In August 1944, she was bombed by an Allied aircraft and sunk only to be re-floated in September 1944. She was sold and broken up in 1945.

Italia class

The Italian navy recovered slowly from the disaster of the Battle of Lissa in 1866, but built some fine ships. Italian naval architects were talented and open to new ideas, while the navy concentrated on quality rather than quantity, and so in the pre-Dreadnought era was able to rival the British and French navies in the Mediterranean. The turret ships *Duilio* and *Dandolo* when laid down in 1873 were faster at 15 knots and more heavily armed with 450mm/ 17.7in muzzle-loaders than any other battleship. Although ugly ships, they were admired by Jacky Fisher, then in command of the Royal Navy's largest warship, *Inflexible*.

In the 1870s, the Italian engineer Benedetto Brin designed two ships, *Italia* and *Lepanto*, which in many ways were the forerunners of the battlecruiser. Different sources describe these ships as large, fast battleships or strategic cruisers. The 430mm/17in guns were at the limits of gun technology, and Brin dispensed with side armour, building the hulls of iron and steel and covering the sides with wood and zinc. Although they each took some nine years to complete and were relatively weakly armoured, these two ships were for many years in the 1880s the largest and fastest in the world. Each was also capable of embarking a division of infantry.

Italia as built had six funnels, three forward and three aft, but was rebuilt in 1905–8 to look like *Lepanto* with just four funnels. The guns were sited in pairs amidships around a central control tower and an elegant military mast. They were later fitted with more quick-firing guns and two additional torpedo tubes. The single pole mast was also replaced and two shorter ones were fitted. Neither, however, saw any action.

Lepanto was stricken in 1914 and then *Italia* in 1921, after a career as a floating battery, a cereal carrier and a depot ship.

Italia class

Class: *Italia, Lepanto.* Launched 1880–3
Dimensions: Length – 122m/400ft 3in
 Beam – 22.5m/73ft 11in
 Draught – 8.7m/28ft 8in
Displacement: 13,897 tonnes/13,678 tons
Armament: Main – 4 x 430mm/17in and
 7 x 150mm/5.9in guns
 Secondary – 4 x 120mm/4.7in guns and
 4 x 355mm/14in torpedoes
Machinery: 24 boiler, 4 shafts, 8,389kW/11,250ihp
Speed: 18 knots
Complement: 669 men

Ruggiero di Lauria class

On March 8, 1880, one of *Duilio's* huge muzzle-loading guns was double-charged in a drill error and blew up. The accident prejudiced the Italian public against large ships and large guns, which members of the government opposed already on the grounds of cost.

The task of designing a successor ship to the Italia class was given to an engineer called Giuseppe Micheli and for once Italian ingenuity failed. Micheli tried various ideas but could only come up with an improved *Duilio* type. The improvements included a forecastle, which the original design had lacked; placing the breech-loading guns in barbettes and better armour, but the class was already obsolete when they were completed in 1888–91.

Francesco Morisini was used as a target and sunk in 1909; her guns were mounted on an Italian monitor used to provide the army with gunfire support. The other two were stricken in 1911. *Andrea Doria* became a floating battery in World War I and was broken up in 1929, but *Ruggiero di Lauria* survived until 1943 as an oil bunker at La Spezia, and was not broken up until 1946.

BELOW LEFT: **The low freeboard of the Ruggiero de Lauria class harked back to former designs and may have only been suitable for the relatively calm waters of the Adriatic.** BELOW RIGHT: **A rare picture of an Italian warship being built on stocks. Given the lack of tide in the Mediterranean and Adriatic it scarcely seems possible that she will reach the sea.** BOTTOM: **Despite their unusual appearance, the Ruggiero di Lauria class were heavily armed ships carrying 430mm/17in guns.**

Ruggiero di Lauria class	

Class: *Ruggiero di Lauria, Francesco Morosini, Andrea Doria*. Launched 1884–5
Dimensions: Length – 100m/328ft 1in
Beam – 19.8m/65ft 1in
Draught – 8.3m/27ft 2in
Displacement: 10,045 tonnes/9,886 tons
Armament: Main – 4 x 430mm/17in and
2 x 150mm/6in guns
Secondary – 4 x 120mm/4.7in guns and
2 x 355mm/14in torpedoes
Machinery: 8 boilers, 2 shafts, 7,898kW/10,591ihp
Speed: 16 knots
Complement: 507 men

LEFT: **This photograph shows the 120mm/4.7in guns run out and trained to starboard as they might be when repelling a torpedo-boat attack.**
ABOVE: **Seen in profile the twin side-by-side funnels merge into one and** *Re Umberto*, **seen here, looks like any other pre-Dreadnought.** BELOW: **Freeboard and its consequent seaworthiness did not impinge much upon Italy's considerations of design, but her architects were open to novel ideas such as single and twin funnels.**

Re Umberto class

Benedetto Brin (1833–98) worked until the age of 40 as a naval engineer. In 1873, the Italian navy minister, Simone Pacoret di Saint Bon, made Brin undersecretary of state, and the two men complemented each other; di Saint Bon had the ideas and Brin accomplished them in his designs for Italian warships. When Brin himself became the navy minister, he developed di Saint Bon's ideas and is credited with creating the first organic scheme for the development of the Italian fleet. He had already designed the turret ships *Duilio* and *Dandolo* and Italy's first battleships, the *Italia* class, when he temporarily abandoned big ship designs in favour of smaller warships.

The Italian warship-building industry was insignificant when Brin took office, but under his guidance it made rapid progress. During his time, he helped create private shipyards and machine shops, and introduced the indigenous manufacture of armour, steel plates and guns. Brin's appointment as minister for foreign affairs in 1892 was probably an over-promotion, but his previous achievements qualify him as the creator of the Italian navy.

Two ships were ordered in 1883, and when Brin became navy minister for the second time he decided to build a third ship of the same class. The layout showed Brin's hand: a tall central mast, and a symmetrical disposition of the funnels and turrets fore and aft. The forward funnels were, however, a pair that sat abreast of each other. In Brin's design he continued to sacrifice armour for speed and armament, and the armoured belt of the Re Umberto class was only 100mm/4in thick. These ships, like many Italian and French ships of the period, were a long time in building and when they were complete, they rapidly became obsolete. Nevertheless all three ships survived World War I.

Re Umberto was laid up in 1912 but was later used as a depot ship and as a floating battery. When the Italian navy planned to force the Austro-Hungarian port of Pola, she was fitted as an assault ship, stripped of her former armament in favour of 75mm/3in guns and trench mortars. The idea was that she should

rush the harbour followed by a flotilla of small craft, but the war ended before this scheme could be put into effect. *Sicilia* became a repair ship and *Sardegna* a depot ship. All three were stricken in the 1920s.

Re Umberto class

Class: *Re Umberto, Sicilia, Sardegna.* Launched 1888–91
Dimensions: Length – 122m/400ft 3in
Beam – 23.4m/76ft 10in
Draught – 9.3m/30ft 6in
Displacement: 13,892 tonnes/13,673 tons
Armament: Main – 4 x 340mm/13.5in and
16 x 120mm/4.7in guns
Secondary – 16 x 6pdr, 10 x 37mm/1.46in guns
and 5 x 450mm/17.7in torpedoes
Machinery: 18 boilers, 2 shafts,
11,180kW/15,000ihp
Speed: 20 knots
Complement: 733 men

Ammiraglio di Saint Bon class

Italian strategists had not fixed on the size or type of ship they wanted, so for their next class of ship they were driven by the government, which wanted ships to be as small and as cheap as possible. So when di Saint Bon died, Brin returned temporarily and he proposed a medium-sized ship with relatively small 255mm/10in guns. The design showed the symmetry of earlier Italian ships and followed the style that the British had started with *Collingwood* and Brin had copied with *Re Umberto*: two twin guns forward and two aft. The ships took some eight years to complete, but not even Brin could not save the design from its inherent weaknesses: the ships were too slow at 18 knots and small, and their freeboard was only 2.7m/9ft. Overall they were too weak to

ABOVE: **Italian naval architects were beginning to be influenced by overseas developments, but *Ammiraglio di Saint Bon* still has the unusual arrangement of a single, central mast.** BELOW LEFT: ***Emanuel Filiberto* at the end of World War I.**

stand in the line of battle and too slow to catch even a cruiser. They saw limited service in World War I and were not broken up until 1920.

Ammiraglio di Saint Bon class

Class: *Ammiraglio di Saint Bon, Emanuel Filiberto.* Launched 1897
Dimensions: Length – 105m/344ft 6in
  Beam – 21.1m/69ft 3in
  Draught – 7.7m/25ft 2in
Displacement: 10,244 tonnes/10,082 tons
Armament: Main – 4 x 255mm/10in and
  8 x 150mm/6in guns
  Secondary – 8 x 55mm/2.24in guns and
  4 x 450mm/17.7in torpedoes
Machinery: 12 boilers, 2 shafts,
  10,664kW/14,300ihp
Speed: 18 knots
Complement: 557/567 men

Regina Margherita class

The Italian navy wanted a ship to match the Austro-Hungarian Habsburg class, and so Brin's last effort was the Regina Margherita class. These were intended to be modern, fast and well-armed ships, even at the expense of armoured protection, as in so many Italian designs. With this class the Italians reverted to a larger battleship design although the result was smaller than other contemporary, foreign battleships. Symmetry was carried to an extreme with two funnels amidships, fore and aft, two matching pole masts, and forward and after combined control towers and bridges. Unlike their

immediate predecessors the Ammiraglio di Saint Bon class, which could burn coal or oil, these ships could only use coal. Brin died while the class was under construction and the second ship was named after him.

On September 27, 1915, while in Brindisi harbour, *Benedetto Brin* suffered a fire and exploded killing 450 of her crew including the Italian admiral, an act which was later blamed upon Austrian saboteurs, but was more likely an internal explosion. On December 11, 1916, *Regina Margherita* was sunk off Valona by mines laid by the successful German submarine minelayer *UC-14*.

ABOVE: **The high sides and massive central superstructure on 13,209 tonnes/13,000 tons displacement showing perhaps some French design influence on** *Regina Margherita*. BELOW: **The ship's company lined up for their photograph.** BELOW LEFT: **A stern view of this fine ship in 1910. In profile they looked like full-grown battleships.**

Regina Margherita class

Class: *Regina Margherita, Benedetto Brin.* Launched 1901
Dimensions: Length – 130m/426ft 6in
 Beam – 23.8m/78ft 2in
 Draught – 8.8m/28ft 11in
Displacement: 13,427 tonnes/13,215 tons
Armament: Main – 4 x 305mm/12in and
 4 x 205mm/8in guns
 Secondary – 20 x 75mm/3in guns and
 4 x 450mm/17.7in torpedoes
Machinery: 28 boilers, 2 shafts.
 16,249kW/21,790ihp
Speed: 20 knots
Complement: 812 men

Regina Elena class

Vittorio Cuniberti succeeded Brin as the leading Italian ship designer and he was tasked with planning a ship with 12 205mm/8in guns, moderate armour and a speed of 22 knots. Cuniberti produced a design with two single 305mm/12in guns in addition to the required 12 205mm/8in guns.

Cuniberti was also first to produce a design for an all-big-gun battleship. However, such a ship was too ambitious for the Italian navy even given its record of innovation. Instead Cuniberti was given permission to publish an article abroad, and in 1903 *Jane's Fighting Ships* printed "An Ideal Battleship for the British Fleet", in which Cuniberti proposed a warship of 17,273 tonnes/ 17,000 tons armed with 12 305mm/12in

guns in single and double turrets, with 305mm/12in armour (which would certainly have been unusual for the Italian navy) and high speed of 24 knots. An article by Cuniberti three years earlier in *Marine Rundschau* entitled "*Ein neuer Schlachtschifftypus*" had gone unnoticed. However, his *Jane's* article was read in London just when the British Admiralty, where Jacky Fisher was First Sea Lord, was considering the lessons learned from the Battle of Tsushima and the design of its next generation of battleships. It is therefore clear that Cuniberti's ideas contributed to the design for Dreadnought.

Meanwhile in Italy, Cuniberti's design for a battleship that was faster than any British or French ship and stronger than

any armoured cruiser became the successful Regina Elena class. Two ships were authorized in 1901 and two more the following year. They were elegant ships with fine lines and scalloped fore-ends to provide a forward arc of fire for the 205mm/8in guns which were all mounted in turrets, with a single turret-mounted 305mm/12in gun at each end, and three tall funnels, although these were later cut down with some positive effect on the ship's speed.

Regina Elena class

Class: *Regina Elena, Vittorio Emanuele, Roma, Napoli.* Launched 1904–7
Dimensions: Length – 132.6m/435ft
  Beam – 22.4m/73ft 6in
  Draught – 7.9m/25ft 11in
Displacement: 12,751 tonnes/12,550 tons
Armament: Main – 2 x 305mm/12in and
  12 x 205mm/8in guns
  Secondary – 16 x 75mm/3in guns and
  2 x 450mm/17.7in torpedoes
Machinery: 28 boilers, 2 shafts.
  14,392kW/19,300ihp
Speed: 22 knots
Complement: 742 men

LEFT: **The Regina Elena class was armed with two single 305mm/12in guns, mounted one forward and one aft.** BELOW LEFT: *Regina Elena, Roma* and *Napoli* on manoeuvres off Venice in 1910. BELOW: *Regina Elena* at anchor at Messina in December 1908 after the earthquake there.

Sissoi Veliki

The Russian navy built a number of powerful, and in some cases innovative, ironclad warships after the Russian War 1854–6. The Russians also participated in every stage of ship evolution from the screw line-of-battle ship, broadside and central battery ship, to the turret ship, coast defence monitor, and coast defence turret ship. They first put 300mm/12in guns in the turret ship *Petr Veliki* (1869) and in the circular coast defence ships *Novgorod* and *Vice Admiral Popov* in 1872–4, and this became the standard armament for successive classes of barbette and turret ships from then on.

In 1892 the Russian navy laid down its first battleship of the modern era at the New Admiralty yard in St Petersburg. *Sissoi Veliki* was a small ship for her armament, presumably intended for operations in the Baltic and to be the largest warship of any navy bordering on the Baltic coast, when the Swedes were still seen as the Russian navy's traditional enemies. However she had a high freeboard, was ocean-going and twice deployed from the Baltic to the Far East.

Sissoi Veliki suffered a serious accident in 1897 when one of her main guns fired before the breech was closed, but she was repaired in time to be part of the allied naval forces off China in 1900 during the Boxer Rebellion. The international fleet consisted of American, Austrian, British, French, German, Italian, Japanese and Russian ships under the command of the British admiral, Sir Edward Seymour. Seymour had landed sailors and marines to defend the embassies in Peking and these had become cut off. As part of the relief operations, the allied fleet bombarded the Taku forts at the entrance to the Peiho River and a squadron of ships forced their way upstream.

Sissoi Veliki's armoured belt was 405mm/16in to 305mm/12in thick and the turret armour 305mm/12in, which were to prove their worth at the Battle of Tsushima on May 27, 1905. She was one of six battleships lost there – the greatest number in any single battle of the steam age. The Russian pre-Dreadnoughts *Sevastopol, Kniaz Suvarov, Osliabia, Borodino, Imperator Alexander III* and

Navarin were sunk by Japanese guns and torpedoes. *Sissoi Veliki* was hit by about 12 large-calibre shells, suffered serious bow damage near the waterline and was torpedoed in the stern, but did not sink until her crew scuttled her.

Sissoi Veliki

Class: *Sissoi Veliki.* Launched 1894
Dimensions: Length – 107.2m/351ft 10in
    Beam – 20.7m/68ft 1in
    Draught – 7.8m/25ft 6in
Displacement: 10,567 tonnes/10,400 tons
Armament: Main – 4 x 305mm/12in and
    6 x 150mm/6in guns
    Secondary – 12 x 3pdr, 18 x 1pdr guns and
    6 x 455mm/18in torpedoes
Machinery: 12 Belleville boilers, 2 shafts,
    6,400kW/8,500ihp
Speed: 16 knots
Complement: 586 men

Admiral Ushakov class

The Admiral Ushakov class were built as part of a Baltic naval arms race, and in particular to counter the Swedish coast defence ships of the Svea and Oden classes. Mounting four 255mm/10in guns on a displacement of under 5,080 tonnes/5,000 tons (and 15 per cent overweight compared to their design) they were hardly suitable for a voyage to the Pacific in 1904–5, although some sources say that these ships were good sea-keepers.

The three ships differed slightly: *Admiral Seniavin* was the heaviest ship and drew more water, while *Admiral General Graf Apraksin* had only one gun fitted in the after turret. The armour on all three ships was only 150mm/6in to 230mm/9in thick.

The gun was unsuccessful: designed for the Russian army and navy, both to be fitted in ships and mounted in coastal batteries, the naval version was too lightly constructed, suffered from weak barrels and thus had poor ballistic qualities. The land version had better ballistic qualities but it had primitive mountings which restricted its rate of fire. Nevertheless four guns were mounted in the Black Sea battleship *Rostislav* in 1898. The Russian army had a battery of these guns at Port Arthur by 1904, and they became the main coast defence guns of the Russian navy until World War I.

At the Battle of Tsushima in 1905 *Admiral Ushakov* fought bravely. She was hit twice below the waterline and once above by Japanese heavy shells, and was left behind by the Russian fleet. The next day, May 28, out of ammunition and surrounded by Japanese armoured cruisers, *Admiral Ushakov* was scuttled by her own crew.

Admiral Seniavin was badly damaged on May 27 and surrendered to the Japanese the next day. Renamed *Mishima,* she remained in service with the Imperial Japanese Navy until 1928. *General Admiral Graf Apraksin* also surrendered, and served as the *Okinoshima* until being scrapped in 1926.

Admiral Ushakov class

Class: *Admiral Ushakov, Admiral Seniavin, General Admiral Graf Apraksin.* Launched 1893–6

Dimensions: Length – 87.3m/286ft 6in
Beam – 15.85m/52ft
Draught – 5.9m/19ft 6in

Displacement: 5,051 tonnes/4,971 tons

Armament: Main – 4 x 255mm/10in and
4 x 120mm/4.7in guns
Secondary – 6 x 3pdr, 10 x 1pdr guns and
4 x 380mm/15in torpedoes

Machinery: 8 boilers, 2 shafts, 4,288kW/5,750ihp

Speed: 16 knots

Complement: 404 men

BELOW: **The proportions of** *General Admiral Graf Apraksin* **make her look like a lake steamer. She was not designed for the oceanic voyage to the Battle at Tsushima in 1905.** RIGHT: *Admiral Seniavin* **at speed. The clouds of smoke reveal the logistic and strategic weakness of these coal-burners.**

121

Petropavlovsk class

Named after important Russian victories on land, the Petropavlovsk class were flush-decked ships with an appreciable tumblehome. Like earlier Russian battleships they were overweight, in this case by about 10 per cent compared to their design. However, they followed what had now become a standard pattern with twin 305mm/12in turrets, one forward, one aft. Eight of the 150mm/6in guns were mounted in turrets and four in a central battery, port and starboard. Like earlier Russian ships they were seemingly well armoured with belts tapering from 305mm/12in to 205mm/8in thick.

All three ships formed part of the Russian First Pacific Squadron based at Port Arthur and were there at the outbreak of the Russo-Japanese War. *Petropavlovsk* struck a mine and blew up on April 13, 1904, with heavy loss of life including the Commander-in-Chief of the Russian Pacific Fleet, Admiral Makarov.

The other ships of the class proved to be much more resilient. At the Battle of the Yellow Sea on August 10, 1904, *Poltava* survived being hit by over a dozen rounds of 305mm/12in and

205mm/8in shells. She was hit again at the siege of Port Arthur with howitzer shells fired by the Japanese army, caught fire and sank. She was raised by the Japanese and commissioned as the *Tango*. In 1916 she was sold back to the Russians and this time named *Tchesma* (the name *Poltava* having already been taken for a Russian Dreadnought-type) and sent to the White Sea. *Sevastopol* was also mined on June 23, 1904, and again on August 23, 1904, but survived both incidents. She sustained several hits during the Battle of the Yellow Sea, and at the siege of Port Arthur, after being hit five times by 280mm/11in shells, sallied from the harbour. Her captain, Essen, took her to a new anchorage outside the harbour but close inshore and there, behind boom defences, she survived nightly attack for seven nights in December 1904 by Japanese torpedo boats. Three torpedoes exploded in her

nets without causing much damage to *Sevastopol*, but a fourth torpedo hit her stern. On January 2, 1905, Essen had *Sevastopol* towed into deep water where he scuttled her.

The Russian ships in the Far East were generally courageously fought, and proved themselves capable of sustaining much damage. The Russian fleet owed its defeats, through the Russo-Japanese War, more to the lack of logistic support than to a want of bravery, until by 1905 morale had also begun to collapse.

Petropavlovsk class

Class: *Petropavlovsk, Poltava, Sevastopol.*
Launched 1894–5
Dimensions: Length – 112.5m/369ft
Beam – 21.3m/70ft
Draught – 7.8m/25ft 6in
Displacement: 11,536 tonnes/11,354 tons
Armament: Main – 4 x 305mm/12in and
12 x 150mm/6in guns
Secondary – 12 x 3pdr, 28 x 1pdr guns,
6 x 455mm/18in torpedoes and 60 mines
Machinery: 12 boilers, 2 shafts,
8,389kW/11,250ihp
Speed: 16.5 knots
Complement: 632 men

BELOW: *Petropavlovsk* and her two sisters formed the Russian First Pacific Squadron and were in the Far East when the Russo-Japanese war broke out. Despite their limitations they fought bravely but were inevitably overwhelmed by the Japanese.

Rostislav

The battleship *Rostislav*, laid down in 1894, is notable for being the first oil-fired battleship in the world, although she was also capable of burning coal. Originally intended to be a copy of the *Sissoi Veliki*, she was supplied with rather unsatisfactory 255mm/10in guns and the Nicolaiev yard on the Black Sea made other changes. Constructed to the same length as *Sissoi Veliki* she emerged with two turrets in the contemporary layout, but with an extra two 205mm/8in guns in the central battery. She also displaced about 1,524 tonnes/1,500 tons less than *Sissoi Veliki*. Although slow and weak, she saw plenty of action in World War I.

Learning the lessons of the Battle of Tsushima, the Russian Black Sea battleship squadron was formed into a single firing-unit of 305mm/12in-gunned ships, from which *Rostislav* was excluded. The fall of her 255mm/10in rounds were so different from the larger shells of the other battleships, and potentially confusing to the fire controller, that she was actually forbidden from firing tactically on the same target.

However, as early as November 1914 *Rostislav* was used to bombard Turkish shore facilities at Zonguldak, and she was present at the first action of World War I when battleships engaged each other. As the Russian Black Sea fleet was returning to Sevastopol on November 18, it was intercepted by the German-manned and Turkish-flagged *Goeben* and *Breslau*. While *Goeben* duelled with the battleship *Evstafi* and her sisters, *Rostislav* engaged the *Breslau* and drove her to the disengaged side of *Goeben*.

Rostislav returned several times in 1915 to bombard facilities and prohibit sea traffic on the south coast of Turkey, and in 1916 she was employed supporting the Russian troops in the Caucasus. On September 2, 1916, while at anchor in the Romanian port of Constanta, she was hit by a bomb dropped from a German seaplane.

At the end of the war *Rostislav* was captured alongside by advancing armies under German command, but retaken by British and French forces supporting the Whites during the Russian revolution.

ABOVE: **In theory the Black Sea in World War I should have been dominated by the German battlecruiser *Goeben*, but the Russian Black Sea Fleet of pre-Dreadnoughts were well handled and were able to operate widely throughout the theatre.**

Her internal machinery had been wrecked, so in November 1920 *Rostislav* was grounded off Kerch as a fixed battery. *Rostislav* survived until 1930 when she was broken up, being the last surviving battleship of the Imperial Russian Navy.

Rostislav

Class: *Rostislav*. Launched 1896
Dimensions: Length – 107.2m/351ft 10in
 Beam – 20.73m/68ft
 Draught - 6.7m/22ft
Displacement: 9,022 tonnes/8,880 tons
Armament: Main – 4 x 255mm/10in and
 8 x 150mm/6in guns
 Secondary – 20 x 3pdr guns and
 6 x 455mm/18in torpedoes
Machinery: 12 boilers, 2 shafts.
 6,488kW/8,700ihp
Speed: 16 knots
Complement: 650 men

Peresviet class

The Peresviet class with their three funnels, length and extended forecastle deck, and French-style tumblehome, French-type turrets, weak armament and miserable speed were thoroughly unsatisfactory. Besides two twin 255mm/10in turrets they had five 150mm/6in guns in casemates port and starboard and a bow chaser. The Peresviet and Osliabia were built by the New Admiralty yard in St Petersburg and Pobieda was built by the Baltic Works in St Petersburg and incorporated some minor changes. The main belt of armour, Russian-made "Harvey-ized" in the first units, and steel alloy in Pobieda, was 95m/312ft long and 2.44m/8ft deep.

Peresviet was seriously damaged at the Battle of the Yellow Sea. The Japanese captured a hill overlooking Port Arthur and used it to spot the fall of shot of the advancing army's 280mm/11in howitzers. Peresviet was hit by at least 23 rounds and was scuttled on December 7, 1904.

The Japanese raised her and named her Sagami. In 1916 Russia needed warships to guard her White Sea ports against the Germans and Sagami was repurchased and given back her old name. However, she ran aground off Vladivostok on May 26, 1916, and stuck fast for two months. Then on January 4, 1917, Peresviet struck a mine laid by the German minelayer U-73 and sank 16km/10 miles from Port Said, this time for good. Few ships can claim to have been sunk twice.

Osliabia was in the Baltic when the Russo-Japanese war broke out, and was sent to the Far East as part of the Russian Second Pacific Squadron. She was sunk by gunfire at the Battle of Tsushima. During the Russo-Japanese War Pobieda struck a mine on April 13, 1904, but the force of the explosion was

largely absorbed by a coal bunker and she was repaired in time to be present at the Battle of the Yellow Sea in August 1904. She was finally sunk on December 7, 1904, at Port Arthur. Despite 21 280mm/11in howitzer hits, the Japanese were able to raise her and bring her into service as the Suwo. She was finally scrapped in 1922.

BELOW: *Pobieda* was mined in 1904 and heavily shelled at Port Arthur. However, she was raised and served on as the Japanese *Suwo* until 1922.

Peresviet class

Class: *Peresviet, Osliabia, Pobieda.* Launched 1898–1900
Dimensions: Length – 132.3m/434ft
  Beam – 21.8m/71ft 6in
  Draught – 7.9m/26ft
Displacement: 12,887 tonnes/12,683 tons
Armament: Main – 4 x 255mm/10in and
  11 x 150mm/6in guns
  Secondary – 20 x 11pdr, 20 x 3pdr,
  8 x 1pdr guns and 5 x 380mm/15in torpedoes
Machinery: 32 Belleville boilers, 3 shafts.
  11,186kW/15,000ihp
Speed: 18 knots
Complement: 752 men

LEFT: **The battleship *Potemkin*, also known under other names, was made famous by Sergei Eisenstein's classic black and white film of the 1905 mutiny onboard which presaged the Russian Revolution. Although she may have flown as many as five different national flags, it is as *Potemkin* that she will always be known.**

Potemkin

The pre-Dreadnought *Kniaz Potemkin Tavricheski* is universally known as the battleship *Potemkin* and for the mutiny which took place aboard on June 25, 1905. Following "Bloody Sunday", when Cossacks had savagely suppressed a protest march on the Winter Palace in St Petersburg on January 22, 1905, the Black Sea port of Odessa remained calm until strikes were called that spring. Socialists had been agitating in the fleet since 1903, but *Potemkin* was regarded as one of the most loyal of ships. However, a mutiny was planned during gunnery exercises, the eventual cause being a refusal to eat maggot-infested meat. *Potemkin*'s captain assured his men that the meat was edible while his second-in-command threatened to shoot 12 sailors chosen at random. There were shouts, small arms were seized and within a few minutes seven officers had been killed and their bodies thrown over the side.

A People's Committee took the ship to Odessa, where the mutineers threatened to bombard the city. However, after several hundred pro-mutiny demonstrators were massacred by Cossacks near the Richelieu Steps,

Potemkin's guns remained silent because the mutineers did not know who to fire on. That night rioting broke out and some 6,000 people were killed by soldiers and looters.

When the barbette ships *Georgi Pobiedonsets* and *Dvenadtsat Apostolov*, and the turret ship *Tri Sviatitelia* approached Odessa, *Potemkin* ordered them to "Surrender or we fire" and the Russian admiral retired to join his commander-in-chief at Tendra Island. When the squadron returned, reinforced by the battleship *Rostislav* and the barbette ship *Sinop*, *Potemkin* steamed out again and this time the barbette ship *Georgi Pobiedonsets* surrendered to mutineers onboard and returned to Odessa with the *Potemkin*.

Over the summer the mutiny subsided and *Potemkin* took refuge in nearby Constanta, Romania, where she was scuttled in shallow water and the crew stole away. By July 11, *Potemkin* had been pumped out and towed back into Russian waters. The mutiny that foreshadowed the Russian Revolution by 12 years was over. In October the Tsar exorcised *Potemkin*'s black history by renaming her *Pantelimon*, and she saw

service in World War I until in April 1917 the Provisional Government renamed her *Potemkin* and, a month later, *Boretz zu Svobodu*. She changed hands several times as independence-seeking Ukrainians, the German army, and counter-revolutionaries occupied Sevastopol. While the British temporarily held Sevastopol, men from the cruiser *Calypso* disabled her engines on April 25, 1919, and in November 1920 the Red Army finally seized control.

Potemkin, immortalized in Sergei Eisenstein's classic silent film *Battleship Potemkin*, was broken up in 1922.

Potemkin

Class: *Kniaz Potemkin Tavricheski*. Launched 1900
Dimensions: Length – 115.4m/378ft 6in
    Beam – 22.25m/73ft
    Draught – 8.2m/27ft
Displacement: 12,784 tonnes/12,582 tons
Armament: Main – 4 x 305mm/12in and
    16 x 150mm/6in guns
    Secondary – 14 x 11pdr guns and
    5 x 380mm/15in torpedoes
Machinery: 22 Belleville boilers, 2 shafts,
    7,904kW/10,600ihp
Speed: 16.5 knots
Complement: 750 men

LEFT: *Retvisan*, another Russian ship which was fought bravely and survived the Russo-Japanese War until sunk by the besieging artillery.

Retvisan

Retvisan	
Class: *Retvisan*. Launched 1900	
Dimensions: Length – 117.9m/386ft 8in	
Beam – 22.2m/72ft 8in	
Draught – 7.9m/26ft	
Displacement: 13,107 tonnes/12,900 tons	
Armament: Main – 4 x 305mm/12in and	
12 x 150mm/6in guns	
Secondary – 20 x 11pdr, 24 x 11pdr, 24 x 2pdr,	
8 x 1pdr guns 6 x 380mm/15in torpedoes	
and 45 mines	
Machinery: 24 Niclausse boilers, 2 shafts,	
12,677kW/17,000ihp	
Speed: 18 knots	
Complement: 738 men	

These two similar ships were ordered from foreign yards as the Imperial Russian Navy built up its three fleets, in the Baltic, the Black Sea and the Pacific. *Retvisan* was a three-funnelled, flush-deck ship, while the *Tsessarevitch*, though similar in length and displacement, had two funnels and her pronounced tumblehome gave away her French origins. They had similar main armament, but *Retvisan*'s 150mm/6in guns were mounted four in casemates and eight in a main deck battery. *Tsessarevitch* had her 150mm/6in guns in turrets and she was slightly more heavily armoured. Undoubtedly they were the best Russian battleships to date, and they were sent to join the

Russian fleet based at Port Arthur. There they were joined by the battleships *Petropavlovsk, Poltava, Sevastopol, Pobieda* and *Peresviet* as well as many cruisers, gunboats and auxiliaries.

Tsessarevitch

LEFT: *Tsessarevitch*, onboard which the Russian Admiral Vitgeft lost his life when a Japanese shell struck the bridge during the Battle of the Yellow Sea in August 1904.

Tsessarevitch	
Class: *Tsessarevitch*. Launched 1901	
Dimensions: Length – 118.5m/388ft 9in	
Beam – 23.2m/76ft 1in	
Draught – 7.9m/26ft	
Displacement: 13,122 tonnes/12,915 tons	
Armament: Main – 4 x 305mm/12in,	
12 x 150mm/6in guns	
Secondary – 20 x 11pdr, 20 x 3pdr guns,	
4 x 380mm/15in torpedoes and 45 mines	
Machinery: 20 Belleville boilers, 2 shafts,	
12,304kW/16,500ihp	
Speed: 18.5 knots	
Complement: 782 men	

Japan broke diplomatic relations with Russia on February 6, 1904, and two Russian ships were sunk at sea on February 8, although war was not declared when on February 8 and 9, Japanese destroyers attempted to "Copenhagen" the Russian ships in Port Arthur, which was un-expecting and gaily lit. Of 20 torpedoes fired, two reached *Retvisan* and *Tsessarevitch*, which ran aground, though both were soon raised and repaired. Despite its disorder the *Tsessarevitch* steamed out the next day to thwart a major Japanese attack.

Later, when the fleets met on August 10, 1904, in the Battle of the Yellow Sea, both sides concentrated fire on the head of the other's line, the battleships *Mikasa* and *Tsessarevitch* respectively. A dozen 305mm/12in rounds crashed into *Tsessarevitch*, killing Rear Admiral Vitgeft and hitting the control tower, causing *Tsessarevitch* to veer out of control. She was later interned in Kiao Chau, a German concession on the Chinese coast.

Retvisan was also hit nearly a score of times but managed to return to Port Arthur where she was besieged with the

rest of the Russian fleet and sunk by howitzers of the Japanese army on December 6, 1904. She was raised and repaired by the Japanese navy and commissioned as the *Hizen*, the only American-built battleship in the steam age to be captured by an enemy or to have flown two flags. She was sunk as a target in 1924.

In World War I, *Tsessarevitch* served in the Baltic and was engaged by the German Dreadnought *Kronprinz* on October 17, 1917, but escaped with only two hits. She was scrapped in 1922.

Borodino class

The five battleships of the Borodino class took the *Tsessarevitch* as their model. However, post-battle analysis of the Russo-Japanese war revealed some serious flaws in the French design. The class had a very pronounced tumblehome, with the hull sides curved sharply inward from the waterline, and they proved to be extraordinarily manoeuvrable, but under certain conditions of flooding the centre of gravity of these ships could change rapidly. This created instability and a large overturning momentum, just as the French battleship, *Bouvet,* demonstrated when she capsized after striking a mine off the Dardanelles in March 1915.

Previous Russian warships, whatever their defects, stood up well to battle damage, and the Borodinos, though their armoured belt was thinner and narrower than in the *Tsessarevitch* prototype, also sustained a great deal of damage before four of them succumbed at the Battle of Tsushima.

Borodino, Imperator Alexander III, Orel and *Kniaz Suvarov* were all at the Battle of Tsushima and in theory these modern ships should have acquitted themselves

well, but material weaknesses and perhaps human exhaustion made these an ill-fated group of ships. The Russians fought their ships hard, but as *Kniaz Suvarov* led the line she became the first target for the Japanese gunners. When her steering gear was damaged, she was forced out of line, and repeatedly hit by shellfire, torpedoed and sank.

Imperator Alexander III took the lead but was soon enveloped in flames and began to list heavily from a hit in the bows. This caused flooding and she later capsized. *Borodino*'s end was even quicker and more dramatic: she suffered a magazine explosion and blew up.

Orel's superstructure was badly damaged and although she survived the day, she surrendered the following day. Once repaired, *Orel* served the Japanese as *Iwami* until being scrapped in 1922.

Only the last ship of the class, *Slava*, was not ready and so did not sail for the Far East. In World War I she fought the German Dreadnought *König* off Moon Sound in the Gulf of Riga on October 17, 1917, when she flooded so much that she grounded and was scuttled by torpedo. The wreck was broken up in 1935.

ABOVE: **The Borodino class was a successful development of *Tsessarevitch* and their presence gave some homogeneity to the Russian line at the Battle of Tsushima. Only *Slava* was not ready in time to steam to the Far East, but she gave a good account of herself in the Baltic in World War I. At Tsushima *Borodino*, seen here, blew up after a shell hit a magazine. *Slava*, a sister ship, had more success against a German Dreadnought in World War I, but ran aground and was sunk by her own side.**

Borodino class

Class: *Borodino, Imperator Alexander III, Orel, Kniaz Suvarov, Slava.* Launched 1901–3
Dimensions: Length – 121m/397ft
  Beam – 23.2m/76ft 2in
  Draught – 8m/26ft 2in
Displacement: 13,733 tonnes/13,516 tons
Armament: Main – 4 x 305mm/12in and
  12 x 150mm/6in guns
  Secondary – 20 x 11pdr, 20 x 3pdr guns and
  4 x 380mm/15in torpedoes
Machinery: 20 Belleville boilers, 2 shafts,
  12,155kW/16,300ihp
Speed: 18 knots
Complement: 835 men

LEFT: **The Russians learned valuable lessons from the Battle of Tsushima and when they next faced battle *Evstafi* and *Ioann Zlatoust* acquitted themselves well.**

Evstafi class

Class: *Evstafi, Ioann Zlatoust.* Launched 1906
Dimensions: Length – 118m/387ft 3in
    Beam – 22.6m/74ft
    Draught – 8.2m/27ft
Displacement: 13,046 tonnes/12,840 tons
Armament: Main – 4 x 305mm/12in,
    4 x 205mm/8in and 12 x 150mm/6in guns
    Secondary – 14 x 11pdr and 6 x 3pdr guns and
    3 x 455mm/18in torpedoes
Machinery: 22 Belleville boilers, 2 shafts,
    8,054kW/10,800ihp
Speed: 16.5 knots
Complement: 879 men

Evstafi class

Generally similar to *Potemkin* and laid down in 1898, these two ships spent some time on the slips while the Russians considered the lessons of the Russo-Japanese War. As a result their armour was improved, especially to the upper deck which was increased to 205mm/8in. The trend towards larger guns was followed and the Evstafis were fitted with 205mm/8in guns. Later in World War I they were also fitted with additional anti-aircraft guns.

The Russian navy as a whole learned other lessons from the Russo-Japanese War, and the Russians developed a system whereby the centre ship of a squadron of three would control the fire of all ships. Equipment and procedures for transmitting the range and correction data between ships were devised and the range-tables for all major guns were revised. New shells with more reliable and predictable trajectories were designed and gun mountings improved, including smoke-extraction fans to keep the turrets clear. With these gunnery improvements and more thorough training, *Evstafi* and *Ioann Zlatoust* formed the core of a squadron which acquitted itself well when it came up against the more recent *Goeben*.

Imperator Pavel class

LEFT: **The last pre-Dreadnoughts of the Russian navy seen at anchor together in the Baltic.**

Imperator Pavel class

Class: *Imperator Pavel, Andrei Peroswanni.*
    Launched 1906–7
Dimensions: Length – 140.2m/460ft
    Beam – 24.4m/80ft
    Draught – 8.2m/27ft
Displacement: 17,679 tonnes/17,400 tons
Armament: Main – 4 x 305mm/12in,
    14 x 205mm/8in and 12 x 120mm/4.7in guns
    Secondary – 4 x 3pdr guns and
    3 x 455mm/18in torpedoes
Machinery: 22 Belleville boilers, 2 shafts,
    13,423kW/18,000ihp
Speed: 17.5 knots
Complement: 933men

These were the last pre-Dreadnoughts to be built for the Imperial Russian navy and showed all the lessons of the Russo-Japanese war. A large number of 205mm/8in secondary guns were mounted in turrets and casemates, and the hulls were completely armoured – even to the removal of scuttles and deadlights. Originally fitted with slender US-style cage or lattice masts, these were cut down to funnel height and replaced with pole masts. They took little part in the Baltic fighting in World War I.

Imperator Pavel, renamed *Respublika* in 1917, was scrapped in 1923. *Andrei Peroswanni* was torpedoed in Kronstadt harbour on August 18, 1919, long after the war in the rest of Europe was over, during an attack by British coastal motorboats. She was scrapped in 1925.

LEFT: **Austro-Hungarian naval architects had some help from their German-speaking cousins, but generally their designs were their own. The Habsburg class were small, well-proportioned vessels.**

Habsburg class

Habsburg class

Class: *Habsburg, Arpad, Babenburg.*
   Launched 1900–2
Dimensions: Length – 114.55m/375ft 10in
   Beam – 19.8m/65ft
   Draught – 7.5m/24ft 6in
Displacement: 8,364 tonnes/8,232 tons
Armament: Main – 3 x 240mm/9.4in and
   12 x 150mm/6in guns
   Secondary – 10 x 12pdr guns and 2 torpedoes
Machinery: 16 boilers, 2 shafts.
   14,307kW/16,000ihp
Speed: 19.85 knots
Complement: 638 men

A ustro-Hungarian provinces in the northern and eastern Adriatic Sea gave the otherwise landlocked empire access to the sea. From the mid-1800s a significant navy was developed, modelled on British lines, and the first ship was a steam frigate ordered from England at the end of the Russian War 1854–6. The first torpedoes were designed and built in Austria, and the Austro-Hungarian navy distinguished itself in fighting the Danes in the North Sea in support of their allies the

Prussians in 1864. The empire, however, had a continental outlook and the navy was starved of funds. Nevertheless, the Austro-Hungarians, although often building only single ships, took part in the development of the battleship from broadside ironclad to centre-battery ship and coast defence ships, sometimes mounting quite large guns.

The three units of the Habsburg class are listed here because, though their guns were less than 255mm/10in, they were heavily armoured, seagoing and

had a significant impact upon the regional balance of power. Although modified before the war, when the superstructure of *Habsburg* was reduced by one deck, they were obsolete by 1914, when Austria-Hungary fought Italy. Although used on isolated operations, as when *Babenburg* shelled the Italian port of Ancona in 1915, by the end of the war their crews had been drafted into the submarine and air services. All three were ceded to Britain in 1920 and scrapped in Italy in 1921.

Erzherzog Karl class

LEFT: **The Erzherzog Karl class was a successful design for a small pre-Dreadnought. Like other ships then building on the slips, they were made obsolescent by the launch of *Dreadnought*. In World War I they were used for bombardment.**

At the end of the war all three ships were seized at Pola by the newly independent state of Yugoslavia, but *Erzherzog Karl* and *Erzherzog Friedrich* were ceded to France and *Erzherzog Ferdinand Max* to Britain, but all were broken up in 1920/1.

Erzherzog Karl class

Class: *Erzherzog Karl, Erzherzog Friedrich,
   Erzherzog Ferdinand Max.* Launched 1903–5
Dimensions: Length – 126.2m/414ft 2in
   Beam – 21.8m/7l ft 5in
   Draught – 7.5m/24ft 7in
Displacement: 10,640 tonnes/10,472 tons
Armament: Main – 4 x 240mm/9.45in and
   12 x 190mm/7.48in guns
   Secondary – 12 x 70mm/2.76in and
   4 x 47mm/1.85in guns
Machinery: 2 shafts, 13,423kW/18,000ihp
Speed: 20.5 knots
Complement: 700 men

T hese were the three largest and last pre-Dreadnoughts of the Austro-Hungarian navy. Like previous designs, they were compact ships, limited by the size of the dockyard facilities at Trieste, though compared to their Italian rivals they were better armoured. They also displayed some advances, and for the first time the secondary guns in their casemates were electrically operated.

Launched in 1903–5, however, the class was rendered obsolete while the ships were being completed by the launch in Portsmouth of *Dreadnought*.

During World War I they were limited to the role of shore bombardment, including a raid on May 24, 1915, on the city and ancient ferry port of Ancona. In early 1918 they were used in helping to suppress a mutiny at Cattaro.

129

Directory of Battleships

World War I

There were very few fleet engagements after the Battle of Trafalgar in 1805, the most studied being the Battle of Tsushima in 1905 between the Japanese and Russians. The annihilation of the Russian fleet altered the balance of power in Europe, which coincided with the resurgence of the USN and the rise of the German navy. Germany had imperial ambitions and though its fleet was only intended for a limited purpose, German naval armament was perceived as a threat by Britain, then the greatest naval power in the world. A deadly arms race started across the North Sea which became a symptom, if not the cause, of World War I. In the event the German warships outside the North Sea were quickly rounded up, and though the Germans adopted tactics intended to defeat the Royal Navy by attrition, they never succeeded. Der Tag, the day when the two fleets would meet in decisive battle, was a disappointment to both sides although the Germans won materially, tactically, and in terms of propaganda. The Germans realized too late that submarine warfare was the only way that they could have won the war at sea.

LEFT: The British built warships for navies throughout the world, although in war they frequently took them over for their own use. The Chilean *Almirante*, seen here, served in World War I as the British HMS *Canada*.

Dreadnought

The change from the mixed calibres of previous designs to the all-big-gun armament, which Cuniberti had advocated and which Fisher adopted, was a direct result of increasing gun ranges and the need for a single calibre whose fall of shot could be distinguished by spotters.

British naval architects were already considering an all-big-gun design when Cuniberti's article was printed in English, and when Admiral Sir Jacky Fisher became First Sea Lord in October 1904 he tasked a committee to look at various arrangements of turrets. The USN had similar proposals under review and their analysis of the Battle of Tsushima would also convince the Japanese. Spotters needed to see the fall of shot in order to calculate range, but the gun range was increasing so much that the splashes of large- and medium-calibre guns could not be told apart. The obvious solution was to fit guns all of the same calibre.

Naval officers were also impressed by the economy of carrying only one outfit of ammunition and spares. However, the greatest improvement in *Dreadnought* was a result of the bold decision to fit four turbine-driven shafts. This was only four years after the Royal Navy had sent its first turbines to sea fitted in destroyers. The decision-making process was marked by Fisher's energy. The Committee on Design met on January 3, 1905, and hy the end of February had made its

TOP: **HMS** *Dreadnought*, which gave her name to the type she founded. In the background is Nelson's *Victory* and coming up the harbour are three submarines which were also part of Fisher's revolution. ABOVE: *Dreadnought*, again with *Victory* in the background, consciously linking the new great ship to the concept of the Royal Navy's supremacy at sea.

recommendations. *Dreadnought* was laid down on Trafalgar Day, October 21, 1905, launched on February 10, 1906, and completed in December of the same year. This was something of a record even for the super-efficient Royal Dockyard of Portsmouth, although it was a little longer than the 12 months that Fisher claimed. Nevertheless, Fisher had energized everybody and everything and deserves much of the credit for her quick build.

LEFT: **With the commissioning of**
***St Vincent* in 1910 there were seven**
Dreadnoughts in the First Division of
the Home Fleet. A. B. Cull's picture
shows the first time that such a
powerful squadron put to sea.
BELOW: **A familiar picture of**
***Dreadnought* just after her launch,**
which nevertheless is unique because
it shows her underwater form. Fisher
had decided among his other
revolutionary ideas to do away with
the ram, although the designers
managed to retain a bulbous shape
which helped streamline the ship.

Her naval architects deserve some credit, too. The decision to fit turbines instead of reciprocating engines saved space and about 1,016 tonnes/1,000 tons of weight and when this was combined with the hull form it allowed *Dreadnought* unprecedented speed, in excess of 20 knots. This had been rigorously tested in the model ship tanks at Haslar. Her sea trials were highly successful. The high forecastle kept *Dreadnought* dry, the wide beam to accommodate turrets on each side of the superstructure kept down the roll and the turbines reduced vibration. Consequently foreign navies immediately wanted to copy her. Nevertheless, the first German Dreadnoughts, the Westfalens, were not ready until 1909, and the first Japanese Dreadnoughts, *Satsuma* and *Aki,* and the first Americans, the South Carolina and Delaware classes, in 1910.

The designers made two mistakes, probably forced upon them by naval officers, among them the gunnery expert and future Commander-in-Chief of the Grand Fleet, John Jellicoe. The two wing turrets had limited arcs of fire; it would have been better to place an extra turret on the centre line and accept the increased weight penalty. As it was, fully loaded she was 3,556 tonnes/3,500 tons more than her designed displacement and *Dreadnought* sat so low that her armoured belt was under water and useless. Also, to provide a convenient support for a derrick to hoist her boats, the foremast with its gun-direction platform was placed aft of the fore funnel. This meant that if smoke or heat haze did not obscure the gun director then the acrid exhaust gases would choke the crew. These defects could not be rectified, although later she was armed with more light guns, her topmasts were cut down and she received a larger gun-direction platform and searchlight control positions.

Dreadnought saw the start of World War I as flagship of the Fourth Battle Squadron, until superseded by the more modern *Benbow*. On March 18, 1915, in the Pentland Firth, she became the first and only battleship to sink a submarine, the German *U-29*. In May 1916 she became flagship of the Third Battle Squadron of the Edward VII class ships at Sheerness, guarding the Thames, and so missed the Battle of Jutland, and on June 14, off Dunnet Head, *Dreadnought* attempted but failed to ram a second submarine. She returned to the Grand Fleet in 1918, was placed in reserve in 1919 and scrapped in 1922. *Dreadnought* was a singleton; she named not a class but a type of ship.

Dreadnought

Class: *Dreadnought.* Launched 1906
Dimensions: Length – 160.6m/527ft
  Beam – 25m/82ft
  Draught – 9.5m/31ft
Displacement: 18,400 tonnes/18,110 tons
Armament: Main – 10 x 305mm/12in guns
  Secondary – 24 x 12pdr guns and
  5 x 455mm/18in torpedoes
Machinery: 18 Babcock and Wilcox boilers,
  4 shafts, 17,375kW/23,300shp
Speed: 21 knots
Complement: 695 men

Bellerophon class

This class was very similar to the *Dreadnought* and the ships were also built very rapidly. Internally the propulsion machinery was the same, but they were also fitted with an inner longitudinal bulkhead designed to localize damage from a torpedo hit, known as a torpedo bulkhead. The tripod foremast was placed over the bridge superstructure and thus clear of funnel gases, but a second tripod mainmast was added with a "fighting top" which was exposed to the fumes of both funnels. While these two masts gave the Bellerophons a more balanced look than *Dreadnought*, the fire control position on the mainmast proved useless and was removed along with the topmasts during the war.

The secondary armament was also improved from 12-pounders (75mm/3in) to 100mm/4in guns. Initially some guns were sited on the main turrets' roofs, but these were later placed in casemates in the superstructure. Other changes during World War I included the removal of torpedo nets and the after torpedo tube, more extensive radio aerials, searchlight platforms, additional anti-aircraft guns,

and funnel caps. By 1918 all three ships had ramps on the A and Y turrets and could fly off either a Sopwith Pup fighter biplane or a Sopwith Strutter reconnaissance aeroplane.

Bellerophon joined the Home Fleet in 1909 and the Fourth Battle Squadron of the Grand Fleet in August 1914, and fought at the Battle of Jutland. Her career was remarkable for two collisions, one with *Inflexible* at Portland in 1911 and one with a merchantman in 1914. She was placed in reserve at the war's end and broken up in 1921.

Superb was flagship of the Fourth Battle Squadron at Jutland. In November 1918 she led the Allied Fleet through the Dardanelles, was paid off in 1919, briefly

TOP: *Bellerophon* underway. The design fault of placing the foremast behind the funnel has been corrected. *Bellerophon*'s jack, not normally flown at sea, appears to indicate she is dressed for some occasion. ABOVE: *Superb* in the Hamoaze at Plymouth. BELOW: *Temeraire* in Plymouth Sound.

a target and broken up in 1921. *Temeraire* followed a similar career, but was used as a seagoing training ship until being scrapped in 1921–2. The war service of these ships proved the soundness of the basic Dreadnought design.

Bellerophon class

Class: *Bellerophon, Superb, Temeraire.*
Launched 1907
Dimensions: Length – 160.3m/526ft
Beam – 25.2m/82ft 6in
Draught – 8.3m/27ft 3in
Displacement: 19,100 tonnes/18,800 tons
Armament: Main – 10 x 305mm/12in guns
Secondary – 16 x 100mm/4in guns and
3 x 455mm/18in torpedoes
Machinery: 18 boilers, 4 shafts,
17,151kW/23,000shp
Speed: 21 knots
Complement: 733 men

St Vincent class

The third class of ships of the basic Dreadnought design followed a trend of gradual improvement and increase in size. Horsepower was increased to offset the rise in displacement and the hull form began to be refined, so the St Vincents were slightly slimmer and longer. As in the Bellerophons the after fire-control position proved useless and was later removed.

A new 305mm/12in gun was introduced with a longer barrel, although this did not prove effective as the higher muzzle velocity shortened the barrel life and reduced accuracy at longer ranges. Pre-war modifications included lowering the topmasts and moving the secondary armament from the main gun roofs. Wartime modifications were similar to the Bellerophons with the addition of funnel caps, searchlight towers and aircraft ramps.

St Vincent was commissioned into the Home Fleet as flagship in 1910, fought at the Battle of Jutland as part of the First Battle Squadron, and was broken up.

The future King George VI served as a Lieutenant on Collingwood at Jutland. Later this class moved from the First to the Fourth Battle Squadron. Collingwood was sold for scrap in 1922. Vanguard followed her sisters into the Home and Grand Fleets and Jutland, and between them these ships fired over 250 305mm/12in rounds at the German High Sea Fleet, and received no hits. On July 9, 1917, Vanguard suffered a violent explosion and sank with appalling speed, killing 804 men. This was later attributed to faulty ammunition.

In this period a number of ships blew up when not in action. Although sometimes attributed to sabotage or other covert enemy action, the cause was invariably the spontaneous combustion of ammunition.

BELOW: **Vanguard (with other Dreadnoughts beyond her) approaching Portsmouth.** RIGHT: **Vanguard followed by another St Vincent class. The artist A. B. Cull has captured the winter weather when these ships operated in the North Sea.**

St Vincent class

Class: *St Vincent, Collingwood, Vanguard.* Launched 1908–9
Dimensions: Length – 163.4m/536ft
  Beam – 25.7m/84ft 2in
  Draught – 7.9m/25ft 11in
Displacement: 19,875 tonnes/19,560 tons
Armament: Main – 10 x 305mm/12in guns
  Secondary – 20 x 100mm/4in guns and
  3 x 455mm/18in torpedoes
Machinery: 18 boilers, 4 shafts,
  18,270kW/24,500shp
Speed: 21 knots
Complement: 718 men

Invincible, Indomitable and Inflexible

One of Fisher's more debatable ideas concerned the armoured cruiser. Fisher wanted a cruiser that was larger and faster than any other cruiser, which could protect trade by hunting down and destroying every other smaller cruiser and could also act either as a heavy scout in pursuit of an enemy or as support of the van of the battlefleet. In official words: "To engage the enemy battlecruisers in a fleet action, or, if none are present, by using their speed to cross the bow of the enemy and engage the van of his battlefleet".

The result was the battlecrusier (so named in 1913) of which the Invincibles were the first. They were long ships so that they could accommodate the number of boilers needed to give them their high speed, and like *Dreadnought* they mounted a uniform large-calibre armament. However, when compared to the battleships they were lightly armoured although externally they looked very similar. Like *Dreadnought* they had twin rudders and four turbine-driven shafts which made them very effective. They were however vulnerable not just against battleships but also against ships of their own type firing large-calibre guns. In the case of the Invincibles the wing turrets, P and Q, had very limited-beam firing arcs. Later in the war *Indomitable* was fitted with flying-off ramps over these turrets.

At the Battle of Jutland the Fifth Battle Squadron had been loaned to the Battlecruiser Fleet and the Invincibles, who formed the Third Battlecruiser Squadron, had been lent to the Grand Fleet. Inevitably Jellicoe placed the three battlecruisers in the line of battle, where they suffered accordingly. Although

Invincible and *Indomitable* disabled the *Wiesbaden* and *Pillau* and hit *Lützow*, when *Invincible* came under sustained fire from the German battleships *Derfflinger, Lützow* and *König*, a shell hit Q turret causing a huge explosion that blew her in half. There were only six survivors from a crew of over 1,000.

Previously *Invincible* had taken part in the first naval engagement of the war, the Battle of Heligoland Bight on August 28, 1914. In November 1914 she had been ordered to sail from Devonport still with dockyard labourers onboard to hunt for Admiral Graf von Spee's squadron in the South Atlantic. On December 8, 1914, she had fought at the Battle of the Falkland Islands, when *Invincible, Inflexible* and their consorts sank the German *Scharnhorst* and *Gneisenau*, the light cruisers *Leipzig* and *Nürnberg*, and two colliers. During the battle *Invincible* was hit 22 times by smaller-calibre shells, but without fatalities.

As a new ship *Inflexible* visited New York in 1909. At the outbreak of World War I she was flagship of the British Mediterranean Fleet and with *Indomitable*, in August 1914, was involved in the unsuccessful hunt for the German battlecruisers *Goeben* and *Breslau*. She joined *Invincible* in the hunt for *Graf Spee* and the Battle of the Falkland Islands. In February and March 1915 she wore out her guns' barrels during bombardments in the Dardanelles, where she was flagship of the British Dardanelles Squadron. On March 18, 1915, *Inflexible* was hit nine times by Turkish batteries and ran on to a mine, needing to be beached for temporary repairs before

going to Malta for full repairs. At the Battle of Jutland she fired 88 305mm/12in rounds and received no damage herself. On August 19, 1916, *Inflexible* was attacked unsuccessfully by the German submarine *U-65*, and on January 31, 1918, she collided with a British submarine in the ironically named Battle of May Island. She was sold for scrap in 1921.

On commissioning *Indomitable* carried the Prince of Wales on a visit to Canada. At the outbreak of World War I she took part in the chase of the *Goeben* and *Breslau*, and in November 1914 participated in a preliminary bombardment of the Dardanelles forts that may have alerted the Turks to future British and allied intentions. She joined the Second Battlecruiser Squadron and fought at the Battle of Dogger Bank on January 24, 1915. There she fired on *Blücher*, closing the range to 5,490m/6,000yd, and received no damage herself. Afterwards *Indomitable* towed *Lion* back to Rosyth. At the Battle of Jutland *Indomitable* fired 175 305mm/12in rounds, hitting *Derrflinger* (three times), *Seydlitz* (once) and the pre-Dreadnought *Pommern*. She was sold for scrap in 1921.

BELOW: The fine photograph of a previous *Inflexible*, taken from the ramparts of the fortress of Malta, shows how far warship design had evolved since the masted turret ship *Inflexible* of 1874–1903.

OPPOSITE AND ABOVE: *Invincible* and her sisters were conceived as fast armoured cruisers, but inevitably in the case of ships with an armament of 305mm/12in guns fleet commanders wanted to place them in the line of battle and they were restyled battlecruisers. The lack of fire control equipment clearly indicates that the heavy guns had outranged the means of laying them accurately – especially in the frequent mists and fogs of the North Sea.

Invincible, Indomitable and *Inflexible*

Class: *Invincible, Indomitable, Inflexible.*
Launched 1907
Dimensions: Length – 172.8m/567ft
Beam – 23.9m/78ft 6in
Draught – 8m/26ft 2in
Displacement: 17,652 tonnes/17,373 tons
Armament: Main – 8 x 305mm/12in guns
Secondary – 16 x 100mm/4in guns and
5 x 455mm/18in torpedoes
Machinery: 31 boilers, 4 shafts,
30,574kW/41,000shp
Speed: 26 knots
Complement: 784 men

LEFT: *Neptune* at anchor and working her boats. She is wearing the flag of the Commander-in-Chief, Home Fleet. ABOVE: *Neptune* at anchor in the fleet anchorage of Scapa Flow during World War I. Note that the after tripod mast and flying bridges have been removed. BELOW LEFT: A period picture postcard showing *Hercules* dressed overall while underway. The Royal Navy was fond of reusing the famous names of its ships, and chose the classic names of earlier wooden-walled battleships, like *Hercules*, to remind the world that Britainnia ruled the waves.

Neptune, Colossus and Hercules

When the American and the Argentine navies built Dreadnoughts which would fire 10 and 12 guns on the broadside, the British staggered their midships turrets, on a longer hull, so that both midships turrets could be fired across the deck. To leave the boats clear and open the firing arcs, a flying bridge was introduced linking the islands of the superstructure.

The roof-mounted 100mm/4in guns were suppressed and placed in the superstructure behind armoured shields. Pre-war a searchlight platform was added, the after control position was removed, the fore funnel heightened and a clinker cowl fitted.

Neptune was the fastest British battleship to date, making nearly 23 knots on trials. She fought at Jutland, where she suffered no damage, and was broken up in 1919. *Colossus* and *Hercules*, the last two 305mm/12in-gunned battleships of the period, were half-sisters to *Neptune*.

Realizing that in battle the wreckage from the flying bridges would fall on P and Q turrets, this was reduced in size, and in 1917 removed completely. The after control position was never fitted but, in a retrograde step, the forward mast and control position were placed abaft the fore funnel. In *Colossus* the 100mm/4in guns in the superstructure were protected by dropping ports; *Hercules* had shields. Pre-war the fore funnel was raised and later the torpedo nets were removed.

Colossus was hit at Jutland by two shells, the only Grand Fleet battleship at Jutland to be damaged. In 1919–20 she was painted in Victorian black, white and buff livery and served as a training ship at Devonport for cadets. She was broken up in 1928. *Hercules* also fought at Jutland. In November 1918 she carried the Allied Naval Commission to Kiel, and was sold for breaking up in 1921.

Neptune

Class: *Neptune*.
Launched 1909
Dimensions: Length – 166.42m/546ft
Beam – 25.9m/85ft
Draught – 8.7m/28ft 6in
Displacement: 19,996 tonnes/19,680 tons
Armament: Main – 10 x 305mm/12in guns
Secondary – 16 x 100mm/4in guns and
3 x 455mm/18in torpedoes
Machinery: 18 Yarrow boilers, 4 shafts,
18,643kW/25,000shp
Speed: 21 knots
Complement: 759 men

Colossus and Hercules

Class: *Colossus, Hercules*.
Launched 1910
Dimensions: Length – 166.4m/546ft
Beam – 25.9m/85ft
Draught – 8.8m/28ft 9in
Displacement: 20,550 tonnes/20,225 tons
Armament: Main – 10 x 305mm/12in guns
Secondary – 16 x 100mm/4in guns and 3 x
535mm/21in torpedoes
Machinery: 18 boilers, 4 shafts,
18,643kW/25,000shp
Speed: 21 knots
Complement: 755 men

Indefatigable class

As successions of Dreadnought-type battleships and battlecruisers were built year on year, their design improved. However this class has been criticized because *Indefatigable* was a near replica of *Invincible*, which had been laid down three years before. *Australia* and *New Zealand* were laid down at the same time as the Lion class battlecruisers, which incorporated all the lessons learned so far, were bigger by 8,128 tonnes/8,000 tons, more heavily armed (340mm/13.5in guns) and better armoured (230mm/9in on the belt), matching the increases in equivalent ships being built in Germany. There is no direct evidence why this should be so, other than speculation that it was done on grounds of dockyard capacity, speed, cost (£1.7 million – *Australia* and *New Zealand* were paid for by their namesake countries) or to produce a second homogeneous division of battleships.

The class were some 6m/20ft longer than *Invincible*, which allowed greater staggering and better arcs of fire to the midships turrets, P and Q. The fore funnel was increased in height to help clear smoke from the bridge and the after control position was initially fitted but soon dismantled. Various light guns were added during the war, and after Jutland, *Australia* and *New Zealand* were given an additional 25mm/1in of armour between P and Q turrets. They also received searchlights, range clocks, and, in 1918, flying-off platforms over the midships turrets. These two ships already differed from *Indefatigable* in their internal arrangement of armour and their bridge layouts, and had 745.7kW/1,000shp more power.

Indefatigable served in the British Mediterranean Fleet and took part in the unsuccessful chase of *Goeben* and *Breslau*. In November 1914 she bombarded Cape Helles in the Dardanelles, before joining the Second Battlecruiser Squadron. At the Battle of Jutland *Indefatigable* was hit by *Von der Tann*. Two rounds entered the after (X) magazine, causing an explosion,

ABOVE: *Indefatigable* was one of three similar battlecruisers. Fast but lightly armoured, she was hit by *Von der Tann* at the Battle of Jutland and blew up. The fundamental weakness of these ships was their lack of armour, but some ships had laid great emphasis on rapid rate of fire (rather than accuracy).

and as *Indefatigable* veered out of line a second salvo hit her forward and she blew up.

Indefatigable class

Class: *Indefatigable, Australia, New Zealand.*
  Launched 1909–11
Dimensions: Length – 179.8m/590ft
  Beam – 24.4m/80ft
  Draught – 7.9m/26ft
Displacement: 18,800 tonnes/18,500 tons
Armament: Main – 8 x 305mm/12in guns
  Secondary – 16 x 100mm/4in guns and
  3 x 455mm/18in torpedoes
Machinery: 32 boilers, 4 shafts,
  32,811kW/44,000shp
Speed: 25 knots
Complement: 800 men

Australia

At the start of World War I the Admiralty in London and the government in Canberra struggled over *Australia*'s deployment. The Australian government wanted *Australia* as a deterrent and defence against a raid by the German East Asiatic Squadron, yet was anxious to strike its own blow in the war. Therefore after mustering the Australian fleet in Sydney, *Australia* escorted Australian and New Zealand troops for the capture of the German colonies of Samoa and New Guinea.

In September 1914 *Australia* steamed east to Fiji. Japan had declared war on Germany and *Australia* was sent to join Japanese ships off California which were intended to prevent the Germans using the Panama Canal. When the news came of the Battle of the Falklands, *Australia* was sent to join the British Grand Fleet at Scapa Flow; as she was too long for the Panama Canal she made passage via Cape Horn in late December 1914.

In the South Atlantic she sank the German merchantman *Eleonore Woermann*, thus ending enemy coaling arrangements. She was made flagship of the Second Battlecruiser Squadron, although following a collision with her sister ship *New Zealand* she missed the Battle of Jutland. Between January 1915 and November 1919 *Australia* steamed some 91,565km/56,908 miles, mostly on the Northern Patrol, the distant blockade of Germany. She became the first aircraft-carrying ship of the Australian navy, using a platform built over the guns from which Sopwith fighters were launched as scouts and to attack Zeppelins.

After her return to Australia in May 1919, she once more became flagship of the Royal Australian Navy and played a leading role in the visit of the Prince of Wales in another battlecruiser, the British *Renown*. However, *Australia* consumed too much of the navy's budget and manpower, and by 1920 she was

ABOVE: *Australia*, paid for and manned by Australians, played an active part in World War I and became a source of pride for the new nation.
BELOW: Following the Washington naval treaty, *Australia* was de-equipped and scuttled in April 1924 off Sydney.

downgraded to a drill ship at Flinders Naval Depot with a secondary role as a fixed defensive battery. In November 1921 she was paid off into reserve.

Australia was included in the tonnage allowed the British Empire under the terms of the Washington Treaty. There were efforts to have her preserved as a monument, but she was stripped, and in April 1924 towed to sea, where the pride of the Australian navy was scuttled, amid much public lament – the battlecruiser *Australia* had been a symbol of the country's burgeoning nationhood.

Australia	

Class: *Indefatigable, Australia, New Zealand.*
    Launched 1909–11
Dimensions: Length – 179.8m/590ft
    Beam – 24.4m/80ft
    Draught – 7.9m/26ft
Displacement: 18,800 tonnes/18,500 tons
Armament: Main – 8 x 305mm/12in guns
    Secondary – 16 x 100mm/4in guns and
    3 x 455mm/18in torpedoes
Machinery: 32 boilers, 4 shafts,
    32,811kW/44,000shp
Speed: 25 knots
Complement: 800 men

New Zealand

In 1909 the Prime Minister of New Zealand decided to set an example to the other British Dominions by offering to fund a "first class battleship" for the Royal Navy. In the event New Zealand paid for an Indefatigable class battlecruiser and a sister ship to *Australia*, which was rather cheaper than the super-Dreadnoughts which were being introduced.

The British Admiralty sent *New Zealand* on a tour of the Dominions in 1913 to show them what could be done, before sending her to join the First Battlecruiser Squadron of the Grand Fleet. There she took part in the Battles of Heligoland Bight and Dogger Bank, and when Beatty's own flagship *Lion* was damaged at Dogger Bank, he transferred his flag to *New Zealand*.

In April 1916 *New Zealand* and *Australia* collided in fog in the North Sea. *New Zealand* was repaired just in time to rejoin the fleet before the Battle of Jutland, but *Australia* missed the great battle. As if to make up for this *New Zealand* fired more rounds at Jutland than any other ship in the battle – a total of 420 305mm/12in shells. In turn she was hit just once by a shell which landed on X turret without major damage or casualties.

In November 1917 *New Zealand* also fought in the Second Battle of Heligoland Bight. Unlike *Australia*, who was manned largely by Australians, there were mostly British and very few New Zealanders in the battlecruiser *New Zealand*. Nevertheless her captain had been presented with a Maori battledress and

it was thought to be unlucky if he did not wear this when going into battle.

In 1919–20 Admiral Jellicoe was sent on a world tour to assess the Empire's needs for defence – the British Admiralty still hankered after an Empire navy and Jellicoe was supposed to report what contributions the Dominions could make. He chose *New Zealand* as his flagship and she was specially modified to provide him with suitable office and living accommodation. It has been reckoned that nearly one-third of the population of her home country saw the battlecruiser *New Zealand* while she was in New Zealand waters. *New Zealand* was scrapped in 1923.

ABOVE: *New Zealand* became Jellicoe's flagship for his 1919 mission to advise on the naval requirements of the British Empire. The photograph shows his specially built quarters on the port side forward of the funnels. ABOVE RIGHT: *New Zealand* bows-on showing the fine lines of this class of ship. LEFT: Visitors' day on *New Zealand*. Although only a handful of the ship's company were in fact New Zealanders, the population of New Zealand took a proprietary interest in the affairs of their ship, and her captain was expected to wear Maori costume when going into action.

New Zealand

Class: *Indefatigable, Australia, New Zealand.* Launched 1909–11
Dimensions: Length – 179.8m/590ft
Beam – 24.4m/80ft
Draught – 7.9m/26ft
Displacement: 18,800 tonnes/18,500 tons
Armament: Main – 8 x 305mm/12in guns
Secondary – 16 x 100mm/4in guns and 3 x 455mm/18in torpedoes
Machinery: 32 boilers, 4 shafts, 32,811kW/44,000shp
Speed: 25 knots
Complement: 800 men

LEFT: **Port bow photograph of one of the Orion class. For some extraordinary reason the foremast has been put back behind the funnel where the gunnery control optics, and their operators, will be affected by the smoke and haze.** BELOW: **A starboard profile of this class of ship, showing the hot fumes which must have made climbing the foremast a noxious experience. Producing four Dreadnoughts a year was about the industrial capacity of Great Britain.**

Orion class

The 305mm/12in, 50-calibre gun had proved inaccurate and caused too much barrel wear, so the 340mm/13.5in gun, not seen since the 1890s, was reintroduced in the Orion class. The lower muzzle velocity and larger shell was successful in reducing instability in flight and increased accuracy, and, with increased elevation of firing, the 340mm/13.5in gun could hit a target at 21,950m/24,000yd. The shell when it arrived was also considerably heavier (635kg/1,400lb) than the 305mm/12in version (567kg/1,250lb).

The Orions incorporated many minor improvements. The awkward arrangement of placing guns midships to fire athwartships was abandoned and all were mounted on the centre line. The forward turrets, A and B, and the after ones, X and Y, were super-firing. On the other hand, blast through the sighting hoods of the lower turrets prevented these guns being fired ahead. Side armour was extended up to the main deck, overcoming the problem that at full load the armoured belt tended to be submerged and therefore useless. The mainmast was reduced to a small pole mast. Bilge keels were fitted to reduce roll.

Once more the foremast and its control position were placed aft of the fore funnel, and the only reason for this can be a continued emphasis on seamanship (the need for a derrick to hoist boats) over gunnery. However, the interference this caused with optics and the hazard to health was much reduced because the funnel served fewer boilers.

When *Thunderer* was fitted with the Scott director aiming system in 1912 and took part in a competitive shoot against *Orion* she scored many more hits.

During World War I the topmasts were reduced and torpedo nets removed, the fire-control platform extended, plating over magazines increased and flying-off platforms fitted over B turret. *Thunderer* had an additional runway over X turret.

Monarch rammed *Conqueror* in December 1914, damaging her bows, and *Revenge* collided with *Orion* causing similar damage. These four ships formed the Second Battle Squadron at the Battle of Jutland, where they fired 198 rounds but neither caused nor sustained any damage. Discarded after the Washington Treaty, *Thunderer* survived until 1926 as a cadet training ship, then, like her sisters in 1922, was broken up.

Orion class	
Class: *Orion, Conqueror, Monarch, Thunderer.* Launched 1910–11	
Dimensions: Length – 177.1m/581ft Beam – 27m/88ft 6in Draught – 7.3m/24ft 1in	
Displacement: 22,560 tonnes/22,200 tons	
Armament: Main – 10 x 340mm/13.5in guns Secondary – 16 x 100mm/4in guns and 3 x 535mm/21in torpedoes	
Machinery: 18 boilers, 4 shafts, 20,134kW/27,000shp	
Speed: 21 knots	
Complement: 752 men	

Lion class

The Lion class battlecruisers were 6 knots faster than the Orion class battleships. To achieve this they had 42 rather than 18 boilers, and were 36.6m/120ft longer. To reduce weight the maximum thickness of armour was reduced from 305mm/12in to 230mm/9in and the super-firing after turret was removed. Nevertheless, the displacement increased by over 4,064 tonnes/4,000 tons to 22,556 tonnes/22,200 tons.

They were handsome ships, known in the fleet as the "Cats", and were the subject of much favourable comment inspired by the Admiralty, which encouraged rumours exaggerating their speed and armoured strength.

When launched *Lion* had the foremast placed between the closely spaced first and second funnels, but the heat was so intense that the crew in the gun-direction platform were stranded. The direction platform was re-sited forward of the fore funnel on a pole mast and this was reinforced by struts, turning it into a tripod.

Lion was Admiral Beatty's flagship in the Battle Cruiser Force. She took part in the Battles of Heligoland Bight, Dogger Bank and Jutland. At Dogger Bank she fired nearly 250 rounds but made only four hits; one on *Blücher*, one on *Derfflinger* and two on *Seydlitz*. In turn she was hit by 16 280mm/11in and 305mm/12in rounds and had to be towed back by *Indefatigable*. She was also damaged at Jutland, and saved from explosion by the heroism of one man who ordered the flooding of a magazine. Q turret was temporarily removed in late 1916. She made numerous other sorties, but was scrapped in 1924.

Princess Royal fought at the Battle of Heligoland Bight before escorting the first Canadian troops across the Atlantic in September 1914, and guarding the North America and West Indies station during the hunt for Admiral Graf von Spee's squadron. She was also in action at Dogger Bank. At Jutland she was hit by *Derfflinger, Markgraf* and *Posen*, but although suffering damage, casualties and on fire, she remained in action. *Princess Royal* was part of the covering force during the Second Battle of Heligoland Bight on November 17, 1917. She was sold for scrap in 1922.

Lion class

Class: *Lion, Princess Royal.*
  Launched 1910–11
Dimensions: Length – 213.4m/700ft
  Beam – 27m/88ft 6in
  Draught – 8.4m/27ft 8in
Displacement: 26,690 tonnes/26,270 tons
Armament: Main – 8 x 340mm/13.5in guns
  Secondary – 16 x 100mm/4in guns and
  2 x 535mm/21in torpedoes
Machinery: 42 boilers, 4 shafts,
  52,199kW/70,000shp
Speed: 27 knots
Complement: 997 men

ABOVE: *Lion*, flagship of Admiral Sir David Beatty's First Battlecruiser Squadron, leads *Princess Royal* to sea and into action on May 31, 1916. LEFT: *Lion* being towed into Armstrong's yard at Newcastle upon Tyne for repairs after the Battle of Jutland. BELOW: The Lion class were graceful ships well equipped with radio, which Beatty did not seem to want to use at Jutland and so lost control of the Fifth Battle Squadron that was allocated to him.

Queen Mary and *Tiger*

Superficially similar to the Lion class, *Queen Mary* incorporated several minor improvements. An additional 3,729kW/5,000shp gave her half a knot extra speed, the armoured belt was modified, and the larger main armament shell gave even greater stability in flight and accuracy, though for a period she could shoot at greater ranges than the guns could be sighted. Wartime modifications included a larger bridge and gun-direction platform with director control in 1915, reduced topmasts, and additional legs for the foremast.

Queen Mary was at the Battle of Heligoland Bight but missed the fighting at Dogger Bank. At Jutland she was another ship of the Battle Cruiser Force which came under fire from the German *Derfflinger*. She had fired about 150 rounds at *Seydlitz* when she was hit on Q turret and shortly afterwards between A and B turrets. The forward magazines exploded and the fore part of the ship disappeared and as she settled, listing to port, a further enormous explosion occurred, barely half an hour after the battle had started.

BELOW: *Queen Mary* and *Tiger* were at first glance the same as the Lion class, but they were half a knot faster and bigger-gunned. BOTTOM: *Tiger* with *Renown* beyond her, steaming at full speed into a heavy swell in the North Sea (1917 or 1918). Together, *Lion*, *Tiger*, *Princess Royal* and *Queen Mary* were known as the Cats.

The Tiger class were half-sisters to *Lion* and *Princess Royal*, together known as the Cats. Externally the difference was the rearrangement of the turrets, Q turret now being placed aft of three equally spaced funnels. For the first time in a British battlecruiser, the secondary armament consisted of 150mm/6in guns. Internally, improved boilers gave *Tiger* 63,385kW/85,000shp, but the speed increase this enabled was disappointing while the fuel consumption increased alarmingly. Protection (230mm/9in maximum armour) was just as poor as in other battlecruisers.

At the Battle of Dogger Bank, *Tiger* exchanged fire with German opponents, and was hit by six large-calibre hits. At Jutland, she was hit 15 times without her ammunition exploding, thus seemingly proving that in ships where the rules of handling ammunition were followed there was less risk of disaster.

Queen Mary

Class: *Queen Mary*. Launched 1912
Dimensions: Length – 214.4m/703ft 6in
Beam – 27.1m/89ft
Draught – 8.5m/28ft
Displacement: 27,200 tonnes/26,770 tons
Armament: Main – 8 x 340mm/13.5in guns
Secondary – 16 x 100mm/4in guns and
2 x 535mm/21in torpedoes
Machinery: 42 boilers, 4 shafts,
55,928kW/75,000shp
Speed: 27.5 knots
Complement: 997 men

Tiger

Class: *Tiger*. Launched 1913
Dimensions: Length – 214.6m/704ft
Beam – 27.6m/90ft 6in
Draught – 8.7m/28ft 6in
Displacement: 28,885 tonnes/28,430 tons
Armament: Main – 8 x 340mm/13.5in guns
Secondary – 12 x 150mm/6in guns and
4 x 535mm/21in torpedoes
Machinery: 39 boilers, 4 shafts,
63,385kW/85,000shp
Speed: 29 knots
Complement: 1,121 men

LEFT: **The four ships of this class formed the newest squadrons of Dreadnought, until** *Audacious* **was sunk by a mine off Northern Ireland in October 1914.** BELOW: *King George V* **lying under a huge crane at Portsmouth and being fitted out after launch. The crane is being used to begin to assemble** *King George V*'s **355mm/14in guns.**

King George V class

This class was similar to the Orions, but with the foremast placed forward of the funnels and modified during World War I, including the fitting of flying-off ramps in 1918. Almost the last of the Dreadnoughts to be built before the outbreak of war, the King George V class was the epitome of the type.

King George V served the war in the Grand Fleet and became a post-war gunnery training ship. She was finally scrapped in 1926 (under the terms of the Washington Treaty) when *Nelson* and *Rodney* were completed.

Ajax served the war in the Grand Fleet and operated in the Black Sea against Russian revolutionaries in 1919. She was scrapped in 1926. *Centurion* also served the war in the Grand Fleet and after operations in the Black Sea was converted to a radio-controlled target ship. She was used as a decoy in World War II and then sunk as a block ship off Normandy in France on June 9, 1944.

In October 1914 the converted German liner *Berlin* laid a minefield off Malin Head on the north coast of Ireland, where the British Grand Fleet was using Loch Swilly as a base whilst the anti-submarine defences of Scapa Flow were being improved. On the morning of October 27, 1914, as she steamed out

on exercises with the other super-Dreadnoughts *Centurion, Ajax, King George V, Orion, Monarch* and *Thunderer*, the *Audacious* struck a mine on her port side amidships, quickly developed a list and lost power. Most of her crew were taken onboard the White Star liner *Olympic. Audacious* slowly settled by the stern and, at nightfall, after the rest of her crew had been rescued, she capsized, there was an explosion, and she sank.

No lives were lost, and the sinking was blamed on the weakness of the longitudinal bulkheads which were buckled in the initial explosion and had allowed floodwater to spread, though it seems that the damage control procedures in the ship could not have been very proficient.

Ludicrously, since the incident had been witnessed by American passengers onboard *Olympic*, the Commander-in-Chief of the Grand Fleet, Jellicoe, persuaded the British Admiralty to try to keep the sinking a secret. While everyone but the British acknowledged the loss, the British kept *Audacious* in the Navy List and reticence on the subject damaged British credibility. *Audacious* was the first loss of a major warship in World War I.

King George V class

Class: *King George V, Centurion, Audacious, Ajax.* Launched 1911–12
Dimensions: Length – 182.1m/597ft 6in
Beam – 27.1m/89ft
Draught – 8.7m/28ft 8in
Displacement: 23,370 tonnes/23,000 tons
Armament: Main – 10 x 340mm/13.5 guns.
Secondary – 16 x 100mm/4in guns and 2 x 535mm/21in torpedoes
Machinery: 18 boilers, 4 shafts, 23,117kW/31,000shp
Speed: 21 knots
Complement: 782 men
Former name of *King George V* was *Royal George*

Iron Duke class

Similar in many respects to the King George V class, the Iron Dukes were 7.7m/25ft longer and 0.3m/1ft wider in the beam. However they were 2,032 tonnes/2,000 tons heavier, mainly because of the increase in the secondary armament from 100mm/4in to 150mm/6in to meet the greater ranges at which torpedo-boats could fire their improved weapons. A large direction platform was fitted on build, and these were also the first battleships to be fitted with anti-aircraft guns – two 12pdr on the after superstructure of *Iron Duke* in 1914. The stern torpedo tubes which had been a feature of design until now were suppressed.

The secondary armament casemates were, however, a problem: the hinged plates that closed off the revolving turrets were vulnerable in any kind of seaway and once washed away or damaged allowed seawater to flood on to the mess decks. The problem was solved by fitting dwarf bulkheads and rubber seals, but the design fault was that the guns were mounted too low in the hull. After Jutland searchlights and increased armour were fitted.

Iron Duke was flagship of the Home Fleet under Admiral Callaghan, and then of the Grand Fleet, under both Jellicoe and Beatty. In 1919–26 she was part of the British Mediterranean Fleet, and bombarded Red Army positions in the Black Sea in support of the White Russians during operations there in 1919–20. While the others of her class were scrapped under the terms of the Washington Treaty, *Iron Duke* was retained in a demilitarized state as a training and depot ship. Demilitarization included removal of B and Y turrets, and

BELOW: *Iron Duke* in 1914 as flagship of the Grand Fleet under Admiral Sir John Jellicoe. *Iron Duke* served on into World War II when she was an accommodation ship at Scapa Flow.

a substantial part of her armour, and limiting her speed, through the removal of boilers, to 18 knots. *Iron Duke* spent World War II at Scapa Flow, with the rest of her armament removed, was damaged by bombs in 1939 and finally sold for scrap in 1946. *Benbow* served her time in the Grand Fleet, joined the British Mediterranean Fleet between 1919 and 1926 and, like others of her class, provided gunfire support for White Russians in the Black Sea in 1919–20, and was sold for scrap in 1931. *Emperor of India*, whose former name was *Delhi*, spent World War I in the Grand Fleet (but missed Jutland because she was in refit), and was in the Mediterranean between 1919 and 1926. She was sunk as a gunnery target in 1931.

Between them the Iron Dukes fired 292 rounds of 340mm/ 13.5in ammunition during Jutland, of which *Marlborough* fired 162. She was torpedoed amidships and a hole 21m x 6m/70ft x 20ft was blown in her side, abreast the boiler rooms, where she was only protected by coal bunkers. Unlike *Audacious* she was able to keep station at 17 knots and did not cease firing until her guns were prevented from bearing by her list. She made her way to the Humber, and after three months' repairs on the Tyne she rejoined the Grand Fleet. *Marlborough* served with the rest of her class in the Mediterranean until 1926, then the Atlantic Fleet until 1929, and was scrapped in 1932.

TOP: *Iron Duke* enters Portsmouth. On the left is *Queen Elizabeth* and on the right is *Victory*. All three ships are flying the St George cross signifying an Admiral in command. ABOVE LEFT: *Emperor of India*, showing how with a following wind the bridge and in particular the gunnery direction platform could be enveloped in smoke and funnel gases. ABOVE: An over-flight of biplanes portends the coming struggle between the surface ship and the aircraft.

Iron Duke class

Class: *Iron Duke, Marlborough, Emperor of India, Benbow*. Launched 1912–13
Dimensions: Length – 189.8m/622ft 9in
 Beam – 27.4m/90ft
 Draught – 8.8m/29ft
Displacement: 25,400 tonnes/25,000 tons
Armament: Main – 10 x 340mm/13.5in guns
 Secondary – 12 x 150mm/6in guns and
 4 x 535mm/21in torpedoes
Machinery: 18 boilers, 4 shafts,
 21,625kW/29,000shp
Speed: 21 knots
Complement: 995 men

Queen Elizabeth class

Though armed and armoured as battleships, the Queen Elizabeth class was fast enough to operate with the Battle Cruiser Force, to which, as the Fifth (Fast) Battle Squadron, they were attached during the Battle of Jutland (except *Queen Elizabeth* herself who was in dockyard hands). They were regarded as the finest battleships of their era. Their 380mm/ 15in guns were one reason for this and another – which her crew appreciated – was that with oil-fired boilers they were cleaner and more spacious than coal-fired ships. The six 380mm/15in guns could deliver a heavier broadside than any five-turret predecessor, and the guns were more accurate and suffered less barrel wear than the 340mm/13.5in. To secure supplies of oil the British government bought shares in Middle Eastern oil companies, thus inadvertently setting the course of foreign policy later in the century.

All five ships were overweight when completed and in practical terms their speed was about 24 knots.

Like other Dreadnoughts they were modified after Jutland and were fitted with range clocks and deflector scales, searchlight towers and additional deck armour. In 1918 all five were fitted with flying-off ramps on B and X turrets.

Although the handling of the Fifth Battle Squadron at Jutland was severely criticized, its participation in the Battle Cruiser Force probably saved Beatty's ships from an even worse mauling. In particular, the Germans were impressed by the accuracy of *Valiant*'s shooting.

Built at Portsmouth, but towed to Fairfield's to be fitted with her engines, as first of class *Queen Elizabeth* had a stern walk and two additional 150mm/6in guns under the quarterdeck, but these were removed in 1915 when they proved wet. Instead single guns with stern arcs were retrofitted port and starboard underneath X turret, as was done in the rest of the class.

TOP: *Queen Elizabeth*, after she had been modernized in the interwar years. The forward tripod had been replaced by a heavy control tower. ABOVE: In peacetime ceremonial duties were part of life on a battleship and here, on *Queen Elizabeth*, seamen and Royal Marines man the side for HM the King, and prepare to salute him in the traditional manner by giving him three cheers.

Queen Elizabeth bombarded forts in the Dardanelles in early 1915, but was recalled to the Grand Fleet although she missed the Battle of Jutland. In 1917, after Beatty had become Commander-in-Chief of the Grand Fleet, he took her for his flagship. Briefly in September 1917 she wore the flag of Admiral Mayo USN. The surrender of the German High Seas

LEFT: **Rough weather when the deck would be out of bounds.** BELOW: **In calm weather the forecastle was a place of work and here *Queen Elizabeth*'s crew are seen preparing to launch paravanes (used to keep mines clear of striking the hull).**

Fleet was signed onboard *Queen Elizabeth* on November 15, 1918. Refitted and then modernized, she served on into World War II.

Repaired after a collision with *Barham* on December 2, 1915, *Warspite* was ready in time for the Battle of Jutland. She fired over 250 rounds, but was hit herself by some 15 305mm/12in rounds. At a critical moment her steering gear failed and *Warspite* steamed a full circle under the German gunfire but the Grand Fleet came up to drive off the Germans before she could be destroyed, and she limped back to Rosyth. Her repairs were just completed when on August 24 she was damaged in another collision, this time with *Valiant*. *Warspite* was partially modernized in 1924–6 and served in World War II.

The Federated States of Malaya paid for a fifth ship, named *Malaya*. She was ready in time for Jutland where she fired 215 rounds and was hit herself eight times by 305mm/12in rounds. *Malaya* visited Cherbourg for celebrations of the peace in April 1919 and in 1920 visited Germany. In 1921 *Malaya* took Prince Arthur of Connaught to India and on to Malaya. She served in the fleet until 1948.

Valiant served with the Grand Fleet throughout World War I and fired 299 rounds at the Battle of Jutland, receiving only slight splinter damage. She was modernized in 1929–30 and rebuilt in 1937–9.

Barham was named after Lord Barham, First Lord of the Admiralty and architect of the Campaign of Trafalgar in 1803–5. In the fighting at Jutland, *Barham* fired 337 rounds and during the "run to the north" came under heavy fire from the German High Seas Fleet. Midshipman Blackett, who subsequently became one of the greatest scientists of the 20th century and winner of the Nobel Prize for Physics in 1948, described this as "our five minutes' hate". It really lasted much longer and was extraordinarily unpleasant. It is estimated that some 500 305mm/12in bricks were fired at the *Barham* and the rest of the squadron. "How we survived with so very few hits I have no idea," Blackett said. "Everyone was very relieved that the Grand Fleet had joined up, for it was exceedingly unpleasant alone."

Like her sisters, *Barham* was modernized from 1931–4, emerging with a single smokestack, enhanced protection against long-range plunging gunfire, and additional anti-aircraft guns, as well as a hangar and catapult for two seaplanes.

In World War II, *Barham* was capsized and blew up after she had been torpedoed by a German U-boat in the Mediterranean. The U-boat was returning from a special forces operation in North Africa when it found itself in the path of the British Mediterranean Fleet making a sortie to the west. The U-boat commander was lucky to get in his snapshot and it hit *Barham* with three torpedoes. The loss of *Barham* was recorded on film and makes for poignant viewing, as well as unique footage.

Queen Elizabeth class

Class: *Queen Elizabeth, Warspite, Valiant, Barham, Malaya.* Launched 1913–15
Dimensions: Length – 196.6m/645ft
Beam – 27.7m/91ft
Draught – 9.5m/31ft
Displacement: 27,940 tonnes/27,500 tons
Armament: Main – 8 x 380mm/15in guns
Secondary – 14 x 150mm/6in guns and 4 x 535mm/21in torpedoes
Machinery: 24 boilers, 4 shafts, 41,759kW/56,000shp
Speed: 25 knots
Complement: 925 men
A sixth ship, to be named *Agincourt*, was cancelled. All ships of the class were extensively rebuilt between the wars, and their anti-aircraft armament improved.

Royal Sovereign class

Although known as the Royal Sovereigns, the British Admiralty referred to these ships as the Revenge class, and in fact *Ramillies* was the first ship to be laid down. Compared to the Queen Elizabeths their speed was reduced to 21 knots, and the 150mm/6in guns placed further aft to keep them drier. The obvious visual difference was the single, large, centrally placed funnel.

Ramillies was built with 2.1m/7ft-wide bulges faired into the hull to absorb the effect of an exploding torpedo. Filled with wood, tubes, oil and water, the bulges weighed an extra 2,540 tonnes/ 2,500 tons, but did not affect speed or fuel consumption, and were retrofitted in others of the class.

Up to this point all Dreadnoughts had had four shafts and twin rudders, but in this class two in-line rudders were fitted, the smaller, forward rudder intended to reduce vulnerability and make hand-steering, in an emergency, easier. In practice, the ancillary rudder proved ineffective and was removed.

When Fisher returned to office in 1914, he had the designs changed from mixed coal and oil to all oil-fired, with the intention of raising the horsepower and

with this the speed to 23 knots. He also had work on three other ships of this class, *Renown*, *Repulse* and *Resistance*, suspended as he wanted to replace them with battlecruisers.

After Jutland pumping and flooding arrangements were extended to cope better with damage, extra armour was placed over the magazines, and flash-tight doors on ammunition routes improved. Searchlight towers, range clocks and deflection scales were also fitted. By 1918 all ships had flying-off ramps over B and X turrets.

Only *Royal Oak* and *Revenge* fought at Jutland. The *Royal Sovereign* was completed in time, but missed the battle through engine problems. *Ramillies*'s completion was delayed after she had damaged her rudder on launch, and she did not join the Grand Fleet until 1917. *Resolution* was completed too late.

Royal Oak was torpedoed by the German U-boat *U-47* at Scapa Flow in 1939. *Royal Sovereign* was transferred to the Soviet Navy in 1944, and renamed *Archangelsk*, to be returned in 1949 when she was broken up. All others survived World Wars I and II and were sold for breaking up in 1948.

ABOVE: The Royal Sovereign class of ships saw much active service in both World Wars of the 20th century, but were already slow ships when completed. BELOW: *Revenge* on a spring cruise in 1934. The effect of the Atlantic swell, even on a 28,450-tonne/28,000-ton battleship, would have been the same whatever the year, even though architects tried to build their ships for North Atlantic conditions.

Royal Sovereign class

Class: *Ramillies, Resolution, Revenge* (ex *Renown*), *Royal Oak, Royal Sovereign.* Launched 1914–16
Dimensions: Length – 190.3m/624ft 3in
  Beam – 27m/88ft 6in
  Draught – 8.7m/28ft 6in
Displacement: 28,450 tonnes/28,000 tons
Armament: Main – 8 x 380mm/15in guns
  Secondary – 4 x 150mm/6in guns and
  4 x 535mm/21in torpedoes
Machinery: 18 boilers, 4 shafts,
  29,830kW/40,000shp
Speed: 21 knots
Complement: 937 men

Erin

The main concern of the Turkish navy in the run-up to World War I was superiority in the Aegean over its former vassal, Greece, and in the Black Sea over its traditional enemy, Russia. To meet these perceived threats, Turkey had ordered several ships in Britain including the new-build super-Dreadnought *Reshadieh*, and *Sultan Osman I* was purchased from Brazil while still in the yard. In addition to two cruisers and four destroyers, none of which were delivered, these ships were paid for in part by public subscription in Turkey. Resentment at their requisition in August 1914 by the Royal Navy, after the crews had arrived to steam them home, helped to bring Turkey into the war on the side

of Germany. As a result the Turkish navy was commanded by a German admiral on the side of the central powers.

Reshadieh (formerly *Reshad V*), renamed *Erin* in the Royal Navy, had the same gun plan as *Orion* and mixed elements of the King George V and Iron Duke class designs, but was slightly shorter and broader. Her extra beam meant that she could not fit into any Royal Navy dry dock and she had to be docked in private yards. She carried a main armament of ten 340mm/13.5in guns in twin turrets in the same layout but her secondary armament consisted of 150mm/6in guns. Her armour was equivalent to her British contemporaries, though she was regarded as rather

Erin

Class: *Erin*. Launched 1913
Dimensions: Length – 170.5m/559ft 6in
  Beam – 27.9m/91ft 7in
  Draught – 8.7m/28ft 5in
Displacement: 23,150 tonnes/22,780 tons
Armament: Main – 10 x 340mm/13.5in guns
  Secondary – 16 x 150mm/6in guns and
  4 x 535mm/21in torpedoes
Machinery: 15 boilers, 4 shafts,
  19,761kW/26,500shp
Speed: 21 knots
Complement: 1,070 men
A second ship of the class, *Reshad-i-Hammiss*, was cancelled.

overcrowded and cramped for accommodation. She was readily recognized by her unusual reverse tripod mast, round funnels, and by Q turret being one deck higher than in her contemporary British designs. *Erin* was given improved fire-control equipment in 1917 and, in 1918, flying-off platforms on B and Q turrets. It is said that Japan's first battlecruiser, *Kongo,* also laid down in 1911 at Vickers, was derived from this design by Sir George Thurston.

Erin spent the war, including the Battle of Jutland, in the Grand Fleet. She was placed in reserve in 1919 and sold to the breakers in 1922, in the era when many ships were culled.

ABOVE: **The Royal Navy's requisitioning of a Turkish battleship which had been partly paid for by public subscription by the Turkish nation, and whose Turkish crew had already been formed, caused much resentment. This helped bring Turkey into the war on the side of Germany.** RIGHT: ***Erin* had a short career. Launched in 1913, she was broken up in 1922. The British Admiralty had a preference for large ships of similar types and equipment-fits: *Erin* had too many unique features to make her economical to retain.**

Agincourt

The battleship *Rio de Janeiro* was ordered by the Brazilian Government in November 1910 and she would have been the ultimate expression of the naval arms race between the Argentine, Brazil and Chile. She was to have been the most powerful warship not just in South America, but in the world, and she was for a time certainly the longest. However she was also a long time building as the Brazilians could not agree amongst themselves what armament to give their ships: various designs were considered between eight 405mm/16in and 14 305mm/12in guns, and eventually the latter was chosen, partly on the grounds of standardization of ammunition stock within the Brazilian fleet and partly under the influence of German advisers who were content with their own 305mm/12in guns. In the meantime Brazil's position in the arms race was costing 25 per cent of the national budget, which became untenable when the price of rubber collapsed and with it the Brazilian economy. In December 1913 *Rio de Janeiro* was sold to Turkey and renamed *Sultan Osman I*. Work recommenced and now included some luxury fittings.

The Turkish Government expected delivery of their new super-Dreadnought in July 1914, and her crew had arrived to take her, and *Reshadieh,* home, but as the delivery time neared Armstrong's were approached by the Admiralty to delay the

ABOVE: *Agincourt* was also destined for the Turkish navy but forcibly taken over by the Royal Navy. The picture on this page shows her as modified for British service, and opposite shows her with the flying bridges and tripod masts with which she was built.

handover of the ship. Then on July 31, 1914, with war imminent, the First Lord of the Admiralty, Winston Churchill, minuted that "Messrs Armstrong should be informed that in view of the present circumstances the Government cannot permit the ship to be handed over to a Foreign Power or to be commissioned as a public ship of a Foreign Government, or to leave their jurisdiction". Next day a company of Sherwood Foresters with fixed bayonets boarded the *Sultan Osman I* and escorted all the Turkish naval personnel off the ship. Money for the new ship had been raised partly by public subscription in Turkey, and her seizure by Britain strengthened the hand of the pro-German faction in the Turkish government. Two months later Turkey was at war with Britain.

Renamed *Agincourt*, her luxurious fittings gave her the nickname of "The Gin Palace" in the Royal Navy and appropriately her first captain and the core of her first crew came from the Royal Yacht. There were individual cabins for the officers and spacious accommodation for the crew but this

had been achieved by eliminating many watertight bulkheads. Like *Erin*, the armoured protection (maximum thickness 230mm/9in) was not up to Royal Navy standards (305mm/12in). The flying bridges – also known as "Marble Arches" – were no longer a feature of British designs and these, along with the tripod mainmast, were removed. To complete her eccentricity the seven turrets were named after the days of the week, Sunday, Monday, Tuesday, Wednesday, Thursday, Friday and Saturday. So unique was *Agincourt*'s appearance that it became common to give stationing orders relative to her.

She was not a success in the Royal Navy: much of her equipment was non-standard and required more frequent visits to the dockyard. The 305mm/12in gun had not been fitted since the Indefatigable battlecruisers, and the single-lever loading arrangements were unusual. Besides concern for control of flooding if torpedoed, it was rumoured that she would break her back or turn turtle if she fired her full broadside.

Nevertheless, at the Battle of Jutland *Agincourt* was one of the first battleships to sight the German High Seas Fleet, and the sight of her 14 guns firing broadsides and enveloping her in a sheet of flame was described as awe-inspiring.

During the war the gunnery direction platform and bridge were enlarged, and searchlight towers around the second funnel were added, together with some extra, light guns.

After the war *Agincourt* was offered for sale to the Brazilian Government, which was not interested; Brazil's challenge to the first navies of the world had ebbed. *Agincourt* was converted to oil-fired boilers and given additional protection, and five turrets (Tuesday to Saturday) were removed so she could be used as a depot ship. However, these plans were dropped and she was scrapped in 1922, along with a great many other ships.

TOP: **As built, originally for the Brazilian government who sold her to the Turks,** *Agincourt* **had a prominent midships Sampson mast and two tripods.**

ABOVE: **Much of her equipment was, literally, foreign to the Royal Navy but such a powerful ship could not be allowed to go overseas into another navy. Subsequently her career in the Royal Navy was foreshortened.**

Agincourt

Class: *Agincourt*. Launched 1913
Dimensions: Length – 204.7m/671ft 6in
    Beam – 27.1m/89ft
    Draught – 8.2m/27ft
Displacement: 27,940 tonnes/27,500 tons
Armament: Main – 14 x 305mm/12in guns
    Secondary – 20 x 150mm/6in, 10 x 75mm/3in
    guns and 3 x 535mm/21in torpedoes
Machinery: 22 boilers, 4 shafts,
    25,354kW/34,000shp
Speed: 22 knots
Complement: 1,115 men

Canada

There is good evidence that during the period running up to World War I the British Admiralty used ships being built in British yards for foreign navies as a reserve. The Chilean Government had ordered two battleships as their response to the South American arms race, to be named *Almirante Latorre* and *Almirante Cochrane*. Turkish battleships being built in Britain had been seized, but Chile was a friendly country where there were large British business

BELOW: **Unlike Turkey whose ships, which were being completed in Britain, were requisitioned, Chile sold her two incomplete battleships to the Royal Navy.**

interests, and she was an important supplier of nitrates for the ammunition industry. As a result *Almirante Latorre* was purchased, though the hint to the Chilean Government that it should follow Australia, Malaysia and New Zealand in paying for a battleship did not work.

Canada was similar to the British Iron Dukes, but 12.2m/40ft longer and 2–3 knots faster, her funnels were taller and thicker, and she had a pole mainmast. In 1918 she had flying-off ramps on B and X turrets. *Canada* joined the Grand Fleet and fought at Jutland and in 1920 she was returned to Chile. In 1914 *Canada*'s sister ship *Almirante Cochrane* had been built up to the

forecastle deck, and in 1918 she was taken in hand and completed as the aircraft carrier *Eagle*.

Canada

Class: *Canada*. Launched 1913
Dimensions: Length – 201.5m/661ft
  Beam – 28m/92ft
  Draught – 8.8m/29ft
Displacement: 29,060 tonnes/28,600 tons
Armament: Main – 10 x 355mm/14in guns
  Secondary – 16 x 150mm/6in guns and
  4 x 535mm/21in torpedoes
Machinery: 21 boilers, 4 shafts,
  27,591kW/37,000shp
Speed: 23 knots
Complement: 1,167 men

LEFT: **The battlecruiser *Renown* was a familiar site off the coast in 1937.**

ABOVE: ***Renown*'s guns had a range of just over 32km/20 miles. Her rate of fire was about one round per minute and it was claimed that each shell could penetrate up to 1.46m/57in of wrought iron.**

BELOW: **All needs were catered for – large galleys and dining rooms, crowded messes and, on most warships, quiet places such as *Renown*'s chapel, seen here.**

Renown class

The Royal Navy had decided against building more battlecruisers when Fisher returned to office as First Sea Lord. He drew lessons from the Battle of the Falklands and to those who said that World War I would be over within a year, he promised to build his new ships quickly enough to participate. Using the material assembled for two Royal Sovereign class ships, Fisher ordered instead two fast battleships. They were 61m/200ft longer and 10,160 tonnes/10,000 tons heavier than previous battlecruisers, and armed with 380mm/15in guns instead of 305mm/12in, but they suffered from the same basic weakness of the battlecruiser concept in that they were too lightly armoured. However they were fast ships, reaching 30 knots, although not their designed speed of 32 knots.

They were also under-gunned on secondary armament. Under Fisher's influence 100mm/4in guns were selected, which even in triple mountings could not deliver the necessary weight of shells, and needed a disproportionately large crew.

Further, they were not delivered until after the weaknesses of the battlecruisers became tragically evident at the Battle of Jutland. Jellicoe, while still Commander-in-Chief of the Grand Fleet, proposed that both ships should be given increased armour as well as other post-Jutland modifications typical of the British Dreadnought fleet. The architects still could not solve the smoke problem and so the fore funnel was also raised 1.8m/6ft to clear the bridge of funnel gases.

At the end of the war they received more armour again. After World War I both ships were extensively refitted and in the inter-war years they were rebuilt, adding another 6,095 tonnes/6,000 tons.

Neither ship saw much action during World War I, although both led busy lives in the inter-war years and also fought in World War II.

Renown class

Class: *Renown, Repulse*. Launched 1916
Dimensions: Length – 242m/794ft
  Beam – 27.4m/90ft
  Draught – 7.8m/25ft 6in
Displacement: 28,095 tonnes/27,650 tons
Armament: Main – 6 x 380mm/15in guns
  Secondary – 17 x 100mm/4in guns and
  2 x 535mm/21in torpedoes
Machinery: 42 boilers, 4 shafts,
  83,518kW/112,000shp
Speed: 30 knots
Complement: 967 men

Courageous, Glorious and *Furious*

Fisher's ill-defined plans to "Copenhagen" the German fleet by forcing an entry into the Baltic gave rise to two extremes of his battlecruiser concept. *Courageous* and *Glorious* were thinly armoured, shallow draught, and fast. The hull was so light that on trials *Courageous* suffered buckling between the breakwater and the forward turret and both ships were strengthened. Fisher hoped to fit a 455mm/18in gun but it was not ready in time. Reckoned by some to be "white elephants", they were tried in a number of different roles. They were fitted with additional torpedoes (although there was no recorded incident of a contemporary Dreadnought successfully firing her torpedoes) and *Courageous* was briefly equipped as a minelayer. A significant advance was made in using small-tube boilers for the first time and double-helical turbines. With 18 Yarrow small-tube boilers they could achieve almost the same horsepower as the Renowns with 42 large-tube boilers.

Courageous and *Glorious* took part in an action against German light cruisers in November 1917. Both were converted to aircraft carriers in the 1920s.

BELOW: ***Courageous**, seen here alongside at Devonport, and **Glorious** were light battlecruisers in which even armament was sacrificed for speed. Eventually both ships were converted to aircraft carriers.*

Furious was similar in size to *Courageous* and *Glorious*, even down to her turret rings, but she had, at last, the 455mm/18in gun in single mountings. She was also slightly beamier. However while nearing completion she was converted to an aircraft carrier. Contrary to popular history, the Admiralty was very air-minded, appreciating the value of aircraft both for reconnaissance and as fighters – particularly after the Royal Naval Air Service's success in shooting down airships. Nearly all battleships were converted to carry flying-off ramps, and the decision was taken to platform over the whole of *Furious*'s forecastle, and suppress the forward turret as one large flying-off ramp. There was space for a hangar under the ramp. Derricks were fitted for hoisting seaplanes onboard, but trials showed that an aircraft like the Sopwith Pup could also be landed on the deck.

The conversion was a limited success and in August 1917 *Furious* was taken in hand for a rebuild which would turn her into a through-deck carrier. The Royal Navy is sometimes accused of being too battleship-minded in the inter-war years and criticized for not paying enough attention to naval aviation, but up to April 1, 1918 (when the RAF was formed), it owned one of the largest air forces in the world and the loss of so many men and machines to the RAF was a serious setback.

TOP: **Another view of** *Courageous*, **this time from the quarter.** ABOVE: *Furious* **also was converted to an aircraft carrier (above left) on board where in the inter-war years the Royal Navy experimented with the first arrester wires (above right). Despite the loss of expertise by the transfer of large numbers of aircraft and airmen to the RAF, the Royal Navy continued to innovate and, despite a lack of modern aircraft, maintained its tactical skill in the use of aircraft. Control of the Fleet Air Arm did not revert to the Royal Navy until just before World War II. Nevertheless, the Fleet Air Arm newly restored to the Admiralty's operational control made rapid progress and distinguished itself well in all theatres of the war, against the German, Italian and Japanese navies.**

Courageous class

Class: *Courageous, Glorious.* Launched 1916
Dimensions: Length – 239.7m/786ft 3in
  Beam – 24.7m/81ft
  Draught – 7.1m/23ft 4in
Displacement: 19,540 tonnes/19,230 tons
Armament: Main – 4 x 380mm/15in guns
  Secondary – 18 x 100mm/4in guns and
  2 x 535mm/21in torpedoes
Machinery: 18 small-tube boilers, 4 shafts,
  67,113kW/90,000shp
Speed: 32 knots
Complement: 828 men

Furious

Class: *Furious.* Launched 1916
Dimensions: Length – 239.7m/786ft 6in
  Beam – 26.8m/88ft
  Draught – 6.4m/21ft
Displacement: 19,826 tonnes/19,513 tons
Armament: Main – 2 x 455mm/18in guns
  Secondary – 11 x 140mm/5.5in guns and
  2 x 535mm/21in torpedoes
Machinery: 18 boilers, 4 shafts,
  67,113kW/90,000shp
Speed: 31 knots
Complement: 880 men

LEFT: *Michigan* at anchor at evening colours. The low light through the lattice masts shows their delicate and elaborate construction. ABOVE: *Michigan* firing a broadside of her 305mm/12in guns during 1912. BELOW: The larger navies were beginning to experiment with replenishment at sea, but operations like this coaling while underway from the bunker ship *Cyclops* to *South Carolina* in 1914 were slow and cumbersome.

South Carolina class

The launch of the British *Dreadnought* with her size, turbine machinery, speed of 21 knots, and main battery of ten 305mm/12in guns shook naval observers everywhere. The USN had already ordered its first all-big-gun ships, but the design was artificially constrained by the US Congress to 16,257 tonnes/16,000 tons, and delayed while the USN absorbed the lessons of the Great White Fleet and of the Battle of Tsushima. In the end, *South Carolina* and *Michigan* were similar to earlier US pre-Dreadnoughts, including in the retention of reciprocating engines.

They did, however, have two novel features: lattice masts and super-firing guns. Apparently the original intention had been to install a gun-direction platform amidships on a flying bridge, but this was dropped in favour of the lattice or cage mast. Experiments had shown that this stood up well to shellfire and reduced vibration at the top of the mast and certainly the gun-direction platform could be carried up higher. This did not always work and in 1918 a heavy gale bent *Michigan*'s mast over. Nevertheless, the lattice mast was retro-fitted into many US pre Dreadnoughts

and became the distinctive recognition mark of future US battleships.

The other novel feature was the super-firing turret. This enabled the full complement of main armament guns to be brought to bear on either beam, giving ships arranged like this a superiority over other Dreadnoughts with guns arranged in echelon or staggered in midships positions. The super-firing gun soon became the norm in every other navy.

South Carolina visited Europe in 1910–11, took part in US interventions in Haiti and Mexico in 1913–14, and spent the rest of World War I on the east coast of the USA. In 1919 she made four round-trips to France, bringing home over 4,000 servicemen, and was scrapped in 1924.

Michigan visited England and France in 1910, and spent the rest of her career in the Atlantic. In spring 1914 she was involved in the Vera Cruz incident when many of her crew served ashore. In World War I she stayed in the western Atlantic, but between January and April 1919 she brought home more than a thousand veterans of the western front. She was scrapped in 1924.

South Carolina class

Class: *South Carolina, Michigan.* Launched 1908
Dimensions: Length – 137.2m/450ft
  Beam – 24.5m/80ft 5in
  Draught – 7.5m/24ft 7in
Displacement: 16,260 tonnes/16,000 tons
Armament: Main – 8 x 305mm/12in guns
  Secondary – 22 x 75mm/3in guns and
  2 x 535mm/21in torpedoes
Machinery: 12 boilers, 2 shafts.
  11,304kW/16,500ihp
Speed: 18.5 knots
Complement: 869 men

LEFT: Quite soon the USN Dreadnoughts like the Delaware class did away with wing turrets and mounted all turrets on the centre line.

Delaware class

Class: *Delaware, North Dakota.* Launched 1909
Dimensions: Length – 155.5m/510ft
  Beam – 26m/85ft 4in
  Draught – 8.3m/27ft 3in
Displacement: 20,707 tonnes/20,380 tons
Armament: Main – 10 x 305mm/12in guns
  Secondary – 15 x 125mm/5in guns and
  2 x 535mm/21in torpedoes
Machinery: 14 boilers, 2 shafts,
  18,640kW/25,000shp
Speed: 21 knots
Complement: 933 men

The Delaware class, reckoned to be the first true Dreadnoughts in the USN, were 25 per cent larger than the previous class, capable of over 20 knots, and their ten centre-line 305mm/12in guns exceeded anything so far built. The secondary armament consisted of 125mm/5in guns, which became the standard size in the USN.

Absorbing more lessons from the Battle of Tsushima, large but fully enclosed conning towers were intended to reduce the exposure of bridge personnel. *Delaware* was fitted with triple-expansion reciprocating engines, while *North Dakota* was turbine-driven. The reciprocating engine proved more efficient and reliable and – the Americans claimed – *Delaware* was the first ship that could steam for 20 hours at full speed without a breakdown. *North Dakota*'s first turbines proved inefficient and better, geared turbines were installed in 1915 delivering 23,340kW/31,300shp.

Delaware served with the British Grand Fleet in the US Sixth Battle Squadron, and was scrapped in 1924. *North Dakota* was reduced to an auxiliary role after World War I and lasted until 1931.

Florida class

LEFT: *Florida*'s after turrets trained out to starboard and ready for action: the men do not appear to be wearing any kind of action clothing and the awning will have to be taken down to prevent blast from the guns from tearing it apart.

Compared to the Delaware class, these ships had an improved 125mm/5in gun with better armour and, once the US Congressional limit had been breached, showed the tendency for US Dreadnoughts to grow in size. Both ships landed seamen and marines during the Vera Cruz crisis in 1914. *Florida* joined the British Grand Fleet at Scapa Flow, and in December 1918 she escorted President Wilson to France and was at New York for the Victory Fleet Review. *Utah* was based in Ireland to cover Allied convoys as they approached Europe. Both ships were modernized in the 1920s when they received bulges, new oil-fired boilers and the funnels were trucked into one. The lattice mainmast was removed and an aircraft catapult fitted over the midships turret. Under the 1930 London Naval Treaty, *Florida* was scrapped and *Utah* was converted to a radio-controlled target ship in 1931. On December 7, 1941, *Utah* was hit by two aerial torpedoes and capsized in the attack on Pearl Harbor, where her wreck can still be seen.

Florida class

Class: *Florida, Utah.* Launched 1909–10
Dimensions: Length – 155.5m/510ft
  Beam – 27m/88ft 3in
  Draught – 8.6m/28ft 3in
Displacement: 22,175 tonnes/21,825 tons
Armament: Main – 10 x 305mm/12in guns
  Secondary – 16 x 125mm/5in guns and
  2 x 535mm/21in torpedoes
Machinery: 12 boilers, 4 shafts,
  20,880kW/28,000shp
Speed: 21 knots
Complement: 1,001 men
Beam increased to 32m/106ft by the addition of anti-torpedo bulges.

LEFT: The outline of USN Dreadnoughts did not change much until some of them were modernized in the 1920s. Here *Wyoming*, taken about 1937, can be compared with ships on the previous page. The most obvious feature is that a pole mast replaces the after cage mast and there is a single funnel.

Wyoming class

> ### Wyoming class
>
> **Class:** *Wyoming, Arkansas.* Launched 1911
> **Dimensions:** Length – 165.8m/544ft
>   Beam – 28.4m/93ft 2in
>   Draught – 8.7m/28ft 7in
> **Displacement:** 26,420 tonnes/26,000 tons
> **Armament:** Main – 12 x 305mm/12in guns
>   Secondary – 21 x 125mm/5in guns and
>   2 x 535mm/21in torpedoes
> **Machinery:** 12 boilers, 4 shafts,
>   20,880kW/28,000shp
> **Speed:** 21 knots
> **Complement:** 1,063 men

Twenty per cent larger again than their predecessors, the Wyomings had two more 305mm/12in guns, and the secondary armament was carried one deck higher. Both ships operated with the British Grand Fleet during World War I and afterwards in the Atlantic and Pacific. After modernization in 1925–7 they emerged with broader beams and thicker deck armour, and their silhouettes changed by single funnels, a pole mainmast and an aircraft catapult.

In 1931 *Wyoming* became a training ship, losing first her armour and six of the main turrets, and, in 1944 when the priority became anti-aircraft training, gaining extra 125mm/5in guns. She was scrapped in 1947.

Arkansas was also used for pre-World War II training, and she supported the occupation of Iceland and escorted convoys in the North Atlantic until refitted in 1942. Emerging with a tripod foremast, she was used for shore bombardment in

support of the Normandy landings and off Southern France in 1944. Between February and May 1945, she supported the landings on Iwo Jima and Okinawa. *Arkansas* was expended during atomic bomb tests at Bikini Island in 1946.

New York class

LEFT: A second modernization in the 1930s gave these and similar ships two tripod masts and a single funnel. The primary career of both ships was inshore bombardment.

supported the Iwo Jima and Okinawa landings in 1945. *New York* was exposed during atomic bomb tests at Bikini Island and in 1948 was sunk as a target off Pearl Harbor. *Texas* is preserved as a memorial at San Jacinto and is the only remaining World War I-era US battleship still in existence.

> ### New York class
>
> **Class:** *New York, Texas.* Launched 1912
> **Dimensions:** Length – 172.2m/565ft
>   Beam – 29.1m/95ft 6in
>   Draught – 8.7m/28ft 6in
> **Displacement:** 27,433 tonnes/27,000 tons
> **Armament:** Main – 10 x 355mm/14in guns
>   Secondary – 21 x 125mm/5in guns and
>   4 x 535mm/21in torpedoes
> **Machinery:** 14 boilers, 2 shafts,
>   20,954kW/28,100shp
> **Speed:** 21 knots
> **Complement:** 1,026 men

The two New Yorks with their 355mm/14in guns were last in the line of the original US Dreadnoughts. Both ships served with the British Grand Fleet in 1917–18. They were modernized in the 1920s, and became the first USN battleships to have tripod masts. However, oil-fired boilers, a single trunked funnel, additional deck armour

and anti-torpedo bulges increased beam and displacement, so that they could no longer make 20 knots. They served throughout World War II, covering convoys in the North Atlantic and supporting the landings in North Africa in November 1942. *Texas* also bombarded targets off Normandy and Southern France in 1944. In the Pacific they

LEFT: *Oklahoma* passing Alcatraz in the 1930s.
BELOW: **Sailors swabbing out the 355mm/14in guns.
The need for this function did not change with the
passing of time.** BOTTOM LEFT: *Nevada* operating a
kite balloon off Cuba in World War I. BOTTOM RIGHT:
Nevada at sea with other battleships in the 1920s.

Nevada class

The Nevadas were the first US battleships to carry a super-firing twin turret over a triple turret, thus contracting the heavy broadside into just four mountings. At the time they were also the most heavily armoured USN battleships, with the upper and lower belts merged into one with a maximum thickness of 340mm/13.5in. They were the first to use oil as their primary fuel and the last to have two shafts. *Nevada* had turbines and Yarrow boilers, while *Oklahoma* was the last USN battleship to have reciprocating steam engines (with Babcock and Wilcox boilers) which gave her a range of 12,875km/8,000 miles. They were originally completed with a large battery of anti-torpedo-boat 125mm/5in guns, but these were very exposed to the sea and were suppressed.

The Nevadas were based in Ireland in World War I, covering troop convoys to Europe. They were modernized in 1927–9, when gun elevation was increased, and two distinctive tripod masts were fitted as well as aircraft catapults. Anti-torpedo bulges increased the beam to 32.3m/106ft and additional anti-aircraft guns were added.

Both ships were sunk in the Japanese attack on Pearl Harbor on December 7, 1941. *Nevada* was the only battleship to get underway and became the main objective of the second wave of Japanese aircraft and was stranded. *Nevada* supported the landings at Attu in May 1943, Normandy and Southern France in 1944, and Iwo Jima and Okinawa in 1945, when she was hit by a suicide plane on March 27 and by shore artillery on April 5. Irradiated at Bikini in 1946, she was sunk off Hawaii.

In 1936 *Oklahoma* evacuated during the Spanish Civil War. At Pearl Harbor she was berthed outboard of the battleship *Maryland* and hit by a large number of aerial torpedoes. She rolled over and sank. Her salvage became a matter of pride but with a gaping hole in her side she was beyond repair. The hulk sank while under tow in 1947.

Nevada class	

Class: *Nevada, Oklahoma.* Launched 1914
Dimensions: Length – 175.3m/575ft
 Beam – 29m/95ft
 Draught – 8.7m/28ft 6in
Displacement: 27,940 tonnes/27,500 tons
Armament: Main – 10 x 355mm/14in guns
Secondary – 21 x 125mm/5in guns and
 2 x 535mm/21in torpedoes
Machinery: 12 boilers, 2 shafts,
 20,880kW/26,000shp (*Nevada*)
 19,700kW/24,800shp (*Oklahoma*)
Speed: 20 knots
Complement: 864 men

LEFT: *Pennsylvania* at sea in May 1934, after her first modernization. One of the most significant features was the replacement of the cage masts by tripods, carrying considerably more fire control equipment than these ships used to have.

Pennsylvania class

Class: *Pennsylvania, Arizona.* Launched 1915
Dimensions: Length – 185.3m/608ft
  Beam – 29.6m/97ft
  Draught – 8.8m/29ft
Displacement: 31,900 tonnes/31,400 tons
Armament: Main – 12 x 355mm/14in guns
  Secondary – 22 x 125mm/5in, 4 x 75mm/3in
  guns and 2 x 535mm/21in torpedoes
Machinery: 12 boilers, 4 shafts,
  23,490kW/31,500shp
Speed: 21 knots
Complement: 915 men

Pennsylvania class

The Pennsylvanias were enlarged Nevadas, with four triple turrets. Reconstructed in 1929–31, they received the usual range of improvements. In addition *Pennsylvania*, designated as a flagship, was given a two-tier armoured conning tower. Both were in battleship row when the Japanese attacked Pearl Harbor. *Arizona* blew up and her remains are now an American national memorial.

Pennsylvania was in dry dock and only slightly damaged. Fitted with a large battery of anti-aircraft guns in late 1942, she supported many amphibious operations and was at the Battle of Surigao Strait on October 25, 1944.

On August 12, 1945, *Pennsylvania* was the last major warship to be hit during World War II. A target ship at atomic bomb tests in 1946, *Pennsylvania* was scuttled in 1948.

New Mexico class

LEFT: An aerial view of *New Mexico* taken in 1919. Compare this photograph of *New Mexico,* more or less as newly completed with distinctive cage masts, and *Pennsylvania* after modernization. All these ships underwent further modernizations after Pearl Harbor in order to combat the threat from the air.

The New Mexico class had three triple turrets of an improved design. Some secondary armament was placed in the bow and stern, but had to be removed because they were too wet, and the remaining 125mm/5in guns were in the superstructure. A clipper bow made for better sea-keeping. Initially two ships were intended, but selling two pre-Dreadnoughts to Greece paid for a third. *New Mexico* had a new propulsion system, which had been trialled in the collier *Jupiter*. This used steam turbines to turn electrical generators, which in turn powered the ship's propellers driven by electric motors. All were rebuilt in 1931–4, receiving new superstructures, modern gun directors, new engines, deck armour and anti-torpedo bulges. All three were in the Atlantic in 1941 and so avoided the attack on Pearl Harbor, but were recalled and participated in many landing operations, and *Mississippi* took part in the Battle of Surigao Strait.

Mississippi was converted to a gunnery training and weapons development ship in 1946, and in the 1950s to a test ship for the USN's first surface-to-air guided missile, Terrier. She was sold for scrap in 1956. *New Mexico* was hit twice by kamikaze planes, but was present in Tokyo Bay when Japan surrendered on September 2, 1945. She was sold for scrap in October 1947. *Idaho* was also present in Tokyo Bay and she was scrapped in November 1947.

New Mexico class

Class: *New Mexico, Mississippi, Idaho.*
  Launched 1917
Dimensions: Length – 190m/624ft
  Beam – 29.7m/97ft 5in
  Draught – 9.1m/30ft
Displacement: 32,510 tonnes/32,000 tons
Armament: Main – 12 x 355mm/14in guns
  Secondary – 14 x 125mm/5in, 4 x 75mm/3in guns
  and 2 x 535mm/21in torpedoes
Machinery: 9 boilers, 4 shafts,
  23,862kW/32,000shp
Speed: 21 knots
Complement: 1,084 men

LEFT: *Kashima* was the last pre-Dreadnought built for the Imperial Japanese Navy, with 305mm/12in and 255mm/10in guns.

Kashima class

Class: *Kashima, Katori*. Launched 1905
Dimensions: Length – 144.3m/473ft 7in
  Beam – 23.8m/78ft 2in
  Draught – 8m/26ft 4in
Displacement: 16,663 tonnes/16,400 tons
Armament: Main – 4 x 305mm/12in and
  4 x 255mm/10in guns
  Secondary – 12 x 50mm/2in guns and
  5 x 455mm/18in torpedoes
Machinery: 20 boilers, 2 shafts,
  11,782kW/15,800shp
Speed: 18.5 knots
Complement: 946 men

Kashima class

These two ships were the last pre-Dreadnoughts built in Britain for the Imperial Japanese Navy, and with one exception represented the last major Japanese warships built anywhere abroad. They were the equivalent of the King Edward VII class. No doubt Japanese officers standing by their ships in Britain would have had plenty of time to study developments in battleship design. The Imperial Japanese Navy had already drawn up plans for an 18,290-tonne/18,000-ton cruiser with 255mm/10in guns, and the lessons of the Russo-Japanese War confirmed to the Japanese their subsequent choice of an all-big-gun ship. *Kashima* and *Katori* saw no action and were broken up in 1924.

Satsuma class

LEFT: *Satsuma*, seen here before her launch, and *Aki* were to be all-big-gun ships but the Japanese ran out of cash to buy all the guns they required.

two half-sisters, and *Aki* had three instead of two funnels. Both ships were disarmed under the terms of the Washington Naval Treaty. They were unsuitable for modernization, and expended as targets in 1924.

Satsuma class

Class: *Satsuma, Aki*. Launched 1906–7
Dimensions: Length – 146.9m/482ft
  Beam – 25.5m/83ft 6in
  Draught – 8.4m/27ft 6in
Displacement: 19,683 tonnes/19,372 tons
Armament: Main – 4 x 305mm/12in and
  12 x 255mm/10in guns
  Secondary – 12 x 120mm/4.7in guns and
  5 x 455mm/18in torpedoes
Machinery: 20 boilers, 2 shafts,
  12,901kW/17,300ihp
Speed: 18.25 knots
Complement: 887 men

The Satsuma class is further proof that the idea of an all-big-gun ship arose in several places at about the same time. These ships had been designed before the Battle of Tsushima and were to be armed with 12 305mm/12in guns. However, impoverished by the Russo-Japanese War, the Imperial Japanese Navy could not afford both the 305mm/12in guns it wanted to buy from Britain and the Curtis turbines from the USA. Hence these ships were completed with a mixed armament, all in turrets.

The Japanese learned quickly, and *Aki* benefited from the lessons learned in building *Satsuma*, and the 120mm/4.7in guns were replaced by 150mm/6in guns as the secondary armament. The Japanese did not have the same problems as the USN in making turbines work in their ships and they quickly abandoned the reciprocating steam engine, though a shortage of oil meant that the Japanese used coal-fired boilers for longer than most navies. There were minor differences in size between these

LEFT: *Tsukuba* and *Ikoma* were the first Japanese-built battlecruisers. They were slow and very lightly armoured, and their small size, less than half the tonnage of battlecruisers being built in Europe and America, meant that they served little tactical operational purpose and were very soon obsolete.

Tsukuba class

The Imperial Japanese Navy had a preference for speed and armament over armour, and this included both large battlecruisers and small ones like *Tsukuba* and *Ikoma*. Built as armoured cruisers (when the Royal Navy introduced the term) these were re-rated as battlecruisers and were ordered to replace earlier pre-Dreadnought battleships. Japanese industry, including shipbuilding, was advancing rapidly and

with these and successor ships they demonstrated their ability to build quickly. Nevertheless, despite their rapid construction, by the time these ships were completed in 1907–8 other navies were building yet bigger and faster battlecruisers. *Tsukuba* was a defect-prone ship and suffered an ammunition explosion in 1917. *Ikoma* was re-armed in 1919 as a training ship before being scrapped in 1924.

Tsukuba class

Class: *Tsukuba, Ikoma*. Launched 1905–6
Dimensions: Length – 137.2m/450ft
  Beam – 23m/75ft 5in
  Draught – 7.9m/26ft 1in
Displacement: 13,970 tonnes/13,750 tons
Armament: Main – 4 x 305mm/12in and
  12 x 150mm/6in guns
  Secondary – 12 x 120mm/4.7in guns and
  3 x 455mm/18in torpedoes
Machinery: 20 boilers, 2 shafts,
  15,287kW/20,500ihp
Speed: 20.5 knots
Complement: 879 men

Ibuki class

LEFT: *Ibuki* and *Kurama* were not much better than the Tsukuba class, and were scrapped in the 1920s, when these ships, and their immediate predecessors, had been taken over by the Dreadnought revolution. All of them were too small, apart from any other consideration, to be of further use in the inter-war years.

Ibuki class

Class: *Ibuki, Kurama*. Launched 1907
Dimensions: Length – 147.8m/485ft
  Beam – 23m/75ft 4in
  Draught – 7.9m/26ft 1in
Displacement: 14,870 tonnes/14,636 tons
Armament: Main – 4 x 305mm/12in and
  8 x 205mm/8in guns
  Secondary – 14 x 120mm/4.7in guns and
  3 x 455mm/18in torpedoes
Machinery: 20 boilers, 2 shafts,
  16,778kW/22,500ihp
Speed: 20.5 knots
Complement: 844 men

The Ibuki class was an improved Tsukuba class. *Ibuki* was delayed because the slips at Kure were occupied and she was re-engineered with turbines. Few Japanese ships saw any action in World War I, but *Ibuki* joined the hunt in

the Pacific for the German East Asiatic Squadron. She also escorted convoys of Australian and New Zealand troops across the Indian Ocean in 1914. Warships also operated in support of the Allies in the eastern Mediterranean.

LEFT: *Fuso* in dry dock at Kure. *Fuso* and *Yamashiro* when completed were powerful, elegant ships, but were rebuilt with thick control towers and single funnels in the 1930s. Unlike the Kashima, Satsuma, Tsukuba and Ibuki classes, which were all too small, the 30,480-tonne/30,600-ton *Fuso* and *Yamashiro* incorporated all the lessons of the Dreadnought revolution and were capable of a worthwhile and significant mid-life update which enabled them to see action in World War II.
BELOW: *Yamashiro* at sea in 1934.

Fuso class

The Fuso class was the first of super-Dreadnoughts with guns greater than 305mm/12in. Reckoned by some to be too lightly armoured for their size, the Japanese applied the lesson they had learned from mine and torpedo damage during the Russo-Japanese War and fitted their ships with much greater subdivision of compartments in order to control this damage.

After World War I both ships acquired additional searchlights and improved gun-direction platforms, and *Yamashiro* received a British-style flying-off ramp on B turret. Both ships were extensively modernized in the 1930s. They were lengthened by some 7.6m/25ft, and their beam increased by over 3.7m/12ft with anti-torpedo bulges. New turbines and space-saving boilers nearly doubled their horsepower from 29,828kW/40,000shp to 55,928kW/75,000shp and increased speed by nearly 2 knots, despite the weight of additional deck armour. The change from coal- to oil-fired boilers also increased the ships' range.

Both ships were equipped with aircraft and a catapult, which was mounted on the quarterdeck in *Yamashiro* and initially over Q turret in *Fuso* until removed to the quarterdeck. The secondary and anti-aircraft armament was improved and the elevation of the main guns increased to 43 degrees, giving the 355mm/14in guns a range of 22km/13.5 miles. In the conversion, the fore funnel was done away with entirely, and the elegant tripod mast of the original design was replaced by towering pagodas containing conning positions, light guns, searchlights, rangefinders and gun direction platforms.

Fuso and *Yamashiro* operated together during World War II, either as the covering force to long-range convoys or awaiting the decisive battle which the Japanese thought the Americans might attempt, as the Russians had 40 years before. They were also sunk together.

At the Battle of Surigao Strait on October 25, 1944, *Fuso* and *Yamashiro* encountered a USN fleet which included the six battleships *Mississippi, Maryland, West Virginia, Tennessee, California* and *Pennsylvania*. *Fuso* was sunk by gunfire and *Yamashiro* succumbed to a massed torpedo attack by USN destroyers – although experts are still arguing as to which ship was sunk first and, in the darkness, how.

Fuso class

Class: *Fuso, Yamashiro*. Launched 1914–15
Dimensions: Length – 203m/665ft
　Beam – 28.6m/94ft
　Draught – 8.7m/28ft 6in
Displacement: 30,480 tonnes/30,600 tons
Armament: Main – 12 x 355mm/14in guns
　Secondary – 16 x 150mm/6in,
　4 x 80mm/3.1in guns and 6 x 535mm/21in
　torpedoes
Machinery: 24 boilers, 4 shafts,
　29,828kW/40,000shp
Speed: 22.5 knots
Complement: 1,193 men

Kongo class

The battlecruiser *Kongo* was the very last Japanese capital ship to be built outside Japan. While *Kongo* was designed and built by Vickers, large components were delivered from Britain to Japan for *Kongo*'s three sister ships. *Kongo* was intended as a model ship for Japanese shipyards to emulate, but her evident success, and superiority over the British Lion class which was building at the same time, inspired the changes which led to the Tiger class.

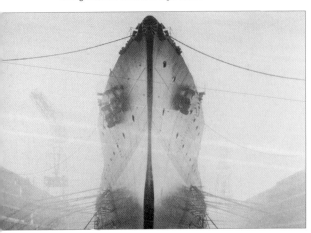

After World War I all four ships were refitted and received pagoda-like control towers, and funnel cowls, and were re-designated as battleships. They were modernized in 1936–7 when the hull was lengthened, and with new machinery they could reach over 30 knots. High speed and heavy guns made the Kongo class useful ships which saw much action in World War II. The Japanese concept was that the Kongos should act as escorts to carrier battle groups. Modifications during World War II to *Kongo* and *Haruna* included the fitting of radar. All ships of the class were sunk in the war.

In December 1941, *Kongo* supported the Japanese invasion of the Malayan Peninsula. She then supported landings in Java, and was part of the force which raided the Indian Ocean. At the Battle of Midway in June 1942, *Kongo* was part of the covering force, and during the Guadalcanal campaign she bombarded Henderson airfield, took part in the Battle of the Santa Cruz Islands and the naval Battle of Guadalcanal. Then in June 1944 she performed her intended function as part of the Japanese carrier escort force at the Battle of the Philippine

TOP: **The battleship *Kongo* from a postcard in the 1920s. Japanese sailors were proud of their ships and wanted postcards to send home. *Kongo* was the last major unit built abroad for the Imperial Japanese Navy, primarily for Japanese constructors to gain experience of the latest British methods. The three other ships of the same class were Japanese-built.** LEFT: **A rare picture of *Kongo* in dry dock at Yokosuka during her reconstruction during the 1930s.**

LEFT: **Four Japanese battleships photographed pre-war:** *Nagato*, *Kirishima*, *Ise* and *Hyuga*. The Japanese fleet was powerful but, as the profiles of these ships show, photographed in the 1930s, it relied on a core of World War I ships which had been modernized and some inter-war ships which had not been built in large batches nor followed the same generational and incremental steps from which American and British battleships had benefited. BELOW: *Haruna* was sunk at Edashima in April 1945 by USN carrier aircraft.

Sea. At the Battle of Leyte Gulf, *Kongo* showed her immense strength, surviving a torpedoing, naval air attacks, and a bombing from high level. However, on November 21, 1944, she was torpedoed by the USN submarine *Sealion*, causing a fire which raged out of control until she blew up and sank. *Kongo* was the only battleship to be sunk by a submarine attack during the war in the Pacific.

Like her sisters, *Kirishima* was modernized in 1927–30, rebuilt in 1935–6, and reclassified as a battleship. She was part of the escort force during the Japanese attack on Pearl Harbor and in spring 1942 part of the fleet that raided the Indian Ocean. Active throughout that year, she received minor damage during a skirmish on November 13. Off Savo Island two nights later she was disabled by the USN battleship *Washington*, during the last ever purely battleship-to-battleship engagement, and was scuttled by her crew.

Haruna was damaged by a mine laid by the German auxiliary cruiser *Wolf* in 1917. In December 1941 she covered the landings in Malaya and in early 1942 she supported the Japanese conquest of the Dutch East Indies. *Haruna* was present at most significant battles throughout 1942: in June she was damaged at the Battle of Midway and in October (with *Kongo*) she devastated Henderson airfield. With the bulk of the Japanese fleet, *Haruna* was held back in Japan for a decisive battle against the US Navy during 1943–4. She was hit by a bomb in June 1944 at the Battle of the Philippine Sea, and also survived the Battle of Leyte Gulf. Damaged by near-misses in October 1944, *Haruna* was finally sunk at Kure by carrier aircraft on July 28, 1945.

Hiei was the only one of her class to be demilitarized under the terms of the Washington Naval Treaty. However, in the 1930s she received the same modernization as her sisters and returned to the Japanese order of battle. She was present at the attack on Pearl Harbor, the invasion of the Dutch East Indies, and the Japanese sortie into the Indian Ocean. During

the campaign off Guadalcanal she showed great resilience, like *Kirishima*, surviving more than 100 hits from the USN cruisers *Portland* and *San Francisco*, and torpedoes from the destroyers *Cushing* and *O'Bannon*. She was finally hit and sunk by high-level bombing on November 13, 1942.

Kongo class

Class: *Kongo, Hiei, Haruna, Kirishima*.
  Launched 1912–13
Dimensions: Length – 215m/704ft
  Beam– 28m/92ft
  Draught – 8.5m/27ft 7in
Displacement: 27,940 tonnes/27,500 tons
Armament: Main – 8 x 355mm/14in guns
  Secondary – 16 x 150mm/6in,
  8 x 80mm/3.1in guns and
  8 x 535mm/21in torpedoes
Machinery: 36 boilers, 4 shafts,
  47,725kW/64,000shp
Speed: 27.5 knots
Complement: 1,221 men

Ise class

These were improved versions of the Fuso class, being slightly longer and larger. The midships P turret was moved and raised into a super-firing position over Q turret, thus making better use of the between decks and enabling an improved machinery room space.

They were modernized in two stages. In 1926–8 the two tripod masts were replaced by a pole mainmast and a pagoda foremast, the fore funnel received a cowl, and a catapult was mounted on X turret (this was removed to the quarterdeck in 1933). Total conversion followed in the 1930s, when they were lengthened, the armour increased, bulges fitted, boilers upgraded, fore funnel suppressed, main gun elevation improved and they received additional light guns.

After the Battle of Midway, both ships were modified into semi-aircraft carriers. The after turrets were suppressed and a short flight deck installed, with two

TOP: *Ise* was launched in 1916 and with her sisters modernized in the 1920s. ABOVE: *Hyuga* sitting on the bottom at Kure after an air attack in 1945. RIGHT: A close-up of B turret. The forward turret is submerged.

powerful catapults, however neither ship seems to have carried aircraft and the concept was never proved.

Hyuga was at the Battle of Midway, and converted to a semi-carrier in 1942–3. However, she saw action as a battleship during the battle for Leyte Gulf. She received some damage and was sent to Kure for repairs, where she was bombed again in March and July 1945. She settled on the bottom on July 24, where she was broken up in 1946.

Ise followed an almost identical career, and was sunk on July 27, 1945.

Ise class

Class: *Ise, Hyuga.* Launched 1916–17
Dimensions: Length – 206m/675ft
  Beam – 28.6m/94ft
  Draught – 8.9m/29ft 1in
Displacement: 31,762 tonnes/31,260 tons
Armament: Main – 12 x 355mm/14in guns
  Secondary – 20 x 140mm/5.5in,
  4 x 80mm/3.1in guns and
  6 x 535mm/21in torpedoes
Machinery: 24 boilers, 4 shafts,
  33,557kW/45,000shp
Speed: 22.5 knots
Complement: 1,360 men

Nassau class

A battleship considerably more powerful than the archetypal pre-Dreadnought was being contemplated by the German navy when the news of Fisher's *Dreadnought* spread abroad. The consequence was a three-year delay while the Germans worked out exactly what Fisher had achieved. The resulting design was the first German Dreadnought, with 12 large-calibre guns in a hexagonal layout of twin turrets. This was not ideal as only a maximum of four turrets could be brought to bear on any one target, but the Germans rationalized that the two turrets on the disengaged side formed a reserve. These ships were easily identified by the two prominent gooseneck cranes carried amidships. The Nassau class rolled dangerously even on a smooth sea and bilge keels had to be fitted.

The class operated as a unit and in April 1916 were part of the covering force during the German bombardment of Scarborough and Yarmouth. At the Battle of Jutland, *Nassau* was hit twice and soon repaired, *Westfalen* and *Rheinland* were both hit once and slightly damaged, and *Posen* was undamaged.

In August and again in October 1916 attempted sorties into the North Sea were frustrated, but in April 1918 *Nassau* progressed as far as the latitude of Stavanger, Norway, before turning back without achieving very much. *Westfalen* was torpedoed by the British submarine *E-23* in August 1916 but repaired.

In 1918 *Westfalen* was sent into the Baltic to assist the Finns in their uprising against the Russians and the ensuing civil war. *Rheinland* accompanied *Westfalen* to the Baltic, but ran aground in April 1918 off the Åland islands. She was salvaged (involving the removal of 6,503 tonnes/6,400 tons of coal, armour, ammunition and guns) three months later and was towed to Kiel where she became a barracks ship.

Posen first entered the Baltic and then accompanied *Nassau* north to Norway. All ships of the class were deleted from the German navy in November 1919. *Nassau* was allocated to Japan, and *Westfalen* and *Posen* were allocated to Britain. All ships of the class were scrapped in 1920–4 under the terms of the Armistice, leaving Germany with only some very obsolete battleships.

Nassau class

Class: *Nassau, Westfalen, Rheinland, Posen.* Launched 1908
Dimensions: Length – 137.7m/451ft 9in
Beam – 26.9m/88ft 5in
Draught – 8.1m/26ft 6in
Displacement: 18,870 tonnes/18,570 tons
Armament: Main – 12 x 280mm/11in guns
Secondary – 12 x 150mm/6in,
16 x 88mm/3.46in guns and
6 x 455mm/18in torpedoes
Machinery: 12 boilers, 3 shafts,
16,405kW/22,000ihp
Speed: 19.5 knots
Complement: 1,008 men

BELOW: **A starboard bow view of the *Westfalen*.**
BOTTOM: **The four ships of the Nassau class, *Nassau*, *Westfalen*, *Rheinland* and *Posen*, alongside, possibly in pre-war Hamburg.**

ABOVE LEFT: **The German battle fleet at sea.** *Oldenburg* **is nearest to the camera.** ABOVE: **Post-war** *Ostfriesland* **was sunk during aerial bombing trials by the USAAF.** LEFT: **The bombing trials were somewhat artificial as the targets were both stationary and not firing back at the bombers. Nevertheless, although it took several attempts by the bombers to get photographic evidence like this, the pictures had a powerful influence on decision-makers in the USA.**

Helgoland class

While retaining the inefficient hexagon layout of the main armament, the Helgolands were a considerable improvement over their predecessors. Compared with the Dreadnoughts building in Britain, they were like most German ships of this period, lighter and beamier. They also had better internal subdivision and greater pumping power, and the German ammunition was safer when hit because it was inclined to burn rather than explode. The Germans retained reciprocating steam engines for longer than the Royal Navy, but this class introduced the 305mm/12in gun to the German navy.

The class acted as a unit, and was part of the covering force for the bombardment of Scarborough and Yarmouth in April 1916, and fought at Jutland in May. *Helgoland* and *Oldenburg* received one hit each and were quickly repaired. *Ostfriesland* hit a mine but was repaired by the end of July. All the

Helgoland-class ships were largely inactive for most of the remainder of the war. After Germany's defeat in World War I, *Helgoland, Ostfriesland, Thüringen* and *Oldenburg* were handed over to Britain, USA, France and Japan respectively.

Interned at Scapa Flow, *Ostfriesland* was not scuttled with the rest of the German High Seas Fleet because she had been moved to Rosyth, prior to being taken over by the USN. She was steamed to New York where she was decommissioned and dry-docked so that USN naval architects could examine her design. She was then expended as a target in July 1921 while at anchor. *Ostfriesland* survived many bomb hits and near-misses. She would probably have avoided any damage if she had been underway and, even if hit, been saved if damage control measures had been taken. Carefully edited film of her eventual sinking was used to help

promote the use of air power. In 1920 *Thüringen* survived an attempted scuttling off Cherbourg by her German crew. In 1920s she was used as a target, then was sold for scrap. A large portion of the hull still remains off the beach at Gavres and continued to be used for target practice until the 1990s.

Helgoland class

Class: *Helgoland, Ostfriesland, Thüringen, Oldenburg.* Launched 1909–10
Dimensions: Length – 167.2m/548ft 7in
  Beam – 28.5m/93ft 6in
  Draught – 8.2m/26ft 11in
Displacement: 22,800 tonnes/22,440 tons
Armament: Main – 12 x 305mm/12in guns
  Secondary – 14 x 150mm/6in,
  14 x 88mm/3.46in guns and
  6 x 510mm/20in torpedoes
Machinery: 15 boilers, 3 shafts,
  20,880kW/28,000ihp
Speed: 20 knots
Complement: 1,113 men

LEFT: *Prinzregent Luitpold* immediately pre-war showing off the range and elevation of her 305mm/12in guns.

Kaiser class

Class: *Kaiser, Friedrich der Grosse, Kaiserin, König Albert, Prinzregent Luitpold.* Launched 1911–12.
Dimensions: Length – 172m/564ft
Beam – 29m/95ft 3in
Draught – 8.3m/27ft 3in
Displacement: 25,095 tonnes/24,700 tons
Armament: Main – 10 x 305mm/12in guns
Secondary – 14 x 150mm/6in guns and 5 x 510mm/20in torpedoes
Machinery: 18 boilers, 3 shafts, 18,640kW/25,000hp
Speed: 21 knots
Complement: 1,088 men

Kaiser class

The Kaisers were the first German battleships to be fitted with turbines and with an oil-burning capability. Like other German ships they had three (rather than the British arrangement of four) propellers. It was intended to provide *Prinzregent Luitpold* with a diesel to drive her central shaft but this was not fitted and the space was left empty. The use of turbines made it easier to mount the midships guns *en echelon*, and with one after turret mounted in a super-firing position the Kaisers – despite having one less turret compared with their predecessors – could still bring one more turret (all five) to bear on either beam.

Kaiser took part in most of the German naval operations of World War I that took place in the North Sea: the bombardments of the English towns on the east cost, the First and Second Battles of Heligoland Bight and the Battle of Jutland, where she was hit twice. In 1917 she also operated in the Baltic. All four sister ships followed similar careers. In addition, *Friedrich der Grosse* was flagship of the German High Seas fleet until March 1917.

König class

LEFT: The *linienschiff König* from a pre-war postcard. The class was new at the time of Jutland, where they saw much fighting, and they also fought in the Baltic.

These ships followed the pattern of operations for the High Sea Fleet and were in the thick of the fighting at Jutland, firing between them some 700 rounds of 305mm/12in munitions. They received hits as follows: *König*, ten; *Grosser Kurfürst*, eight; *Markgraf*, five. *Kronprinz* escaped undamaged. *König* went on to destroy the Russian battleship *Slava* on October 17, 1917, in the Baltic. Commander Noel Laurence in the British submarine *J-1* has the distinction of

being the only submariner to hit two battleships in one go, when he fired a salvo of torpedoes at *Kronprinz* and *Grosser Kurfürst* on November 5, 1916, but in neither case was the damage fatal. *Kronprinz* was renamed *Kronprinz Wilhelm* in 1918.

Grosser Kurfürst holds something of a record for accidents: she collided with *König* in December 1914, ran aground in 1917, collided with *Kronprinz* also in 1917, hit a mine in the same year,

damaged herself entering Wilhelmshaven in 1918, and ran aground off Heligoland on May 30, 1918.

All ships of both the Kaiser and König classes were interned at Scapa Flow and scuttled on June 21, 1921. They were then broken up from the 1930s onwards.

König class

Class: *König, Grosser Kurfürst, Markgraf, Kronprinz (Wilhelm).* Launched 1913
Dimensions: Length – 177m/580ft
Beam – 29m/96ft
Draught – 8.4m/27ft 6in
Displacement: 25,910 tonnes/25,000 tons
Armament: Main – 10 x 305mm/12in guns
Secondary – 14 x 150mm/6in guns and 5 x 510mm/20in torpedoes
Machinery: 18 boilers, 3 shafts, 25,350kW/34,000hp
Speed: 21.5 knots
Complement: 1,100 men

Bayern class

LEFT: *Baden* seen here pre-war as fleet flagship. Neither ship was available in time for *Der Tag* (the Battle of Jutland) and they were the last Dreadnought battleships to be completed for the German Kaiser's navy. Others were planned and even laid down, but all were cancelled. ABOVE: *Bayern* had a relatively short life. She was laid down in 1914, launched in 1915 and scuttled in 1919. BELOW LEFT: *Bayern*, showing the German three-shaft arrangement, being towed to the breakers in 1935. BELOW: *Bayern* was mined in the Gulf of Riga in 1917.

This class introduced the 380mm/15in gun to the German navy as well as double-ended super-firing turrets, which meant that with just four twin turrets, all guns could fire over wide arcs on the beam. The German navy considered fitting triple turrets, but after studying the Austro-Hungarian battleships of the Viribus Unitis class, they decided against it on the grounds of weight, ammunition supply, rate of fire, torque and loss of fighting capability should one turret be hit. Instead the Germans opted for the larger-calibre gun. The two outer shafts were turbine-driven, and the centre line shaft was diesel-driven.

Bayern and *Baden* missed the Battle of Jutland but *Bayern* supported German landings in the Gulf of Riga in October 1917 against Russian-held positions. Ten German battleships were opposed by two Russian pre-Dreadnoughts, cruisers and three small British C-class submarines. Off Moon (Muhu) in the northern entrance to the gulf *Bayern* and *Grosser Kurfürst* hit mines on October 12, and *Bayern* suffered serious flooding through her forward underwater torpedo flat.

However, on October 17, the battleships *König* and *Kronprinz* damaged the Russian pre-Dreadnought *Slava* so badly that she had to be scuttled, and hit *Grazdanin* (formerly *Tsessarevitch*) which retired to the east and north. The badly flooded *Bayern* did not reach Kiel until October 31. She was scuttled at Scapa Flow and broken up in 1934–5. *Baden* took over from *Friedrich der Grosse* as flagship of the German High Fleet. She saw no action and was scuttled at Scapa Flow but beached by the British before she could sink, and eventually expended as a target during battleship practice in 1921.

Two slightly larger ships, *Sachsen* and *Württemberg*, were laid down in 1913 and 1914 but not completed and broken up on the slips in 1921.

Another class of fast battleship, this time with 420mm/16.5in guns, was designed but work on these ships was never started.

Bayern class

Class: *Bayern, Baden.*
  Launched 1913-15
Dimensions: Length – 179.8m/589ft 10in
  Beam – 30m/98ft 5in
  Draught – 8.4m/27ft 8in
Displacement: 28,525 tonnes/28,074 tons
Armament: Main – 8 x 380mm/15in guns
  Secondary – 16 x 150mm/6in,
  8 x 88mm/3.46in guns and
  5 x 600mm/23.6in torpedoes
Machinery: 14 boilers, 3 shafts.
  35,794kW/48,000shp
Speed: 21 knots
Complement: 1,187 men

Von der Tann

Starting in 1908 the Hamburg shipyard of Blohm and Voss built a series of successful battlecruisers, the first ship in response to the British Invincible class being *Von der Tann*.

This first German battlecruiser was bigger all-round than the *Invincible*, and more heavily armoured. Anti-roll tanks were originally fitted but these proved ineffective and bilge keels were installed instead and the additional space was used for extra fuel. *Von der Tann* was also the first German capital ship to have turbines. Although the speed was about the same, her endurance was greater. The secondary armament (150mm/6in) was heavier than the *Invincible*'s (100mm/4in), and the German 280mm/11in main gun was almost as good as the British 305mm/12in, while the British ammunition was inferior. Although the midships turrets were placed *en echelon*, they were far enough inboard to have a good arc of fire on the opposite beam, and in most situations the broadside consisted of eight guns as compared to *Invincible*'s six. German ships generally had more thorough damage control arrangements, and so *Von der Tann* was a much better design and a superior warship to the Invincibles.

Von der Tann was present at most of the major naval engagements of World War I, starting with the Battle of Heligoland Bight in August 1914. She bombarded the English towns of Yarmouth on November 3, 1914, Scarborough on December 16, 1914, and Lowestoft on April 24, 1915.

At Jutland *Von der Tann* engaged *Indefatigable,* where one salvo caused an explosion in X magazine and another hit *Indefatigable*'s forecastle, whereupon she blew up, after only a quarter of an hour of the first phase of the battle. By comparison *Von der Tann* was also hit but withstood the damage. Two 380mm/15in and two 340mm/13.5in rounds put two turrets out of action and damaged two others, and she was without her main armament for one hour and fifteen minutes, but she was fully repaired by August 1916.

Her other sorties were less successful and late in 1916 and again in 1917 she required repairs to her turbines. She was scuttled with the rest of the German High Seas Fleet, but raised in 1903 and broken up at Rosyth in 1931–4.

BELOW: *Von der Tann* photographed in 1910 before she was handed over to the German navy. She was reckoned to be a considerably better fighting ship than any British battlecruiser, primarily because she could withstand more damage. RIGHT: *Von der Tann* under tow to the breakers. Some of the work was contracted abroad and these tugs, in the mid 1930s, are flying the Nazi swastika.

Von der Tann

Class: *Von der Tann*. Launched 1909
Dimensions: Length – 171.7m/563ft 4in
  Beam – 26.6m/87ft 3in
  Draught – 8.1m/26ft 6in
Displacement: 19,370 tonnes/19,064 tons
Armament: Main – 8 x 280mm/11in guns
  Secondary – 10 x 150mm/6in,
  16 x 88mm/3.46in guns and
  4 x 455mm/18in torpedoes
Machinery: 18 boilers, 4 shafts.
  32,513kw/43,600shp
Speed: 24.75 knots
Complement: 923 men

Moltke and *Goeben*

Moltke and *Goeben* were further improvements over *Von der Tann*, being slightly larger, with a streamlined hull form and, as with *Von der Tann*, bilge keels replaced the anti-rolling tanks. The main improvement and external difference was an additional super-firing after turret, bringing the broadside up to a possible ten 280mm/11in guns.

Moltke was present at most surface actions in World War I, took part in the bombardment of the English east coast and was torpedoed twice. She was hit forward by a torpedo fired by Lieutenant Commander Noel Lawrence of *E-1* (who would later torpedo *Kronprinz* and *Grosser Kurfürst* while in command of the submarine *J-1*) on August 19, 1915, in the Gulf of Riga but the damage was slight. On April 25, 1918, during a sortie by the German High Seas Fleet, *Moltke* lost a propeller, damaged the water inlet of one of her condensers and an engine room was flooded. She was under tow by *Oldenburg* when she was torpedoed by *E-42*; nevertheless she reached Germany and was repaired. Scuttled at Scapa Flow, *Moltke* was raised in 1927 and broken up in 1927–9.

Goeben was flagship of the German Mediterranean division and was visiting Trieste when World War I broke out. Under the command of Admiral Souchon she made a feint against French troop convoys assembling in North Africa and then made a dash for the Bosphorus, chased unsuccessfully by the British *Indomitable* and *Indefatigable*. Once she arrived at Constantinople she was sold to Turkey, to replace capital ships which the British had confiscated, and played a major role in turning the balance of power in the region. The renamed *Yavuz* saw active service in the Black Sea, including some of the few engagements between pre-Dreadnoughts and Dreadnoughts, and she sank the British monitors *Raglan* and *M-28* on January 20, 1918, but ran into a minefield. She survived until 1974.

TOP: **The battlecruiser *Moltke*, photographed pre-war.** ABOVE: ***Moltke* being towed under the Forth Bridge on her way to the breakers at Rosyth.**

Moltke class

Class: *Moltke, Goeben*. Launched 1910
Dimensions: Length – 186.5m/611ft 11in
  Beam – 29.5m/96ft 10in
  Draught – 9m/29ft 5in
Displacement: 22,979 tonnes/22,616 tons
Armament: Main – 10 x 280mm/11in guns
  Secondary – 12 x 150mm/6in,
  12 x 88mm/3.46in guns and
  4 x 510mm/20in torpedoes
Machinery: 24 boilers, 4 shafts,
  38,776kW/52,000shp
Speed: 25.5 knots
Complement: 1,053 men

LEFT: **The damaged Seydlitz, down by the bows, after the Battle of Jutland. Despite the damage she was able to return to Germany for repair, before eventually being scuttled at Scapa Flow and raised for scrap in 1928.**

Seydlitz

Class: *Seydlitz*. Launched 1912
Dimensions: Length – 200.5m/657ft 11in
Beam – 28.5m/93ft 6in
Draught – 8.2m/26ft 11in
Displacement: 24,989 tonnes/24,594 tons
Armament: Main – 10 x 280mm/11in guns
Secondary – 12 x 150mm/6in,
12 x 88mm/3.46in guns and
4 x 510mm/20in torpedoes
Machinery: 27 boilers, 4 shafts,
46,979kW/63,000shp
Speed: 26.5 knots
Complement: 1,068 men

Seydlitz

Blohm and Voss continued their incremental changes to their battlecruisers. *Seydlitz* was larger again than the Moltke class and had a raised forecastle and the forward turret was one deck higher. Anti-rolling tanks still featured, but were not used. Like her predecessors *Seydlitz* had tandem rudders, but the forward rudder was ineffective and all these ships had excessively large turning circles. The British obtained the plans for *Seydlitz*

although they were not influenced by them. At the Battle of Dogger Bank *Seydlitz* received two or three 340mm/13.5in hits from *Lion* that caused a rapid fire that burned out both after turrets. During the raid on Lowestoft she struck a mine and shipped nearly 1,524 tonnes/1,500 tons of sea water.

At Jutland, *Seydlitz* fired on *Queen Mary* and helped to sink her. She also received a score of large-calibre hits herself and was torpedoed twice by the

destroyer *Petard* (or maybe *Turbulent*). Both after turrets were again burned out, and she shipped 5,385 tonnes/5,300 tons of water, increasing her draught to 14m/46ft. However, like other German designs which had good subdivision, *Seydlitz* proved capable of sustaining much damage. She reached Germany and was repaired at Wilhelmshaven. She was interned, scuttled at Scapa Flow and then raised for scrap in November 1928.

Derfflinger class

LEFT: *Lützow*, **one of the three Derfflinger class, was sunk at the Battle of Jutland in 1916. This proved to be the exception and other ships, such as *Seydlitz* above, proved to be very resistant to British firepower in battle.**

Flush-decked and with a pronounced sheer which became characteristic of later German warships, the Derfflingers had two super-firing turrets at each end. At the Battle of Dogger Bank *Derfflinger* was hit by three 340mm/13.5in shells, causing superficial damage. At Jutland she fired on *Queen Mary* and *Invincible*, which both blew up, but *Derfflinger* was hit by a score of heavy rounds, including ten 340mm/13.5in shells from *Revenge*. Both after turrets were put out of action,

fires started and she was flooded, but she was repaired by October 1916. She was interned, scuttled and raised at Scapa Flow in 1934 and her remains were finally scrapped in 1948.

At Jutland *Lützow* is credited with sinking *Invincible*, and probably the cruiser *Defence*, but took at least 24 heavy shells and was badly damaged. Her crew was rescued by a German torpedo boat who then torpedoed *Lützow*, which sank in two minutes.

Hindenburg was completed too late for Jutland, saw little action and was scuttled at Scapa Flow. She was broken up in 1931–2.

Derfflinger class

Class: *Derfflinger, Lützow, Hindenburg*.
Launched 1913–15
Dimensions: Length – 210.4m/690ft 3in
Beam – 29m/95ft 2in
Draught – 8.3m/27ft 3in
Displacement: 26,600 tonnes/26,180 tons
Armament: Main – 8 x 305mm/12in guns
Secondary – 12 x 150mm/6in,
4 x 88mm/3.46in guns and
4 torpedoes of various sizes
Machinery: 18 boilers, 4 shafts,
46,979kW/63,000shp
Speed: 26.5 knots
Complement: 1,112 men
Hindenburg's displacement was 26,938 tonnes/
26,513 tons. *Hindenburg* was 2.44m/8ft longer.
The secondary armament and size of torpedoes
varied across the class.

Courbet class

The French navy was late in entering the Dreadnought race, and then built these four low-profile racy-looking ships, though following French procurement methods each was built at a different yard. Armed with twelve 305mm/12in guns, the forward and after guns were in super-firing turrets but the two wing turrets could only fire on their respective beams. Unlike the Dreadnought prototype, they also carried a substantial battery of medium-calibre guns. The thickness of the armour was generally less in these ships than in equivalent American and British battleships, but a minimum of 180mm/7in armour was carried well below the waterline. Originally they also carried a small outfit of mines: however, though some battleships were used as minelayers, it was not a happy combination of functions. The medium-calibre armament was suppressed in the 1920s and 1930s when these ships were also fitted with new boilers and the funnel arrangements were altered. In 1918 *Courbet* carried an observation balloon, and in 1920 *Paris* experimented with an aircraft ramp over B turret.

Jean Bart was completed in time to carry the French President on a pre-war state visit to St Petersburg in July 1914. In accordance with joint British and French naval plans, all four ships were employed in the Mediterranean during World War I, and on August 16, 1914, were involved in a battle off the Albanian coast in which the Austro-Hungarian cruiser *Zenta*

BELOW: **In 1940 some of the French fleet escaped to England. This close-up of** *Courbet* **shows British sailors cheering for the camera. After** *Courbet* **reverted to the Free French navy, she was grounded as an anti-aircraft battery off Ouistreham during the Normandy landings.**

LEFT: Although they were a long time building and obsolescent when complete, the Courbet class (except for *France* which was wrecked in 1922) lasted until World War II. BELOW: The funnel arrangements and tall thin pole of military masts were reminiscent of some Italian designs of battleships. The layout lacks control equipment and rangefinders high over the ship, which nearly every other navy found essential for operations. These ships were not risked in the North Sea against the German High Sea Fleet.

was sunk. *Jean Bart* was heavily damaged by the Austro-Hungarian submarine *U-12* in the Strait of Otranto in December 1914 and repaired at Malta. These modern ships were not risked during the Dardanelles campaign, but in 1919 *Jean Bart* took part in operations in the Black Sea against the Bolsheviks. *France* ran aground in Quiberon Bay in 1922 and was wrecked. *Jean Bart* (renamed *Ocean* in 1937) was scuttled in Toulon, used by the Germans as a target, and sunk by the Allies in 1944. *Paris* and *Courbet* saw action against the advancing German army in 1940, and were interned in Britain after the fall of France. *Paris* was offered to the Free Polish navy as a depot ship and finally scrapped in Brest in 1956. *Courbet* was a hulk, powered by an old railway locomotive lashed to her deck, when she was scuttled as a block ship off Ouistreham on the eastern edge of the Normandy landings where she was repeatedly attacked by German manned-torpedoes.

The French navy's operations in World War I were to convoy troops from North Africa to metropolitan France, then to counter the Italian and Austro-Hungarian fleets in the Mediterranean.

Courbet class

Class: *Courbet, Jean Bart, France, Paris.*
Launched 1911–12
Dimensions: Length – 158.5m/520ft
Beam – 27.89m/91ft 6in
Draught – 8.99m/29ft 6in
Displacement: 22,545 tonnes/22,189 tons
Armament: Main – 12 x 305mm/12in guns
Secondary – 22 x 135mm/5.4in guns and
4 x 455mm/18in torpedoes
Machinery: 24 boilers, 4 shafts, power
20,880kW/28,000shp
Speed: 20 knots
Complement: 1,085 men

When Italy joined the allies the French were released to support the allied landings at Gallipoli, while the Italians guarded the Austro-Hungarians. The Royal Navy was responsible for closing the Channel and North Sea to the Germans.

Bretagne class

These ships were developments of the Courbet class, but as French resources were increasingly directed towards her army, their completion was delayed and they saw little action during World War I.

The heavy guns were 340mm/13.5in, but instead of wing turrets they carried a centre-line midships turret which could fire on either beam. Unlike the Courbet class they were regularly modernized in the 1920s and 30s, during which they were converted to oil-burning, and the torpedo tubes and minelaying capability were suppressed. The after funnel was also raised. After trials in these ships with balloons and ramps in the 1930s, *Lorraine*'s funnel was also moved aft and the midships turret removed so she could carry up to four aircraft.

All three ships operated with the British Mediterranean Fleet in early 1940. However, after the fall of France, the British demanded that the French navy should agree to measures of internment or disarmament to stop them falling into German hands, and when the French admiral at Mers-el-Kebir could not agree, *Provence, Bretagne* and other warships

were shelled on July 3, 1940, by the British battleships *Hood, Barham* and *Resolution*. *Bretagne* blew up with large loss of life. *Provence* was sunk and then salvaged by the French, and taken to Toulon where she was scuttled in 1942 by patriotic Frenchmen. She was then raised by the Germans so that her guns could be installed in coastal batteries, and finally broken up in 1949.

In July 1940 *Lorraine* was in the British naval base of Alexandria, where she agreed to internment, and subsequently joined the Free French navy at Dakar in 1943. She took part in the Allied landings in southern France in 1944, bombarding French soil, and in 1945 in the reduction of a remaining German stronghold, near the mouth of the Gironde. She was scrapped in 1954.

The *Vasilefs Konstantinos* (also *Re Constantino*) was built in France for the Greek navy in 1914. She was very similar in design to the Provence class, and with the outbreak of war she was taken over by the French navy and given the name *Savoie* but never completed.

TOP: **French shipbuilding programmes were often leisurely and the *Bretagne* class took four years to complete, 1912–16.** ABOVE: **One of the class at a speed trial in 1914. The class saw little action in the war. Two ships suffered under the guns of the British, and a third ship was used to bombard southern France and ports along the French Atlantic coast.**

Bretagne class

Class: *Bretagne, Provence, Lorraine.*
  Launched 1913
Dimensions: Length – 164.9m/541ft
  Beam – 26.9m/88ft 3in
  Draught – 8.9m/29ft 2in
Displacement: 23,600 tonnes/23,230 tons
Armament: Main – 10 x 340mm/13.5in guns
  Secondary – 22 x 135mm/5.4in guns and
  4 x 455mm/18in torpedoes
Machinery: 24 boilers, 4 shafts,
  21,625kW/29,000shp
Speed: 20 knots
Complement: 1,124 men

Normandie class

In the midst of growing tension in Europe, France announced an ambitious programme in 1912 to achieve a strength of 28 battleships by 1922. It was envisaged that this would be reached by building battleships, and battlecruisers or fast battleships, in divisional numbers, of two and even three units per year. However, with the outbreak of World War I, France placed her priority for resources on her army and the Royal Navy was left to guard the northern flank of the allied armies on the Channel and North Sea coast. With this nearly all work on designing or building capital ships in France slowed to a stop.

Construction of five ships of the Normandie class began in 1913 and 1914. The French had also designed a quadruple 340mm/13.5in turret, which was planned for this class, and adoption of which would have enabled French designers to reduce the length and weight of the armoured citadel. This class would therefore have had three turrets, one each forward, midships and aft. Work continued as far as to allow the hulls to be launched, but thereafter they were robbed of their equipment, the boilers were taken for smaller warships and the guns for the army. Some of these guns were captured by the German army and turned against their builders. The hulls of *Normandie, Languedoc, Flandre* and *Gascogne* languished uncompleted for many years until the Washington Naval Treaty sealed their fate and they were deleted in 1922 from the French order of battle and scrapped. Work on *Vendée* recommenced in 1918 and after some experiments she was completed as the aircraft carrier *Béarn* in 1927.

Normandie class

Class: *Normandie, Vendée, Flandre, Gascogne, Languedoc.* Not launched
Dimensions: Length – 194.5m/638ft 2in
  Beam – 29m/95ft 2in
  Draught – 8.65m/28ft 5in
Displacement: 29,465 tonnes/29,000 tons
Armament: Main – 16 x 340mm/13.5in guns
  Secondary – 24 x 135mm/5.4in guns and
  6 x 455mm/18in torpedoes
Machinery: 21 or 28 boilers, 4 shafts,
  23,862kW/32,000shp
Speed: 23 knots
Complement: 1,200 men

BELOW: **None of the Normandie class was completed, but one hull was taken to convert to France's first aircraft carrier, *Béarn*. She was too small and slow to be successful, although after conversion in World War II by the Americans she finished her career as a submarine tender, finally broken up in 1967.**

LEFT: As a design, *Dante Alighieri* was clearly in the line of succession of Cuniberti's elegant proposals for the all-big-gun ship, and one which was copied by the Russian navy. This aerial photograph gives a very good idea of Cuniberti's concept: a relatively clear upper deck without large numbers of secondary or tertiary guns, and the main guns able to bear over wide angles of fire. BELOW: Firing a broadside from the midships two turrets.

Dante Alighieri

The Italian warship designer Vittorio Cuniberti had already designed a number of ships for the Italian navy when he had published an article in *Jane's Fighting Ships* on what he thought would be the ideal battleship for the Royal Navy. This ship had 12 305mm/12in guns in single and double turrets and secondary armament was to consist of 75mm/3in guns. Cuniberti also placed emphasis on speed, sacrificing armour if need be, and proposed a ship which has a displacement of 17,273 tonnes/17,000 tons.

However, Admiral Fisher took up Cuniberti's all-big-gun idea in Britain, while Cuniberti and the Italian navy were still building distinctly pre-Dreadnought ships like the Vittorio Emanuele class. These were small battleships (13,209 tonnes/13,000 tons) with two single 305mm/12in guns in fore and aft mountings and a range of medium- and small-calibre guns. These ships were laid down in 1901–5 and although completed they took some six years each to build while the Italians absorbed intelligence about *Dreadnought*.

The Italian Government joined the Dreadnought race by authorizing the *Dante Alighieri* in 1907, although she was not laid down until 1909. The Cuniberti-designed ship had 12 305mm/12in guns, all on the centre line, one forward and one aft, and two amidships. A novel feature of the design was that the guns were for the first time in any navy placed in triple mountings. This arrangement enabled the boiler rooms to be widely separated and the engine room to be placed in the centre of the ship. *Dante Alighieri* also had two in-line rudders and four shafts. When completed she was capable of 24 knots and reckoned to be the fastest battleship in the world, although critics suggested that the armour was too light.

Dante Alighieri's only noteworthy action in World War I was the bombardment of Durazzo in the Adriatic during the army's struggle with the Austro-Hungarians. She was modified in 1923 and given a tripod foremast, taller

fore funnels and an aircraft ramp on C turret, but was scrapped in 1928.

The type was copied by the Russians in both their Gangut and Imperatrica Marija classes.

Dante Alighieri

Class: *Dante Alighieri*. Launched 1910.
Dimensions: Length – 158m/518ft 5in
  Beam – 26.6m/87ft 3in
  Draught – 8.8m/28ft 10in
Displacement: 19,835 tonnes/19,522 tons
Armament: Main – 12 x 305mm/12in guns
  Secondary – 20 x 120mm/4.7in,
  13 x 75mm/3in guns
  3 x 455mm/18in torpedoes
Machinery: 23 boilers, 4 shafts,
  26,360kW/35,350shp
Speed: 24 knots
Complement: 950 men

Conte di Cavour class

These three ships were the epitome of Cuniberti's ideas. They carried a main armament of 305mm/12in guns and 18 120mm/4.7in guns in casements around the superstructure as defence against torpedo boats. The arrangement of the heavy guns was novel. The Italians adopted the principle of super-firing guns and placed a twin turret above a triple turret forward and aft, and also a triple turret amidships on the centre line, giving the unusual number of 13 main armament guns. This was only one gun less than the then most heavily armed ship in the world, the Brazilian 14-gun *Rio de Janeiro* (later the British *Agincourt*), but in two fewer turrets.

Critics again thought that these ships were too lightly armoured, and that, in the tradition of Italian warship building, too much had been sacrificed for speed. This was tacitly acknowledged in the inter-war years when heavier armour and the Pugliese system was fitted, but by then the output of the machinery had also been increased from 22,371kW/ 30,000hp to 67,113kW/90,000hp.

Conte di Cavour and *Giulio Cesare* were modified in the 1920s after the Washington Naval Treaty. The foremast

was moved to a better position, before the fore funnel (a mistake the British had made in *Dreadnought* by placing the mast where it would be wreathed in funnel smoke) and both ships were fitted with catapults for aircraft. In one more demonstration of innovation in Italian design, the catapult was placed on the forecastle and the aircraft stored on the roof of the A turret.

Leonardo da Vinci sank as a consequence of an internal magazine explosion in 1916 at Taranto harbour, and although she was raised, was scrapped in 1921. This explosion was blamed on saboteurs, but it is more likely that it was one more in a series resulting from unstable ammunition. Neither *Conte di Cavour* nor *Giulio Cesare* saw any action in World War I, and they were so

TOP: **The silhouette was transformed when the Conte di Cavour class was modernized in the 1930s.** ABOVE: *Giulio Cesare*, **followed by** *Conte di Cavour*, **off Naples for the Italian fleet review of 1938.** BELOW LEFT: **A rare picture of** *Conte di Cavour* **flying off her aircraft from the forecastle-mounted catapult.**

largely rebuilt, starting in 1933, and their appearance changed, that they also appear under separate entries in *Battleships of World War II*.

Conte di Cavour class

Class: *Conte di Cavour, Giulio Cesare, Leonardo da Vinci.* Launched 1911
Dimensions: Length – 168.9m/554ft 1in
Beam – 28m/91ft 10in
Draught – 9.3m/30ft 6in
Displacement: 23,360 tonnes/22,992 tons
Armament: Main – 13 x 305mm/12in guns
Secondary – 18 x 120mm/4.7in,
13 x 75mm/3in guns and
3 x 455mm/18in torpedoes
Machinery: 20 boilers, 4 shafts,
23,324kW/31,278shp
Speed: 22.2 knots
Complement: 1,197 men

Caio Duilio class

Similar in layout to the Conte di Cavour class with their two tall funnels and tripod mast mounted before each, these two ships had the trademark 13 heavy guns mounted in five turrets, and retained the medium guns in casements, but increased the calibre from 120mm/4.7in to 150mm/6in. This increased the displacement by 2,032 tonnes/2,000 tons without any serious adverse affects upon the speed of about 21 knots. Other Italian features included two in-line rudders. Neither ship saw action during World War I.

From 1926 onwards they carried an aircraft launched from a rail over the forecastle, and the familiar arrangement of rangefinders in Italian ships whereby they were mounted vertically one over the other revolving around the forward conning tower. Caio Duilio was damaged by an internal explosion in 1925, and with the Andrea Doria was rebuilt in the years 1937–40.

In 1914 Italy also ordered four larger battleships (29,465 tonnes/29,000 tons) *Francesco Morosini, Francesco Caracciolo, Cristoforo Colombo* and *Marcantonio Colonna* but work on these ships came to a halt during World War I. They were intended to be fast battleships, similar to but faster than the British Queen Elizabeth class, and a direct response to the Austro-Hungarian Ersatz Monarch class which were building in Triestino. The 380mm/15in guns intended for these ships were used in several monitors.

Under the Washington Naval Treaty Italy was allowed 71,120 tonnes/70,000 tons and plans were drawn up for three 23,370-tonne/23,000-ton 380mm/15in-gun battleships in 1928. This was partly in response to news of the French Dunkerque class, but eventually a larger design was chosen which became the Vittorio Veneto class.

TOP: *Caio Duilio* as she appeared in World War I, showing the classic lines of a Dreadnought battleship and her similarity to the contemporary British designs. ABOVE: Photographed in about 1912, the guns have been installed but the builders have not yet left or removed their mess.

Caio Duilio class

Class: *Caio Duilio, Andrea Doria.* Launched 1913
Dimensions: Length – 165.8m/544ft 1in
  Beam – 28m/91ft 10in
  Draught – 9.4m/30ft 10in
Displacement: 23,324 tonnes/22,956 tons
Armament: Main – 13 x 305mm/12in guns
  Secondary – 16 x 150mm/6in, 19 x 75mm/3in
  guns and 3 x 455mm/18in torpedoes
Machinery: 20 boilers, 4 shafts.
  22,371kW/30,000shp
Speed: 21 knots
Complement: 1,198 men

Gangut class

This class was a compromise. Whilst the Tsar wanted these ships, his Duma did not and the naval staff favoured a design by Cuniberti but a technical committee preferred a Blohm and Voss design. The German design was opposed on principle and John Brown and Co. from Britain was brought in to re-work the drawings. The resulting ship was a Baltic-Dreadnought, close to Cuniberti's original ideas. British (Yarrow) boilers instead of French (Belleville) boilers gave a speed of 24.5 knots on trials, at the expense of some armour and although the armour was thinner it was spread over the full hull. Ice-breaking bows were also fitted.

All four ships formed part of the Russian First Battleship Brigade based in the Baltic, where they conducted a series of minor operations until they came under Bolshevik control during the Russian Revolution, and were demobilized at Kronstadt in 1918.

Petropavlovsk engaged Royal Navy destroyers in May 1919, during British intervention in the Russian civil war, and on August 17 she was sunk by torpedoes from British coastal motor boats which raided Kronstadt harbour. She was raised and modernized

between 1926–8 and participated in the 1937 fleet review at Spithead as *Marat*. In 1939 *Marat* bombarded Finnish positions, and in 1941 was hit by German long-range artillery and aerial bombs while alongside at Kronstadt, where she settled on the bottom. Partially repaired in January 1944, she was used as a fixed battery to fire on German army positions south of Kronstadt. She was renamed *Petropavlovsk* in 1943, and broken up in about 1953.

Poltava caught fire in 1922, sank and was plundered for spares for her sisters. Repairs were commenced on her under the name of *Frunze* in 1926–8 but she was hulked again in the 1930s. Her remains were sunk at Leningrad in 1941 and she was broken up in the 1950s.

Sevastopol operated with *Gangut* during World War I, and was modernized in 1928 as *Parizhkaya Kommuna*. While on passage to the Black Sea she was forced into Brest for repairs in 1929. She was modernized again in 1936–9 and during World War II bombarded the seaward flank of the advancing German army. She reverted to her old name in 1942, and was broken up in the late 1950s.

ABOVE: *Gangut* at anchor. A comparison with the aerial picture of *Dante Alighieri* shows how similar these ships are to the original Italian design. Considering their length and variety of service, these were successful and long-lived ships which withstood a great deal of damage.

Gangut was refitted in 1926–8 and 1931–4, and renamed *Oktyabrskaya Revolyutsiya*. In World War II she duelled with Finnish and then German positions, and on September 23, 1941, was hit by several bombs. Repaired at the Baltic Shipyard, she was ready to bombard the flank of the retreating German army in 1944. She was finally broken up in 1959.

Gangut class

Class: Gangut, Petropavlovsk, Poltava, Sevastopol. Launched 1911
Dimensions: Length – 180m/590ft 6in
Beam – 26.6m/87ft 3in
Draught – 8.4m/27ft 6in
Displacement: 23,735 tonnes/23,360 tons
Armament: Main – 12 x 305mm/12in guns
Secondary – 16 x 120mm/4.7in guns and
4 x 455mm/18in torpedoes
Machinery: 25 boilers, 4 shafts.
31,319kW/42,000shp
Speed: 23 knots
Complement: 1,126 men

Imperatritsa Mariya class

Similar to the Ganguts but adapted for operations in the Black Sea, the Russian naval staff wanted bigger guns to counteract the battleships ordered in Britain for Turkey. However, to avoid delay in acquiring 355mm/14in guns, 305mm/12in main armament was accepted. John Brown and Co. advised in their construction as with the Ganguts. A heavier armoured belt was provided, but the problem of blast from the main guns affecting the secondary armament in its casemates was not resolved. There were minor differences between these ships when completed, and a bewildering series of name changes.

Imperatritsa Mariya bombarded the Turkish and Bulgarian coasts in 1915 and 1916 and on July 22, 1916, fought the ex-German Turkish-flagged light cruiser *Breslau*. On October 20, 1916, she suffered an internal explosion, whilst alongside in Sevastopol. Sabotage was suspected, but the most likely cause was a spontaneous explosion of unstable ammunition. The wreck was raised in 1918 and broken up in 1922.

Imperator Alexander III was not completed until after the Russian Revolution in February 1917, when she was renamed *Volya*. In April 1918, for a few months, she flew the flag of the independent state of Ukraine, but on October 1, 1918, she was seized by the Germans and renamed (perhaps mistakenly) *Volya*. In 1919 she sailed briefly under the British flag, and during the war between the Red and White Russians she fought on the side of the Whites under the name of *General Alekseev*. She was steamed to Bizerta, where the French government offered to give her up to the newly installed Soviet rulers of Russia, but she was sold for scrapping in 1924 and finally broken up in 1936.

Imperatritsa Ekaterina Velikaya (ex *Ekaterina II*) also undertook bombardment operations, and she fought the ex-German battlecruiser *Goeben* on January 7–8, 1916, and the light cruiser *Breslau* on April 4–5, 1916. In April 29, 1917, she was renamed *Svobodnaya Rossiya* and under this name she again fought *Breslau* on June 24–5, 1917. Under the terms of the armistice she should have been handed over to the Germans but escaped from Sevastopol to Novorossijsk where she was sunk by torpedoes from the destroyer *Kerch* on June 18, 1918.

Imperatritsa Mariya class

Class: *Imperatritsa Mariya, Imperator Alexander III, Ekaterina II.* Launched 1913–14
Dimensions: Length – 167.8m/550ft 6in
Beam – 27.3m/89ft 6in
Draught – 8.4m/27ft 6in
Displacement: 22,960 tonnes/22,600 tons
Armament: Main – 12 x 305mm/12in guns
Secondary – 20 x 130mm/5.1in guns and
4 x 455mm/18in torpedoes
Machinery: 20 boilers, 4 shafts.
19,761kW/26,500shp
Speed: 21 knots
Complement: 1,220 men
Imperator Alexander III renamed *Volya* and *Ekaterina II* renamed *Imperatritsa Ekaterina Velikaya. Ekaterina II* was slightly longer and larger than her sisters.

ABOVE: *Imperator Alexander III*, seen here from a distance, entered service after the February 1917 revolution in Russia, when she was renamed *Volya*. *Volya* later flew the flag of independent Ukraine and later still under White Russian authority she was known as *General Alexieff*. LEFT: *Volya* also spent some time under German and then British control as revolution raged around the Black Sea. The clean lines and minimum of superstructure, with the emphasis on keeping free the big guns' arcs of fire, show the influence of Italian design. Under German control she was briefly known as *Volga*.

LEFT: **Although the Bolsheviks renamed** *Imperator Nikolai I* **in 1917 and called her** *Demokratiy*, **she was never finished.**

Imperator Nikolai I

Intended as a fourth ship of the Imperatritsa Mariya class, *Imperator Nikolai I* was a larger ship all round, which enabled her designers to give her increased armour. She was built on the Black Sea and intended to counter the acquisition by Turkey of the *Rio de Janeiro* (which became the British *Agincourt*) from the Brazilian navy. Although 355mm/14in and even

400mm/16in guns were contemplated for this ship, the guns never became available. In any case, *Imperator Nikolai I* was not completed: she fell into German hands in 1918 and into the Allies' hands in 1919. Although the Germans started to break her, construction was later recommenced until the Allies decided to demolish her to prevent her being commissioned by the Reds.

Imperator Nikolai I

Class: *Imperator Nikolai I.* Launched 1916
Dimensions: Length – 188m/616ft 9in
　Beam – 28.9m/94ft 9in
　Draught – 9m/29ft 6in
Displacement: 27,740 tonnes/27,300 tons
Armament: Main – 12 x 305mm/12in guns
　Secondary – 20 x 130mm/5.1in guns and
　4 x 455mm/18in torpedoes
Machinery: 20 boilers, 4 shafts.
　19,243kW/27,300shp
Speed: 21 knots
Complement: 1,252 men

Borodino class

The Russian battleships and battlecruisers all had a similar silhouette, except that in the Borodino class the forward triple turret was carried one deck higher on an extended forecastle. The forward secondary guns in their casemates were still wet, and suffered from blast effects by continuing

to be placed beneath the main turrets. As World War I developed the Russians had difficulty in sourcing equipment for the Borodino class, especially the turbines. None were completed. Consideration was given to converting the most advanced ship, *Izmail*, to an aircraft carrier but all were broken up.

Borodino class

Class: *Borodino, Izmail, Kinburn, Navarin.*
　Launched 1915–16
Dimensions: Length – 221.9m/728ft
　Beam – 30.5m/100ft
　Draught – 10.2m/33ft 6in
Displacement: 33,020 tonnes/32,500 tons
Armament: Main – 12 x 355mm/14in guns
　Secondary – 24 x 130mm/5.1in guns and
　6 x 535mm/21in torpedoes
Machinery: 25 boilers, 4 shafts,
　50,708kW/68,000shp
Speed: 26.5 knots
Complement: 1,250 men

LEFT: **Like other nations, the Russians named ships after famous victories on land. Borodino, sunk in 1905 was to have been replaced by one of four ships built at St Petersburg, but they were overwhelmed by the Russian revolution and never completed. Except in the Black Sea, the Russian navy never recovered from its defeat at the Battle of Tsushima.**

Radetzky class

These ships, the last of the Austro-Hungarian pre-Dreadnoughts, were designed by Siegfried Popper. Popper wanted to build an all-big-gun ship but could not fit the necessary gun layout into a ship of less than 16,257 tonnes/16,000 tons to which he was constrained by the size of the available docks.

Although small and seemingly over-armed for their displacement, the Radetzkys were well suited to warfare in the Adriatic, even if their active service was against shore targets rather than against other warships. Some speed was given up for increased armour, which was similar to British Dreadnoughts, while they were not much slower than their Italian equivalents. Popper emphasized underwater protection, and when underwater explosive experiments failed to inform him, he devised a satisfactory mathematical model for his design of an armoured double bottom.

Erzherzog Franz Ferdinand was named after the Austrian crown prince whose assassination at Sarajevo marked the start of World War I.

Radetzky was at the British Coronation Review in 1911 and all three ships of the class made training cruises in the eastern Mediterranean in 1912. In 1913 they formed part of an international squadron which demonstrated in the Ionian against the Balkan War.

In the spring of 1914 Zrinyi made a training cruise with the two new Dreadnoughts, Viribus Unitis and Tegetthoff, in the eastern Mediterranean and visited Malta.

In the opening moves of World War I, the Radetzkys covered the German Admiral Souchon's escape from the Adriatic, and bombarded Montenegro and Ancona and other coastal targets, but after the summer of 1915 they took little active part in the war.

Austro-Hungary wanted to give her fleet to the Yugoslavs in order to keep it out of Italian hands but Erzherzog Franz Ferdinand was interned at Venice. However Yugoslav officers steamed Radetzky and Zrinyi from Pola. On sighting a superior Italian force, the two battleships hoisted American flags and

ABOVE: Not many pictures of the Austro-Hungarian fleet have survived: this is Radetzky photographed in 1911. Her only action was the bombardment of Ancona in Italy. She fell, briefly, into Yugoslav hands at the end of the war, but was allocated to the USA and scrapped in Italy.

sailed south down the Adriatic coast to Split, where a flotilla of USN submarine chasers accepted their surrender. However, all three ships were eventually ceded to Italy and scrapped in 1920–6.

Radetzky class

Class: *Erzherzog Franz Ferdinand, Radetzky, Zrinyi*. Launched 1908–10
Dimensions: Length – 137.44m/450ft 11in
 Beam – 24.59m/80ft 8in
 Draught – 8.15m/26ft 9in
Displacement: 14,740 tonnes/14,508 tons
Armament: Main – 4 x 305mm/12in guns
 Secondary – 8 x 240mm/9.4in,
 20 x 100mm/4in guns and
 3 x 455mm/18in torpedoes
Machinery: 12 Yarrow boilers, 2 shafts.
 14,765kW/19,800ihp
Speed: 20.5 knots
Complement: 876 men

Tegetthoff class

The Tegetthoff class was the Austro-Hungarian response to news of the building of the Italian Dreadnought, *Dante Alighieri*. Although German experts had been consulted, the design was all-Austrian and the decision to fit triple turrets was influenced more by the desire to match the Italians. When financial authority for these ships was slow in forthcoming, the Austrian Commander-in-Chief, Admiral Montecuccoli, took out a personal loan for these ships, some months before parliament approved their construction.

The ships were compact, yet strongly armed and armoured. Their main weaknesses were the lack of reserve displacement and poor underwater protection, which led to the loss of two ships of the class.

In June 1918, Admiral Horthy planned a major raid on the Otranto barrage, in coordination with the Austro-Hungarian army. His battleships left Pola in two poorly protected groups: *Viribus Unitis* and *Prinz Eugen* on June 8, and *Szent Istvan* and *Tegetthoff* the next evening. *Szent Istvan's* engines gave her trouble, reducing speed and making excessive smoke, and she was intercepted in the early hours of the morning by two Italian torpedo-boats on an unrelated mission

off the island of Premuda. *Szent Istvan* was hit with two torpedoes and the bulkhead between the boiler rooms collapsed. She quickly flooded and within three hours she had capsized. The sinking was filmed from *Tegetthoff*, making it one of the rare sequences of a battleship being sunk. The planned bombardment was aborted and the Austro-Hungarian navy returned to harbour for the last time.

On October 6, 1918, the Austrian emperor gave the Austro-Hungarian navy to the National Council of Slovenians, Croats and Serbs, and the fleet allegedly hoisted the Croatian flag. That night, while the end of the war was celebrated ashore and afloat, two Italian divers placed mines under the brightly lit *Viribus Unitis*, which blew up at dawn. Four days later Italian troops entered Pola and captured *Tegetthoff* and *Prinz Eugen*.

ABOVE: **One of the Tegetthoff class at speed. She was named after one of the few Austro-Hungarian naval leaders.** LEFT: ***Szent Istvan* was sunk by Italian torpedo-boats in 1918 and settled slowly, giving sufficient time for her loss to be filmed from her sister ship, *Tegetthoff*, and for some unique and poignant footage to be captured.**

Prinz Eugen was ceded to France and expended in underwater explosive tests as a bomb target and finally sunk by the guns of the French battleships *Jean Bart*, *Paris* and *France*. *Tegetthoff* was ceded to Italy and broken up in 1924–5.

In 1914–16 the Austro-Hungarian navy laid down four improved Tegetthoff ships, but these were never launched.

Tegetthoff class

Class: *Viribus Unitis, Tegetthoff, Prinz Eugen, Szent Istvan.* Launched 1911–14
Dimensions: Length – 151m/495ft 5in
    Beam – 27.3m/89ft 8in
    Draught – 8.9m/29ft
Displacement: 20,334 tonnes/20,013 tons
Armament: Main – 12 x 305mm/12in guns
    Secondary – 12 x 150mm/6in,
    18 x 65mm/2.6in guns and
    4 x 535mm/21in torpedoes
Machinery: 12 boilers, 4 shafts
    (*Szent Istvan* 2 shafts). 20,134kW/27,000shp
Speed: 20.5 knots
Complement: 1,087 men

LEFT: *Drottningen Victoria* is seen here during her sea trials in 1921. The photograph shows her as newly completed, but all three ships were modernized before World War II. ABOVE: Perhaps the most unusual flying accident occurred in 1939 when an aircraft crashed into the foremast of *Gustav V*. BELOW: An unusual photograph of a torpedo firing trial in 1893. Many battleships carried torpedoes in underwater tubes which were never photographed.

Sverige class

By the beginning of the 20th century Sweden possessed a large fleet although some of the hulls were elderly. Even the *John Ericsson*, which was almost 50 years old, having been upgraded three times, was still available. Between 1900 and 1905 the Swedish navy decided to build three classes of coast defence ships, Dristigheten, Oscar II and five ships of the Åran class.

However, Sweden's traditional enemy was Russia and larger ships were needed to increase the enemy's risk by forcing her to commit her own battleships in the event of an invasion. After considering a range of designs the so-called F-boat was decided upon in 1911, only for a change of government in 1912 to cancel the order on economic grounds. A remarkable battleship-club was started that rapidly raised more than enough money to build the first ship of a new class, and the government had little option but to thank the people and begin construction of *Sverige*.

The second and third ships of this class, *Drottningen Victoria* and *Gustaf V*, although ordered during World War I, were not completed until 1921 and 1922. The design of the later ships also changed slightly, they were larger and had two shafts instead of four and icebreaking stems instead of rams. After successive modernization all three ships differed from each other, all were given heavy tripod masts, but in *Gustaf V* the two funnels were combined into one, while *Sverige* was given an S-shaped fore funnel, and *Drottningen Victoria* retained her upright funnels. There were different arrangements of gun directors, and at each modernization the anti-aircraft weaponry was improved. Coal-fired boilers were also replaced by oil.

Swedish battleships successfully helped to safeguard their neutrality in two world wars, and the fate of other navies meant that for many years in the 20th century the Swedish navy was master of the Baltic, but by 1957 the Swedish battleships had been decommissioned. All that remains of Sweden's battleship ambitions are various guns which were set up in fixed defensive batteries.

Sverige class

Class: *Sverige, Drottningen Victoria, Gustaf V.*
Launched 1915–18
Dimensions: Length – 120.9m/396ft 8in
Beam – 18.6m/61ft
Draught– 6.2m/20ft 4in
Displacement: 7,240 tonnes/7,125 tons
(*Sverige* 6,935 tonnes/6,825 tons)
Armament: Main – 4 x 280mm/11in guns
Secondary – 8 x 150mm/6in, 6 x 75mm/3in guns
and 2 x 535mm/21in torpedoes
Machinery: 12 boilers, 2 shafts,
17,830kW/23,910shp
Speed: 22.5 knots
Complement: 427 men

De Zeven Provincien

While armed and armoured like a small battleship, *De Zeven Provincien* was in fact the last of the long line of Dutch coast defence ships. *De Zeven Provincien* saw little action in World War I, in which the Netherlands were neutral, and in 1912 was sent to the Dutch East Indies, the vast archipelago which later became Indonesia.

When a mutiny broke out onboard in 1933, *De Zeven Provincien* was bombed by a Dutch seaplane which hit her forecastle, killing 23 men. In 1935–6 she was used as a training ship, and in 1937 she was substantially modified and re-commissioned under the name *Soerabaia*. *De Zeven Provincien* was badly damaged in a Japanese air attack on February 18, 1942, and scuttled a few days later.

Meanwhile, a Dutch Royal Commission in 1912–13 recommended the building of a new fleet for the Royal Netherlands Navy to defend the Netherlands, protect her colonies and police the East Indies. The fleet would have included nine battleships of about 20,320 tonnes/20,000 tons and capable of 21 knots, armed with 340mm/13.5in guns. The number of ships was determined by the perceived need to maintain a squadron in the Far East, a squadron in home waters, and a reserve. It was a long-term, rolling programme which envisaged the earlier ships being replaced by more modern ships over a 30-year period.

The Dutch got as far as asking German and British firms for proposals when World War I broke out and these

plans were abandoned. The leading design was by Germaniawerft and provided for a ship of 21,000 tonnes/20,668 tons, 21 knots, and armed with eight 340mm/13.5in, 16 150mm/6in and 12 75mm/3in guns.

De Zeven Provincien class

Class: *De Zeven Provincien.* Launched 1909
Dimensions: Length – 101.5m/333ft
    Beam – 17.1m/56ft
    Draught – 6.2m/20ft 3in
Displacement: 6,635 tonnes/6,530 tons
Armament: Main – 2 x 280mm/11in and
    4 x 150mm/6in guns
    Secondary – 10 x 75mm/3in guns
Machinery: 8 boilers, 2 shafts,
    5,966kW/8,000ihp
Speed: 16 knots
Complement: 452 men

ABOVE: **The Dutch contemplated building a proper battleship, but only managed a coast defence ship, which they armed with 280mm/11in guns. She survived from 1910 to 1942.** LEFT: **One of the smallest post-Dreadnoughts to appear in these pages,** De Zeven Provincien **saw much of her service in the Dutch East Indies, where she was scuttled to prevent her falling into Japanese hands.** De Zeven Provincien **lies in the line of development between the pocket battleship and the monitor.**

España class

These three small battleships were built in Spain to British plans and largely under the supervision of British architects. The intention of their ingenious design was to incorporate the Dreadnought principles of an all-big-gun warship into the size of a pre-Dreadnought battleship. This was typical of a long tradition that British designers could be so adventurous with designs for foreign navies while at home the Admiralty was much more cautious about innovation. At less than 16,257 tonnes/16,000 tons they were the smallest and slowest Dreadnoughts and the variant was not copied elsewhere.

Their eight 305mm/12in guns were mounted in one turret forward and aft and two midships turrets mounted *en echelon*. The secondary armament was mounted in casemates. Distinctive recognition features were the boats mounted on the roofs of the midships turrets, the single upright funnel almost in the centre of the ship, and two tall tripod masts.

España ran aground off Morocco in 1923 and her large-calibre guns were salvaged but the wreck was broken up in the heavy surf which pounds that coast almost continually throughout the year.

Jaime I was not completed before the outbreak of World War I, when Britain was unable to supply further material. In 1923–5 she took part in what was known as the Riff revolt and was hit from a shore battery. In the Spanish Civil War she fought on the side of the Republicans, and bombarded Ceuta and Algeciras, but she was bombed in Malaga in 1936 and further damaged by an internal explosion in 1937. She was finally scrapped in 1939.

Alfonso XIII, which took the name *España* in 1931, declared for the Nationalists in the Spanish Civil War and bombarded Bilbao in April 1937, but soon afterwards hit a mine and was sunk – though at the time the Nazis claimed one of their aircraft had been involved.

Three more ships of a class named *Reina Eugenia* were supposed to be laid down during World War I, but plans were abandoned in favour of more affordable cruisers and destroyers. During World War II Franco approved a plan to build four modern battleships but financial weakness prevented this being taken up.

TOP: **A handsome picture of one of the España class (probably the renamed *Alfonso XIII* which was renamed *España* after the name ship had been wrecked) which shows a passing resemblance to Italian and Russian designs and faithfulness to Cuniberti's concepts.** ABOVE: *España* declared for the nationalist government and was sunk by a mine off Santander. At the time the Germans thought that Basque government aircraft were responsible for the loss.

España class

Class: *España, Jaime I, Alfonso XIII.*
Launched 1912–14
Dimensions: Length – 132.58m/435ft
Beam – 24m/78ft 9in
Draught – 7.77m/25ft 6in
Displacement: 15,700 tonnes/15,453 tons
Armament: Main – 8 x 305mm/12in guns
Secondary – 20 x 100mm/4in guns
Machinery: 12 boilers, 4 shafts.
11,558kW/15,500shp
Speed: 19.5 knots
Complement: 854 men

Kilkis and *Lemnos*

Kilkis and *Lemnos* were both 13,209-tonne/13,000-ton battleships, originally built as two of the Mississippi class pre-Dreadnoughts completed in 1908 for the USN. Their place might properly be regarded as belonging to an earlier period, but they had careers that spanned both World Wars of the 20th century. The Greeks and Turks fought at sea in the Balkan Wars 1912–13, which saw the first use of aviation in modern warfare and the first use of submarine torpedo attack.

The Hellenic navy consisted of ships bought in from several navies, and two battleships were ordered, one from Germany and the other from France, but neither ship was finished. The American 355mm/14in guns intended for a German-built ship named *Salamis* were purchased for the British Abercrombie class monitors, and the unfinished *Salamis* was not scrapped until 1932. An unnamed French-built battleship of 23,369 tonnes/23,000 tons was to have been similar to the Provence class.

However, Greece did purchase two pre-Dreadnoughts from the USA in 1914, while Turkey hoped to acquire modern battleships from Britain. *Kilkis*, the name ship of the class, was taken over at Newport News, Virginia, in July and served in the Royal Hellenic Navy until 1932 when she became a training ship. *Lemnos* was in the Mediterranean on a training cruise with USN midshipmen when she was handed over.

The *Lemnos* was originally the *Idaho* and she was amongst the Greek naval ships temporarily seized by France in 1916 during a constitutional crisis in Greece. *Lemnos* was active in Turkish waters during the chaotic period following the end of World War I, but went out of active service during the 1930s and was retained as a hulk. *Kilkis* and her sister ship *Lemnos* became two of the longest-surviving pre-Dreadnoughts until they were both sunk at Salamis by German dive-bombers on April 23, 1941, during the German invasion of Greece. The wrecks were salvaged for scrap in the 1950s.

LEFT: *Kilkis* and *Lemnos* retained the lattice masts which the USN had fitted before World War I. Apart from two Argentinian battleships built to order in the USA, they were the only USN battleships to pass out of American service and to fly a foreign flag.
ABOVE: Both ships were sunk by German aircraft while at anchor at Salamis in 1941. The picture was taken from a German bomber as it dived on *Kilkis* at anchor. The ships had not been modernized and were no match for modern air power.

Kilkis class

Class: *Kilkis* (ex *Idaho*), *Lemnos* (ex *Mississippi*). Launched 1905
Dimensions: Length – 116.4m/382ft
Beam – 23.5m/77ft
Draught – 7.5m/24ft 8in
Displacement: 13,210 tonnes/13,000 tons
Armament: Main – 4 x 305mm/12in,
8 x 205mm/8in and 8 x 180mm/7in guns
Secondary – 12 x 75mm/3in guns and
2 x 535mm/21in torpedoes
Machinery: 8 boilers, 2 shafts,
7,457kW//10,000ihp
Speed: 17 knots
Complement: 744 men

Yavuz Sultan Selim

The Turks had two old German pre-Dreadnought battleships, *Kurfürst Friedrich Wilhelm* and *Weissenburg,* which had been modernized and renamed as *Heireddin Barbarossa* and *Turgut Reis* and saw active service in World War I. *Heireddin Barbarossa* was sunk by the British submarine *E-11* in the Sea of Marmara on August 8, 1915. *Turgut Reis* survived as a hulk until she was broken up in 1956–7.

The Turks made several attempts to improve their battleship strength by purchasing ships in Britain. However, *Resadiye* was confiscated by the Royal Navy and commissioned as *Erin*, and two other ships of this class, *Mahmud Resad V* and *Fatik* were cancelled. *Sultan Osman I* (ex *Rio de Janeiro*) was also taken over as *Agincourt.*

Consequently, when the German battlecruiser *Goeben* and the cruiser *Breslau* escaped from the British Mediterranean Fleet, arriving off Istanbul on August 10, 1914, it was natural that the Turks were interested in acquiring these ships. *Goeben* transferred to the Turkish flag six days later, while retaining most of her German crew and thereafter led perhaps the busiest and longest life of any ship of the period.

Goeben was twice bested by the Russian Black Sea pre-Dreadnought squadron. On November 18, 1914, and again in May 1915, she exchanged fire with *Evstafi*, which hit *Goeben*, whereupon the German-Turkish ship again had to use her speed to avoid being outgunned by the Russian squadron.

On January 20, 1918, this time in the Dardanelles, *Goeben* sank the British monitors *Lord Raglan* and *M-28* but as the German-Turkish ships shaped a course for Lemnos island, *Breslau* hit a mine, and while *Goeben* attempted a tow *Goeben* hit three mines herself, while *Breslau* hit several more and sank rapidly. *Goeben* then ran aground on Nagara Point, where she was attacked by British seaplanes from *Ark Royal,* but the bombs used were too small to be effective. The British submarine *E-14* was diverted from her patrol in the Otranto Straits but by the time she arrived, *Goeben* had been towed off by *Turgut Reiss*.

Yavuz survived under the Turkish flag until 1973–6 when she was broken up shortly before her diamond jubilee – one of the longest surviving ships of her era.

LEFT: **The German battlecruiser** *Goeben* **was sold to the Turks in 1914 and is here seen under a prominent Turkish flag, although the German crew remained onboard to man her. She was not finally handed over to the Turkish authorities until November 1918.**

BELOW: **Under her new owners – whatever the nationality of the crew –** *Yavuz Sultan Selim* **took part in many actions in the Black Sea. In 1918, during a brief sortie from the Black Sea, she sank the British monitor** *Raglan.*

Yavuz Sultan Selim ☪

Class: *Yavuz* (as *Goeben*). Launched 1910
Dimensions: Length – 186.5m/611ft 11in
  Beam – 29.5m/96ft 10in
  Draught – 9m/29ft 5in
Displacement: 22,979 tonnes/22,616 tons
Armament: Main – 10 x 280mm/11in guns
  Secondary – 12 x 150mm/6in,
  12 x 88mm/3.46in guns and
  4 x 510mm/20in torpedoes
Machinery: 24 boilers, 4 shafts,
  38,776kW/52,000shp
Speed: 25.5 knots
Complement: 1,053 men

Rivadavia class

In the 1870s the Argentine navy consisted of a few cruisers, and although *La Plata* (1874), *Los Andes* (1874), *Libertad* (1890), and *Independencia* (1891) were classed as coast defence battleships they were small and poorly armed. Only *Patagonia* (1885), a protected cruiser built in Italy, had a single gun of 255mm/10in size and she was reconstructed in 1909 as a survey ship. However, when Argentina's quarrel with Chile over boundaries in Patagonia and territorial limits in the Beagle Channel was settled (for the time being) by British arbitration in 1902, the British thoughtfully wrote into the treaty clauses concerning the limitation of naval arms. The Royal Navy bought two pre-Dreadnought battleships from Chile which were under construction in Britain and Argentina sold two cruisers to Japan which were building in Italy.

In 1904 the Brazilian Government decided upon a programme of naval expansion, and Argentina asked foreign companies to tender plans for new battleships. Fore River won the competition and the ships became the

only Dreadnoughts built in the United States for a foreign navy. Although the Argentine decision was based on technical and financial grounds, there was another, unintended consequence of choosing American yards. Unlike orders placed by foreign nations in European yards where the ships being built were taken over by the warring powers, American neutrality during the early years of World War I allowed a timely delivery of both Dreadnoughts. As a result Argentina got her warships, whereas Brazil and Chile did not.

They were a combination of ideas from capital ship design, with battleship and battlecruiser features, good protection, significant armament and relatively high speed. The superimposed turret arrangement was American, and the wing turrets showed British design influence. The secondary 150mm/6in battery was attributed to German influence as were the triple shafts, but engine-room and boiler-room layout was similar to the Italian Dante Alighieri class. The forward cage mast was entirely American.

ABOVE: *Rivadavia* and *Moreno* were possibly the only major warships to be built in the USA for export. Their design incorporated features from American, British, German and Italian naval architecture. This picture shows the profile after modernization.

Both ships underwent modernization in the 1920s. In 1937 *Moreno* attended the Coronation Review at Spithead while *Rivadavia* tactfully visited Brest, and later both ships visited Wilhelmshaven. Neither ship fired her guns in anger during World War II, and in 1956 they were stricken from the navy list.

Rivadavia class

Class: *Rivadavia, Moreno.* Launched 1911
Dimensions: Length – 181.3m/594ft 9in
  Beam – 30m/98ft 4in
  Draught – 8.4m/27ft 8in
Displacement: 28,388 tonnes/27,940 tons
Armament: Main – 12 x 305mm/12in guns
  Secondary – 12 x 150mm/6in, 16 x 100mm/4in
  guns and 2 x 535mm/21in torpedoes
Machinery: 18 boilers, 3 shafts,
  29,455kW/39,500shp
Speed: 22.5 knots
Complement: 1,130 men

Minas Gerais class

Minas Gerais and *Sao Paulo* were the most powerful warships in the world when completed. They were built amid rumours that they were destined for another power, or for the Royal Navy, and had two super-firing turrets fore and aft and two wing turrets. The Brazilian Government ordered them even before the first Dreadnought was commissioned. The only outdated thing about these ships was that they were powered by reciprocating engines and not turbines. As a direct consequence the USA started to court Brazil as a pan-American ally, but a downturn in the economy and a mutiny halted the Brazilian Dreadnought programme. Therefore, when Brazil declared war on the Central Powers in 1917 and promised to send her battleships to join

the Grand Fleet at Scapa Flow, both ships were in need of refit. *Sao Paulo* was sent to New York in June 1918 to be modernized, and though her refit outlasted the war, *Minas Gerais* was also sent north and completed her refit in 1923.

Minas Gerais was modernized in 1934–7, but *Sao Paulo* was judged to be in too poor a condition to justify the cost. Neither ship saw action in World War II. *Sao Paulo*, en route to Britain for breaking, broke her tow in the North Atlantic in 1951 and was never seen again. *Minas Gerais* was towed to Italy to be broken up in 1954.

In 1910 Brazil ordered a yet more powerful warship, which would have been the largest in the world. However a mutiny in the navy had undermined public support for buying Dreadnoughts, and eventually *Rio de Janeiro* was sold to Turkey as *Sultan Osman I*, and was about to be steamed away from Britain when the Royal Navy confiscated her under the name of *Agincourt*. In 1921 Great Britain offered to sell *Agincourt* back to Brazil but after consideration the idea was rejected.

The Brazilians contemplated a fourth Dreadnought, to be known as *Riachuelo*, and four designs were considered for a battleship of 32,005 tonnes/31,500 tons

TOP: *Sao Paulo* as built and photographed at Rio de Janeiro in 1918. ABOVE: *Minas Gerais*, date unknown, but showing features of World War I, the range clock, and World War II, what appear to be radar domes. BELOW LEFT: *Minas Gerais* in 1909. The structure apparently extending to port and starboard are in fact spans of the bridge over the River Tyne in England, where this was photographed.

to 36,580 tonnes/36,000 tons with main batteries of 355mm/14in, 380mm/15in or 405mm/16in guns. Construction was never started and the idea was dropped on the outbreak of World War I.

Minas Gerais class

Class: *Minas Gerais, Sao Paulo.* Launched 1908–9
Dimensions: Length – 165.5m/543ft
   Beam – 25.3m/83ft
   Draught – 7.6m/25ft
Displacement: 20,378 tonnes/19,281 tons
Armament: Main – 12 x 305mm/12in guns
   Secondary – 22 x 120mm/4.7in and
   8 x 3pdr guns
Machinery: 18 boilers, 2 shafts,
   17,524kW/23,500shp
Speed: 21 knots
Complement: 900 men

Almirante Latorre class

As part of the South American naval arms race, Chile ordered two Dreadnoughts to counter the ships that the Argentine had built in face of the perceived threat from Brazil. The first ship was named *Valparaíso*, then *Libertad*, and thirdly *Almirante Latorre*. Work on *Almirante Latorre* started in 1911, but ironically work could not start on *Almirante Cochrane* until the Brazilian *Rio de Janeiro* had left the slip. The design was similar to the British Iron Duke class but with 355mm/14in guns in lieu of 340mm/13.5in, however neither ship was delivered to the Chileans.

At the outbreak of World War I the Royal Navy purchased *Almirante Latorre* from its ally and renamed her *Canada*, and for a while considered purchasing *Almirante Cochrane* to be renamed *India*. Being less advanced, work was halted on *Almirante Cochrane* until 1917, when she was taken in hand to be finished as

the aircraft carrier *Eagle*. *Almirante Latorre* (*Canada*) was modified at the end of the war and flying-off ramps were fitted over B and X turrets.

Chile finally took over *Canada* and gave her back her original name. The Chilean navy also wanted their second Dreadnought and asked for *Eagle* to be reconverted, but they were offered instead the battlecruiser *Inflexible*. This was refused and the Chileans settled for just one capital ship and several minor war vessels.

Almirante Latorre was modernized in Devonport in 1929–31 and converted to oil-fired boilers. Anti-torpedo bulges were fitted which raised her beam to 31.4m/103ft, and she was given new gunnery control systems. An Italian-designed catapult was fitted on the quarterdeck. She remained in service until 1958 when she was towed to Japan to be broken up.

TOP: *Almirante Latorre* in 1913. Soon after this photograph she was purchased by the Royal Navy and renamed *Canada*. ABOVE: *Almirante Cochrane* at the time of her launch. In 1917 the uncompleted hull was purchased and finished by the British as the aircraft carrier *Eagle*.

Almirante Latorre class

Class: *Almirante Latorre* (as *Canada*), *Almirante Cochrane*. Launched 1913
Dimensions: Length – 201.47m/661ft
  Beam – 28.04m/92ft
  Draught – 8.84m/29ft
Displacement: 29,060 tonnes/28,600 tons
Armament: Main – 10 x 355mm/14in guns
  Secondary – 16 x 150mm/6in guns and
  4 x 535mm/21in torpedoes
Machinery: 21 boilers, 4 shafts,
  27,591kW/37,000shp
Speed: 23 knots
Complement: 1,167 men

Directory of Battleships

World War II

The battleship, which had benefited from every kind of advance in technology in the 19th century, was threatened in the next century by two new weapons: the submarine and the aeroplane. The oldest and most powerful navy in the world, the Royal Navy realized this and at the start of World War I had not only the largest fleet of battleships but also the largest fleet of modern submarines. The Royal Navy was also the first to experiment with taking aircraft to sea and by 1918 the Royal Naval Air Service was one of the largest air forces in the world. Even as these new weapons increased in numbers and effectiveness, the battleship held sway up to the beginning of World War II. Throughout the war there were sporadic clashes between British and Italian, British and German, and American and Japanese capital ships. However tactics and operations involving aircraft evolved so rapidly that by 1942 the aircraft carrier rather than the battleship was regarded as the new capital ship of the fleet. By the end of World War II such battleships as remained were not being replaced, though a few lingered on in active service with the USN.

LEFT: American battleships in line ahead in the 1940s – still the optimum formation for bringing the maximum number of guns to bear upon an enemy, whatever technical changes had taken place over the previous century.

Hood

When commissioned in 1920 *Hood* was the largest warship in the world, and between the wars she became an icon not just for the Royal Navy, but for the British Empire. *Hood* was generally regarded, in respect of the combination of fighting power, speed and protection, to be the most powerful ship in the world. She was also thought to be one of the most beautiful. During a ten-month world cruise in 1923–4 *Hood*, with the battlecruiser *Repulse* and their escorts, visited the British dominions and crossed the Pacific to the USA and Canada, reminding the world that the Royal Navy was still the most impressive in the world.

Hood was ordered in response to the wartime German 28-knot Mackensen class battlecruisers, none of which were commissioned. Her design was modified in light of the lessons learned from the loss of battlecruisers *Queen Mary*, *Indefatigable* and *Invincible* at the Battle of Jutland, and extra armour was added. Although usually referred to as a battlecruiser, *Hood* was really a fast battleship and an improved version of the Queen Elizabeths, with the same main armament of eight 380mm/15in guns, a sloped armoured belt and improved torpedo protection. Nevertheless, magazine protection remained one of her weak spots and her deck armour was only 75mm/3in thick. Small-tube boilers and a longer hull-form gave *Hood* a speed of 31–2 knots, 7 knots faster than the Queen Elizabeths. However, the extra weight made her sit lower in the water than designed and she had a

ABOVE: *Hood* was made famous by her inter-war world cruise when she was admired for her handsome looks. She was sunk by the German battleship *Bismarck* after a few minutes' fight.

tendency to dig in, fore and aft, in any seaway and at speed. Four ships of the same class were originally ordered, but work on *Hood*'s three sisters, who were to be named *Rodney*, *Howe* and *Anson*, was halted in 1917.

Hood was modernized twice, once in 1929 and again in 1939. There were proposals to remove or reduce the 610-tonne/600-ton conning tower and make further improvements to her deck armour, but World War II came too soon to allow this.

Hood, marked with red, white and blue stripes to indicate her neutrality, was part of the international force which intervened in the Spanish Civil War. On St George's Day, 1937, *Hood* covered a convoy of three British merchant ships as they delivered food to the besieged population of Bilbao and evacuated refugees, training her guns on the Spanish Nationalist cruiser *Almirante Cervera* as she did so.

At the outbreak of World War II *Hood* was with the Home Fleet at Scapa Flow, taking part in the chase of *Scharnhorst* and *Gneisenau*, and escorting convoys in the North Atlantic. In June 1940 she was attached to Force H, the British force established at Gibraltar after the collapse of France and their commitment to defend the western Mediterranean. On July 3,

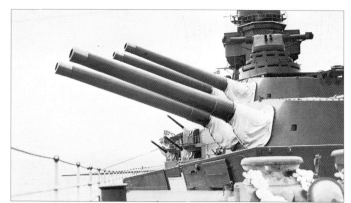

RIGHT: *Hood*'s main 380mm/15in guns and secondary armament trained out to starboard. BELOW: Two sailors demonstrating loading drill on a 100mm/4in anti-aircraft gun. BELOW RIGHT: Nearly all battleships of the period had underwater torpedo tubes. Although much vaunted they were little used. BOTTOM RIGHT: *Hood*'s crew of nearly 1,500 men required mass-catering on her mess deck.

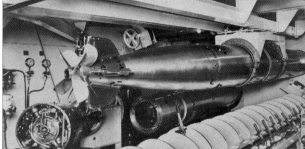

1940, Force H opened fire on the French fleet at Mers-el-Kebir where the battleship *Bretagne* was blown up and *Provence* and *Dunkerque* were badly damaged.

In May 1941 *Hood* and the new *Prince of Wales* formed Vice Admiral Holland's Battle Cruiser Force sent to intercept the even newer German battleship *Bismarck* and the heavy cruiser *Prinz Eugen* as they made their breakout into the Atlantic. The Germans were found by the patrolling cruisers *Norfolk* and *Suffolk* and shadowed on radar. Reports by wireless enabled Holland to bring his ships into action on the morning of May 24 in the Denmark Strait, between Iceland and Greenland. Both sides opened fire shortly before 06.00 hours but as Holland closed the range *Bismarck*'s fifth salvo hit *Hood* amidships, starting a fire in her 100mm/4in ammunition. The fire spread to the main magazine, causing a catastrophic explosion which tore through the ship, breaking her hull in several places. Only three of her 1,418 ship's company survived.

The news shocked the British and the Prime Minister Winston Churchill ordered that "*Bismarck* must be sunk at all costs". The German ship had been damaged in the brief exchange of shot with *Hood* and *Prince of Wales*; two days later she was crippled by aircraft from the carrier *Ark Royal*, wrecked by the battleships *King George V* and *Rodney* on the morning of May 27, and finally despatched by torpedoes. Revenge was complete and commerce raiding by German surface warships was brought to an end.

Hood

Class: *Hood*. Launched 1918
Dimensions: Length – 262m/860ft
   Beam – 32m/105ft
   Draught – 8.7m/28ft 6in
Displacement: 43,355 tonnes/42,670 tons
Armament: Main – 8 x 380mm/15in guns
   Secondary – 12 x 140mm/5.5in, 4 x 100mm/4in
   guns and 6 x 535mm/21in torpedoes
Machinery: 24 boilers, 4 shafts.
   107,381kW/144,000shp
Speed: 31 knots
Complement: 1,477 men

Queen Elizabeth – modernized

The Queen Elizabeth class was reconstructed between the wars, emerging from the modernization with a single funnel, improved deck armour, additional anti-aircraft guns, and a hangar and catapult for two seaplanes.

In 1941 *Queen Elizabeth* joined the British Mediterranean Fleet at Alexandria where on December 19, 1941, she and *Valiant* were attacked by Italian frogmen. Both ships settled on an even keel and the extent of the damage was kept secret. *Queen Elizabeth* was repaired at Norfolk, Virginia, and *Valiant* at Durban in 1943, and later both ships bombarded Japanese positions in the Dutch East Indies. *Queen Elizabeth* was scrapped in Scotland in July 1945.

Valiant was modernized in 1929–30 and again in 1937–9, and in World War II served in every theatre of war: she took part in the Norway campaign in Spring 1940; she exchanged fire with the French battleship *Richelieu* at Dakar in September 1940 during an operation to put De Gaulle in power there; she fought at the Battles of Cape Matapan in March and Crete in May 1941; and provided covering fire during the Allied landings on Sicily in July and at Salerno in September 1943. In August 1944, *Valiant* was in dry dock at Trincomalee in Ceylon (now Sri Lanka) when the dock collapsed. She was never fully repaired and was sold for scrap in 1948.

At the Second Battle of Narvik in April 1940 *Warspite* led a flotilla of destroyers into the fjord where eight German destroyers and a U-boat were sunk. At the Battle of Calabria in July 1940, a single shot from *Warspite* hit the Italian battleship *Giulio Cesare* at nearly 24km/15 miles range and the Italian fleet retreated, however *Warspite* was too slow to catch up. At the Battle of Matapan in March 1941, *Warspite* sank two heavy cruisers. In the battle for Crete she was bombed and was sent to Puget Sound for repairs. In 1942 she was flagship of Force A in the Indian Ocean which brushed with Admiral Nagumo's Japanese fleet. She was hit by a German glider bomb during the Allied landings at Salerno in 1943, putting X turret out of action. Nevertheless, she bombarded the coast during the Normandy landings and again at Walcheren in 1944. *Warspite* was sold for scrap in early 1947, but broke her tow and ran aground in Mounts Bay, Cornwall, where she was eventually broken up.

On December 28, 1939, *Barham* was torpedoed by *U-30*, but repaired in Liverpool. She joined the Mediterranean Fleet and at the Battle of Matapan, she sank the Italian cruiser *Zara* and the destroyer *Alfieri* on the night of March 28, 1941. In May of that year, *Barham* was again severely damaged off Crete and repaired at Durban. Finally her luck ran out and on November 25, 1941, she was torpedoed by *U-331*. The German submarine was returning from having landed a small patrol to blow up a railway bridge on the Egyptian coast and her meeting with the *Barham* was by chance, her commanding officer doing well to get in a snap attack. *Barham* was hit by three torpedoes and within five minutes had rolled over to port,

LEFT: **An aerial view of one of the Queen Elizabeth class at anchor in Weymouth Bay: the number of small craft alongside and the work on deck hint at the logistic effort which each battleship needed, even in peacetime.** BELOW: **A multiple pom-pom or "Chicago piano" was retrofitted to many battleships for anti-aircraft defence. Note that the seamen wear knives on lanyards as their ancestors did in the age of sail.**

Queen Elizabeth class

Class: *Queen Elizabeth, Warspite, Valiant, Barham, Malaya.* Launched 1913–15
Dimensions: Length – 197m/645ft 9in
Beam – 27.6m/90ft 6in
Draught – 8.8m/28ft 9in
Displacement: 27,940 tonnes/27,500 tons
Armament: Main – 8 x 380mm/15in guns
in four twin turrets
Secondary – 16 x 150mm/6in, 2 x 75mm/3in
and 4 x 3pdr guns
Machinery: 24 boilers, 4 shafts.
55,928kW/75,000shp
Speed: 25 knots
Complement: 925 men
All ships of the class were extensively rebuilt
between the wars, and anti-aircraft
armament improved.

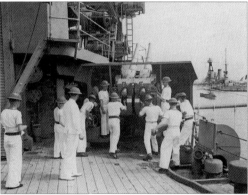

one or more of her magazines blew up and she sank with the loss of more than two-thirds of her crew. Cunningham acknowledged that the sinking of *Barham* was a most daring and brilliant performance on the part of the U-boat. He described the sinking:

> I saw the Barham, *immediately astern of us, stopped and listing heavily over to port. The poor ship rolled nearly over on to her beam ends, and we saw men massing on her upturned side. A minute or two later there came the deep rumble of a terrific explosion as one of her main magazines blew up. The ship became completely hidden in a great cloud of yellowish-black smoke, which went on wreathing and eddying high into the sky. When it cleared away the* Barham *had disappeared. There was nothing but a bubbling, oily-looking patch on the calm surface of the sea, dotted with wreckage and the heads of swimmers. It was ghastly to look at, a horrible and awe-inspiring spectacle when one realized what it meant.*

TOP: **The end of *Barham*, torpedoed off Sollum on November 25, 1941.** ABOVE LEFT: **A gun crew at a drill while at anchor in Alexandria, 1940. The French battleship in the background would later be demilitarized.** ABOVE: **Even a 30,481-tonne/ 30,000-ton battleship could be moved by the waves. If the length matched the frequency of a wave, even a large ship could be moved like this.**

Malaya alone did not receive the second major refit like her sisters. She was at the Battle of Calabria, and then employed on escort duties in the North Atlantic. In March 1941, while escorting convoy SL67, *Malaya*'s aircraft spotted *Scharnhorst* and *Gneisenau* off the Cape Verde Islands, which turned away. Later she was torpedoed off the coast of West Africa by *U-106* and steamed to the USA for repairs. She ended her life moored in a Scottish loch as a stationary target for the RAF and was scrapped in 1948. *Malaya*'s ship's bell hangs in the East India Club, London.

Royal Sovereign class

Also known as the Revenge class, these ships were progressively modernized during their lives. *Revenge* and *Royal Oak* were the only ships of this class at the Battle of Jutland. They were envisaged as smaller versions of the Queen Elizabeths, designed to use coal or oil to fire the boilers. During and immediately after World War I the class received anti-torpedo bulges which increased their beam to 31m/102ft, director fire-control for the secondary armament, and flying-off ramps over B and X turrets. In the inter-war years various 150mm/6in guns were removed and replaced by 100mm/4in high-angle anti-aircraft guns. By 1939 the torpedo tubes and aircraft platforms were removed and anti-aircraft armament increased by two and later three octuple 2pdr mountings. Also the deck armour over the magazines was increased to 100mm/4in thickness. *Resistance*, *Renown* and *Repulse* were cancelled in 1914, but the steel which had been assembled for the latter two was used for two new battlecruisers of the same names. As a class they were too slow to be effective in World War II.

Ramillies and *Revenge* were deployed to Izmir during the brief Turko-Greek war after World War I. In 1939 *Ramillies* escorted troop convoys in the Channel and in 1940 in the Indian Ocean. On August 18, 1940, she bombarded Bardia, and in November fought at the Battle of Cape Spartivento while transferring from Alexandria to Gibraltar. She was escorting convoy HX106 when she was sighted by *Scharnhorst* and *Gneisenau* on February 8, 1941, and they turned away.

In May 1941 she took part in the hunt for *Bismarck*. By May 1942 she was back in the Indian Ocean where she bombarded Diego Suarez, but on May 20 she was torpedoed by a Japanese midget submarine. Repaired at Durban and at

TOP: *Royal Sovereign* entering Malta in April 1935. Malta was the kingpin of British strategy in the central Mediterranean where the British had had interests since the 1600s. ABOVE: Three pictures on these two pages show the different camouflage schemes in use. These were intended not to disguise the ships but to fool the enemy's optical rangefinders. Here *Resolution* is in wartime camouflage in May 1942.

Devonport, *Ramillies* bombarded German positions during D-Day and the Allied landings in southern France. She was sold for scrapping in 1948.

Revenge carried British bullion reserves to Canada in 1939 and escorted Canadian troopships back to England. In September 1940 *Revenge* bombarded Cherbourg to interrupt German preparations for Operation Sealion, the invasion of Britain. *Revenge* sailed from Halifax, Nova Scotia, to participate in the hunt for *Bismarck*. After a year in the Indian Ocean, *Revenge* returned home to be taken out of service and was sold for scrap in 1948.

Resolution also took bullion to Canada. During the Norway Campaign on May 18, 1940, she was hit by a large bomb which penetrated three decks, but was soon repaired. As part of Force H she bombarded the French fleet at Mers-el-Kebir on July 3, 1940. She took part in operations against the Vichy French at Dakar when she was torpedoed by the French submarine *Bévéziers*. When repairs at Portsmouth became impossible because of German air raids she was sent to Philadelphia. *Resolution* then escorted troop convoys in the

Royal Sovereign class

Class: *Ramillies, Resolution, Revenge* (ex-*Renown*), *Royal Oak, Royal Sovereign.*
Launched 1914–16
Dimensions: Length – 190m/624ft
Beam – 27m/88ft 6in
Draught – 8.7m/28ft 6in
Displacement: 28,450 tonnes/28,000 tons
Armament: Main – 8 x 380mm/15in guns
Secondary – 14 x 150mm/6in guns and
4 x 535mm/21in torpedoes
Machinery: 18 boilers, 4 shafts.
29,828kW/40,000shp
Speed: 21 knots
Complement: 908–997 men

TOP: *Ramillies* in another camouflage scheme in 1943. ABOVE LEFT: *Royal Sovereign* in camouflage and now with radar fitted in 1943. ABOVE: *Royal Sovereign* in dry dock pre-war and clearly showing her hull shape. The availability of dry docks had strategic influence throughout the battleship era, and floating docks like this were important targets. When a floating dock collapsed in Trincomalee during World War II, the battleship in the dock was severely damaged.

Indian Ocean, but by early 1944 had become a training ship and was scrapped, also in 1948.

Royal Sovereign was in the Home Fleet during 1939 and on Atlantic convoy duty in 1940–1. She was part of the British Mediterranean Fleet at the Battle of Punto Stilo on July 18, 1940, when Cunningham, with the battleships *Warspite*, *Malaya*, *Royal Sovereign*, and the carrier *Eagle*, met the two Italian battleships *Giulio Cesare* and *Conte di Cavour*. *Warspite* hit *Giulio Cesare* at long range, but Cunningham was hampered by the slow speed of *Malaya* and *Royal Sovereign*, though he pursued the Italians to within 80km/50 miles of the coast of Calabria. *Royal Sovereign* spent 1942–3 refitting in the USA after just one month in the Indian Ocean and then returned home. On May 30, 1944, *Royal Sovereign* was loaned to the Soviet navy and renamed *Arkhangelsk*. She was returned in 1949 and subsequently scrapped.

Royal Oak was sunk at Scapa Flow on October 14, 1939, by the German submarine *U-47*, when 833 men were killed, the wreck subsequently being preserved as a war grave. Recently, divers have worked on the wreck to prevent leaking oil tanks causing pollution.

One 380mm/15in gun from *Resolution* and another from *Ramillies* are displayed outside the Imperial War Museum in London.

Battle of Cape Spartivento

Operation Collar aimed to pass a fast convoy eastward through the Mediterranean, which Admiral Somerville with Force H from Gibraltar would cover with the battlecruiser *Renown* and the carrier *Ark Royal*. Meanwhile aircraft carriers of the British Mediterranean Fleet would raid targets as far apart as Tripoli and Rhodes, and pass the battleship *Ramillies* through the Mediterranean from east to west. Despite their setback at Taranto earlier in November 1940, the Italian navy was still a significant force, and when *Ramillies* was about to join Force H off the coast of southern Sardinia, Somerville encountered a superior Italian fleet including the battleships *Vittorio Veneto* and *Giulio Cesare* and several cruisers.

The Battle of Cape Spartivento, or Tuelada as it is known to the Italians, started with Somerville chasing towards the Italians, but he was hampered by the slow speed of *Ramillies*, and though shots were exchanged at long range, the British could not overhaul the faster enemy. Air strikes also failed to slow the Italians down. The battle ended when Somerville felt obliged to turn back from the Italian coast to protect the convoy. Curiously the British Admiralty ordered a board of enquiry for not continuing the pursuit of the Italians, but Somerville was exonerated.

LEFT: *Nelson* **in the Thames for the Silver Jubilee in 1977. Ships of the fleet were anchored at various ports in the Thames to show themselves off to their public. The odd layout of these ships gave them a peculiar profile from wherever they were viewed.**
ABOVE: *Nelson* **and** *Rodney* **at sea together, bristling with guns.**

Nelson and *Rodney*

The Royal Navy had various proposals for fast battleships or battlecruisers at the end of World War I, and *Nelson* and *Rodney* were lineal descendants of remarkable ships planned under the designation "G3". These plans were cancelled following the Washington Naval Treaty, but revived as heavy battleships incorporating the lessons learned in the war. However, the restriction on displacement to 35,560 tonnes/ 35,000 tons standard (a measure now defined for the first time by treaty) was in part responsible for their unusual layout of guns, which was intended to reduce the length of the armoured belt. The planned 119,312kW/160,000shp giving 30 knots was also reduced and they had only a quarter of that horsepower and the low speed of barely 23 knots.

The design aimed to produce the heaviest armament and best protection possible for the least displacement. They were amongst the best armoured of all British battleships with an internal belt of armour 305–355mm/12–14in thick, inclined at 15 degrees to the vertical and extending from A turret to the after 150mm/6in guns. The armoured deck was 165mm/6.5in over the magazines and 95mm/3.75in thick over the machinery, not including the 25mm/1in plating underneath.

The internal bulges were designed to withstand a 340kg/ 750lb warhead, and comprised an empty outer chamber, a water-filled chamber, a 38mm/1.5in torpedo bulkhead inboard and another compartment to limit flooding if the torpedo

bulkhead was strained. *Nelson*'s armour was further increased in 1937–8. Triple drum boilers enabled the actual number of boilers to be reduced to eight.

The three triple turrets were all forward of the superstructure, with B turret at a higher level than A and C. The 150mm/6in guns on either beam repeated this arrangement. In World War II a large number of smaller-calibre guns were added, especially the octuple 2pdr known as a "Chicago piano" and single 20mm/0.79in guns. Initially the 405mm/16in guns suffered some mechanical problems which compared badly to the tried and tested British 380mm/15in gun, and the power-operated 150mm/6in and 120mm/4.7in guns were slow. The performance of all these guns had improved by the outbreak of World War II.

Some other navies copied features of *Nelson* and *Rodney*. On rebuild the USN's *Idaho, Mississippi* and *New Mexico* were given tower masts, the French *Dunkerque* and *Strasbourg* were given Nelson-like gun layouts, and the Japanese and Russian navies also toyed with similar designs.

In October 1939 when Germany tried to repeat a World War I tactic by sailing the battlecruiser *Gneisenau* and other ships to draw the Home Fleet within U-boat range, *Nelson* and *Rodney* with *Hood, Repulse, Royal Oak* and the carrier *Furious* searched but made no contact with the enemy. When the armed merchant cruiser *Rawalpindi* was sunk on November 23

ABOVE LEFT: The triple 405mm/16in guns of *Nelson* and her ship's company preparing for inspection. ABOVE RIGHT: *Nelson's* main armament at maximum elevation. LEFT: *Rodney*, an Admiral class battleship of 1884, showing how far battleship design had come in 50 years. BELOW: *Rodney* ammunitioning with 405mm/16in shells, a slow, cumbersome, manpower-intensive task and the techniques were little improved since the days of sail.

by *Scharnhorst* and *Gneisenau*, *Nelson* was one of the ships which prevented their breakout into the Atlantic, but returning to base she was damaged by a mine laid by *U-31* off Loch Ewe. Once repaired, *Nelson* joined Force H and was part of the escort for most of the important Malta-bound convoys in 1941 and 1942, although on September 27, 1941, during Operation Halberd, she was damaged by an Italian aircraft torpedo. *Nelson* was repaired well in time for Operation Torch, the Allied landing in North Africa in November 1942 and in July 1943. Together with *Rodney*, *Warspite* and *Valiant*, she was part of a fleet of over 2,500 American and British warships assembled for the invasion of Sicily.

One of the bombarding ships during the Normandy landings, *Nelson* was damaged by a mine on June 18, 1944. Repaired in Philadelphia, she briefly saw action in the Far East before becoming a training ship. She was used as a target ship in 1948 and scrapped in 1949.

Rodney had a similar wartime career to *Nelson*, except she took part in the Norway Campaign in 1940, where she was hit by a large bomb which penetrated three decks but did not explode. Her most famous action was the sinking of *Bismarck*. On May 27, 1941, *King George V* and *Rodney* caught up with the crippled German battleship and opening fire at about 08.45 reduced *Bismarck* to a wreck in an hour and a half, thus revenging the loss of *Hood*.

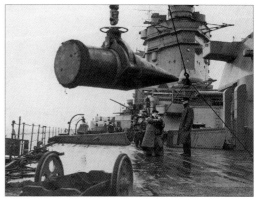

Nelson and *Rodney*

Class: *Nelson, Rodney*. Launched 1925
Dimensions: Length – 216m/710ft
 Beam – 32m/106ft
 Draught – 10m/33ft 6in
Displacement: 33,848 tonnes/33,313 tons
Armament: Main – 9 x 405mm/16in guns
 Secondary – 12 x 150mm/6in, 6 x 120mm/4.7in
 guns and 2 x 620mm/24.5in torpedoes
Machinery: 8 boilers, 2 shafts.
 33,557kW/45,000shp
Speed: 23 knots
Complement: 1,314 men
Rodney was larger at 33,370 tons and both ships at deep load were well over 40,000 tons

King George V class

The King George V class were designed just as the inter-war naval treaties expired, and the Royal Navy needed modern fast ships to match the German *Bismarck* and *Tirpitz*. The critical path for construction lay through the manufacture of guns, which the British had been trying to limit to 355mm/14in as they thought this the optimum size to fit into a treaty-sized 35,560-tonne/35,000-ton hull. The arrangement of two quadruple turrets, fore and aft, and a double turret in B position was a trade-off between armament and armour.

The secondary armament consisted of a new 130mm/5.25in dual-purpose gun mounted in eight twin power-operated turrets, and the other, lighter close-range anti-aircraft weaponry was upgraded during the war by fitting eight-barrelled pom-poms and 20mm/0.79in guns. Some ships were fitted with a rocket, which fired a trailing wire and an explosive

BELOW: **King George VI visiting the battleship named after his father "in northern waters" during World War II. A comparison (see opposite) with a similar view of an earlier ship of the same name shows how far warship construction and equipment had advanced in 20 years.**

charge, but this proved more dangerous to the firer than to any enemy aircraft. Armoured protection was better than in the Nelsons, including the anti-torpedo bulges being divided into a sandwich, the middle layer being used for fuel or water. They had four shafts each driven by an independent set of machinery, and space-saving Admiralty pattern three-drum boilers. Speed to catch the enemy was important, and the class was designed to reach 27.5 knots, 6 knots faster than *Nelson* and *Rodney*.

As a class they were commissioned in the war, decommissioned in the late 1940s and scrapped in 1957–8, a life of about 16 years. *King George V* was completed in October 1940 and in March 1941 covered a commando raid on the Lofoten islands. She then covered convoys in the North Atlantic and Arctic and, on May 27, 1941, while flagship of the British Home Fleet, she brought *Bismarck* to bay. Churchill had ordered that *Bismarck* must be sunk at all costs and suggested that this might mean towing *King George V* home, but the order was as unnecessary as it was unusual. She gave gunfire support during the landings on Sicily and at Salerno in 1943,

King George V class

Class: *King George V, Prince of Wales, Duke of York, Anson, Howe.* Launched 1939–40
Dimensions: Length – 227m/745ft
  Beam – 31m/103ft
  Draught – 8.9m/29ft
Displacement: 37,316 tonnes/36,727 tons
Armament: Main – 10 x 355mm/14in guns
  Secondary – 16 x 130mm/5.25in and
  32 x 2pdr guns
Machinery: 8 boilers, 4 shafts.
  82,027kW/110,000shp
Speed: 28 knots
Complement: 1,422 men

ABOVE FAR LEFT: **An aerial view of one of the class underway.** ABOVE LEFT: **King George VI is seen here inspecting his father's namesake.** LEFT: **By comparison the World War I battleship called *King George V* (scrapped in the 1920s) had torpedo nets, very little fire control equipment when first built, and a stern gallery which was a design feature left over from the days of sail. Radar, of course, was not available until World War II.**

and in December brought Churchill home from the Tehran Conference. *King George V* was refitted before joining the British Pacific Fleet in October 1944, and was in Tokyo Bay at the Japanese surrender on September 2, 1945.

Duke of York was ready for service in November 1941, was employed on Arctic convoys, and covered the landings in North Africa in October 1942. In December 1943 she was covering convoy JW55B when the German battlecruiser *Scharnhorst* sortied from her lair in the Norwegian fjords. On December 26, in appalling weather, *Duke of York*'s radar-controlled guns scored several hits on *Scharnhorst*, enabling the escorting cruisers to torpedo the German battlecruiser. *Duke of York* was flagship of the British Pacific Fleet at the Japanese surrender.

Howe covered Arctic convoys until May 1943, but in July she transferred to the Mediterranean for the invasion of Sicily. In 1944 she became flagship of the British Pacific Fleet during the Okinawa campaign, in the new role for the battleship of bombardment and providing an anti-aircraft umbrella for the fleet. In June 1945 she was sent into dock at Durban and so missed the Japanese surrender. *Anson* covered Arctic convoys until June 1944, when she was sent to Plymouth for refit. In

April 1945 *Anson* and the *Duke of York* sailed for the Far East and on August 30, 1945, *Anson* helped liberate Hong Kong two days before the formal Japanese surrender at Tokyo. *Anson* never fired her 355mm/14in guns in anger.

When *Bismarck* escaped from the Norwegian fjords into the Atlantic she was intercepted, on May 24, 1941, in the Denmark Strait by *Hood* and *Prince of Wales*. *Hood* blew up after a brief engagement. *Bismarck* shifted her fire on to *Prince of Wales* and damaged her, but not before *Prince of Wales* had hit *Bismarck,* causing damage and fuel leaks which led eventually to the German ship's demise.

In August 1941, *Prince of Wales* took Churchill across the Atlantic to meet President Roosevelt in Newfoundland, where together they drafted the first Atlantic Charter. Later that year *Prince of Wales* together with *Repulse* formed Force Z at Singapore, which sailed to stop Japanese troops landing on the Malay coast. On December 10, 1941, Force Z was overwhelmed by Japanese bombers and torpedo aircraft: they were the last two American or British capital ships in the Pacific. Following Pearl Harbor, air power, which the British Fleet Air Arm had done so much to develop in the Mediterranean, had truly come of age.

Lion class and *Vanguard*

This four-ship class of battleships was an enlarged version of the King George V class and was contemplated pre-war with two ships, *Lion* and *Temeraire*, being laid down in 1939. Under the London Naval Treaty these ships would have had 405mm/16in guns on a 45,720-tonne/45,000-ton displacement. Similar in layout and silhouette the Lion class would have had a transom stern, an armoured conning tower and a pole mainmast. The turbines and boilers were arranged as in *King George V*, but the 405mm/16in gun would have been a development over *Nelson*'s guns, with a shell 15 per cent heavier. Construction was suspended on the outbreak of World War II and cancelled in 1943–4. The Royal Navy realized very early that the era of the battleship was drawing to a close.

Vanguard was the last battleship to be built for the Royal Navy. Built on Clydebank, she was launched on November 30, 1944, but did not serve in the war. She was the biggest British battleship with a deep load displacement of 51,820 tonnes/51,000 tons. Her guns were reputedly those of *Glorious* and *Courageous* and had been in storage since the 1920s when it was decided to convert the ships to aircraft carriers.

The heavy anti-aircraft armament was what might be expected for war in the Pacific, but soon after the end of World War II many of the single 40mm/1.57in guns were removed. In 1947, when *Vanguard* took part in a royal tour to South Africa by King George VI, the anti-aircraft mounting above B turret was replaced by a reviewing platform.

Vanguard was refitted at Devonport in 1947–8, and then used as a training ship at Portsmouth where she became something of a fixture. She was sold for scrapping in 1960, and thousands of people gathered to wave farewell to this icon of British sea power on August 6. As *Vanguard* was being towed out through the narrow entrance to Portsmouth harbour, she broke free of her tugs and threatened to crash into a public house on the Portsmouth side and cut through the Custom House jetty. However she ran aground. She was towed off later that day, and finally scrapped at Faslane just a few miles from Clydebank where she was built. This was the end of an era. For reasons of cost, manpower, technical advance and operations, the world's greatest navy gave up the construction of battleships forever.

ABOVE: *Vanguard*, the last battleship of a long line in the Royal Navy – although outwardly different, she was similar to the King George V class. TOP LEFT: A handsome picture of *Vanguard* from the air. TOP RIGHT: *Vanguard* from the stern, a view which the architect seems to have neglected, but the transom stern was intended to increase her length and, with a pronounced sheer to the bow, to give her better seagoing qualities. RIGHT: *Vanguard* dressed overall and beautifully framed.

Vanguard

Class: *Vanguard.* Launched 1944
Dimensions: Length – 248m/814ft 4in
  Beam – 33m/108ft
  Draught – 9.4m/30ft 9in
Displacement: 45,215 tonnes/44,500 tons
Armament: Main – 8 x 380mm/15in guns
  Secondary – 16 x 130mm/5.25in and
  73 x 40mm/1.57in guns
Machinery: 8 boilers, 4 shafts.
  96,941kW/130,000shp
Speed: 30 knots
Complement: 1,893 men

Colorado class

Four ships were ordered in 1916 and were completed in the 1920s, apart from *Washington*, which was never finished, and represented the first 405mm/16in battleships of the USN. Apart from the size of the guns, the design and layout of the Colorado class were an evolution of the Tennessee class, and like all USN battleships were characterized by lattice masts. *Maryland* was the first American battleship to be fitted with a catapult. Later these ships carried three catapults, two on the quarterdeck and one on X turret.

Modernization for all three ships was approved in 1939, but rising tension worldwide delayed this until 1941. Modernization had started at Puget Sound on *Colorado*, when *Maryland* and *West Virginia* were sunk at Pearl Harbor, but both were raised and also went to Puget Sound for their delayed modernizations. They emerged in 1942 with additional armour and anti-torpedo bulges. Further refits during the war progressively improved the radars, gunnery directors and anti-aircraft armament.

Colorado returned after her refit to Pearl Harbor in August 1942. From December 1942 to September 1943 she was deployed in the New Hebrides and the Fiji islands as part of a blocking force against further Japanese expansion. In November 1943 she provided gunfire support for the American landings on Tarawa, and was then sent back to the USA for a further upgrade. During early 1944 *Colorado* covered landing operations at Kwajalein, Eniwetok, Saipan, Guam and Tinian. At Tinian on July 24, shore batteries found her range and she

ABOVE: *Colorado* passes under the Golden Gate bridge into San Francisco in 1945. This iconic scene was repeated many times over – and continues to be so – but for many ships at the end of World War II it was also a last scene as the USN was run down and ships placed in reserve during the post-war period.

was hit 22 times. Repaired on the West Coast, *Colorado* arrived in Leyte Gulf where on November 27 she was hit by two kamikazes. Many of the ship's crew were killed or wounded and the attack caused extensive damage. Nevertheless, a few days later she bombarded Mindoro in December before going to Manus Island for temporary repairs. Off Luzon in January 1945, *Colorado* bombarded Japanese positions in Lingayen Gulf where she was hit once more. In April and May 1945 *Colorado* covered the invasion of Okinawa and in August and September was in Tokyo Bay. At the end of the war, in a repeat of the use of USN battleships after World War I, *Colorado* made "magic carpet" voyages, bringing over 6,000 troops home. She was placed in reserve in 1947 and sold for scrapping in 1959.

At Pearl Harbor *Maryland* was berthed inboard of *Oklahoma* and thus was protected from the fury of the attack. Although hit by bombs she was able to steam to Puget Sound after temporary repairs. The pattern of employment for all this class of ships was dictated by their age and lack of speed, and since they were too slow to operate with the aircraft carriers, *Maryland*, though repaired at Puget Sound in two months, missed the main actions of the Battle of Midway. Later

TOP LEFT: A Colorado class battleship, with storeships alongside, is preparing for her next action. This picture is reminiscent of many others: battleships with their huge crews were hungry beasts with a constant demand for stores. ABOVE: *Maryland* firing point-blank during the bombardment of Tarawa.
LEFT: *Colorado* firing her 405mm/16in guns to starboard, sometime in the 1940s. Note how the technique of lattice mast construction has been retained. BELOW: Skills like signalling with flags survived even the age of the battleship. One sailor is sending semaphore and another is reading a message: in ideal conditions this method could be used at the extremes of visibility.

Maryland joined *Colorado* in protecting the routes to Australia through the Fiji islands and the New Hebrides. Her main role during the extensive amphibious campaigning in the Pacific was to provide gunfire support, as she did at Tarawa in the Gilberts, at Kwajalein Atoll in the Marshalls and at Saipan.

On June 22, 1944, while at anchor off Saipan, a Japanese aircraft missed *Pennsylvania* but torpedoed *Maryland*, opening a gaping hole in her side. Nevertheless she was repaired at Pearl Harbor within two months and was ready to cover beach clearance operations in the Palau islands.

On October 25,1944, *Maryland* took part in the Battle of Surigao, part of the larger Battle of Leyte Gulf, when the Japanese battleships *Fuso* and *Yamashiro* tried to force the straits. The Japanese were detected by a layered defence of torpedo boats, destroyers, cruisers and battleships, and the remnants of the Japanese force were then annihilated by naval aircraft.

In November *Maryland* was hit by a kamikaze plane which crashed between A and B turrets. Again repaired at Pearl Harbor, *Maryland* was back for the Okinawa campaign, where on April 7, a kamikaze plane hit her, this time on X turret causing heavy casualties, especially amongst the exposed 20mm/0.79in gunners. *Maryland* was sent back to Puget Sound for permanent repairs and was there on VJ-Day. On the "magic carpet" run she brought back more than 8,000 troops. Placed in reserve in 1947, *Maryland* was scrapped in 1959.

Colorado class (continued)

At Pearl Harbor on December 7, 1941, *West Virginia* lay in battleship row, berthed outboard of *Tennessee*, where in the first waves of attack she was hit by seven 455mm/18in aircraft torpedoes in her port side and two bombs. The bombs caused fires and the detonation of ammunition, wrecking two of *West Virginia*'s aircraft and setting light to their aviation fuel. The torpedoes badly damaged the port side but prompt damage control prevented her capsizing. *West Virginia*'s captain was killed by shrapnel from a bomb landing on *Tennessee*. *West Virginia* settled on an even keel and fires drove her crew off the ship: others were trapped below decks and suffered a lingering death. The fires were only subdued after 24 hours and she was refloated six months later to be rebuilt at Puget Sound over the next two years.

Like her sisters, the lattice masts were removed, a new superstructure was fitted and a very large number of 40mm/1.57in and 20mm/0.79in anti-aircraft guns fitted. The 125mm/5in guns in casemates were also replaced by dual-purpose 125mm/5in guns in turrets. The two funnels were trunked into one, giving *West Virginia* a very different silhouette to other ships of the class.

At the Battle of Surigao *West Virginia* led *Maryland*, *Mississippi*, *Tennessee*, *California* and *Pennsylvania* in a line that, for the last time in history, crossed the T of the enemy's line, and sank the Japanese battleship *Fuso*. Other operations included covering the landings in Lingayen Bay and the invasions of Iwo Jima and Okinawa, finishing in Tokyo Bay on August 31, 1945. After this *West Virginia* played host to thousands of visitors for Navy Day on October 27 in San Diego,

ABOVE: **A dramatic picture of *Maryland* in the thick of action in November 1944. The action was not at night, but the brightness of the explosion on *Maryland*'s forecastle has resulted in the film being under-exposed. Nevertheless, the melodramatic mood of the picture is accurate.**

and was part of the "magic carpet" bringing home thousands of US servicemen. The "Wee Vee" was decommissioned in the late 1940s and sold for scrapping in 1959.

The Battle of Leyte Gulf

This action arose from a Japanese attempt to interrupt American troop-landings there. A Northern Decoy Force with four carriers (but not many aircraft) and two partially converted battleship-carriers steamed south from Japan. A Centre Strike Force including five battleships closed Leyte Gulf from the north-west through San Bernadino Strait, while a Southern Strike Force including two battleships closed from the south-west through the Surigao Straits in a pincer.

On October 24, in the Battle of Sibuyan Sea, the Centre Strike Force was attacked by aircraft of the US Third Fleet, and the giant battleship *Musashi* was sunk. Next the Northern Decoy Force succeeded in luring the Third Fleet north leaving the San Bernadino Strait open, with only escort carriers and old battleships of the US Seventh Fleet to protect the landings.

Overnight on October 24/25, the Southern Strike Force of the battleships *Fuso* and *Yamashiro* entered the Surigao Strait where they suffered successive attacks from smaller ships, during which *Yamashiro* was lost. When *Fuso* met six US battleships formed into line she too was sunk.

LEFT: *West Virginia* on fire and aground after being torpedoed in battleship row, Pearl Harbor, 1941. BELOW: After the Japanese attack, *West Virginia* was raised and repaired and she is seen here in dry dock, June 1942. The recovery and repair of ships after the Japanese attack on Pearl Harbor became a matter of pride for the USN, even after it was realized that aircraft carriers were needed more than battleships.

ABOVE: The incomplete battleship *Washington* in 1922. She was destined to be sunk in experiments during 1924. The name was used in a new ship of a subsequent class.

Early on October 25, the remains of the Centre Strike Force with four battleships steamed through the San Bernardino Strait to attack the escort carriers and accompanying destroyers of the Seventh Fleet. Japanese surface ships and kamikaze aircraft sank or destroyed two escort carriers and several smaller ships, but just when the Centre Strike Force should have smashed the amphibious shipping, the Japanese turned away.

Meanwhile at the Battle of Cape Enga, aircraft of the US Third Fleet sank all the main units of the Northern Decoy Force, *Chitose*, *Chiyoda*, *Zuiho* and *Zuikaku*. Centre Strike Force, having failed in its objective, escaped from the returning US Third Fleet.

Colorado class

Class: *Maryland, Colorado, Washington, West Virginia*. Launched 1920–1
Dimensions: Length – 190m/624ft
  Beam – 29.7m/97ft 5in
  Draught – 9.2m/30ft 2in
Displacement: 33,123 tonnes/32,600 tons
Armament: Main – 8 x 405mm/16in guns
  Secondary – 12 x 125mm/5in, 8 x 75mm/3in guns and 2 x 535mm/21in torpedoes
Machinery: 8 boilers, 4 shafts. 19,985kW/26,800shp
Speed: 21 knots
Complement: 1,083 men

North Carolina class

The name North Carolina was taken from a ship ordered in 1917, laid down in 1920, but cancelled under the terms of the Washington Naval Treaty.

In the new *North Carolina* the armament was increased from 355mm/14in to 405mm/16in during their design, but too late to alter other features of the class. However, for the first time in a USN ship the guns were arranged two forward and one aft, with secondary armament in turrets. There were no scuttles in the hull and habitability suffered accordingly. Their hulls had to be strengthened after both ships experienced severe vibrations on trials and during World War II both were refitted, when they received enclosed bridges, improved radars, and a very large number of anti-aircraft guns. Post-war there were proposals to convert *North Carolina* and *Washington* into satellite launch ships, helicopter ships, or fast-replenishment ships but these came to nothing.

North Carolina was the first of her class to be built after the expiry of the Washington Naval Treaty in 1936. She was regarded as the first of the modern battleships, receiving so much publicity that she was nicknamed "Showboat".

When the Pearl Harbor attack took place *North Carolina* was undergoing trials off the East Coast of America. She entered the Pacific in June 1942 and covered the landings at Guadalcanal and Tulagi in August 1942. The USN had developed the concept of battle groups consisting of carriers and battleships, in which long-range strike capability was provided by the carrier's aircraft and the purpose of the battleship was as an anti-aircraft battery. In this role, *North Carolina* was on the screen of the aircraft carrier *Enterprise* during the Battle of the Solomons, August 23–25. During this

ABOVE: *North Carolina* photographed in 1941. The USN battleships of this class were the first to be built after the expiry of the Washington Treaty. This picture shows *North Carolina* as she was designed and built, but very soon afterwards she was taken in hand again and fitted with a massive anti-aircraft armament, radars and improved fire-control systems.

engagement *North Carolina* claimed to have shot down between seven and fourteen Japanese aircraft in one eight-minute action. On September 6, 1942, *North Carolina* was torpedoed by a Japanese submarine but she was repaired at Pearl Harbor and ready for action in November.

From then on *North Carolina*'s actions read like a roll call of the American island-hopping advance through the Pacific: Tarawa, Makin, Kwajalein, Majuro, Truk, Marianas, Palau, Yap, Ulithi, Woleai, Ponape, Satawan, New Guinea, Wake, Saipan and the Battle of the Philippine Sea.

In 1945 during preparations for the landings on Okinawa, *North Carolina* played the battleship's dual role of providing heavy bombardment and an anti-aircraft umbrella. On April 6 while under attack by kamikaze aircraft she was hit by friendly fire and needed repairs at Pearl Harbor before joining a carrier battle group for the attack on the Japanese home islands. In the final days of the assault she bombarded factories near Tokyo, and she landed seamen and marines ashore for "preliminary occupation duty".

North Carolina provided the "magic carpet" for troops on passage between Okinawa and the US East Coast, made one training cruise for midshipmen and was then deactivated. In 1961 she was given to the people of North Carolina, where she is now a museum ship at Wilmington.

LEFT: *North Carolina*'s launch in June 1940. ABOVE: *Washington*, equipped with all her wartime additions. BELOW LEFT: *North Carolina* on her maiden voyage, but apparently not yet fully fitted, showing off the elevation of her guns.

North Carolina class

Class: *North Carolina, Washington.* Launched 1940
Dimensions: Length – 222m/728ft 9in
  Beam – 33m/108ft 4in
  Draught – 10m/33ft
Displacement: 38,086 tonnes/37,484 tons
Armament: Main – 9 x 405mm/16in guns
  Secondary – 20 x 125mm/5in, 16 x 28mm/1.1in
  and 12 x 13mm/0.5in guns
Machinery: 8 boilers, 4 shafts.
  90,230kW/121,000shp
Speed: 28 knots
Complement: 1,880 men

A battleship named *Washington* was ordered in 1916 but cancelled in 1921 when the hull was already built, and she was sunk as a target in 1924. In the early part of 1942 the new battleship *Washington* was deployed in the North Atlantic and Arctic with the British Home Fleet. On May 1, *King George V* rammed the British destroyer *Punjabi*, cutting her in two, and *Washington* passed between the sinking halves while *Punjabi*'s depth charges exploded beneath her. *Washington* escaped with only a minor leak and whip damage to her fire-control radars.

In August 1942 *Washington* entered the Pacific, and on the night of November 14–15 took part in a battle off Savo Island. The Japanese were trying to reprovision their positions at Guadalcanal when *Washington* and *South Dakota* met the Japanese battleship *Kirishima* in a night action. *Kirishima* concentrated her fire on *South Dakota* who was forced to retire, but was badly damaged by *Washington*'s accurate radar-controlled gunnery and had to be scuttled the next

morning. This was the only battleship-to-battleship action that took place during World War II.

Washington was involved in another collision in February 1943 when she rammed *Indiana*, crumpling her bows. A temporary bow was fitted at Pearl Harbor and she was sent to Puget Sound for permanent repair. From then on *Washington* formed part of various carrier battle groups and took part in the Battle of the Philippine Sea in June 1944 when together with six other battleships, four heavy cruisers, and 14 destroyers she formed the screen.

Like other battleships, *Washington*'s anti-aircraft armament was steadily improved throughout the war until by the end she sported 15 x quadruple 40mm/1.57in, 1 x quadruple 20mm/0.79in, 8 x twin 20mm/0.79in, and 63 x single 20mm/0.79in guns. *Washington*'s last refit carried her through VJ-Day and she made only one brief sortie into the Pacific before being sent to Europe to bring troops home. She was decommissioned in 1947, and scrapped in 1961.

South Dakota class

This class generally resembled the North Carolinas but were shorter and more heavily armoured as they were designed to provide protection against 405mm/16in shells, but on the same displacement as the earlier ships, and with the same speed and armament. Two ships were planned and two more added to the programme at the outbreak of World War II in Europe. Underwater, the outboard propeller shafts were encased in fins and the inboard shafts were placed entirely between the fins. Overall the design was rather cramped, causing problems of habitability between decks and operationally for the placing of anti-aircraft guns around the superstructure. All four ships were ready for service in 1942.

During the war the 28mm/1.1in and 13mm/0.5in anti-aircraft guns were replaced with larger numbers of 40mm/1.57in and 20mm/0.79in weapons. In addition, the radar suite was upgraded and the bridges were enclosed. Like other battleships post-war plans were made for conversion to missile ships, satellite launch ships, helicopter assault ships, and fast replenishment ships, but none of these ideas came to fruition.

South Dakota was fitted as a force flagship and her conning tower was one level higher than other ships of the class, compensating for the extra weight by having two fewer 125mm/5in guns and an extra pair of quadruple 28mm/1.1in guns. She made an inauspicious start on September 6, 1942, when she struck an uncharted pinnacle in Lahai Passage and suffered extensive damage to her hull needing several weeks of repairs at Pearl Harbor.

In October 1942 South Dakota was part of a battle group centred on the carriers Enterprise and Hornet which met a much larger Japanese carrier force preparing for a major assault on Henderson Field. In what became known as the

TOP: *South Dakota* taken on August 9, 1943. In this picture *South Dakota*'s anti-aircraft armament has been greatly increased over her original design. ABOVE: *South Dakota* in line astern somewhere in the Pacific in 1945. There was no other formation in which the number of guns bearing on a target could be maximized.

Battle of Santa Cruz, Hornet was sunk and Enterprise was temporarily put out of action while the Japanese carrier Shokaku was damaged. While protecting Enterprise during the third wave of air attacks, South Dakota was hit on her A turret by a 227kg/500lb bomb, but she was also credited with having shot down 26 Japanese planes.

On October 30, South Dakota and the destroyer Mahan were in collision and South Dakota's bows crumpled, requiring a repair at Noumea. However, by November 13, 1942, she was able to join the battleship Washington and four destroyers for a night sweep off Guadalcanal, while a Japanese flotilla consisting of the battleship Kirishima, several cruisers and destroyers were approaching to bombard Henderson Field.

In the moonlight of November 14/15, the enemy were sighted from South Dakota at a range of 16,550m/18,100yds. Washington opened fire shortly before South Dakota and the salvoes from both ships straddled the Japanese. South Dakota then fired on another target until it disappeared from her radar screen. As South Dakota's after main turret fired on a third target, it demolished her own planes, whilst her 125mm/5in

TOP LEFT: **Colours on the last evening as** *South Dakota* **is decommissioned (the guns under the dome are already "mothballed").** ABOVE: *South Dakota* **manoeuvring while under air attack from a Japanese Kamikaze aircraft.** FAR LEFT: **The guns of** *Indiana* **on commissioning day, April 30, 1942.** LEFT: **One of the South Dakota class firing her broadside at a shore target. Despite all the investment in battleships, this and anti-aircraft defence was, at the end of their era, their principal role.**

guns engaged targets close inshore, thought to be enemy destroyers. *South Dakota* was then illuminated by searchlight at about 5,485m/6,000yds from ships as they cleared Savo Island, and she came under fire from several warships including the battleship *Kirishima*, taking considerable damage. A fire started in the foremast, she lost power temporarily, her radios failed, her radars and radar plot were demolished, and, as she turned away from the onslaught, she lost track of her consort. *Washington* continued the engagement, damaging *Kirishima* so badly that the Japanese scuttled her next morning. The Americans lost three destroyers, the Japanese cruisers *Takao* and *Atago* were hit and, besides *Kirishima*, the destroyer *Ayanami* was also scuttled.

South Dakota was again repaired at Noumea and she was sent to New York for refit in December 1942. For a few months she operated in the North Atlantic as convoy escort before returning to the Pacific in September 1943, where the actions she was involved in were the familiar roll-call of the American advance across the Pacific. On June 19, 1944, the first day of the Battle of the Philippine Sea, the battleship escorts were

placed so as to be able to continue supporting the army and marines on Saipan while being prepared to intercept a Japanese surface force which was known to be approaching from the west. *South Dakota* was hit during a heavy air raid by a 227kg/500lb bomb which penetrated the main deck, causing minor material damage but over 50 casualties. However, her damage control was sufficient to keep her in action until she was sent to Puget Sound for repair in July.

In May 1945, while loading ammunition from a stores ship, an explosion caused a fire and her magazines were flooded to prevent further damage. Then on July 14, *South Dakota* bombarded the Kamaishi Steel Works on Honshu, the first time that the home islands of Japan had been attacked by ships since the Royal Navy had bombarded Shimonseki and Kagoshima in the 19th century.

South Dakota was in Tokyo Bay for the formal Japanese surrender, leaving there on September 20, 1945, to be refitted in Philadelphia in 1946. In 1962, after 15 years in reserve, she was sold for scrapping. A wave of nostalgia meant that other ships of her vintage were preserved as museum ships.

South Dakota class (continued)

Indiana operated in the Pacific throughout World War II. From November 1942 to October 1943 she was part of a fast battle group based around the carriers *Enterprise* and *Saratoga* as the Americans advanced through the Solomons. In November 1943 she was part of the force which re-took the Gilbert Islands, and in January 1944 she bombarded Kwajalein for eight days prior to the landings there. However, on February 1 *Indiana* collided with the battleship *Washington* and needed repairs to her starboard side at Pearl Harbor.

In the Battle of the Philippine Sea, she bombarded Saipan on June 13–14 and on June 19 as four large air raids attacked the American ships, *Indiana* helped the other escorts and the carrier-based fighters shoot down 100 of the enemy in what was called the "Great Marianas Turkey Shoot". In the next months she bombarded targets on Palau and the Philippines, was refitted at Puget Sound, resumed her bombardment role at Iwo Jima and Ulithi, and screened the carriers during raids on Tokyo in February 1945. Between March and June 1945 she supported carrier operations against Japan and Okinawa,

BELOW: **The USN took part in amphibious operations in Europe as well as the Pacific. Here the *Massachusetts* prepares for Operation Torch off the coast of North Africa.**

riding out a terrible typhoon in June. In August she bombarded targets on the Japanese home islands, and on September 5 entered Tokyo Bay. Later she formed part of the Pacific Reserve Fleet until being sold for scrap in 1962. *Indiana*'s mast is erected at the University of Indiana in Bloomington and her anchor is on display at Fort Wayne.

Massachusetts was commissioned in May 1942 and supported the Allied landings in North Africa, Operation Torch, in November 1942. On November 8, off Casablanca, she silenced the guns of French battleship *Jean Bart* and sank two French destroyers. *Massachusetts* was then deployed to the Pacific, first covering the route through the Solomons to Australia, and then in November 1943 escorting the carrier strikes on the Gilbert Islands. In December she shelled Japanese positions on Nauru and in January she bombarded Kwajalein. Other operations followed at Truk, Saipan, Tinian, Guam and again at Truk, and she was at the Battle of Leyte Gulf in October 1944.

Massachusetts experienced the tremendous typhoon in December 1944, with winds estimated at 120 knots, in which three destroyers foundered. In June 1945 she passed through the eye of a typhoon with 100-knot winds. In July and August 1945 she shelled targets on the Japanese mainland, probably

firing in anger the last 405mm/16in shell of World War II on August 9. Since 1965, "Big Mamie", as she is known, has been a museum ship at Fall River, Massachusetts.

Alabama formed part of the British Home Fleet, based in Scapa Flow from May to August 1943, while British battleships were employed in the Mediterranean in support of the Allied landings on Sicily. In June, Alabama and her sister ship covered the reinforcement of Spitzbergen. In July, Alabama feinted at southern Norway aiming to reinforce German beliefs of a threatened landing there, and perhaps to lure the German battleship Tirpitz from her lair in the fjords.

By late 1943 Alabama was in the thick of the fighting in the Pacific, including the Battles of the Philippine Sea and Leyte Gulf, and the bombardment of Japan itself. On August 15, 1945, when the Japanese capitulated, Alabama's seamen and marines were among the first American forces to land.

Her war was over when she had retrieved her crew on September 5, in Tokyo Bay, and taken 700 members of the USN's construction battalion home from Okinawa, arriving in San Francisco on October 15, 1945. In 1962 Alabama became a museum ship at Mobile, Alabama.

TOP LEFT: **The brand-new Alabama in camouflage in December 1942.**
TOP RIGHT: **A stoker puts on a burner of one of Alabama's boilers.** ABOVE FAR LEFT: **A close-up of one of Alabama's 405mm/16in guns.** ABOVE LEFT: **Another view of the business end of Alabama.** ABOVE RIGHT: **Old and new technology. Two fire control radars, a direction-finding loop, and signal flags. Flag signals, under the right circumstances, were still a reliable and adequate means of sending orders.**

South Dakota class

Class: *South Dakota, Indiana, Massachusetts, Alabama.* Launched 1941–2
Dimensions: Length – 207m/680ft
 Beam – 33m/108ft
 Draught – 10.7m/35ft
Displacement: 38,580 tonnes/37,970 tons
Armament: Main – 9 x 405mm/16in guns
 Secondary – 20 x 125mm/5in and
 numerous lighter guns
Machinery: 8 boilers, 4 shafts.
 96,941kW/130,000shp
Speed: 27.5 knots
Complement: 1,793 men

LEFT: **Post-war much of the tertiary armament of anti-aircraft guns was removed to produce the clean lines of *Iowa*.** BELOW: **The business of ammunitioning ships did not however end. After a series of disastrous explosions earlier in the century caused by unstable ammunition, it was now normally inert, but was still stowed quickly.**

Iowa class and *Iowa*

The Iowas were the last class of battleships to be completed for the USN and were considered to be the best, certainly the fastest, and with their long forecastles, cowled funnels and relatively low silhouettes, among the most handsome of all their type. They were conceived as stretched versions of the South Dakotas, their length (60m/200ft longer) giving them 5 to 6 knots extra speed (despite an increase of 10,160 tonnes/ 10,000 tons standard displacement) and making them capable of protecting a force of fast carriers against the swift Japanese Kongo class battlecruisers.

The USN invoked the so-called escalator clause of the London Naval Treaty to exceed the 45,720-tonne/45,000-ton limit, and eventually the full load displacement of these ships was 58,460 tonnes/57,540 tons. Four ships were planned and two more added in January 1941 after the Japanese attack on Pearl Harbor in the previous month.

Although designed to counter Japanese heavy cruisers and battlecruisers, their principal roles were as command ships, in-shore bombardment, and, of course, operating in fast carrier battle groups as air defence ships for which they were fitted with a huge number of anti-aircraft guns (the actual numbers

varied from ship to ship). They underwent the same World War II modifications as other American battleships, including improved electronics, an enlarged and enclosed bridge and yet more anti-aircraft guns.

They were prestigious vessels capable of a number of tasks, but like nearly every other Dreadnought their war complement was much greater than their peacetime complement. *Iowa*, for example, carried 1,000 more men than her given number of 1,921. They were thus expensive ships to maintain in service and though recalled to service in Korea, Vietnam and the Gulf War for their bombardment capability, they were frequently placed in reserve.

When *New Jersey* was recalled for the Vietnam War, where the air threat was minimal, even though all of the 40mm/1.57in and 20mm/0.79in guns were removed, she still needed a complement of over 1,500 to man the main armament and the steam plant. Even when fitted with eight quadruple armoured boxed launchers for Tomahawk cruise missiles and four quadruple canisters for Harpoon surface-to-surface missiles, their very high manpower costs could not be justified. However, in testimony to the powerful iconic status of these

Iowa class

🇺🇸

Class: *Iowa, New Jersey, Missouri, Wisconsin, Illinois, Kentucky.*
Launched 1942–50
Dimensions: Length – 270m/887ft
  Beam – 33m/108ft
  Draught – 11m/36ft 2in
Displacement: 48,880 tonnes/48,110 tons
Armament: Main – 9 x 405mm/16in guns
  Secondary – 20 x 125mm/5in, 80 x
  40mm/1.57in and 50 x 20mm/0.79in guns
Machinery: 8 boilers, 4 shafts.
  158,088kW/212,000shp
Speed: 33 knots
Complement: 1,921 men

ABOVE: *Iowa* firing her main armament. LEFT: The fire and smoke of a broadside. There was noise too. RIGHT: The blast effect can clearly be seen on the surface of the sea. There was always a risk of self-inflicted damage from blast. These two aerial photographs show, by the flattening of the water around *Iowa*, how far the blast effect reached.

ships, even in the late 1990s some of them were notionally held in reserve, though there was very little probability of them returning to service.

Besides Tomahawk and Harpoon missiles and modern close-in weapons systems, other options included designating them as BBGs or guided-missile battleships but it was realized that the missiles were unlikely to withstand the blast effects of the 405mm/16in guns. They were not modernized for the Korean War, but in the 1980s the electronics were upgraded, the catapults and aircraft were replaced with limited helicopter facilities, and drone launch and recovery systems were fitted. The aircraft crane was suppressed and habitability was improved. They were not, however, refitted as flagships.

As a class they were finally decommissioned in 1990–2. *New Jersey* and *Wisconsin* both still had reserve status in 1996, but *New Jersey* was stricken in 1999 to allow her to become a museum at Camden, New Jersey, and *Wisconsin* is a "museum-in-reserve" at Norfolk, Virginia. *Missouri* is a museum at Pearl Harbor, and *Iowa*, who has been robbed for spares for the other ships, lies at Suisun Bay, California, awaiting preservation.

Iowa was specially fitted as a flagship and her conning tower was one deck higher than her sisters, who nevertheless proved equally capable of the role. She was damaged by grounding on her trials and repaired at Boston. She took President Franklin D. Roosevelt to Casablanca in 1943 on his way to the Tehran Conference, and when she had brought him back she transferred to the Pacific where she operated in support of fast-carrier task forces for the remainder of the war. *Iowa* also bombarded the Japanese home islands in July 1945 and she entered Tokyo Bay with the occupation forces on August 29, 1945.

Iowa was placed in reserve in 1949, re-commissioned in 1951–8, and made one deployment in the Korean War when she bombarded North Korean positions. She was modernized and commissioned again in 1984, but in 1989 her B turret was damaged by an internal explosion, and the centre gun was never restored. Despite being used for spares, she was reinstated on the register of naval vessels in 1999, but after years lying at Philadelphia she was towed to California to be a museum. Besides the Mikasa in Japan, and some shipwrecks, all the preserved battleships of the modern era are in the USA.

New Jersey

The second *New Jersey*, and the first of three similar ships built in the same yard, was launched at the Philadelphia Naval Shipyard on the anniversary of the Japanese attack on Pearl Harbor. She transited the Panama Canal in January 1944 to join the US Fifth Fleet which was in the Ellis Islands, preparing for the assault on the Marshall Islands. Her first employment was screening a carrier task force as they flew strikes against Kwajalein and Eniwetok. On January 31, the Fifth Fleet landed troops on two atolls, the undefended Majuro and the bitterly defended Kwajalein. The stubborn Japanese defence continued well into the month, while US forces assaulted another atoll, Eniwetok, on January 17. When the Japanese threatened to mount relief operations by forces based at Truk 1,127km/700 miles away, *New Jersey*, now flagship of the Fifth Fleet, led a raid which successfully disrupted their operations.

In June *New Jersey* supported the American invasion of the Marianas. The Japanese fleet was ordered to annihilate the American invasion force, which led to the Battle of the Philippine Sea, also known as the "Marianas Turkey Shoot" because the Japanese lost so many of their aircraft. *New Jersey*'s role was in providing anti-aircraft close support to the

ABOVE: **USN battleships survived post-war and ships such as *New Jersey*, seen here with a modern suite of electronics, was used to bombard shore targets during the Vietnam War. Here *New Jersey*, photographed in March 1960, is seen firing on targets near Tuyho in central South Vietnam.**

carriers. The loss of some 400 aircraft, three carriers and many trained pilots was a disaster for the Japanese. Following this *New Jersey* became flagship of the Third Fleet as fast carrier task forces struck at targets throughout the theatre of war. In September the targets were in the Visayas and the southern Philippines, then Manila and Cavite, Panay, Negros, Leyte and Cebu. Raids on Okinawa and Formosa (now Taiwan) to debilitate enemy air power began in October in preparation for landings at Leyte.

This invasion brought about the last major sortie of the Imperial Japanese Navy in a three-pronged attack. In the Battle of Leyte, a Northern Decoy Force of carriers, though nearly bereft of aircraft, and two battleships succeeded in drawing away ships which should have been protecting the invasion beaches. This allowed the Japanese Centre and Southern Strike Forces to close Leyte Gulf through the San Bernardino Strait. Both were heavily damaged, but the Centre Strike Force,

RIGHT: *New Jersey* in the Pacific in November 1944. Compare the suite of aerials with those on the opposite page. BELOW: Long Beach Naval Shipyard, California. Overhead view of the aft deck of the battleship *New Jersey* in dry dock while undergoing refitting and reactivation. BELOW RIGHT: The perspective of this photograph emphasizes the long bow of this class of ships even more.

New Jersey

Class: *Iowa, New Jersey, Missouri, Wisconsin, Illinois, Kentucky.* Launched 1942–50
Dimensions: Length – 270m/887ft
  Beam – 33m/108ft
  Draught – 11m/36ft 2in
Displacement: 48,880 tonnes/48,110 tons
Armament: Main – 9 x 405mm/16in guns
  Secondary – 20 x 125mm/5in, 80 x
  40mm/1.57in and 50 x 20mm/0.79in guns
Machinery: 8 boilers, 4 shafts.
  158,088kW/212,000shp
Speed: 33 knots
Complement: 1,921 men

despite losing the giant battleship *Musashi*, entered the area of amphibious operations. Meanwhile *New Jersey* had gone north and although the Third Fleet sank the decoy force, the landings were at risk. *New Jersey* returned south at full speed, but the Centre Strike Force too had turned back and made its escape. Japan now intensified its suicide attacks and on October 27, in the mêlée which characterized mass kamikaze attacks, *New Jersey* damaged a plane, which crashed into the carrier *Intrepid* while anti-aircraft fire from *Intrepid* sprayed *New Jersey*.

In December 1944 *New Jersey* was part of the Lexington task force which attacked Luzon and then experienced the same typhoon which sank three destroyers.

New Jersey continued her roles at Iwo Jima and Okinawa and off Honshu before a refit at Puget Sound, and from September 17, 1945, to January 28, 1946, she was guardship in Tokyo Bay. Notably, by the end of the war, her anti-aircraft armament consisted of 20 x quadruple 40mm/1.57in, 8 x twin 20mm/0.79in, and 41 x single 20mm/0.79in guns.

Between periods in reserve *New Jersey* saw much post-war action. She twice deployed to Korea, in the familiar role of giving gunfire support ashore, though on several occasions the

Koreans reached her with their own shore batteries, and she also operated with Allied warships, notably the British cruiser *Belfast* and the Australian carrier *Sydney* in October 1951.

In the 1960s she was refitted for the Vietnam War, and in operations off the coast of Vietnam *New Jersey* fired some 3,000 405mm/16in shells.

New Jersey was also uniquely engaged in support of US marines in Beirut in February 1984 when she fired nearly 300 rounds into the surrounding hills. Proponents of the battleship argued that they still had a viable role and that with armour more than 305mm/12in thick in many places even an Exocet-type missile would bounce off.

In 1986 *New Jersey*'s deployment in the Pacific was used to support the case for the battleship battle group concept and the battleship modernization programme was validated. Consequently in 1987–8 *New Jersey* visited Korea prior to the Olympic Games, and Australia during the bicentennial there, and exercised in the Indian Ocean and the Gulf. She was decommissioned for the last time in 1991 at Bremerton, which had seen so many battleships during World War II. *New Jersey* opened as a museum ship and memorial in October 2001.

Missouri

Missouri, or the "Mighty Mo", was not ready until the very end of 1944. Her first operations were to escort the carriers of Task Force 58 on strikes on the Japanese islands, and to bombard Iwo Jima. In March 1945 she opened the Okinawa campaign by bombarding the island. During the Battle of the East China Sea, on April 7, Missouri was escorting the carriers of the US Fifth Fleet which sank the giant Japanese battleship *Yamato*, a cruiser and four destroyers.

In June and again in July *Missouri* and other ships bombarded Japanese industrial targets on the home islands, and by the end of July the Japanese no longer had control over their own sea and air space. On August 10, the Japanese sued for peace and while negotiations were underway the Commander-in-Chief of the British Pacific Fleet, Admiral Fraser, conferred an honorary knighthood on Admiral Halsey on August 16. On August 21, *Missouri* landed 200 men for duty with the initial occupation force and she entered Tokyo Bay on August 29, where the surrender took place onboard on September 2, 1945.

In the months immediately after the war, *Missouri* attended celebrations in New York, carried the remains of the Turkish ambassador to the USA to Istanbul, and balanced this with a

ABOVE RIGHT: *Missouri* in action. The area of disturbed water indicates the extent of the blast from the guns. There were similar blast effects on the upper deck of the ship. BELOW: *Missouri* experienced war in the Pacific and was heavily engaged post-World War II as well. She is now preserved as a museum ship.

visit to Greece. This Mediterranean deployment, lasting until the spring of 1946, was the beginning of a long-term USN commitment to defend the region against Soviet expansion and marked an early stage in the Cold War.

Following this, on September 2, 1947, President Truman celebrated the signing of the Inter-American Conference for the Maintenance of Hemisphere Peace and Security. This extension of the 19th-century Monroe doctrine marked the decline of British naval influence in the region. Truman and his family returned to the USA in *Missouri*.

On January 17, 1950, *Missouri* spectacularly ran aground in Hampton Roads, her momentum carrying her three ship-lengths out of the main channel and lifting her some 2m/7ft above the waterline. She was re-floated two weeks later.

The Korean War was business as usual for *Missouri*. In September 1950 she bombarded shore targets and from

Missouri

Class: *Iowa, New Jersey, Missouri, Wisconsin, Illinois, Kentucky.* Launched 1942–50
Dimensions: Length – 270m/887ft
Beam – 33m/108ft
Draught – 11m/36ft 2in
Displacement: 48,880 tonnes/48,110 tons
Armament: Main – 9 x 405mm/16in guns
Secondary – 20 x 125mm/5in, 80 x
40mm/1.57in and 50 x 20mm/0.79in guns
Machinery: 8 boilers, 4 shafts.
158,088kW/212,000shp
Speed: 33 knots
Complement: 1,921 men

TOP: **The fine long bows which were features of this generation of USN battleships.** ABOVE: **USN sailors and marines witness the Japanese surrender ceremony onboard the battleship *Missouri* in Tokyo Bay.** RIGHT: **The orderly scene around the table of the signing ceremony contrasted sharply with how it must have looked to the Japanese, with USN sailors and marines hanging from every vantage point in the ship.**

then until March 1951 her duties alternated between more bombardments and air defence of carrier task forces. On December 23, 1950, she gave gunfire support to the Hungnam defence perimeter as the last US troops were evacuated.

After two midshipmen's training cruises and a refit which lasted until January 1952, *Missouri* returned to Korea, where her last bombardment was against targets in the Kojo area on March 25, 1953. She was placed in reserve in February 1955, where she remained for nearly 30 years. In 1984–6 she was refitted to help make up the 600-ship USN and in the autumn of 1986 sent on a circumnavigation, following the track of the Great White Fleet. When she emerged from refit her 20 125mm/5in guns had been reduced to 12 and replaced with 32 Tomahawk cruise missiles and 16 Harpoon surface-to-surface missiles. All the 40mm/1.57in and 20mm/0.79in anti-aircraft

guns had been suppressed. In the late 1980s *Missouri* was based in the Pacific, deployed to the Gulf area during an incipient crisis there, and took part in numerous exercises.

After Iraq invaded Kuwait on August 2, 1990, *Missouri* was sent via Hawaii and the Philippines to the Gulf. On January 17, 1991, *Missouri*'s mission was yet again shore bombardment, but this time the weapons used were 28 Tomahawk cruise missiles. In February *Missouri* also used her 405mm/16in guns, the first time they had been fired in anger for nearly 40 years.

At Pearl Harbor on December 7, 1991, *Missouri* took part in a commemoration of the 50th anniversary of the attack there, and she was decommissioned for the last time on March 31, 1992. In 1998 the "Mighty Mo" was given to the USS *Missouri* Memorial Association and opened as a museum ship on January 29, 1999.

LEFT: **A standard aerial three-quarters bow-on shot of** *Wisconsin* **in the Hampton Roads, showing the battleship in its ultimate state of development. Heavy guns are in place, but a considerable secondary and tertiary armament has been added to give the ship better defence against smaller surface ships and, of course, aircraft.** ABOVE: **Three of the USN's four remaining Dreadnoughts in reserve at Philadelphia Navy Yard during 1967: from left to right,** *Wisconsin, New Jersey* **and** *Iowa.* **The end of an era, even for the USN, is at hand.**

Wisconsin

The new *Wisconsin* joined the Pacific War in October 1944, screening the fast carriers during operations against the Philippines, Formosa, Lingayen Gulf and French Indo-China. After bombarding Manila on December 18th *Wisconsin* and the fleet were caught by a typhoon when the ships were short of fuel and light in the water; three destroyers were sunk. Her next operation was the occupation of Luzon and anti-aircraft escort for the air strikes on Formosa, Luzon and the islands of Nansei Shoto in January 1945. She also made a sweep of the South China Sea, in the hope that Japanese heavy ships might be met at sea. In February, when Task Force 58 attacked the Japanese home island, under the cover of bad weather *Wisconsin* escorted the main body of ships, and she was at Iwo Jima also in February and Okinawa in March 1945.

When the 66,040-tonne/65,000-ton battleship *Yamato* attacked the American invasion fleet off Okinawa on April 7, she was sunk by carrier planes and *Wisconsin* was not called into action. Meanwhile the US fleet came increasingly under attack from kamikaze aircraft making suicide dives, and on April 12 it was estimated that about 150 enemy aircraft were destroyed in the "divine wind" as *Wisconsin* kept most of the kamikazes away from their targets. In June *Wisconsin* rode out a typhoon, while two carriers, three cruisers and a destroyer

suffered serious weather damage. Operations against Japan resumed on June 8, when the Japanese air effort was already broken. Consequently on July 15 *Wisconsin* was able to close with the coast and bombard steel mills and refineries on Hokkaido, and industrial plant on Honshu, even closer to Tokyo. Battleships of the British Pacific Fleet joined the bombardment.

When *Wisconsin* anchored in Tokyo Bay on September 5, she had already steamed over 160,900km/100,000 miles during her short career. In the immediate post-war period *Wisconsin* provided the "magic carpet" for returning US servicemen, paid visits to South America and cruised with midshipmen embarked to Europe until 1947.

Wisconsin spent two years in reserve until required for the Korean War, where she replaced her sister ship *New Jersey* as flagship of the Seventh Fleet. Operations included screening the carrier attack forces, and as the air threat diminished, frequently joining the "bombline" to provide gunfire support to forces ashore. Targets included artillery positions, bunkers, command posts, harbours, railways, shipyards and trench systems, and on one occasion the illumination with star-shell of an enemy attack. On March 15, 1952, one of *Wisconsin*'s last missions in the Korean War was to destroy a troop train, but she in turn was hit by four 150mm/6in rounds from a shore

Wisconsin

Class: *Iowa, New Jersey, Missouri, Wisconsin, Illinois, Kentucky.* Launched 1942–50
Dimensions: Length – 270m/887ft
Beam – 33m/108ft
Draught – 11m/36ft 2in
Displacement: 48,880 tonnes/48,110 tons
Armament: Main – 9 x 405mm/16in guns
Secondary – 20 x 125mm/5in, 80 x
40mm/1.57in and 50 x 20mm/0.79in guns
Machinery: 8 boilers, 4 shafts.
158,088kW/212,000shp
Speed: 33 knots
Complement: 1,921 men

TOP: *Wisconsin* **refuelling a destroyer underway in February 1945.** ABOVE: **An informal band concert onboard.** RIGHT: **The beginning of the end of one of the class, whose guns have been cut off but not yet hoisted away for recycling.**

battery. Three seamen were injured but little material damage was done. On April 4 and 5 at Guam, as a test, *Wisconsin* became the first Iowa class battleship to enter a floating dock.

Wisconsin remained in commission throughout the 1950s, alternately employed in training and on exercises, and showing the flag in the Atlantic and Pacific. On May 6, 1956, *Wisconsin* collided with the destroyer *Eaton* in a heavy fog. The long, relatively thin bows of these ships were graceful, but a weakness of the design meant that the collision badly damaged *Wisconsin*. In order to hasten repairs the 109-tonne/ 120-ton, 20.7m/68ft-long bow of the uncompleted *Kentucky* was brought by barge from Newport News to Norfolk, welded in place in a remarkable 16 days, and on June 28 she was ready.

What was thought to be *Wisconsin*'s last deployment in 1956–7 consisted of a midshipmen's training cruise and exercises, visiting Western Europe, the West Indies and the Mediterranean. When *Wisconsin* joined the reserve fleet in 1958, it was the first time since 1895 that the USN had had no battleship in commission. With *Iowa*, she remained at Philadelphia for 26 years until refitted to help make up the Reagan era's 600-ship navy. The 125mm/5in guns were replaced by surface-to-surface missiles and the 40mm/1.57in and 20mm/0.79in guns by 20mm/0.79in radar-controlled,

automatic Phalanx guns. On a typical training cruise she would embark up to 700 midshipmen from colleges across the USA, and visit ports in northern Europe or the Mediterranean and the West Indies. On her penultimate cruise *Wisconsin* sailed from Norfolk on June 19, 1957, transited the Panama Canal, crossed the Equator and visited Chile, whilst on her last cruise she visited the Clyde in Scotland in September and Brest in France. The USN decommissioned *Wisconsin* in 1990, but she was almost immediately required for the 1990–1 Gulf War. With *Missouri*, *Wisconsin* bombarded targets north of Khafji in Saudi Arabia, on Faylaka Island and in Kuwait City.

She was decommissioned for the final time on September 30, 1991, and after languishing in the navy yard *Wisconsin* was berthed in 2000 in downtown Norfolk as a museum ship.

Kentucky and *Illinois*

LEFT: *Kentucky* and *Illinois* were never completed. The bow of *Kentucky* was used to repair *Wisconsin*, and although redesigned several times while building, the hull never progressed much beyond the stage seen here.

Two other ships of the Iowa class were ordered. Originally *Kentucky* and *Illinois* were to have been of the new Montana type but the USN opted for an existing design, the Iowa.

Kentucky was laid down in March 1942 but, when in June the priority for construction became large numbers of landing craft, the double bottom section of the ship was launched and towed away. Work resumed in December 1944 but proceeded slowly and in 1947, when nearly half-finished, work stopped again, restarted briefly in 1948 and stopped again. The hull was re-launched in 1950 to clear the dock for repairs to *Missouri* after her grounding.

Kentucky was redesigned several times in the late 1940s and 1950s, and was designated as BBG-1, a missile-firing ship. However, her bow was cut off in May 1956 to repair *Wisconsin* after her collision. A replacement bow was built but never fitted. She was scrapped in 1959 when her engines and boilers were salvaged and installed in two fast combat-support ships.

The order for *Illinois* was cancelled in 1945, at the end of World War II.

Alaska class

LEFT: Although designated in the USN as CB, indicating a cruiser, these ships carried 305mm/12in guns and were battleships in all but name. They were not, however, regarded as a successful type.

Although armed with 305mm/12-in guns, the Alaska class was more like the heavy cruisers, or "pocket battleships" built without treaty limits, than regular, heavily armoured battleships. They were built to counter the threat of Japanese commerce raiders, a threat that never materialized.

Alaska entered the Pacific theatre in December 1944, when her primary task was to provide an anti-aircraft fire screen for the fast-carrier task forces formed around the fleet carriers *Yorktown*, *Intrepid*, *Independence* and *Langley*. *Alaska*'s secondary role was to direct fighters. *Alaska* destroyed her first kamikaze on March 18, 1945, but also shot down a friendly aircraft. Next day she escorted the heavily damaged carrier *Franklin* out of the fray. On March 27, in her third role, she also bombarded targets on Okinawa. After a busy summer she made a sweep into the East China Sea in July to find that it was empty of enemy ships, and then in August operated against the Japanese mainland.

However, in September, October and November 1945 *Alaska* supported the landing of occupying troops at Inchon in Korea and Tsingtao in China, who took over from Japanese garrisons.

Alaska was expensive in manpower, and by the end of the war there were plenty of cruisers which could perform her roles. She went into reserve in 1946–7 and was never reactivated, being sold for scrap in 1960.

Guam, who operated mainly with *Alaska* in the Pacific, was likewise placed in reserve in 1947 and sold for scrapping in 1961. It was proposed to convert *Hawaii* to a guided-missile ship and then to a command ship, but she was never finished.

Alaska class

Class: *Alaska, Guam, Hawaii.* Launched 1943–5
Dimensions: Length – 246.5m/808ft 6in
  Beam – 27.8m/91ft 1in
  Draught – 9.7m/31ft 10in
Displacement: 30,257 tonnes/29,779 tons
Armament: Main – 9 x 305mm/12in guns
  Secondary – 12 x 125mm/5in, 56 x
  40mm/1.57in and 34 x 20mm/0.79in guns
Machinery: 8 boilers, 4 shafts.
  111,855kW/150,000shp
Speed: 33 knots
Complement: 1,517 men

Montana class

The USN planned five ships of the Montana class: they would have been 282m/925ft long and 37m/121ft in the beam and, freed of treaty limits, the size grew quickly from 45,700 tonnes/ 45,000 tons to over 60,950 tonnes/ 60,000 tons displacement. With 8 boilers generating 128,260kW/172,000shp their designed speed was 28 knots. Originally 455mm/18in guns were considered but the USN settled for 12 405mm/16in guns in four triple turrets. A new large-calibre 125mm/5in gun was planned and they would have had a plethora of 40mm/ 1.57in and 20mm/0.79in guns.

Heavily armoured and bulged, they would not have fitted through the Panama Canal at the time and money was included in the budget to build new locks along the waterway.

Construction work was halted in April 1942, on the grounds of steel shortages, and *Montana*, *Ohio*, *Maine*, *New Hampshire* and *Louisiana* were cancelled on July 21, 1943. The Battle of Midway had shown, as had in different ways the war at sea in the Atlantic and the Mediterranean, that the future need was for aircraft carriers. Consequently the planned Montana class of battleships was cancelled and their place in the USN's construction plans was taken by six carriers of the Midway class.

ABOVE: **The Montana class were cancelled in 1943 when it was realized that the war in the Pacific would be fought principally by aircraft carriers.**
LEFT: **Design progressed as far as this fine model of 1941. The Montana class would obviously have been large ships – although presumably the anti-aircraft armament would have been enhanced before entering the war in the Pacific.**

Nagato and *Mutsu*

Built between 1917 and 1920 the Nagato class were the first all-Japanese-designed warships, the first to be fitted with 405mm/16in guns, and at the time among the fastest battleships in the world. At this stage of international relations the Japanese still had access to British technology and were able to learn the lessons of Jutland: *Nagato* and *Mutsu* were regarded as equivalent to the British Queen Elizabeth class.

Both were modified in 1924 and rebuilt in 1934–5. A characteristic of *Nagato*'s appearance was the six-legged mast festooned with platforms. However, smoke from the fore funnel interfered with the gunnery control positions and in 1921 a tall cowl was added. Later, at the first conversion, the fore funnel was given a distinctive S-shape. Various positions were tried for aircraft ramps and catapults, which aid the dating of photographs.

In 1934 the horizontal armour was reinforced, anti-torpedo bulges were fitted and extended beyond the armoured citadel, the torpedo tubes were removed and there were various additional platforms built around the foremast. New engines and boilers were fitted which allowed there to be one massive central funnel, and the length was increased by extending the stern 8.7m/28.5ft. The heavy guns were given greater elevation (and thus range) and numerous lighter guns were added. Finally an aircraft catapult and crane were added at the weather deck or X turret deck level.

ABOVE: Designed during World War I but completed in the 1920s, *Nagato* is seen here during her early trials. The massive conning tower is clearly Japanese, but Japanese naval architects had been trained in Britain, and there are still traces of that influence in *Nagato*'s profile, particularly her upright funnels.

In 1941 *Nagato* was Yamamoto's flagship during the attack on Pearl Harbor. She also took part in the Battles of Midway, the Philippine Sea, and Leyte Gulf.

In May and June 1942 Yamamoto with some 150 ships set out to occupy Midway Island and the western Aleutians, hoping to draw out the US Pacific Fleet to its destruction. As Dutch Harbor in the Aleutians was being invaded by the Japanese, the main carrier battle raged in the south between groups of aircraft carriers. Four Japanese carriers were lost: *Akagi*, *Hiryu*, *Kaga* and *Soryu*, on June 4 and 5, and the American *Yorktown* was badly damaged and sunk by a Japanese submarine on June 7. Yamamoto had spread his forces too widely, and although outnumbered the Americans had been able to concentrate their forces better. The Battle of Midway was the first major victory for the USN in the Pacific. Afterwards the Japanese still had the most ships, including aircraft carriers, but the industrial muscle of the USA would soon change this. So, when *Nagato* and the Japanese fleet retreated from Midway, it marked the high tide of attempts to secure the perimeter of their conquests.

Nagato class

Class: *Nagato, Mutsu.* Launched 1919–20
Dimensions: Length – 216m/708ft
Beam – 29m/95ft
Draught – 9m/30ft
Displacement: 34,340 tonnes/33,800 tons
Armament: Main – 8 x 405mm/16in guns
Secondary – 20 x 140mm/5.5in, 4 x 80mm/3.1in
guns and 8 x 535mm/21in torpedoes
Machinery: 15 oil-burning and 6 mixed-firing
boilers, 4 shafts. 59,656kW/80,000shp
Speed: 26.5 knots
Complement: 1,333 men

Two years later the Battle of the Philippine Sea was also fought at long range and although it involved *Nagato*, as well as four other Japanese battleships, these retreated after disastrous losses of Japanese aircraft.

However, during the Battle of Leyte Gulf, on October 25, 1944, *Nagato* was one of four battleships of the Japanese main Centre Strike Force which passed through the San Bernadino Strait into the amphibious area of operations. There at the Battle of Samar, *Nagato* sank the escort carrier *Gambier Bay* and three destroyers. Kamikaze aircraft also sank the escort carrier *St Lo*, but instead of wreaking havoc among the amphibious shipping, the Centre Strike Force retired through the San Bernadino Strait.

Nagato having been damaged by aircraft bombs off Samar was temporarily repaired, but did not see action again. She was bombed at Yokosuka on July 18, 1945, and badly damaged, and when the Japanese surrendered she was the last surviving battleship afloat. Her end was ignominious: while under tow to Bikini atoll she and her escort broke down and drifted for two days. She had developed a leak and was listing

TOP: *Nagato* or *Mutsu* after her refit of 1924 and before the 1933–4 refit.
ABOVE LEFT: The Japanese fleet leaving Brunei on October 22, 1944, en route to their defeat at the Battle of Leyte: from right to left, *Nagato*, *Musashi*, *Yamato* and cruisers. ABOVE RIGHT: The Japanese *Nagato* seen in the late 1930s preparing for aircraft operations by hoisting a biplane on to a launching ramp on B turret. However, once the war started such aircraft were mostly dispensed with and battleships relied on their carrier escorts for aerial reconnaisance.

and needed three weeks' repairs before she could complete her voyage. However, she survived the first (atmospheric) nuclear test, codename Able, with fairly minor damage, but sank from massive hull damage after the second (underwater) test, codename Baker, on July 25, 1946.

Mutsu was paid for by popular subscription, much of it raised in schools. She survived the cuts imposed on the Japanese Navy by the Washington Treaty, and took part in the attack on Pearl Harbor, the Battle of Midway and the Solomons campaign. However, on June 8, 1943, whilst in Hiroshima Bay, an explosion in the after magazine blew *Mutsu* in two. The cause has never been satisfactorily explained.

Kaga and *Tosa*

After the Russo-Japanese War the Imperial Japanese Navy, with much of its fleet obsolescent notwithstanding its victory at Tsushima, developed the concept of the 8-8 fleet. The Japanese had already thought of the all-big-gun ship when they received news from Portsmouth of Fisher's *Dreadnought* and their 8-8 concept laid emphasis on large, fast battleships. Their idea was that there were ages of ships, the first in the front line, the second operational but aging, and the third in reserve. The concept was that they would have two squadrons of eight ships, each less than eight years old, backed by ships of the other ages. This plan, with variations due to changes of government, finance and international tension, was maintained until the Washington Naval Conference. Meanwhile the Japanese concept had become the 8-8-8 plan, one squadron of ships of each age, and this called for more battleships and four battlecruisers by 1928. Japan was spending more than one-third of her national budget on naval construction, and it is unlikely that she could have achieved the 8-8-8 plan, but she was resentful at the limits imposed by the Washington Naval Treaty in 1921–2.

The treaty called for the cancellation of *Kaga* and *Tosa*, both laid down in 1920. They were conceived as high-speed battleships with the same speed as the Nagatos but with the main armament increased to ten 405mm/16in guns with an X

and a Y turret. When cancelled in 1922 under the Washington Naval Treaty, *Tosa* was used for explosives trials and sunk as a target ship in 1925.

Kaga was also cancelled under the treaty, but before she could be broken up, Japan was struck by an earthquake which severely damaged the battlecruiser *Amagi*, scheduled for conversion into an aircraft carrier, and the decision was made to rebuild *Kaga* instead.

The carrier *Kaga* participated in the attack on Pearl Harbor on December 7, 1941, and also in naval operations against Rabaul and Port Darwin in 1942. She was sunk at the Battle of Midway on June 5, 1942.

The Japanese Navy had a tradition of innovation in battleship design, and many proposals were equal to, and sometimes better than, their foreign contemporaries. When *Nagato* was commissioned in the 1920s and *Yamato* in 1941 they were each in their time the world's most powerful battleship. In the 1920s a class of four fast battleships was planned which would have been about 50,000 tonnes/tons and armed with 450mm/18in guns, but these ships were cancelled under the Washington Treaty.

TOP: *Mutsu, Ise* (before her wartime conversion) and *Fuso* in line of battle showing their massive control towers which were characteristic of Japanese battleships after refit in the 1930s. ABOVE: *Kaga* was modernized in 1936. ABOVE RIGHT: *Kaga* was completed as an aircraft carrier.

Also a class of large cruisers, like the USN Alaska class, with 150mm/12in or 360mm/14in-guns was envisaged. The Japanese navy had an astonishing ability to redesign and rebuild capitals ships, even given the shortage of raw materials which was the *causus belli* of the attack on Pearl Harbor and the war in the Pacific. During the war resources were shifted from battleships to aircraft carriers, though it was a shortage of experienced pilots as much as any material or technological failure which brought about Japan's defeat.

Kaga class

Class: *Kaga, Tosa.* Launched 1921
Dimensions: Length – 231.5m/760ft
 Beam – 30.5m/100ft
 Draught – 10m/33ft 1in
Displacement: 40,540 tonnes/39,900 tons
Armament: Main – 10 x 405mm/16in guns
 Secondary – 20 x 140mm/5.5in,
 4 x 80mm/3.1in guns and
 8 x 610mm/24in torpedoes
Machinery: 12 oil and 4 mixed-fired boilers, 4
 shafts. 67,859kW/91,000shp
Speed: 26.5 knots
Complement: 1,333 men

Yamato class

Japanese war plans were for a pre-emptive strike which would sweep aside the weak opposition of the British, Dutch and French forces (who in the event were preoccupied with the war in Europe), to capture Wake and Guam, and to build and defend a perimeter around a zone of co-prosperity ruled by Japan. The Japanese wanted a quick peace with the USA, but if this was not going to be possible they reckoned that, with the USN exhausted and having suffered attrition during its passage across the Pacific, the Imperial Japanese Navy could meet the USN in a decisive battle close to its home base and annihilate it.

The Japanese navy studied Tsushima and Jutland but not the U-boat campaign of World War I. Little attention was paid to the convoying of Japanese merchant ships or to the attack upon shipping on America's long, vulnerable supply lines, and no plans were made for a long or defensive war. Furthermore, despite the success of carrier aviation at Pearl Harbor, they did not foresee the influence which carrier-borne aircraft would have on the war in the Pacific or have sufficient reserves of aircraft and pilots.

Nevertheless, the plan worked at first, although the attack on Pearl Harbor was counterproductive. Tactically it was a failure because the USN carriers were at sea and escaped

ABOVE: *Yamato,* fitting out at Kure in September 1941, is seen here with her huge 455mm/18in guns in place. Japanese shipbuilding facilities had not progressed as much as their ship design and completion of the Yamato class to this stage was a considerable feat of ingenuity and logistics.

damage. Politically it brought the USA into the war on the side of Britain, and it underestimated the strength of American rage and resolve. Industrially Japan could not match the unprecedented American construction programmes which turned out ships and aircraft and trained men at extraordinary rates. When by the end of 1942 Japanese and American naval losses were about the same (two battleships and four large aircraft carriers), the USN could have been expected to replace their ships whereas the Imperial Japanese Navy, which was already suffering shortages when the war started, could not compete despite desperate efforts.

However, if Japanese plans to consolidate and defend an area of influence in the Far East were to have any chance of success, a navy was needed superior to any rival, and this included the USN. When the Geneva Disarmament Conference broke down, Japan announced its intention to withdraw from the 1922 and 1930 naval treaties when they expired in 1936 and planning started on the giant battleships of the Yamato

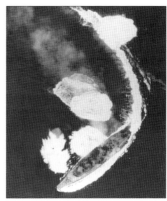

LEFT: *Yamato*'s death throes after being attacked by USN aircraft in the East China Sea in April 1945. BELOW LEFT: *Yamato* at speed in December 1941. BELOW: *Yamato* manoeuvring to avoid air attack. By the end of the war USN fliers had been trained in huge numbers, and had the confidence of experience and superior aircraft, so that the Japanese surface fleet was no match for US naval aviation.

class. These ships were built in great secrecy, not excepting a 360-tonne/400-ton camouflage net to cover *Musashi* who at over 31,750 tonnes/35,000 tons was the largest ship to date launched from a slipway. *Yamato* and *Shinano* were built in new or specially enlarged docks, and a purpose-built heavy lift ship was needed to bring the guns and mountings to the shipyard. They were the largest battleships ever built, with the largest guns. Each mounting weighed over 2,270 tonnes/2,500 tons, and their range, at 45 degrees elevation, was 42,940m/ 46,960yd or 23 nautical miles. Their armour was supposed to give protection against 455mm/18in shells or a bomb dropped from 4,575m/15,000ft. The armoured belt was inclined at 20 degrees and below it was an inclined anti-torpedo belt: the weight and thickness of armour was impressive, though trials showed that the connection between the two belts was weak and the bulkheads were insufficiently elastic.

After many tank tests and competitive designs, there was an element of provocation in the final choice: it was reckoned that the largest ship which could pass through the Panama Canal was about 57,000 tonnes/63,000 tons, so if the USN was to

out-build the Imperial Japanese Navy it would have to forgo the advantage of being able to swing its ships between the Atlantic and the Pacific, or widen the canal.

Yamato, the name ship of the class, was built at Kure naval dockyard. Commissioned in December 1941, just over a week after the start of the Pacific war, *Yamato* served as flagship of the Japanese Combined Fleet at the critical battles of 1942, including the Battle of Midway. This battle however was fought between the carrier groups; the battleships of the Japanese main force did not come into action and indeed the opposing fleets never saw each other.

She spent most of 1943 based at Truk and on December 24, 1943, was torpedoed by the American submarine *Skate,* requiring repairs which lasted until April 1944.

Like other Japanese and American battleships of the period, *Yamato*'s anti-aircraft battery was hugely increased before she took part in the Battle of the Philippine Sea in June. Again this was a carrier battle, in which Japanese naval air power was annihilated, and the battleships did not come into action and retreated upon Okinawa.

235

Yamato class (continued)

At the Battle of Leyte Gulf in October 1944 *Yamato* was part of the Japanese Centre Force, four surviving battleships and eight cruisers, which despite losing *Yamato*'s sister ship, *Mushashi*, in the Sibuyan Sea, pressed on into the actual Gulf on October 25. She helped to sink the escort carrier *Gambier Bay* and three destroyers by gunfire. The Centre Force was attacked several times by USN aircraft off the island of Samar, and just when it seemed the invasion forces must be destroyed, the Japanese admiral lost his nerve and retreated back through the San Bernardino Strait.

Yamato received little damage during the Battle of Leyte Gulf, and in Japan in November 1944 was fitted with yet more anti-aircraft guns. She was attacked by USN carrier planes in March 1945, and again slightly damaged. In April she took part in the suicidal Operation Ten-Go, intended to ruin the American invasion of Okinawa. On April 7, 1945, in the Battle of the East China Sea, some 320km/200 miles north of Okinawa, *Yamato* was attacked by a massive force of carrier planes from the USN Fifth Fleet and sunk.

Yamato's remains were located in 1985: she lies split in two at a depth of 305m/1,000ft. Her bows from B turret forward are upright, but the rest is upside down with a large hole close to the after magazines.

Musashi, sister ship of *Yamato*, was built at Nagasaki and commissioned in August 1942. The Japanese still conceived a decisive battle with the main fleet of the USN and in 1943 and 1944 *Musashi* was based at Truk to cover the threat of an American advance. Later she moved to Palau and on March 29, 1944, was torpedoed by the American submarine *Tunny*, needing repairs in Japan. *Musashi*'s anti-aircraft firepower was increased and in June 1944 she took part in the Battle of the Philippine Sea. Her last battle was during the Leyte Gulf campaign. *Musashi* was one of five battleships which formed the Centre Strike Force which, without carrier air support, intended to destroy the American landings on the Pacific coast of Leyte. On October 24, 1944, approaching from the west through the archipelagic Sibuyan Sea, and south of Luzon, *Musashi* and her consorts were attacked by American carrier aircraft. She was hit by 19 torpedoes and 17 bombs and though her armour enabled her to withstand more damage than any other ship might have done, several hours after the last attack she capsized and sank.

BELOW: ***Musashi*** caught leaving Brunei in October 1944, on what was to be the last major coordinated sortie by the Imperial Japanese Navy. Without aircraft carriers and naval air power to protect her, ***Musashi*** and her sisters were doomed.

Construction on *Shinano* as a battleship was stopped in 1942, and instead she was completed as an aircraft carrier in late 1944. However, while on trials, she was torpedoed and sunk by the American submarine *Archerfish* on November 29, 1944, as the USN blockade of Japanese waters increased.

Hull number 111 was intended to be a fourth Yamato class but construction on her was suspended in 1941 because of a shortage of skilled labour and materials, and cancelled in 1942; parts were used in three other ships.

Prior to World War II the Imperial Japanese Navy drew up plans for heavy cruisers or battlecruisers which would have been similar to the American Alaska class, and for a class of super-Yamatos, but all these plans were dropped for an emergency construction programme of aircraft carriers.

Yamato class

Class: *Yamato, Musashi, Shinano*, No. 111. Launched 1940–4
Dimensions: Length – 256m/839ft 9in
Beam – 37m/121ft
Draught – 10.5m/34ft
Displacement: 63,315 tonnes/62,315 tons
Armament: Main – 9 x 455mm/18in guns
Secondary – 12 x 155mm/6.1in,
12 x 125mm/5in and 24 x 25mm/1in guns
Machinery: 12 boilers, 4 shafts.
111,855kW/150,000shp
Speed: 27 knots
Complement: 2,500 men

LEFT: *Musashi* under air attack in the Sibuyan Sea. Cloud off the mountains and blue sky contrast sharply with death from the skies. BELOW: The Emperor Hirohito with officers of the battleship *Musashi* in 1943. Not even an emperor's support could help his navy once the USN had begun to exact its revenge for Pearl Harbor.

LEFT: **The so-called "pocket battleships" proved to be useful commerce raiders and tied up many British resources in the early months of World War II, but by mid-1942 they were either sunk or blockaded.** BELOW LEFT: *Admiral Graf Spee* **on launch. Launches of ships for the new German navy became opportunities for parade and display by the Nazi party.**

Deutschland (Lützow) and *Admiral Scheer*

The Treaty of Versailles which ended World War I imposed a displacement restriction on German warships of 10,160 tonnes/10,000 tons. In the 1920s the German navy tried to design an effective capital ship within this limit, varying the armament, armour, length and beam. The possibility of a heavy monitor for coastal defence or a large cruiser were examined and rejected, and eventually the design of a pocket battleship emerged. Weight was saved by using an all-welded construction, and the use of diesel engines gave good range and relatively high speed. The resulting ships were more powerful than any cruiser and faster than any battleship but there was no operational concept which justified these ships: the design was a matter of political and technical compromise. They were, however, well suited for commerce raiding.

Deutschland led an eventful life and survived World War II despite being frequently damaged, including being bombed by Republican aircraft off Ibiza on May 29, 1937, during the Spanish Civil War. *Deutschland* sailed prior to the outbreak of

World War II to a station off Greenland, where she sank two small ships and took another prize, and returned to the Baltic in mid-November, being renamed *Lützow* while still at sea. She took part in the German invasion of Norway, where she was hit by Norwegian coastal batteries on entering Oslo Fjord.

Whilst returning to Germany for repairs she was torpedoed by the British submarine *Spearfish* on April 11, 1940, and severely damaged. Later, while still under repair at Kiel, she was hit by a bomb which failed to explode during a raid by the Royal Air Force.

Then on June 13, 1941, *Lützow* was hit by an air-launched torpedo while en route to Norway, requiring her to return to Kiel for more repairs the next day. She eventually returned to Norway in May 1942, but ran aground and underwent more repairs in Germany. However, in December 1942 *Lützow*, the cruiser *Hipper* and their escorts attacked convoy JW51B off Bear Island and were driven off by a much weaker British squadron. When Hitler learned this he raged for an hour and a half on the theme that capital ships were a waste of men and material, during which time Grand Admiral Raeder "rarely had the opportunity to comment". The subsequent order to draw up plans for decommissioning the German big ships was a turning point in the war for the German navy and Raeder resigned after 14 years in office.

During 1943–5 *Lützow* was used in the Baltic, bombarding the seaward flank of the Soviet army, where on April 16, 1945, *Lützow* was badly damaged during an RAF bombing raid and she settled on the bottom. Her crew fought her as a fixed battery, firing on the advancing Soviet forces, until they blew her up on May 4, 1945. She was salvaged by the Russians and broken up in 1948–9.

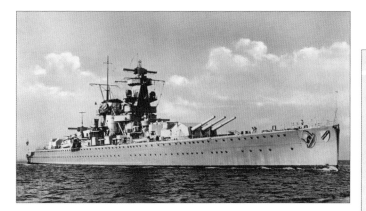

Deutschland class

Class: *Deutschland, Admiral Scheer, Admiral Graf Spee.* Launched 1931–4
Dimensions: Length – 186m/610ft 3in
  Beam – 21.6m/70ft 10in
  Draught – 5.8m/19ft
Displacement: 11,890 tonnes/11,700 tons
Armament: Main – 6 x 280mm/11in guns
  Secondary – 8 x 150mm/6in,
  6 x 105mm/4.13in, 8 x 37mm/1.46in,
  6 x 20mm/0.79in guns and
  8 x 535mm/21in torpedoes
Machinery: 8 diesels, 3 shafts.
  40,268kW/54,000hp
Speed: 28 knots
Complement: 619–1,150 men

Deutschland was renamed *Lützow* in 1939. Two more ships of the Deutschland class, as well as *Admiral Scheer* and *Admiral Graf Spee* (see over) were started but their material was used to build *Scharnhorst* and *Gneisenau*.

ABOVE LEFT: **Originally launched as *Deutschland*, Hitler later ordered her name to be changed to *Lützow* because he feared the loss of a ship with such a talismanic name.** LEFT: **A detail of *Deutschland* when newly completed, and being admired by onlookers.** BELOW: **Seamen of *Deutschland* receiving training in traditional skills in this photograph dated 1935. Oared craft were retained throughout the 20th century by all navies.**

Like *Deutschland*, *Admiral Scheer* saw service off Spain, and bombarded Almeria on May 31, 1937, in retaliation for the bombing of *Deutschland*. On September 4, 1939, *Admiral Scheer* was bombed in the Schillig Roads; she was also bombed on July 20, 1940, and again escaped damage. In October 1940 *Admiral Scheer* broke out into the North Atlantic where she was attacked by the armed merchant cruiser *Jervis Bay*. *Jervis Bay* was lost together with five ships of convoy HX84, but the remainder of the convoy scattered. *Admiral Scheer* then raided in the Atlantic and Indian Oceans, sinking 16 ships totalling 100,644 million tonnes/99,059 million tons until she returned, undetected, to Kiel on April 1, 1941.

In the summer of 1942 *Admiral Scheer* was part of the threatening fleet of German surface ships that sortied briefly during the debacle of convoy PQ17. She made one more sortie, sinking the Soviet icebreaker *Sibirjakov* on August 26, 1942, and bombarding the Russian coast, before going into a prolonged refit in November 1942. From November 1944 to March 1945 she was employed in coastal operations in the Baltic against the advancing Soviet army. Her luck finally ran out on April 9, 1945, when she was bombed and capsized. She was broken up *in situ,* 1948.

239

Admiral Graf Spee

Like her sisters, *Admiral Graf Spee* saw limited action off the coast of Spain during the Spanish Civil War. She sailed from Germany on August 21, 1939, to take up her station in the South Atlantic where together with her forays into the Indian Ocean she sank nine ships of 50,893 tonnes/50,089 tons. More than 20 British and French warships in eight groups were formed, each reckoned to be sufficient to despatch any raider of the pocket battleship type, and battleships and cruisers were deployed to act as escorts to ocean-going convoys in the North Atlantic. Thus, one objective of the German raider policy, to scatter and tie down enemy naval forces, was achieved.

The hunting groups were ordered to keep radio silence, which meant the Admiralty in London would not necessarily know about their movements, although they were ordered not to stray very far from concentrations of merchant ships. The Admiralty's orders foresaw that local commanders would need rather more than usual latitude to disregard any order they received, and to use their initiative.

At dawn on December 13, 1939, Force G under Commodore Henry Harwood found the *Admiral Graf Spee* off the River Plate. The battle which followed showed that the Royal Navy had learned a great deal since Jutland. After meeting his

captains in "Nelson style" onboard his flagship, Harwood gave his orders on the eve of battle in crisp sentences: "My policy with three cruisers in company versus one pocket battleship. Attack at once by day or night. By day act in two divisions ... by night ships will normally remain in company in open order." The three cruisers, the British 205mm/8in-gun cruiser *Exeter*

BELOW: *Admiral Graf Spee* attended the British Coronation Fleet Review at Spithead in 1937. Two years later, if *Admiral Graf Spee* had been flying her aircraft for dawn reconnaissance off the River Plate in December 1939, she might have avoided the searching British cruisers. RIGHT: On launch at Wilhelmshaven on June 30, 1934.

and the 150mm/6in-gun cruisers *Ajax* and the New Zealand *Achilles* had not operated together before, yet the following morning, no further tactical orders were necessary as the ships split into two divisions to divide the fire of their superior enemy.

Although *Exeter* in particular took terrible punishment from *Graf Spee*'s 280mm/11in guns, she did not blow up, as some of the battlecruisers at Jutland had done: the Royal Navy had clearly re-learned some key lessons about damage control and ammunition handling.

Exeter attacked from the south while the two light cruisers, *Ajax* and *Achilles*, worked around to the north acting as one division. *Admiral Graf Spee* concentrated her heavy armament on *Exeter,* putting her two after turrets out of action and forcing her to retire to the Falklands for repairs, while the two light cruisers dodged in and out of range of *Admiral Graf Spee*'s guns. *Admiral Graf Spee* does not seem to have been well handled and by 08.00, with only superficial damage, she broke off action and headed for the neutral port of Montevideo in Uruguay. She entered Montevideo at midnight with the two light cruisers hard on her heels, and there by diplomatic means she was maintained for several days while other British hunting groups headed for the area. By December 17 the only reinforcement which had arrived was the heavy cruiser *Cumberland* who, whilst refitting at the Falklands, had by a quirk of radio propagation heard the gunnery control signals and correctly interpreted that her presence was needed.

However, Langsdorff, the captain of the *Admiral Graf Spee*, had convinced himself that the entire Royal Navy was waiting for him and, having landed his crew, he scuttled his ship off Montevideo and committed suicide. His funeral was attended by some of the British merchant seamen he had held captive.

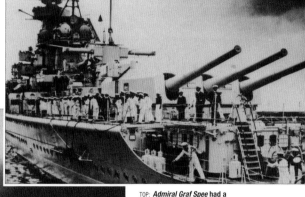

TOP: **Admiral Graf Spee** had a relatively low silhouette and consequently her secondary range-finder lacked height.
ABOVE: **Photographed at Montevideo where she had taken refuge after the Battle of the River Plate, Admiral Graf Spee** does not show much sign of damage. LEFT: **Admiral Graf Spee** was scuttled because her captain feared the arrival of British reinforcements to the cruisers who had driven him into port.

Scharnhorst and *Gneisenau*

The original requirement for these two ships was that they should have the same speed and armament as the Deutschland class pocket battleships, but on a larger displacement – 19,305 tonnes/19,000 tons, allowing for heavier armour. The German navy's view was that if such a vessel was limited to 280mm/11in guns, then they should have a third triple turret, making the displacement 26,415 tonnes/26,000 tons. Hitler rejected this because he still did not want to break the Versailles Treaty and so provoke Britain. However, the Anglo-German Naval Agreement of 1935 allowed for two *panzerschiffe* of 26,415 tonnes/26,000 tons each armed with 280mm/11in guns. The agreement also allowed a maximum calibre of 406mm/16in and Hitler ordered the ships to be built with 380mm/15in guns, but the 280mm/11in triple turrets were available and it would have taken some time to develop a new turret. These new turrets were fitted to *Bismarck* and *Tirpitz* and although it was intended to up-gun *Scharnhorst* and *Gneisenau*, war prevented this. Both ships were refitted with the clipper or Atlantic bow on the eve of World War II, and during the war the close-range armament was increased. Two catapults were fitted, one high over the boat deck and the other on the roof of C turret which was removed pre-war.

Scharnhorst sank the armed merchant cruiser *Rawalpindi* in November 1939 but her planned breakout into the Atlantic was thwarted. On April 9, 1940, during the invasion of Norway she fought a brief battle with the battleship *Renown* but escaped in a snowstorm. On June 8, she sank the carrier *Glorious* and two

TOP: **The Germans designed elegant and powerful-looking ships such as *Scharnhorst*.** ABOVE: ***Scharnhorst*'s sister ship *Gneisenau*.**

destroyers, but the *Acasta* managed a torpedo hit which opened a large hole and flooded her. She was attacked by carrier-borne aircraft but escaped again to Kiel for repairs. In January 1942 *Scharnhorst* succeeded in breaking out into the Atlantic and sank several ships. She was hunted by British battleships but eluded them and reached Brest safely on March 23, 1942, after 60 days at sea and steaming 28,950km/18,000 miles. She was under repair for most of 1943 but in September she bombarded Spitsbergen and in December sallied to attack the Russia-bound convoy JW55B, when on December 26, 1943, she was overwhelmed by the

Scharnhorst class

Class: *Scharnhorst, Gneisenau.* Launched 1936
Dimensions: Length – 235m/770ft 8in
    Beam – 30m/98ft
    Draught – 8m/27ft
Displacement: 35,400 tonnes/34,841 tons
Armament: Main – 9 x 280mm/11in guns
    Secondary – 12 x 150mm/6in,
    14 x 105mm/4.13in, 16 x 37mm/1.46in and
    8 x 20mm/0.79in guns
Machinery: 12 boilers, 3 shafts.
    123,041kW/165,000shp
Speed: 32 knots
Complement: 1,669 men

TOP: *Scharnhorst* firing her main armament. TOP RIGHT: **A view of one of the** *schlachtschiff* (battleship) *Gneisenau's* **machinery rooms.** ABOVE: **Captain Ciliax, then commanding** *Scharnhorst***, inspecting his ship's company pre-war. During the war he would make his fame in a German squadron, including leading these two ships, on the Channel Dash.**

battleship *Duke of York* and the cruisers *Belfast*, *Jamaica* and *Norfolk* and sunk with heavy loss of life.

For much of the war *Gneisenau* operated with *Scharnhorst*. However, on June 20, 1940, she was torpedoed by the submarine *Clyde* and only at the end of the year returned to Kiel for repairs. She broke out into the Atlantic with *Scharnhorst* in January to March 1942, and while in Brest was bombed many times, without serious damage. After being bombed by the RAF in November 1942 *Gneisenau* was taken in hand for the long-anticipated up-gunning. However, work was stopped in early 1943 and her armament used ashore. Three 280mm/11in guns were installed near the Hook of Holland and six in Norway. She was finally scuttled at Gdynia in 1945 and broken up between 1947 and 1951.

Scharnhorst and *Gneisenau* are best known for their Channel Dash or Operation Cerberus. Hitler was convinced that the British were going to invade Norway and personally ordered the Ugly Sisters, as the RAF knew them, home. Taking advantage of foul weather in the English Channel and by a combination of good luck and British failures, the Germans sailed on February 12, 1943, and evaded notice until they were about to enter the Straits of Dover. It was a bad day for the British, relieved only by the incredible bravery of the men of 825 Naval Air Squadron, led by Lieutenant Commander Eugene Esmonde, who was awarded a posthumous VC, for a "forlorn hope" attack in their *Swordfish*.

The dash by German warships up the English Channel was a humiliation for the British. *Scharnhorst* twice hit mines, and *Gneisenau* escaped only to be bombed at Kiel. A serious threat to allied shipping in the Atlantic was over and the German naval commander, Raeder, recognized that he had won a tactical victory but suffered a strategic defeat. The British could now concentrate their efforts against the German surface fleet, whose threat to shipping in the Atlantic had been diminished.

Bismarck

Design work on Germany's first fully-fledged battleships, with armament and armour equivalent to foreign capital ships, began in the early 1930s. Initially this class was supposed to be of 35,560 tonnes/35,000 tons displacement but the design was modified several times, even on the slipway, and after the Anglo-German naval treaty it was recognized that their standard displacement would be nearer 45,200 tonnes/45,000 tons, and eventually their deep load displacement exceeded 50,800 tonnes/50,000 tons.

The actual design was conservative, a development of World War I Baden design, with a main armament of eight 380mm/15in guns in twin turrets, two forward and two aft. Her secondary battery of six twin-turreted 150mm/6in guns were intended for use against destroyers, and her mixed anti-aircraft battery included guns of three different sizes: 105mm/4.1in, 37mm/1.46in and 20mm/0.79in was regarded as inadequate for World War II, given the developments there had been in naval aviation.

Bismarck was, however, very heavily armoured, again along the lines of the Baden class, and her broad beam gave her stability and made her a good, steady gun platform. Her 30-knot speed made for a fast battleship, but the steam plant was fuel-hungry and thus limited range, a defect which the German navy hoped to overcome by fitting diesel engines in all future designs. *Bismarck*'s keel was laid down in July 1936 and even after launch modifications continued, which took two years and included the fitting of a new clipper or Atlantic bow. As a result she was not ready until late in 1940.

ABOVE: *Bismarck* was hit by *Prince of Wales* during their brief battle on May 24, 1941, causing flooding forward which slowed the German ship down. She is seen here from *Prinz Eugen*, shortly before *Bismarck* feinted to the north to allow *Prinz Eugen* to escape. The Royal Navy thought, temporarily, that *Bismarck* was making back towards Norway, but soon resumed the chase to the south. Next, *Bismarck* was attacked from the air.

Germany naval strategy was to avoid set-piece battles with the Royal Navy and to conduct a war on commerce, using surface raiders, both warships and disguised merchant ships, and U-boats. The intention was both to disperse British forces, to force merchant ships into inefficient convoys and then to disrupt the convoy patterns, as well as to destroy shipping. Under this plan battleships and cruisers were to evade the British blockade and break out into the Atlantic, and eventually the Indian and Pacific Oceans. The heavy cruisers *Admiral Hipper* and *Prinz Eugen*, the pocket battleships *Lützow*, *Admiral Graf Spee* and *Admiral Scheer*, the battlecruisers *Scharnhorst* and *Gneisenau*, and, of course, *Bismarck* were faster than most British battleships. This posed a serious threat which was taken very seriously by the Royal Navy and also by the French navy while it was still active in World War II. Germany's strategy was not successful while her navy could be blockaded in the North Sea, but after the fall of France in June 1940, when the German fleet had access to the French Atlantic ports, the strategic balance changed. In December 1940 and early 1941 German surface raiders sank 47 merchant ships, and U-boats sank many more.

Bismarck

Class: *Bismarck, Tirpitz.* Launched 1939
Dimensions: Length – 248m/813ft 8in
    Beam – 36m/118ft 1in
    Draught – 8.5m/28ft 6in
Displacement: 42,370 tonnes/41,700 tons
Armament: Main – 8 x 380mm/15in guns
    Secondary – 12 x 150mm/6in,
    16 x 105mm/4.13in, 16 x 37mm/1.46in and
    12 x 20mm/0.79in guns
Machinery: 12 boilers, 3 shafts.
    102,907kW/138,000shp
Speed: 29 knots
Complement: 2,092–2,608 men

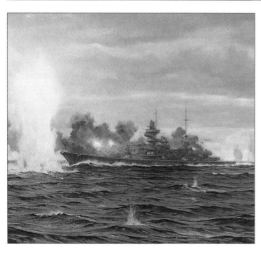

TOP: **Hitler making the Nazi salute towards** *Bismarck,* **though oddly there does not seem to be anyone on the upper deck to return the compliment.** ABOVE : *Bismarck* **was finally overwhelmed by the British Home Fleet.** ABOVE RIGHT: *Bismarck* **photographed from** *Prinz Eugen* **during the encounter with** *Hood.*

In May 1941 the German navy sent *Bismarck* and the heavy cruiser *Prinz Eugen* on a raid into the Atlantic. The movement was spotted but in bad weather the Germans got into the Denmark Strait, where they were shadowed by two British cruisers. On May 24, 1941, during a brief battle between the two Germans and the British *Prince of Wales* and *Hood, Hood* blew up and *Prince of Wales* was damaged. *Bismarck* however was hit by 355mm/14in shells from *Prince of Wales* which caused her to lose fuel and contaminated several bunkers with salt water. *Prinz Eugen* was detached into the Atlantic while *Bismarck* headed for Brest. Next, presaging the new

relationship between battleship and aircraft which would change naval warfare forever, a strike by nine aircraft from the aircraft carrier *Victorious* hit *Bismarck* with one torpedo, but the damage was slight.

For two days *Bismarck* escaped detection while the hunting British fleet cast to the north, thinking that *Bismarck* might have been returning to Norway. However, she was spotted by the American pilot of a RAF flying boat and in the evening of May 26, and in appalling weather, the aircraft of the carrier *Ark Royal* crippled *Bismarck* by wrecking her steering gear and jamming her rudder. At dawn the next day the battleships *King George V* and *Rodney* opened fire on the German ship at a range of 14,630m/16,000yds, and in an hour and a half *Bismarck* was reduced to a blazing wreck. She was torpedoed and sank some 555km/300 nautical miles west of Ushant. Of her crew of 2,222 men only 110 survived the sinking.

Tirpitz

The sister ship of *Bismarck*, *Tirpitz* was commissioned in February 1941, when she operated in the Baltic on trials and training, and was engaged in support of Operation Barbarossa, the German advance into Russia. However, in January 1942 *Tirpitz* was sent to Norway: Hitler was obsessed that "the fate of the war will be decided in Norway", and throughout the war kept large forces there. Here *Tirpitz* acted like a fleet-in-being and in turn consumed British effort and imagination in plans for her destruction.

One of *Tirpitz*'s few offensive actions was Operation Rösselsprung or "knight's move", a planned attack on convoy traffic in June and July 1942. It was spoilt when three destroyers escorting the German Battle Group I, consisting of *Tirpitz* and the heavy cruiser *Admiral Hipper*, grounded outside Altenfjord. The pocket battleship *Lützow*, belonging with *Admiral Scheer* to Battle Group II, was also stranded and needed repairs in Germany. Both battle groups turned back

BELOW: *Tirpitz* underway for her sea trials in 1941. Her sister ship *Bismarck* had a career which could be measured in months. *Tirpitz*'s career lasted only a handful of years and she saw little action, although her presence as fleet-in-being in a lair in a Norwegian fjord and the threat she represented, in particular to Arctic convoys to Russia, tied up huge resources.

when the Germans suspected an attack by submarines and carrier aircraft. However, when the British Admiralty dispersed the convoy PQ17, 19 of the 36 merchant ships were subsequently lost to German aircraft or U-boats.

At the end of 1942 there was a failed attempt to attack *Tirpitz* at her anchorage by miniature submarines and two-man torpedoes known as chariots, carried into the fjords by a Norwegian fishing boat. The bombing of *Gneisenau* showed that it was unsafe for *Tirpitz* to return to Germany and so she was refitted in the fjords, where in March 1943 she was joined by *Prinz Eugen*, *Scharnhorst* and *Lützow*. On September 8, 1943, *Tirpitz* and *Scharnhorst* bombarded Spitsbergen, which was to be the last time *Tirpitz* fired her main armament in anger.

Back in Kaafjord, the Royal Navy mounted Operation Source in September 1943, an attack using X-craft towed into position by parent submarines. Shortly after 08.00 on September 21, two violent explosions underneath *Tirpitz* forced her upwards several feet. All power was lost and she settled with a list to port. The damage was severe: there were splits in the bottom of the hull, buckling and distortion; a generator room was flooded and electrical generators lifted off their mountings; the propeller shafts were jammed and A and X turrets jumped off their roller paths.

ABOVE: **Hitler inspecting the parade before the launch of *Tirpitz* on April 1, 1939. Top left is the hull of *Tirpitz* showing the bilge keel which ran each side of the length of the ship.** TOP RIGHT: ***Tirpitz* in her lair with smokescreens put up to obscure her from the air during attack by the Fleet Air Arm.** RIGHT: **Sunk at last after several raids, *Tirpitz* turned turtle and was scrapped *in situ*, by a Norwegian company. Some portions of her still lie on the bottom of the fjord in her last berth.**

During the winter of 1943–4 the Germans repaired *Tirpitz*, who, despite receiving further shock damage by Soviet bombers in February, was able to begin manoeuvring trials in the following spring. There then began a series of attacks by carrier aircraft of the Royal Navy.

The first of these, Operation Tungsten, comprised the battleships *Duke of York* and *Anson*, the carriers *Victorious*, *Furious*, *Searcher*, *Pursuer* and *Emperor* and a large number of cruisers and destroyers. Fleet Air Arm Barracuda torpedo-bombers, Wildcats and Hellcats struck on April 3, 1944, just as *Tirpitz* was weighing anchor for post-repair trials. The first attack lasted barely a minute and scored six direct hits, and a second attack a few minutes later scored eight direct hits: there were other probable hits and the aircraft descended to strafe *Tirpitz* as well. By 08.00 all the aircraft but three had landed on their carriers.

Similar attacks were cancelled as a result of bad weather, but on July 17, 1944, Operation Mascot scored a near-miss despite improved anti-aircraft defences and *Tirpitz* was only saved from further damage by an effective smokescreen. Nevertheless, *Tirpitz*'s much-delayed sea trials on July 31 and August 1, 1944, were her last.

In August a series of operations all codenamed Goodwood using the carriers *Indefatigable*, *Formidable*, *Furious*, *Nabob* and *Trumpeter* started. Goodwood III on August 24, 1944, was

the heaviest and most determined so far, and even the Germans admired the British skill and dexterity in flying. The effect of all these attacks was to render *Tirpitz* unserviceable from September 1943 onwards.

Finally, on September 15, 1944, 33 Lancaster bombers, which had been pre-positioned in Russia, attacked using 5,445kg/12,000lb bombs nicknamed Tallboys. By now the German anti-aircraft fire included a barge firing next to her 380mm/15in guns, but despite this one bomb hit *Tirpitz* and exploded underneath, flooding the forward part of the ship and shaking much of her machinery off its mountings. *Tirpitz* was towed to shallower water where on November 12 she was again attacked by Lancaster bombers dropping Tallboys. There were two direct hits and several near-misses and an internal explosion, whereupon *Tirpitz* rolled over to port and capsized with heavy loss of life.

Tirpitz was broken up *in situ* between 1949 and 1957 by a Norwegian company.

Tirpitz

Class: *Bismarck*, *Tirpitz*. Launched 1939
Dimensions: Length – 248m/813ft 8in
  Beam – 36m/118ft 1in
  Draught – 8.5m/28ft 6in
Displacement: 42,370 tonnes/41,700 tons
Armament: Main – 8 x 380mm/15in guns
  Secondary – 12 x 150mm/6in,
  16 x 105mm/4.13in, 16 x 37mm/1.46in and
  12 x 20mm/0.79in guns
Machinery: 12 boilers, 3 shafts.
  102,907kW/138,000shp
Speed: 29 knots
Complement: 2,092–2,608 men

LEFT: **A stern view of** *Dunkerque*, **showing the hangar for her aircraft – then quite an advanced feature of warship design.** ABOVE: **The French battleships** *Strasbourg* **and** *Dunkerque* **at their berth in Mers-el-Kebir in Algeria (then a French colony), where they had taken refuge after the fall of France. While at berth they were attacked by the Royal Navy in July 1940, after the French had refused British proposals to ensure that their fleet would not fall into the possession of the Nazis.**

Dunkerque and *Strasbourg*

These two ships, built as part of France's battleship tonnage allowed by the Washington Naval Treaty, were like the British Nelson class in having all of their main armament forward. France was allowed a total battleship displacement of 177,800 tonnes/175,000 tons under the treaty. Smaller and cheaper ships were sought, but the French navy eventually settled on a design of 26,925 tonnes/26,500 tons, partly in response to the heavy cruisers built in Germany and the new Italian battleships which were known to be in progress. The treaty allowed guns of up to 380mm/15in, but on grounds of economy France chose a new calibre of 330mm/13in.

Other novel features included a large number of medium-calibre and anti-aircraft guns in quadruple mountings and a purpose-built aircraft hangar aft. A prominent feature of these ships was a control tower consisting of three separate structures rotating on a common axis and weighing more than 86 tonnes/85 tons.

In 1939 *Dunkerque* was part of Force I, one of several British and French forces formed to hunt down German raiders in the Atlantic and Indian Oceans. In December she carried French gold to Canada for safekeeping and returned escorting Canadian troop convoys to Britain. After the fall of France, she was badly damaged twice while alongside at Mers-el-Kebir, after senior French officers had refused British proposals to neutralize their fleet to prevent it being used by the Nazis. Consequently the Royal Navy bombarded the port on July 3 and British aircraft attacked on July 6 to stop French warships falling into Nazi hands. After emergency repairs she was taken to Toulon, where on November 27, 1942, she was sabotaged by loyal Frenchmen and stranded in her dry dock for the next three years. She was finally sold for scrap in 1956.

Strasbourg was also involved in the 1939 hunt for the German pocket battleship *Admiral Graf Spee*, which was raiding in the South Atlantic. She suffered a similar fate to *Dunkerque*: although only lightly damaged by British shelling at Mers-el-Kebir, she was scuttled by the French at Toulon on November 27, 1942, and despite attempts at salvage, was sunk again by US aircraft in August 1944 during Allied landings in the south of France. She was sold for scrap in 1955.

Dunkerque class

Class: *Dunkerque, Strasbourg.*
Launched 1935–6
Dimensions: Length – 214.5m/703ft 9in
Beam – 31m/102ft
Draught – 8.7m/28ft 6in
Displacement: 26,925 tonnes/26,500 tons
Armament: Main – 8 x 330mm/13in guns
Secondary – 16 x 130mm/5.1in,
8 x 37mm/1.46in and 32 x 13mm/0.52in guns
Machinery: 6 boilers, 4 shafts.
83,891kW/112,500shp
Speed: 29.5 knots
Complement: 1,431 men

LEFT: *Richelieu* at Dakar in 1941. *Richelieu* exchanged shots with the British *Resolution*, and her sister ship *Jean Bart* exchanged shots with the USN *Massachusetts*. BELOW: *Richelieu*, having fought the British at Dakar, declared for the Free French, was refitted in New York and fought alongside the British in the Far East.

Richelieu class

After the Anglo-German naval agreement and the abrogation or expiry of the Washington Naval Treaty, France considered herself free to expand her navy. The Richelieu class represented a further development of the Dunkerque class, but was 10,160 tonnes/10,000 tons larger, with 380mm/15in guns, and a speed of 2 to 3 knots faster.

Richelieu and *Jean Bart* escaped from France. *Richelieu* benefited from being completed in New York and gaining from USN experience in the Pacific. *Jean Bart*, which carried very heavy anti-aircraft armament, was damaged during the Allied landings in North Africa and work to complete her did not recommence until 1946. A novel feature of the design included blowers to mix cold fresh air with the hot flue gases and so minimize the effect upon fire-control optics.

Before completion *Richelieu* was moved from Brest to Dakar, where on July 8, 1944, she was damaged by aircraft from the British carrier *Hermes* and again between September 23 and 25 during a duel with the battleship *Resolution*. Once taken over by the Free French navy she sailed for New York where she was finally completed, and in November 1943 began operations with

the British Home Fleet. In 1944 and 1945 she operated with the British East Indies Fleet and then the British Pacific Fleet, visiting Toulon in September 1944 and returning to Cherbourg in March 1946. She was broken up in Italy in 1968.

The incomplete *Jean Bart* escaped from St Nazaire and evaded the advancing Germans in June 1940, eventually reaching Casablanca. There, in November 1942 during Allied landings in North Africa, she exchanged fire with the USN battleship *Massachusetts* and received several gunfire and bomb hits. She was towed to Brest after the war and completed in 1955. *Jean Bart* took part in the Suez campaign in 1956, was decommissioned in the 1960s and scrapped in Japan in 1969.

Clémenceau was only 10 per cent complete when France was overrun by the Germans and she was declared war booty. The hull section was floated out of

dock but never worked on again and was sunk in a US air raid in 1944. *Gascogne* was never started.

A final class of battleships, *Alsace*, *Normandie*, *Flandre* and *Bourgogne* was proposed for 1940 onwards but not actually implemented.

Richelieu class

Class: *Richelieu, Jean Bart, Clémenceau, Gascogne.*
Launched 1939–40
Dimensions: Length – 247.8m/813ft
Beam – 33m/108ft 3in
Draught – 9.65m/31ft 7in
Displacement: 35,560 tonnes/35,000 tons
Armament: Main – 8 x 380mm/15in guns
Secondary – 9 x 150mm/6in, 12 x 99mm/3.9in,
8 x 37mm/1.46in and 16 x 13mm/0.52in guns
Machinery: 6 boilers, 4 shafts.
111,855kW/150,000shp
Speed: 32 knots
Complement: 1,670 men
Jean Bart was fitted with bulges and had a beam of 35.5m/116ft.

LEFT: *Conte di Cavour* and *Guilio Cesare* were
modernized in the 1930s. The reconstruction
amounted to a complete rebuild which totally
changed their profile, as well as adding 10.3m/34ft
to their length.

Conte di Cavour class (1933)

Starting in 1933 *Conte di Cavour* and *Giulio Cesare* were completely rebuilt. A new bow section added more than 9m/30ft to their length. New oil-fired boilers and turbines driving two shafts, reduced from four, delivered three times more horsepower. This, with the longer hull ratio, produced 6 knots of extra speed. The midships turret was suppressed and the ships were given a completely new superstructure. The 305mm/12in main armament was replaced by 320mm/12.6in guns, and the armoured protection increased. Horizontal armour was increased to 135mm/5.3in and vertical armour around the turrets by an additional 50mm/1.97in. The Pugliese system was installed in which fuel tanks ran the length of the ship, and these contained a large empty cylinder intended as a shock absorber to minimize a hit on or below the waterline.

Conte di Cavour took part in the action off Punto Stilo on July 9, 1940, also known as the Battle of Calabria, when the British battleships *Malaya*, *Barham* and *Royal Sovereign* chased the Italian fleet to within sight of the coast of Calabria. Battles such as this helped to establish the superior morale of the British battlefleet under Cunningham's aggressive command. There followed other largely unsuccessful actions against the British fleet and various Malta convoys. On November 11, 1940, Swordfish torpedo-bombers from the British carrier *Illustrious* attacked the Italian fleet in the harbour of Taranto and *Conte di Cavour* was sunk by a torpedo. Raised and towed to Trieste for repairs, she was sunk again by the Italians to prevent her falling into German hands, only to be raised by the Germans but sunk again by the USAAF in 1945. She was scrapped in 1951.

Giulio Cesare was hit by a 380mm/15in-shell from the British *Warspite* during the Battle of Punto Stilo. She took part in the action near Cape Teulada in November 27, 1940, against Force H and the battleships *Renown* and *Ramillies*, and was engaged against British cruisers and destroyers at the First Battle of Sirte on December 17, 1941.

By early 1942 *Giulio Cesare* was reduced to the status of a training and barracks ship. Allocated to the Soviet Union as war reparations, she became the *Novorossijsk*, but was lost in 1955 as a result of striking a mine in the Black Sea.

Leonardo da Vinci was sunk by a magazine explosion in 1916, attributed (probably wrongly) to Austrian saboteurs. Although she was refloated and it was planned to refit the hull, she was scrapped in the 1920s.

Caio Duilio class (1937)

Like their near sisters, the Conte di Cavour class, these ships were completely rebuilt under Mussolini's regime in Italy. The hull was lengthened by inserting a new bow section, and they were given an all-new propulsion plant, driving two shafts. These measures together gave them 6 knots of extra speed, up to 27 knots. The midships turret was removed and they were given new superstructures. The main armament was increased to 320mm/ 12.6in calibre, the secondary armament of 12 135mm/5.3in guns was mounted in four triple turrets, and they also carried numerous lighter anti-aircraft guns. Armour was also increased and they received the Pugliese protection system.

Caio Duilio re-entered service in July 1940 and thereafter was involved in a number of unsuccessful skirmishes against the British Mediterranean Fleet. During the attack on Taranto by aircraft of the Royal Navy's Fleet Air Arm she received one torpedo hit but remained afloat and the following month was at sea on North Africa convoy duties. On December 17, 1941, she fought a brief and unsuccessful action with British cruisers and destroyers in what became known as the First Battle of Sirte. She was surrendered to the Royal Navy on September 9, 1943, when the Italian government signed an armistice with the Allies, and scrapped in 1957.

Andrea Doria was also unsuccessful against the British Mediterranean Fleet, although regularly employed on convoy protection duties to and from North Africa and in attempts to disrupt British convoys to Malta. She escaped damage during the British attack on Taranto harbour on November 11, but did join Caio Duilio in the unsuccessful action at the First Battle of Sirte. Andrea Doria was surrendered to the Royal Navy at Malta on September 9, 1943, and scrapped in 1957.

Caio Duilio class

Class: *Caio Duilio, Andrea Doria.* Launched 1913
Dimensions: Length – 186.9m/613ft 2in
    Beam – 28m/91ft 10in
    Draught – 9.5m/30ft 10in
Displacement: 21,590 tonnes/23,800 tons
Armament: Main – 10 x 320mm/12.6in guns
    Secondary – 12 x 135mm/5.3in,
Machinery: 8 boilers, 2 turbines.
    59,859kW/87,000shp
Speed: 27 knots
Complement: 1,490 men
The specifications given here are for the ships as they were rebuilt in the 1930s.

ABOVE: **Detail of the port quarter of *Andrea Doria*.** LEFT: **The Caio Duilio class and the Conte di Cavour class were similar ships when first built, with tall funnels, even taller tripod masts and a midships turret, as seen here. Contrast this with the 1930s rebuild opposite, which gave the ships of these two classes a much lower profile. The length was increased too and with more efficient machinery, which nearly tripled the horsepower, the speed was increased in both classes by some 6 knots. Improved armour increased displacement by some 2,032tonnes/2,000 tons.**

Vittorio Veneto class

These handsome battleships were the first to be built by Italy after the Washington Naval Treaty, and were partly a response to the French *Dunkerque* and *Strasbourg*. Clearly the Italians were intent upon breaching the treaty limit of 35,560 tonnes/35,000 tons, and at full load these ships displaced more than 45,720 tonnes/45,000 tons. The guns were 380mm/15in, rather than the 405mm/16in which were permitted by treaty, which was due to the limited capacity of the Italian ordnance industry. However they were long guns capable, in theory, of a range of 42,062m/46,000yds.

With the exception of the 120mm/4.7in guns which were old Armstrong weapons, all the guns were of a new design, and, given the environment in which these ships would operate, the anti-aircraft armament was increased during the war.

The armour which was up to 350mm/13.8in thick was intended to defeat 380mm/15in shells at 16,000m/17,500yds, and there was complex subdivision inside the hull, including the Pugliese system. This consisted of a torpedo bulkhead

ABOVE: **Italian design at its best, *Vittorio Veneto* was built in 1934–40 and scrapped in 1948–51.** BELOW LEFT: **The Vittorio Veneto class were beamy, well-thought-out ships intended for war in the Mediterranean. With its mix of new and modernized battleships and the ability to operate under the cover of aircraft from numerous shore airfields, the Italian navy had the material to dominate the Mediterranean. However, in early encounters Cunningham and his British Mediterranean Fleet established their superior morale.**

which curved inboard and downward to meet the outer bottom. Within this was a compartment containing an empty longitudinal drum which was manufactured under pressure thus absorbing the force of any explosion, however, poor construction technique was blamed for the system not proving as effective in action as was hoped.

As they often showed in battle with the British, this class of ship was capable of high sustained speed. A quarterdeck catapult could launch three reconnaissance planes or, as the war progressed, three fighters. In September 1941 *Littorio* became the first Italian battleship to be fitted with radar.

Vittorio Veneto was the busiest of the Italian battleships. Completed in April 1940, she escaped damage during the attack on Taranto, and was flagship of the Italian fleet during the Battle of Cape Matapan in March 1941. Here she was hit during a torpedo attack by *Formidable*'s aircraft, but was not slowed sufficiently to allow Cunningham in *Warspite* with the British Mediterranean Fleet to catch up. She then underwent repairs until August 1941. Her main employment was as distant cover for Axis Africa-bound convoys and the interdiction of British Malta-bound shipping. On November 8, 1941, the cruisers *Aurora* and *Penelope*, forming the British Force K, sallied from Malta and snapped up a convoy supposedly under the *Vittorio Veneto*'s protection. Then on December 14, 1941, the British submarine *Urge* torpedoed the *Vittorio Veneto* and she required repairs which lasted until early 1942. In June 1943

TOP: *Littorio* (formerly *Italia*) was badly damaged at Taranto in November 1940 by the British Fleet Air Arm. ABOVE: *Roma* on her launch in 1940.
LEFT: *Roma* having entered the war against the British was on her way to surrender at Malta when she was bombed by her erstwhile allies, the Germans, and sunk.

she was bombed while at La Spezia. After being surrendered to the British at Malta in September 1943, she was interned at Suez and then returned to Italy, being scrapped in 1948.

Littorio, as she is better known, was damaged in Taranto by three torpedoes delivered by Swordfish aircraft from the British carrier *Illustrious*. She sank by the bows and remained under repair at Taranto until August 1941. At the Second Battle of Sirte on March 22, 1942, she made a determined attempt to interdict a four-ship convoy protected by British cruisers and destroyers under the command of Admiral Philip Vian, but was driven off by superior tactics, including the use of smokescreens and torpedo attack. She was renamed *Italia* on July 30, 1943, after the overthrow of Mussolini, and was badly damaged on September 9, 1941, by German glider bombs but survived. After internment at Alexandria, she was returned to Italy in 1947 and scrapped.

Roma was bombed in La Spezia in June 1942 as she was nearing completion. Repaired, she sailed in September 1943 with the Italian fleet to its surrender under the guns of Malta, but was struck by a German glider bomb and sank with heavy losses. *Impero* was never completed and was taken over by

the Germans at the Italian armistice; she was bombed and sunk in Trieste in 1945, and scrapped in 1950. With the loss of all its battleships at the end of World War II, Italy's attempt to join the first rank of navies was brought to an end, despite leading some of the stages of battleship development and designing some very graceful ships.

Vittorio Veneto class

Class: *Vittorio Veneto, Italia* (ex *Littorio*),
Roma, Impero. Launched 1937–40
Dimensions: Length – 224m/735ft
Beam – 32.75m/107ft 5in
Draught – 9.6m/31ft 5in
Displacement: 41,377 tonnes/40,724 tons
Armament: Main – 9 x 380mm/15in guns
Secondary – 12 x 155mm/6.1in,
4 x 120mm/4.7in, 12 x 90mm/3.54in,
20 x 37mm/1.46in and 16 x 20mm/0.79in guns
Machinery: 8 boilers, 4-shaft geared turbines.
96,940kW/130,000shp
Speed: 30 knots
Complement: 1,830–1,950 men

Sovyetskiy Soyuz class

Under the Soviet second five-year plan (1933–7) the old Imperial shipyards at Leningrad and Nikolayev were modernized. In 1938 the *Sovyetskiy Soyuz* was laid down at the Baltic shipyard, known in the Soviet era as the Ordzhonikidze Shipyard (No. 189), and *Sovyetskaya Ukraina* at the Andre Marti Shipyard (No. 198) at Nikolayev on the Black Sea. New yards were also built in the Arctic and the Far East, as well as inland on canals which could be used to take unfinished hulls to the coast for completion. One of the new yards was Shipyard No. 402 at Molotovsk (now Severodvinsk) on the White Sea, where the construction hall was big enough to take two super-battleships of the Sovyetskiy Soyuz class side by side.

After World War I, the Soviet Union was not regarded as a naval power and had not been invited to any of the inter-war naval arms conferences. Stalin apparently studied the strategic writings of the American naval officer, Mahan, who urged

nations (in his case the USA) to obtain a navy for geo-strategic purposes, and wanted a navy for the Soviet Union for reasons of self-esteem as much as for national security. The Soviet Union therefore became a late signatory of the London Naval Treaty and in 1937 signed a bilateral Anglo-Soviet Naval agreement. Stalin ordered his agents to purchase whatever was needed from his capitalist enemies for the Soviet naval programme, and they eventually obtained plans bought from Italy, who had supplied the Imperial Russian Navy, to help work up their own version of a super-Dreadnought. Blueprints were also purchased from the USA, despite objections from the USN, and in 1940 the Soviet navy sought help from Nazi Germany.

The initial Soviet plan was to build a fleet of 16 battleships and 12 heavy cruisers and corresponding numbers of other warships during the next two five-year plans. It is doubtful whether the Soviets ever had the technology to achieve this

LEFT: Soviet plans to build battleships in the inter-war years came to nothing. However the Soviets did acquire the Italian *Giulio Cesare* as war reparation in 1948. Italian naval officers and men refused to steam *Giulio Cesare* to Russia, and so she had to be manned with a civilian crew. BELOW: The British also lent *Royal Sovereign* between 1944 and 1949, seen here flying the Soviet flag.

Sovyetskiy Soyuz class

Class: *Sovyetskiy Soyuz, Sovyetskaya Ukraina, Sovyetskaya Byelorussiya, Sovyetskaya Rossiya.* Not launched.

Dimensions: Length – 271m/889ft
Beam – 38.7m/127ft
Draught – 10.1m/33ft 2in

Displacement: 60,099 tonnes/59,150 tons

Armament: Main – 9 x 405mm/16in guns
Secondary – 12 x 150mm/6in,
8 x 100mm/4in and 32 x 37mm/1.46in guns

Machinery: boilers, 3 shafts turbo-electric.
172,257kW/231,000shp

Speed: 28 knots

plan or any of its subsequent alterations and it certainly did not have the finance. However four Sovyetskiy Soyuz class battleships were authorized in 1938 and construction of three of them was started. All three were overtaken by war.

The design bore a passing resemblance to the Italian Vittorio Veneto class, with two triple turrets forward, B turret super-firing over A, and an after turret in a tall barbette. They also had a tall tower superstructure forward of two large upright funnels. The Italian Pugliese system of underwater protection was also adopted. None of these ships were completed, and all were broken up in the 1940s.

From May 1944 to February 1949 the Soviet navy was lent the British battleship *Royal Sovereign* under the name of *Arkhangelsk*, pending delivery of an equivalent Italian battleship as part of the Soviet Union's share of war reparations. She was used to escort Arctic convoys, but became something of a target for German U-boats, including an attack by Biber midget submarines, and spent much of the time behind anti-submarine nets. She was returned to Britain in 1949 and broken up.

As for the Sovyetskiy Soyuz class itself, these were by far the largest Russian warships designed, but the German invasion prevented their completion, and the post-war shipyards lacked the capacity and the political direction to continue to build battleships. The name ship of the class, *Sovyetskiy Soyuz*, was well advanced when war broke out, but between 1941 and 1944 most of the armour was removed for use elsewhere in the Soviet war economy. Post-war she was cut into sections and scrapped. Work on the second ship, *Sovyetskaya Ukraina*, was almost 75 per cent complete when the German army occupied Nikolayev on August 16, 1941. When the German army evacuated the city in 1944 they damaged the building slip and the ship, preventing her completion. No progress was made with the other two ships of the class, *Sovyetskaya Byelorussiya* and *Sovyetskaya Rossiya*.

By the end of World War II the Soviet navy still had not recovered from its parlous state after the Battle of Tsushima, and the world had to wait until the Cold War, when it briefly flourished under Admiral Gorshkov.

CRUISERS

IMAGE: **An aircraft takes off from a Duquesne class ship.**

The History of Cruisers

Operating alone on long, distant commissions, cruisers bred commanding officers of independence and initiative, resourceful and ready to use marines or bluejackets to extend the reach of the ship herself. History is rich in such incident but, with progressive imperial stability, cruiser operations became more closely tied to those of the battle fleets as European relationships cooled.

The wide variety of cruisers in 1914 highlights the difficult compromises necessary to produce the correct balance of armament, protection and propulsive power. With considerable success, they assumed the roles of sailing frigates in patrolling, reconnaissance, tracking and reporting. During World War II, their long range and independence exploited good intelligence to hunt down the enemy's auxiliary raiders and the supply ships upon which they depended.

In wartime, the major threat to cruisers turned out to be not other cruisers but aircraft and submarines. The answer to the former was the guided missile, and it was the rapid development and proliferation of these that signalled the demise of the conventional cruiser. Today's ideals are technological excellence and lean crews.

LEFT: **The turn of the 20th century marked the peak of British maritime supremacy. Here, the crew of a three-master, snubbing at her anchor, cheer the passage of an armoured cruiser, a product of the Naval Defence Act, in full Victorian livery.**

Early cruisers

The origins of the term "cruiser" lay more in a ship's function than in its type. In general, it was applied to ships too small to lay in a line of battle and which were engaged on independent duties. A cruiser might, thus, be a frigate scouting or reconnoitering on behalf of a battle fleet, a corvette engaged in the policing of distant stations, a sloop safeguarding commerce from the depredations of privateers or even a cutter patrolling to counter a lucrative smuggling trade. These and similar duties greatly occupied the Royal Navy of the early 19th century and it is not surprising, therefore, that the service was responsible for many of the developments that eventually refined the cruiser into specific types.

By the middle of the 19th century, in the absence of major wars, the most important duty of cruisers was the policing of colonial territorial waters, generally "showing the flag" and deterring local belligerents with aspirations to disrupt any part of a worldwide British trade network from acting.

Where improvements in iron construction and in propulsion machinery were being applied to the battle fleet on a continuous basis, change came slowly to the colonial cruisers for very practical reasons. One was that early examples of this new machinery was inefficient, burning large quantities of coal, of which the ships could stow little and at a time when the full network of imperial coaling stations had yet to be established. Ships might spend many years on a single station, being serviced in the region and rotating crews at specified intervals. Such vessels needed a high degree of reliability and long

TOP: **The combined mass of all-metal hulls, machinery and bunkers, and heavier guns, enforced the end of the multi-decked warship. HMS** *Warrior* **and** *Black Prince*, **designed to lay in a line-of-battle, were, nonetheless, single-deckers and therefore technically large frigates.** ABOVE: **Despite the technical advances of ships such as the above, guns were still mounted on the broadside. The 254mm/10in gun shown fired explosive shells, but was still mounted on a wooden carriage with old-style breechings to contain its recoil.**

endurance, so their machinery was regarded as auxiliary to sail, under which they spent the greater part of their time. Often referred to as "captains under God", their commanding officers in these days of slow communications were of necessity accustomed to making decisions without reference to higher authority, and were accustomed to independent action.

This apparent reluctance to change also resulted from the fact that colonial cruisers frequently worked in extreme climates, usually tropical but occasionally in high latitudes.

A wooden vessel was infinitely more comfortable for her crew than an early "iron pot" which, poorly insulated, sweated unhealthily. Even when iron construction became more general, it remained common for colonial cruisers to be of so-called "composite construction", i.e. wood planked on an iron frame. A further incentive was that a copper-sheathed wooden hull fouled less quickly in tropical waters than an iron one, a consideration of some significance with respect to both speed and to the remote possibilities of regular dry-docking on distant stations. Finally, the woodworking trades still comprised a high proportion of a dockyard's manpower, and the scarcer metal workers were more efficiently employed on major warships.

In 1860 there were 34 screw frigates and corvettes, 76 screw sloops and 24 "gun-vessels" in the Royal Navy's establishment. Many were unprotected, others described as "ironclad" by virtue of the addition of a waterline belt, typically of 114mm/4.5in of wrought iron backed by 660mm/26in of teak. This was rarely tested in action.

Guns were fewer but had increased in size considerably. Typically, there were eight 100pdr muzzle-loading smooth bores, disposed four to each broadside. They were concentrated amidships in what was termed a "central battery", protected by sides and transverse bulkheads, again of 114mm/4.5in iron backed by teak.

Fully rigged and typically of 3,251 tonnes/3,200 tons displacement, a screw corvette would have steam reciprocating machinery developing some 1,305kW/1,750ihp. With a clean hull this might be good for nearly 12 knots. Her complement of up to 270 would include a marine detachment and/or a company of bluejackets well-trained in military skills to be used for intervention ashore as required.

In Pacific territories, an administrator might have responsibility for scores of widely scattered islands, and the station cruiser afforded him not only transport but underpinned his authority. Many a British vice-consul, overtaken by a local insurrection, has owed his life to the timely arrival of the Navy.

TOP: **Iron screw corvettes were diminutives of the frigates usually lacking a deck over the broadside battery. Here, the *Active* of 1869 leaves Portsmouth under sail, passing the famous *Victory*, all-wood, obsolete and representative of the "Old Navy".** ABOVE: **The *Swiftsure* of 1870 carried ten 229mm/9in, muzzle-loading, rifled shell guns. In order to protect these with the thickest feasible armour, they were concentrated into an amidships, two-deck redoubt, this type of vessel becoming known as a "central battery" ship.** BELOW: **Also carrying her heaviest weapons amidships, the French *Victorieuse* shows differences from her British equivalents. Note the use of sponsons to gain a measure of axial fire, the short forecastle, and the vestigial navigating bridge forward of the funnel.**

The influence of the American Civil War

During their long years of war against Great Britain, the French employed large numbers of privateers which, given legitimacy by Letter of Marque, preyed to great effect on British commercial shipping. From 1861, with the onset of civil war, American Union ships quickly blockaded the ports of the Confederate South, which resulted in the latter responding by the licensing of approximately 80 privateers. Although these succeeded in taking many Union prizes it proved impossible to realize their value by condemnation before a prize court. The South's own ports were blockaded and those of all major maritime powers were unavailable because, by the 1856 Declaration of Paris, privateering had been declared illegal in International Law. As the only available option was now to sink any capture, the profit motive disappeared and with it the majority of would-be privateers. These now turned instead to the risky but highly lucrative trade of blockade-running.

Driven more by altruism than by the prospect of personal gain, however, some Confederate skippers continued to cause considerable disruption to Union shipping. Notable among these was Captain Raphael Semmes, who commanded the *Alabama,* one of a pair of fast screw sloops built to disguised account by the British firm of Laird. In a wide-ranging two-year cruise Semmes took 69 prizes but finally, in June 1864, was obliged to call at the French port of Cherbourg for essential machinery repairs. Upon leaving port, the *Alabama* was met by the protected Union ship *Kearsarge* and destroyed in a protracted gunnery duel.

Between them, the *Alabama* and other notable raiders, such as the Laird-built *Florida* and the *Shenandoah*, accounted for about five per cent of Northern shipping. Although it made

no difference to the eventual outcome of the war, it caused the Union to lay down several fast cruising vessels capable of hunting down the fastest raider. Built of wood, with some iron reinforcement, these differed from ship to ship but collectively, were known by the name of the lead ship, *Wampanoag*. For the sake of endurance they were fully rigged but their *raison d'être* was speed, and nearly one half of their lean hulls was devoted to machinery. The *Wampanoag* herself could sustain a then world record speed of 16.7 knots. Her four outsized funnels and three masts made for a very impressive appearance and, to the particular interest of Britain and France, both of whom had profited considerably from the war, it was let known that the function of the ships was, primarily, to apprehend Confederate raiders but, in the case of foreign intervention, to raid enemy commerce.

Completed after the cessation of hostilities, the Wampanoags proved to have weak hulls, and their machinery unreliable and expensive to operate (not least because of the

ABOVE: **Under the command of Captain Raphael Semmes, the** *Alabama* **became the most successful Confederate raider. All such cruisers must, however, return to port at some stage for essential repairs and maintenance. As with many raiders yet to come, this would prove to be her undoing.**

LEFT: **At the time of the Civil War, America still depended upon Europe, both as a source of specialist heavy engineering and as an important market for its goods. Merchantmen carrying the latter, vital to finance the war, were vulnerable to commerce raiders such as the Confederate** *Alabama*.

LEFT: Concerned by the success of commerce raiders during the American Civil War, the British Admiralty began to replace its many wooden frigates with large iron frigates with considerable speed for the day. Typified by the *Inconstant* of 1868, they proved to be too expensive.

ABOVE RIGHT: Last of the Confederate raiders, the *Shenandoah* wreaked havoc on the Union-based whaling industry in the Northern Pacific. Difficulties in apprehending her led directly to the United States acquiring naval basing rights in the Samoan Islands. LEFT: Although nowhere near as spacious as this impression suggests, the *Merrimack*'s slope-sided topside construction is evident. Two of her eight 229mm/9in Dahlgren rifled breech-loaders are shown. Despite her superior firepower, her celebrated duel with the turret-equipped *Monitor* proved inconclusive. BELOW: Best known of the big Union wood-built cruisers was the *Wampanoag*, typifying the type that the *Inconstant* (above) was designed to counter. Although setting an early world speed record of nearly 18 knots, she was so expensive to operate that she worked almost exclusively under sail.

necessary number of stokers). Congress, which saw little justification for a fleet at all, saw even less for these ships but, nonetheless, the fact that they could out-run anything that they could not out-fight caused considerable concern in British and French naval circles, who both built in direct response.

Recognizing that the long wooden hulls of the Americans lacked longitudinal stiffness, both countries countered with large iron frigates. Launched in 1868, the British lead ship was the *Inconstant*, whose 5,873 tonnes/5,780 tons considerably exceeded the *Wampanoag*'s 4,283 tonnes/4,215 tons. Despite that, she was unprotected and, as contemporary iron plate had a bad reputation for shattering when struck by heavy shot, she was sheathed externally in timber. About a knot slower than the American, the *Inconstant* was, nevertheless, by far the better ship. Two variants, the larger *Shah* and smaller *Raleigh*, were also built but all proved expensive to run in peacetime.

Much delayed by the 1870–71 war with Prussia, the French produced the *Duquesne* and *Tourville*. Where the British ships mounted their ten heavy guns broadside in central batteries, the French located some weapons in sponsons to give a measure of end-on fire.

In order to afford some protection, these large iron frigates were designed with coal bunkers flanking their machinery spaces.

The origins of the protected cruiser

Completed in 1875, the British unprotected frigate *Shah* was deployed as flagship of Commander-in-Chief, Pacific, Rear Admiral Algernon de Horsey. Accompanied by the unarmoured wooden screw corvette *Amethyst*, she arrived in Callao, Peru, in May 1877 to find that, following a mutiny aboard, the Peruvian turret-ship (or monitor) *Huascar* was taking armed action against foreign interests. Intent on her capture, de Horsey came up with her off Ilo on May 29.

The *Huascar* had been built by Laird 12 years previously and, in contrast with the British ships' mainly broadside armament, mounted two 254mm/10in weapons, firing 136.3kg/300lb projectiles, in a revolving turret. Her armoured belt varied between 114mm/4.5in and 64mm/2.5in in thickness, while the turret armour was 140mm/5.5in thick. Her stem was also reinforced for ramming.

Far larger, the *Shah* mounted two 229mm/9in, sixteen 178mm/7in and eight 64-pounder guns, the *Amethyst* adding fourteen more 64-pounders.

Refusing a summons to surrender, the *Huascar* sought shallow water, obliging her deeper-draught adversaries to fire, for the most part, at long range. During a three-hour action the *Huascar* tried once, unsuccessfully, to ram the *Shah*, while her inexperienced gunners failed to score a single hit.

For their part, the British ships made 70–80 hits from between 1,372m/1,500yds and 2,286m/2,500yds. Of all these, only one pierced the *Huascar*'s armour. During the action the *Shah* launched a Whitehead torpedo, the first such instance, but missed, due to its inaccuracy and low speed.

TOP: Like the Confederate *Alabama*, the Peruvian turret ship *Huascar* was British-built. Taken over by renegade elements, she was intercepted in a policing action by the British iron frigate *Shah*. In the only big-ship action fought by the Victorian Navy, the *Shah* failed to sink the pirate. ABOVE: Benedetto Brin, the great Italian constructor, pioneered the vaulted protective deck, crowned by a cellular layer, as a lighter and more effective alternative to vertical side armour. Laid down in 1877–78, his battleships *Lepanto* (seen here) and *Italia* dispensed completely with belt armour.

De Horsey thus failed to apprehend the renegade, while his actions caused misgivings at home for, had the *Huascar* been competently handled, she would have given the British the choice of retreating or being sunk. Clearly, cruising ships required protection but, due to their weight, vertical side belts were out of the question. However, the great Italian constructor, Benedetto Brin, was designing battleships with a new, and lighter, means of protection, already partially adopted by the British Admiralty in the turret battleship *Inflexible*, completed in 1881 and a command of the redoubtable John Fisher.

LEFT: **The French protected cruiser *Tage* here demonstrates a "harbour furl" (or "harbour stow") whereby her square canvas is gathered to the centre of the yard, a method which allows the sails to dry. Her three funnels are indicative of the number of boilers necessary even for auxiliary machinery.** ABOVE: **The British *Inflexible* of 1876 swiftly adopted Brin's ideas. She was not, of course, a cruiser but note here the low freeboard hull with unarmoured ends, and the powerfully armoured citadel with the two twin 406mm/16in muzzle-loader turrets placed *en echlon*.**

Brin reasoned that no side armour could withstand hits from the huge 432mm/17in guns that he was specifying. He therefore abandoned it entirely in favour of thinner horizontal protection, made lighter through using not-too-reliable steel plate. The "horizontal" protective deck was actually vaulted, its 76mm/3in plate abutting a ship's sides some 1.83m/6ft below the designed waterline. Above it, a flat unarmoured deck was located some 1.52m/5ft above the waterline. The space between these decks was subdivided into small compartments, or cells, some coal-filled, some void.

At ranges then considered practicable, projectiles followed fairly flat trajectories. Any penetrating the side, or shell, plating about or below the waterline would contact the convex curvature of the protective deck at a very shallow angle and be deflected upward, to expend their energy within the cellular layer. Despite some resultant flooding, it was unlikely that this would be sufficient to submerge the upper level of the cellular structure. Compartments above and below the cellular level would not, therefore, be flooded, the ship retaining adequate buoyancy and stability.

For cruising ships, the Admiralty began by partially adopting the idea, initially in the first-of-class *Comus* of 1878. Being far smaller than the *Inflexible*, her protective system was also on a smaller scale. The protective deck, flat rather than curved, was 38mm/1.5in in thickness, and located only 0.91m/3ft below the waterline, extending over only the central machinery spaces and magazines. The cellular structure was only a half-deck in depth but screened down either side by coal-filled bunker spaces. The *Comus* had a steel frame clad with iron plate, the latter being wood-sheathed and coppered as was customary for colonial cruisers.

ABOVE: **Last of the sailing corvettes built for the Royal Navy, the C-types (*Cordelia* here) were also the first with all-metal hulls. Steel-framed, iron-clad, and wood-sheathed, they had a 38mm/1.5in steel protective deck over their machinery.**
BELOW: **First French cruiser to be built with a protective deck, the *Sfax* of 1884 slightly pre-dated the *Tage* (top left) and her sister *Cécille*. She was capable of a then-respectable 17 knots and with the *Tages* comprised the commerce-raiding squadron. Note how the heavy rig is no longer used for sailing.**

With this class of 11 ships, a new breech-loading 152mm/6in gun made its appearance. The final pair, *Calliope* and *Calypso*, mounted four of them in sponsons, French-style, to improve axial fire.

265

Early belted and armoured cruisers

There is rarely a definitive solution to the problems posed by warship design and, despite Benedetto Brin's concept of horizontal protection attracting one school of design, another still preferred and justified vertical protection. This, in what were still considered "line-of-battle ships", was necessarily massive. Faster than such vessels, a "cruiser" would logically decline action and her protection could be on a lighter scale. The question was one of how best to apply it. A given weight of armour could be spread fairly thinly over full length vertical belts, more thickly over shorter belts that protected only vital areas, or distributed in a compromise of vertical belting and protective deck. As a result two types developed; the "belted" and the "armoured" cruiser, although the latter term was often used to describe either type.

The Russians are credited with building the first belted cruisers with the launch of the *General Admiral* in 1873 and the *Minin* in 1878. Their full-length belts were, respectively, 152mm/6in and 178mm/7in thick, leaving the gun batteries, one level above, unprotected. The *General Admiral*'s six 203mm/8in main battery weapons were breech-loading rifles (BLRs) and were concentrated in an amidships box with high bulwarks. The four corner guns could be traversed to fire either ahead or on the beam. In contrast, the *Minin* adopted French ideas with pronounced tumblehome and her four 203mm/8in BLRs located in four quarter sponsons, the weapons being capable of limited traverse to enable them to fire ahead or to work on the beam or axially for the purpose of chase fire.

TOP: **Russia's *General Admiral* had a shallow armoured belt protecting the waterline over its entire length. Just discernible is the open-topped box redoubt amidships, the ship's six 9.1-tonne/9-ton guns firing over a low armoured bulkhead only 0.76m/30in in height.** ABOVE: **The *Shannon* (if this is indeed her, for she was completed with a vertical stem) was the Royal Navy's first armoured cruiser. Her waterline belt stopped 18.3m/60ft from the stem, terminating in a 229mm/9in bulkhead. An armoured deck continued forward. Except for forward fire, the battery was unprotected.**

The launch of the *General Admiral* resulted in the laying-down of the *Shannon*, Britain's first armoured cruiser although, as this term was not yet generally accepted, she was classed as a "broadside armour-belted cruising ship with the status of a Second Class battleship", terminology, which reflected the still uncertain purpose of such vessels.

In both armament and armour, the *Shannon* was interesting. Of her seven 229mm/9in muzzle-loading rifles (MLRs), six were in the open and fired broadside, while the seventh, beneath the poop deck, could traverse sufficiently to fire through embrasures on either quarter. For the purposes of pursuit, two 254mm/10in MLRs fired forward through a transverse iron bulkhead. Up to 229mm/9in thick, this also served to protect the gundeck from raking fire from ahead (betraying tactical thinking from the still-recent sailing ship era).

The ship's belt armour, of similar thickness, extended from right aft to the transverse bulkhead, which continued down two levels to close it off. The belts were roofed by a 38mm/1.5in thick protective deck, one level beneath the gundeck. Forward of the lower edge of the bulkhead a 76mm/3in protective deck sloped downward, terminating in reinforcement for the ram. For further protection, this deck was overlaid by deep (if inaccessible) coal bunkers.

Over-ambitious and overweight, the *Shannon* was judged to be too weak to serve in a battle line yet too slow to be an effective cruising ship. This appears to have been anticipated prior to her launch as her two follow-ons, *Nelson* and *Northampton*, were laid down at 40 per cent larger by displacement. Their belts extended over only the centre section of the hull but were closed off by armoured bulkheads at either end. The extra power required twin shafts, each fitted with two propellers, which imposed considerable drag when the ships were under sail.

Powerful rivalry still existed between the British and French navies and, despite the reservations of the former toward the large armoured cruisers, the French followed suit in 1882 with the launch of the *Vauban* and *Duguesclin*. These displaced about 5,995 tonnes/5,900 tons compared with *Northampton*'s 7,722 tonnes/7,600 tons, and differed in having their armour disposed in a similar way to that of their recently completed battleship *Amiral Duperré*. Their belts were full length but shallow, leaving a margin to provide protection for four barbette-mounted 240mm/9.5in breech-loading rifles (BLRs). Barbette mountings left the guns exposed but, lacking heavy overhead shielding, permitted the weapons to be mounted higher above the waterline.

ABOVE: **Together with her near-sister *Vettor Pisani*, the Italian Navy's *Carlo Alberto* was not completed until 1898. Her side belt was of 152mm/6in plate amidships, tapering to 114mm/4.5in at the extremities. The main protective deck was 152mm/6in thick, with a 51mm/2in secondary deck above.**

BELOW: ***Nelson* and *Northampton* (shown) were larger derivatives of the *Shannon*. The deep embrasure was for one of the four symmetrically disposed 18.3-tonne/18-ton guns which fired axially through armoured bulkheads. Eight 12.2-tonne/12-ton guns fired on the beam through the unarmoured side above the belt. Compare the rigging with that of the *Alberto* (above).**

ABOVE: **A further solution to deploying four heavy guns was afforded by the French *Amiral Duperré*. Two single 343mm/13.5in, 48.8-tonne/48-ton guns were barbette-mounted on sponsons forward of the funnels, with two more on the centreline further aft and covered by a light spar deck.**

LEFT: **The Nelsons had "soft", or unarmoured, ends in order to concentrate protection amidships. Loss of buoyancy in the ends, if holed in action, was minimized by utilizing them for water-excluding spaces along the waterline, such as coal bunkers and water tanks.**

The Naval Defence Act of 1889

The Royal Navy of the 1870s and 1880s was a service in transition. Its well-organized, well-proven fleet of wooden, broadside-armed sailing ships had been assailed by technological development. How best to absorb and combine developments such as iron or steel, horizontal or vertical steam engines, paddles or screws, barbettes or turrets, muzzle or breech loaders? Each development attracted enthusiasts and in one form or another, these technologies found their way into new vessels, even if only for evaluation. The net result was an eclectic range of oddities and one-offs that lacked any sort of coherence and which were a logistical nightmare.

Technological development was not, of course, limited to Great Britain and growth in foreign fleets, particularly those of France and Russia, was a matter of some concern. To maintain battle fleets at home and in the Mediterranean, and to cover its worldwide imperial commitments, the Navy required adequate numbers of effective fighting ships; these it now obviously lacked.

The full extent of the Navy's weaknesses was first highlighted during 1884 in a series of articles in the influential Pall Mall Gazette, and the resulting public interest was skilfully exploited by interested parties. One such person was the junior Sea Lord, the then Captain Lord Charles Beresford, who prepared a detailed memorandum for the Board of Admiralty

> "Most of what you see is mere ullage." Admiral Hewitt describing the Royal Navy's ships at the 1887 Golden Jubilee Review

TOP: **Between 1899 and 1902 the new protected cruiser HMS *Crescent* acted as flagship on the Royal Navy's then North America and West Indies Station. Wearing a courtesy ensign, admiral's flag and jack, she is seen leading a squadron at an American review at Bar Harbor, Maine.** ABOVE: **Although rather similar in appearance to the Crescents, *Blake* and *Blenheim* (seen here) were rather larger, mounting a second 234mm/9.2in gun in lieu of a couple of broadside 152mm/6in guns. She is pictured in the uniform grey livery adopted from 1902, and disarmed, is serving as a depot ship, probably during World War I.**

demonstrating the complacency engendered by long years of freedom from major maritime war. For example, since the abolition of the old Navy Board there was no organization to oversee the conduct of war. Neither was there any intelligence-gathering service, nor a plan for the direction of merchant shipping in war, or for the transport and strategic stockpiling of essentials such as coal and ammunition.

To the Admiralty's embarrassment, this highly confidential assessment found its way into the columns of the same Pall Mall Gazette, raising public interest still further. Ever the opportunist, Beresford resigned his position on the Board early in 1888 to use his parallel occupation as Member of Parliament

ABOVE: **HMS *Blanche* was one of the four Barracouta-class Third Class cruisers which spent much of their lives in the Channel and Atlantic fleets, sometimes leading a division, or half flotilla, of torpedo boats. Note the navigating bridge, located aft, and what appears to be auxiliary canvas, bent on the after side of the masts.** RIGHT: **Destroyed by an internal explosion while visiting the Cuban capital, Havana, the USS *Maine* became the catalyst for the war against Spain. An armoured cruiser, she mounted two twin 254mm/10in turrets, the forward offset to starboard, as seen here, the after to port.**

> 'There is no doubt that, had we gone to war with France
> in those days, we might well have been swept off the face of
> the globe... The Naval Defence Act saved the country."
> **Admiral Bacon in *A Naval Scrap Book***

to lobby the Navy's case for coherent, planned expansion. From so controversial a figure, who attracted both detractors and supporters in equal measure, the Service might have appreciated less support, but he was certainly effective.

Less obvious, but equally influential, was an 1887 report by the Assistant Controller, William White (later Sir William, Director of Naval Construction), anticipating the need to replace 72 warships during the ensuing four years. Where it was customary for the Chancellor of the Exchequer to inform the First Lord of what he could expect by way of annual vote, it was apparent that what was now required was a fully funded, multi-year construction plan. Needless to say, the Treasury baulked.

Then, early in 1889, a committee of three adjudicating flag officers reported unfavourably on the conduct of recent naval manoeuvres. It highlighted the poor performance of various types of ship and went on to exceed its brief in a reasoned redefinition of the purpose and scope of British sea power. The Royal Navy, it stated, was "altogether inadequate to take the offensive in a war with only one Great Power". The fleet, in fact, needed the strength to take on a combination of the next two largest fleets, the so-called Two Power Standard.

Between them, Beresford, White and the adjudicators could take credit for the Government appreciating the gravity of the situation and funding what was passed as the Naval Defence Act of 1889.

ABOVE: **Wearing the jack of the Kaiserliche Marine, the *Victoria Louise* was classed as a heavy cruiser. Note the stepped arrangement of the secondary 15cm/5.9in weapons, maintained right through to the final Scharnhorsts.** LEFT: **The Victorian Royal Navy was noted for "spit and polish" in preference to target practice, evidenced by this view of the after 234mm/9.2in gun aboard the *Edgar*. A reliable weapon, weighing about 23.4 tonnes/23 tons, the 9.2 fired a 172kg/380lb projectile. With only two guns per ship, a slow rate of fire, and no fire control, the weapon was not very effective.**

Among 70 new warships to be spread between the 1889–94 Programmes were no less than 42 cruisers. Of what were already being termed the First, Second the Third Classes they brought much-needed standardization, creating a force against which foreign fleets had to measure themselves. The bulk were constructed in White's reorganized and newly efficient royal dockyards.

The formal adoption of the Two Power Standard gave the Royal Navy an exact size but, with developments abroad, it would prove to be too expensive a goal to maintain.

First, Second and Third Class protected cruisers

All of the Defence Act cruisers, irrespective of class, would be "protected", as opposed to "armoured" or "belted". This was the result of an assessment of the preceding armoured cruisers, whose protection had generally followed that of contemporary battleships, and which had not been considered successful. Leading the way with these were the *Imperieuse* and *Warspite*, a pair which, completed in 1886 and 1888 respectively, were greatly influenced by the new French Marceau-class battleships, many of whose features they copied on a smaller scale. Difficult to classify, they were known officially as "armour-plated steel barbette ships" but, in adopting a partial 254mm/10in belt and 38–76mm/1.5–3in protective deck, they came out near 1,016 tonnes/1,000 tons overweight. This was serious for, of the 2.4m/8ft depth of the belt, 1m/3.25ft should have given above-water protection. As it was, the upper edge of the belt was near the waterline, so that the ships depended mainly on their coal bunkers and protective deck for protection.

While the *Imperieuse* and *Warspite* were building, the seven-ship Orlando class was laid down. These were designed at 5,690 tonnes/5,600 tons compared with *Imperieuse*'s 8,636 tonnes/8,500 tons yet they still carried a pair of guns of the same 234mm/9.2in calibre. This class, too, was belted and, as the general rule of thumb for vertical armour was to make it of

ABOVE: Lead ship of a class of seven, *Orlando* was a "belted" cruiser which, for her length, carried a heavy armament. Her forward 234mm/9.2in and five starboard 152mm/6in guns, all in open shields, are clearly visible. Note how the forward and after 152mm/6in weapons are sponsoned to supplement axial, or "chase" fire.

similar thickness to the primary gun calibre, they carried the same 254mm/10in belt over two-thirds their length. This was closed by 305mm/12in transverse bulkheads, roofed by 50mm/2in plate and continued to either end in the form of a 76mm/3in protective deck. It is small wonder that, with a full load of fuel aboard, their belt was totally submerged.

None of the Orlandos was ever tested in action, so their limitations remained unexposed. In service they were judged to be a success, being fitted with innovative horizontal triple-expansion machinery delivering a speed of 18 knots. It was apparent, however, that too much was being attempted on too limited a displacement. Nonetheless, by accepting a displacement of approximately 6,706 tonnes/6,600 tons and a slight reduction in speed, the Americans followed suit with the *Maine*, launched in 1888. Mounting four 254mm/10in guns in two echeloned twin turrets, she looked the part, being often referred to as a "Second Class battleship". The French, however, had reservations, and were preparing a revised design which would point armoured cruiser development in a new direction.

LEFT: In the mid-1880s the torpedo was still something of a novelty weapon. With six fixed above-water tubes, firing on the beam, forward, amidships and aft, the seven Archers were classed as "torpedo cruisers". High bulwarks and many boats obviously made loading these fragile weapons a tricky process. ABOVE: The eight Astraeas (*Hermione* seen here) were enlarged and improved Apollos. Despite her imposing appearance she mounts only a single 152mm/6in gun forward and aft, and eight 119mm/4.7in guns firing on the beam. Both classes were worn out and obsolete by 1914.

ABOVE: Nearly 50 Third Class cruisers were built in the 20 years after 1885 for the purposes of commerce protection. The *Pallas* (shown here) of 1890 led a nine-ship class of which five were transferred to the Royal Australian Navy. The final 11 (Pelorus class) had a reduced armament. BELOW RIGHT: French influence was evident in the *Warspite*, which carried the new 234mm/9.2in at either end and on the beam, necessitating pronounced tumblehome. BELOW: Of the 21 Apollos built in 1890–91, only eight survived to serve during World War I, seven of them converted to minelayers. The *Retribution*, shown here, was scrapped in 1911. Several of the class were expended as blockships, notably at Zeebrugge and Ostend.

Even before the completion of the Orlandos, expert opinion in Britain had swung in favour of the protected cruiser in offering a more balanced design. All cruisers resulting from the 1889 Act were thus of the protected type, resulting in a hiatus in armoured cruiser production. For extended range, British cruisers required large coal bunkers, while increased magazine space was needed because guns of 152mm/6in calibre and below now fired fixed ammunition as "quick-firers". Cruisers had, in any case, no business fighting armoured ships, so weight earlier devoted to belts was better allocated to coal and ammunition. This premise was satisfactorily proven in the building of the 9,297-tonne/9,150-ton *Blake* and *Blenheim*, launched in 1889 and 1890 respectively.

The largest cruisers ordered as a result of the 1889 Act were the nine Edgar-class vessels which, at 7,468 tonnes/7,350 tons, were slightly scaled-down Blakes. Rated First Class, they were intended for duties attached to the battle fleet. Two groups of Second Class cruisers were also built, comprising eight Hermiones of 4,430 tonnes/4,360 tons and no less than 21 Apollos of 3,455 tonnes/3,400 tons. Ships of either class could make about 20 knots and the function of both was primarily trade protection. Finally, there were four 2,621-tonne/2,580-ton Pallas-class cruisers, tacked on to a further five built to serve the Australian states. Rated Third Class, the British units were intended for colonial duties.

All the new ships adhered to a basic cruiser layout established with the Orlandos, with a large gun forward and aft complemented by six, eight or ten smaller weapons firing from protected broadside casemates.

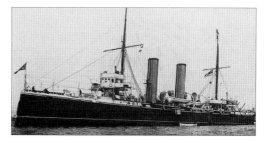

271

Cruisers and naval brigades

A major duty for a Victorian colonial cruiser was to be able to put ashore fully trained and equipped "bluejacket" contingents suitable to meet any reasonable degree of unrest. All ranks were given regular military-style training – small arms drill twice weekly and, once per week, drill with cutlass, field guns and landing parties.

Irrespective of the size of a ship's contingent, it was termed a "naval brigade". With a crew even larger than that of a contemporary battleship, a large armoured cruiser would be expected to be able to field a fully self-supporting force of 400 men. Of these, 200 seamen and 80 marines would be organized in four or five companies of riflemen. Eighty seamen and marine artillerymen would be responsible for two 76mm/3in 12-pounders and one machine gun, all on wheeled mountings. In addition there were pioneers and ammunition carriers, medical staff and stretcher bearers, armourers, signallers and buglers. What amounted to about half the ship's complement was commanded by up to 20 officers. In the absence of such a force, their ship would need to be withdrawn temporarily from frontline duties. A Third Class cruiser would muster an equally self-contained force of about half the above size. Ships were sometimes immobilized in order to provide more men.

> "By ten o'clock the 100 bullocks and 60 horses were spanned-in to the guns and wagons. Commander Limpus reported that he was ready. I sounded the advance from the Town Hall, the band played 'A Life on the Ocean Wave', and the little army started." Captain Percy Scott's own account of the Navy's departure from Durban

For those deployed at the "sharp end", the long era of *Pax Britannica* could be anything but peaceful. Naval interventions were numerous and quite often on a considerable scale, as was the case when a massive Afrikaner incursion into Natal precipitated the Second Boer War in October 1899. The British had anticipated this event, so that the Royal Navy's South Africa squadron was reinforced by the timely arrival of the two large "white elephants" *Powerful* and *Terrible*. The former, her crew looking forward to home leave following a three-year China Fleet commission, had instead been diverted to Mauritius to collect a half-battalion of British troops for passage to Durban. Interestingly, these ships were credited with 22 knots, but this nine-day run, averaging 595km/370 miles per day, or about 13.4 knots, was considered a good sustained performance.

ABOVE: **The appropriately named armoured cruiser *Good Hope* laying in Table Bay during the South African War. In July 1907 the vessel became the flagship of the gunnery enthusiast Admiral Sir Percy Scott. Her secondary 152mm/6in shooting was then "without parallel in the British Fleet". Seven years later she was destroyed by gunfire at Coronel.**

Commanding the *Terrible*, which arrived at Cape Town on October 14, was Captain Percy Scott, a passionate gunnery specialist. On his own initiative he put ashore several of the ship's long-barrelled 76mm/3in 12-pounders and oversaw the dockyard's mounting them on improvised carriages for transport up-country.

A considerable British military force quickly found itself invested in the town of Ladysmith. Its field artillery was outranged by that of the Boers and the Navy was requested to provide the means of redressing the balance.

Within 24 hours, Scott had landed two 119mm/4.7in guns and had them fitted to carriages. These, together with their 20.4kg/45lb ammunition, sailed immediately for Durban in the *Powerful*. From there, a 284-strong brigade from the cruiser travelled with the guns directly to the Ladysmith area in two special trains, the final stretch under enemy fire. The two 119mm/4.7in guns, accompanied by four 12-pounders and four Maxims, found themselves immediately in action at Lombard's Kop. The enemy repulsed, the guns were then relocated in the town's defences, the 12-pounders in a battery, the 119mm/4.7in guns individually. All were capable of being moved at short notice.

Ammunition was short, and the sailors often found themselves serving as infantry, but the Navy's excellent

ABOVE LEFT: **All "bluejackets" of Victoria's navy were trained in military arts and usually relished the prospect of a "run ashore" to offset the routine of life afloat. It can only be noted, however, that, to marksmen as skilled as the Boers, the white uniforms made their practice considerably easier.** ABOVE: **The US Navy, too, was ready and able to land armed contingents to maintain or restore law and order, as evidenced by this party from the cruiser *Philadelphia* in Samoa. The United States sought basing rights in the island, but their interests clashed with the more colonial objectives of Great Britain and Germany.**

gun-laying endlessly disrupted the Boers' own batteries and troop concentrations. This contributed greatly to the effort of keeping the town in British hands until finally relieved in February 1900.

Scott, meanwhile, had satisfied Army requests for a 152mm/6in gun on a field mounting, together with several 119mm/4.7in guns on flat railway wagons. There was also an improvised armoured train, complete with searchlight.

By September 1900, when hostilities ended, the *Terrible* had already replaced the *Powerful* on the China station – just in time to become deeply involved in the Boxer Rebellion. Having exchanged their khaki battle dress for the more familiar blue, the contingents from the two cruisers were replaced by those from others, notably the *Forte, Philomel* and *Tartar.*

LEFT: **As far back as 1882 the Royal Navy had improvised an armoured train in the course of the Egyptian campaign. Less than 20 years later similar trains were used in South Africa. This short-barrelled 406.4kg/8cwt, 76mm/3in 12-pounder is well protected but apparently rather limited in traverse.** ABOVE: **Percy Scott, then commanding the *Terrible* at the Cape, records that "we had on board long-range 12-pounder guns, specially supplied for use against torpedo boats". Mounted on "a pair of Cape wagon wheels and an axle tree" they looked "rather amateurish" but outranged anything available to either side.**

273

Later armoured cruisers

British reservations on belted and armoured cruisers were not shared by the French. Trials using new medium-calibre, quick-firing (QF) guns had impressed them with the damage that could be inflicted upon unprotected topsides. Such punishment would effectively disable a protected cruiser engaged on commerce raiding, a strategy important to the French. They established that a fairly modest thickness of armour would defeat or greatly reduce the effect of QF weapons and so, in 1890, launched the 6,604-tonne/6,500-ton *Dupuy de Lôme*, whose hull was totally clad in 100mm/3.9in armour from 1m/3ft 3in below the designed waterline right up to main deck level. To emphasize her role, the French reversed usual practice by locating a heavy 194mm/7.64in gun on either side in the waist and three smaller 164.7mm/6.48in firing axially at either end. Satisfactory arcs of fire were obtained by the use of exaggerated tumblehome, which also saved some topside weight but reduced the ship's stability range.

The *Dupuy de Lôme*'s immediate successors, the four 4,775-tonne/4,700-ton *Admiral Charners* of 1892–94 and the slightly larger *Pothuau* of 1895, reverted to a more orthodox armament layout.

The Russian cruiser *Rurik* was launched in 1892, but completed at a leisurely rate. At approximately 11,122 tonnes/10,923 tons she was nearly twice the size of the *Dupuy de Lôme*. Probably well-placed rumour credited her with an impressive range of 30,577km/19,000 miles, a threat against

ABOVE: **Of the ten-strong Monmouth class of armoured cruiser only the nameship became a war casualty. The *Kent* (shown here) is passing the Downs as a sailing merchantman engages a tow for the London Docks. She gained fame at the Falklands in 1914 by overhauling and sinking the German cruiser *Nürnberg*.**

commerce that the British could not ignore. In response, they launched in 1895 the then-enormous 14,427-tonne/14,200-ton *Powerful* and *Terrible*. Although classed as protected cruisers they were considerably larger than contemporary battleships, with the forecastle deck extending right aft. The resulting high freeboard made them good seaboats while giving sufficient depth to mount an impressive sixteen 152mm/6in secondary weapons in double-decked casemates. They were inordinately expensive to operate and their 4-knot advantage over the *Rurik* and her two follow-on vessels was bought at the expense of protection.

In total contrast to the *Dupuy de Lôme* the Americans launched the one-off *New York* in 1891 to a sound, unfussy design that put a twin 203mm/8in turret forward and aft, and a single 203mm/8in on either side of the waist. She was followed by the slightly larger *Brooklyn* of 1895, which continued the "lozenge" layout but mounted four twin turrets.

With the Powerfuls, however, the British had started a trend that led directly to the apotheosis of the armoured cruiser. Their 48 boilers demanded four funnels, whose impressive silhouette prompted a French series that began with the six-funnelled

Jeanne d'Arc of 11,329 tonnes/11,150 tons, launched in 1899, and finished, 18 ships later, with the two Waldeck-Rousseaus of 14,072 tonnes/13,850 tons in 1907–08. All had boiler spaces and, therefore, funnels, split into two distinctive groups. Early units continued the practice of mounting a heavy gun at either end, with an essentially broadside-mounted secondary battery. Later vessels moved to single-calibre armament, mostly turret-mounted.

By using more effective and thinner nickel and chrome-based cemented armour, the British returned to the armoured cruiser with the six Cressys of 1899–1901. Between then and 1906 they built 35 ships in steadily escalating size, culminating with the 14,834-tonne/14,600-ton Minotaurs, which carried four 234mm/9.2in guns in two twin centreline turrets, and ten 191mm/7.5in guns in single turrets sided in the waist.

With the six Californias of 1904 the Americans produced powerful equivalents. Although these were followed by the slightly smaller trio of Charlestons, size then increased again to the four impressive 14,733-tonne/14,500-ton Tennessees, with four 254mm/10in guns and sixteen 152mm/6in guns.

Although the "naval race" with Germany was, by 1906, having a great effect on British capital ship policy, this was not true with respect to armoured cruisers. Of these, the Germans had but half a dozen reckonable units. The two pairs of Prinz Adalberts (1901–02) and Roons (1903–04) had four 21cm/8.2in and ten 15cm/5.9in guns apiece, but their two 11,786-tonne/11,600-ton derivatives, the Scharnhorsts, mounted a formidable eight 21cm/8.2in and six 15cm/5.9in guns.

Development came to an abrupt halt in March 1908 with the completion of the *Invincible*, the first battlecruiser. Larger, faster, more heavily armed, she made the armoured cruiser obsolete overnight.

ABOVE: Showing her ram forefoot as she pitches in a swell, the Cressy-class *Euryalus* looks all of her 12,193 tonnes/12,000 tons. Detail on the starboard side of her hull is clearly visible, including the two-level casemates of the secondary 152mm/6in guns. Note the row of ventilators paralleling the funnels and the docking bridge aft. BELOW: Battlecruisers, such as the prototype *Invincible*, were not really cruisers but fast, virtually unprotected battleships for use in opposed reconnaissance. Against armoured cruisers they were deadly, but they were themselves vulnerable to heavy-calibre gunfire.

LEFT: *Scharnhorst*, and her sister *Gneisenau*, represented the latest and best of German armoured cruiser design in 1914. That they were overwhelmed by the 305mm/12in gunfire of battlecruisers appeared to vindicate Fisher's dictum that speed and firepower were sufficient protection in themselves. BELOW: The six American Pennsylvanias of 1903–04 carried four 203mm/8in and fourteen 152mm/6in guns on a 14,072-tonne/13,850-ton displacement. For a further 711 tonnes/700 tons, the four following Tennessees carried four 254mm/10in and sixteen 152mm/6in weapons. All, including the Pennsylvania-class *California*, were renamed after cities, this ship becoming *San Diego*.

Scouts and the origins of the light cruiser

The British Admiralty's practical experience with steam turbines began with the destroyer *Viper* in 1899. Following successful service in several significant merchant vessels, it was then decided to install this type of machinery in a cruiser. Existing Third Class protected cruisers were limited by their triple expansion reciprocating engines so that minor increases in speed were only possible by designing longer and finer hulls. One of the final groups of such ships, the Topaze class, was selected to evaluate steam turbine propulsion, the *Amethyst* being thus completed in 1904. Although an inefficient direct-drive, un-geared installation, it still developed some 22 per cent more power, delivering an extra 1.5 knots.

At about the same time, a case was made for a new type of small cruiser, a Scout, capable of assisting in a traditional close blockade by assuming the sailing frigate's role of watching the enemy's harbours. Destroyers were also developing rapidly and it was envisaged that flotillas of 24 such craft would make mass torpedo attacks on an enemy battle line. To control such a pack a senior officer would need to be embarked on a larger craft, capable of keeping pace while carrying heavier quick-firing (QF) guns to deter any counter-attack by enemy destroyers. It was mainly with this role in mind that the Admiralty had four pairs of scouts built, to a similar specification but individual design of the manufacturing yards. The preferred result was the Armstrong-built *Amethyst* design, completed in 1905. This displaced 2,713 tonnes/2,670 tons and could make 25.5 knots with reciprocating machinery. For service requirements, the Admiralty had this basic design stretched to 3,353–3,505 tonnes/3,300–3,450 tons, the

TOP: **Both British and German fleets produced series of effective "fleet" cruisers named after their respective towns. Earlier British classes, such as the Bristols (*Gloucester* seen here) had a protective deck. With the generally short range encounters that developed, the later classes were fitted with belts.** ABOVE: **The eight Arethusas (*Aurora* seen here) were smaller than the fleet cruisers, and intended to work with the then-usual large destroyer flotillas. Particularly associated with the Harwich Force, they led to the numerous "C" class of light cruiser. Note the sturdy tripod mast.**

resulting Boadicea and Active classes making 26 knots with turbines, and carrying up to ten 102mm/4in guns.

Although fewer, the German Third Class protected cruisers were similar to their British counterparts, and formed the basis of their first group of "Towns" in 1904–05. Then, at a rate of two or three hulls per year, they evolved rapidly, with steam turbines being generally adopted in 1909. Their 10cm/3.9in guns were greatly superior to the 102mm/4in of the British ships and they also had a 50mm/2in protective deck, which the contemporary Boadiceas lacked.

In 1910–11, therefore, the British completed the five Bristols, some 15.2m/50ft longer than a Boadicea and with

displacement increased from 3,455 tonnes/3,400 tons to 4,877 tonnes/4,800 tons. This allowed the ten 102mm/4in guns to be complemented by a pair of single 152mm/6in weapons that were better able to stop a destroyer. In addition, they had a partial 50mm/2in protective deck and, with 25 per cent more power and partial oil firing, a maximum speed of 26 knots.

The British "Towns", like their German equivalent, comprised a series of continuously evolving groups. They totalled 18 ships, of which the final trio, the Birminghams of 1915–16, displaced 5,527 tonnes/5,440 tons and mounted nine 152mm/6in guns. Interestingly, they exchanged a protective deck for a 76mm/3in side belt, capable of stopping a 10cm/3.9in projectile and indicative of the expectation of close-range action.

The Birminghams could make 25.5 knots but, for their successors, the Staff Requirement was 30 knots. The resulting Arethusas were smaller and finer-lined; although nominally 27-knot ships, they were good for 29 knots if forced. Already termed "light cruisers", they had a 25mm/1in protective deck worked in, similar to the latest German practice. This, in addition to an armoured belt, technically made them small armoured cruisers.

From the Arethusas evolved the first group of the extensive C-class which, in a series of related sub-classes, comprised 30 ships, themselves slowing evolutionary improvements.

Of the original pure "scout cruiser", little more was seen. Exceptions were the trio of American Chesters of 1907 and the later, and much enlarged, Omahas. During World War II, the Italians introduced their handsome *Capitani Romani*, described officially as *esploratori oceanici*, while the Germans commenced work on their the uncompleted *spähkreuzer* (reconnaissance cruisers).

ABOVE: Designed more specifically to operate individually as scouts, the USS *Chester* (shown here) and her two sisters were given unusually high freeboard to assist in maintaining speed in a seaway. Not intended for serious fighting, their armament and protection was very light. BELOW: Completed in 1918, the Kölns represented the ultimate stage of development of the German "Towns". They had both belt and protective deck, 15cm/5.9in guns in place of 10.5cm/4.1in and geared steam turbines. Confusingly, later ships repeated names of those sunk earlier, the previous *Köln* being lost at Heligoland Bight. BOTTOM: The only successors to the US Navy's Chester-class scouts were the ten Omahas of 1920–24. Twice as large and 10 knots faster, they had a powerful chase armament of six forward-firing 152mm/6in guns. These were disposed in a twin gunhouse and four single casemates.

The pursuit of the *Goeben*

As Europe stumbled toward war in 1914 the British Mediterranean Fleet, commanded by Admiral Sir Berkeley Milne, comprised one squadron each of battlecruisers, armoured cruisers and light cruisers together with 16 destroyers. Allied with the French these would have to meet the combined strength of the Austro-Hungarian and Italian navies together with a German contingent bound by the planned Triple Alliance. Germany's contribution was just two ships but, of these, the battlecruiser *Goeben* had firepower and speed that outclassed any British or French ship in the Mediterranean.

The First Lord of the Admiralty, Winston Churchill, was well aware of this point and, on July 30, six days before war erupted, gave Milne broad instructions which stated, specifically: "Do not at this stage be brought to action against superior forces, except in combination with the French …"

On August 1, the *Goeben* and the light cruiser *Breslau* were at Brindisi. To shadow them, Milne despatched two battlecruisers, while Rear Admiral Ernest Troubridge was sent with his four armoured cruisers to patrol the Otranto Strait at the entrance to the Adriatic.

> "Being only able to meet *Goeben* outside the range of our guns and inside his, I have abandoned the chase with my squadron…"
> Troubridge to Milne, timed 04:49 hours, August 7, 1914

TOP: HMS *Chatham* was one of only four light cruisers available to Admiral Sir A. Berkeley Milne's Mediterranean Fleet in August 1914. The picture shows how her fine lines demand a multitude of timber shores to stabilize her when stemmed in dry dock, here only partly emptied. ABOVE: Consort to the *Goeben* was the light cruiser *Breslau*, also completed in 1912. The escape of the pair to Constantinople, and their continued existence, ostensibly under the Turkish flag, was a source of continuing concern during the Anglo-French Dardanelles campaign, as a foray was constantly threatened.

Arriving at Messina on August 2, the German Rear Admiral Wilhelm Souchon received the disappointing news that Italy, after all, intended to remain neutral. Without waiting to complete with coal, he departed with some urgency. His absence was quickly noted and reported to Milne by the light cruiser *Chatham*. Troubridge was promptly ordered westward, leaving only the *Gloucester* and destroyers to watch Otranto. Indecisive, Milne then ordered Troubridge to return, and the *Chatham* to join the battlecruisers in their search.

ABOVE: The island harbour of Mudros was the major base for British and French forces during the operations around the Dardanelles. The Cressy-class armoured cruiser is either *Bacchante* or *Euryalus*. Used for reconnaissance and spotting, the airship is a non-rigid Sea Scout "blimp" of the RNAS. RIGHT: The dogged but, ultimately, unsuccessful Allied campaign on the Gallipoli peninsula resulted in a continuous stream of troop convoys to and from the theatre. Having evaded German cruisers, such as the *Emden*, in the Indian Ocean, these Anzac troops now had to be protected from the *Goeben*.

Souchon, meanwhile, anticipating a declaration of war with France, headed for North Africa in order to disrupt the recall of French military forces. News of war with both France and Russia came on August 3, and, early next morning, the *Goeben* bombarded the embarkation port of Philippeville, while the *Breslau* attacked Bona. The operation was brief and limited but inflicted psychological damage.

Souchon was now informed of a new German alliance with Turkey and ordered to Istanbul (then Constantinople). Needing coal, he made for Messina but, at 10:30 hours on August 4, encountered the British battlecruisers. Not yet at war, the British made to shadow the Germans but unable to match their speed, were quickly shaken off. At midnight, a British ultimatum to Germany expired and the two nations were at war.

Early on August 5, Souchon arrived again at Messina but, as a belligerent, was allowed only an insufficient 24 hours to coal his ship. He duly sailed on August 6, passed the *Gloucester,* watching the southern end of the strait, and headed eastward. As Austria-Hungary had not yet declared war, his situation was precarious. Occasionally harried by the *Breslau*, the *Gloucester* successfully trailed the fugitives as far as Cape Matapan before being ordered back due to lack of coal.

Although much slower, Troubridge's armoured cruisers had been well placed to make an interception. Uncertain, however, of exactly what constituted a "superior force", he desisted. In doing so he almost certainly avoided a Coronel-style defeat, but his action resulted in Court Martial proceedings.

Milne was now thoroughly confused by conflicting Admiralty telegrams regarding Austria-Hungary's participation. For 24 hours the hunt for Souchon lost momentum, allowing the Germans to take aboard emergency coal at an Aegean rendezvous. Unaware of Souchon's true destination, Milne disposed his forces to safeguard the Greek coast, enabling the enemy to safely enter the Dardanelles on the evening of August 9, to the consternation of the Admiralty.

ABOVE: Much in her original condition, the *Goeben* is seen here under Turkish colours as the *Yavuz*. She served until the 1960s and, as the sole surviving example of a major World War I combatant, should have survived as a museum ship. Despite widespread protest, however, she was scrapped. BELOW: Another of Milne's light cruisers, the *Gloucester* under the command of Captain Howard Kelly, performed a classic cruiser role in shadowing and reporting the progress of the Germans. Alone, and occasionally exchanging fire with the *Breslau*, she desisted only when bunkers became low.

There followed the charade of the two German ships taking Turkish names and colours, and their crews donning Turkish uniform. They proved to be a considerable nuisance to Russian interests in the Black Sea, but although a continuous threat to Anglo-French operations in the eastern Mediterranean, they mounted only one damaging raid. This, in turn, proved disastrous for them, the ex-*Breslau* being sunk by mines and the *Goeben* fortunate to regain sanctuary following heavy mine damage.

Coronel and the Falklands

Most significant of the detached German naval forces in August 1914 was the East Asiatic Squadron, based at the Chinese enclave of Tsingtao. Commanded by the very able Vice Admiral Graf von Spee, it comprised the latest armoured cruisers *Scharnhorst* and *Gneisenau*, and the light cruisers *Emden*, *Leipzig* and *Nürnberg*.

Once Japan entered the war supporting Britain in accordance with its treaty obligations, von Spee knew that Tsingtao would be indefensible so, already on a Pacific cruise, his squadron never returned. Detaching the *Emden* to conduct war against commerce in the Indian Ocean he, and the remainder of squadron, headed eastward toward South America, his progress marked by sudden raids on islands in quest of coal and provisions. Eluding the British, Commonwealth and Japanese warships that were seeking him, von Spee linked up with a further cruiser, *Dresden*, at Easter Island on October 12.

The only British force in South American waters was a scratch group commanded by Rear Admiral Christopher Cradock. Its two armoured cruisers, *Good Hope* and *Monmouth*, unlike the German ships, had only recently been mobilized. Their crews consisted largely of reserves and new recruits. Cradock also had the pre-Dreadnought *Canopus* but, believing her too slow to fight an action, neglected to concentrate on her. Aware of von Spee's progress, he sent ahead his only modern cruiser, the *Glasgow*, to seek intelligence upon which he could base his next move.

On October 31, the German admiral learned that *Glasgow* was at the small Chilean port of Coronel and, believing her

TOP: **Flagship of Read Admiral Christopher Cradock's South American Squadron, the armoured cruiser *Good Hope* had been recently commissioned with a large proportion of reservists. Not efficiently "worked-up", she was totally outclassed by von Spee's seasoned cruisers.** ABOVE: **Von Spee's nemesis at the Falklands, the battlecruiser *Inflexible* leads the armoured cruiser *Minotaur* and two others. The two battles proved little more than the old dictum that "a good big 'un will always beat a good little 'un".**

unsupported, moved to intercept. When, late the following day, he made contact, he found her in company with the *Good Hope*, *Monmouth* and the armed liner *Otranto*. Although the *Canopus* was 300 miles distant, Cradock immediately detached the *Otranto* and sought action.

His situation was hopeless from the outset. His big ships had had little gunnery practice and in heavy seas they were unable to work the guns in their lower casemates. They were further disadvantaged by being sharply etched against the afterglow of the sun sinking behind them, while their opponents were near-invisible against the darkening eastern horizon.

RIGHT: **Cradock had the obsolete battleship** *Canopus* **in support. However he was more concerned with bringing von Spee to action than in falling back on the veteran, which was a day's steaming distant. His decision cost the Royal Navy its first defeat in a century.**

Within 100 minutes both *Good Hope* and *Monmouth* had been sunk without survivors but von Spee's big ships, although unscathed, had shot off over 40 per cent of their ammunition, which would not be replenished.

Although courageous, Cradock had, in the circumstances, acted foolishly. Sixteen hundred had perished in what had been the Royal Navy's first defeat in over a century. At the Admiralty the new First Sea Lord, Fisher, acted decisively with his political superior, Churchill, and in great secrecy detached three battlecruisers from Jellicoe's Grand Fleet. Von Spee was obviously headed homeward and to guard against the possibility that he would use the newly opened Panama Canal, the *Princess Royal* was sent to North American waters. It was thought more likely however that he would double the Horn and be tempted by the large coal stocks maintained on the Falkland Islands. Vice Admiral Sir Doveton Sturdee was therefore despatched with the *Invincible* and the *Inflexible*, collecting en route the cruisers *Bristol*, *Carnarvon*, *Cornwall*, *Kent* and the Coronel survivor, *Glasgow*.

Sturdee arrived at Port Stanley on December 7, and was still engaged in coaling when, less than 24 hours later, von Spee approached. Berthed in the harbour was the *Canopus*, and a speculative 305mm/12in salvo from her deterred the enemy, who made off into open ocean.

The British were quickly in pursuit and, in unusually clear conditions, steadily overhauled the fugitives. *Inflexible* opened fire at 12:50 and, half an hour later, von Spee ordered his light cruisers to scatter *sauve qui peut*. Each, however, attracted its own pursuer and, long out of dock, were caught and destroyed, only the *Dresden* escaping.

In destroying the *Scharnhorst* and *Gneisenau*, Fisher's revolutionary battlecruiser concept was totally vindicated, their superior speed and firepower overwhelming von Spee's gallant defence and by extension signalling the obsolescence of the armoured cruiser.

TOP: **The captain of the** *Gneisenau* **was reportedly at odds with von Spee over the latter's decision to attack the Falklands. As it was, the German cruisers, long out of dock, were neither able to out-run nor out-gun Sturdee's battlecruisers.** ABOVE: **HMS** *Bristol*, **with an engine opened for repair, nearly missed the Falklands action. She was eventually despatched together with an auxiliary to round up von Spee's accompanying colliers who it was feared conveyed a landing force to occupy the islands.**

ABOVE: **Sole German survivor of the Falklands action, the** *Dresden* **went to ground in the maze of waterways around the Magellan Strait. When eventually run to earth in Chilean territorial waters, British cruisers ignored neutrality laws to effect her destruction.** BELOW: **Sisters of the ill-starred** *Monmouth*, *Cornwall* **(seen here) and** *Kent* **both participated at the Falklands. In company with the** *Glasgow*, **survivor of Coronel, the** *Cornwall* **sank the** *Leipzig*, **while** *Kent* **overhauled and disposed of the** *Nürnberg*.

281

Blockade and the Tenth Cruiser Squadron

At 03:00 hours on August 2, 1914, Rear Admiral Dudley de Chair broke his flag aboard the cruiser *Crescent* at Portsmouth. One hour later an Admiralty telegram ordered him to take his Tenth Cruiser Squadron (10th CS) to Scapa Flow "with all despatch". Its task on declaration of hostilities would be to initiate a sea blockade of Germany. Maintaining a permanent patrol line from the Orkneys to the Norwegian coast, it would first snare any returning German-flag shipping and then, as this inevitably diminished, intercept neutrals attempting to break the blockade with the intention of confiscating contraband cargo.

"Contraband" is not an exact term but here is understood to mean any goods that would directly benefit the enemy military or Germany's capacity to wage war. Cargoes destined for the civil population were exempt although successive British Orders-in-Council considerably extended the list of what constituted contraband.

The Admiralty's objective was to make all neutral shipping proceed via the restricted Dover Strait where it could be efficiently regulated. The official view was that any proceeding via the northern route had some reason for evasion. The British assumption of a right to stop and search caused widespread resentment among neutrals, particularly the United States. In deference to the latter, the content of forthcoming Orders-in-Council were first discussed with them.

De Chair's ships, Crescent- and Edgar-class cruisers dating from 1893–94, were among the navy's oldest. "Short-legged", mechanically unreliable, crowded, wet and uncomfortable, they proved totally unable to cope with the first northern autumnal gales. Badly damaged, some barely surviving, they were exchanged in November 1914 for the first of what would be a total of about two dozen ex-passenger liners. Armed with old 152mm/6in guns, these were far better able to cope with the

> "If anything more strikingly demonstrating the value of sea power can be given [than the work of the 10th CS], I do not know of it."
> Speech by Sir Eric Geddes, First Lord of the Admiralty, on opening the post-war Sea Power exhibition

ABOVE: Neutrals could be encountered anywhere in British waters, and here a destroyer is preparing to send away her seaboat to examine a Nederland Line passenger vessel.

endless storms of these northern latitudes. They had capacious bunker capacity and comfortable accommodation, not only for their own crews but also for the many extra hands required to form "prize crews" for the purpose of taking neutrals into the examination anchorages at Kirkwall or Lerwick. A ship might have a dozen or more armed parties away at any time and not expect to recover them for weeks on end. Their transfer by open boat could be hazardous, so the ships, known officially as Armed Merchant Cruisers (AMCs), carried Newfoundlanders, who were second-to-none in the art of small boat handling.

LEFT: Like the *Alsatian*, flagship of the Tenth Cruiser Squadron, the 10,754grt *Virginian* belonged to the Allan Line, later subsumed into Canadian Pacific. She and the *Victorian* were the first steam-turbine passenger liners on the North Atlantic service. BELOW: Two P&O liners served in the blockade service, the 9,500-tonne/9,350-ton *Moldavia*, dating from 1903, and the 10,885grt *Mantua* of 1909. The *Moldavia* is seen embarking peacetime passengers by tender.

ABOVE: **Admiral de Chair's flagship, *Crescent*, and the supporting Edgar-class cruisers were among the oldest in the navy, and manifestly unsuited to protracted patrols in Northern waters. Breakdowns, structural damage and casualties persuaded the Admiralty to retire the ships in favour of armed liners.**

That the blockade was hurting the enemy was evident in his continual complaints regarding its legality, and his trying to justify the employment of still-illegal unrestricted U-boat warfare as a consequence.

The AMCs were not escorted, and it was a constant mystery why the Germans never specifically targeted them. Several, however, were lost to torpedo, others through stress of the unremittingly foul northern weather.

From March 1916 the 10th CS was under the command of Rear Admiral Reginald Tupper. His workload began to be eased at about this time through the introduction of the so-called Navicert, a certificate issued by naval authority to a ship and cargo at its port of origin, identifying the eventual end-user and obviating the requirement for further search.

Further relief came in April 1917. American ships and cargoes, particularly cotton, had been something of a delicate issue, now solved by that nation becoming a combatant. Neutral shipping was in business to make a profit and, for the most part, would trade with either camp. The endless British problem, therefore, was how to stifle the flow to the enemy without causing diplomatic opprobrium, while at the same time realizing that "playing safe" reduced the value of the blockade.

In round figures, nearly 13,000 interceptions were made. Some 2,000 of these proceeded voluntarily for examination and a further 1,800 went under armed guard. It was believed that about 650 ships evaded the patrols, but this represented just 5 per cent of movements.

The loss of materials to Germany was debilitating, civilian morale suffering further from the feeling of encirclement. Indeed, as the government tended to blame the blockade in order to disguise its own failings, this impression was exacerbated.

ABOVE: *St. George* was the odd one out, being the only Edgar not involved with 10th CS, having been converted to a destroyer depot ship pre-war. By coincidence, she had been an earlier appointment of de Chair, when he was a commander and she was flagship C-in-C, South Atlantic.

RIGHT: Designed for the long-haul Australasian service, Orient liners were comfortable and of great endurance. Four, including the *Orvieto*, seen here, served with the Tenth Cruiser Squadron, the *Otway* being lost by torpedo.

German experience in World War I

In August 1914, there existed enormous potential for German cruisers to damage Allied commercial shipping. The British Admiralty believed that the time-honoured defensive measure of convoy had been made redundant by the advent of steam propulsion. Traffic thus followed well-defined routes, which created focal points of high shipping density. Despite advice for caution, commercial considerations encouraged masters to deviate little from normal peacetime routine.

To support cruiser warfare, however, Germany lacked the British advantage of worldwide bases and coaling stations. Extended operations would depend upon how reliably cruisers could obtain coal and provisions and, if required, ammunition and repair facilities. As a result, well before the war probable theatres were identified and a representative – vice consul, commercial attaché or equivalent – appointed to organize

ABOVE: Detached from von Spee's squadron at the outbreak of war the *Emden*, under her resourceful commanding officer, von Müller, pursued a brief but successful raiding career in the Indian Ocean. Her boldness was typified by a surprise bombardment of oil storage tanks at Madras (now Chennai) on September 22, 1914. BELOW LEFT: Von Müller's decision to destroy the cable station on Cocos Island sealed the *Emden*'s fate. A radioed alarm brought the Australian cruiser *Sydney* (shown here) quickly to the scene. A Chatham-class cruiser, her eight 152mm/6in guns totally outclassed the German's ten 10.5cm/4.1in weapons.

requirements. Despite international law regarding supply to combatants by neutrals, high profit would always justify high risk for some operators.

Reflecting their lack of experience in maritime warfare, the Germans in fact had only modest plans in place, initially involving only three regular cruisers and a handful of auxiliaries. In the Indian Ocean, the light cruiser *Emden* had been detached from the German East Asiatic Squadron to conduct a campaign against commercial shipping. For three months her commanding officer, Karl von Müller, skilfully evaded hunting forces by constantly changing his location. The *Emden* took 23 prizes, totalling over 100,000 gross registered tons (grt) with all captured personnel being scrupulously well-treated before being transferred to neutral ships. Inevitably von Müller was apprehended, his nemesis on November 9 being the Australian cruiser *Sydney.*

ABOVE: Pictured at Dar-es-Salaam, where she was German East Africa station ship, the *Königsberg* complicated matters in the Indian Ocean by embarking on a commerce-raiding cruise while the *Emden* was still at large. Fortunately, she went to ground in the Rufiji delta, where the Royal Navy blockaded and destroyed her. RIGHT: As a variation on commerce raiding, the Germans used commercial ships as minelayers from the outset. The very first shots of the naval war were fired on August 5, 1914, when the cruiser *Amphion* and two destroyers of the Harwich Force intercepted and sank the *Königin Luise* (shown in the foreground).

The light cruiser *Karlsruhe* was in the Caribbean. Being a new ship, fresh out of dock, she outpaced intercepting British cruisers on two occasions. Like the *Emden*, she supplemented her supplies from prizes which she used to extend her line of search. Her commander, Köhler, operated primarily in the teeming focal point off north-eastern Brazil, accounting for 16 ships of some 73,000grt before the *Karlsruhe* was destroyed by an internal explosion on November 4, 1914.

The third German light cruiser at large was the *Königsberg*, based in East Africa. She had taken but one prize when, reputedly short of coal, she holed-up in the fetid, shallow delta of the Rufiji River to await supplies. Searching British cruisers intercepted her collier, learned of her location and blockaded her until she could be destroyed by indirect bombardment.

Included in this first wave of raiders were several auxiliary cruisers mostly passenger liners armed by appointment in August 1914. In total they accounted for a further 100,000grt of Allied shipping but led a limited, fugitive existence. Within months, those not intercepted and sunk were compelled by mechanical problems to seek sanctuary and internment in neutral ports, where they remained for the duration.

An unquantifiable bonus for the Germans was the very considerable disruption caused to trade through a raider being at large and the number of regular warships removed from other duties for the purpose of hunting her down.

Although the U-boat soon became the principal means by which the Germans conducted their campaign against commerce, auxiliary cruisers continued to be used to considerable effect. Regular warships had proved to be over-ambitious in the role, as ordinary merchantmen with concealed armament aroused little suspicion and were inexpensive to

BELOW: Converted from a merchantmen, the successful German raider *Möwe* laid mines off Cape Wrath in January 1916. These claimed the pre-Dreadnought *King Edward VII*, seen here. That sovereign had stipulated that she should always be a flagship; this had been her first voyage as a "private" ship.

convert and to operate. Most successful was the *Möwe* whose mines, laid early in 1916, accounted for several ships including the pre-Dreadnought battleship *King Edward VII*. During a later foray she accounted for a record 25 ships of some 123,000grt. Another auxiliary *Wolf,* actually cruised for a single period of 15 months without being apprehended. Making considerable use of a small embarked floatplane, she sank about 114,000grt.

Experience gained during 1914–18 enabled the Germans to prepare an even more formidable campaign during World War II, conducted almost exclusively by auxiliary cruisers supported by a well-organized force of supply ships.

285

Goodenough at Jutland

On May 31, 1916, as Jellicoe's Grand Fleet and Scheer's High Seas Fleet headed for the clash that would be Jutland, each was preceded, at a distance of 48–63km/ 30–40 miles, by its respective battlecruiser force. Their task was armed reconnaissance and they, in turn, had light cruiser screens pushed out ahead and around.

Admiral Beatty's "eyes" were the 13 ships of the First, Second and Third Light Cruiser Squadron (LCS) which were disposed on a line of bearing as the whole formation headed SSE. At 14:20 hours, the easternmost cruiser, *Galatea*, sighted what proved to be Admiral Hipper's advance force. Against standing instructions, all nine of the First and Third LCS peeled off to investigate. This left just Commodore William ("Barge") Goodenough's Second LCS in company. Wearing his broad pendant in the *Southampton*, he led *Birmingham*, *Nottingham* and *Dublin*.

Correctly suspecting the presence of a larger enemy force, Beatty pressed on to the south. Goodenough was positioned on his starboard bow while the remainder, on rejoining, fell in on the port quarter. At 15:40 Hipper's battlecruisers were sighted and the light cruisers kept to Beatty's disengaged side as a vicious and prolonged gun duel developed. In the course of this, as Hipper sought to entice Beatty's squadron on to Scheer's greater force, two British battlecruisers, *Indefatigable* and *Queen Mary*, blew up catastrophically.

This exchange was still in progress when, at 16:30, the *Southampton*, some three miles ahead, sighted and reported "sixteen battleships with destroyers disposed around them". This was Jellicoe's first warning of Scheer's approach. Beatty immediately reversed course to lure the German forces in turn on to the Grand Fleet. Goodenough, however, held on toward Scheer in order to confirm his earlier observation. As the Second LCS closed the enemy battle fleet at a combined speed of about 45 knots, not a shot was fired for, end-on, the enemy was uncertain of his identity. With the range at just 10,973m/12,000yds, Goodenough's commander said "If you're going to make that signal, sir, you'd better make it now. You may never make another…"

That done, at 16:48, the Second LCS turned away. In doing so it presented its distinctive profiles, attracting a storm of fire. There began an hour and more of misery as the older battleships at the German rear, their 28cm/11in guns unable to range the British capital ships, used the trailing Goodenough for practice. Deluged with water and shell fragments, the cruisers survived by "chasing the salvoes", or weaving to confuse the enemy gun-layers. These manoeuvres also caused Goodenough's navigating officer's dead reckoning to be increasingly in error, influencing the Commodore's reports.

LEFT: Having received over 20 heavy calibre shell hits and at least one torpedo, the German battlecruiser *Seydlitz* arrived back at Wilhelmshaven with an estimated 5,385 tonnes/5,300 tons of water aboard and her two after turrets burned out. Note how the roof and guns of the forward turret have also been removed. BELOW LEFT: German heavy calibre guns fired a total of 3,597 recorded rounds at Jutland, of which 122 scored direct hits. British figures were 4,480 and 123 respectively. Commodore Goodenough's *Southampton* took 21 hits, one 28cm/11in, two 15cm/5.9in and the remainder 10cm/3.9in. BELOW: On a day notable for poor signalling and reporting, comprehension and initiative, "Barge" Goodenough and the Second Light Cruiser Squadron were an exception, doing all that could reasonably have been expected of them.

> "I never knew before how much protection there is in a canvas screen."
> *Southampton*'s Navigating Officer, "Paddy" Ireland, to Commodore Goodenough as the cruiser was under continuous 28cm/11in shell fire

At 18:15 hours the great battle line of the Grand Fleet came into sight across the northern horizon and it soon became Scheer's turn for discomfort. As the battle became general Goodenough tucked his squadron in at the rear of the British line, firing on the enemy's light units as opportunities were presented.

Scheer's priority was now to extricate himself and, in conditions of fitful visibility, he succeeded admirably. As darkness fell, the British, still in battle formation, were effectively between the Germans and their base, however during the night Scheer's forces moved through the tail of Jellicoe's line resulting in violent clashes.

Stationed to the west of the Grand Fleet battleships, Goodenough suddenly encountered the enemy's Fourth Scouting Group, whose half-dozen light cruisers were under 805m/880yds distant. Both sides opened with searchlights and rapid salvoes. The *Southampton* sank the *Frauenlob* with a torpedo but, brightly illuminated, was in turn swept by fire. To an earlier hit by a spent 28cm/11in shell was now added two by 15cm/5.9in shells and about 18 by 10cm/3.9in shells. The ship's 76mm/3in belt resisted the smaller projectiles but fragments scythed the upper-deck and exposed gun crews. Her communication aerials destroyed, she signalled *Nottingham* by lamp: "My wireless is shot away. Answer calls for me and report the action."

ABOVE: The presence of considerable numbers of obsolescent fighting units suggests that Admiral Scheer really did not expect to fight a major battle. Having already extinguished a potentially serious fire caused by two 152mm/6in hits, the *Frauenlob* capsized following a torpedo hit from *Southampton*. BELOW: At Jutland, the *Canterbury* (shown) and *Chester* were attached to *Hood*'s devastated Third Battle Cruiser Squadron. The *Chester* would be heavily damaged but *Canterbury* attached herself to the Third Light Cruiser Squadron. Despite a busy day, she escaped with just one hit.

The demise of the armoured cruiser

As related earlier in this book, armoured cruisers had by the 1880s developed into a type of Second Class battleship, the true capital ship having the maximum practicable armament and protection, being complemented by large cruisers with medium-calibre weapons, lighter protection and higher speed.

Not convinced of the benefits of the latter expensive ships, the British Admiralty concentrated in the Naval Defence Act classes on protected cruisers of more modest size.

The French, however, persisted in building large and fast cruisers aimed primarily at war on commerce. Newly developed Krupp cemented steel armour with its improved stopping power permitted much thinner and lighter protection and so the Admiralty reverted to vertical belt armour in addition to protective decks. As a result, the British armoured cruiser was reborn.

Necessary speed translated into many boilers, many boilers into length. Extra length permitted extra displacement and the adoption of the 234mm/9.2in gun forward and aft. These, with

ABOVE: **Some of the last pre-Dreadnought battleships, the King Edward VII class of 1903–05 (shown here) were about 138.4m/454ft in length. Contemporary Devonshire-class armoured cruisers were nearly 6.1m/20ft longer. The latter were 4 knots faster but mounted only 191mm/7.5in rather than 305mm/12in main-calibre guns. Their vertical protection was proof against only cruiser gunfire.**

casemated, 152mm/6in guns along either beam, followed the armament layout of contemporary capital ships. It was then but a short step to the proposal of using armoured cruisers as a fast wing of the battle fleet, tasked with conducting reconnaissance in force, finishing off damaged enemy ships and even engaging smaller enemy capital ships.

Once accepted as an element of the battle fleet as opposed to commerce protection, the armoured cruiser rapidly increased in size and cost. Compare, for instance, the armoured cruiser *Black Prince* and the battleship *King Edward VII*, launched 1903/04:

> "She tore past us with a roar, rather like a motor roaring up hill on low gear, and the very crackling and heat of the flames could be heard and felt. She was a mass of fire from foremast to mainmast, on deck and between decks. Flames were issuing out of her from every corner…"
> Eyewitness account from destroyer *Spitfire* of *Black Prince*'s final moments, Jutland night action

	King Edward VII	Black Prince
Displacement	15,881 tonnes/15,630 tons	13,717 tonnes/13,500 tons
Length overall	138.2m/453ft 9in	154m/505ft 6in
Armament	4x305mm/12in	6x234mm/9.2in
	4x234mm/9.2in	10x152mm/6in
	10x152mm/6in	
Complement	777	789
Cost (£)	1.38 million	1.20 million

In terms of cost and manning, the two types were almost equal and, at a time when naval strength was commonly measured by the yardstick of capital ship numbers, more armoured cruisers simply meant fewer battleships.

Controversy was resolved with the launch in 1907 of the first of Fisher's revolutionary battlecruisers (initially termed "large armoured cruisers"). With eight 305mm/12in guns and a 3-knot speed advantage these were the natural predators of armoured cruisers, which were effectively made obsolete. However, as only four of the new "Town"-class light cruisers were in service in 1914, existing ships still had their part to play.

Action soon found them wanting. In heavy seas at the battle of Coronel, the *Good Hope* was unable to use her lower casemated 152mm/6in guns to defend herself. (Four years later, the 13,920-tonne/13,700-ton American *San Diego* flooded and foundered when her lower casemates were submerged by a list of only 9.5 degrees.) Under ideal conditions, the 234mm/9.2in gun was a reliable and accurate weapon, but in action, just two barrels and no fire control greatly degraded this potential.

At the Falklands, Fisher's battlecruiser concept was triumphantly vindicated when Sturdee's two battlecruisers used their speed and gun range to destroy von Spee's two crack armoured cruisers almost at leisure.

Jutland marked the end of the armoured cruiser as an integrated battle fleet unit. In accordance with Grand Fleet Battle Orders to "push on and gain touch with the enemy's

battle fleet", Arbuthnot's First Cruiser Squadron succeeded only too well. At just 7,315m/8,000yds in indifferent visibility it was swept by fire from Scheer's mainforce, the *Defence* blowing up and the *Warrior* foundering later. This vulnerability to heavy-calibre gunfire was underlined when a third, *Black Prince*, blew up from a pre-Dreadnought's gunfire in a nocturnal clash.

In contrast, the new light cruisers proved remarkably resistant. None was sunk at Jutland although several were hard hit (e.g. *Southampton* by one 28cm/11in, two 15cm/5.9in and eighteen 10cm/3.9in shells; *Chester* by seventeen 15cm/5.9in shells; *Castor* by about ten 15cm/5.9in and 10cm/3.9in shells, etc). By the end of the war British armoured cruisers were mostly relegated to trade protection and service on distant stations. Ironically their nemesis, the battlecruiser, had likewise been discredited in the supreme test of major action.

ABOVE: The one-off *Blücher* was built by the Germans on the basis of faulty intelligence regarding the capability of the then-secret British battlecruisers. Really an armoured cruiser, she was nonetheless attached to Hipper's battlecruiser squadron and paid the price at Dogger Bank.

TOP: **Dating from 1901–03, Cressy-class armoured cruisers (*Euryalus* seen here) were no longer fit for front-line duty during World War I. The class was somewhat unfairly damned when three, not comprehending the new rules of submarine warfare, were destroyed together by one boat.** ABOVE: **The final class of armoured cruiser built for the Royal Navy were the three Minotaurs of 1908 (*Shannon* seen here). Into their slender 158.2m/519ft hulls were packed two twin 234mm/9.2in turrets and 10 single 191mm/7.5in turrets, the latter sided in the waist. Capable of only 23 knots, they were rendered obsolete by the battlecruiser.** ABOVE LEFT: **With the six Pennsylvanias of 1903–04 and the four Tennessees of 1904–06, the US Navy's armoured cruisers were every bit the equal of their British counterparts. With the decision to reserve "State" names for battleships, all were "demoted", the *California* (CA.6) becoming the *San Diego*, seen here.**

Inter-war treaties and their effect on cruiser development

Following World War I the victorious nations lapsed into an insupportable capital ship "naval race". The reasons for this were various, but included American suspicions of Japanese intentions in the western Pacific, the determination by the American "big fleet" lobby to bring about a US fleet "second to none" (which upset the British, still committed to a Two Power Standard in fleet strength) and the perennial rivalry between France and Italy in the Mediterranean.

To halt the enormously expensive capital ship construction programmes that resulted, representatives of the five nations met in Washington in 1921–22. Although the resulting treaty, binding until 1936, was aimed primarily at capital ships, it was also the first of several to fundamentally affect the cruiser category, in terms of numbers, size and armament.

With the peace, the Royal Navy had scrapped all pre-war cruisers but, although this left about 50, most were of the small "fleet" type, in which endurance had been subordinated to speed and firepower. For peacetime operation the service needed rather larger ships, for trade protection, whose characteristics were diametrically opposite. At Washington, therefore, Britain refused to accept limitations on the number of cruisers "not connected with or required for fleet action".

The treaty limited individual cruiser size to 10,160 tonnes/10,000 tons displacement, carrying guns of no greater than 203mm/8in calibre. Both parameters were in excess of anything yet constructed (excepting the discredited and discontinued armoured cruiser) and had the unintended effect that each signatory began to build up to them. With

no global tonnage limit agreed, a new "treaty cruiser" race developed. These ships, too, were extremely expensive. The Royal Navy had to build them to avoid being out-classed but they soaked up scarce funding while being unnecessarily large for required purposes.

Great Britain lobbied hard to limit the 203mm/8in treaty cruiser but attempts at compromise failed at Geneva in 1927. In 1930, therefore, the London Naval Conference tried again, this time successfully. Its subsequent treaty defined a cruiser as a surface ship of war, other than a capital ship or aircraft carrier, exceeding 1,880 tonnes/1,850 tons and carrying guns exceeding 130mm/5.1in calibre. In deference to British requirements for small "fleet" cruisers and larger "trade" cruisers, the treaty sub-categorized them into ships carrying guns of greater or less than 155mm/6.1in calibre.

Global limitations were placed on overall cruiser tonnage and also on each of the two sub-categories, popularly termed "heavy" and "light" cruisers. Agreed ceilings were as follows:

	Heavy cruisers tonnes/tons	Light cruisers tonnes/tons	Total tonnes/tons
British Commonwealth	149,156/146,800	195,284/192,200	344,440/339,000
United States	182,888/180,000	145,803/143,500	328,691/323,500
Japan	110,140/108,400	102,062/100,450	212,201/208,850

As can be seen, the larger proportion of the British allocation was for light cruisers, any number of which could be built within the total agreed tonnage. In heavy cruisers, the

LEFT: **Having been allied to Great Britain and the United States during World War I, Japan felt slighted by what she felt was a meagre tonnage allowance permitted under the Washington Treaty. *Chokai* was one of 16 powerful cruisers constructed as a substitute for capital ships.**

ABOVE: Naval occasion – the complement of HMAS *Australia* formally drawn up during a royal review at Spithead. The spacious proportions of the County-class cruisers are evident. Comfortable ships, they were ideal for independent cruiser operations.
BELOW: Late treaty restrictions on light cruisers reduced the number allowed to the Royal Navy. Numbers were maximized by reducing individual displacements to a minimum. The four Arethusas were really Improved Leanders less one twin turret, and represented the minimum effective size. The nameship is shown here.

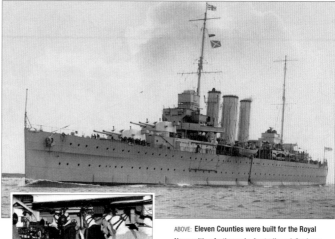

ABOVE: Eleven Counties were built for the Royal Navy, with a further pair, *Australia* and *Canberra* for the expanding Royal Australian Navy. *Australia*, here seen as a flagship, had a busy time during World War II, her three funnels apparently making an irresistible target for Japanese kamikazes. INSET LEFT: The Vickers-pattern 152mm/6in gun, used in British light cruisers, was a relatively simple but reliable weapon, firing a 45.4kg/100lb projectile. In full flash gear and gas mask, a loading number is seen ramming home the separate charge. BELOW: The American Brooklyn-class light cruisers with 15 guns were built in direct response to Japanese developments. After 1945 they were the only American light cruisers to be transferred to foreign flags, Argentina, Brazil and Chile each receiving a pair. This is the Brazilian *Tamandaré*, ex-USS *St. Louis* (CL.49).

actual number of hulls was stipulated, consensus following tough bargaining. By the end of 1936, it was agreed, the United States could build 18, the British Commonwealth 15 and Japan 12.

The London Treaty was, in its entirety, to remain in force for no longer than the end of 1936, when the remaining clauses of the Washington Treaty also lapsed. With the mid-1930s seeing an accelerating pace of rearmament, a Second London Naval Conference was convened in good time with the hope of maintaining some control over construction. In the subsequent treaty, signed in March 1936, there were several articles of critical importance relating to cruiser design. Individual displacements were now to be limited to only 8,128 tonnes/8,000 tons. Until January 1, 1943, guns of greater than 155mm/6.1in calibre were forbidden. One can see in these parameters, for instance, the origins of the British "Crown Colony" class and its derivatives which, on that displacement, mounted an ambitious twelve 152mm/6in guns in four triple turrets, later reduced to three.

The treaty also divided light cruisers into two sub-categories, i.e. greater or less than 3,048 tonnes/3,000 tons displacement, with either carrying guns of up to 155mm/6.1in calibre. This covered new classes of "super-destroyer", favoured particularly by the French.

The River Plate action

Dubbed "Pocket Battleships" by the popular press, Germany's Deutschland-class armoured ships were built for commerce raiding. Cruising at 13 knots, their range was greater than 30,578km/19,000 miles. Well-protected, mounting six 28cm/11in and eight 15cm/5.9in guns, they were destined to out-fight anything that they could not out run.

Supported by a dedicated supply ship, the *Admiral Graf Spee* sailed for the South Atlantic before hostilities commenced and, by December 7, 1939, she had destroyed nine merchantmen. Then, having evaded a total of eight hunting groups, she made for the shipping focal point off the estuary of the river Plate, which separates Argentina from Uruguay. Here, early on the December 13, she encountered Commodore Henry Harwood's South American Division. Wearing his broad pennant in the light cruiser *Ajax*, he had in company her sister, *Achilles* (largely New Zealand-manned) and the small 203mm/8in cruiser *Exeter*. It was unfortunate that his largest unit, the 203mm/8in *Cumberland*, had been detached to the Falklands.

On a summer morning the three British cruisers immediately adopted Harwood's stated plan of splitting the enemy's fire by operating in two divisions. When first sighted, the German was to the north-west of the British and headed toward them on an approximately south-easterly course. As the range was about 17,374m/19,000yds, both sides opened fire immediately. *Exeter* turned on to a westerly heading to get

ABOVE: **This impression of the River Plate action implies a close-range encounter. Harwood, however, with ships of superior speed, selected ranges to divide the enemy's fire and to keep at a distance where smaller calibre guns would still be effective against armour. Not an easy compromise.** ABOVE RIGHT: **A boat crew from the *Graf Spee* assists the ship in coming to a buoy in this pre-war shot. Note the "Wappen", or arms, of the original Vice Admiral Maximilian Reichsgraf von Spee, who died with the *Scharnhorst* at the Falklands in December 1914.**

on to the *Graf Spee*'s starboard flank, while the two light cruisers worked up to full speed to work around to the north of the enemy to engage him from the opposite side. As they worked across the *Graf Spee*'s bows, they successfully headed her off, her course being quickly changed to east and then under smoke to the north-west.

The German commanding officer, Captain Langsdorff, initially divided his fire as Harwood intended, but soon realized that the *Exeter* constituted the major threat. Concentrating on her with his 28cm/11in main battery, he quickly hit her three times, putting "B" turret out of action and causing the ship to be conned from the emergency after steering position. To ease the pressure, *Exeter* fired torpedoes but was hit three times more. After some 35 minutes she had one turret left operable and, with an increasing list from flooding, was barely able to stay in the action.

By now, *Ajax* and *Achilles*, the former with her aircraft spotting, had closed the enemy, only lightly opposed by the *Graf Spee*'s secondary armament. They were hitting freely although their 152mm/6in projectiles bounced "like turnips" from the German's armour. In contrast, the *Exeter*'s three hits on the *Graf Spee* had penetrated deeply.

> "As things turned out, I am delighted that you did not have the *Cumberland* with you – even if you had sunk the *Graf Spee*, it would not have been so glorious an affair."
> Personal letter to Harwood from the First Sea Lord, Sir Dudley Pound, January 11, 1940

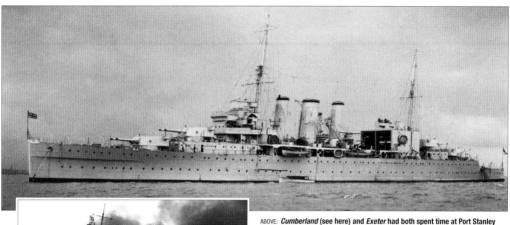

ABOVE: *Cumberland* (see here) and *Exeter* had both spent time at Port Stanley in the Falklands for essential maintenance. *Cumberland* was still there when Harwood's ships sighted the enemy but sailed immediately. She arrived off the River Plate as reinforcement, having steamed at full power for 36 hours.

LEFT: In one of the best-remembered images of World War II, the gutted wreck of *Graf Spee* burns out in shallow water off Montevideo. Two secondary 15cm/5.9in guns are visible by the wrecked funnel and, far right, the barbette of the after triple 28cm/11in turret has been displaced by a magazine explosion.

BELOW: HMS *Achilles* was one of only two cruisers fully manned by New Zealanders. Endorsed by Commodore Harwood, their Commanding Officer's report read that "New Zealand had every reason to be proud of her seamen during their baptism of fire." Four died and three were injured.

Langsdorff made extensive use of smoke and course changes to upset the light cruisers' gun-laying and, having effectively put the *Exeter* out of action, began to concentrate fire on the lighter ships. These undoubtedly saved the *Exeter* from destruction, although the *Ajax* was caught by a 28cm/11in shell which immobilized two turrets, half her main armament.

Better to observe the scattered action, Captain Langsdorff had forsaken his armoured control position for the exposed fore top, where he was lightly wounded by splinters and probably concussed by blast. To the puzzlement of the British, he maintained a wavering westerly heady directly for neutral South American waters. His ship had suffered three 203mm/8in and eighteen 152mm/6in hits but with the exception of a large hole right forward, she was not significantly damaged. His 35 dead and 60 wounded weighed heavily on the German commander, however, who made for Montevideo in Uruguay, trailed at a respectful distance by Harwood's two light cruisers.

As a belligerent, Langsdorff was allowed 24 hours in a neutral port but, to effect repairs and seek medical assistance, a further 72 hours were granted. The British Admiralty, meanwhile, was despatching every possible warship to the area. Langsdorff knew that he had no chance of fighting his way back to Germany. Politically, internment was not an option so, having gained Berlin's sanction, he sailed into the Plate on the December 17 and destroyed his ship by exploding the magazines.

ABOVE: Both *Ajax* (here) and *Achilles* came close to torpedoing the *Graf Spee* as her attention was distracted by *Exeter*. A single 28cm/11in hit put both *Ajax*'s after turrets out of action but her fire, although rapid, was of an accuracy affected by sudden, necessary and radical changes of course.

293

Armed merchant cruisers in World War II

Inter-war treaty limitations and political parsimony combined to guarantee that the Royal Navy entered the new war with too few cruisers. On the pre-war assumption that the United Kingdom would experience no shortfall in mercantile tonnage, the Admiralty therefore planned to plug the gap with 50 Armed Merchant Cruisers, or AMCs. These were requisitioned by October 1939, their cargo capacity immediately being lost to the nation.

In time of war, passenger liners are valuable particularly as troop carriers and, too complex to be built at such a time, needed to be husbanded carefully. Six, however, had already been lost by the time of the fall of France in June 1940. The 41 of the type taken by the Admiralty were required for long-range patrolling and to give convoys a measure of defence against attack by surface raiders. For armament, they were given aged 152mm/6in and 119mm/4.7in guns retained from discarded cruisers of World War I.

> "An immense expense and also a care and anxiety." First Lord of the Admiralty (Winston Churchill) to First Sea Lord (Admiral of the Fleet Sir Dudley Pound) on the subject of AMCs. January 1940

ABOVE: Pre-war, the *Worcestershire* was one of the stately Bibby Line four-masters providing a liner service to India and Burma. In her wartime guise of Armed Merchant Cruiser (AMC) she has landed two masts and had her funnel shortened. She has both air and surface search radar and six antique 152mm/6in guns.

Under some pressure, the Admiralty released nine but allocated no less than 25 to a Northern Patrol. As in the previous war, it was aimed at contraband control, and the interception of returning enemy merchantmen and outgoing raiders. It was successful in both. During the first four months of hostilities over 300 neutrals were sent in for examination but when, in November 1939, the AMC *Rawalpindi* sighted the fast German battleships *Scharnhorst* and *Gneisenau*, she could do little more than raise the alarm and demonstrate how to die bravely. Her warning caused the enemy to abandon his planned foray but patrolling AMCs then proved vulnerable to U-boat attack, losing six more of their number during 1940.

To reduce this rate of attrition, AMCs were based on Halifax, Nova Scotia, from the end of the year. From here they escorted eastbound convoys as far as meridian 25 degrees West before refuelling in Iceland and patrolling the Denmark Strait in the course of their return.

LEFT: **A unit of the patrol line in the Faeroes-Iceland gap, the ex-P&O liner** *Rawalpindi* **encountered the German battleships** *Scharnhorst* **and** *Gneisenau* **in November 1939. Although the AMC was quickly destroyed, her report of the enemy's position caused him to abandon his planned Atlantic foray.**
ABOVE: **The German auxiliary cruiser** *Thor*, **which sailed in June 1940, encountered the AMCs** *Alcantara* **in July and** *Carnarvon Castle* (seen here) **in the December. Both British ships suffered considerable damage but were not able to inflict sufficient to cause the enemy to abandon his cruise.**
LEFT: **Sole escort to a 37-ship Atlantic convoy when it was attacked by the "pocket battleship"** *Admiral Scheer*, **the** *Jervis Bay* **sold her life dearly, buying sufficient time to allow her charges to scatter. As a result, losses were limited to just five merchantmen.**
BELOW: **Protracted cruises by German auxiliary raiders depended greatly upon meeting regularly with supply ships and tankers. One of these,** *Weser*, **was destroyed by the Canadian AMC** *Prince Robert* (seen here) **off Mexico in September 1940.**

By February 1940 the Admiralty had 46 AMCs, mostly ex-passenger liners, in commission and spread between Halifax, Freetown (West Africa), the Mediterranean, and the Indian and Pacific Oceans.

Armed with obsolete weapons removed from long-scrapped warships, and with only the most rudimentary fire control, it was obvious that what the Naval Staff termed "indispensable auxiliaries" were unable to engage even the weakest of enemy raiders on anything approaching equal terms. Yet, deployed to intercept just this category of opponent, the ex-Royal Mail liner *Alcantara* encountered the German *Thor* off the Brazilian coast in July 1940. Badly damaging the British ship, the *Thor* escaped to continue her cruise. Still in the South Atlantic in the December, she met up with the AMC *Carnarvon Castle*, with a similar result. Both AMCs had been totally outranged, but little could be done to improve matters, better equipment being unavailable.

AMCs also continued to escort convoys. Sole escort for 37 merchantmen, the *Jervis Bay* found herself fighting off the *Admiral Scheer* in November 1940. Selling her life dearly, she bought sufficient time for her charges to scatter with the loss of only five. Her commanding officer was awarded the Victoria Cross.

Unstinting valour could not disguise the vulnerability of the AMC, underlined when the *Thor*, on her second cruise, easily destroyed the *Voltaire*.

Increasing numbers of escorts permitted a July 1941 reorganization of the North Atlantic. Here, and soon afterwards on the West African station, AMCs were withdrawn for other duties, more suited to their purpose.

With the build-up of American and Canadian troops in the United Kingdom, and the resumption of the Allied offensive, troopship capacity became inadequate and so, during 1942, a further dozen AMCs reverted to this role. Of the remaining 23, all returned to troopship duties during 1943–44 save those retained for specialist service, such as heavy repair and depot ships, or Landing Ships, Infantry (LSIs).

Having exchanged their bright peacetime liveries for grey Admiralty "crabfat", the liners fought their war courageously and at considerable cost but were never considered the equals of a regular warship and proved ultimately to be more valuable in the role for which they had been originally designed — people carrying. Most survived to give long post-war service.

The German raiders

Experience during World War I, particularly with the *Wolf* and *Möwe*, proved to the German Navy that innocently disguised, armed merchantmen made more effective commerce raiders than warships. The latter were more expensive, ever in short supply, demanded large crews and needed frequent dockyard attention. On the other hand, a merchantman's designed cargo capacity could accommodate fuel and stores for considerable endurance, while through paint and canvas, she could quickly assume a false identity before shifting location.

During World War II, despite the service being under strength, surface warships still conducted a number of raiding cruises, leading directly to the loss of the *Graf Spee* and the *Bismarck*. Plans existed, however, for the conversion of 26 auxiliary raiders. In the event, only half of these were actually taken in hand, of which nine made cruises.

The intention was for them to operate in more remote theatres, such as the South Atlantic and Indian Oceans, where Allied shipping, particularly British, was plentiful but where regular German surface combatants could not safely venture. Both Japan and Soviet Russia (until June 1941) rendered considerable assistance. Further support was given by a network of German supply ships stationed at remote oceanic locations. The major function of these was the replenishment of long-range U-boats to extend their patrols still further but they could also offer limited mechanical assistance.

Merchantmen selected for conversion comprised good-quality tonnage from the major companies, notably Hamburg-Amerika, Norddeutscher Lloyd and Hansa lines. Typically of 7,000–8,000grt, although some were considerably smaller, they

TOP: **Typifying the innocent appearance of German auxiliary cruisers, the** *Orion* **appears to be any nondescript, disruptively painted merchantman. Formerly the** *Kurmark* **of Hamburg-Amerika she mounted six 15cm/5.9in guns and, in total, was credited with sinking 61,342grt of Allied shipping.** ABOVE: **The usual quarry for an auxiliary raider was the independently routed merchantman, normally encountered in remote areas of ocean not covered by the regular convoy network. Any attempt by a victim to transit an "RRR" raider warning would result in heavy fire and casualties.**

varied greatly in appearance, some being steam propelled, others motorships. Their ingeniously concealed armament usually included six 15cm/5.9in guns and two to six torpedo tubes. Most carried two floatplanes to extend their search horizon, and several hundred mines, which were planted in small clutches at focal points, positions calculated to cause maximum loss and disruption.

Badly delayed by the unusually severe winter of 1939–40, the first raiders, *Atlantis* and *Orion*, sailed in March and April 1940. During May and June the *Widder*, *Pinguin* and *Thor* also broke out successfully. Last of the "first wave", the *Komet*, which had been fitted out at Murmansk, was escorted by Soviet icebreakers to gain the Pacific by the northern route.

The raiders' commanding officers were selected from older regular personnel, usually with considerable experience of the merchant service. Their normal mode of operation was to close with a selected victim, disclose their identity and demand complete compliance, particularly that no radio be used. Any defiance was met by 15cm/5.9in gunfire into the bridge structure. British Admiralty instructions, however, were that a ship was to transmit a raider warning before submitting, an

LEFT: The AMC *Carnarvon Castle*'s attempt to apprehend the German raider *Thor* resulted in her receiving heavy damage. Guns issued to AMCs were, as seen here, aged weapons removed from long-scrapped warships of an earlier war. Fire control was also rudimentary. ABOVE: Following resupply from the auxiliary raider *Kormoran*, a U-boat (*U-124*) strikes down a torpedo. *Kormoran* was disguised as the Japanese freighter *Sakito Maru*, with the Rising Sun flag displayed on each side of the hull and authentic Japanese markings which they had taken with them from Germany.

ABOVE LEFT: The final encounter between the *Kormoran* and the Australian cruiser *Sydney* took place about 241.4km/150 miles south-west of Carnarvon, Western Australia. On abandoning ship, one of the *Kormoran*'s boats capsized but the remainder safely made the Australian coast, where the survivors were made prisoner. ABOVE: Cadet O'Hara on the SS *Stephen Hopkins*, a US Liberty ship engaging the German auxiliary cruisers *Stier* with *Tannenfels* on fire on September 27, 1942. BELOW: Suspicious of the *Kormoran*, which was disguised, the fully alert *Sydney* unwisely took position on her beam and at less than a mile's range. She was suddenly swept by gunfire and torpedoes. Answering in kind, she inflicted mortal damage on the raider but headed away, never to be seen again.

order that resulted in the death of many courageous radio officers, who transmitted despite warnings.

The "second wave" comprised the raiders *Stier*, *Kormoran* and *Michel* together with the *Thor*, making a further cruise. They were the last as, by 1943, the interlocking Allied patrol and escort system made such operations increasingly difficult, not least for the targeted supply network.

The majority of raiders were destroyed, but their experience was varied. Three (*Komet*, *Atlantis* and *Pinguin*) were intercepted and sunk by British warships. Another, *Kormoran*, engaged in a duel with the Australian cruiser *Sydney*, an exchange that resulted in the destruction of both. The *Stier* was likewise sunk in a mutually destructive duel, this time with the American merchantman *Stephen Hopkins*, which defended herself valiantly with a single 127mm/5in gun. The *Thor* proved to be something of a scourge for the weakly armed British Armed Merchant Cruisers (AMCs), fighting off and badly damaging first the *Alcantara*, then the *Carnarvon Castle*, before finally sinking a third, the *Voltaire*. She was, herself, destroyed by explosion while refitting in Yokohama.

Despite the huge disruption caused by German merchant raiders (Italian and Japanese hardly figured), they accounted for only 133 ships of about 830,000grt, about 3.8 per cent of total war losses. Most successful was the *Atlantis* with 22 ships of about 146,000grt.

LEFT: **HMS *Exeter*'s Walrus amphibian secured and ready for hoisting aboard. Visible are the two starboard-side 102mm/4in guns on high-angle mountings and capable of long-range barrage fire against aircraft. By World War II aircraft were already too fast to be accurately tracked by such weapons.** ABOVE: **Virtually useless against attacking aircraft, the quadruple 12.7mm/0.5in machine gun was still being widely specified for newbuildings into World War II. Together with the 2-pounder "pompom" cannon and high-angle 76mm/3in 12-pounders they comprised a range of standard weapons that fell far short of satisfactory.**

The introduction and development of the anti-aircraft cruiser

Although by the end of World War I 76mm/3in guns on high-angle (HA) mounts had made a general appearance to provide an anti-aircraft capability, they lacked any sort of fire control and were virtually useless. To combat a high-flying bomber the problem was complex. Firstly, a gun with the necessary elevation and a high sustained rate of fire was required. This then needed to be linked to a control system capable of measuring an aircraft's present and predicted position. Manual estimation quickly proved to be too slow.

The 1930s saw the introduction of small multiple automatic weapons (for example the British 12.7mm/0.5in machine-gun and 2-pounder pompom, and the American 28mm/1.1in gun) for close-range defence but, for longer ranges, medium-calibre guns were required. Here, the British preference was for the

102mm/4in, whose 13.6–15.9kg/30–35lb fixed ammunition could be rapidly handled by hand. The Americans retained their trusted 127mm/5in gun, whose 24.9kg/55lb projectile tested the ability of strong men on a continuous basis.

New British light cruisers (i.e. 152mm/6in) of the 1930s were so strapped by treaty-imposed tonnage restrictions that only four 102mm/4in guns could be accommodated. The adoption of the very successful twin mounting reduced the space required for these but doubled the weight per gun. In those pre-radar days, the American 127mm/5in 38-calibre could range to the useful limits of visibility while still having a capacity against surface or shore targets.

As the 1930s progressed, the British Admiralty became concerned that neither convoys nor battle groups had sufficient anti-aircraft (AA) escorts. For the former, programmes of sloops and escort destroyers were put in hand, both classes armed with the ubiquitous twin 102mm/4in Mark XIX mounting. However, only the most recent of fleet destroyers had guns of high elevation, and with the desire for a steadier platform it was decided to convert the better of the elderly C-class cruisers for

LEFT: **In a post-war exercise HMS *Cleopatra*, a surviving Dido-class AA cruiser, puts up an impressive barrage against an attacking aircraft. Air-to-surface guided weapons were already in the inventory, however, against which even fast and accurate gunnery was largely ineffective.**

ABOVE: **A well-proven standard weapon, the American 127mm/5in 38 had a higher rate of fire than the British 133mm/5.25in, making their Atlanta-class cruisers (*Oakland* shown here) more effective against air attack than the Royal Navy's Didos. With gunhouses located on three levels, both types had high profiles.**

ABOVE RIGHT: **Twenty years old, the Royal Navy's C-class cruisers found a new and effective role converted into the first dedicated AA cruisers. Units such as *Curlew*, seen here, were given four twin 102mm/4in high-angle mountings with full director control. Ironically, the ship was destroyed by aircraft attack in 1940.**

an AA role. Their 152mm/6in and torpedo armament were landed in favour of 102mm/4in HA guns with full director control. They were effective but only six were converted before they were superseded by better, purpose-built ships.

During 1935 it had been decided that a new 133mm/5.25in projectile would be the best compromise between rapid HA fire and ship-stopping capability. Guns of this calibre mounted in twin turrets and capable of an 80-degree elevation were installed in the specialized Dido-class cruisers that followed. Considered a true dual-purpose weapon, the 133mm/5.25in gun comprised the entire designed medium-calibre armament for the ship which, uniquely, was designed with three forward mountings.

The commissioning of the Didos conveniently coincided with the introduction of radar. Although still primitive, its improved approximation of heights and ranges allowed the ships to use their armament effectively to the limit of its range. In practice, however, the 36.3kg/80lb fixed ammunition proved to be too heavy for rapid handling.

As the 133mm/5.25in gun was considered to be a light weapon, the Didos, themselves small, were given five twin mountings for maximum barrage fire. The weight of the three

forward turrets severely taxed the ships' generally light construction, so that most landed their "C" guns in favour of automatic weapons.

Much the same design philosophy governed the American Atlanta class. These were originally configured around no less than sixteen 127mm/5in 38-calibre guns, disposed in six centreline and two wing mountings. Together with radar gun direction, the proximity fuse provided the greatest improvement in the ability to cause damage of AA fire, as the projectile no longer had to actually hit a target to destroy it. Despite this huge advantage, the hitting power of the kamikaze saw the *Atlantis*'s wing turrets and torpedo tubes landed in favour of more 40mm/1.57in guns.

The aerial threat during World War II progressed from high level and dive bombing to radio-controlled glider bombs and suicide kamikazes. These last two threats needed to be completely disintegrated and not just disabled in order to stop the attack. The main post-war innovation was to temporarily exchange small-calibre automatic weapons for 76mm/3in, radar-laid guns as an interim measure while the first surface-to-air missile (SAM) systems were being developed.

LEFT: **The 40mm/1.57in Bofors and the 20mm/0.79in Oerlikon designs were the most effective AA weapons of World War II, and were produced under licence in huge numbers in the United States. A weakness of the quadruple 40mm/1.57in, as is here apparent, was the requirement for so many to feed it ammunition.**
ABOVE: **Experience in the Pacific was that low-level torpedo aircraft would synchronize their attack with dive bombers, splitting the available defensive fire. As seen here, a single aircraft would draw huge volumes of barrage fire. Proximity fusing was possible only in 76mm/3in projectiles and larger.**

The *Bismarck* pursuit

Although broad, the Denmark Strait between Iceland and Greenland is constricted by a permanent but variable icefield. It is in this area that the relatively warm Gulf Stream forms fogs and mirages on encountering the ice chill, which results in treacherously shifting visibility.

On May 23, 1941, the British heavy cruisers *Suffolk* and *Norfolk* were patrolling these difficult waters. Their purpose was to detect any attempt by the new German battleship *Bismarck*, accompanied by the heavy cruiser *Prinz Eugen*, to break through into the open Atlantic. Having sailed from Norway two days earlier, they were expected at any time.

From the rugged north-western extremity of Iceland a defensive minefield narrowed the strait further but the cruisers kept near the ice edge, where conditions were at their most variable and radar most useful. As no air patrols could be flown, the British were keeping an extra sharp watch to avoid being surprised.

At 19:22, in a clear patch, *Suffolk* suddenly made visual contact with the enemy at about 10,973m/12,000yds. *Norfolk* then emerged from a fogbank even more closely, to be greeted by a couple of warning salvoes. Using their extra speed and the patchy visibility to advantage, the two gained position on the quarters of the enemy. Following at high speed, they transmitted regular positional reports to Admiral Tovey who was endeavouring to intercept with the Home Fleet.

Well ahead of Tovey was Vice Admiral Holland in the battlecruiser *Hood*, accompanied by the new battleship

TOP: *Suffolk*'s great asset was her effective new radar. In the capricious fog of the Denmark Strait, this allowed her and the *Norfolk* to trail the enemy from a safer distance. The appearance of the Counties was not improved by the unsightly hangar and the weight-saving measure of cutting down the quarterdeck.
ABOVE: Having given her pursuers the slip, the *Bismarck*'s fate was decided through a sighting by a Coastal Command Catalina. Known to its American builders as a PBY, its design dated back to 1933 but, proving enormously versatile, it flew throughout World War II. More than 3,300 were built.

Prince of Wales. Vectored in by the cruiser's reports, these made contact at about 05:50 on May 24. Rear Admiral Wake-Walker, with the cruisers, anticipated his task complete and, from 24km/15 miles, watched the heavy ships engage. When, at about 06:00, the *Hood* blew up and the *Prince of Wales* was obliged to retire, his responsibilities became even greater as Tovey was still 482km/300 miles distant.

LEFT: **The Abyssinian Crisis and Spanish Civil War saw the *Hood* retained in the Mediterranean as flagship, her planned modernization never being undertaken. By far the largest and most imposing vessel in the Royal Navy at that time, her loss was keenly felt.** ABOVE: **A Southampton-class cruiser such as the *Sheffield* is seen here in typical Atlantic conditions. Water could be driven through the smallest of apertures, creating electrical faults or flooding, and it was common practice to train the forward turrets abaft the beam in such conditions.** BELOW: **Against a dour Arctic sky, a silhouetted *Prinz Eugen* is seen loosing a salvo as heavy-calibre British shells fall to the right. The very similar profiles of *Prinz Eugen* and *Bismarck* led to some confusion with the British gunlayers, leading to doubt as to which ship was actually being engaged.**

ABOVE: **In perhaps the finest action picture ever of a battleship, the *Bismarck*'s own gunfire puts her in sharp relief. Her after turrets are trained on their extreme forward bearing as she engages the British ships, then on her port bow. Most of the action was fought on this bearing as *Hood* tried to close the range.**

ABOVE: **A pre-war impression of *Norfolk*, painted for Far Eastern service. In days before air-conditioning, the great hulls of the Counties, with well-ventilated mess decks, high deckheads and wood-sheathed weather decks, made them very suitable and popular ships for tropical use.**

Unknown to Wake-Walker, the *Bismarck* had sustained damage sufficient to persuade her flag officer, Vice Admiral Lütjens, to abandon his foray and to make for a port in occupied western France.

During the night of May 24/25 the carrier *Victorious* mounted an unsuccessful air strike and Lütjens made several aggressive feints in an endeavour to shake off his trackers. These, of necessity, maintained a respectful distance and changes of course were frequent. At about 03:00 on May 25, Lütjens finally broke contact with his pursuers by making a radical change of heading, quickly detached the *Prinz Eugen* and made for Brest.

At this point Tovey was some 161km/100 miles adrift, but other British units were closing in. Urgent searches were mounted to re-establish contact, but it was not until 10:30 on May 26 that a PBY (Catalina) sighted the *Bismarck*, now just 1,127km/700 miles short of the sanctuary of Brest.

Interception was now only possibly by Vice Admiral Somerville's Force H, battling northward from Gibraltar in a rising gale. Somerville sent the cruiser *Sheffield* ahead to establish visual contact, but she was still 32km/20 miles short when the *Ark Royal*'s first air strike arrived. In appalling weather conditions, they attacked the *Sheffield* in error. By dint of furious manoeuvre the cruiser survived unscathed and, maintaining station, acted as a waypoint for the second strike. This put two torpedoes into the fugitive at about 21:00 on May 26, slowing her sufficiently to enable Tovey to engage at first

light with the battleships *King George V* and *Rodney*. Their heavy gunfire reduced the *Bismarck*'s topsides to a flaming shambles but, at the close ranges being employed, her hull was immune to fatal damage. Tovey's ships now very low on fuel pulled away, leaving the helpless hulk to be despatched by torpedo. This duty fell to a further cruiser, the *Dorsetshire*, which completed the task clinically with two torpedoes on one side and one on the other. Just 16km/10 miles distant was the *Norfolk*, which had seen the task through from the outset.

LEFT: The amphibious landing on Guadalcanal, August 7, 1942, was the first of any size in the Pacific. Very much a shoestring operation, it was initially virtually unopposed. Within 48 hours, the USS *Chicago*, seen here covering the landing, would be fighting for her life.

BELOW: A Japanese impression of the Battle of Savo Island with, probably, the *Quincy* (left) and *Astoria* hopelessly ablaze. The ferocity and skill of the Imperial Japanese Navy in night-fighting came as an unpleasant surprise to the Allies, who had to embark on a steep learning curve.

Savo Island

Commanded by Rear Admiral Richmond K. Turner, American amphibious forces hit Guadalcanal and neighbouring Tulagi in the Solomons on August 7, 1942. Japanese response was immediate; Vice Admiral Mikawa Gunichi sailing from Rabaul with five heavy and two light cruisers. His objective was to destroy the landing by attacking the vulnerable amphibious warfare ships laying off-shore. The operation proper had been covered by a three-carrier force under Vice Admiral Frank Jack Fletcher who controversially withdrew on the following day. This left Turner protected by a force of six heavy and two light cruisers and 13 destroyers. Two heavy and one light cruiser were Australian and the force's senior officer was Rear Admiral V.A.C. Crutchley VC of the Royal Navy.

Mikawa had to travel 966km/600 miles and, in the course of August 8, he was sighted at least twice. The reports, however, took 11 hours to reach Turner while the assessment of the enemy force was such that it was thought to only be capable of a daylight attack, which was anticipated for August 9.

Turner and Crutchley had little reason for alarm and made precautionary night dispositions, the 15 transports being herded into a guarded anchorage off Tulagi. The direction of Mikawa's advance was from the north-west down the 29km/18-mile-wide channel between Guadalcanal and Florida Island. This approach was divided by the round, 5km/3 mile-diameter island of Savo, a brooding volcanic cone towering to nearly 500m/547yds.

Crutchley, with Turner's agreement, divided his heavy cruisers to patrol north and south of Savo, placing the light cruisers further back to cover the approach to Tulagi. Beyond Savo, two radar-equipped picket destroyers patrolled across the strait.

> "It is difficult for me to understand how events could have occurred as they did, but it seems best to face facts." Turner to Crutchley in a preliminary assessment of the battle, August 12, 1942

Mikawa's plan was simple, to sweep in to the south of Savo, overwhelm the covering force with torpedo salvoes and gunfire, destroy the amphibious fleet and to "hightail it" out to the north of Savo to be well beyond Fletcher's carrier aircraft range before daylight.

Feeling secure against night attack, Crutchley and his flagship, the *Australia*, were absent with Turner when, at about 01:00 on August 9, the Japanese in line ahead swept past the picket destroyers without being noticed. If this was not serious enough, Mikawa's cruiser-launched floatplanes had been over-flying the amphibious force area for about 90 minutes without causing undue suspicion.

These suddenly dropped flares, throwing the cruisers *Canberra* and *Chicago* of the southern force into sharp relief. Still unsuspected, the leading Japanese ships snapped on searchlights, their instantaneous 203mm/8in salvoes following torpedoes already in the water. Blasted by two dozen hits and two torpedoes, the Australian was never in the fight. Her colleague, *Chicago*, took one hit each from shell and torpedo but, totally bewildered by what was happening, failed to warn the northern force of three cruisers.

As Mikawa swept around Savo his line lost cohesion in the darkness and confusion. Now effectively in two groups, it hit the northern force from two sides simultaneously. Smothered at close range by an enemy that they barely saw, the *Astoria*, *Quincy* and *Vincennes* were fatally damaged within minutes.

The *Chokai*, Mikawa's flagship, had suffered a single hit but this, to the charthouse, appeared to affect the Admiral's judgement. With his primary objective, the amphibious fleet, now virtually undefended, he now feared dawn retribution from Fletcher's carriers (in fact now almost beyond strike range). Throwing his chance of achieving annihilation to the wind, Mikawa led his squadron away, unmolested, into the velvety blackness of the tropic night.

Behind, he left four Allied cruisers sunk or sinking and over 1,000 Allied seamen dead. The action lasted barely an hour. Only the *Chicago* survived.

A subsequent enquiry absolved the Allied commanders of negligence but noted that their forces had not yet acquired that level of aggression and war-awareness that divided defeat from victory. That could, and would, be achieved only by constant action against a still underestimated, but able and resourceful, enemy who excelled at night-fighting.

TOP: **Seen here probably on builder's trials in the Clyde in 1927, the Australian cruiser *Canberra* was lost at Savo Island, literally without firing a shot. Even as she responded to the sudden appearance of Mikawa's force she was swamped by gunfire, taking "at least 24 shells" as the Japanese swept past.**

ABOVE: **As built, the Japanese *Kako* mounted her 20cm/7.87in guns in single turrets, as seen here. They were later twinned. As Mikawa's triumphant force withdrew, it passed the veteran American submarine S-44 which, from 640m/700yds, sank the *Kako* with four torpedoes.**

LEFT: **Within the complex organization of the Imperial Japanese Navy, Vice Admiral Mikawa Gunichi was senior officer of the Outer South Seas Force of the Eighth Fleet. At Savo Island his judgement was faulty in that although he defeated the Allied cruiser force, he failed to destroy the transports, his primary objective.**

ABOVE: **Kinugasa (seen here) and *Aoba* were improved versions of the *Kako* and *Furutaka*, the four usually operating as a division. The *Kinugasa* was the tail-ender of the Chokai group, as the *Furutaka* became separated in the confusion. She suffered only four killed and one wounded.**

LEFT: **Just two months before she was lost at Savo Island, the cruiser *Astoria* was one of those acting as escort to the carrier *Yorktown* at Midway. With that carrier disabled, and later sunk, Admiral Fletcher transferred his flag temporarily to the *Astoria*.**

303

LEFT: After World War II the US Navy disposed of its surviving pre-war tonnage. Of the nine Brooklyn-class light cruisers of 1936–38, only one had become a war casualty. Two more were scrapped and two each were transferred to Argentina, Brazil and Chile. ABOVE: Under the Argentinian flag, the *Boise* (CL.47) became the *9 de Julio* and the *Phoenix* (CL.46) the *17 de Octubre*. Following political upheavals she was renamed *General Belgrano* in 1956 (seen here) after Don Manuel Belgrano, hero of national independence and designer of the national flag.

Phoenix/Belgrano – the life and death of a Pearl Harbor veteran

Four of the large new Brooklyn-class light cruisers were present in Pearl Harbor when the Japanese struck on December 7, 1941. Three were in the crowded Navy Yard but the fourth, *Phoenix* (CL.46), was anchored in the East Loch. Fortunate in not being made a torpedo target she made to get under way along with other ships. A signal from the flagship initially prohibited movement but, once this was countermanded, the *Phoenix* was able to slip down past Ford Island and the gutted wreckage of "Battleship Row" to gain the relative safety of the open sea.

Despite going on to serve at all the main southern amphibious landings, including Hollandia, Leyte, Lingayen and Mindoro, *Phoenix* survived the war. Prematurely aged by hard service, she, together with her sister *Boise*, was transferred in 1951 to Argentina. She assumed the name 17 *de Octubre* but, five years later with the collapse of the Peron regime, she was renamed for General Belgrano, hero of national independence.

Her life proceeded uneventfully until, in April 1982, Argentina invaded the long-claimed British Falkland Islands. Making clear her intention of recovering the territory, Britain quickly despatched a naval task force and declared a 644km/400-mile diameter Maritime Exclusion Zone (MEZ) about the islands. Ahead of the task force, unseen and unadvertised, sped three nuclear attack submarines (SSNs). These, *Spartan*, *Splendid* and *Conqueror*, arrived between April 12 and April 19.

The considerable Argentine military presence on the islands was largely dependent upon supply by sea. A plethora of

LEFT: **Survivor's view of the *Belgrano* foundering following two torpedo hits from the nuclear submarine HMS *Conqueror*. The sinking caused a political storm but, militarily, was absolutely correct in the establishment of moral superiority. The Argentine surface fleet gave no further trouble.**

LEFT: **The second Argentine cruiser,** *9 de Julio,* **(seen here), was deleted in 1979 and probably used as a source of spares to keep the 40-year-old** *Belgrano* **functioning. Although conventionally armed, the** *Belgrano* **had overwhelming firepower in comparison with that of the British warships.**

targets was thus available to the SSNs but the Royal Navy was bound by the principle of "minimum force" and, for the moment, rules of engagement permitted no attack. Nonetheless, although the British government insisted on terming the dispute a "conflict" rather than a "war", it was traditional naval strategy to hit first and to hit hard in order to establish a moral ascendancy over an adversary (compare with Heligoland Bight 1914 and Calabria 1940).

On May 1 the situation changed when intercepted signal traffic indicated that the Argentinian Navy was contemplating a major attack on the British task force. The latter, operating to the north-east of the islands, beyond the reach of enemy mainland-based air, found itself between two hostile task groups. To its north-west was one based on a carrier deploying A-4 Skyhawks. To its south-west, and skirting the MEZ, was a second, comprising the *Belgrano* and Exocet-armed escorts. The cruiser, although now elderly, shipped fifteen 152mm/6in guns which comfortably out-ranged the 114mm/4.5in armament of the British.

The Argentinians hoped that carrier-based air strikes with A-4s (superior in performance to the British Harriers) would cause damage and disorder from which the *Belgrano* group could take advantage.

Early on May 2 the two S-boats had located the carrier's escorts but not the carrier, their prime target. Meanwhile to the south of the islands the *Belgrano* group was being tracked by the *Conqueror*. London assessed the cruiser to be a direct threat and, despite her not having entered the MEZ and having turned on to a westerly course, ordered her sinking. The *Belgrano* had turned away on learning that due to lack of wind, the carrier air strike could not be mounted.

Unrushed, the *Conqueror* closed to within 1.6km/1 mile before putting two torpedoes into the Argentinian which, poorly

TOP RIGHT: **HMS** *Conqueror* **was the first nuclear hunter-killer ever to sink a ship in anger. She used the elderly Mk8 torpedoes on the grounds of a close attack (under one mile) and for the odd reason that they would have "a better chance of penetrating the cruiser's armour and anti-torpedo bulges."** ABOVE: *Phoenix* **attempts to escape, passing Pearl Harbor's blazing oil tanks. In company with the** *Detroit,* **she was first ordered back to her berth before finally getting out to sea. She fired over 80 rounds of 127mm/5in against attacking Japanese aircraft and managed to escape damage.**

prepared, had no hope of survival. The British submarine easily evaded the depth charges expended by hopeful escorts but, despite her also not interrupting their subsequent life-saving efforts, a total of 321 were lost in the sinking.

The anti-war lobby in Britain subsequently made a maximum of political capital for the sinking yet, militarily, it was correct in signalling unequivocally to the Argentinians the consequences of any attempt at direct naval intervention. For the remainder of the short war, the Royal Navy was untroubled by the Argentinian surface fleet, which tended to remain in waters judged too shallow for the operation of SSNs.

305

The cruiser after 1945

Unable to win a war at sea fought by conventional means, Germany and Japan turned to the unconventional. As early as 1943 the Luftwaffe was deploying guided bombs against shipping while, during the following year, the less technologically advanced Japanese dispensed with the requirement for sophisticated guidance systems by employing suicide pilots. Either method was potentially lethal and highly accurate. Rapid-fire, radar-laid proximity-fused weaponry was the first response but the long-term solution lay in the surface-to-air missile (SAM), capable of eliminating such a threat at a safe distance.

First-generation SAM-systems were very demanding of space, with bulky missiles and handling arrangements and the need to direct each missile from launch to contact. Cruiser-sized hulls were required and although many nearly new war-built hulls were available, they did not lend themselves to easy conversion.

By the early 1950s, two viable American SAMs had emerged in the long-ranged Talos and medium-range Terrier. Accommodating the former required deep hull penetration and was expensive. Terrier, more compact, could be housed in a superstructure, although even this was bulky.

Reflecting the still-necessary flexibility of a cruiser, these early conversions were "single-ended", retaining their original forward gun armament. Their considerable extra "kudos" as

TOP: *California* (CGN.36) leads *Virginia* (CGN.38) with, possibly, *South Carolina* (CGN.37) to her starboard, and supported by *Leahy/Belknaps*. An all-nuclear navy appeared a possibility during the 1970s but, despite being able to steam indefinitely, nuclear warships still require regular topping-up with stores, ammunition and victuals. ABOVE: Following experience of air attack in World War II, and with the additional threat of Soviet Cold War developments of maritime bombers equipped with stand-off, air-to-surface missiles, Western fleets concentrated first on producing effective surface-to-air missiles, such as the 16.1km/10-mile ranged American Tartar. BELOW LEFT: Designed initially without guns, the *Long Beach* (CGN.9) later had a pair of single 127mm/5in 38 guns added, visible in the waist. The early Talos and Terrier missile systems were replaced by Standard, and Harpoon was added. Early plans to carry Polaris were not pursued.

missile carriers quickly made them popular as flagships, exacerbating the problem of inadequate accommodation space. With aircraft carriers needing to maximize volume devoted to aircraft, it was expected that area missile defence would be furnished by an escorting cruiser, although the latter was still expected to be flexible enough to operate independently in more traditional roles.

Despite the difficulties, the Americans produced the three Albany-class double-enders, incorporating both Talos and Terrier, and with a gun armament confined to just two 127mm/5in 38s. The two systems were also sold abroad but the resulting foreign conversions were few.

ABOVE: When the Royal Navy's long-anticipated new attack carrier was cancelled in the early 1970s, a class of dedicated escorts was cancelled with her. HMS *Bristol*, the Type 82 prototype, alone survived. She had combined steam and gas-turbine propulsion and was designed around the Sea Dart SAM system.

ABOVE: "If a ship *looks* right, she usually *is* right." So runs the old tag and, unfortunately, the elaborate American missile cruiser conversions never "*looked right*". The 1960s rebuilds, such as the *Albany* double-ender, proved that purpose-designed vessels were ultimately better value for money.

RIGHT: Theoretically capable of 20 rounds per minute per barrel, the 152mm/6in guns of the British Tiger class were, mechanically, highly complex. Obsolete as all-gun cruisers, the ships were converted to carry ASW helicopters.

ABOVE: France's last remaining conventional cruiser, *Colbert*, had been converted to a command ship by the early 1980s, serving as flagship for the Toulon-based Mediterranean Fleet. In this role she carried no gun larger than a 100mm/3.9in. BELOW: Missile systems are very demanding of space, and cruisers need to be designed around them. The Russian *Slava* of 1982 can accommodate 16 large SSM launchers forward, with eight vertical-launch silos for SAMs in the gap abaft the funnel.

Major World War II operations had highlighted the requirement for headquarters or task command ships. The considerable equipment and staff associated with their extensive command and control functions were located in mercantile hulls during the war but, for the peace, demanded the new concept of the "command cruiser", for which only purpose-design could really be satisfactory.

The cash-strapped British government was slow to introduce these new types of ship. An ambitious design for an 18,289-tonne/18,000-ton single-ender came to nought. Conventionally armed, unconverted cruisers found their way remorselessly to the scrapyards, while the three new Tigers, although completed with sophisticated, fully automatic 152mm/6in and 76mm/3in weapons, were obsolete before they were commissioned.

In place of the Sea Slug-armed 18,289-tonne/18,000-ton vessel and the large Type 82 escort for the projected new carrier, the Royal Navy received the County-class cruiser-sized destroyers. The Type 82s were terminated at one ship while the promised "command cruiser", following much inter-service and political wrangling, found final form in the *Invincible*, an ASW helicopter carrier in all but name.

Just a few good examples of the conventional cruiser were built post-war, notably pairs by France, the Netherlands and Sweden. Its last group, however, had to be the planned 24-strong Sverdlovs of the Soviet Russian fleet. At about 15,749 tonnes/15,500 tons and gun-armed they were fine ships and, although anachronistic, caused NATO planners problems in the area of trade protection.

For the US Navy, the extension of nuclear propulsion to surface ships removed the cruiser even further from its traditional concepts. The monstrous, all-missile *Long Beach* proved to be an evolutionary dead-end while her nuclear-powered escorts, although termed "frigates", were the size of earlier cruisers. Although they were eventually rerated "cruisers", their extra expense proved unjustifiable.

New technologies and mission changes have, for the moment, seen the end of the traditional cruiser, replaced by large, multi-function fleet escorts equipped with three-dimensional radar and a variety of missiles. This has been made possible by electronic micro-miniaturization, which has greatly increased potential without the parallel explosion in ship size.

Directory of Cruisers

Pre-World War I

In the period up to 1914 the cruiser emerged as a warship category in its own right. Its development was inevitably greatly influenced by the enormous technical advances of the era. From the cumbersome and heavy cylindrical boiler developed the water-tube types, lighter and more efficient. Compound armour advanced to proprietary "cemented" steels, giving greater protection for less weight. Horizontal and vertical steam reciprocating engines gave way to the smooth-running, compact steam turbine.

Our early examples are still sailing warships with auxiliary power, armed, mainly on the broadside, with muzzle- and breech-loading, smooth-bore and rifled shell guns. By 1914 we see 27-knot cruisers armed with quick-firing weapons, designed either to operate with the fleet or against commerce. During this period, armoured cruisers, as large and as costly as contemporary battleships, are still seen by some as a viable alternative. Cheaper and faster, protected cruisers emerged as the best "general purpose" type, equivalent to the old 74-gun Third Rate.

LEFT: Small masted cruisers, such as the *Condor* of 1898, were the backbone of the Royal Navy's Pacific cruising fleet. Of several closely related classes, they were usually of composite construction, with iron or steel framing, clad in wood. The lower hull was sheathed in copper.

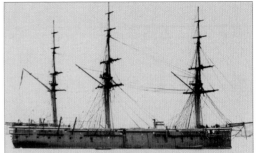

Royal Oak, Hector and *Zealous*

A French order for four, steam-driven ironclads, placed in 1858, triggered immediate British reaction. Iron protection, however, was first added only to gundecks and machinery. Only with the *Royal Oak*, completed in 1863, was armour extended to a belt, above and below the waterline. Converted from a 91-gun two-decked Second Rate while under construction, she emerged as a "wooden-hulled iron frigate" as, eventually, did her six sisters.

Conversion involved lengthening by 6.4m/21ft and the plate, full-length over gundeck and waterline, was 64–114mm/ 2.5–4.5in in thickness. She was completed with eleven 178mm/7in, breech-loading rifled guns (BLRs) and twenty-four 30.8kg/68lb cannon. The great combined weight of plate and artillery, spread over the entire length,

imposed great hogging stresses on a timber-framed hull. She was, therefore, rearmed in 1867, with four 203mm/8in and twenty 178mm/7in guns (all of them muzzle-loaders). All except four of the latter calibre were concentrated around the centre of the ship.

Although technically a frigate, she was still considered to be "of the line", but her machinery was of low power, and she still relied mainly upon her full sailing rig. Effectively, she was a second-rate liner, with further third-rates (slower and weaker) ranked below her.

The *Zealous*, another converted two-deck 91-gunner, typified these latter ships. Experience had shown the problems attendant upon lengthening, so she retained her original dimensions. To save weight at the extremities, she had a full-length armoured belt, but sixteen

ABOVE LEFT: The *Royal Oak* as rearmed. Sheathed with 50–114mm/2.5–4.5in armour plate on her wooden frame, she and her near sisters were able to accommodate only one tier of heavy guns, technically making them frigates. The *Royal Oak* was faster under sail than under power. Note the canvas windsail ventilators. ABOVE: Unlike the *Royal Oak*, the *Zealous* was not lengthened on being converted from a two-decker. Her wooden frame was less strained by the concentration of sixteen of her twenty 178mm/7in MLRs in a central citadel. Note her funnel is lowered like that of the *Royal Oak*.

of her twenty 178mm/7in MLRs were concentrated amidships. Side armour on the gundeck was limited to this area, closed off at either end with a 76mm/3in transverse bulkhead.

Iron-on-wood was never satisfactory and the Admiralty was, at this time, hesitantly moving to iron-on-iron framing (the big Warriors were, as yet, incomplete). *Hector* and *Valiant*, completed in 1864 and 1868, heralded the new style.

ABOVE: Still new, the *Hector* in 1864 with funnel raised. Like the *Royal Oak* (above), she is barque-rigged, but with double topsails. She was the first Royal Navy ship to be built and engined by the same firm (Napier).

Royal Oak (as rearmed)

Built: Chatham Dockyard
Commissioned: May 28, 1863
Displacement: 6,451 tonnes/6,350 tons (designed); 7,112 tonnes/7,000 tons (full load)
Length: 83.2m/273ft (bp)
Beam: 17.4m/57ft
Draught: 7.4m/24ft 3in (normal)
Armament: 4 x 203mm/8in MLR and 20 x 178mm/7in MLR guns
Machinery: 2-cylinder, horizontal, single-expansion engine, 6 box boilers, 1 shaft
Power: 2,760kW/3,700ihp for 12.5 knots
Endurance: 559 tonnes/550 tons (coal) for 4,075km/2,200nm at 5 knots
Protection: 76–102mm/3–4in (belt), 76–114mm/ 3–4.5in (gundeck)
Complement: 585

LEFT: Naval occasion: the *Inconstant* with masts manned and dressed overall. Her ungainly lines are improved by the fine Victorian livery. Retired to serve as a static training ship in 1898, her iron hull was not scrapped until 1956. ABOVE: A good view of the *Shah* under both sail and steam. The ship gained fame in 1877 when, with the corvette *Amethyst*, she engaged the Laird-built pirate ironclad *Huascar* off Ilo, Peru. In the course of the action, *Shah* launched the first Whitehead torpedo in anger. It missed.

Inconstant, *Shah* and *Raleigh*

Civil War experience led the Americans to build the fast cruiser/commerce destroyers of the Wampanoag type. As is not uncommon, their actual performance was somewhat exaggerated but, although this was suspected by the British Admiralty, the ships posed sufficient threat to warrant a suitable response.

Thus, the *Inconstant*, was laid down in 1866 as the first of a new type of large "iron screw frigate". Speed, seaworthiness and endurance demanded a considerable length of hull and, in contrast to the longitudinally weak, wooden structure of the Wampanoags, the new ship was of all-iron construction. To reduce fouling (and, thus, to maintain speed and to increase time between dockings), the hull was sheathed in a double layer of oak, coppered from boot-topping downward. Design margins were very tight, so that the sheathing and deep, flanking coal bunkers constituted the ship's sole protective system. This method of protection was undoubtedly influenced by the British Admiralty's deep misgivings about the shattering effect of shot on iron plate.

Because of these doubts, the *Inconstant* was given an unusually large number of heavy-calibre weapons, to enable her to conduct a gunnery duel at ranges where she would incur little damage. Her mainly broadside armament was located on two levels, and she was given full ship-rig. Bunkers were sufficient for 43 days' steaming at 5 knots but only 54 hours at full speed.

Inconstant's great cost (for the day) was exacerbated by the new techniques involved in her construction. The second-of-class, *Shah*, was beamier and steadier, with greater bunker capacity and with a lighter armament. She proved to be 16 per cent cheaper but, despite this, the third and last of the type, *Raleigh*, was shorter, slower, yet more lightly armed and, generally, less capable for her designated role.

Inconstant, *Shah* and *Raleigh*

	Built	Commissioned
Inconstant	Pembroke Dockyard	August 1869
Raleigh	Chatham Dockyard	June 1874
Shah	Portsmouth Dockyard	December 1875

Inconstant (as built)

Displacement: 5,873 tonnes/5,780 tons
Length: 102.8m/337ft 4in (bp)
Beam: 15.3m/50ft 4in
Draught: 7.5m/24ft 7in (maximum)
Armament: 10 x 229mm/9in MLR and 6 x 178mm/7in MLR guns
Machinery: 2-cylinder, horizontal, single-expansion, trunk engine, 11 boilers, 1 shaft
Power: 5,490kW/7,360ihp for 16.2 knots
Endurance: 764 tonnes/750 tons (coal) for 5,149km/2,780nm at 10 knots
Protection: Nominal
Complement: 600

ABOVE: Smallest of the large iron frigates, *Raleigh* was more economical to man, consequently spending much of her life as a station flagship. She was reputedly the last Royal Navy ship to round the Horn under canvas and was scrapped in 1905.

Volage and Bacchante classes

Admiralty policy regarding the large, iron screw frigates was never made particularly clear. Assuming, however, that they were intended both to accompany high-value convoys and to patrol distant trade routes, it made sense to complement them with a smaller class of vessel, capable of undertaking similar tasks more cheaply in nearer waters. As more accurate detail of the American building programme emerged, it became apparent that their vaunted "commerce destroyers" were, in practice, not quite the threat that they had appeared. The Admiralty thus reduced its own programme, but did not stint on the quality of the remaining ships.

The *Volage* and *Active* were laid down in 1867, the year after the *Inconstant*, and described as "iron screw corvettes". This description was accurate inasmuch as the ships, besides being significantly smaller, carried their mainly broadside armament on an open upper deck, protected only by high bulwarks. Both had iron hulls, sheathed in a single layer of oak, but attracted considerable criticism in being slower than the big frigates and, therefore, less effective in their cruising role.

It will be noted that, in line with British practice of the time, all were equipped with muzzle-loading rifles (MLRs). Early unfortunate experience with breech-loading (BL) guns had brought about a reversion to MLRs, but the obvious and increasing advantages of BL guns saw them generally reintroduced in the late 1870s. The two Volage-class corvettes were thus, as part of a general fleet programme, later rearmed.

The *Volage* design was improved for the following three Bacchantes. Although only 3.1m/10ft longer, these carried a far heavier armament, the gundeck being covered to protect gun crews from falling

ABOVE LEFT: This photograph gives a clear view of the *Euryalus* in Mediterranean livery tended by the customary flotilla of Maltese dghaisamen. Both she and the *Bacchante* were straight-bowed.

ABOVE: *Boadicea* at Calcutta with awnings rigged. Her knee bow differentiates her from her two sisters. Although her class carried their armament on a covered gun deck, they were classed as corvettes, rather than frigates, owing to their limited complement and, thus, flexibility.

debris. They varied considerably in detail and, despite having the more advanced compound engine, they were slower again than the Volage pair.

Volage and Bacchante classes

	Built	Commisssioned
Active	Thames Iron Shipbuilding Co, Blackwall	March 1871
Volage	Thames Iron Shipbuilding Co, Blackwall	March 1870
Bacchante	Portsmouth Dockyard	July 1879
Boadicea	Portsmouth Dockyard	May 1877
Euryalus	Chatham Dockyard	June 1878
Highflyer	Portsmouth Dockyard	Cancelled

Volage (as built)

Displacement: 3,129 tonnes/3,080 tons
Length: 82.3m/270ft (bp)
Beam: 12.8m/42ft 1in
Draught: 6.6m/21ft 6in (maximum)
Armament: 6 x 178mm/7in MLR and 4 x 160mm/6.3in MLR guns
Machinery: 2-cylinder, horizontal, single-expansion trunk engine, 5 box boilers, 1 shaft
Power: 3,379kW/4,530ihp for 15.3 knots
Endurance: 427 tonnes/420 tons (coal) for 3,426km/1,850nm at 10 knots
Protection: Nominal
Complement: 340

LEFT: Pictures of Victorian cruisers, such as the *Volage* seen here, are not so common. Full plain sail is supplemented by studding sails on the weather side. Smaller than the Bacchantes, both the *Active* and *Volage* had knee bows.

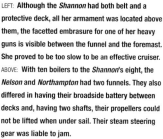

LEFT: **Although the *Shannon* had both belt and a protective deck, all her armament was located above them, the facetted embrasure for one of her heavy guns is visible between the funnel and the foremast. She proved to be too slow to be an effective cruiser.** ABOVE: **With ten boilers to the *Shannon*'s eight, the *Nelson* and *Northampton* had two funnels. They also differed in having their broadside battery between decks and, having two shafts, their propellers could not be lifted when under sail. Their steam steering gear was liable to jam.**

Shannon and Nelson class

As the *Inconstant* was to the US Navy, so was the *Shannon* to the Russian, each the response to a perceived threat. Innovative designers, the Russians in 1873 launched the *General Admiral,* a new-style "belted cruiser" mounting six heavy guns in a central battery. Her design eschewed the usual protective deck in favour of a 152mm/6in armoured belt. British response was immediate, the *Shannon* being laid down even as the Russian was being launched.

In being equipped with both belt armour and protective deck, the *Shannon* may be assumed to be the first British armoured cruiser. Although extending fully aft, the belt terminated well short of the bows, being closed-off by a transverse bulkhead. Both upper and lower edges of the belts linked to protective decks, together creating an armoured box.

The *Shannon*'s battery was above the armour, devoid of cover other than that provided by reinforced bulwarks. Her two 254mm/10in MLRs fired forward along the facets, while three 229mm/9in MLRs fired on each broadside. A seventh 229mm/9in gun was located beneath the poop, firing astern.

Originally classed as a Second Class battleship, but capable of little over 12 knots, she was generally considered to be neither cruiser nor capital ship.

In recognition of the *Shannon*'s anticipated shortcomings, the two larger Nelsons were commenced just one year later. They adopted twin boilers (evidenced externally by two funnels), which enabled the steering gear to be located below the armoured deck.

A short belt left both bow and stern "soft", while creating a central armoured box, above which was a covered box battery. From its four corners, 254mm/10in guns could train either axially or abeam, while four 229mm/9in weapons fired on each broadside.

Like the *Shannon*, the Nelsons were considered over-expensive for their purpose, and could not be afforded in useful numbers.

LEFT: **Later in her existence, the *Nelson* is seen with reduced, "military" rig and with large fighting tops added to fore- and mizzen-masts, supporting quick-firing guns. By the time of this photograph (the 1890s), she was reduced to trooping and training duties.**

Shannon and Nelson class

	Built	Commissioned
Shannon	Pembroke Dockyard	July 19, 1877
Nelson	Elder, Glasgow	July 26, 1881
Northampton	Napier, Glasgow	July 26, 1881

Shannon (as built)

Displacement: 5,542 tonnes/5,455 tons
Length: 79.2m/260ft (bp)
Beam: 16.5m/54ft
Draught: 6.8m/22ft 3in (mean)
Armament: 2 x 254mm/10in MLR, 7 x 229mm/9in MLR and 6 x 20lb BL guns
Machinery: 4-cylinder, horizontal compound engine, 8 boilers, 1 shaft
Power: 2,513kW/3,369ihp for 12.3 knots
Endurance: 589 tonnes/580 tons (coal) for 4,186km/2,260nm at 10 knots
Protection: 152–229mm/6–9in iron, backed by 254–330mm/10–13in teak (belt); 38–76mm/1.5–3in (decks)
Complement: 450

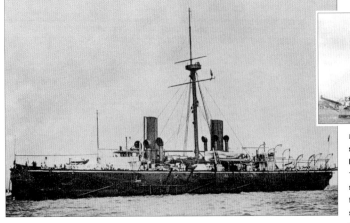

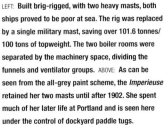

LEFT: **Built brig-rigged, with two heavy masts, both ships proved to be poor at sea. The rig was replaced by a single military mast, saving over 101.6 tonnes/ 100 tons of topweight. The two boiler rooms were separated by the machinery space, dividing the funnels and ventilator groups.** ABOVE: **As can be seen from the all-grey paint scheme, the *Imperieuse* retained her two masts until after 1902. She spent much of her later life at Portland and is seen here under the control of dockyard paddle tugs.**

Imperieuse class

Further building of large armoured cruisers by the Russians, and a deterioration of Anglo-Russian relations, resulted in the British Admiralty producing the two Imperieuse-class "steel barbette ships". They were intended to work on distant stations where they were more likely to be involved in a ship-on-ship gunnery duel than in a line action.

Recent French practice had been to arrange four heavy guns lozenge-style, i.e. one forward, one aft and one on either beam. The beam-mounted guns were located on shallow barbettes, sponsoned out over sides fashioned with pronounced tumblehome. This enabled (in theory at least) three of the four guns to bear forward, aft, or on either beam. Lighter than turrets, barbettes permitted higher freeboard. These two cruisers

became the only British warships to adopt these features.

Four of the new 234mm/9.2in BL guns (which would prove to be very reliable weapons) were mounted in open shields on the revolving armoured turntables of the barbettes. A full-length, but non-continuous, protective deck was stepped up by one level over the extent of the shallow amidships belt, roofing in above the machinery and boiler spaces.

Faulty design calculations saw the ships badly overweight. They were, however, the last armoured ships designed with square rig. In this case, the two-masted brig rig proved so inefficient that it was removed. Further weight was saved by the suppression of four of the intended ten 152mm/6in guns of the broadside secondary battery. Through being constructed of steel, the

ships' structure was already somewhat lighter than it would have been had it been made of iron. The protective deck was raised one level in way of machinery.

Relieved of two heavy masts and a bowsprit, the appearance of the pair was radically changed, with a single mast stepped amidships, between the funnels. Although castigated failures, both enjoyed long careers.

Imperieuse class

	Built	Commissioned
Imperieuse	Portsmouth Dockyard	September 1886
Warspite	Chatham Dockyard	June 1888

Imperieuse class

Displacement: 8,655 tonnes/8,500 tons (full load)
Length: 96m/315ft (bp)
Beam: 18.9m/62ft
Draught: 8.3m/27ft 3in (maximum)
Armament: 4 x 234mm/9.2in BL and 10 x 152mm/6in BL guns; 6 x 457mm/18in torpedo tubes (6x1)
Machinery: 2 x 3-cylinder inverted compound engines
Power: 7,460kW/10,000ihp for 16.75knots, 12 boilers, 2 shafts
Endurance: 1,148 tonnes/1,130 tons (coal) for 12,965km/7,000nm at 10 knots
Protection: 254mm/10in with 254mm/10in teak backing (belt); 51–203mm/2–8in (protective deck); 203mm/8in (barbettes)
Complement: 555

LEFT: **In this view of the *Warspite*, the French-style tumblehome of the sides is visible. This enabled the amidships sponson-mounted 234mm/9.2in guns to theoretical fire along the ship's axis. In practice, the effects of gun blast greatly reduced the useful arcs of the weapons.**

ABOVE LEFT: Painted for tropical duty, the *Calliope* lays to a buoy in Portsmouth harbour. Not apparent is the unusual combination of materials used in her construction – steel framed and iron plated, sheathed in wood and with underwater sections coppered. ABOVE: Ceremony played a great part in the life of the average colonial cruiser, as here with the *Comus*, seen in Canadian waters. The *Comus* was the only one of her class to have a uniform 152mm/6in breech-loading battery. LEFT: Seen undergoing repairs to her propeller shaft, the *Conquest* shows her underwater detail to advantage. Note the heavy wooden rudder and the parallel-sided aperture for the lifting screw.

Comus and Calypso classes

During the 1870s, the French were still perceived to be Britain's most likely naval adversary. The Royal Navy was responsible for safeguarding Britain's teeming merchant shipping but, generally discounting convoy as being irrelevant to steam-powered ships, it was difficult to plan to counter a determined *guerre de course* (war against commerce), where raiders might be fast armed merchantmen. Even if not commandeered for fleet work, the handful of large "armoured cruisers" available could offer little effective cover on distant trade routes.

The answer was sought in larger numbers of small cruisers, individually smaller and more affordable than the *Volage* type, and of considerable endurance. Thus were conceived the Comus-class corvettes, later regraded "Third Class cruisers".

Designed to operate alone, they were expected to be able to fight and to withstand damage. On their limited displacement, belt protection could not be considered, so the Comus class became the first extended series of protected cruiser, with a light protective

deck 0.91m/3ft below the designed waterline, overlaid with a 1.22m/4ft deep subdivided (or "cellular") layer. Machinery spaces were flanked by coal bunkers, while the hull was given a double layer of teak sheathing, the bottom sections coppered.

For endurance, all were given a three-masted ship or barque rig, and were among the last Royal Navy ships to use sail on a regular basis.

As early 152mm/6in BL guns proved unsatisfactory, most of the class spent

the greater part of their careers armed with MLRs. Recognizing the trials of long, tropical commissions, the Admiralty did much to improve habitability, particularly with efficient ventilation and adequate sanitary facilities.

The enlarged pair of Calypsos, displacing 2,814 tonnes/2,770 tons, were built in parallel and were armed from the outset with 152mm/6in and 127mm/5in BL guns. They were the last type of fully rigged corvette to be built for the Royal Navy, signalling the demise of sail.

Comus and Calypso classes

	Built	Commissioned
Canada	Portsmouth Dockyard	May 1, 1883
Carysfort	Elder, Glasgow	September 15, 1880
Champion	Elder, Glasgow	December 7, 1880
Cleopatra	Elder, Glasgow	August 24, 1880
Comus	Elder, Glasgow	October 23, 1879
Conquest	Elder, Glasgow	April 18, 1885
Constance	Chatham Dockyard	October 3, 1882
Cordelia	Portsmouth Dockyard	January 25, 1887
Curaçoa	Elder, Glasgow	February 24, 1880
Calliope	Portsmouth Dockyard	January 25, 1887
Calypso	Chatham Dockyard	October 19, 1885

Comus class (with revised armament)

Displacement: 2,418 tonnes/2,380 tons
Length: 68.5m/224ft 8in (bp)
Beam: 13.6m/44ft 6in
Draught: 5.9m/19ft 3in (normal)
Armament: 2 x 178mm/7in MLR and 12 x 64pdr MLR
Machinery: 3 x 4-cylinder horizontal compound engine, 6 boilers, 1 shaft
Power: 1,865kW/2,500ihp for 13 knots
Endurance: 478 tonnes/470 tons (coal) for 6,075km/3,280nm at 10 knots
Protection: 127mm/5in (protective deck)
Complement: 265

LEFT: **A graceful knee bow differentiates the** *Iris* **from her sister. In this picture she still has her foremast crossed in her original barquentine rig. Her proportions were particularly pleasing, her underwater form being an early example of refinement through tank-testing.** ABOVE: *Iris* **with her later, light rig. Their fine form meant that they could not carry any great press of sail, but with over half their length devoted to boilers and machinery they achieved a very high speed for their day.**

Iris class

Although not incorporating the innovative protective deck system of the *Comus* that followed them, the *Iris* and her sister were significant in cruiser evolution. Not yet defined as a category, cruisers tended still to be in concept either reduced battleships or colonial police craft. Particularly with the latter, hulls were necessarily optimized more for their qualities under sail than for speed. To counter any determined French war against commerce, the Admiralty now required moderately armed, but fast, cruisers. Thus, the Iris design, dating from 1875, was that of a "fast corvette" but was referred to officially as a "despatch vessel", a misleading label almost certainly designed to disguise its true function.

Lightness of construction, a fine form, and plenty of power characterized the design. Lightness was bought by constructing each vessel completely out of still-expensive steel, which exhibited equal strength with iron for about 15 per cent less material. Carefully tank-tested (a further recent innovation), the hull had a slim length/breadth (L/B) ratio of 6.52 (cf. *Comus*'s L/B = 5.06). Propulsion was by twin screws, the engines being horizontal compound units, low enough to be accommodated below the waterline. Their only real protection was afforded by the deep flanking coal bunkers.

Although initially fitted with a light barquentine rig, they soon had this removed. The fineness of the hull precluded the two engines being installed conventionally, side-by-side. They therefore occupied adjacent spaces, separated by a watertight bulkhead and driving shafts of unequal length. As the boiler spaces were also subdivided, the whole contributed greatly to the ships' potential survivability.

Propeller design was still in its infancy and it was only after several changes that the pair realized their true capability, comfortably exceeding 18.5 knots, the fastest of their time.

Iris had a clipper bow, the *Mercury* a straight stem. Both were later termed Second Class Cruisers.

Iris class

	Built	Commissioned
Iris	Pembroke Dockyard	April 1879
Mercury	Pembroke Dockyard	September 1879

LEFT: **Seen in tropical livery, the** *Mercury* **still has her original heavy sailing rig and is pierced for her original, old-style armament of ten 64pdr muzzle-loaders. She was rearmed twice more before finishing her career as a depot ship. She was not scrapped until 1919.**

Iris (as built)

Displacement: 3,342 tonnes/3,290 tons (normal); 3,790 tonnes/3,730 tons (full load)
Length: 91.4m/300ft (bp); 101m/331ft 6in (oa)
Beam: 14m/46ft
Draught: 6.2m/20ft 6in (maximum)
Armament: 10 x 64pdr MLR (later, 13 x 127mm/5in BL)
Machinery: 2 x 4-cylinder, horizontal, direct-acting compound engines, 12 boilers, 2 shafts
Power: 4,476kW/6,000ihp for 17.5 knots
Endurance: 793 tonnes/780 tons coal for 8,150km/4,400nm at 10 knots
Protection: Nominal
Complement: 275

LEFT: *Leander* finished her career with a 16-year spell as a depot ship. The distinctive three pairs of cowl ventilators remain but, of her original rig, only the mainmast here survives, complete with W/T extension. The new stump foremast is set vertically and she has gained two light derrick posts aft. ABOVE: Seen in the early years of the 20th century, the *Amphion* is in her final (schooner) rig. The most forward and after guns on each broadside were located in sponsons giving them a measure of axial fire.

Leander class

Also initially rated "despatch vessel", but reclassed as Second Class cruisers while under construction, the four Leanders took the *Comus*'s protected cruiser concept a stage further. The latter had a thin, flat deck, located below the (normal) waterline, surmounted by a cellular layer extending above the waterline. The Leanders had a much thicker deck which extended only over the machinery spaces. There was no cellular layer but the protective deck, flat for over half its width, sloped at about 25 degrees along either side. The flat was just above the waterline and the slopes terminated some 0.91m/3ft below it. The idea was that close-range, flat-trajectory shot, hitting about the waterline, would be deflected upward. Of the two

schemes, that of the *Comus* probably offered better survivability, but was more space-consuming. As they were never equally tested in action, no meaningful comparison may be drawn.

Interestingly, the Admiralty Board was itself divided, with the chosen Leander design being an improved Iris. Installed power and speed were less, but considerably greater bunker space more than doubled its endurance, an important factor in commerce protection. Twin screws also gave redundancy in the event of damage.

Like the *Iris*, the Leanders were fitted initially with a light barquentine rig, removed at the first major refit, probably because of their reputation for tenderness when not under a press of sail.

Being built later than the *Iris*, the Leanders benefited by being armed from the outset with 152mm/6in BL guns. Ten were carried, five along either side of the upper deck. This was itself transitional in that the centre three fired on the broadside, with only the end weapons able to train anything like axially. In addition, the ships were credited with carrying up to 16 smaller weapons, a mix of Nordenfelts, Gardners and Gatlings.

Leander class

	Built	Commissioned
Amphion	Pembroke Dockyard	August 10, 1886
Arethusa	Napier, Glasgow	September 29, 1887
Leander	Napier, Glasgow	May 29, 1885
Phaeton	Napier, Glasgow	April 20, 1886

Leander (as built)

Displacement: 3,789 tonnes/3,730 tons (normal); 4,369 tonnes/4,300 tons (full load)
Length: 91.4m/300ft (bp); 96m/315ft (oa)
Beam: 14m/46ft
Draught: 6.2m/20ft 6in (mean)
Armament: 10 x 152mm/6in BL guns
Machinery: 2 x 2-cylinder, horizontal, direct-acting compound engines, 12 boilers, 2 shafts
Power: 4,103kW/5,500ihp for 16.5 knots
Endurance: 1,032 tonnes/1,016 tons (coal) for 20,372km/11,000nm at 10 knots
Protection: 38mm/1.5in (partial-protective deck)
Complement: 280

ABOVE: **Although of the same design as the *Amphion* (above) the *Arethusa* appears longer and lower by virtue of her earlier Victorian livery. She still has her canvas bent on. The light bowsprit is probably an aid to handling the old-fashioned stocked anchor.**

Torpedo cruisers

ABOVE: **Third Class protected cruisers, the Barracoutas incorporated the novelty of two 356mm/14in torpedo tubes, both above-water. Their main armament remained their six 119mm/4.7in guns. Note that the navigating bridge was abaft the mainmast, and that the hull had both raised forecastle and poop.**

The French Navy's "Jeune École" movement, exploring the possibilities of torpedoes in conjunction with small warships, influenced the Royal Navy in directions other than in simply developing antidotes. One result was the so-called "torpedo cruiser", a small Third Class cruiser designed to work with the battle fleet, covering it against enemy torpedo boats while, itself, having the means to inflict injury if the opportunity arose. The application required an agile vessel armed with torpedoes and with numerous quick-firing (QF) guns capable of stopping a torpedo boat.

A first attempt produced the two 1,605-tonne/1,580-ton Scouts of 1886–87 with a single 356mm/14in torpedo tube forward and further "launching apparatus" in the waist. Only later fitted with 119mm/4.7in QF guns, they were not successful in that they were poor sea-keepers and, at 16.5 knots, too slow.

Built in parallel were the eight larger Archer-class ships. Unlike the Scouts, which were fitted only with a pair of

military masts, the Archers reverted to a three-masted, fore-and-aft auxiliary sailing rig. Also too slow, and reputed to be sluggish seaboats, over-armed with six 152mm/6in BL guns, they found a useful role in colonial duties.

In 1888, as the last Archers were being completed, the keels were laid of the four Barracoutas. They were more closely related to the Scouts but, although similarly classed as Third Class protected cruisers, changed the former's horizontal reciprocating machinery for more efficient, but higher profile, vertical, triple-expansion engines. Their protective deck was heavier and, for small ships, innovative in running full length.

As cruisers, the concept proved to be a design dead-end, primarily because the power-to-weight ratio of reciprocating machinery was not in favour of small, fast hulls. Evolution continued, nonetheless, through the development of smaller "torpedo gunboats" of the Gossamer, Alarm and Dryad classes, totalling 30 units.

Torpedo cruisers

	Built	Commissioned
Fearless	Barrow Iron Shipbuilding	July 1887
Scout	Thomson, Clydebank	October 1886
Archer	Thomson, Clydebank	December 1888
Brisk	Thomson, Clydebank	March 20, 1888
Cossack	Thomson, Clydebank	January 1, 1889
Mohawk	Thomson, Clydebank	December 16, 1890
Porpoise	Thomson, Clydebank	February 12, 1888
Racoon	Devonport Dockyard	July 1888
Serpent	Devonport Dockyard	March 1888
Tartar	Thomson, Clydebank	June 30, 1891
Barrosa	Portsmouth Dockyard	June 1890
Barracouta	Sheerness Dockyard	March 1891
Blanche	Pembroke Dockyard	February 1891
Blonde	Pembroke Dockyard	July 1891

Barracouta (as built)

Displacement: 1,609 tonnes/1,580 tons (normal)
Length: 67m/220ft (bp); 71m/233ft (oa)
Beam: 10.7m/35ft
Draught: 4.6m/15ft (mean)
Armament: 6 x 119mm/4.7in guns;
   2 x 356mm/14in torpedo tubes
Machinery: 3-cylinder, triple-expansion engines,
   4 boilers, 2 shafts
Power: 2,238kW/3,000ihp for 16.5 knots
Endurance: 163 tonnes/160 tons (coal) for
   6,297km/3,400km at 10 knots
Protection: 25–51mm/1–2in (protective deck)
Complement: 160

LEFT: *Barrosa* alongside. The aperture for the starboard, hull-mounted torpedo tube is forward of the brow ("gangway"). Note the 119mm/4.7in gun, trained to starboard, and the shuttered embrasure for a 3pdr. Note also the twinned, "torpedo-boat" type funnels, the large cutting davit for the anchor, and the bow ornament.

Vulcan

In 1883 the French Admiral Théophile Aube "father" of the Jeune École made, on the strength of one experience, the ambitious statement that his tiny 46-ton torpedo boats were capable of operating "self-sufficiently" and of navigating the Mediterranean or Atlantic alone. This arrant nonsense led to his navy specifying escorting gunboats and larger "defensive" torpedo craft to protect capital ships at sea.

Less than impressed by French claims, the British Admiralty was already evaluating larger, rival designs stemming from yards such as Yarrow, Thornycroft and White. Production also began on "Second Class torpedo boats", small craft designed to be carried aboard parent ships in place of earlier spar torpedo-armed picket boats. Lacking endurance and seaworthiness, these would be put afloat in the vicinity of the enemy.

This concept was first essayed in the *Hecla*, purchased on the stocks as a mercantile hull in 1878 and already converted to a naval auxiliary. Commanded 1881–84 by the redoubtable Captain (later Admiral of the Fleet) A.K.

Wilson, the "unhandy" *Hecla* was described by him as being a combination of armed transport and "torpedo store ship", carrying also mines, cables and six Second Class torpedo boats with facilities for their support.

With Wilson as its champion, the idea was deemed successful enough for Portsmouth Dockyard to lay down the purpose-designed *Vulcan* in 1888. The ship was an orthodox protected cruiser except for her light, and primarily defensive, armament of 119mm/4.7in QF guns and the extensive stowage aft for six Second Class torpedo boats. These were located on trolleys, which were rail-transferred to within the operating radius of either of two 20.3-tonne/20-ton Elswick-supplied hydraulic gooseneck cranes.

Rapid development in torpedo craft saw the *Vulcan* quickly made obsolete. Reduced to a depot-ship, then training-ship status, her long-lived hull existed until 1955.

ABOVE: **Despite her fine lines, the *Vulcan* was rarely able to make 20 knots. This picture clearly shows the complication of the anti-torpedo net protection. The cap in the stem covers two of the ship's six torpedo tubes.** LEFT: **A torpedo boat typical of the type designed to be carried by major warships, to be set afloat in close proximity to an enemy line. The torpedo launching gear is visible amidships. Note the protected cupola for the helmsman and the turtle-decked forward end.**

ABOVE: **Dominated by her two enormous, 20.3-tonne/20-ton gooseneck cranes, the *Vulcan* is seen in all-grey Edwardian livery. She still retains her Bullivant nets but has lost her original ornate bow ornament. Most of her career was spent as depot ship or torpedo school vessel.**

Hecla and *Vulcan*

	Built	Commissioned
Hecla	Harland & Wolff, Belfast	October 1878
Vulcan	Portsmouth Dockyard	July 1891

Vulcan (as built)

Displacement: 6,726 tonnes/6,620 tons (normal)
Length: 106.6m/350ft (bp); 113.6m/373ft (oa)
Beam: 17.7m/58ft
Draught: 6.9m/22ft 6in (maximum)
Armament: 8 x 119mm/4.7in QF guns; 6 x 356mm/14in torpedo tubes; 6 x Second Class torpedo boats each carrying 2 x 356mm/14in torpedoes
Machinery: Vertical, triple-expansion engines, 4 boilers, 2 shafts
Power: 8,975kW/12,032ihp for 16.5 knots
Endurance: 1,016 tonnes/1,000 tons (coal) for 22,224km/12,000nm at 10 knots
Protection: 51–127mm/2–5in (protective deck)
Complement: 430

Bramble, Condor and Cadmus classes

LEFT: Colonial sloops retained their sailing rig for a considerable period. Here, the *Fantome* is rigged as a barquentine, canvas bent-on. Note the navigating bridge is located aft, also the conspicuous cowl ventilators, essential for the cooling of machinery spaces in the tropics. The spacious stern accommodation harks back to earlier days. ABOVE: Unlike the *Fantome*, the Condor-class *Mutine* is rigged as a barque. Despite their considerable draught, sloops of these classes were valuable during World War I in the Mesopotamia campaign, before being superseded by shallow-draught river gunboats. *Mutine* survived until 1932 as an RNVR drill-ship, being superseded by purpose-built shallow-draught river gunboats.

All "cruisers", in the then-prevailing sense of the word, were a late-Victorian collection of ship types described variously as corvettes, sloops and gun vessels or gunboats. Differences between these categories were far from clear cut and, until they were all eventually regraded Third Class cruisers, the primary significance of a category lay in its determination of the rank of commanding-officer and, hence, a ship's establishment. All were built for, or found their vocation in, colonial service.

Of those considered here, the smallest were the four Brambles which, at only 721 tonnes/710 tons displacement, were categorized First Class gunboats. They carried just two 102mm/4in and four 12pdr QF guns and were commanded by a Lieutenant. Following over 60 built of wood or of composite (wood planking on iron-framed) construction, these were the first boats of all-steel build. For smaller hulls, steel offered lighter construction, although this was offset by the sheathing

and coppering specified to retard fouling while on tropical service.

The Brambles were not equipped with sailing rig, so their bunker capacity limited their endurance, although machinery was also becoming more efficient and reliable. Sail training in the Royal Navy was also being scaled-down, so crews with these skills were becoming more difficult to assemble.

Where the Brambles had no true protection, the larger Condor and Cadmus classes had sufficient displacement to work in a protective deck over the extent of the boiler and machinery spaces. Longer than the Brambles by 7.3m/24ft and 9.1m/30ft respectively, they were still about the same length shorter than the earlier Comus- and Calypso-class steel corvettes and were, therefore, classed as "sheathed steel sloops". As such, they rated a Commander in command, in contrast to a corvette's Captain.

Designed for long commissions on distant stations, the steel sloops were fitted initially with sailing rig but, during their long careers, all had it removed.

LEFT: The *Condor* dries sails in the warmth of a Mediterranean port. A later commission saw her based on the Canadian Pacific coast. In December 1901 she left Esquimalt for Honolulu only to be immediately overwhelmed by a severe storm. Wreckage was found, but no survivors. Her heavy rig may well have contributed to her loss.

Bramble, Condor and Cadmus classes

	Built	Commissioned
Bramble	Potter, Liverpool	June 1900
Britomart	Potter, Liverpool	June 1900
Dwarf	London & Glasgow	August 1899
Thistle	London & Glasgow	April 1901
Condor	Sheerness Dockyard	November 1, 1900
Mutine	Laird, Birkenhead	1900
Rinaldo	Laird, Birkenhead	1900
Rosario	Sheerness Dockyard	May 1899
Shearwater	Sheerness Dockyard	1900
Vestal	Sheerness Dockyard	1900
Cadmus	Sheerness Dockyard	1904
Clio	Sheerness Dockyard	1904
Espiegle	Sheerness Dockyard	1901
Fantome	Sheerness Dockyard	1902
Merlin	Sheerness Dockyard	1902
Odin	Sheerness Dockyard	1902

Cadmus (as built)

Displacement: 1,087 tonnes/1,070 tons (normal)
Length: 56.4m/185ft (bp); 64m/210ft (oa)
Beam: 10.1m/33ft
Draught: 3.4m/11ft 3in (normal)
Armament: 6 x 203mm/4in QF guns
Machinery: 3-cylinder, vertical, triple-expansion engines, 4 boilers, 2 shafts
Power: 1,044kW/1,400ihp for 13.3 knots
Endurance: 7,408km/4,000nm at 10 knots
Protection: 25–38mm/1–1.5in (partial protective deck)
Complement: 130

LEFT: **Although built with forced draught for their boilers, the Merseys still needed to have their funnels increased in height, as seen here on the *Severn*. This did not assist their reputation as heavy rollers, leading to their original sailing rig being removed.**

Mersey class

If it is accepted that the *Iris* and *Mercury* were the ancestors of modern cruiser design, then the four Leanders, laid down about five years later, were their first derivatives. With the same major hull dimensions as the straight-stemmed *Mercury*, they floated more deeply due to the addition of a partial protected deck. Constructed of 38mm/1.5in plate, this extended over only the boiler and machinery spaces, but the resulting extra displacement cost about 1 knot in maximum speed. To protect the machinery and to keep the weight of the deck at an acceptable height, horizontal, double-acting compound (i.e. double-expansion) engines were again specified.

Although the Leanders mounted ten 152mm/6in guns in the same arrangement as those aboard an Iris, they were all far more effective breech-

loaders (BLs). The class was originally fitted with a barquentine rig (i.e square-rigged on foremast, fore-and-aft on main and mizzen) but, as it contributed to heavy rolling, it was later removed.

Rated Second Class protected cruisers, the Leanders were followed immediately by the four, further-improved Merseys. Good, evolutionary design saw these have a lower displacement on the same major dimensions despite having a full-length protective deck. They were also faster on much the same power.

The Merseys were the first cruisers built without a sailing rig, their consequent lack of bowsprit enabling a curved, ram bow to be adopted. Unusually the designers managed to exhaust their 12 boilers through a single funnel.

At about this time, the Admiralty's talented constructor William White,

who had been associated with all these projects, left government employment to join Armstrong's at Elswick. He favoured small cruisers that sacrificed a measure of protection for improved speed and firepower. His legacy was to give the Merseys a single, over-large 203mm/8in BL gun on both forecastle and poop.

Mersey class

	Built	Commissioned
Forth	Pembroke Dockyard	July 1889
Mersey	Chatham Dockyard	June 1887
Severn	Chatham Dockyard	February 1888
Thames	Pembroke Dockyard	July 1888

Mersey class (as designed)

Displacement: 4,114 tonnes/4,050 tons (full load)
Length: 91.4m/300ft (bp); 96m/315ft (oa)
Beam: 14m/46ft
Draught: 5.9m/19ft 6in (full load)
Armament: 2 x 203mm/8in BL and
  10 x 152mm/6in BL guns; 2 x 356mm/14in
  torpedo tubes
Machinery: 2-cylinder, horizontal, direct-acting,
  compound engines, 12 boilers, 2 shafts
Power: 4,476kW/6,000ihp for 18 knots
Endurance: 914 tonnes/900 tons (coal) for
  16,205km/8,750nm at 10 knots
Protection: 51–76mm/2–3in (protective deck)
Complement: 325

LEFT: **From 1903 until 1920 the *Thames* served as a depot ship for submarines, as seen here. She was then sent to Simonstown as a training ship, finally being scuttled offshore after a career of over 60 years. Note the semaphore arms at the mainmast head.**

LEFT: **Compared with her sister *Aurora* (below), the *Orlando* appears to have a more generous freeboard, an impression accentuated by her shorter funnels. The white ribband above the boot-topping shows, however, that she is "light", probably lacking both bunkers and ammunition.**

Orlando class

Having been created, the modern cruiser was now the subject of some indecision. The introduction of quick-firing armaments had suggested the likely riddling of a ship's hull and topsides. Assuming that resultant flooding was well-controlled, it appeared likely that these relatively small-calibre projectiles might lack a lethal punch, hence the *Mersey*'s carrying of a pair of 203mm/8in weapons, capable of piercing the belt of any cruiser antagonist.

As, however, these larger weapons were yet by no means universal, it could still be argued that the provision of a vertical belt, which would keep enemy projectiles out altogether, was preferable to a protective deck system, which would merely contain damage inflicted. The argument for the latter arrangement lay in its lightness.

Therefore, when the successor to the *Mersey* was being considered, sketch designs were prepared with alternatives of belt or protective deck. Somewhat surprisingly, the former was selected, probably influenced by current French and Russian designs of armoured cruiser, their most likely perceived opponents.

The new class, the seven Orlandos, were actually "armoured cruisers" in that their shallow, part-length belt was itself overlaid with a full-length protective deck. Probably with an eye to the available number of dry docks worldwide, the same hull length was again adopted, although beam was increased by a generous 3m/10ft. Despite this, the extra weight of protection, together with a heavy and over-ambitious 234mm/9.2in gun at either end, brought each to at least 406

tonnes/400 tons overweight, submerging the belt and totally negating its benefit.

Built with short funnels, which were soon lengthened, the Orlandos set the style for British cruisers over many subsequent classes. Their secondary 152mm/6in guns, later converted to QF, were carried at an effective height, sponsoned for chase-fire. Although their masts were crossed by heavy yards, they were not designed for sailing.

Orlando class

	Built	Commissioned
Aurora	Pembroke Dockyard	July 1889
Australia	Napier, Glasgow	December 11, 1888
Galatea	Napier, Glasgow	March 1889
Immortalité	Chatham Dockyard	July 1889
Narcissus	Earle, Hull	July 1889
Orlando	Palmer, Jarrow	June 1888
Undaunted	Palmer, Jarrow	July 1889

Displacement: 5,690 tonnes/5,600 tons (designed); 6,110 tonnes/6,000 tons (full load)
Length: 91.4m/300ft (bp)
Beam: 17.1m/56ft
Draught: 6.9m/22ft 6in (full load)
Armament: 2 x 234mm/9.2in and 10 x 152mm/6in BL guns; 6 x 457mm/18in torpedo tubes (6x1)
Machinery: 3-cylinder, triple-expansion engines, 4 boilers, 2 shafts
Power: 6,338kW/8,500ihp for 18 knots
Endurance: 914 tonnes/900 tons (coal) for 14,816km/8,000nm at 10 knots
Protection: 254mm/10in (partial belt); 51–76mm/2–3in (protective deck)
Complement: 490

ABOVE: **Greatly improved in appearance and in boiler efficiency by longer funnels, the Orlandos established the general form of many subsequent British cruisers. *Aurora* is seen at the 1897 Diamond Jubilee Fleet Review.**

Medea and Barham classes

For a short spell in 1883–85, William White broke his Admiralty career to work for Armstrong's at Elswick. At a time when cruiser design was in an important formative phase, therefore, there existed a strong cross-influence between "pusser" designs and those of what would become a long line of influential "Elswick cruisers".

Laid down in 1887, the five-strong Medea class were a cross between scaled-down Merseys and the Elswick-designed Italian cruiser *Dogali*. Originally classified as Second Class cruisers, they were regraded Third Class while under construction. Intended to be a small and inexpensive type to be built in numbers for trade protection, they proved to be too limited, despite carrying six 152mm/6in BL (later QF) guns.

Of the five, *Medea* and *Medusa* were equipped with vertical compound engines, the remainder with horizontal-

acting machinery. The latter trio were also wood-sheathed and coppered, making them slightly slower.

The Medeas, in turn, provided the basis for the Admiralty-designed Katoombas trio, commenced by Elswick in 1888 to Australian account.

White also produced a stretched version of his *Barracouta* design, intended to realize 19.5 knots on double the installed power. This could only be achieved under forced draught conditions where, even with fast and expert stoking, boilers and machinery were subjected to great stress, accidents and failures being common.

The two resulting cruisers, *Barham* and *Bellona*, were completed in 1889–90, but already looked dated with their two widely spaced funnels alternating with the three masts of a now-anachronistic sailing rig. When achieved, their designed speed was assisted by their

slim form, their 85.3m/280ft by 10.7m/35ft hulls giving a length/breadth (L/B) ratio of about 8.0, compared with the *Medea*'s 6.36. Their main armament was restricted to a manageable six 119mm/4.7in QF weapons.

Medea and Barham classes

	Built	Commissioned
Magicienne	Elder, Glasgow	February 11, 1880
Marathon	Elder, Glasgow	July 1889
Medea	Chatham Dockyard	May 1889
Medusa	Chatham Dockyard	June 1889
Melpomene	Portsmouth Dockyard	July 1889
Barham	Portsmouth Dockyard	July 1891
Bellona	Hawthorn Leslie, Hebburn	July 1891

Medea (as built)

Displacement: 2,844 tonnes/2,800 tons (full load)
Length: 80.7m/265ft (bp)
Beam: 12.8m/42ft
Draught: 5m/16ft 6in (normal)
Armament: 6 x 152mm/6in BL guns; 2 x 356mm/14in torpedo tubes
Machinery: 2-cylinder, vertical compound engines, 6 boilers, 2 shafts
Power: 6,711kW/9,000ihp for 18.8 knots
Endurance: 406 tonnes/400 tons (coal) for 14,816km/8,000nm at 10 knots
Protection: 25–51mm/1–2in (protective deck)
Complement: 220

LEFT: **Many of the "Naval Defence Act" cruisers were modified to other roles in later life. *Iphigenia*, seen here and her sister *Intrepid* were "chummy ships", built together at the same yard, converted to minelayers (note the stern apertures) in 1910, and both expended, together with their sister *Thetis*, to block Zeebrugge canal entrance in April 1918.**

Pearl, Apollo and Astraea classes

The three Katoomba-type cruisers built at Elswick for Australian service were to form the first three of a new Pearl class of Third Class protected cruisers, essentially improved Medeas with an all-QF armament of eight 119mm/4.7in guns. Two more were constructed on Clydebank to complete the five-strong Australian squadron.

Following national agitation regarding the effective strength of the Royal Navy, Parliament passed the Naval Defence Act in 1889, providing for 70 new warships. At the same time, the so-called Two Power Standard was adopted, setting the Royal Navy's strength at equal to at least a combination of the next two most powerful fleets.

A first result was that four more Pearls were built for the Royal Navy. These were followed by 11 slightly enlarged and faster Pelorus class, spread over three programmes of the later 1890s.

No less than 29 Second Class protected cruisers were to be ordered, of which 21 were Apollos and the remainder of the larger Astraea class. The construction of so many Apollos represented huge confidence in a design which, at 3,455 tonnes/3,400 tons, was little more than an enlarged Medea. The layout remained the same, with a raised forecastle and poop, upon each of which was mounted a single, centreline,

152mm/6in gun. In the waist, behind high bulwarks at upper deck level, were located 119mm/4.7in QF guns, all essentially broadside weapons.

In their day, the Apollos were considered successful, if lightly armed. The eight follow-on Astraeas displaced a further 975 tonnes/960 tons and had a thicker protective deck. They were also flush-decked, allowing them to better maintain speed in adverse conditions and also to carry their eight 119mm/4.7in QF guns at a greater height.

Obsolete by World War I, these classes nonetheless played useful, if expendable, roles. Four were used as blockships at Ostend and Zeebrugge.

Apollo class

Displacement: 3,455 tonnes/3,400 tons (normal)
Length: 91.4m/300ft (bp), 95.8m/314ft 6in (oa)
Beam: 13.3m/43ft 8in
Draught: 5.5m/18ft; (maximum)
Armament: 2 x 152mm/6in QF and 6 x 119mm/4.7in QF guns; 4 x 356mm/14in torpedo tubes
Machinery: 3-cylinder, vertical, triple-expansion engines, 4 boilers, 2 shafts
Power: 6,898kW/9,250ihp for 20 knots
Endurance: 544 tonnes/535 tons coal for 16,668km 9,000nm at 10 knots
Protection: 25–51mm/1–2in (protective deck)
Complement: 270

Pearl, Apollo and Astraea classes

	Built	Commissioned
Katoomba (ex-*Pandora*)	Armstrong, Elswick	March 24, 1891
Mildura (ex-*Pelorus*)	Armstrong, Elswick	March 18, 1891
Ringarooma (ex-*Psyche*)	Thomson, Clydebank	February 3, 1891
Tauranga (ex-*Phoenix*)	Thomson, Clydebank	June 4, 1891
Wallaroo (ex-*Persian*)	Armstrong, Elswick	March 31, 1891
Pallas	Portsmouth Dockyard	July 1891
Pearl	Pembroke Dockyard	October 1892
Philomel	Devonport Dockyard	November 10, 1891
Pheobe	Devonport Dockyard	March 1892
Aeolus	Devonport Dockyard	January 6, 1894
Andromache	Chatham Dockyard	December 1891
Apollo	Chatham Dockyard	April 1892
Brilliant	Sheerness Dockyard	April 1893
Indefatigable	London & Glasgow	April 1892
Intrepid	London & Glasgow	November 1892
Iphigenia	London & Glasgow	May 1893
Latona	Vickers, Barrow	April 1891
Melampus	Vickers, Barrow	December 1891
Naiad	Vickers, Barrow	January 1893
Pique	Palmer, Jarrow	March 1893
Rainbow	Palmer, Jarrow	January 1893
Retribution	Palmer, Jarrow	May 1893
Sappho	Samuda, Poplar	February 1893
Scylla	Samuda, Poplar	April 1893
Sirius	Armstrong, Elswick	April 1892
Spartan	Armstrong, Elswick	July 1892
Sybille	Stephenson, Hebburn	May 1894
Terpsichore	Thomson, Clydebank	April 1892
Thetis	Thomson, Clydebank	April 1892
Tribune	Thomson, Clydebank	May 1892
Astraea	Devonport Dockyard	November 5, 1890
Bonaventure	Devonport Dockyard	July 5, 1894
Cambrian	Pembroke Dockyard	September 1894
Charybdis	Sheerness Dockyard	January 14, 1896
Flora	Pembroke Dockyard	March 1895
Forte	Chatham Dockyard	January 1895
Fox	Portsmouth Dockyard	April 14, 1896
Hermione	Devonport Dockyard	January 14, 1896

LEFT: This image of *Dido* gives an idea of the complexity of warship rigging even into the new century. Although never designed for canvas, they have lengthy topmasts to elevate the W/T aerials, whose gaff appears at the main top. The topmasts are stayed to crosstrees, sailing-ship fashion, and the yards have footropes.

ABOVE: The rather weak original armament of the Eclipses is evident in this picture of the *Juno*. Although she carries five 152mm/6in guns it will be obvious that, from this angle, only two of them, i.e. that on the forecastle and the sponsoned weapon by the forward funnel, can bear. Fortunately, there was sufficient margin to upgrade the six waist 119mm/4.7in guns to 152mm/6in ordnance.

Eclipse class

The long run of Apollos and Astraeas was criticized endlessly for its light armament although, in fairness, the ships were designed as inexpensive trade protection cruisers rather than combatants. As is usual, however, the advantages offered by a larger type became obvious and, even before the completion of the Astraeas, the larger Eclipses were being laid down.

These answered the critics in mounting five 152mm/6in guns. One of them was installed on the raised forecastle which was added to improve seakeeping. This was flanked by a further pair firing forward along facets at upper-deck level. Two more 152mm/6in guns were sided on the quarterdeck. In the waist, six 119mm/4.7in guns alternated with 12pdr weapons. In 1902 the 119mm/4.7in guns were upgraded to 152mm/6in ordnance, for a respectable total of 11. This followed the design of the Highflyer class derivatives, equipped with eleven 152mm/6in QF guns from the outset.

Single, open mountings such as these made for poor layouts, the Eclipses being able to command a six-gun broadside with, axially, just two bearing aft and three, theoretically, forward.

Despite a unit cost half as large again as that of an Apollo, the Eclipses were criticized for having no greater speed. Their heavier protection contributed toward a significantly greater draught, seen as inhibiting their versatility. However, they did have greater endurance and were better armed.

Unfortunately the class was always compared with the Elswick-designed cruisers, but, as was usual for minor fleets, they were untested by real action and battle damage, enjoying long and uneventful careers. Although the Admiralty view was that the Elswick ships had inferior survivability, they nonetheless boasted speeds of better than 23 knots and firepower including combinations of 203mm/8in and 152mm/6in weapons on similar dimensions and displacement.

Still able to provide useful second-line service during World War I, the class disappeared in the course of the huge cull of warships in the early 1920s.

LEFT: *Venus* in a wartime guise with her larger 152mm/6in waist guns in evidence. Note the addition of the spotting top. Initially a unit of the 11th Cruiser Squadron in Irish waters, she moved during 1915 to the Red Sea and the Persian Gulf before transferring with three sisters to the East Indies Station.

Eclipse class

	Built	Commissioned
Diana	Fairfield, Glasgow	1897
Dido	London & Glasgow	1898
Doris	Vickers, Barrow	1898
Eclipse	Portsmouth Dockyard	1897
Isis	London & Glasgow	1898
Juno	Vickers, Barrow	1897
Minerva	Chatham Dockyard	1897
Talbot	Devonport Dockyard	1896
Venus	Fairfield, Glasgow	1897

Eclipse (as designed)

Displacement: 5,689 tonnes/5,600 tons (normal)
Length: 110.9m/364ft (wl); 112.8m/370ft 4in (oa)
Beam: 16.5m/54ft
Draught: 7m/23ft (maximum)
Armament: 5 x 152mm/6in QF and 6 x 119mm/4.7in QF guns; 3 x 457mm/18in torpedo tubes
Machinery: Inverted, 3-cylinder, triple-expansion engines, 8 boilers, 2 shafts
Power: 7,308kW/9,800ihp for 20 knots
Endurance: 1,016 tonnes/1,000 tons (coal) for 12,964km/7,000nm at 10 knots
Protection: 38–76mm/1.5–3in (protective deck)
Complement: 420

LEFT: **Although less than 20 years old at the outbreak of World War I the then-colossal pair, *Powerful* (seen here) and *Terrible* played no active part, appearing vulnerable in any perceived role. Both were reduced to a training role post-war. Note the hull discontinuity caused by the double-level casemate.** ABOVE: **Her impressive size and the achievements of her "naval brigade" made the *Terrible* familiar to the public through numerous depictions. This one, in her later grey livery, shows her detail accurately and well. Note the characteristic funnel grouping.**

Powerful class

The great Russian cruisers *Rurik* and *Rossia* took from 1891 to 1898 to build. Their potential as commerce destroyers, although greatly exaggerated, resulted in the British Admiralty's equally massive response, the two Powerfuls, completed within the same timeframe.

Although the two Russians proved to be capable of only about 18 and 20 knots, respectively, the two British ships were designed for 22, a speed exceeded by both. This, together with the requirement to safely carry up to 3,048 tonnes/3,000 tons of coal in order to give them unprecedented range ("Why?" asked critics, pointing out that Great Britain, unlike Russia, was blessed with a worldwide network of coaling stations) resulted in an enormous hull, for which the required power demanded 48 of the new Belleville water-tube boilers, located in eight separate spaces.

Over 30.5m/100ft longer than a contemporary battleship, a Powerful demanded over 80 more crewmen. By any yardstick, they were expensive to operate. By contemporary critics they were excoriated because, as protected cruisers, they could not be included in a line of battle. This common but dangerous line of thought, equating size to battle worthiness, culminated in the total discrediting of both armoured and battlecruisers.

Their relatively light armament featured double-decked casemates for the first time, housing the twelve, later sixteen, 152mm/6in secondary weapons. This introduced the unhealthy trend of locating half the secondary armament at middle-deck level, too low to be of use in adverse conditions.

Temperamental, unreliable and expensive, both were non-operational by 1914. *Terrible*, however, under the

command of Percy Scott, "father" of Royal Naval gunnery, had made her mark ashore. Superbly organized, her naval brigade made invaluable contributions in both the South African (Boer) War in 1899 and at the Boxer Rebellion of 1900.

Powerful class

	Built	Commissioned
Powerful	Vickers, Barrow	1898
Terrible	Thomson, Clydebank	1898

Terrible (as rearmed in 1903)

Displacement: 14,529 tonnes/14,300 tons (normal); 19,203 tonnes/18,900 tons (full load)
Length: 152.3m/500ft (bp); 163.9m/538ft
Beam: 21.6m/71ft
Draught: 9.4m/31ft (maximum)
Armament: 2 x 234mm/9.2in and 16 x 152mm/6in QF guns; 4 x 457mm/18in torpedo tubes
Machinery: 4-cylinder, triple-expansion engines, 48 boilers, 2 shafts
Power: 18,642kW/25,000ihp for 22 knots
Endurance: 3,048 tonnes/3,000 tons (coal) and 406 tonnes/400 tons (oil) for 12,964km/7,000nm at 14 knots
Protection: 76–152mm/3–6in (protective deck); 51–152mm/2–6in (casemates)
Complement: 895

LEFT: **Not a flattering picture of *Powerful*, but one that emphasizes her enormous, machinery-packed length. Note how, excepting the single 234mm/9.2in guns at either end, the weather deck is clear of armament, all secondary and tertiary guns being casemated.**

LEFT: **A rather nice depiction of *Alabama* under manoeuvring canvas only. She is cleared for action as her nemesis approaches. Her battle ensign is, correctly, the famous "Stars and Bars", the Confederacy's first national flag. Semmes' decision to duel with the *Kearsarge* was noble, but foolhardy.** ABOVE: **Little more than a fragile, if fast, armed merchantman, the *Alabama* was successful as long as she struck suddenly and moved quickly on, avoiding armed confrontation. Her tactics were thus those of successful raiders ever since.**

Alabama and *Trenton*

Waging war on the maritime commerce of an opponent can be very effective for the weaker adversary. For the Confederacy during the American Civil War, however, it enjoyed only brief success as privateering had recently been declared illegal under international law, effectively removing the profit motive.

Most famous of the raiders was the *Alabama*, a fast, three-masted, screw ship-sloop built in Great Britain by Laird of Birkenhead. Under her resourceful commander, Raphael Semmes, she roamed worldwide, claiming 69 prizes between August 1862 and June 1864. Seeking to rectify mechanical problems, Semmes entered the French Port of Cherbourg. Here his ship was blockaded, then sunk by the Union warship *Kearsarge*.

The *Alabama* and her fellow raiders did not affect the outcome of the war but had considerable impact on naval

thought. Several navies subsequently built large cruisers, both as raiders and raider-antidotes.

Laid down in 1875, the wooden screw corvette *Trenton* was among the first American cruisers to adopt a, later-standard, "city" name. For a decade, her typical peacetime cruiser routine saw commissions in the Mediterranean, the Far East and South America.

She was refitting in New York when news came of deteriorating relationships between American, British and German officials engaged in seeking concessions in the Pacific territory of Samoa. The American consul in the capital, Apia, requested American warship presence to counteract that of three Germans already there. In March 1889 the *Trenton* duly arrived, rendezvousing with the screw sloop *Vandalia* and *Nipsic*. Also present was the British cruiser *Calliope*.

With little warning, the ships were embayed by hurricane-force winds, only the *Calliope* managing to fight her way to the relative safety of open water. The remainder were sunk or stranded, the *Trenton* and *Vandalia* being wrecked with the loss of 49 lives. The shock loss of these and the German ships led to a rapid agreement for a tripartite condominium.

Alabama

Built: Laird, Birkenhead
Commissioned: August 24, 1862
Displacement: 1,066 tonnes/1,050 tons (normal)
Length: 67m/220ft (wl)
Beam: 9.6m/31ft 8in
Draught: 5.4m/17ft 8in (normal)
Armament: 1 x 110lb, 1 x 68pdr and 6 x 32pdr guns
Machinery: Steam reciprocating engine
Speed: 13 knots
Complement: 145

LEFT: **Although referred to as a "corvette", the *Trenton* carried most of her armament below deck. On the upper deck, right forward, she had a pair of breech-loading chase guns. Like the big 203mm/8in muzzle-loader, right aft, these were mounted on racers, enabling them to be fired on the beam as well.**

Trenton

Built: New York Navy Yard
Commissioned: February 14, 1877
Displacement: 3,860 tonnes/3,800 tons (normal)
Length: 77.1m 253ft (wl)
Beam: 14.6m/48ft
Draught: 6.2m/20ft 6in (normal)
Armament: 11 x 203mm/8in MLR and 2 x 20pdr BLR
Machinery: Steam reciprocating engine
Power: 2,313kW/3,100ihp
Speed: 14 knots
Complement: 477

LEFT: The Union's response to the fast Confederate raiders was a group of wood-built frigates in which the designer, Benjamin Isherwood, sacrificed everything for speed. Although capable of a then world record speed of 18 knots, they burned too much fuel for their limited bunker capacity.
ABOVE: The launch of the *Madawaska* in 1865. Like the Union Navy's monitors, these large cruisers were given indigenous Indian names. During the time of the Civil War, there was considerable pride engendered in the "New" Navy, but this quickly evaporated in the expensive rehabilitation after hostilities ceased.

Wampanoag

The success of the *Alabama* and others as commerce raiders stimulated the Union Government to build a series of what were intended to be "super cruisers", capable of both hunting down commerce raiders or, if needs be, acting in a similar role.

The seven ships, commenced in 1863, are loosely referred to as the Wampanoag class, after the lead ship, but they were of various designs and sizes. All were completed after the Civil War had finished and one not at all.

The concept centred upon speed. To destroy merchant shipping, they had to catch it, so they were relatively lightly armed and devoid of any protective feature other than strategically located coal bunkers. On meeting any hostile warship, they were to use their speed to decline action.

Created by a noted clipper designer, the *Wampanoag*'s lines were fine, her hull long, both for potential speed and to accommodate the boilers and machinery, whose combined weight absorbed 1,219 tonnes/1,200 tons of the ship's 4,283 tonnes/4,215 tons displacement and, indeed, almost exactly half her length.

The ship's length was considerable in relation to its depth. Built in wood, the hull lacked longitudinal and torsional stiffness and, although its structure was augmented by metal plates, braces and ties, it worked badly.

She was, however, fast, achieving a reported near-18 knots maximum, and averaging 16.7 knots over a 38-hour trial. Her narrow-gutted hull permitted inadequate bunker space, a situation not improved by her equally inadequate auxiliary sailing rig. Chase fire, an important factor in pursuit, was also lacking owing to the fine lines.

The actual menace posed by large raiders was over-estimated, but could not be ignored, the British Admiralty responding with the large iron frigates *Inconstant* and *Shah*.

Renamed *Florida* in 1869, the *Wampanoag* was reduced to extended reserve status, thence serving in auxiliary roles until her disposal in 1885.

LEFT: Probably originally equipped with a bowsprit, the *Wampanoag* was considerably altered later in life to make her less expensive to run. She was also renamed *Florida*. With her considerable length, relative lack of depth and heavy point loading, her wooden hull worked badly and was destined for a short existence, however well maintained.

Wampanoag (as designed)

Built: New York Navy Yard
Commissioned: September 17, 1867
Displacement: 4,283 tonnes/4,215 tons (normal)
Length: 108.1m/355ft (wl)
Beam: 13.8m/45ft 2in
Draught: 5.8m/19ft (normal)
Armament: 10 x 203mm/8in, 2 x 100pdr, 2 x 24pdr and 1 x 60pdr pivot gun
Machinery: Steam reciprocating engines, 1 shaft
Power: 2,313kW/3,100ihp
Speed: About 18 knots
Protection: None
Complement: Unknown

LEFT: The authorization of the "ABCD Squadron" in 1883 marked the foundation of the "modern" American Navy. Designed to a handy size, they were large enough to be employed independently yet not of a scale that would be difficult to justify to a hostile Treasury. The *Atlanta* had considerably less freeboard than suggested here and later landed her heavy brig sailing rig.

The "ABCD Squadron"

Although it marked the beginning of what was known as the New Navy, the "ABCD Squadron" reflected the United States' then design inexperience by being obsolescent on completion. The nation was firmly opposed to the creation of a battle fleet, but the Naval Advisory Board, itself exposed to partisan argument and attack from the various naval support bureaux, recognized the requirement for cruisers to "show the flag", representing American interests abroad and, in time of war, to conduct operations against enemy commerce.

In practice, war could be envisioned only against Great Britain, whose maritime strength was overwhelming. What few distant coaling stations were available to American ships would

probably rapidly be denied them by the British, so sailing rig remained essential to endurance, underlined by the fact that American propulsion machinery design was still inferior to that of Europe.

Approved in 1883, the squadron comprised the 3,048 tonne/3,000-ton sisters *Atlanta* and *Boston*, the 4,572 tonne/4,500-ton *Chicago* and the unarmoured "despatch boat" *Dolphin*. All three cruisers were constructed of steel, with a partial 38mm/1.5in protective deck.

Although available ordnance included a newly introduced 152mm/6in QF (or RF ["rapid fire"] in American parlance) the heavier projectile of the older 203mm/8in BL was preferred. This being a heavy weapon for smaller ships the Atlantas had to accept the weight-saving of low-freeboard fore-and-afterdecks in order to

mount a single barrel at either end. The larger *Chicago* mounted four such, located in prominent, sided sponsons, whence they commanded a measure of end-on fire without interfering with the heavy, three-masted barque rig, which was greatly reduced in an 1898 modernization.

Only the *Chicago* was twin-screwed, but her original machinery, itself replaced by 1898, was archaic and, being of high profile, vulnerable to damage.

The *Atlanta* was stricken in 1912, the others serving in auxiliary roles throughout World War I.

The "ABCD Squadron"

	Built	Commissioned
Atlanta	Roach, Chester, Pa.	July 19, 1886
Boston	Roach, Chester, Pa.	May 2, 1887
Chicago	Roach, Chester, Pa.	April 17, 1889
Dolphin	Roach, Chester, Pa.	December 8, 1885

Chicago (as built)

Displacement: 4,572 tonnes/4,500 tons (normal)
Length: 99m/325ft (wl); 101.9m/334ft 4in (oa)
Beam: 14.7m/48ft 3in
Draught: 6.1m/20ft 2in (normal)
Armament: 4 x 203mm/8in BL, 8 x 152mm/6in QF and 2 x 127mm/5in QF guns
Machinery: 2-cylinder, compound, overhead beam engines, 14 boilers, 2 shafts
Power: 3,730kW/5,000ihp for 14 knots
Endurance: 1,168 tonnes/1,150 tons (coal) for 11,112km/6,000nm at 10 knots
Protection: 38mm/1.5in (protective deck over machinery only)
Complement: 300

ABOVE: **Considerably larger than the Atlantas, the *Chicago* was completed with a three-masted barque rig, that was removed in an 1898 modernization. Note how her four 203mm/8in breech-loaders are located in conspicuous sponsons to avoid interference with the sailing rig. Her broadside secondary armament is carried very low. Explosive shells made open gundecks such as this very vulnerable.**

LEFT: **Seen coaling at Malta during her delivery voyage, the *Naniwa* is painted in a livery not dissimilar to that of the Royal Navy. There would be several changes. Note how the two 26cm/10.2in guns are mounted on barbettes with no real overhead protection. Light shields would be added later.**

Naniwa class

The two Naniwas were members of the extended Elswick group of protected cruisers derived from the generic *Esmeralda*, completed in 1884. The American cruiser *Charleston* was also built to a closely related design.

William White, then working for Armstrong, modified George Rendel's original concept by increasing freeboard, enabling the full-length protective deck to be arched to above the (normal) waterline. Damage to much of its area would therefore, in theory, cause less flooding below. A further safety feature, by no means universal at that time, was the provision of a double bottom, extending from the forward to the after magazine space.

The extra freeboard, besides improving seakeeping, also increased the command of the two 26cm/10.2in guns, mounted singly in barbettes, forward and aft. Three sponsons along each side at upper deck level carried 15cm/5.9in guns. All were specified by

the Japanese to come from the German firm of Krupp. During 1900 the 15cm/5.9in weapons were replaced by Armstrong-built 152mm/6in QF guns; then, in 1902, the 26cm/10.2in guns were likewise replaced.

Although the machinery was of the low-profile, but relatively inefficient horizontally reciprocating type, the *Naniwa*'s trial speed of 18.77 knots placed her among the fastest of contemporary cruisers.

Both saw service in the Sino-Japanese and Russo-Japanese wars. Action at the Yalu and at Tsushima saw both survive considerable damage, and both were involved in the sinking of the Russian *Rurik*. Contemporary reports spoke well of their robustness and general performance, although their stability range was questionable.

The *Naniwa* was wrecked in June 1912, while the *Takachiho*, by then reduced to auxiliary duties as a transport and minelayer, was torpedoed and sunk

ABOVE: **The *Naniwa* seen here after the conclusion of the war with Russia in a new "tropical" colour scheme. By now the ship had been rearmed with a uniform eight 152mm/6in guns from Armstrong. The centreline guns have open shields, to be proved vulnerable at Tsushima, the broadside weapons are here trained outboard.**

in the course of the seizure of the German enclave and base of Tsingtao in October 1914, early in World War I.

Naniwa class

	Built	Commissioned
Naniwa	Armstrong, Elswick	December 1, 1885
Takachiho	Armstrong, Elswick	March 26, 1886

Naniwa (as built)

Displacement: 3,784 tonnes/3,725 tons (normal)
Length: 91.4m/300ft (bp); 97.5m/320ft (oa)
Beam: 14m/46ft
Draught: 5.6m/18ft 6in (normal)
Armament: 2 x 26cm/10.2in and 6 x 15cm/5.9in guns; 4 x 356mm/14in torpedo tubes
Machinery: Horizontal compound (double-expansion) engines, 6 boilers, 2 shafts
Power: 5,294kW/7,100ihp for 18 knots
Endurance: 812 tonnes/800 tons (coal) for 16,668km/9,000nm at 13 knots
Protection: 51–76mm/2–3in (protective deck)
Complement: 340

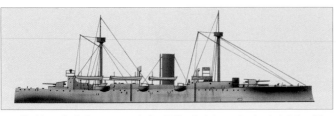

ABOVE: **Elswick gave the Naniwas a generous freeboard. This not only improved seakeeping but allowed the guns to be mounted higher. Internally, it permitted the centre of the vaulted protective deck and its openings to be above normal waterline, a great advantage if damaged in action.**

Unebi

Japan was keen to acquire expertise from the West sufficient to establish a domestic and independent warship-building capability. Commodore Matthew Perry's expedition and the ensuing 1854 Treaty of Kanagawa gave the United States an initial advantage as a source of that expertise, an advantage lost in 1861, when the Americans descended into a self-absorbing civil war.

The Dutch had enjoyed a small, but continuous presence in Japan's closed society but now found themselves elbowed aside by more ruthless French and British interests. The latter quickly had naval advisors on the spot and was making arrangements to train Japanese naval officers in Britain. The French, however, had the more immediate material success. Between 1865 and 1876 they created the major dockyard at Yokosuka from scratch, trained a largely local workforce, and then appointed the noted constructor Emile Bertin as superintendent to teach the Japanese the arts of steel shipbuilding.

Although Elswick won the order for the two Naniwas, the French built the protected cruiser *Unebi* over the same timescale. The British pair mounted, typically, a single large-calibre gun on the centreline at either end. The French opted for four, rather smaller 24cm/9.5in weapons, which demanded four large, sided sponsons. These, in turn, required the extravagant tumblehome typical of contemporary French ships.

In contrast to the Naniwas, with their light, "military" masts, the *Unebi* was given a heavy three-masted barque rig. Despite this, she had far finer proportions (L/B of 7.53, compared with a Naniwa's 6.52). Not only did she have a more archaic appearance but she also had an inferior endurance, her sailing rig being hardly auxiliary.

For the long delivery voyage, the Naniwas had the advantage of the network of British coaling stations. Less fortunate, the *Unebi* relied more on sail. In October 1887 she disappeared, still engaged on her maiden trip.

TOP: **Although launched a year after the Naniwas, the *Unebi*, with her heavy rig, looks anything but contemporary with them. Seen here in a French port prior to delivery, she has sails bent on to the yards but appears to have her bowsprit run in. Note the exaggerated ram bow.** ABOVE: **Standing rigging required that the *Unebi*'s main armament was sponson mounted. This governed hull configuration, and the effect of the tumblehome would be to reduce stability as the ship heeled under a press of sail.**

Unebi

Built: Soc. des Forges et Chantiers, le Havre
Commissioned: December 3, 1886
Displacement: 3,688 tonnes/3,630 tons (normal)
Length: 97.9m/321ft 6in (bp)
Beam: 13m/42ft 10in
Draught: 5.7m/18ft.9in (normal)
Armament: 4 x 24cm/9.5in BL and 6 x 15cm/5.9in BL guns; 4 x 381mm/15in torpedo tubes
Machinery: 3-cylinder, horizontal, triple-expansion engines, 6 boilers, 2 shafts
Power: 4,476kW/6,000ihp for 16 knots
Endurance: 10,371km/5,600nm at 10 knots
Protection: 51–76mm/2–3in (protective deck)
Complement: 280

Itsukushima class

Despite the unexplained disappearance of the le Havre-built *Unebi* while on her delivery voyage, the Japanese quickly ordered a further pair of protected cruisers from France. However, the latter's shipbuilding industry had been greatly retarded by government policies, and the only yard able to accept the order was Forges et Chantiers de la Mediterranée, which was the company that owned the nation's largest military gun manufacturer, Canet.

The result demonstrated the intimate and interconnected nature of the industry at that time, for the ships were designed by Emile Bertin (newly appointed head of Yokosuka Navy Yard), while the ships' primary weapons came from Canet (whose eponymous founder had learned his trade at Armstrong) and their secondary weapons from Armstrong, whose small, quick-firing guns were superior to the French product.

With no concession to elegance, the ships carried a single 32cm/12.6in gun which, on a displacement of 4,282 tonnes/4,215 tons, was so disproportionate as almost to warrant the term "monitor". The lead ship,

ABOVE: **With their single 32cm/12.6in Canet gun, the three Itsukushimas were, perhaps, as much monitor as cruiser. Of idiosyncratic French design, they had minimal superstructure, dominated by a lofty, stiff tripod mast bearing spotting tops. Excepting a single 119mm/4.7in gun right aft, the remaining armament was all broadside-mounted aft of amidships, crew accommodation being concentrated forward.**

Itsukushima, had a high-freeboard hull, with a full-width deckhouse that ran for 60 per cent of the ship's after length. The single, primary weapon was mounted forward on a shallow barbette, with the secondary guns mounted within and on the deckhouse. A miniscule bridge structure was located immediately before the single funnel. Abaft the funnel was a single, oversized tripod mast.

The second unit, *Matsushima*, had her 32cm/12.6in gun located aft. Consequently, she was more built-up forward and, aft, was one level lower. The third ship, *Hashidate*, was Japan's first-ever domestically built armoured ship. She was a copy of the *Itsukushima* and took six years to build.

Both French-built units survived quite severe action damage during the war with China, the main criticism being

applied to the secondary broadside batteries, whose guns were not separately screened. *Matsushima* was lost by magazine explosion in 1908, probably due to unstable cordite.

Itsukushima class

	Built	Commissioned
Hashidate	Yokosuka Navy Yard	June 1894
Itsukushima	Soc. des Forges et Ch. de la Mediterranée, la Seyne	August 1891
Matsushima	Soc. des Forges et Ch. de la Mediterranée, la Seyne	March 1891

Itsukushima class (as built)

Displacement: 4,282 tonnes/4,215 tons (normal)
Length: 89.8m 294ft 11in (bp); 99m/325ft (oa)
Beam: 15.5m/51ft
Draught: 6.3m/20ft 8in (mean)
Armament: 1 x 32cm/12.6in and 11 x 119mm/4.7in QF guns; 4 x 381mm/15in torpedo tubes
Machinery: 3-cylinder, horizontal, triple-expansion engines, 6 boilers, 2 shafts
Power: 4,028kW/5,400ihp for 16.5 knots
Endurance: 690 tonnes/680 tons (coal) for 11,112km/6,000nm at 10 knots
Protection: 38mm/1.5in (protective deck); 305mm/12in (turret)
Complement: 430

Yoshino

B eing a successful series, constructed for numerous flags, the "Elswick Cruiser", although varying considerably in detail according to customer specification, was of a general form that was continuously improved. When, therefore, the Japanese sought tenders for a 4267-tonne/4,200-ton vessel, Armstrong only had to modify the form of the *Nueve de Julio*, just laid down to Argentinian account.

The Japanese were already developing the strategy of using cruiser forces as earlier fleets would use battle squadrons. Units such as the Itsukushimas, with their heavy guns, would form the slower, core force, while others such as the *Yoshino*, incorporating speed with an all-quick-firing armament, would constitute a fast wing, scouting, reporting and herding an opponent into the maw of the heavy artillery. (The Imperial Japanese Navy was still using coherent cruiser groups with devastating effect as late as 1942–43.)

Laid down in 1892, *Yoshino* continued the Elswick preference for raised forecastle and poop, separated by an open waist with high bulwarks, sections of which could be lowered to expose the broadside armament. Four 152mm/6in QF guns were carried, one each forward, aft, and two in sided sponsons, allowing them firing arcs from ahead to 60 degrees abaft the beam. Fighting tops, with light guns and searchlights, were a feature.

TOP LEFT: **Typically Elswick in appearance, the** *Yoshino* **makes a fine show under full power. The critical eye, however, would note how wet she is forward, even in a flat calm, while the wave form, with its deep hollow does not look very efficient.** TOP RIGHT: **Elswick had a reputation for plenty of guns, but note how the 47mm/1.85in weapons, here with their apertures open, are so low as to be unusable at speed, as in the picture to the left. The sponson of the starboard wing 152mm/6in gun can be seen in line with the forward funnel.** ABOVE: **This full, starboard-side view of the** *Yoshino* **gives a good idea of the layout of a contemporary light cruiser, with raised forecastle and poop, and an open waist from which the secondary armament fires through broadside apertures. The rudimentary navigating bridges, with plenty of glazing, are uncomfortably close to the main armament. The volume of coal smoke was inevitably related to speed.**

Like the Argentinian, the *Yoshino* incorporated an unusually thick protective deck and, of higher power, was briefly the world's fastest cruiser. Expected to be opposed by enemy torpedo boats and destroyers, she received an unusually large number (22) of 3pdr QF guns located, inter alia, in the bridge structure, mast fighting tops and, near uselessly, at lower-deck level.

The *Yoshino* played a notable role (against Armstrong-built Chinese ships) at the Yalu in 1894 but, during operations against the Russians outside Port Arthur in 1904, she sank following a collision, confirming Admiralty suspicions regarding the survivability of Elswick cruisers.

Yoshino

Built: Armstrong, Elswick
Commissioned: July 1893
Displacement: 4,247 tonnes/4,180 tons (normal)
Length: 109.7m/360ft (bp); 118.2m/388ft (oa)
Beam: 14.2m/46ft 6in
Draught: 5.2m/17ft (normal)
Armament: 4 x 152mm/6in QF and 8 x 119mm/4.7in QF guns; 5 x 457mm/18in torpedo tubes
Machinery: 4-cylinder, triple-expansion engines, 12 boilers, 2 shafts
Power: 11,745kW/15,750ihp for 22.5 knots
Endurance: 1,026 tonnes/1,010 tons (coal) for 16,668km/9,000nm at 10 knots
Protection: 44–114mm/1.75–4.5in (protective deck)
Complement: 375

333

LEFT: On much the same specification as that of the *Yoshino*, the Japanese wanted to upgrade the main armament to a pair of 203mm/8in weapons on the *Kasagi* (shown here) and *Chitose*. Their American builders wisely increased length and beam to accommodate them. The canvas was very much a "get-you-home" addition.

Takasago and Kasagi class

Expanding to meet the demands of the war against China, the Japanese Navy acquired the Elswick-built *Esmeralda* from Chile in 1894. Now ten years of age, she displaced only 2,327 tonnes/2,290 tons but had a full protective deck and an over-ambitious armament of a 29.4-tonne/29-ton, 254mm/10in gun at either end. This, and six 152mm/6in secondary weapons, left no margin for raised forecastle and poop. Renamed *Izumi*, she was valued for her big guns but, although influential in her day, she was a poor seaboat and was quickly reduced to auxiliary duties.

Following the war, the Japanese embarked on a replacement and expansion programme. Armstrong benefited through a contract to build an improved *Yoshino*, while two American

yards received orders for near-copies, reputedly in recognition of their having remained neutral during the recent war with China.

The seakeeping qualities of the *Yoshino* had not been above criticism and for the new ship, named *Takasago*, Armstrong were required to replace four 152mm/6in guns with two 203mm/8in weapons, and eight 119mm/4.7in QF guns with ten. This represented an increase in topside weight from 44.7 tonnes/44 tons to 51.8 tonnes/51 tons. On a hull of the same length, Armstrong compensated with an extra 0.3m/1ft of beam. Although still fast, the *Takasago* was a heavy roller. Inadequate subdivision resulted in her rapid foundering on being mined in 1904, although, at that date, damage control procedures were rudimentary.

The two American yards, building the *Kasagi* and *Chitose*, were allowed some flexibility in interpretation of the basic specification. Although obliged to retain the same scale of protection and armament as the *Takasago*, both opted for longer and beamier hulls. This resulted in (normal) displacements being increased by about 762 tonnes/750 tons and 610 tonnes/600 tons respectively. Their installed power was reduced, as was endurance and maximum speed, by nearly one knot. By not being designed to such tight margins, however, the two were probably the better ships.

ABOVE: The early "peacetime" livery of Japanese warships tends to conceal hull detail while the white-painted topside detail merges with a pale background. Despite her diminutive size, the *Takasago* was sufficiently protected to resist 203mm/8in gunfire but note how, due to stability considerations, the fighting tops are carried low. LEFT: When work was light, Armstrong would lay down a speculative cruiser, in this case a sister to the *Takasago*. The Japanese did not purchase her, however, and she became the Chilean *Chacabuco*. Note her boats are in the water and the boat boom rigged.

Takasago and Kasagi class

	Built	Commissioned
Takasago	Armstrong, Low Walker	April 1898
Chitose	Union Ironworks, San Francisco	March 1899
Kasagi	Cramp, Philadelphia	December 1898

Takasago (as built)

Displacement: 4,226 tonnes/4,160 tons (normal); 5,344 tonnes/5,260 tons (full load)
Length: 109.7m/360ft (bp); 118.2m/388ft (oa)
Beam: 14.2m/46ft 6in
Draught: 6.2m/20ft 6in (full load)
Armament: 2 x 203mm/8in guns, 10 x 119mm/4.7in QF, and 10 x 76mm/3in (12pdr) QF guns; 5 x 457mm/18in torpedo tubes
Machinery: 4-cylinder, vertical, triple-expansion engines, 8 boilers, 2 shafts
Power: 11,745kW/15,750ihp for 22.5 knots
Endurance: 1,041 tonnes/1,025 tons (coal) for 10,186km/5,500nm at 10 knots
Protection: 64–114mm/2.5–4.5in (protective deck)
Complement: 425

Azuma

The Sino-Japanese War of 1894–95 proved to the Japanese that discipline, practised manoeuvre and overwhelming firepower were essential to sea supremacy. As a result, the naval academy and the fleet itself were subject to considerable and urgent expansion. The thoroughness with which this was undertaken was apparent a decade later, when Japanese squadrons trounced those of the Russians, propelling their nation into the front rank of world naval powers, and consequent national rivalries.

The 1896–97 post-war naval acquisition programme had attracted considerable funding, of which little could be absorbed by the nascent domestic shipbuilding industry.

Armoured cruisers commended themselves particularly to the Japanese who used them rather as a squadron of fast Second Class battleships. Whether for speed of delivery, or to evaluate the relative quality of national construction techniques, is not clear, but the orders for six armoured cruisers of about 10,160 tonnes/10,000 tons displacement were split between Great Britain (*Asama* and *Tokiwa*, *Izumo* and *Iwate* from Armstrong at Elswick), Germany (*Yakumo* from AG Vulcan, Stettin) and the French-built *Azuma*.

Identical specifications governed speed, protection and armament, the latter introducing twin 203mm/8in BL turrets forward and aft. Perhaps the most distinctive feature of the *Azuma* was her lack of "Frenchness", there being no hint

TOP: **Of the six armoured cruisers built in Europe at the turn of the century to Japanese account, the only French-sourced ship,** *Azuma*, **could be identified by her unequally spaced funnels. Originally, as here, the funnels were half-cased, later being replaced by three slender, higher funnels and lighter masting.** ABOVE: **Effectively the Second Class battleships of their day, the armoured cruisers carried their twelve 152mm/6in secondary armament on two levels, eight in casemates, four in open mountings. By twinning the four 203mm/8in guns of the primary armament in turrets, space was saved but at the cost of a lower rate of fire.**

of the customary exaggerated ram bow profile, pronounced tumblehome or substantial, sponsoned gun positions. Only in the unequal funnel spacing could her likely origin be suspected.

Protection was capital-ship style, with a complete waterline belt of Harvey nickel steel, 178mm/7in amidships tapering to 89mm/3.5in at either end. Between the limits of the 203mm/8in magazines a 127mm/5in belt extended one level further upward to protect the underside of the 152mm/6in secondary casemates. The protective deck was of 76mm/3in plate.

Prominent during the Russo-Japanese War, all six armoured cruisers survived until the end of World War II, latterly in non-combatant roles.

Azuma (as built)	

Built: Soc. des Chantiers de la Loire, St. Nazaire
Commissioned: July 1900
Displacement: 9,428 tonnes/9,280 tons (normal); 10,130 tonnes/9,950 tons (full load)
Length: 131.5m/431ft 6in (bp); 137.8m/452ft 5in (oa)
Beam: 18.1m/59ft 3in
Draught: 8.5m/28ft (full load)
Armament: 4 x 203mm/8in BL (2x2), 12 x 152mm/6in QF (12x1) and 12 x 76mm/3in QF (12x1) guns; 5 x 457mm/18in torpedo tubes
Machinery: 4-cylinder, triple-expansion engines, 24 boilers, 2 shafts
Power: 13,422kW/18,000ihp for 21 knots
Endurance: 1,219 tonnes/1,200 tons (coal) for 12,964km/7,000nm at 10 knots
Protection: 89–178mm/3.5–7in (belt); 76mm/3in (protective deck); 160mm/6.3in (turrets)
Complement: 720

LEFT: **Much influenced by the British "Towns", the Chikumas' distinctive bow profile set them apart. Note how the adoption of stockless, or close-stowing, anchors reduced greatly the foredeck clutter. The *Hirado*'s two very lofty masts were to elevate W/T aerials to gain range in the Pacific. The mast on the far left belongs to another ship.**

Chikuma class

It was a measure of the progress being made by the Japanese shipbuilding industry that two of the three Chikumas could be contracted out to private yards. Although experience relied heavily on the still-completing Tones, the new ships were greatly influenced by the Royal Navy's Weymouth class. Nearly 30m/100ft longer than a Tone, a Chikuma had no increase in beam and, with a 50 per cent increase in installed power, could make 26 knots, an improvement of about 3 knots. All were fitted with steam turbines but, for evaluation purposes, these were of different types. This resulted in the *Yahagi* having four shafts, the others two.

Like the British Towns, the Chikumas adopted a uniform 152mm/6in main armament. With a raised forecastle and poop hull form, they mounted a centreline

gun at either end, their remaining six being sided in the waist. Four of these were slightly sponsoned to theoretically allow axial fire, although this was inhibited in practice by the effect of blast over-pressure on adjacent structures.

Care was taken over the ships' appearance, the stem having less curvature than that of the Tones, and with the latter's unusual stern profile replaced by a western-style "cruiser" stern. Of elegant proportions, the four funnels stood nearly vertical, complementing the lofty masts. The latter were necessary to extend radio transmission ranges over the vast Pacific Ocean.

Sixteen boilers were distributed over four adjacent boiler rooms, each of which was exhausted by one funnel. The spaces were roofed by the protective deck, of which the horizontal, axial

section was some 45.7cm/18in above the waterline, the thickened slopes abutting the shell plating some 1m/3ft below it. Subdivided coal bunkers both covered and flanked the machinery spaces as added protection.

All were reduced to auxiliary status before World War II, the *Hirado* and *Yahagi* being scrapped only in 1947.

Chikuma class

	Built	Commissioned
Chikuma	Sasebo Navy Yard	May 17, 1912
Hirado	Kawasaki, Kobe	June 17, 1912
Yahagi	Mitsubishi, Nagasaki	July 27, 1912

Chikuma (as built)

Displacement: 4,470 tonnes/4,400 tons (standard); 5,120 tonnes/5,040 tons (full load)
Length: 134m/440ft (bp); 144.7m/475ft (oa)
Beam: 14.2m/46ft 8in
Draught: 5.1m/16ft 8in (mean)
Armament: 8 x 152mm/6in QF and 4 x 76mm/3in QF guns; 3 x 457mm/18in torpedo tubes
Machinery: Direct-drive steam turbines, 16 boilers, 2 shafts
Power: 16,778kW/22,500shp for 26 knots
Endurance: 1,148 tonnes/1,130 tons (coal) and 305 tonnes/300 tons (oil) for 18,520km/10,000nm at 10 knots
Protection: 22–57mm/0.88–2.25in (protective deck)
Complement: 430

LEFT: **Otherwise identical, the *Yahagi* had four, rather than two, shafts. The 16 boilers could burn either coal or oil. Coal, however, comprised about 80 per cent of the bunkers, probably because of its value as protection, although they had both vertical belt and protective deck. The Chikumas were Japan's first steam turbine cruisers.**

Chiyoda

The loss of the brand-new *Unebi* in 1887 came as a profound shock to the developing Japanese Navy. Although further orders were still placed in France, that for the *Chiyoda*, the *Unebi*'s replacement, went to Clydebank. Larger warships for the Royal Navy were by now being designed without sailing rig but the Japanese, with differing priorities, again specified it. The ability to proceed under sail still greatly increased cruising endurance, while teaching further mariners the art. Where the *Unebi* had a heavy barque rig, however, the *Chiyoda* had a lighter, mainly fore-and-aft barquetine rig. The three lower masts were, nonetheless, capped with substantial fighting tops, in which rapid-fire automatic weapons were mounted. These, together with the rig, were removed in 1902, when light topmasts with W/T gaff were substituted.

Shorter, but with the same beam, the *Chiyoda* would not have had to resist the *Unebi*'s press of sail. Lacking the latter's French tumblehome, her waterplanes would have been fuller offering greater resistance to heeling. An unknown with respect to the *Unebi* at the time of her sinking was the degree of depletion of her coal bunkers, and its effect on her stability.

A critical element in the *Unebi*'s stability also had to be her relatively heavy armament. Four Krupp 24cm/9.5in guns were located at upper deck level, a combined weight of 77.2 tonnes/76 tons even without their sponsons. Also mounted at the same height were seven 15cm/5.9in weapons, representing a further 28.4 tonnes/28 tons.

Reportedly, the Japanese wanted to burden the *Chiyoda* with 32cm/12.6in French-built Canets, to achieve commonality with the new Itsukushimas. At 39.6 tonnes/39 tons apiece, such weapons were grossly out of scale on a 2,439-tonne/2,400-ton

ABOVE LEFT: **The liner-like proportions of the** *Chiyoda*'s **hull indicate her status as a training ship. Her final seven years or so were spent as a submarine depot ship, a role suited to her internal capacity.** ABOVE: **Later a common feature of British-built cruisers, the knuckle was unusual at this early date. The large catting davit shows that she still retains old-style stocked anchors.**

vessel, and Brown's wisely opted for a uniform armament of ten 119mm/4.7in QF guns, a total weight of only 20.3 tonnes/20 tons, 80 per cent of which was borne on a level lower than in the *Unebi*.

Chiyoda	

Built: Brown, Clydebank
Commissioned: December 1890
Displacement: 2,439 tonnes/2,400 tons (normal)
Length: 91.4m/300ft (bp); 94.4m/310ft (oa)
Beam: 12.8m/42ft
Draught: 4.3m/14ft (normal)
Armament: 10 x 119mm/4.7in QF guns; 3 x 457mm/18in torpedo tubes
Machinery: Vertical, triple-expansion engines, 6 boilers, 2 shafts
Power: 4,178kW/5,600ihp for 18 knots
Endurance: 427 tonnes/420 tons (coal) for 14,816km/8,000nm at 10 knots
Protection: 114mm/4.5in belt; 25–38mm/1–1.5in (protective deck)
Complement: 350

LEFT: **Note how the rigging differs in each of the pictures of Chiyoda. The short lower masts and very light topmasts indicate that sailing under canvas was never a serious proposition. The heavy tops were removed in the 1902 updating.**

LEFT: The *Marco Polo* makes an impressive sight as she negotiates the swing bridge to enter the inner port at Taranto. Note the very large fighting tops, each carrying two 37mm/1.46in guns. The port side catting davit is swung out, ready to release an emergency anchor.

Marco Polo

During the late 1880s, British constructors reached the conclusion that, for cruisers, "protected" was superior to "armoured". Before the improved Harvey and Krupp armour plate became available, protection in any realistic thickness was thought to be simply too heavy to cover an adequate area of the hull. On a limited displacement, a thick armoured belt was necessarily shallow and, with the ship in full load condition (or overweight), the belt could easily be submerged and of little use as intended. The 5,690-tonne/5,600-ton Orlandos were thus the last Royal Navy armoured cruisers until construction of the type was resumed in the late 1890s with the 12,193-tonne/12,000-ton Cressys.

Bucking the above trend, however, the Italian *Marco Polo* was a "one-off", an example of a small armoured cruiser (4,572 tonnes/4,500 tons), laid down in 1890 and completed in 1894. She thus bears comparison with contemporary British protected cruisers. The seven Astraeas, completed 1894–95, displaced only 224 tonnes/220 tons less, were 1.8m/6ft shorter, but 38cm/15in greater in the beam. Although more generously proportioned, the British ships could nonetheless make 19.5 knots on 6,711kW/9,000ihp where the Italian was good for only 17 knots with 7,460kW/10,000ihp. "Superiority" was thus a straight trade-off between, on the one hand, speed and, on the other, protection/firepower. Here, the *Marco Polo* was the better.

Both had a 51mm/2in protective deck, the Italian having a 100mm/3.9in belt in addition. Where an Astraea mounted two 152mm/6in and eight 119mm/4.7in guns, the *Marco Polo* had six and ten respectively, in similar disposition.

Obsolete by World War I, the Astraeas served only on distant stations or in auxiliary roles. Likewise, the *Marco Polo* saw no real action and, later in the war, was relegated to troop transportation. Stripped of her belt armour she served successively under the names of *Cortellazzo*, *Europa* and *Volta* before being scrapped in 1922.

ABOVE: Seen here at La Spezia in January 1898, the *Marco Polo* is about to depart on her first deployment to the Far East. She had been serving as flagship of the "flying division". Note the low waist, with two 152mm/6in and three 119mm/4.7in guns in shields firing over a high bulwark on either side.

Marco Polo

Built: Cantiere di Castellammare di Stabia
Commissioned: July 21, 1894
Displacement: 4,572 tonnes/4,500 tons (normal); 4,917 tonnes/4,840 tons (full load)
Length: 99.7m/327ft 3in (bp); 106m/348ft (oa)
Beam: 14.7m/48ft 3in
Draught: 6.2m/20ft 4in (full load)
Armament: 6 x 152mm/6in and 10 x 119mm/4.7in guns; 5 x 450mm/17.7in torpedo tubes
Machinery: Vertical, triple-expansion engines, 4 boilers, 2 shafts
Power: 7,460kW/10,000ihp for 17 knots
Endurance: 620 tonnes/610 tons (coal) for 10,742km/5,800nm at 10 knots
Protection: 100mm/3.9in (belt); 51mm/2in (protective deck)
Complement: 394

Giovanni Bausan class

For navies accustomed to slow ironclads, with heavy sailing rigs and broadside armament, George Rendel's design for the Chilean *Esmeralda* appeared nothing short of revolutionary. Offering a combination of speed, protection and hitting power on a relatively modest displacement, the "Elswick cruiser" promised to be a comparatively inexpensive solution to the needs of many fleets.

Armstrong sold the concept to the Italians directly from the drawing board, the *Esmeralda* herself not yet having been launched when the slightly longer *Bausan* was laid down.

Not surprisingly, the two were very similar, although the Italian differed externally in having a prominent gooseneck boat crane fitted in lieu of the more usual boat derrick. Where the *Esmeralda* had British-style open fighting tops for the location of light automatic weapons, the *Bausan* had enclosed tub-like tops.

The armament, a major selling point, was similar, with a 254mm/10in breech-loading gun, mounted in an open-backed gunhouse atop a barbette, at both ends. In place of the Chilean's six 152mm/6in

ABOVE: **Where the *Marco Polo* (opposite) has raised forward and end sections and a low waist, the *Bausan* has a raised centre section with relatively low freeboard forward and aft, giving her a "hogged" appearance. The big cutter is being rigged under the boat crane and hammocks are being aired forward.**

BL guns, the Italian substituted continental-pattern 15cm/5.9in weapons, later replaced. They were sided similarly along the raised central superstructure deck, located on shallow sponsons to increase their arcs.

Although she exhibited the common Elswick failing of inadequate freeboard, a shortcoming ever more evident as ships gathered weight in the course of their careers, the *Bausan* was received enthusiastically as the Italian Navy's first protected cruiser. She was followed by four near-sisters, built between three domestic yards.

During the late 19th century they supported the fleet during the acquisition of Italian territory in North Africa and along the Red Sea coast. In 1912 there was a brief war with Turkey. By 1914, all of the class had been relegated to auxiliary or training roles, their armaments reduced in varying degrees.

Giovanni Bausan class

	Built	Commissioned
Giovanni Bausan	Armstrong, Elswick	May 10, 1885
Etna	Cantiere di Castellammare di Stabia	December 3, 1887
Stromboli	Venice Navy Yard	March 21, 1888
Vesuvio	Orlando, Livorno	March 16, 1888
Ettore Fieramosca	Orlando, Livorno	November 16, 1889

Giovanni Bausan (as designed)

Displacement: 3,121 tonnes/3,072 tons (normal); 3,322 tonnes/3,270 tons (full load)
Length: 84.1m/276ft 1in (bp); 89.3m/293ft 2in (oa)
Beam: 12.8m/42ft
Draught: 5.9m/19ft 4in (full load)
Armament: 2 x 254mm/10in BL and 6 x 15cm/5.9in BL guns; 3 x 356mm/14in torpedo tubes
Machinery: Horizontal compound (double-expansion) engines, 4 boilers, 2 shafts
Power: 4,827kW/6,470ihp for 17 knots
Endurance: 559 tonnes/550 tons (coal) for 9,260km/5,000nm at 10 knots
Protection: 38mm/1.5in (protective deck)
Complement: 267

LEFT: **The American Wampanoag-class raiders bought about a British response in large, Inconstant-type frigates. Despite the vulnerability of these to smaller, but armoured, ships, the French followed suit with the two Tourvilles and the similar *Duguay-Trouin*. Note the tumblehome and the prominent sponsons housing 19cm/7.5in breech-loaders.**

Tourville class

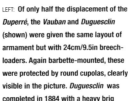

ABOVE: *Amiral Duperré* **was an 11,278-tonne/ 11,100-ton armoured ship, launched in 1879. She was designed around four 34cm/13.5in breech-loaders. These were mounted singly on open barbettes with shields. Two of these are visible, sided forward of the bridge; the others were on the centreline, further aft. Sixteen 14cm/5.5in weapons were also carried, 14 of them on the broadside.**

The threat posed to commerce by the American Wampanoags resulted in the British building large frigates such as the *Inconstant*. Because these needed to be fast, they had long unarmoured hulls, and endurance was provided by a full sailing rig allowing them to operate on distant stations.

Finally, to subdue an enemy raider, once apprehended, a powerful armament was necessary. The resulting, very expensive warships were still, however, not able to engage smaller, but armoured warships.

Although much criticized, the type was also thought appropriate for the French Navy. Delayed by the Franco-Prussian War, the *Tourville* and *Duquesne* were funded under the 1872 Programme, followed by the smaller *Duguay-Trouin*. Like the British, the French found such ships too expensive to build and operate in any number.

All were of composite construction (i.e. wood on iron-frames) and the main armament of the Tourvilles comprised seven 19cm/7.5in breech-loading guns.

All were located on the upper deck, the chase gun being mounted axially to fire through the stem from a cramped location directly beneath the bowsprit. The remaining six were sided in sponsons, which permitted greater firing arcs while positioning them outside the mass of standing rigging.

One level down, on the middle deck, fourteen 14cm/5.5in BL guns were placed conventionally to fire on the broadside. In contrast to the old, pure sailing ships, the heavier guns were mounted at the higher level, while the scope for the middle-deck, broadside guns to run in or recoil was limited by the centreline casings that enclosed the boiler uptakes. These would also have impeded gun crews in serving their guns efficiently.

Such "transitional" designs illustrate the difficulties faced by designers in reconciling conflicting requirements of machinery, armament and sailing rig.

Tourville class

	Built	Commissioned
Duquesne	At. et Ch. de la Gironde, Bordeaux	1878
Tourville	At. et Ch. de la Mediterranée, La Seyne	1878
Duguay-Trouin	At. et Ch. de la Manche, Cherbourg	1879

Tourville

Displacement: 5,563 tonnes/5,476 tons (normal)
Length: 101.6m/333ft 5in (wl)
Beam: 15.3m/50ft 3in
Draught: 7.7m/25ft 4in (normal)
Armament: 7 x 19cm/7.5in BL and 14 x 14cm/ 5.5in BL guns
Machinery: Steam reciprocating, 1 shaft
Power: 5,595kW/7,500ihp for 17 knots
Bunker: 813 tonnes/800 tons (coal)
Protection: None
Complement: 550

LEFT: **Of only half the displacement of the *Duperré*, the *Vauban* and *Duguesclin* (shown) were given the same layout of armament but with 24cm/9.5in breech-loaders. Again barbette-mounted, these were protected by round cupolas, clearly visible in the picture. *Duguesclin* was completed in 1884 with a heavy brig rig and long bowsprit. Only the larger apertures in the side are gun ports.**

340

ABOVE: **At the time the ultimate in "fierce face" warships, the *Dupuy de Lôme*'s hull was protected over its complete area to main deck level. The single 194mm/7.64in gun, flanked by single 164.7mm/6.48in weapons, is visible at either end, as are the amidships 164.7mm/6.48in guns. Despite her overall weight, she had also massive tower masts.**

Dupuy de Lôme

The earliest ironclads were just that – wooden warships hung with vertical plate to keep out enemy shot. Within a couple of decades, however, concepts had advanced to include protective deck systems and the limiting of armour to the maximum thickness of plate over the minimum of vital areas. No one method was ideal; each having its adherents and detractors.

In line with the philosophy of the in-vogue Jeune École movement, the French Navy planned a new cruiser/commerce destroyer. Recent experiments, carried out against an old ironclad, had shown that the effect of a hail of fire from the new, small-calibre quick-firers could disable a warship as surely as heavy shot piercing her armour.

The new ship, a one-off, reflected this. Most commerce raiders were fast, but unprotected, intended to decline action with warships. The *Dupuy de Lôme* was slower, but intended to stand her ground.

Named after one of France's most influential constructors, she was an extraordinary looking vessel, flush-decked with high freeboard and an elongated plough bow. On a relatively modest displacement, the French were able to clad her entire above-water hull area in 100mm/3.9in plate. Internally, there was a 38mm/1.5in vaulted protective deck, covered with a cellular level, and with a splinter deck below it. Machinery was kept compact and below the armour by adopting low-height machinery with triple-screw propulsion.

A long, continuous superstructure deck was terminated in a short forecastle. Both forward and aft there were three individually turreted 164.7mm/6.48in guns. Amidships, single turreted 194mm/7.64in guns projected out on sponsons on both sides.

As with many innovative ships, the *Dupuy de Lôme* was never tested in action, but started a fashion in armoured cruisers to which Great Britain was eventually obliged to subscribe. The contemporary Edgar-class protected cruisers were considered to be the French ship's equal.

ABOVE: **The extraordinary bow form was not designed as a ram but rather, with the elongated stern, a means of increasing waterline length in order to improve hydrodynamic efficiency. The *Dupuy de Lôme* is seen here with her original three funnels and her wetness is evident.**

Dupuy de Lôme

Built: Brest Naval Dockyard
Commissioned: 1892
Displacement: 6,513 tonnes/6,410 tons (normal)
Length: 114.2m/375ft (wl)
Beam: 15.7m/51ft 6in
Draught: 7.2m/23ft 6in (normal)
Armament: 2 x 194mm/7.64in BL and 6 x 164.7mm/6.48in BL guns; 4 x 356mm/14in torpedo tubes
Machinery: Steam reciprocating, 3 shafts
Power: 10,440kW/14,000ihp for 19.5 knots
Bunkers: 914 tonnes/900 tons (coal)
Protection: 100mm/3.9in (sides); 38mm/1.5in (protective deck)
Complement: 515

LEFT: **Seen here in her original configuration, the** *Foudre* **is equipped with a complex gantry system associated with the stowage of her eight torpedo boats. The arrangement contrasts interestingly with that of HMS** *Vulcan* **whose construction inspired that of the** *Foudre.* **Note the inflated observation balloon right aft.** ABOVE: *Foudre* **was converted to an aviation ship in stages. Here, she has lost most of her gantry system but gained her topside seaplane hangar. Later, her bridge was moved further aft and a flying-off platform added over the bows, served by a long derrick stepped to a repositioned foremast.**

Foudre

A French response to the British cruiser *Vulcan*, the *Foudre* was launched in October 1895. Described as a "torpedo depot ship", she was built with a light conventional armament, her main offensive power being vested in eight torpedo boats. These were 18.3m/60ft in length, displacing 14.2 tonnes/14 tons, and were stowed topside, beneath a complex gantry designed for positioning on deck, their setting afloat and their recovery.

For lightness, the boats were to have been constructed of aluminium, but a prototype deteriorated so rapidly in contact with salt water that all were built in steel.

At her after end the *Foudre* had a facility for operating gas-filled, tethered observation balloons, a precursor of her

eventual role. Like the British, the French found the "torpedo depot ship" impractical but, unsuitable for conversion to a conventional cruiser, the *Foudre* became initially a repair ship and then an ocean minelayer in 1910. She had, however, retained her original extensive workshop facilities, and these resulted in her being selected to become the French Navy's first aviation ship.

During 1911, all torpedo boat arrangements were stripped out, the ship's three distinctive, close-spaced funnels raised, and a garage-like hangar installed aft. This work was completed in March 1912, 17 months after Eugene Ely's pioneering flight from an American warship.

The *Foudre*'s hangar was built to accommodate seaplanes, to be flown

from the water. In 1914 this was supplemented by a take-off platform erected over the ship's foredeck. Despite the ship's rather inadequate speed of 19.5 knots, this platform saw the French Navy's first-ever shipboard take-off in May 1914.

With the take-off platform removed in favour of further seaplane facilities, the *Foudre* joined British aviation ships for operations in support of the Dardanelles campaign. Subsequently, however, she proved to be more useful as a fleet repair ship. She was scrapped in 1922, much altered from her original configuration.

LEFT: **A couple of years after** *Foudre's* **completion, she was equipped with facilities for stowing, inflating and towing an observation balloon, to extend her visual range prior to the launching of her torpedo boats. The latter being unsuccessful, the ship was relegated to auxiliary roles for several years prior to her conversion to an aviation ship.**

Foudre

Built: At. et Ch. de la Gironde, Bordeaux
Commissioned: 1896
Displacement: 6,065 tonnes/5,970 tons (normal); 6,188 tonnes/6,090 tons (full load)
Length: 115.9m/380ft 6in (wl); 118.9m/390ft 4in (oa)
Beam: 20.2m/66ft 2in
Draught: 5.3m/17ft 6in (normal)
Armament: 8 x 100mm/3.9in and 4 x 65mm/2.56in guns
Machinery: Vertical, triple-expansion engines, 24 boilers, 2 shafts
Power: 8,579kW/11,500ihp for 19.5 knots
Endurance: 853 tonnes/840 tons (coal) for 11,112km/6,000nm at 10 knots
Protection: 100mm/3.9in (protective deck)
Complement: 430

Stosch and Geier classes

Typical of corvettes, they featured a raised forecastle and poop, and an open waist. They carried eight 10.5cm/4.1in guns, two each forward and aft, with four sided in the waist.

Obsolescent by 1914 some were still serving on distant stations. The *Geier* left East Africa, sailing to the western Pacific (and taking a prize) before entering American Honolulu for internment. The *Cormoran*, refitting at Tsingtao, transferred her guns and crew to an auxiliary raider.

Following German unification, General (later Admiral) Albrecht von Stosch oversaw the transition of the Royal Prussian Navy into the Imperial German Navy. Until 1888 the service was administered by the army, and Stosch established many of its institutions.

Although its early armoured vessels were either built in Great Britain, or depended upon British design and components, less sophisticated warships were constructed domestically. Among these was a class of six Kreuzerfregatten, launched 1877–79 and named after military notables, including Stosch.

The ships were of composite construction, with zinc-sheathed wood on iron framing. All were ship rigged, with armament carried on the broadside. With considerable endurance, the class was comparable with the British *Comus*, and

contributed usefully to Germany's many colonial acquisitions of 1884–85. These included South-West and East Africa, Togo and Cameroon, New Guinea, the Bismarck Archipelago and the Marshall Islands. In later obsolescence the ships served as training and accommodation vessels, the *Gneisenau* being lost in 1900.

The empire established, the German Navy built a series of Stationskreuzer, equivalent in form and function to British corvettes. Smaller than the Kreuzerfregatten, and typified by the six Bird class, they were steel-built and sheathed in wood to upper deck level. To reduce fouling this was overlaid in muntzmetal. They were given a lighter, three-masted barquentine rig but, by 1914, this had been reduced to a handier, two-masted brig rig. Serving as a mining hulk, *Seeadler* blew up in 1917.

Stosch and Geier classes

	Built	Commissioned
Bismarck	Norddeutscher Schiffbau AG, Kiel	1878
Blücher	Norddeutscher Schiffbau AG, Kiel	1878
Gneisenau	Danzig Dockyard	1880
Moltke	Danzig Dockyard	1878
Stein	AG Vulcan, Stettin	1880
Stosch	AG Vulcan, Stettin	1878
Bussard	Danzig Dockyard	1890
Condor	Blohm & Voss, Hamburg	1892
Cormoran	Danzig Dockyard	1893
Falke	Kiel Dockyard	1891
Geier	Wilhelmshaven Dockyard	1895
Seeadler	Danzig Dockyard	1892

Stosch class

Displacement: 2,565 tonnes/2,525 tons to 3,139 tonnes/3,090 tons (normal)
Length: 72.2m/237ft (wl); 82.3m/270ft (oa)
Beam: 13.7m/45ft
Draught: 5.5m/18ft 2in (normal)
Armament: 10 x 15cm/5.9in BL and 2 x 8.8cm/3.46in QF guns; 1 x torpedo tube
Machinery: 3-cylinder, single-expansion reciprocating engine, 4 boilers, 1 shaft
Power: 1,900kW/2,550ihp for 13 knots
Endurance: 325 tonnes/320 tons (coal) for 3,611km/1,950nm at 10 knots
Protection: None
Complement: 410

RIGHT: With an easily manageable barquentine rig, twin-shaft and triple-expansion steam propulsion, the Geier class were useful colonial sloops, carrying a designed eight 10.5cm/4.1in guns. The *Seeadler*, seen here, gave her name to the magnificent natural harbour in the Admiralty Islands, strategically important during World War II, during the reconquest of New Guinea.

LEFT: **A rather dramatic, but accurate, depiction of the *Victoria Louise* as completed, with three funnels and a heavy forward "battle mast". The design and armament layout was sound, being refined through successive classes until World War I. The "plough" bow profile was a characteristic of German armoured cruisers.**

Kaiserin Augusta and Victoria Louise class

Kaiser Wilhelm's ambitions in *Weltpolitik* resulted in frequent demands to increase the size of his fleet. Envious of the Royal Navy, he was all too aware that it could afford to out-build him at any time. His navy needed modern cruisers, yet limited budgets were biased toward capital ship construction. Where the British could build various types of cruiser, the Germans therefore sought to construct a multi-purpose ship, versatile enough to work with the fleet, on colonial duties or in commerce protection.

Launched in 1892, the one-off *Kaiserin Augusta* was, despite her 6,147-tonne/6,050-ton displacement, classed as a Kreuzerkorvette. A protected cruiser, she followed the example of the French *Dupuy de Lôme* in adopting triple-screw propulsion. Again, this was to decrease the bulk of individual engines in order to house them below armour.

The ship was capable of over 21 knots, but her four 15cm/5.9in guns were rather restricted in being located in sided casemates, forward and aft. Eight 10.5cm/4.1in weapons were sided in sponsoned casemates in the waist.

The *Kaiserin Augusta*'s slender hull proved to be weak, requiring extensive remedial structural stiffening. Her successors, the five-strong Victoria Louise class, were shorter, beamier and deeper in the hull. Altogether more capable, they paid the price in being 3 knots slower.

A single 21cm/8.2in gun was carried forward and aft, with eight 15cm/5.9in guns in casemates, four of them at middle-deck level, too low to be of any real use. Later weight reduction saw two 15cm/5.9in guns landed, the three funnels reduced to two (only half-cased) and the heavy tubular foremast reduced to a light pole. Their high profile caused marked leeway.

By 1914 all five were reduced to accommodation ships and all, except the *Victoria Louise*, were scrapped by about 1921. The exception served until 1923 as the mercantile *Flora Sommerfeld* at a time when merchant tonnage was scarce.

Kaiserin Augusta and Victoria Louise class

	Built	Commissioned
Kaiserin Augusta	Germania, Kiel	1892
Freya	Danzig Dockyard	1898
Hansa	AG Vulcan, Stettin	1898
Hertha	AG Vulcan, Stettin	1898
Victoria Louise	AG Weser, Bremen	1898
Vineta	Danzig Dockyard	1899

Victoria Louise class (as built)

Displacement: 5,750 tonnes/5,660 tons (normal); 6,595 tonnes/6,491 tons (full load)
Length: 109.1m/358ft 2in (wl); 110.6m/363ft 1in (oa)
Beam: 17.4m/57ft 1in
Draught: 6.9m/22ft 8in (mean)
Armament: 2 x 21cm/8.3in, 8 x 15cm/5.9in and 10 x 8.8cm/3.46in guns; 3 x 450mm/17.7in torpedo tubes
Machinery: 4-cylinder, triple-expansion engines, 18 boilers, 3 shafts
Power: 7,460kW/10,000ihp (for 18 knots
Endurance: 965 tonnes/950 tons (coal) for 6,852km/3,700nm at 10 knots
Protection: 40–100mm/1.57–3.9in (protective deck)
Complement: 440

ABOVE: **Bearing the prestigious name of *Kaiserin Augusta*, Germany's first armoured cruiser proved less than successful, her long, shallow hull lacking stiffness. She mounted a dozen 15cm/5.9in guns, none of them on the centreline, with two firing aft through the unusually configured stern. During World War I she acted as a gunnery training ship. She was the first triple-screwed ship in the Imperial fleet.**

LEFT: *The Prinz Heinrich* was an improved *Fürst Bismarck*, both of them being one-offs in the development of the best balance of qualities for an armoured cruiser. With reduced protection and only two heavy guns she was, therefore, faster. The arrangement of the secondary armament, amidships, was innovative. ABOVE: Compared with *Prinz Heinrich*, the *Fürst Bismarck* (seen here) had cylindrical battle masts and was one deck lower amidships. Her secondary 15cm/5.9in turrets are more scattered, necessitating a greater weight of armour for the same scale of protection. Note how coal smoke disperses rapidly.

Fürst Bismarck, Prinz Heinrich and Prinz Adalbert class

The *Victoria Louise* was reckoned a Second Class (or "Overseas") cruiser and thought too light for fleet work. The *Fürst Bismarck*, laid down in 1896 was, therefore, armoured with both belt and protective deck (100–200mm/ 3.9–7.87in and 50mm/2in respectively). Considerably larger at 10,862 tonnes/ 10,690 tons, she nonetheless retained her predecessors' excellent seakeeping and manoeuvring characteristics, with high-freeboard forecastle, cutaway keel and triple shafts. Twin 24cm/9.4in turrets were located forward and aft, and ten 15cm/5.9in guns were distributed on three levels in a mixture of casemates and single turrets.

In terms of fighting power, the *Fürst Bismarck* was a great step forward but her speed of only 18 knots left her no margin over that of the capital ships with which she was intended to operate.

With a reduced specification, therefore, the *Prinz Heinrich* was laid

down in 1898. Distinguishable through her extra level amidships and slender, pole masts (in place of the *Fürst Bismarck*'s cylindrical structures), she had a single 24cm/9.4in gun at either end and ten 15cm/5.9in weapons. Her major dimensions were much the same but her belt thickness was halved. Her displacement was reduced by some 1,626 tonnes/1,600 tons and, with installed power increased by about 11 per cent, she showed an improved speed of 20 knots.

Two years later, the two Prinz Adalberts showed further refinement on a hull whose dimensions were still limited by existing facilities. On a slightly increased displacement, twin 21cm/8.2cm gun turrets were located forward and aft, the protective deck was thickened and power was increased by a further 13 per cent. The same number of boilers was provided but these were now arranged in three spaces, necessitating a third funnel.

Both Prinz Adalberts became war casualties in the Baltic. The others, having served as school ships were scrapped in 1919–20.

Fürst Bismarck, Prinz Heinrich and Prinz Adalbert class

	Built	Commissioned
Fürst Bismarck	Kiel Dockyard	1900
Prinz Heinrich	Kiel Dockyard	1902
Friedrich Carl	Blohm & Voss, Hamburg	1903
Prinz Adalbert	Kiel Dockyard	1904

Prinz Adalbert (as built)

Displacement: 9,235 tonnes/9,090 tons (normal); 10,033 tonnes/9,875 tons (full load)
Length: 124.9m/410ft (wl); 126.5m/415ft 3in (oa)
Beam: 19.6m/64ft 4in
Draught: 7.8m/25ft 7in (normal)
Armament: 4 x 21cm/8.3in (2x2), 10 x 15cm/5.9in (10x1) and 12 x 8.8cm/3.46in (12x1); 4 x 450mm/17.7in torpedo tubes (4x1)
Machinery: 3-cylinder, triple-expansion engines, 14 boilers, 3 shafts
Power: 12,677kW/17,000ihp for 20.5 knots
Endurance: 1,635 tonnes/1,610 tons (coal) and 180 tonnes/177 tons (oil) for 12,500km/6,750nm at 10 knots
Protection: 80–100mm/3.15–3.9in (belt); 40–80mm/1.57–3.15in (protective deck); 30–150mm/1.18–5.9in (turrets)
Complement: 528

LEFT: **Following on quickly, the two Prinz Adalberts increased displacement to combine the best features of their two predecessors. Existing dockyard facilities prevented any significant increase in dimensions but a revised boiler arrangement permitted an improved speed. The increased number of searchlights is due to the German Navy's advocation of night engagements.**

Roon class

Laid down in 1902–03, the *Roon* and *Yorck* (sometimes rendered *York*) were the last of a group of six Grosser Kreuzer that were tightly defined by length, the first of which was the *Fürst Bismarck*. Largely repeats of the *Prinz Adalbert*, they were only about 1.3m/4ft 3in longer but were able to accommodate two further boilers. Sixteen were now divided between four spaces, each with a funnel. They were given a further 0.5m/1ft 7in in beam but this was compensated with a thinner protective deck in order to realize 21 knots. Armament was essentially similar in both scale and layout.

By this time, the Imperial German Navy had developed a distinctive national style with a general air of purpose; masts and funnels were strongly vertical, the freeboard generous, and possessing an unmistakeable profile with its pronounced ram bow and "cruiser" stern. Triple-shaft propulsion was retained for, although the resulting machinery was heavier, it was of lower profile. Power transmitted per shaft was also less, permitting small-diameter propellers. This was a point of some significance as German ships had, perforce, to operate continually in very shallow water.

It says much for the pace of naval development, forced along by the "Dreadnought effect", that these fine cruisers should, by 1914, be deemed second-line units. The *Yorck* was, however, involved in the support of a battlecruiser bombardment of Great Yarmouth in November 1914. On her return to the Jade, she blundered into a "friendly" minefield. Striking two mines, she capsized, sinking with loss of 336 crew members.

Previously active against the Russian Baltic Fleet, the *Roon* was disarmed during 1916 with the intention of converting her to carry and operate a reported 8–10 seaplanes. For this service a replacement armament of just six 15cm/5.9in guns was planned. The project was never progressed and the ship was scrapped in 1920.

ABOVE LEFT: **Shipping a total of 16 boilers in four spaces, the *Roon* and *Yorck* (see here) added a fourth funnel. Their retention of reciprocating machinery required triple shafts and made for considerable vibration at higher speeds. The half-cased funnels, a weight-saving measure, became something of a German cruiser trademark.** ABOVE: **This impression of *Yorck* emphasizes her generous freeboard and rounded sheer strake. Note the twin 21cm/8.3in turret and the armoured conning tower immediately above it. The speed with which she capsized on being mined was a severe blow to morale.**

Roon class

	Built	Commissioned
Roon	Kiel Dockyard	1906
Yorck	Blohm & Voss, Hamburg	1905

Roon class

Displacement: 9,682 tonnes/9,530 tons (normal); 10,434 tonnes/10,270 tons (full load)
Length: 127.3m/417ft 10in (wl); 127.8m/419ft 6in (oa)
Beam: 20.2m/66ft 4in
Draught: 7.8m/25ft 5in (mean)
Armament: 4 x 21cm/8.3in (2x2) and 10 x 15cm/5.9in (10x1) and 14 x 8.8cm/3.46in (14x1) guns; 4 x 450mm/17.7in torpedo tubes (4x1)
Machinery: 3-cylinder, triple-expansion engines, 16 boilers, 3 shafts
Power: 14.168kW/19,000ihp for 21 knots
Endurance: 1,595 tonnes/1,570 tons (coal) and 211 tonnes/207 tons (oil) for 7,778km/4,200nm at 12 knots
Protection: 80–100mm/3.15–3.9in (belt); 40–60mm/1.57–2.4in (protective deck); 30–150mm/1.18–5.9in (turrets)
Complement: 550

ABOVE: **The Roons, of which the nameship is seen here, were the last to mount the upper tier of secondary weapons in turrets. This feature differentiates them clearly from the pair of Scharnhorsts, that followed. Already dated by 1914, she was destined for conversion to a seaplane carrier, but the work was never completed. The mainly coal-fired boilers were fitted with auxiliary oil sprayers.**

Minin, Vladimir Monomakh and Pamyat Azova

The 1880s were a period of strained relationships between Russia and Great Britain, and as a result the former's naval developments were of particular interest to the Royal Navy. Two prototype "belted cruisers", the 4,674-tonne/4,600-ton *General Admiral* and *Gerzog Edinburgski* had been launched in 1873–75 followed, three years later, by the greatly improved *Minin*.

Where the earlier ships were of the central-citadel type, with six large pivot guns firing over a low, reinforced parapet, the *Minin* mounted four 203mm/8in weapons, Russian-built breech-loaders in prominent sponsons, enabling two to bear forward and two aft. Of the twelve 152mm/6in weapons, eight fired on the broadside, two forward and two aft. The *Minin* had been planned originally as a turret ship but the disastrous sinking of the British *Captain* caused a redesign. Batteries on all three ships were unprotected, but all ships had a full-length 152mm/6in or 178mm/7in waterline belt.

The *Vladimir Monomakh* of 1882 was an improved *Minin*. Of much the same size, she repeated the armament layout but was constructed of steel rather than iron. Forty per cent more power required twin screws and produced a further 3 knots. Obsolete at Tsushima in 1905, she was sunk while escorting the fleet's transports.

Launched in 1887, the *Pamyat Azova* was a further development, refined for speed. Despite her longer and finer hull (115m/377ft x 15.2m/50ft compared with the *Monomakh*'s 90.4m/296.5ft x 15.8m/52ft), she was of little more displacement. Her belt was of 229mm/9in plate but

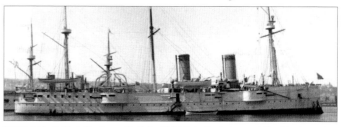

TOP LEFT: **Originally fitted with a heavy ship rig, the** *Minin* **later had her tophamper lightened to a barque rig, as here. Despite the rather disparaging comments of those who had visited her, the** *Minin*'s "big frigate" **format worried a British Admiralty responsible for trade protection.** TOP RIGHT: **In comparison with the 13-knot, single-screw** *Minin*, **the** *Pamyat Azova* **was a relative flyer, with twin screws driving her at 18 knots. Less heavily but still adequately armed, she would have posed the greater menace being more able to decline engagement. Her armour belt was very shallow, probably submerged in the ship's deep condition.** ABOVE: **Although slightly smaller, the** *Vladimir Monomakh* **was an improved** *Minin*. **She carried a deep full-length belt of slightly thinner armour but her more powerful machinery drove her twin shafts for an extra 2.5 knots. All her secondary weapons fired on the broadside, only her prominently sponsoned 203mm/8in guns enjoying axial fire. The sponsons appear vulnerable to damage by slamming.**

shallow and terminating short of bow and stern. It was backed by a largely flat 64mm/2.5in protective deck. Only two 203mm/8in guns were carried, with power increased by over 50 per cent to give 18 knots.

Reduced to depot ship status, she was torpedoed and sunk in the course of the attack on Kronstadt by British Coastal Motor Boats (CMBs) in August 1919.

General Admiral, Gerzog Edinburgski, Minin, Vladimir Monomakh and Pamyat Azova

	Built	Commissioned
General Admiral	Baltic Yard, St. Petersburg	1876
Gerzog Edinburgski	Baltic Yard, St. Petersburg	1878
Minin	Baltic Yard, St. Petersburg	1881
Vladimir Monomakh	Baltic Yard, St. Petersburg	1885
Pamyat Azova	Baltic Yard, St. Petersburg	1891

Minin

Displacement: 5,845 tonnes/5,740 tons (normal); 6,250 tonnes/6,140 tons (full load)
Length: 90.9m/298ft 6in (bp)
Beam: 15m/49ft 3in
Draught: 7.7m/25ft 3in (normal)
Armament: 4 x 203mm/8in BL and 12 x 152mm/6in BL guns
Machinery: Steam reciprocating engine, 1 shaft
Power: 4,476kW/6,000ihp for 13.5 knots
Bunkers: 1,222 tonnes/1,200 tons (coal)
Protection: 178mm/7in (full length belt)
Complement: 450

Bogatyr

During the late 1890s the Russian Navy, having concentrated on the acquisition of large armoured cruisers, was deficient in smaller, protected cruisers. In 1898 a common specification was sent to six builders resulting in contracts for the three best competing designs. In addition to the *Bogatyr*, from AG Vulcan, Krupp built the *Askold* and Cramp (Philadelphia) the *Varyag*.

Of the three, the *Bogatyr* was shortest but beamiest. Her protective deck was of 51mm/2in plate, compared with the others' 76mm/3in, but her funnel uptakes were better protected. Where her competitors' twelve 152mm/6in guns were largely in open mountings protected only by shields, the *Bogatyr* housed four guns in twin turrets and

four in casemates, with only the remaining four in open mountings. This refinement increased displacement considerably but the contract speed was still attained comfortably.

The advantages of protection for gun crews were proven conclusively in the course of the Russo-Japanese War, when reports spoke constantly of those serving open mountings being scythed down by hails of splinters, and crushed by falling rigging.

Being attached to the Vladivostok squadron, the *Bogatyr* was spared the debacle of Tsushima, although it is noteworthy that, of the six Russian protected cruisers present, only one, the oldest, was sunk. Three of these, however, sought internment at Manila.

From the outset of World War I, Russian and German naval forces contested the Baltic. The *Bogatyr*'s minelaying capacity was well-utilized, but her most telling contribution to the war came as early as August 26, 1914. When the German cruiser *Magdeburg* was stranded on the Estonian coast, the timely arrival of the *Bogatyr* and another cruiser obliged the former's crew to blow up their ship. In their haste, they neglected to destroy their code books. These quickly found their way into British hands and subsequently proved to be of inestimable value, the fact of their compromise being kept secret.

Bogatyr (as built)

Built: AG Vulcan, Stettin
Commissioned: 1901
Displacement: 6,751 tonnes/6,645 tons (normal)
Length: 127m/416ft 9in (bp)
Beam: 16.6m/54ft 6in
Draught: 6.3m/20ft 9in mean
Armament: 12 x 152mm/6in (2x2/8x1) and 12 x 76mm/3in (12x1) guns; 6 x 450mm/17.7in torpedo tubes (6x1)
Machinery: Triple-expansion reciprocating engines, 2 shafts
Power: 15,100kW/20,250ihp for 24 knots
Bunkers: 1,118 tonnes/1,100 tons (coal)
Protection: 51mm/2in (protective deck); 89–127mm/3.5–5in (turrets)
Complement: 580

ABOVE: The *Bogatyr* as delivered, and probably painted for Black Sea service. Note that, in contrast to the World War I picture (above), she carries light anti-torpedo nets and more complex masting. Her hull has both raised forecastle and poop, each carrying a twin 152mm/6in turret flanked by a single, casemated 152mm/6in gun at a lower level.

Rurik

The first of three large, domestically constructed cruisers, the *Rurik* combined firepower with, for the day, considerable speed. The potential of such ships for commerce raiding concerned the British Admiralty to the extent that it produced the two Powerfuls. These were large enough to operate in Far Eastern waters, but great length was the key parameter for all such ships, influencing maximum practicable speed and the volume within which the necessary machinery had to be accommodated. Also a factor in displacement, it thus influenced the limits of armour.

For extended endurance, the *Rurik* was given a heavy barque rig whose windage, even without sails spread,

influenced both speed and ship motion. Because of the standing rigging, the ship's four 203mm/8in guns were mounted in sided sponsons, two forward, two aft. They shared the upper deck with six 119mm/4.7in QF guns which, likewise, were protected only by shields. On the main deck, the secondary armament comprised sixteen 152mm/6in QF weapons of which twelve were mounted in an open, broadside battery, devoid of any screens between the weapons.

About the waterline the *Rurik* had a thick, but shallow, composite belt backed by a flat protective deck. It was to penetrate such belts that larger British cruisers carried a pair of 234mm/9.2in guns. In practice, this was too few.

ABOVE: **Although her size commanded much respect, the *Rurik* shows her vulnerability in the huge expanse of unprotected hull. Her shallow belt extended from the forward embrasure as far aft as the mizzen mast but, on full load displacement, it barely extended above the the waterline, a very common failing.**

When inspected by the foreign technical press in 1895, the *Rurik* impressed with her firepower but also with the sheer vulnerability of her gunnery positions. Their dismissal of the ship as something of a "paper tiger" proved to be warranted. At the Battle of Ulsan in August 1904 she, as the smallest of the three Russian cruisers, attracted the heaviest Japanese fire. Holed aft, beyond the limit of the belt, her steering flat was flooded, with water penetrating progressively forward. With nearly 500 dead and wounded, her topsides a ruin, she was finally scuttled.

ABOVE: **In dark livery, the odd cross-section of the *Rurik*'s centre body is here well caught by the light. Reminiscent of "turret" merchant ships, the upper hull has been reduced in beam, to both reduce topweight and to improve the arcs of fire of her still essentially broadside armament.**

Rurik

Built: Baltic Yard, St. Petersburg
Commissioned: 1895
Displacement: 11,122 tonnes/10,923 tons (normal)
Length: 120.8m/396ft 6in (bp)
Beam: 20.4m/67ft
Draught: 7.9m/26ft (normal)
Armament: 4 x 203mm/8in BL, 16 x 152mm/6in QF and 6 x 119mm/4.7in QF guns
Machinery: Steam reciprocating engines, 2 shafts
Power: 9,880kW/13,250ihp for 18.5 knots
Bunkers: 2,032 tonnes/2,000 tons (coal)
Protection: 127–254mm/5–10in (composite armour belt); 64mm/2.5in (protective deck)
Complement: 770

Rossia and *Gromoboi*

B uilt as improved Ruriks, the *Rossia* and the *Gromoboi* were, likewise, designed to operate as long-endurance raiders. To this end, they could stow an enormous 2,540 tonnes/2,500 tons of coal, sufficient to steam from St. Petersburg to Vladivostock without refuelling. They were also built with a three-masted, barquentine sailing rig, an encumbrance later replaced with two orthodox masts. Again, however, its legacy was to oblige the ships' four 203mm/8in guns to be located in sponsons to avoid standing rigging.

Near, but not exact, sisters, they were some 1,219 tonnes/1,200 tons greater than the *Rurik*. They carried a similar scale of armament but, being considerably longer, were able to arrange it more safely. Of the two, the *Rossia*'s layout was the weaker, showing little improvement on that of the *Rurik*. In order to increase the training arcs of the sponsoned 203mm/8in guns, the ship's

sides were given considerable tumblehome. They were pierced with five 152mm/6in gun-ports per side. Her belt was as shallow as the *Rurik*'s.

Completed two years later, the *Gromoboi* (whose odd-sounding name means Thunderer) was greatly improved in having armour extended to upper deck level over that length of the sides that included the gun positions. Six 152mm/6in guns, individually casemated, fired on each broadside. Those farthest forward and aft shared two-storey casemates with the 203mm/8in weapons. To compensate for her extended vertical protection, the *Gromoboi* had a thinner protective deck.

Triple-screw ships, they never achieved their intended 20 knots although, at the Battle of Ulsan, in which the *Rurik* was lost, they survived only by out-running the pursuing Japanese armoured cruisers. Each ship received two dozen and more hits and, while their

ABOVE: The *Gromoboi* differed from the *Rossia* in the double-level casemates abreast the bridge, the upper housing a 203mm/8in gun, the lower one the twelve main deck 152mm/6in weapons. Her original three-masted rig is more decorative than functional.

armour was nowhere pierced, the carnage on the unprotected upper levels was appalling. Being based at Vladivostock, neither was at Tsushima.

Rossia and *Gromoboi*

	Built	Commissioned
Gromoboi	Baltic Yard, St. Petersburg	1900
Rossia	Baltic Yard, St. Petersburg	1898

Rossia (as built)

Displacement: 12,325 tonnes/12,130 tons (normal)
Length: 143.8m/472ft (wl); 146.2m/480ft (oa)
Beam: 20.9m/68ft 6in
Draught: 8m/26ft 3in (normal)
Armament: 4 x 203mm/8in, 16 x 152mm/6in QF and 6 x 119mm/4.7in QF guns; 6 x 450mm/17.7in torpedo tubes
Machinery: Vertical, triple-expansion engines, 32 boilers, 3 shafts
Power: 10,812kW/14,500ihp for 19 knots
Endurance: 2,545 tonnes/2,500 tons (coal) for 35,188km/19,000nm at 10 knots
Protection: 102–203mm/4–8in (belt), 64mm/2.5in (protective deck)
Complement: 725

LEFT: Originally rigged like her near-sister *Gromoboi*, the *Rossia* was greatly improved in appearance by alterations effected when repairing heavy damage sustained during the war with Japan. She is seen here attending the 1911 Coronation review at Spithead. Note the elaborate configuration of her hull to improve firing arcs.

Almirante Oquendo class

Launched from 1890, the three Oquendos were, for their size, heavily armed and armoured. They were, however, badly designed. Their belt, at an impressive 300mm/11.8in in thickness, was so heavy that it was limited to only about 1.7m/5ft 7in in depth, over two-thirds the hull length. It was roofed by a flat, protective deck which, raised to cover the engine crowns, sloped only at either end, towards bow and stern.

The hull had a flush upper deck, into which, forward and aft, was recessed a 270mm/10.5in barbette. These each supported a 28cm/11in breech-loading gun, covered by a shallow, dome-shaped cupola of only 76mm/3in thickness.

Between the two barbettes, the central section of the ships was ringed by deep, but unarmoured, bulwarks. Behind were located ten 14cm/5.5in guns. Six of these fired broadside,

through ports; the other four were sponsored for axial fire.

One level below, the middle deck housed a battery of quick-firers, both 57mm/2.24in Nordenfelts and 37mm/1.46in Hotchkiss. Firing through small, shuttered ports, these occupied a largely open-plan internal space.

Probably to save weight, both upper and middle decks were of wood planking laid directly on to the ships' beams, without steel underlay. This was a critically weak feature, but the Oquendos were designed before the Battle of the Yalu (1894) reminded the naval world of the hazards of fire.

During the short Spanish-American War of 1898, all three Oquendos, together with the Italian-built *Cristobal Colon*, were blockaded by a more powerful American squadron in the bottle-necked Santiago de Cuba. Ordered to break out,

the Spanish were destroyed piecemeal in a long pursuit. Ravaged by fire, their deck burned away, their armour unpierced but their unprotected topsides wrecked, each in turn was run aground to prevent further useless loss of life.

Almirante Oquendo class

	Built	Commissioned
Almirante Oquendo	Anglo-Spanish Shipbuilding Co, Bilbao	1892
Infanta Maria Teresa	Anglo-Spanish Shipbuilding Co, Bilbao	1891
Viscaya	Anglo-Spanish Shipbuilding Co, Bilbao	1893

Almirante Oquendo

Displacement: 7,010 tonnes/6,900 tons (normal)
Length: 103.6m 340ft (oa)
Beam: 19.8m/65ft
Draught: 6.6m/21ft 6in (normal)
Armament: 2 x 28cm/11in BL and 10 x 14cm/5.5in BL guns; 8 x 356mm/14in torpedo tubes
Machinery: Vertical, triple-expansion engines, 2 shafts
Power: 9,694kW/13,000ihp for 20 knots
Protection: 305mm/12in (partial belt); 51–76mm/2–3in (protective deck); 267mm/10.5in (barbettes)
Complement: 460

LEFT: The mercantile-style counter stern of the *Reina Regente* was structurally weaker than the more usual, rounded "cruiser" stern, and exposed the rudder more readily to damage. BELOW: The low-freeboard forward and after ends of the design were, presumably, a weight-saving measure, but probably resulted in a higher centre of gravity.

Reina Regente class

The Oquendo-class armoured cruisers were built by an Anglo-Spanish company, and their not un-British character may well have been further influenced by the three Reina Regentes, built shortly before. Somewhat smaller protected cruisers, these were launched between 1887 and 1893. Armstrong, at Elswick, had lobbied hard for the contract but their proposal was not accepted. (It wasn't wasted effort, being used as the basis for the design of the USS *Baltimore*). The specified armament for the preferred design by Thomson, on Clydebank, may also have been influenced by Armstrong's reputation for "plenty of guns". This, while displacing only 5,029 tonnes/4,950 tons, carried four 24cm/9.5in and six 12cm/4.72in guns.

Like the Oquendos, the Reina Regentes were flush-decked, and mounted all significant armament at upper-deck level. All guns were on open mountings, protected by shields. The 24cm/9.5in weapons were sided, forward and aft. The high amidships bulkhead was given a feature, broken by gun-ports through which the 12cm/4.72in and 6pdr guns fired in broadside.

Only the lead ship was British-built, the other pair was of domestic construction. The design was orthodox, with a full-length, vaulted protective deck. The only unusual feature was that the ram bow was complemented by a mercantile-style counter stern.

The *Reina Regente* disappeared, with all aboard (reportedly 402) on or about March 10, 1895, apparently foundering through stress of weather south-east of Cape Trafalgar. An official inquiry reached the conclusion that,

while running light on bunkers and stores, she was rendered unstable by virtue of her heavy armament.

Although relatively new ships her two sisters were retained in home waters during the 1898 war with the United States. They were regarded as being too "defective in design and speed" to allow them to be despatched to Cuba.

A replacement cruiser, unarmoured but carrying the name *Reina Regente* was completed in 1908.

Reina Regente class

	Built	Commissioned
Alfonso XIII	Ferrol Dockyard	1893
Lepanto	Cartagena Dockyard	1895
Reina Regente	Thomson, Clydebank	1888

Reina Regente (as built)

Displacement: 5,029 tonnes/4,950 tons (normal)
Length: 97m/318ft 6in (oa)
Beam: 15.4m/50ft 6in
Draught: 6.1m/20ft (normal)
Armament: 4 x 24cm/9.5in Bland 6 x 12cm/4.72in QF guns; 5 x 350mm/14in torpedo tubes
Machinery: Vertical, triple-expansion engines, 2 shafts
Power: 8,579kW/11,500ihp for 20 knots
Bunkers: 1,118 tonnes/1,100 tons (coal)
Protection: 75–120mm/2.95–4.7in (protective deck)
Complement: 275

ABOVE: The *Alfonso XIII* clearly shows the major design drawback of all guns, primary and secondary, being carried in open mountings, exposing their crews to blast and fragments.

LEFT: **Seen dressed overall for, presumably, a royal visit, the *Emperador Carlos V* was, by a considerable margin, the largest cruiser in the Spanish Navy, 15.2m/50ft longer than the solitary battleship, *Pelayo*.** ABOVE: **The design of the 28cm/11in Honoria gun mountings exposed a considerable amount of the 450mm/17.5in barbette, theoretically immune to the largest guns then at sea. The ship's belt, however, was proof against only cruiser gunfire.**

Emperador Carlos V

Launched in 1895, some four years after the *Oquendo*, the *Carlos V* (*Carlos Quinto*) made an interesting comparison. The former was an armoured cruiser, with a shallow, 305mm/12in belt and a 58mm/2.3in protective deck, while the latter, a protected cruiser, had no belt as such but a deck of up to 152mm/6in thick. Carrying similar armaments, and both powered for 20 knots, the protected cruiser was the heavier by some 2,134 tonnes/2,100 tons. One reason was that the *Carlos V* was about 12.2m/40ft longer, as was the central, high-bulwarked redoubt. Unarmoured on the earlier ships, both the bulwark and the middle-deck plating below it were of 51mm/2in plate. Six 14cm/5.5in QF guns fired through ports in the bulwark. Two

more, together with four 10cm/3.9in guns, fired through middle deck ports. The upper deck 14cm/5.5in weapons were in open mountings with shields.

The protective deck on the Oquendos was largely flat, but that on the *Carlos V* sloped from above to well below the waterline. Above and below it were deep coal bunkers, which flanked the machinery and boiler spaces.

Except for her disappointingly low maximum speed, the *Carlos V* should have made a better fighting ship than the Oquendos, although all were plagued by unreliable ammunition. It is perhaps fortunate that her qualities were never tested in the war in the United States.

With the commencement of hostilities, she was first ordered to raid commerce on the US Eastern Seaboard. However,

this was quickly changed to head eastward with auxiliaries to reinforce the Philippines. Countermanded again, she was then ordered to return to home waters to meet the threat posed by a rumoured American squadron. This confusion illustrates the difficulty of meeting worldwide commitments with an inadequate navy.

Following the war with the United States, her peaceful seagoing career lasted until 1927, following which she served for five years as an accommodation ship before being scrapped.

Emperador Carlos V

Built: Cadiz Dockyard
Commissioned: 1897
Displacement: 9,398 tonnes/9,250 tons (normal);
    10,058 tonnes/9.900 tons (full load)
Length: 115.8m/380ft (bp); 123.3m/404ft 8in (oa)
Beam: 20.4m/67ft
Draught: 8.7m/28ft 6in (full load)
Armament: 2 x 28cm/11in, 8 x 14cm/5.5in and
    4 x 10cm/3.9in guns; 2 x 350mm/14in torpedo
    tubes
Machinery: 4-cylinder, triple-expansion engines,
    12 boilers, 2 shafts
Power: 13,800kW/18,500ihp for 20 knots
Bunkers: 2,082 tonnes/2,050 tons (coal)
Protection: 64–152mm/2.5–6in (protective deck);
    51mm/2in (upper sides – partial); 254mm/10in
    barbettes
Complement: 555

ABOVE: **Note how the ship's proportions are enhanced by terminating the black hull paint at upper deck level. The white central battery comprised eight 14cm/5.5in guns of French manufacture.**

LEFT: **Laying to a mooring buoy, the** *Kaiser Franz Josef I* **shows her barbette-mounted 24cm/9.5in guns to advantage. The side-casemated 15cm/5.9in weapons were carried too low to be of practical use.** BELOW: **Equivalent in size and protection to a contemporary British Astraea, the** *Franz Josef I* **carried a much heavier-calibre armament. By 1914 they were obsolescent.**

Kaiser Franz Josef I class

In August 1914 the dual monarchy of Austria-Hungary possessed the world's eighth-largest fleet. On the last day of October 1918 its ships hauled down their colours and the service ceased to exist. Despite having Europe's third-largest population, the empire claimed no foreign territory, so that a blue-water navy was always hard to justify when what was really required was an adequate defence force to protect the long eastern coastline of the Adriatic.

Under Wilhelm von Tegetthoff, the victor of Lissa, the navy had achieved direction but, following his premature death in 1871, its fortunes lapsed under the lacklustre Sterneck, and it built little of note.

Two protected cruisers, *Kaiser Franz Josef I* and *Kaiserin Elisabeth* were launched in 1889–90. Although small, they were built with single 24cm/9.5in

guns in barbettes forward and aft. Of their six 15cm/5.9in weapons, two were sided in open mountings on upper-deck sponsons and the remainder in casemates at middle-deck level, their barrels a bare three metres above the (normal) waterline.

Both were modernized in 1904–06, losing their oversized guns (and being demoted from "Grosser" to "Kleiner Kreuzer"). In their place, two further 15cm/5.9in pieces were acquired. These were 40-calibre Skodas, superior to the others, which were of the older, 35-calibre Krupp design. Both ships had their funnels raised considerably.

Together with a handful of minor German warships, the *Kaiserin Elisabeth* found herself in the beleaguered German enclave at Tsingtao in 1914. During the three-month siege, her two best guns

and some smaller pieces, together with 120 men, were landed to assist in defence. Unable to escape, the ship was scuttled a few days before the base capitulated to an Anglo-Japanese force.

The *Kaiser Franz Josef I* was restricted to local defence at Cattaro (now Kotor). Ceded to France in 1919, she sank while under tow.

Kaiser Franz Josef I class

	Built	Commissioned
Kaiser Franz Josef I	Stabilimento Tecnico Triestino, Trieste	July 2, 1890
Kaiserin Elisabeth	Pola Dockyard	November 24, 1892

Kaiser Franz Josef I (as built)

Displacement: 4,115 tonnes/4,050 tons (normal)
Length: 98m/321ft 8in (bp); 103.8m/340ft 9in (oa)
Beam: 14.8m/48ft 7in
Draught: 5.6m/18ft 4in (normal)
Armament: 2 x 24cm/9.5in and 6 x 15cm/5.9in guns; 4 x 450mm/17.7in torpedo tubes
Machinery: Horizontal, triple-expansion engines, 4 boilers, 2 shafts
Power: 6,341kW/8,500ihp for 19 knots
Endurance: 671 tonnes/660 tons (coal) for 5,926km/3,200nm at 10 knots
Protection: 57mm/2.2in (protective deck)
Complement: 435

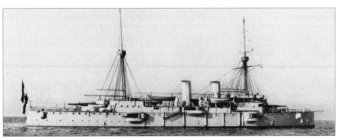

ABOVE: **Seen in a 20th-century overall grey paint scheme, the** *Kaiserin Elisabeth* **could be differentiated by her foremast, crossed with two yards. She was unfortunate in being caught and destroyed at Tsingtao in 1914.**

LEFT: All three pictures on this page show the ship in her original state, prior to her 1910 rebuilding and rearming. The deep forward facets and all sponsoned casemates would be removed.

ABOVE: The massive tubular "battlemasts" were also exchanged for light poles in order to reduce topweight, but nothing was done to improve the inadequate forward freeboard.

Kaiserin und Königen Maria Theresia

Because Austria-Hungary was an empire encompassing a dual monarchy, Maria Theresia was both Empress and Queen, accounting for the unwieldly name borne by an armoured cruiser launched in 1893. Interestingly, the name, as generally written, would have appeared even more ungainly, for the standard abbreviation for both "Kaiserin und Königen" and the warship prefix of "Kaiserlich und Königlich" (i.e. Imperial and Royal) was "KuK". The name would thus be rendered KuK KuK Maria Theresia.

The belt armour fronting the protective deck was very shallow. A considerable amount of 100mm/3.9in plate was applied to the levels above it, in the areas of the forward and aft barbettes and casemates, as well as the amidships casemates. There were also transverse bulkheads of the same thickness enclosing what was referred to as a "citadel". Topside weight was further increased by two lofty "battlemasts", heavy tubular structures.

As built, the ship carried a 24cm/9.5in gun on the barbettes at either end. Of the eight 15cm/5.9in weapons, four were mounted in protruding casemates, and four in open mountings atop the citadel.

During 1909 the 24cm/9.5in guns and heavy barbettes were removed in favour of two 19cm/7.5in pieces in enclosed gunhouses. Further weight was saved by replacing the battlemasts with light poles. The 15cm/5.9in armament was relocated to accommodate sixteen 4.7cm/1.85in QF guns within and atop the citadel.

These fired 1.5kg/3.3lb projectiles and were for repelling torpedo craft.

Making only 19.35 knots on her initial trials nearly 20 years earlier, the KuK Maria Theresia was, by 1914, slower than even the fleet's remaining pre-Dreadnoughts. She was first based at Sebenico (now Sibenik) in a coastal defence role. By 1917, she was at Pola (now Pula), acting as accommodation ship for the crews of its growing German submarine flotilla. She was scrapped in 1920 following an undistinguished career.

Kaiserin und Königen Maria Theresia (as built)

Built: Stabilimento Tecnico Triestino, Trieste
Commissioned: March 24, 1895
Displacement: 5,202 tonnes/5,120 tons (normal)
Length: 106.7m/350ft 3in (bp); 114m/374ft 2in (wl)
Beam: 16.2m/53ft 2in
Draught: 6.5m/21ft 4in (normal)
Armament: 2 x 24cm/9.5in BL and
  8 x 15cm/5.9in QF guns;
  4 x 450mm/17.7in torpedo tubes
Machinery: Horizontal, triple-expansion engines, 10 boilers, 2 shafts
Power: 7,274kW/9,750ihp for 19 knots
Endurance: 752 tonnes/740 tons (coal) for 6,482km/3,500nm at 10 knots
Protection: 100mm/3.9in (citadel sides); 57mm/2.2in (protective deck)
Complement: 485

ABOVE: Another picture of the ship in her original paint scheme, the white area of which emphasized the height of the unarmoured central superstructure. The barbette-mounted main-calibre guns were later exchanged for lighter weapons in round mountings.

LEFT: The imposing appearance of the *Kaiser Karl VI* belies her displacement of less than 7,112 tonnes/7,000 tons. Her single 24cm/9.5in guns, forward and aft, were less effective than they looked as only two barrels, without proper fire control, were insufficient to sustain accurate fire at extended ranges. BELOW LEFT: At about 20 knots, the wave profile created by the *Sankt Georg* indicates a rather inefficient hull form. The sponsored secondary and tertiary armament must have been the cause of much wetness in heavy weather. The permanent awnings amidships were presumably to cool the machinery spaces.

Kaiser Karl VI and *Sankt Georg*

An improved version of the *KuK Maria Theresia*, the *Kaiser Karl VI* was laid down the year after the former's commissioning. For a further 5m/16ft 5in in length she could carry the same armament as well as accommodate an extra 33 per cent boiler capacity, enabling her to comfortably exceed her designed 20-knot speed.

Less bulky topside than her predecessor, the *Karl VI* carried her two 24cm/9.5in guns in turrets, rather than barbettes. A retrograde step was to locate all 15cm/5.9in secondary armament at middle-deck level. All were accommodated in armoured casemates, with two each firing axially forward and aft along facets in the hull. The others were paired amidships in extraordinarily large, sponsoned casemates which must have pounded severely in poor conditions.

Upon the *Karl VI*'s completion, she, too, was followed by an improved derivative. Identifiable by her three thicker funnels, the *Sankt Georg* (St. George) was longer by a further 3m/9ft 10in, also well exceeding her contract speed. Her belt armour was thinned by 10mm/0.4in and protective deck thickened by 5mm/0.2in.

Although the disposition of the armament was similar, its power was considerably enhanced at the expense of introducing a third major calibre. The two 24cm/9.5in guns were now sited in a twin turret forward, the after turret accommodating a single 19cm/7.5in. Four 15cm/5.9in weapons fired axially forward and aft, as before, but the large sponsoned amidships casemates now housed two more 19cm/7.5in barrels per side. A greater proportion of the

Sankt Georg's firepower was thus carried very close to the waterline. While unsatisfactory for oceanic operations, it was probably justifiable in the more benign conditions to be expected in the Adriatic.

Neither ship saw significant action, probably contributing to their crews being in the forefront of the fleet mutiny of spring 1918. Both were scrapped in 1920.

Kaiser Karl VI and *Sankt Georg*

	Built	Commissioned
Kaiser Karl VI	Stabilimento Tecnico Triestino, Trieste	May 23, 1900
Sankt Georg	Pola Dockyard	July 21, 1905

Sankt Georg (as built)

Displacement: 7,315 tonnes/7,185 tons (normal); 7,555 tonnes/7,420 tons (full load)
Length: 117m/384ft (bp); 122m/400ft 6in (wl)
Beam: 18.8m/61ft 9in
Draught: 6.5m/21ft 4in (normal)
Armament: 2 x 24cm/9.5in (1x2), 5 x 19cm/7.5in (5x2) guns and 4 x 15cm/5.9in (4x1) guns; 2 x 450mm/17.7in torpedo tubes
Machinery: Vertical, triple-expansion engines, 12 boilers, 2 shafts
Power: 11,372kW/15,250ihp for 22 knots
Endurance: 804 tonnes/790 tons (coal) for 8,334km/4,500nm at 10 knots
Protection: 210mm/8.25in (belt); 65mm/2.5in (protective deck); 210mm/8.25in (turrets); 135–150mm/5.3–5.9in (casemates)
Complement: 630

LEFT: **Much of the long, lean hull of the *Admiral Spaun* is devoted to no less than 16 boilers. Unlike her improved derivatives, she had four shafts, their turbines located between the aftermost funnel and the mainmast. Note how little impact the ship's seven 10cm/3.9in guns have on her overall appearance.**

Admiral Spaun and Zenta class

Designed to carry seven tubes, the three Zenta-class "torpedo cruisers" were of a size, and contemporary with, the British Pelorus class. They carried eight 12cm/4.72in guns to the British ships' eight 102mm/4in, at the cost of a slightly beamier form and about a half-knot in speed. One centreline gun was carried forward and aft, with three on either side in the waist, mounted inside shutters. A sailplan was included.

Modernization saw the turtleback forecastle given a more orthodox sheer strake, while the waist guns were lowered one level, with a spardeck above. The masting was reduced and five torpedo tubes landed. One of these had fired through the stern, the profile of which was modified.

The eight British scout cruisers, commissioned in 1905 were influential

but, although fast, lacked size and endurance. Intended to undertake a similar role, the *Admiral Spaun* was somewhat larger. Her boilers developed 50 per cent more power and, being later, the ship had the benefit of steam turbines, with their greatly superior power-to-weight ratio. Capable of 27 knots, the *Spaun* and her three improved derivatives were heavily used during the sea war in the Adriatic.

All the type were badly under-armed, with guns of only 10cm/3.9in calibre. There was a wartime intention to upgrade the battery to five 15cm/5.9in guns but they could not be taken out of service long enough to effect the improvement.

The older *Spaun* was scrapped in 1920 but the three derivative were assimilated into the French and Italian

fleets. The *Novarra* became the French *Thionville*, the *Helgoland* and *Saida* the Italian *Brindisi* and *Venezia* respectively.

Admiral Spaun and Zenta class

	Built	Commissioned
Aspern	Pola Dockyard	May 29, 1900
Szigetvar	Pola Dockyard	September 30, 1901
Zenta	Pola Dockyard	May 28, 1899
Admiral Spaun	Pola Dockyard	November 15, 1914
Helgoland	Ganz & Danubius, Fiume	August 29, 1914
Novarra	Ganz & Danubius, Fiume	January 10, 1915
Saida	Cantiere Naval Triestino, Monfalcone	August 1, 1914

Improved Spaun class (as built)

Displacement: 3,592 tonnes/3,535 tons (normal); 4,491 tonnes/4,420 tons (full load)
Length: 125.2m 411ft (bp); 130.6m/428ft 8in (wl)
Beam: 12.8m/42ft
Draught: 5.3m/17ft 3in (full load)
Armament: 9 x 10cm/3.9in guns; 6 x 450mm/17.7in torpedo tubes
Machinery: Direct-drive steam turbines, 16 boilers, 2 shafts
Power: 19,090kW/25,600shp for 27 knots
Endurance: 865 tonnes/850 tons (coal) for 2,963km/1,600nm at 24 knots
Protection: 60mm/2.4in (partial belt); 20mm/0.8in (protective deck)
Complement: 330

ABOVE: **The distinction of firing the opening shots of World War I in the Adriatic fell to the *Szigetvar* (shown here) and her sister, *Zenta*. Her war ended ignominiously with mutiny, downgrading as obsolete to an accommodation hulk, cession to Great Britain as reparation and immediate scrapping in Italy.**

Directory of Cruisers

World War I

Traditional cruisers and their roles were greatly affected by World War I for, although British maritime superiority was assured by the Grand Fleet, the actual outcome of the conflict came to depend upon the defence of trade against an entirely unpredicted submarine threat.

In the early days, British cruisers proved highly vulnerable to U-boat attack but, for the Germans, employment of regular cruisers as commerce raiders proved a wasted resource, they being superseded by cheaper and more effective auxiliary raiders.

Where Germany's few modern armoured cruisers were deployed in distant operations, they proved doughty opponents, but those British examples closely integrated with the battle fleet fared badly by being brought within range of hostile capital ships.

Emerging supreme from war experience were the fleet cruisers typified by the "Towns" of both sides and the British "C" class. Fast and well-armed, they dominated war-emergency building programmes, proving to be tough and well able to absorb punishment.

LEFT: **Commenced during 1896 as a speculative venture, Armstrong at Elswick sold the *Asama* and her sister, *Tokiwa*, to Japan in the following year. Note the early cylindrical, twin 203mm/8in turrets, two-level 152mm/6in casemates and anti-torpedo nets.**

LEFT: **Completed in 1900, the Second Class protected cruiser *Highflyer* remains linked to the sailing navy through her complex masting, the old-style fidded topmasts being supported by crosstrees and futtock shrouds. Although at anchor, she is wearing no jack and her forward end has apparently been "cleared".**

BELOW: **Shorter and beamier than the Highflyers, the four Arrogant type were designed for great manoeuvrability, being among the last ships intended to deliberately ram opponents. For this function they had strengthened bows and twin rudders. The *Gladiator* is seen here as a new ship. Their original mixed armament was changed to a uniform 152mm/6in during 1903–04.**

Arrogant and Highflyer classes

Both classes were categorized as "Second Class cruisers". All four Arrogants were laid down in Royal Dockyards during 1895–96 and were among the last ships designed to use their rams tactically. For this, good manoeuvrability was essential, the ships being designed with a length-on-beam (L/B) ratio of only 5.6, with pronounced cut-ups and large rudder area.

Three funnels and a forest of ventilators defined the extent of the boiler spaces and the normal use of natural draught. The lofty masts included topmasts, fidded and braced, still in sailing-ship fashion. Both were crossed by a pair of yards, and supported fighting tops equipped with small quick-firing Maxim guns.

Following criticisms of inadequate armament, their six waist 119mm/4.7in guns were upgraded to 152mm/6in weapons in about 1903–04, making a total of ten 152mm/6in guns.

Of the class, *Vindictive* earned fame on the Zeebrugge and Ostend raids of 1918. The *Gladiator*, ironically, was sunk by collision in the Solent during 1908.

Ordered under the 1896–97 Estimates, the three Highflyers were essentially three-funnelled Eclipses. At 9.1m/30ft longer than the Arrogants, and with L/B increased to about 6.5, they could make nearly 2 knots more on the same power. Like the Arrogants, they exchanged their six waist 119mm/4.7in guns for 152mm/6in ordnance to give a total of eleven, only six of which could fire in broadside.

Being "protected", the two classes had full-length, vaulted armoured decks, increased in height in way of the tall engine assemblies. Deep wing coal bunkers served as side protection in lieu of an armoured belt. As was then common, the bottoms were wood sheathed and coppered to reduce fouling.

The *Hermes* was the first Royal Navy ship to be adapted (1913) for the carriage and operation of seaplanes. On August 26, 1914, her sister, *Highflyer*, entered territorial waters to sink the 13,950grt NDL liner *Kaiser Wilhelm der Grosse*, which was operating as an armed raider.

Arrogant and Highflyer classes

	Built	Commissioned
Arrogant	Devonport Dockyard	1898–99
Furious	Devonport Dockyard	1898–99
Gladiator	Portsmouth Dockyard	1898–99
Vindictive	Chatham Dockyard	1898–99
Hermes	Fairfield, Glasgow	1900–01
Highflyer	Fairfield, Glasgow	1900–01
Hyacinth	London & Glasgow	1900–01

Highflyer class (as built)

Displacement: 5,740 tonnes/5,650 tons (standard)
Length: 106.6m/350ft (bp); 113.6m/373ft (oa)
Beam: 16.5m/54ft
Draught: 6.4m/21ft (normal)
Armament: 5 x 152mm/6in (5x1), 6 x 119mm/4.7in (6x1) and 9 x 12pdr (9x1) guns; 2 x 457mm/18in torpedo tubes (fixed, submerged) (2x1)
Machinery: 2 sets 4-cylinder vertical, triple-expansion engines, 18 boilers, 2 shafts
Power: 7,460kW/10,000ihp, 19.5 knots
Endurance: 584 tonnes/575 tons (coal) for 10,186km/5,500nm at 10 knots
Protection: 36–76mm/1.5–3in (protective deck)
Complement: 457

LEFT: **Longer than a Highflyer by 3m/10ft, but no less than 4.23m/14ft narrower in the beam, the Third Class protected Gem (or Topaze)-class ships were intended to be a handy, fast and lightly armed type, useful for fleet work. While still too slow for the task, the Gems (*Sapphire* seen here) were forerunners of the Towns.**

Topaze class

All major fleets, from time to time, produced so-called "scout cruisers", but the results were rarely successful. In the period under consideration this was because these necessarily small ships could not incorporate the machinery required for the stipulated speed. Their nemesis, large armoured cruisers, were littler slower and were able to maintain speed in conditions that would slow a scout cruiser.

During 1903–04 the British Admiralty launched four pairs of very small scouts, which would prove to be more appropriate as destroyer leaders, and the quartet of Topaze-class ships (known as Gems), which, slightly larger, proved to be the starting point for the "fleet (or light) cruiser".

Rated as "Third Class cruisers", the four were given a very light, 102mm/4in armament and as high a power as was possible on the displacement. Thus where, for instance, the earlier Highflyers were given about 1.77ihp/ton displacement, the *Topaze* could boast nearer 4.33ihp/ton. The resulting speed advantage, however, was little better than 2 knots, an insufficient margin for an effective scout.

The recently patented Parsons steam turbine had, meanwhile, been applied with some success, first commercially, then by the Admiralty for comparative trials in destroyers. It was now decided that comparison would be scaled-up to cruiser size, and the Topaze-class *Amethyst* would thus be the first major warship to be turbine-driven. Compared with triple-expansion machinery, the turbine offered vibration-free running

and greater compactness (although the latter virtue was offset by the need to have separate turbines for cruising and for high-speed use, and ideally, for going astern).

Amethyst proved successful, not only being about 1.3 knots faster than her fastest sister, but burning only two-thirds the fuel. By 1914, however, they had been superseded by turbine-driven classes, beginning with the Boadiceas, the first true light cruisers.

Topaze class

	Built	Commissioned
Amethyst	Armstrong, Elswick	1904–05
Diamond	Laird, Birkenhead	1904–05
Sapphire	Palmer, Jarrow	1904–05
Topaze	Laird, Birkenhead	1904–05

Amethyst

Displacement: 3,048 tonnes/3,000 tons (normal)
Length: 109.7m/360ft (bp); 113.8m/373ft 6in (oa)
Beam: 12.2m/40ft
Draught: 4.4m/14ft 6in
Armament: 12 x 102mm/4in (12x1) and 8 x 3pdr (8x1) guns; 2 x 457mm/18in torpedo tubes (2x1)
Machinery: Direct-drive steam turbines, 10 boilers, 3 shafts
Power: 7,308kW/9,800shp for 21.8 knots (trials 23.6 knots)
Bunkers: 305 tonnes/300 tons (coal)
Protection: 25–50mm/1–2in (protective deck)
Complement: 300

ABOVE: **It will be noticed from the pictures above that the Gems adopted the new-style stockless anchor. While this greatly simplified getting under way, the forecastle party of the *Diamond* appear to be catting the port anchor. All surviving World War I, the Gems were scrapped in 1920–21.**

361

Blake, Crescent and Edgar classes

Rated First Class cruisers, these were products of the 1889 Naval Defence Act. Earlier cruisers, incorporating both belt and protective deck, had grown over-large, with little or no speed advantage over contemporary battleships. By dispensing with heavy belt armour, the two Blakes could accommodate more powerful machinery.

Occupying nearly two-thirds of the ships' length, machinery and boilers were designed to develop 14,914kW/20,000shp for 22 knots. Four triple-expansion, inverted-cylinder engines, each in its own compartment, were coupled in pairs to drive the two shafts. Unfortunately, the big double-ended boilers gave problems under forced draught conditions and the ships were usually limited to only 11,186kW/15,000shp and 20.5 knots.

Their armament followed the layout adopted for capital ships, with the main-calibre guns mounted forward and aft, and the secondary battery sided in the waist, both in open mounts on the upper deck and in newly adopted casemates at main deck level. The forward 234mm/9.2in gun was located on a short forecastle deck.

Otherwise generally well-regarded, the pair attracted criticism with respect to their near half-million pound unit cost. About 25 per cent cost saving was therefore effected in the following Edgars. Although obviously related, they were of about 1,676 tonnes/1,650 tons less displacement and more lightly protected. Shorter by about 4.6m/15ft, they were

ABOVE: **In order to improve their speed over their predecessors', the two Blakes were considerably increased in size in order to accommodate the necessary machinery. They dispensed with a side belt but shipped a powerful single 234mm/9.2in gun at either end. The *Blake*'s 152mm/6in guns are carried at a good height.**

also finer and, in addition to their lack of forecastle, this adversely affected their heavy-weather performance in early service on the Northern Blockade. They nevertheless acquitted themselves well during the 1915 Dardanelles campaign, for which they were suited and where weather conditions were benign.

Perhaps already uncertain of the Edgars' low forward freeboard, the designer incorporated a low forecastle in two further ships (*Crescent* and *Royal Arthur*) and, interestingly, suppressed the forward 234mm/9.2in gun in favour of a pair of sided 152mm/6in weapons.

Blake, Crescent and Edgar classes

	Built	Commissioned
Blake	Chatham Dockyard	February 2, 1892
Blenheim	Thames Ironworks, Blackwall	May 26, 1894
Edgar	Devonport Dockyard	March 2, 1891
Endymion	Earle, Hull	May 26, 1894
Gibraltar	Napier, Glasgow	November 1, 1894
Grafton	Thames Ironworks, Blackwall	October 18, 1894
Hawke	Chatham Dockyard	May 16, 1893
St. George	Earle, Hull	October 25, 1894
Theseus	Thames Ironworks, Blackwall	January 14, 1896
Crescent	Portsmouth Dockyard	February 22, 1894
Royal Arthur	Portsmouth Dockyard	March 2, 1893

Edgar (as built)

Displacement: 7,468 tonnes/7,350 tons (normal)
Length: 109.7m/360ft (bp), 113.3m/371ft 9in (oa)
Beam: 18.3m/60ft
Draught: 7.2m/23ft 9in (normal)
Armament: 2 x 234mm/9.2in (2x1), 10 x 152mm/6in (10x1) and 12 x 6pdr (12x1) guns; 4 x 457mm/18in torpedo tubes (4x1)
Machinery: 2 sets inverted, triple-expansion engines, 5 boilers, 2 shafts
Power: 8,950kW/12,000ihp for 20.5 knots
Endurance: 864 tonnes/850 tons (coal) for 5,556km/3,000nm at 18 knots
Protection: 127mm/5in (protective deck); 152mm/6in (casemates)
Complement: 545

LEFT: **Four Edgars were greatly modified for the 1915 Dardanelles campaign. The *Endymion*, stemmed in a Malta dry dock, shows her enormous bulges and the gallows added to allow her to tackle defensive nets in mine- and submarine-infested waters. Her original ram bow is also in evidence.**

The 1904 Scouts

Planning for a naval war focused on the North Sea, the Admiralty issued a broad specification in May 1902 for a new type of small cruiser, lightly armed but fast, suitable for watching enemy ports as well as leading a large destroyer flotilla of the time.

Unusually, the Admiralty solicited individual designs, for ships of under 3,048 tonnes/3,000 tons, from six shipbuilders. Those from four – Armstrong, Fairfield, Laird and Vickers – were accepted, and each firm was contracted to build a pair of ships for comparative trials. Broad statistics of those built are shown in the table below.

Externally, the Armstrong design stood out by virtue of its four funnels, the remainder having only three. All had a raised forecastle to improve seakeeping, that of the Vickers ships having curved, "turtle-deck" sheer strakes. All featured a single lofty mast to facilitate radio communication. Originally, the first-of-class bore the name *Eddystone*, but the Admiralty renamed all as listed below.

Although the Admiralty had stipulated reciprocating machinery rather then steam turbines, all achieved the required 25 knots. Informed opinion, however, found "£275,000" hard to justify for such small ships, with an armament of only 12pdr guns with limited endurance.

As if to underline the truth of this, Armstrong, the favoured firm, almost immediately went on to build two near-repeats for Brazil. Turbine-driven, they were 1.5 knots faster and were armed with ten 119mm/4.7in guns. Not surprisingly, then, as the war widened from the North Sea, the bulk of the group were rearmed with nine 102mm/4in ordnance. Acting as convoy escorts, beyond their envisaged roles, the Armstrong-built ships were, by 1918, each carrying one or two 152mm/6in guns in addition to the remaining 102mm/4in weapons.

1904 Scouts

	Built	Commissioned
Adventure	Armstrong, Elswick	November 6, 1905
Attentive	Armstrong, Elswick	February 7, 1905
Foresight	Fairfield, Glasgow	1905–06
Forward	Fairfield, Glasgow	1905–06
Pathfinder	Laird, Birkenhead	1905–06
Patrol	Laird, Birkenhead	1905–06
Sentinel	Vickers, Barrow	1905–06
Skirmisher	Vickers, Barrow	1905–06

Armstrong vessels (as built)

Displacement: 2,682 tonnes/2,640 tons (normal); 2,957 tonnes/2,910 tons (full load)
Length: 113.9m/374ft (bp); 120.3m/395ft (oa)
Beam: 11.7m/38ft 3in
Draught: 3.7m/12ft 3in (normal)
Armament: 10 x 12pdr (10x1) and 8 x 3pdr (8x1) guns; 2 x 457mm/18in torpedo tubes (2x1)
Machinery: 2 sets vertical, triple-expansion engines, 12 boilers, 2 shafts
Power: 11,819kW/15.850ihp (max) for 25 knots
Endurance: 458 tonnes/450 tons (coal) for 5,556km/3,000nm at 10 knots
Protection: 18–50mm/0.7–2in (protective deck)
Complement: 286

	Displacement (tonnes/tons)	Length (bp) (m/ft)	Beam	Power (kW/ihp)	Trials speed (knots)
Armstrong	2,682/2,640	114.3/375	11.7m/38ft 3in	11,819/15,850	25.42
Fairfield	2,906/2,860	111.3/365	11.9m39ft 2in	11,186/15,000	25.16
Laird	2,947/2,900	112.8/370	11.8m/38ft 9in	12,267/16,450	25.06
Vickers	2,926/2,880	109.7/360	12.2m/40ft	13,050/17,500	25.07

LEFT: **Vickers' contribution included *Skirmisher*, here undergoing builder's trials. She has the general appearance of a large destroyer and it was with the larger, later destroyers, such as the Rivers, that the scouts mainly worked. Their use as leaders declined as successive classes of destroyer became faster.**

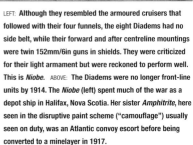

LEFT: Although they resembled the armoured cruisers that followed with their four funnels, the eight Diadems had no side belt, while their forward and after centreline mountings were twin 152mm/6in guns in shields. They were criticized for their light armament but were reckoned to perform well. This is *Niobe*. ABOVE: The Diadems were no longer front-line units by 1914. The *Niobe* (left) spent much of the war as a depot ship in Halifax, Nova Scotia. Her sister *Amphitrite*, here seen in the disruptive paint scheme ("camouflage") usually seen on duty, was an Atlantic convoy escort before being converted to a minelayer in 1917.

Diadem and Monmouth classes

Launched 1898–1900, the eight-ship Diadem class was of an intermediate size between the 14,428 tonne/14,200 ton Powerfuls of 1895 and the 9,297 tonne/9,150 ton *Blakes* of 1890. Protected cruisers, they were ordered in two groups. Where earlier classes had been given single 234mm/9.2in guns at either end (weapons virtually useless in the absence of proper fire control), the Diadems had a homogeneous armament of sixteen 152mm/6in guns. Four of these were paired in open mountings, forward and aft. The remainder were in casemates, four at the upper deck level and eight on the main deck. Apart from the last being located too low to be of use in any sort of sea, the whole layout was typical of its day in permitting only ten guns of sixteen to fire in broadside. The main deck guns were relocated to the upper deck in 1916.

Much controversy at this time attended the design and choice of boilers. Thus, the first group (*Andromeda*, *Argonaut*, *Europa* and *Niobe*) could generate 12,304kW/16,500ihp for 20.5 knots, while the second, with improved steam conditions, developed 13,423kW/18,000ihp for an extra quarter knot.

The Diadems were imposing in their appearance but they were much criticized for their lack of vertical protection. Improving steels enabled the following, and very similar, Cressys to be given both belt and protective deck. The German *Fürst Bismarck*, contemporary with the *Diadem*, was superior for on a displacement some 508 tonnes/500 tons less, she combined a 50mm/2in deck with a belt of up to 200mm/7.8in. Her armament also comprised four 24cm/9.5in guns and twelve 15cm/5.9in guns, of which only four were at main deck level.

ABOVE: The *Andromeda* prior to World War I. Because of their imposing size, they could be employed as station flagships, the flag officer enjoying the privilege of the secluded sternwalk. Note the after bridge, and how close to the water the lowest casemates are located. RIGHT: The *Andromeda* as built. One contributory factor to half the armament being set so uselessly low is apparent here, the substantial mass of the torpedo net being stowed on a shelf in line with the deck above. Reduced to a training hulk in 1913, she was not scrapped until 1956.

By 1914 the Diadems were obsolete, although at least three undertook Atlantic patrols. *Amphitrite* and *Ariadne* landed most of their armament in their conversion to large minelayers, in which role the latter was torpedoed and sunk.

Provided for in the 1898 to 1900 Estimates, the ten Monmouths, or "Counties", were answers to the French Klébers. Of very similar dimensions to the Diadems they mounted two fewer guns but were fitted with both belt and protective deck, and installed power that should have been sufficient for 23 knots. Several failed to attain contract speed until fitted with redesigned propellers. Controversy still surrounded boiler design and some of the class were therefore fitted with 24 boilers of Babcock and Wilcox design, others with 31 Bellevilles units.

Their belt was of 102mm/4in plate, tapering to 50mm/2in at either extremity, where it was closed off with a 76mm/3in transverse bulkhead. Vertically, it extended over the lower and main decks, forming a box roofed by the 30mm/1.2in main deck and floored with the vaulted protective deck.

A new departure was to mount the forward and after centreline 152mm/6in guns in paired, electrically operated turrets. As with the propulsion machinery, these could cause trouble and were cramped.

As with most contemporary British armoured cruisers, the Monmouths had generous freeboard, and their seakeeping was considered excellent. This, however, was slightly offset by their fine entry, necessary to achieve the design speed.

Of the ten, *Bedford* was lost by stranding in 1910, but the remainder of the class proved valuable during World War I. The nameship, poorly manned and exercised, was sunk with all hands at Coronel in 1914. Two of her sisters, however, were in the squadron that avenged her loss at the Falklands shortly afterwards. Of these, the *Kent*, which had made only

21.7 knots on her original trials, burned wooden furniture to boost power and to overhaul the fleeing *Nürnberg*. In the process of pursuing and sinking the fugitive, the *Kent* suffered nearly forty 10.5cm/4.1in hits. These caused little but cosmetic damage, the crew suffering only four fatalities.

ABOVE: **Popularly known as the County class, the Monmouths were designed as a smaller and more economical type of armoured cruiser, to be deployed either with the battle fleet or on trade protection. Although elderly, the class was heavily used during World War I. *Donegal*, seen here, was scrapped in 1920.**

ABOVE: **The Monmouths' belt armour was dimensioned to resist 15cm/5.9in shellfire but the nameship was sunk at Coronel by heavier 21cm/8.3in projectiles. In the ensuing battle off the Falklands the *Kent*, seen here, absorbed no less than 38 hits, from the *Nürnberg*'s 10.5cm/4.1in guns. Her superior protection and heavier firepower inevitably resulted in the German's destruction.**

ABOVE: **This view of the *Berwick* clearly shows the twin 152mm/6in forward turret, the first such mounting on British cruisers and not known for their reliability. The complexity and vulnerability of the W/T rigging is apparent. Riding to two anchors, the ship is using a mooring swivel to prevent crossed cables, or "foul hawse".**

Diadem and Monmouth classes

	Built	Commissioned
Andromeda	Pembroke Dockyard	1900
Argonaut	Fairfield, Glasgow	1900
Europa	Brown, Clydebank	1899
Niobe	Vickers, Barrow	1899
Amphitrite	Vickers, Barrow	1900
Ariadne	Brown, Clydebank	1900
Diadem	Fairfield, Glasgow	1899
Spartiate	Pembroke Dockyard	1902
Bedford	Fairfield, Glasgow	1903
Berwick	Beardmore, Glasgow	1903
Cornwall	Pembroke Dockyard	1905
Cumberland	London & Glasgow	1904
Donegal	Fairfield, Glasgow	1903
Essex	Pembroke Dockyard	1903
Kent	Portsmouth Dockyard	1903
Lancaster	Armstrong, Elswick	1904
Monmouth	London & Glasgow	1903
Suffolk	Portsmouth Dockyard	1904

Later Monmouths (as built)

Displacement: 10,159 tonnes/9,900 tons (normal)
Length: 134m/440ft (bp); 141.2m/463ft 6in (oa)
Beam: 20.2m/66ft 4in
Draught: 7.5m/24ft 6in (normal)
Armament: 14 x 152mm/6in (2x2/10x1) and 10 x 12pdr (10x1) guns; 2 x fixed submerged 457mm/18in torpedo tubes
Machinery: 2 sets vertical, triple-expansion engines, 31 boilers, 2 shafts
Power: 16,405kW/22,000ihp for 23 knots
Bunkers: 1,788 tonnes/1,760 tons (coal)
Protection: 50–102mm/2–4in (belt); 18–50mm/0.75–2in (protective deck); 100–127mm/4–5in (turrets)
Complement: 500

Cressy, Drake and Devonshire classes

Developments in the manufacturing of armour plate, first by Harvey (1891), and then by Krupp (1895), had a significant effect on warship design. During the previous decade, "compound" armour comprised a hard steel face plate hot-rolled on to a tough iron back plate. Harvey's process "cemented" or face-hardened the outer surface of a homogeneous steel plate. Krupp went further by incorporating small quantities of elements that improved the plate's resistance to penetration or to shattering.

In round figures, Harvey had one-and-a-half times and Krupp twice the stopping power of compound armour. For the designer this meant that the same level of protection could be provided at only half the weight. An alternative was to provide a belt in addition to an armoured deck, signalling the return of the armoured cruiser.

The first result was the Cressy type, upgraded Diadems that readopted the 234mm/9.2in ordnance at either end, had a thinner (50–76mm/2–3in against 64–102mm/2.5–4in) protective deck but had a 152mm/6in belt of Krupp steel, 3.5m/11ft 6in in depth. Long in manufacture, armour plate was expensive and, where a Diadem cost £582,000, a Cressy cost £780,000.

ABOVE LEFT: **The six Cressys were effectively Diadems redesigned with a belt. This was possible because of the introduction of Krupp "cemented" (surface hardened) armour which had higher resistance to penetration. This picture shows the *Sutlej*. Note the size of the forward 234mm/9.2in gun in its fully enclosed turret.** ABOVE: **The side belt of the Cressys came no higher than the lower edge of the lower gun casemates, leaving a vast, unprotected acreage, well depicted in this picture of *Aboukir*. In the event, she was simply despatched by submarine torpedo, a form of attack that post-dated her designer's experience.**

Ironically, for the three ships lost, these improvements availed them nothing. Just seven weeks after the outbreak of war, with submarine warfare an unknown quantity to either side, the *Aboukir*, *Cressy* and *Hogue* were despatched by one U-boat with four torpedoes. For the ship designer, it posed a new set of problems, for the thickest of armour was no defence against torpedoes, designed to strike below it.

If the Cressys are viewed as a response to the successful Italian Garibaldis and to the French *Montcalm*, their successors, the Drakes, were designed with the French *Jeanne d'Arc* in mind. This required a 2-knot improvement in speed, necessitating a 43 per cent increase in power, a 14 per cent

ABOVE: **Although having four funnels, the Devonshires (the nameship seen here) were improved Monmouths rather than improved Drakes (opposite). Their shorter funnels gave them a less-stately, more business-like appearance. Note the three forward-firing, fully enclosed 191mm/7.5in guns, with a higher rate of fire than a 234mm/9.2in weapon, and harder hitting than a 152mm/6in gun.**

ABOVE: **In profile, the British armoured cruisers became difficult to differentiate. The Devonshires (*Roxburgh* seen here) were the first to have 191mm/7.5in turrets flanking the bridge, but retained the two-level 152mm/6in casemates abreast the mainmast. Note the adoption of distinguishing funnel bands, although all were later given disruptive paint schemes.**

increase in length and a 35 per cent increase in cost. The result was imposing, but so large that considerable effort was made to reduce their profile and target area.

By virtue of making all 152mm/6in gun casemates double-tiered, the Drakes carried 16 secondary weapons against the Cressys' 12. Also, where the latter's belt terminated below the bridge in a 127mm/5in transverse bulkhead, that of the *Drake* was continued right to the bows at a reduced thickness of 50mm/2in, as flooding forward quickly reduced stability.

They were among the first British warships to incorporate wood treated to reduce fire risk and to have their coal bunkers, an important part of the ships' protective system, subdivided to minimize the effect of a torpedo rather than shellfire. Again, a touch of irony is added by the "fire-proofing" for, at Coronel, the Drake-class *Good Hope* was sunk by German gunfire and was, by their account, "already burning from fore to aft, presenting the unique spectacle of a sheet of flame upon a sea lashed by the tempest".

If the Cressys and Drakes represented a response to the perceived threat posed by foreign contemporaries, the Monmouths were a more moderate design aimed at the actual responsibility of commerce protection. A Monmouth was two-thirds the cost of a Drake, so it is not surprising that this otherwise maligned class of ten should have been extended by an improved batch. These were the Devonshires, a more heavily armed class of six laid down in 1902.

Although resembling Drakes, Devonshires were considerably smaller at 10,923 tonnes/10,750 tons. They were 3.1m/10ft longer than Monmouths, 0.6m/2ft greater in beam, and they were similarly powered and therefore a little slower. The belt was thickened by 50 per cent, and four 191mm/7.5in guns added, two centreline singles, forward and aft, and two more, turreted, in place of the previous forward casemates. One of two lost was the *Hampshire*, carrying Lord Kitchener.

TOP: **Not so obvious in this depiction, the four Drakes were identifiable by their four two-level casemates on each side, housing a formidable secondary armament (on paper, at least) of sixteen 152mm/6in guns. Note how the Victorian livery allowed for considerable flexibility in paint schemes.**

ABOVE: **The lack of a white upper strake on the *Leviathan* (top) as compared with the *Aboukir* (opposite) resulted from a reduction in freeboard, a conscious effort being made by designers to reduce the large overall target area of the ship. One result was to lower the lower casemates still further. At Coronel, the ill-starred *Good Hope*, seen here, was unable to use any of her lower 152mm/6in guns.**

ABOVE: *Hogue*, seen here, was another of the Cressys. Their large number of 152mm/6in quick-firers were intended to smother an opponent, to reduce his capability to respond. The large 234mm/9.2in gun at either end was there to inflict the final, armour-piercing blow. With only two guns and no proper fire control, however, the 234mm/9.2in ordnance was inaccurate.

Cressy, Drake and Devonshire classes

	Built	Commissioned
Aboukir	Fairfield, Glasgow	1902
Bacchante	Brown, Clydebank	1902
Cressy	Fairfield, Glasgow	1901
Euryalus	Vickers, Barrow	1904
Hogue	Vickers, Barrow	1902
Sutlej	Brown, Clydebank	1902
Drake	Pembroke Dockyard	1902
Good Hope	Fairfield, Glasgow	1902
King Alfred	Vickers, Barrow	1903
Leviathan	Brown, Clydebank	1903
Antrim	Brown, Clydebank	1905
Argyll	Scott, Greenock	1906
Carnarvon	Beardmore, Glasgow	1905
Devonshire	Chatham Dockyard	1905
Hampshire	Armstrong, Elswick	1905
Roxburgh	London & Glasgow	1905

Drake class

Displacement: 14,326 tonnes/14,100 tons (normal)
Length: 152.3m/500ft (bp); 161.3m/529ft 6in (oa)
Beam: 21.6m/71ft
Draught: 8.2m/27ft (mean)
Armament: 2 x 234mm/9.2in (2x1), 16 x 152mm/6in (16x1) and 12 x 12pdr (12x1) guns; 2 x fixed 457mm/18in torpedo tubes (2x1)
Power: 23,490kW/31,500ihp for 23 knots
Endurance: 1,270 tonnes/1,250 tons (coal) for 6,019km/3,250nm at 19 knots
Protection: 76–152mm/3–6in (belt); 50–76mm/2–3in (deck); 127–152mm/5–6in (turrets and casemates)
Complement: 900

LEFT: **The two Black Princes (*Duke of Edinburgh* shown here) virtually qualified as Second Class battleships. The great length necessary to accommodate machinery for 23 knots gave them a beam sufficient to mount four 234mm/9.2in wing turrets in the waist. Compared with these, her casemated 152mm/6in weapons look insignificant.**

Black Prince, Warrior and Minotaur classes

By 1902, the prestige of the armoured cruiser was soaring. Big, powerful, expensive, looking every inch a warship, she was proposed by some, who were forgetting what she was designed for, to be suitable for laying in a line of battle. Effectively a Second Class battleship, she was to develop even further under Watts, the newly appointed Director of Naval Construction (DNC).

At the time of the changeover in DNC, the Devonshires were introducing the 191mm/7.5in gun as the armoured cruiser's primary weapon. The Board of Admiralty, however, considered it too light for ships of this size, and, for the following class, required not only the 234mm/9.2in gun but six of them to be disposed in single turrets in the "hexagonal" layout then much in favour. Despite the Cressys having already demonstrated that a casemated, main deck battery of 152mm/6in secondary guns was unworkable in any sea, it was to be retained as easier to control. Too late to rectify, the Monmouths' 102mm/4in belt had been shown in tests to be unable to stop a 152mm/6in shell, so a minimum of 152mm/6in over vital areas was specified.

Although water-tube boilers were by now becoming generally accepted, the Admiralty insisted on including a proportion of the old cylindrical type, as being more economical at cruising speeds. This mix affected the overall length although, compared with the Drakes, the next pair (*Black Prince* and *Duke of Edinburgh*) were 7.3m/24ft shorter but 0.76m/2.5ft greater in the beam.

In order that the forward 234mm/9.2in wing turrets, mounted at upper deck level, could fire ahead, the forecastle was narrow and facetted, allowing the sea to sweep the upper deck along its length. One level below was the broadside 152mm/6in battery which, predictably, proved to be so ineffectual that, having survived Jutland, the *Duke of Edinburgh* had her guns relocated to the upper deck and the casemates plated over.

The situation was rectified in what should have been the final four of the class but which, on account of differences, became known as the Warriors. These used the same hull and had six 234mm/9.2in guns in the same hexagonal layout but, in place of the casemated 152mm/6in battery, had four 191mm/7.5in weapons arranged in single turrets at upper deck level, two per side.

In terms of firepower, speed and protection, British armoured cruisers compared well with their foreign contemporaries until, as the Warriors were all reaching launch stage, there were reports that the US Navy was progressing from the mixed 203mm/8in and 152mm/6in armament of the Pennsylvanias to 254mm/10in and 178mm/7in guns in the four new Tennessees (also known as Washingtons). Used by only two ships in the Royal Navy, the 254mm/10in gun was not

LEFT: **Last of the three classes depicted on these pages, the Minotaurs carried the majority of their armament quite low. Casemates were dispensed with in favour of single turrets, the forbidding row of five 191mm/7.5in guns along either side being their distinguishing feature. The *Defence*, shown here, was lost with all hands at Jutland, having come within range of the enemy battle line.**

favoured and, as the penetrative power of the reliable 234mm/9.2in projectile was only slightly inferior, this calibre was retained for the final trio of armoured cruisers, the Minotaurs. In these, the hexagonal layout was abandoned. Only four 234mm/9.2in guns were carried, but in twin turrets located on the forecastle and quarter deck. Along the waist at upper-deck level were no less than five single 191mm/7.5in turrets per side. They also had an all-water tube boiler outfit.

Despite a further increase in physical size and displacement, the Minotaurs could have only the same scale of protection and their massive dispersed armament, with its separate requirements for safe ammunition paths, resulted in a somewhat congested design. A 17 per cent increase in installed power was also required to give the same speed.

Bristling with armament, the armoured cruiser had been progressed as far as was possible. The Minotaurs were completed in 1908, the same year in which the British themselves made the type obsolete with the entry into service of the *Invincible*, first of the battlecruisers.

ABOVE: **An excellent picture of the Warrior-class *Natal* shows an armament midway between the *Black Prince* and the *Warrior*. The single 234mm/9.2in gun at either end is flanked by two more, making six in total. The 152mm/6in casemated guns have been replaced by turreted 191mm/7.5in guns, two on either side. The *Natal* was destroyed in 1915 at Cromarty by a magazine explosion.**

Black Prince, Warrior and Minotaur classes

	Built	Commissioned
Black Prince	Thames Ironworks, Blackwall	January 1906
Duke of Edinburgh	Pembroke Dockyard	March 1906
Achilles	Armstrong, Elswick	March 1907
Cochrane	Fairfield, Glasgow	February 1907
Natal	Vickers, Barrow	1907
Warrior	Pembroke Dockyard	1907
Defence	Pembroke Dockyard	April 1908
Minotaur	Devonport Dockyard	March 1908
Shannon	Chatham Dockyard	March 1908

Minotaur class

Displacement: 14,834 tonnes/14,600 tons (normal); 16,400 tonnes/16,100 tons (full load)
Length: 149.3m/490ft (bp); 158.1m/519ft (oa)
Beam: 22.7m/74ft 6in
Draught: 7.9m/26ft (normal)
Armament: 4 x 234mm/9.2in (2x2), 10 x 191mm/7.5in (10x1) and 16 x 12pdr guns; 5 x 457mm/18in fixed torpedo tubes
Machinery: 2 sets vertical, triple-expansion engines, 23 boilers, 2 shafts
Power: 20,134kW/27,000ihp for 23 knots
Endurance: 1,018 tonnes/1,000 tons (coal) and 763 tonnes/750 tons (oil) for 15,093km/8,150nm at 10 knots
Protection: 76–152mm/3–6in (belt); 38–50mm/1.5–2in (protective deck), 178–203mm/7–8in (turrets)
Complement: 755

ABOVE: **Having received 21 hits at Jutland, 15 of them from major-calibre projectiles, the *Warrior* slowly foundered while under tow. Hampered by their limited speed – all were powered by reciprocating machinery – armoured cruisers proved deficient in their major role of opposed reconnaissance.**

LEFT: **The Boadiceas and closely similar Actives of 1909–13 were the forerunners of the numerous Town classes. Their design was possible through the adoption of the steam turbine, itself compact but also requiring fewer engine room staff, hence less accommodation. The *Blanche* was attached to the Grand Fleet's 4th Battle Squadron.**

Boadicea, Active and "Town" classes

Already regarded by the Royal Navy as a developing threat at the turn of the century, the German Navy began to commission a series of what the British classed as "Third Class cruisers". Between 1900 and 1904 ten of these steadily improved vessels were completed. Although generally stated to be unarmoured they had a thin protective deck and mounted ten 10.5cm/4.1in guns that totally outclassed the much-criticized 12pdr of the four pairs of British scout cruisers launched in 1904.

Germany then increased the size slightly and, at a rate of about two per year, began building their derived "Town"-class cruisers. Also carrying ten 10.5cm/4.1in guns, and with thicker protection, these steadily increased in displacement in order to incorporate more powerful machinery which, by 1908, drove

them at up to 24 knots. Except for their triple-expansion machinery, these were a superior type to which the Royal Navy had no direct equivalent. Britain's first response was the three Boadiceas, launched in 1908–09. Although their turbines gave them a knot or so advantage, both of their six 102mm/4in guns and their protection were inferior.

They were followed in 1911–12 by the three very similar Actives, which mounted ten 102mm/4in guns apiece. Although there appears to be no reason why the Boadiceas should not have been similarly upgunned, only the *Blonde* was rearmed.

Both the Boadicea and Active classes were primarily destroyer leaders. Their 14.1kg/31lb, 102mm/4in projectiles were inadequate even to stop a destroyer and, for working directly with the battle fleet, there was a requirement for an equally fast vessel, but somewhat larger both to retain a margin over the battle fleet, even in poor weather conditions, and to carry the more potent 152mm/6in gun.

With the need recognized in good time, the first group of British "Towns" began to be launched in 1909. In the first five, the Bristols, ten waist-mounted 102mm/4in guns were supplemented by a single 152mm/6in forward and aft in a dual-calibre layout that mirrored that of contemporary armoured cruisers, complete with difficult fire control.

The Bristols were the first of four groups of "Towns" that represented the beginning of a divergent line of development, i.e. "fleet cruisers" aimed specifically at offensive reconnaissance. Their main characteristics are shown below.

ABOVE: **The Southampton-class ships, the Australian-flagged *Melbourne* (seen here) and *Sydney* both served with the Royal Navy for much of World War I. Slightly finer-lined than the Birminghams, which followed, they carried only one forecastle gun and were the first with the new-profile bow.**

	Launched	Displacement tonnes/tons	Armament	Dimensions m/ft
Bristol (x5)	1909–10	4,877/4,800	2 x 152mm/6in; 10 x 102mm/4in	138 x 14.4/453 x 47
Weymouth (x4)	1910–11	5,334/5,250	8 x 152mm/6in	137 x 14.8/450 x 48.5
Southampton (x7)	1911–12	5,487/5,400	8 x 152mm/6in	137 x 14.9/450 x 48.8
Birmingham (x3)	1913	5,527/5,440	9 x 152mm/6in; 1 x 76mm/3in	139.2 x 15.2/456.8 x 50

Three more Southamptons (*Brisbane*, *Melbourne* and *Sydney*) and the Birmingham-class *Adelaide* served with the Royal Australian Navy, both the *Adelaide* and *Brisbane* being home-built. Completed late, *Adelaide* differed in detail.

Although all of these groups were of pre-war construction, their protection evolved to meet the perceived threat. Thus the first two had protective decks, the third was double-skinned by way of machinery spaces, while the Birminghams added a full-length belt capable of stopping a 10.5cm/4.1in projectile.

The "Towns" were very heavily used throughout World War I, during which period the only two losses (*Falmouth* and *Nottingham*) were due to submarine torpedo. Several, particularly *Southampton* and the broadly similar *Chester*, survived severe damage by gunfire. *Chester*, and her sister *Birkenhead*, were being built to Greek account when taken over by the Royal Navy. Their main difference lay in their 140mm/5.5in armament, whose 37.6kg/83lb shells were more easily handled than the 45.4kg/100lb, 152mm/6in projectile.

In the course of the war most had their foremast converted to a tripod to reduce vibration in the fire control top. The "Towns", specifically *Weymouth*, were the first Royal Navy light cruisers to be fitted with flying-off platforms for fighter aircraft.

ABOVE LEFT: **A forecastle view of the Bristol-class** *Glasgow*. **Escaping from the debacle of Coronel in November 1914, the ship gained revenge shortly afterward, assisting in sinking the** *Leipzig* **at the Falklands and, later, the** *Dresden*. **Note the heavy, cast shield of the 152mm/6in gun.** ABOVE: **The five Bristols (***Newcastle* **seen here) were the first of the Towns, being considerably stretched, four-shaft Actives. They were alone in having a short forecastle and mixed armament, with 102mm/4in secondaries.**

"Town" classes

	Built	Commissioned
Bristol	Brown, Clydebank	1910
Glasgow	Fairfield, Glasgow	1910
Gloucester	Beardmore, Glasgow	1910
Liverpool	Vickers, Barrow	1910
Newcastle	Armstrong, Elswick	1910
Dartmouth	Vickers, Barrow	1911
Falmouth	Beardmore, Glasgow	1911
Weymouth	Armstrong, Elswick	1911
Yarmouth	London & Glasgow	1912
Chatham	Chatham Dockyard	1912
Dublin	Beardmore, Glasgow	1913
Southampton	Brown, Clydebank	1913
Brisbane	Cockatoo, Sydney	1915
Melbourne	Cammell Laird, Birkenhead	1913
Sydney	London & Glasgow	1913
Birmingham	Armstrong, Elswick	1914
Lowestoft	Chatham Dockyard	1914
Nottingham	Pembroke Dockyard	1914
Adelaide	Cockatoo, Sydney	1922

Birmingham class

Displacement: 5,527 tonnes/5,440 tons (normal)
Length: 131.9m/430ft (bp), 139.2m/456ft 9in (oa)
Beam: 15.1m/49ft 6in
Draught: 4.8m/15ft 10in (normal)
Armament: 9 x 152mm/6in guns (9x1);
    2 x 533mm/21in fixed torpedo tubes (2x1)
Machinery: Direct-drive steam turbines,
    12 boilers, 2 shafts
Power: 18,643kW/25,000shp for 25 knots
Bunkers: 1,184 tonnes/1,165 tons (coal),
    239 tonnes/235 tons (oil)
Protection: 50–76mm/2–3in (belt); 38mm/1.5in
    (protective deck)
Complement: 435

ABOVE: **Serving alongside the Italian Navy in the Adriatic, a weather-worn** *Weymouth* **enters Grand Harbour, Malta. Closely following the Bristols, the four Weymouths carried eight 152mm/6in guns, three forward, one aft, and two on either side in the waist, protected by high bulwarks. Note the stump mainmast.**

LEFT: **Where the Towns were designed to operate with the fleet, the rather smaller Arethusas were given a higher speed for working primarily with destroyers in the North Sea. With protection on an equal scale to the Towns, they proved remarkably tough.**

Arethusa and C-classes

Smaller than the "Towns", the Arethusas continued the line of development begun with the Boadicea and Active groups. Larger than the scouts, fast enough to act as destroyer leaders, and with a 76mm/3in belt capable of stopping a 10.5cm/4.1in shell at close range, they proved effective. They were intended to support the battle fleet by leading destroyer attacks against that of the enemy, while also acting to break-up any similar attack on his part. To fulfill this role they were fitted with a dual-calibre armament of rapid-firing 102mm/4in to deal with destroyers and a few 152mm/6in to deter the attentions of any cruiser covering them.

Comparatively small, however, these ships were lively, making them poor gun platforms and causing difficulty with the manual loading of 45.4kg/100lb, 152mm/6in shells. Metacentric height and, to some extent, stability, therefore had to be deliberately reduced to increase roll period and steadiness. The general adoption of oil-firing contributed to the problem, as oil tanks tended to be carried lower than coal bunkers, lowering the centre of gravity and increasing stiffness.

A large increase in installed power gave them a sea speed of 27 knots, which could be comfortably exceeded. Commodore Tyrwhitt, taking over the new *Arethusa* in 1914, wrote enthusiastically: "She's a regular flyer and a ripper ..." With the

ABOVE: **As long as a Town, but considerably narrower, the C-class cruisers were essentially slightly enlarged Arethusas. Extremely successful, the type developed quickly through several sub-types. *Champion* belonged to the two-funnelled Cambrian class.**

ship heavily damaged at the Heligoland Bight, he temporarily wore his flag in the Town-class *Lowestoft*. "[She was] a size larger than the *Arethusa*", he commented, "but slower and rather too big for my job ... We destroyer folk have ways and customs which are quite unknown to the big ships." Obviously, the Admiralty had it about right.

Following on were the six Carolines, first of the successful C-class which, in half-a-dozen variants, eventually ran to 28 ships. Two further Carolines (*Calliope* and *Champion*) were used to trial different arrangements of gearing.

ABOVE: **Gunnery practice with the 152mm/6in ordnance on *Champion*'s forecastle under the watchful eye of the "Chief GI" (gunnery instructor). Note the light gun shield, compared with those on the Towns, the bridge-wing semaphores and the canvas-screened chart table.**

ABOVE: **The Caledon type, completed in 1917, was given an all-centreline armament of five 152mm/6in guns. This broadside by *Calypso* shows how they were disposed. Sturdy tripod masts allowed vibration-free observation and spotting. Tall mainmasts were not required for North Sea operations.**

The Carolines carried eight 102mm/4in guns, sided in the waist and on the forecastle deck. Contrary to historical precedent, the two 152mm/6in weapons were in centreline, in a superfiring disposition, pointing aft. By 1918, the forecastle 102mm/4in gun had mostly been exchanged for additional 152mm/6in ordnance.

Where the Carolines inherited the eight-boiler and three funnel arrangement of the Arethusas, the six follow-on Cambrians benefited from improved technology having only six boilers and two funnels. They were, otherwise, repeats.

In 1916, Armstrong completed the *Centaur* and *Concord*. Incorporating material assembled from deferred Turkish warships, they differed in mounting an all-centreline armament of five 152mm/6in guns. They also had two high-angle (HA) 76mm/3in weapons and a fire control top. The latter necessitated a substantial tripod mainmast, which was eventually fitted to all.

The four Caledons of 1917 were repeats on slightly enlarged hulls, followed by the five Ceres type. These had their bridge structure moved a little further aft in order to permit a second 152mm/6in gun to be located to superfire the forecastle weapon. With increasing topside weight, beam was increased by 0.46m/1ft 6in to improve stability.

The final group, five Carlisles, were similar but, in order to reduce wetness, increased forward freeboard with the so-called "trawler bow".

From 1934 the surviving thirteen Cs were slated for conversion to anti-aircraft cruisers. *Coventry* and *Curlew* were duly rebuilt as prototypes in 1935–36. Lack of funds and priority then slowed the programme until it was overtaken by World War II. Only nine were eventually converted. Their armament varied, with differing mixes of single and twin 102mm/4in high-angle (HA) and multiple 2pdr pompoms, together with the requisite directors and early radar. Five were sunk during World War II, three of them, ironically, by aircraft.

BELOW: **Nine later C-class were converted to anti-aircraft cruisers. The *Curacoa*, see here, is carrying eight high-angle 102mm/4in in twin mountings, and a pompom. Note the two directors, full radar outfit and tripod mainmast.**

ABOVE: **Still fitted with a light-pole foremast, the 1915-built *Cleopatra* belongs to the early, three-funnelled Caroline group. During a Harwich Force operation in 1916, she rammed an enemy destroyer, cutting her in two. In such close-fought encounters, the ships' 76mm/3in side belt proved its worth.**

Arethusa and C-classes

	Built	Commisssioned
Arethusa	Chatham Dockyard	August 11, 1914
Aurora	Devonport Dockyard	September 5, 1914
Galatea	Beardmore, Glasgow	December 10, 1914
Inconstant	Beardmore, Glasgow	January 4, 1915
Penelope	Vickers, Barrow	December 10, 1914
Phaeton	Vickers, Barrow	February 3, 1915
Royalist	Beardmore, Glasgow	March 21, 1915
Undaunted	Fairfield, Glasgow	August 29, 1914
Caroline	Cammell Laird, Birkenhead	December 4, 1914
Carysfort	Pembroke Dockyard	June 8, 1915
Cleopatra	Devonport Dockyard	June 1, 1915
Comus	Swan Hunter, Tyne	May 21, 1915
Conquest	Chatham Dockyard	June 1, 1915
Cordelia	Pembroke Dockyard	January 3, 1915
Calliope	Chatham Dockyard	June 15, 1915
Champion	Hawthorn Leslie, Tyne	December 20, 1915
Cambrian	Pembroke Dockyard	May 31, 1916
Canterbury	Brown, Clydebank	May 9, 1916
Castor	Cammell Laird, Birkenhead	November 12, 1915
Constance	Cammell Laird, Birkenhead	January 26, 1916
Centaur	Vickers, Barrow	August 16, 1916
Concord	Vickers, Barrow	December 18, 1916
Caledon	Cammell Laird, Birkenhead	March 6, 1917
Calypso	Hawthorn Leslie, Tyne	June 21, 1917
Carradoc	Scotts, Greenock	June 15, 1917
Cassandra	Vickers, Barrow	June 29, 1917
Cardiff	Fairfield, Glasgow	June 25, 1917
Ceres	Brown, Clydebank	June 1, 1917
Coventry	Swan Hunter, Tyne	February 21, 1918
Curacoa	Pembroke Dockyard	February 18, 1918
Curlew	Vickers, Barrow	December 14, 1917
Cairo	Cammell Laird, Birkenhead	October 14, 1919
Calcutta	Vickers, Barrow	August 10, 1919
Capetown	Cammell Laird, Birkenhead	April 10, 1922
Carlisle	Fairfield, Glasgow	November 16, 1918
Colombo	Fairfield, Glasgow	June 18, 1919

Carlisle group (as built)

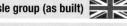

Displacement: 4,760 tonnes/4,685 tons (normal); 5,338 tonnes/5,254 tons (full load)
Length: 129.5m/425ft (bp); 137.5m/451ft 6in (oa)
Beam: 13.3m/43ft 6in
Draught: 4.4m/14ft 6in (normal)
Armament: 5 x 152mm/6in (5x1) and 2 x 76mm/3in HA (2x1) guns; 8 x 533mm/21in torpedo tubes (4x2)
Machinery: Geared steam turbines, 6 boilers, 2 shafts
Power: 22,371kW/30,000shp for 28 knots
Endurance: 950 tonnes/935 tons (oil) for 10,927km/5,900nm at 10 knots
Protection: 38–76mm/1.5–3in (belt); 25mm/1in (partial protective deck)
Complement: 330

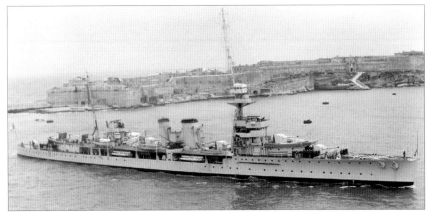

LEFT: **A little larger but otherwise very similar to the late C-type, the D-type *Dauntless* here clearly shows the differences. Superfiring single 152mm/6in at both ends are supplemented by two more on the centreline, before and abaft the funnels. Two quadruple torpedo tube mountings replace four triples.**

D-class

Unlike the British, the Germans upgraded light cruiser gun calibre in one step, without any mixed-calibre armaments. As early as 1914, the two Regensburgs introduced an all-15cm/ 5.9in armament and, although the layout meant that only five of their seven weapons could fire in broadside, this out-classed the early British C-class.

In the D-class, therefore, the British produced a stretched C-type; its extra 6.1m/20ft permitted an extra centreline 152mm/6in gun. In profile, a "D" appeared very similar to a Carlisle but with a larger gap between forefunnel and bridge, where the extra gun was located on the centreline.

In reality, however, both bridge and funnels had been moved aft. Set about 12.2m/40ft further from the bows, the bridge experienced less violent vertical motion while its one-level extra height made it dryer. Extra protection and the substitution of triple for twin torpedo

tubes necessitated a 0.6m/2ft increase in beam. As the same C-class machinery was to be fitted, speed loss was minimized by optimizing shaft speed and propeller design.

Conventional bows were fitted to the first group of three (*Danae, Dauntless* and *Dragon*), with the last five taking the unlovely "trawler" bow to further reduce wetness. Four further ships were cancelled at close of hostilities.

A 1936 proposal to rearm all eight as AA cruisers (but with twin 114mm/ 4.5in HA guns as opposed to the Cs' 102mm/4in armament) came to nothing. However, a one-off conversion was undertaken on the *Delhi* during 1941, in order to allow the Royal Navy to evaluate the US Navy's then-new 127mm/5in 38 weapon, of which five single mountings were fitted. They were not adopted.

Where the C-class AA conversions proved useful both in home and Mediterranean waters, the unconverted

Ds had limited potential during World War II, not least because of their endurance. Only *Dunedin* was lost.

D-class

	Built	Commissioned
Danae	Armstrong, High Walker	June 22, 1918
Dauntless	Palmers, Tyne	December 2, 1918
Dragon	Scotts, Greenock	August 16, 1918
Delhi	Armstrong, High Walker	June 7, 1919
Despatch	Fairfield, Glasgow	June 30, 1922
Diomede	Vickers, Barrow	October 7, 1922
Dunedin	Armstrong, High Walker	October 20, 1919
Durban	Scotts, Greenock	October 31, 1921

D-class

Displacement: 5,233 tonnes/5,150 tons (normal); 5,893 tonnes/5,800 tons (full load)
Length: 135.6m/445ft (bp); 143.9m/472ft 6in (oa)
Beam: 14.2m/46ft 6in
Draught: 4.6m/15ft (normal)
Armament: 6 x 152mm/6in (6x1); 2 x 76mm/3in HA (2x1) and 2 x 2pdr pompom (2x1) guns; 12 x 533mm/21in torpedo tubes (4x3)
Machinery: Geared steam turbines, 6 boilers, 2 shafts
Power: 29,828kW/40,000shp for 29 knots
Endurance: 1,077 tonnes/1,060 tons oil for 12,408km/6,700nm at 10 knots
Protection: 38–76mm/1.5–3in (belt); 25mm/1in (partial protective deck)
Complement: 450

LEFT: **At speed in North Sea conditions, smaller cruisers could be very wet. For this reason, the final six C-class ships (Carlisle type), and five of the eight completed Ds, were given so-called "trawler" bows. These significantly increased forward freeboard but did nothing for the ships' appearance. *Durban* is seen here.**

FAR LEFT: **In response to rumours that the enemy was constructing extra-fast cruisers, the Department of Naval Construction rapidly produced a stretched D-class cruiser with two sets of machinery. The extra length of the resulting E-class (*Enterprise* seen here) also permitted a seventh gun, 16 torpedo tubes, and an aircraft to be carried.**
ABOVE: **Abaft the funnels the E-class, seen here on *Emerald*, carried a revolving platform from which, wind-over-deck permitting, a biplane fighter/reconnaissance aircraft such as the Fairey Flycatcher could simply lift off. Note that the mainmast is offset to port to accommodate this.**

E-class

Developed directly from the D-class, the Es thus harked back to the Arethusas yet, in the case of the *Enterprise*, also looked forward to the cruisers of World War II by dint of being fitted with a prototype of the later-standardized 152mm/6in twin turret.

The class's origins lay in an urgent response to the rumoured new, high-speed German cruisers which were believed to be nearing completion. These turned out to be no more than the Brummers which were completed in 1916 in some secrecy but capable of an unexceptional 28 knots.

The Admiralty's demand for a 34-knot cruiser was quickly realized by the considerable extrapolation of a D-type. Tests indicated that a hull of 20 per cent greater length and marginally increased L/B ratio (9.82 against 9.57) could make 33 knots light with 59,656kW/80,000shp.

This was achieved by incorporating two sets of machinery being built for the new destroyer-leaders. Externally, this arrangement resulted in a return to three funnels, set battlecruiser-style with a pronounced gap between the second and third.

Although large and fast, the Es, of which only two were ever completed, and those long after the war, were armed with seven 152mm/6in guns. *Emerald* mounted her two forward weapons as superimposed singles, the *Enterprise* in the prototype twin turret.

Completed with four triple torpedo tube mountings, both ships were soon given quadruples. Their 16 tubes constituted the largest such armament of any British warship.

Between the mainmast and after funnel, as built, there was a revolving, flying-off platform for a float plane. During

the 1930s a catapult was substituted, causing the mainmast to be relocated forward of the after funnel. The funnels were also increased in height.

With World War II and a proliferation of personnel and electronics, the forecastle deck was extended aft and the masts converted to tripods.

E-class

	Built	Commissioned
Emerald	Armstrong, High Walker	January 14, 1926
Enterprise	Brown, Clydebank	March 31, 1926
Euphrates	Fairfield, Glasgow	Cancelled

Emerald (as built)

Displacement: 8,636 tonnes/8,500 tons (normal); 9,602 tonnes/9,450 ton (full load)
Length: 163m/535ft (bp); 173.6m/570ft (oa)
Beam: 16.6m/54ft 6in
Draught: 5m/16ft 6in (normal)
Armament: 7 x 152mm/6in guns (7x1), 2 x 102mm/4in HA and 2 x 2pdr pompom guns; 12 x 533mm/21in torpedo tubes (4x3)
Machinery: Geared steam turbines, 8 boilers, 4 shafts
Power: 59,656kW/80,000shp for 33 knots
Endurance: 757 tonnes/745 tons (oil) for 14,816km/8,000nm at 15 knots
Protection: 38–76mm/1.5–3in (belt); 50mm/1in (partial protective deck)
Complement: 560

LEFT: **Because of their size and range, the two E-class were much employed between the wars in the Indian Ocean and the Far East. *Enterprise* is seen here in those stations' usual colour scheme of white hull and buff funnels. The knuckle became a feature of British cruiser design.**

LEFT: **Apparently attending a 1930s Kiel Navy Week (note the German K-class cruisers), the *Frobisher* is in a festive mood. All her boats are swung out but not lowered, her liberty men going ashore in a German naval launch. Note how the anchor is catted prior to securing to the buoy.** ABOVE: ***Frobisher* is seen here with early World War II modifications. She now mounts only five main-calibre weapons but has gained high-angle armament and modern directors. Note the light tripod mainmast, radar outfit and disruptive paint scheme.**

Hawkins class

Construction of true "cruisers", built to operate independently, effectively halted in the Royal Navy when the first battlecruiser ran trials in 1908, making obsolete the current line of large cruiser development. From 1907, however, the burgeoning German Navy had been building an evolving line of "Town"-class cruisers which could, and would, be pre-positioned on distant stations in order to operate against commerce in war. Intelligence suggested that these ships would be complemented by larger cruisers with improved all-round capability, including larger-calibre guns. From 1912, therefore, the Admiralty conducted studies for a range of counters with varying combinations of size, speed, armament – and cost. Gun calibre had to be balanced against rate of fire and the 191mm/7.5in gun – used until 1908 for armoured cruisers – emerged favourite.

As the rumoured German ships turned out to be just that, the British "reply"

never materialized. With war in 1914, however, the cruiser problem proved very real. The first wave of commerce-raiding German cruisers was dealt with comparatively quickly, but the Admiralty was sufficiently concerned in 1915 about a resumption to re-examine the studies.

The Board's required combination of qualities demanded a displacement approaching 10,160 tonnes/10,000 tons, with a price tag that saw just four ordered, with a fifth some months later. Known officially as "Improved Birminghams" (a title so tenuously true as to suggest deliberate obfuscation to conceal their true function), the Hawkins class carried seven 191mm/7.5 guns, five on the centreline, two sided in the waist. Different in concept to smaller "fleet" cruisers, they carried only six torpedo tubes, two fixed, and four trainable. For extended endurance, cruising turbines were fitted, while four of the twelve boilers were coal-fired. As the reported enemy threat again failed

to materialize, most of the class were completed post-war. The fifth ship, *Cavendish*, was renamed *Vindictive* and completed as an aircraft carrier.

Hawkins class

	Built	Commissioned
Cavendish	Harland & Wolff, Belfast	September 21, 1918
Effingham	Portsmouth Dockyard	July 10, 1925
Frobisher	Devonport Dockyard	September 20, 1924
Hawkins	Chatham Dockyard	July 23, 1919
Raleigh	Beardmore, Glasgow	February 17, 1920

Hawkins class (as designed)

Displacement: 10,465 tonnes/10,300 tons (normal); 12,575 tonnes/12,350 tons (full load)
Length: 172.1m/565ft (bp); 184.3m/605ft
Beam: 17.7m/58ft
Draught: 5.3m/17ft 3in (normal)
Armament: 7 x 191mm/7.5in (7x1), 10 x 76mm/3in (10x1) and 2 x 2pdr pompom (2x2) guns; 6 x 533mm/21in torpedo tubes (2x2, 2x1)
Machinery: Geared steam turbines, 12 boilers, 4 shafts
Power: 44,742kW/60,000shp for 30 knots
Bunkers: 1,504 tonnes/1,480 tons (oil); 874 tonnes/860 tons (coal)
Protection: 38–76mm/1.5–3in (belt); 25–38mm/1–1.5in (partial protective deck)
Complement: 665

RIGHT: **Seen between the wars in Far East colours, the *Hawkins* shows the typically under-armed appearance of the class. Only the *Effingham* was fully modernized, losing the after funnel with its prominent searchlight towers and gaining an all-152mm/6in armament.**

New York (CA.2) and *Brooklyn* (CA.3)

American big-ship design of the late 19th century exhibited both foreign influence and strong individualism. Authorized in 1888, the armoured cruiser *New York* was required to operate both as a unit of a battle squadron and as a commerce destroyer. Good protection and armament were thus required to be allied to speed and endurance.

On a high-freeboard hull whose forward and after ends showed considerable French influence, six 203mm/8in guns were disposed in a twin, centreline turret forward and aft, and single wing mountings under shields in the waist. To reduce weight, barbettes projected down only one deck, but with smaller-diameter armoured tubes continuing down to the handling spaces.

Unusually, each of the two shafts was driven by two steam reciprocating engines working in tandem. Individual engines could thus be built lower and, therefore, more easily protected. For economic cruising, the leading unit could be disconnected, but a drawback, exposed in action, was that the ship had to be stopped to recouple it.

While only 76mm/3in on the flat, the *New York*'s protective deck slopes were 152mm/6in thick. Above it was a "cellular", or closely subdivided deck. The belt, at only 102mm/4in, was relatively light, but ran full length.

ABOVE: **Best-remembered for wearing Schley's flag at the Battle of Santiago in 1898, the *Brooklyn* (CA.3) showed considerable German influence, not least in the masting and the bow and stern profiles. Clearly visible is the pronounced tumblehome, which enabled the wing turrets to bear axially.**

To free the name for a new battleship, she was renamed *Saratoga* in 1911. As this name, in turn, was required for a new battlecruiser, she was further renamed *Rochester* in 1917, under which name she existed until 1938.

The *Brooklyn*, which followed some four years later from the same yard, took the design further. A better-protected and most imposing vessel, with commanding freeboard and height of funnels, she showed increasing German influence, including tubular "battlemasts". A forecastle was added to further improve seakeeping, and the 203mm/8in gun wing mountings were twinned. To improve their potential for axial fire they were located, French-style, on armoured sponsons projecting from hull sides with pronounced tumblehome.

New York (CA.2) and *Brooklyn* (CA.3)

	Built	Commissioned
Brooklyn (CA.3)	Cramp, Philadelphia	December 1, 1896
New York (CA.2)	Cramp, Philadelphia	August 1, 1893

Brooklyn (as built)

Displacement: 9,363 tonnes/9,215 tons (normal); 10,232 tonnes/10,070 tons (full load)
Length: 122m/400ft 6in (wl); 122.6m/402ft 6in (oa)
Beam: 19.7m/64ft 9in
Draught: 7.3m/24ft (normal)
Armament: 8 x 203mm/8in (4x2); 12 x 127mm/5in (12x1); 5 x 457mm/18in fixed torpedo tubes (5x1)
Machinery: 4 vertical steam reciprocating engines, 7 boilers, 2 shafts
Power: 11,931kW/16,000ihp for 20 knots
Endurance: 914 tonnes/900 tons (coal) for 9,445km/5,100nm at 10 knots
Protection: 76–203mm/3–8in (belt); 76–152mm/3–6in (protective deck); 156–203mm/6.5–8in (barbettes)
Complement: 560

ABOVE: **Earlier than the *Brooklyn*, the *New York* (CA.2) was slightly smaller but better protected. Because of only a moderate tumblehome, however, she could only accommodate single 203mm/8in guns in the waist, and these in vulnerable open mountings. The larger casemated guns were of 102mm/4in calibre.**

LEFT: *California* (CA.6) of 1904 seen here in Pacific Fleet colours. In terms of protection, as well as the effectiveness of their new-pattern 203mm/8in guns, these heavy cruisers were rated the equivalent of older battleships, hence their "state" names. Note the mix of stockless and close-stowing anchors.

BELOW: Recognizing the impracticalities of aircraft taking-off from warships, the US Navy was a pioneer of shipboard catapults. The *West Virginia* (CA.5), renamed *Huntington* in 1916, was the second to be fitted with a quarterdeck catapult, together with a kite-balloon facility.

Pennsylvania class (CA.4–9)

Victory over Spain in the war of 1898 gave the United States responsibility for significant territorial acquisition in the Caribbean and the western Pacific. Deficient in ships with the necessary endurance, however, the US Navy benefited from congressional approval for naval expansion. This included armoured cruisers, a type then of universal interest, being as large as contemporary battleships but trading armament for speed. Protection, due to Harvey armour, was not significantly sacrificed.

With limited practical experience upon which to draw, the designers of the six Pennsylvanias showed considerable technical boldness. Completed from 1905, they bear comparison with the contemporary British Duke of Edinburghs. Of a similar length, but slightly finer, the Americans displaced about 1,016 tonnes/1,000 tons more. Protection was on a very similar scale but, where the British shipped a primary battery of six 234mm/9.2in guns, the Americans, very satisfied with four 203mm/8in weapons, mounted them in twin turrets on the centerline forward

and aft. Ten 152mm/6in quick-firing (QF) guns, five per side, were located behind armour in a main-deck broadside battery. Four more of the weapons were mounted at the corners of the citadel at upper-deck level.

The prestige attached to these ships is indicated by the "state" names that were bestowed. Although somewhat under-armed, they were looked upon as Second Class battleships, to the extent that most eventually received a battleship-style cage foremast.

During World War I, however, all were renamed with more conventional "city" names. In 1918, the *San Diego* (ex-*California*) betrayed the basic frailty of the design by succumbing to a single mine.

Early in the application of aviation to its battle fleet, the US Navy used the *Huntington* (ex-*West Virginia*) in experiments with seaplane catapults and aerostats. None of the class was ever proved in action and, following some service as auxiliaries, the five survivors were scrapped in 1930–32, by which time they were totally obsolete.

Pennsylvania class (as built)

Displacement: 14,070 tonnes/13,850 tons (normal); 15,576 tonnes/15,330 tons (full load)
Length: 152.9m/502ft (wl); 153.5m/503ft 11in (oa)
Beam: 21.2m/69ft 7in
Draught: 7.3m/24ft (normal)
Armament: 4 x 203mm/8in (2x2), 14 x 152mm/6in (14x1) and 18 x 76mm/3in (18x1) guns; 2 x 457mm/18in fixed torpedo tubes (2x1)
Machinery: 2 vertical, triple-expansion engines, 30 boilers, 2 shafts
Power: 17,150kW/23,000ihp for 22 knots
Bunkers: 914 tonnes/900 tons (coal – normal), 2,032 tonnes/2,000 tons (coal – maximum)
Protection: 89–152mm/3.5–6in (belt); 38–102mm/1.5–4in (protective deck); 38–156mm/1.5–6.5in (turrets)
Complement: 825

Pennsylvania class (CA.4–9)

	Built	Commissioned
California (CA.6) (*San Diego*, 1914)	Union Ironworks, San Francisco	August 1, 1907
Colorado (CA.7) (*Pueblo*, 1916)	Cramp, Philadelphia	January 19, 1905
Maryland (CA.8) (*Frederick*, 1916)	Newport News	April 18, 1905
Pennsylvania (CA.4) (*Pittsburgh*, 1912)	Cramp, Philadelphia	March 9, 1905
South Dakota (CA.9) (*Huron*, 1920)	Union Ironworks, San Francisco	January 27, 1908
West Virginia (CA.5) (*Huntington*, 1916)	Newport News	February 23, 1905

Tennessee class (CA.10–13)

In order to achieve a desired establishment of ten modern armoured cruisers, the US Navy followed the Pennsylvanias with the four similar Tennessees, Concerned at tendencies of growth in successive classes, Congress imposed a 14,733-tonne/14,500-ton displacement limit. However, as they were to be equipped with far-weightier 254mm/10in gun twin turrets in place of the *Pennsylvania*'s 203mm/8in ordnance, and speed was to remain the same, there would have to be compromise. Improved boiler technology helped by allowing 16 boilers in place of the earlier 30. Space could thus be utilized more economically in terms of areas to be protected.

A greater proportion of the available displacement was devoted to armour although, except on casemates and turrets (strictly, gunhouses), it tended to be spread farther and more thinly. Thus, the belt was more extensive, but 25mm/1in was shaved from its maximum thickness. For the protective deck, slopes and flat were also reduced in weight. The upper-deck 76mm/3in battery, previously unprotected, received 51mm/2in armour.

The rule of thumb for capital ships was that the belt should have a thickness equal to the calibre of the main armament, and we see here, in the armoured cruiser, a warship far better able to inflict punishment than to absorb it.

With the 1917 entry of the United States into World War I, all the big cruisers were heavily involved in the escort of Atlantic convoys. For this protracted, generally low-speed duty the ships had not only to fill all available coal bunkers for a capacity of 2,032 tonnes/ 2,000 tons, but also to carry half as much again as deck cargo. Their consequent increased draught made the secondary 152mm/6in battery unworkable. Most guns were thus removed and their embrasures plated over.

Wrecked during 1916, the hull of the *Memphis* (ex-*Tennessee*) survived until 1937, while the *Seattle* (ex-*Washington*) served as an auxiliary until 1946.

ABOVE: **Purely experimental, as it prevented use of the after turret, an improved catapult was fitted to the *North Carolina* (CA.12) in 1916. Piloting a Curtiss AB-3 flying boat, Godfrey de C. Chevalier used it to make the first under-way take-off on July 12, as seen here.**

ABOVE: **An interesting view of the after 254mm/10in gun turret of the *Washington* (CA.11). Firing is being simulated with an optical aid, rigged temporarily. Three screens are aligned with the sighting hoods, and shielded mirrors are attached to each gun barrel. Note the tompion, or plug, fitted to the gun muzzle.**

ABOVE: **Although superficially similar, the Tennessees could be distinguished from the Pennsylvanias by their much larger 254mm/10in gun turrets and more complex bridge structure. All except the *Maryland* of the Pennsylvania class received battleship-style cage foremasts before World War I.**

Tennessee class (CA.10–13)

	Built	Commissioned
Montana (CA.13) (*Missoula*, 1920)	Newport News	July 21, 1908
North Carolina (CA.12) (*Charlotte*, 1920)	Newport News	May 7, 1908
Tennessee (CA.10) (*Memphis*, 1916)	Cramp, Philadelphia	July 17, 1906
Washington (CA.11) (*Seattle*, 1916)	New York Shipbuilding	August 7, 1906

Tennessee class (as built)

Displacement: 14,733 tonnes/14,500 tons (normal); 16,125 tonnes/15,870 tons (full load)
Length: 152.9m/502ft (wl); 153.7m/504ft 5in (oa)
Beam: 22.2m/72ft 11in
Armament: 4 x 254mm/10in (2x2); 16 x 152mm/6in (16x1); 22 x 76mm/3in (22x1); 4 x 533mm/21in fixed torpedo tubes (4x1)
Machinery: 2 vertical, triple-expansion engines, 16 boilers, 2 shafts
Power: 17,150kW/23,000ihp
Bunkers: 914 tonnes/900 ton (coal – normal); 2,032 tonnes/2,000 tons (maximum)
Protection: 51–127mm/2–5in (belt); 25–89mm/1–3.5in (protective deck); 51–229mm/2–9in (turrets)
Complement: 855

LEFT: The US Navy's Cruiser 2 was the *Charleston*, whose Elswick design was similar to that of the Japanese *Naniwa*. Designed to carry two 254mm/10in guns, the Americans preferred 203mm/8in ordnance but, due to their lack of availability, initially fitted twin 152mm/6in weapons. The *Charleston* never carried sailing rig.

Newark and *Charleston* (Cruisers 1 & 2)

Toward the close of the 1880s the US Navy embarked on an expansion program which taxed its resources to such an extent that, to act as the design basis for a group of protected cruisers, plans for the Japanese *Naniwa* were purchased from Armstrong at Elswick.

The *Newark*, which became Cruiser 1 of the so-called New Navy, was a typical late-Victorian warship, whose inefficient machinery needed to be backed up by a full sailing rig to confer any reasonable standard of endurance. Her heavy three-masted rig, the last aboard any American warship, precluded centerline armament, so all twelve 152mm/6in guns were mounted broadside. Four each side were sited in projecting sponsons to give an element of near-axial fire.

Although the rig was in contravention of the wishes of the General Board, it gave the ship considerable "presence", and she was fitted as a flagship, with extra accommodation below a raised poop deck.

Modernization in 1898 saw the sailing rig removed and all 152mm/6in guns replaced by newer models. Sold out in 1913, she acted as a quarantine hulk until 1926.

Her only sister, *San Francisco* (Cruiser 5), was rearmed with modern 127mm/5in weapons in 1910 and converted for minelaying, serving during World War I and then as an auxiliary through to 1939.

The *Charleston* (Cruiser 2) was a further, but slightly smaller, variation on the design. From the outset she was fitted with two light pole masts with fighting tops. This rig permitted a single 203mm/8in gun to be located on the centerline, forward and aft, with six 152mm/6in guns mounted broadside in sponsons. As the major weapons were delivered late, the ship carried a temporary armament of four further 152mm/6in guns. Her machinery was of an already obsolete compound, or double-expansion design. She was lost by grounding during 1899.

ABOVE: The last US warship designed with sail, the *Newark*, or Cruiser 1, is seen here prior to 1898, when the rig was reduced. The twelve 152mm/6in guns are all on the broadside, eight of them in distinctive, open-sided sponsons to give a degree of near-axial fire.

Newark (as completed)

Displacement: 4,149 tonnes/4,083 tons (normal)
Length: 94.4m/310ft (wl); 99.8m/327ft 7in (oa)
Beam: 15m/49ft 2in
Draught: 5.7m/18ft 9in (normal)
Armament: 12 x 152mm/6in (12x1) guns;
    6 x 356mm/14in torpedo tubes
Machinery: Steam, triple-expansion engines,
    4 boilers, 2 shafts
Power: 6,339kW/8,500ihp for 18 knots
Endurance: 864 tonnes/850 tons (coal) for
    15,371km/8,300nm at 10 knots
Protection: 51–76mm/2–3in (protective deck);
    51mm/2in (casemates)
Complement: 384

Newark, *San Francisco* and *Charleston* (Cruisers 1, 2 & 5)

	Built	Commissioned
Newark (Cruiser 1)	Cramp, Philadelphia	February 2, 1891
San Francisco (Cruiser 5)	Union Ironworks, San Francisco	November 15, 1890
Charleston (Cruiser 2)	Union Ironworks, San Francisco	December 26, 1889

Baltimore and *Philadelphia* (Cruisers 3 & 4)

Built in parallel with the three previous cruisers were two others of much the same size and capability. These, too, had their basis in an Elswick design. The 5,029-tonne/4,950-ton Spanish protected cruiser *Reina Regente* was launched in 1887, for which Armstrong had unsuccessfully tendered. However, their proposed design was well-gunned and superior to the *Charleston* in carrying four 240mm/ 9.5in guns (sided both forward and aft) and six 120mm/4.72in guns in broadside sponsoned casemates. Duly acquired, the design was translated by Cramp into the *Baltimore* (Cruiser 3), with a mix of 203mm/8in and 152mm/6in guns on the same layout.

With several variations of cruiser on virtually the same displacement, it is evident that the General Board was experimenting to find the type best-suited to its needs. Thus, built on the same hull dimensions, the *Philadelphia* (Cruiser 4) had a uniform armament of twelve 152mm/6in guns. Her layout comprised two sided 152mm/6in guns forward and aft, with four broadside guns on each side, of which the farthest forward and farthest aft were prominently sponsoned for the purpose of providing a degree of near-axial chase fire.

The arrangement aboard the *Baltimore* was obviously less than satisfactory for, following her active involvement in the war against Spain, it was modified to that of the *Philadelphia*.

Both ships were obsolete by 1910 but, where the *Philadelphia* embarked on a new career alternating as a receiving ship and prison hulk that lasted until 1927, the *Baltimore* was reprieved to be converted during 1913–14 into a

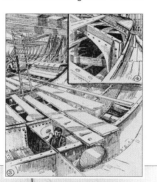

minelayer, armed with just four 127mm/ 5in guns. Involvement in laying the 70,263 mines comprising the great Northern mine barrage was followed by long service as an auxiliary until her final disposal in 1942.

TOP: **An enormous freeboard and a forest of ventilators marked the very similar *Baltimore* and *Philadelphia* (Cruisers 3 and 4 respectively). *Baltimore*'s four 203mm/8in guns are sponsoned on forecastle and poop, and the 152mm/6in secondary armament in the waist. Note the very small bridge structure and the token fighting tops.** LEFT: **A nice sketch of the *Philadelphia* under construction. Note the continuous longitudinals and intercostal transverse members. The fitter is working in what will be the double bottom. The inset shows the vaulted framing that supports the protective deck.** BELOW LEFT: **Her jack struck, the *Philadelphia* is under way, but with hammock covers still airing and the accommodation ladder down. She differed from the *Baltimore* by having a homogeneous 152mm/6in armament. Note the personnel on the open navigating bridge with the armoured conning tower beneath.**

Baltimore (as built)

Displacement: 4,470 tonnes/4,400 tons (normal); 4,677 tonnes/4,593 tons (full load)
Length: 99.8m/327ft 6in (wl); 102.1m/335ft (oa)
Beam: 14.8m/48ft 6in
Draught: 5.9m/19ft 6in (normal)
Armament: 4 x 203mm/8in (4x1) and 6 x 152mm/6in (6x1) guns; 5 x 356mm/14in torpedo tubes (5x1)
Power: 8,020kW/10,750ihp for 19 knots
Endurance: 864 tonnes/850 tons (coal) for 13,334km/7,200nm at 10 knots
Protection: 64–102mm/2.5–4in (protective deck); 51mm/2in (casemates)
Complement: 345

Baltimore and *Philadelphia* (Cruisers 3 & 4)

	Built	Commissioned
Baltimore (Cruiser 3)	Cramp, Philadelphia	January 7, 1890
Philadelphia (Cruiser 4)	Cramp, Philadelphia	July 28, 1890

Olympia (Cruiser 6)

Approved in 1890, the Second Class protected cruiser *Olympia* was conceived with an eye to commerce raiding, with a consequent high speed and long endurance.

Four 203mm/8in guns were again favoured for their penetrative power, but the weight of two twin armoured "barbette turrets" was significant to the ship's design. A 102mm/4in secondary battery was proposed to compensate for this extra weight but was rejected as being too light. Weapons of 152mm/6in, on the other hand, with projectiles of over three times the weight, were considered to have too low a rate of fire. The 127mm/5in weapon that was adopted as a compromise proved to be so satisfactory that it has remained a standard calibre to

the present day. All ten 127mm/5in guns were located in armoured casemates in a superstructure configured to permit a measure of chase fire.

On a four-hour speed trial, the *Olympia*'s "vertical-inverted, direct-acting, triple-expansion engines" developed a reported 12,593kW/17,363ihp for a speed of 21.69 knots against a service maximum of 20 knots.

The ship gained fame as the flagship of Commodore Dewey in the rout of the Spanish squadron at Manila on May 1, 1898. As with the *Baltimore*, however, the 203mm/8in pieces did not perform as well as expected in action and, in a 1901–03 modernization, the ship landed one turret, together with her four torpedo tubes, of which she had one

fixed in both bow and stern and one trainable on either side in the waist.

After this date, *Olympia*'s main employment was in sea training for midshipmen. By World War I, her value was limited, but she received a uniform armament of ten 127mm/5in guns. Her early fame saw her retained long after her useful life had expired and, after long years as a static auxiliary, she was sold out in 1957 to be restored to her original appearance as a museum ship.

ABOVE: **Honoured for her role as flagship at the 1898 Battle of Manila, the *Olympia* (Cruiser 6) survives in perpetuity as a museum ship. Unusually, side decks run the length of the central superstructure, which houses the 127mm/5in secondary armament. Two of her fighting tops have been removed.**

Olympia (as built)

Built: Union Ironworks, San Francisco
Commissioned: February 5, 1895
Displacement: 5,588 tonnes/5,500 tons (normal); 6,005 tonnes/5,910 tons (full load)
Length: 103.3m/339ft (wl); 104.8m/344ft 1in (oa)
Beam: 16.2m/53ft
Draught: 6.6m/21ft 6in (normal)
Armament: 4 x 203mm/8in (2x2) and 10 x 127mm/5in (10x1) guns; 4 x 457mm/18in torpedo tubes
Machinery: Steam, triple-expansion engines, 4 boilers, 2 shafts
Power: 10,070kW/13,500ihp for 20 knots
Endurance: 1,168 tonnes/1,150 tons (coal) for 25,000km/13,500nm at 10 knots
Protection: 51–121mm/2–4.75in (protective deck); 89–114mm/3.5–4.5in (turrets)
Complement: 420

Cincinnati class (Cruisers 7 & 8)

Described as "scout cruisers", the two Cincinnatis, completed in 1894, were contemporary with the British Apollo-class equivalents. Their superstructure, minimized to reduce profile, comprised little more than a two-level bridge, a single pole mast and two lofty funnels. Mainmasts, stump and full-height, were added later to spread W/T aerials.

One 152mm/6in gun was carried on the foredeck, while ten 127mm/5in weapons were disposed, four each side in casemates and two sided on the quarterdeck. At main deck level, the casemated pieces could have been of little use with any sea running. Two were later removed and the forward gun replaced by a further 127mm/5in.

Four torpedo tubes (one visible in the stem above the waterline) were included, although fitting of all appears doubtful. They launched the Howell torpedo, being adopted as the US Navy's standard. Engine-less and trackless, the weapon derived its propulsive energy from a heavy flywheel, run up to high speed before launch. The gyroscopic action of the flywheel maintained trim, while a heavy pendulum detected course changes and corrected them through a rod attachment with the rudders. The Howell torpedo reportedly carried a 43.5kg/96lb warhead some 365.8m/400yds at 25 knots.

As scouts, the ships' modest speed was against them, but they spent busy lives, spanning two maritime wars. In that against Spain, the *Raleigh* was present at the Manila action, while her sister participated in the blockade of Cuba. Typical of cruisers of their time, they were involved in policing operations, quelling unrest in Haiti, Nicaragua, Guatemala, San Domingo (now the Dominican Republic) and Panama. *Cincinnati* assisted in the aftermath of two natural disasters – the 1903 Mont Pelée eruption in Martinique and the 1917 San José earthquake in Guatemala. Employed in second-line operations during World War I, both were sold for scrapping in 1921.

ABOVE LEFT: **Although only capable of a moderate 19 knots, the *Cincinnati* and the *Raleigh* (seen here) were built as scout cruisers. A single 152mm/6in gun is located on the foredeck, with eight of her ten 127mm/5in guns in casemates. Freeboard is good for a ship of her size.** ABOVE: **On April 27, 1898, in the course of the blockade of Cuba, the *Cincinnati* and *New York* exchanged fire with the shore batteries covering the port of Matanzas. Note how upper-deck gun crews are completely unprotected from blast and fragments.**

Cincinnati class (Cruisers 7 & 8)

	Built	Commissioned
Cincinnati (Cruiser 7)	Brooklyn Navy Yard	June 16, 1894
Raleigh (Cruiser 8)	Norfolk Navy Yard	April 17, 1894

Cincinnati class (Cruisers 7 & 8)

Displacement: 3,373 tonnes/3,320 tons (normal); 3,698 tonnes/3,640 tons (full load)
Length: 91.4m/300ft (wl); 93.3m/306ft 2in (oa)
Beam: 12.8m/42ft
Draught: 5.5m/18ft (normal)
Armament: 1 x 152mm/6in and 10 x 127mm/5in (10x1) guns; 4 x 356mm/14in torpedo tubes
Machinery: Steam, triple-expansion engines, 2 shafts
Power: 7,460kW/10,000ihp for 19 knots
Endurance: 565 tonnes/556 tons (coal) for 16,020km/8,650nm at 10 knots
Protection: 12.7–51mm/0.5–2in (protective deck)
Complement: 310

ABOVE: **With her very lofty funnels, *Cincinnati* (Cruiser 7) appears newly completed. Two, more solid, masts were quickly added shortly thereafter. In 1918 the mainmast was reduced to a stub sufficient to support the W/T aerials. By then, the bow torpedo tube had also been removed.**

LEFT: **With her two relatively short funnels, symmetrically disposed masts and line of boats, the *Minneapolis* (Cruiser 13) could pass muster at a distance or in poor visibility as a passenger liner, a considerable advantage if operating as a commerce raider. She never served as such.**

Columbia class (Cruisers 12 & 13)

Civil war experience of blockade running and commerce-raiding made a lasting impression on American naval thought, reflected in the building of the two Columbias. These were to be fast enough to catch the fastest of transatlantic passenger liners while being fitted with bunkers sufficient for protracted operations.

At a time when American cruisers were powered for, at most, 20 knots, these were designed for 22.5 knots although only officially for 21. Hydrodynamic laws being what they are, this apparently modest increase in speed demanded an enormous increase in power. Inevitably, this solution lay in a long hull of which much (in this case, 53 per cent of waterline length) was devoted to boilers and machinery.

The required 15,658kW/21,000ihp was, for the first time, transmitted via three shafts, apparently due to limitations in shaft, rather than propeller manufacture. The three vertical reciprocating engines occupied separate spaces, those driving the wing shafts being side by side, divided by a longitudinal bulkhead, and ahead of the centerline unit. For extended endurance, or maintenance, one or other unit could be shut down.

The height of these "cathedral" engines was such that they projected through the protective deck, their tops requiring protection by an armoured glacis. An odd feature of the design was that it was intended to utilize three funnels, but *Columbia* had four and *Minneapolis* two.

The nameship made 22.8 knots on trials in 1894 (but the Cunard Line *Lucania*, in the same year, made an Atlantic crossing at an average 22 knots).

As built, the armament included two 152mm/6in chase guns on the foredeck and one 203mm/8in gun on the afterdeck to deter pursuers. This was later exchanged for two further 152mm/6in weapons.

The Columbias probably influenced the decision to build the two British Powerfuls and the French *Chateurenault*, respectively launched and laid down in 1895.

LEFT: **Designed as a commerce destroyer, *Columbia* (Cruiser 12) was unusual in having a single 203mm/8in gun on her afterdeck to deter pursuit. Two 152mm/6in guns on the foredeck were sufficient to tackle her intended quarry. Note the very tall masts for long-range W/T reception.**

Columbia class (as built)

Displacement: 7,824 tonnes/7,700 tons (normal)
Length: 125.5m/412ft (wl); 125.8m/413ft 1in (oa)
Beam: 17.7m/58ft 2in
Draught: 6.9m/22ft 6in (normal)
Armament: 1 x 203mm/8in, 2 x 152mm/6in (2x1), and 8 x 102mm/4in (8x1) guns; 4 x 356mm/14in torpedo tubes (4x1)
Machinery: 3 steam, triple-expansion engines, 10 boilers, 3 shafts
Power: 15,658kW/21,000ihp for 22.5 knots
Endurance: 2,164 tonnes/2,130 tons (coal) for 47,226km/25,500nm at 10 knots
Protection: 38–64mm/1.5–2.5in (protective deck)
Complement: 465

Columbia class (Cruisers 12 & 13)

	Built	Commissioned
Columbia (Cruiser 12)	Cramp, Philadelphia	April 23, 1894
Minneapolis (Cruiser 13)	Cramp, Philadelphia	December 13, 1894

Denver class (Cruisers 14–19)

The six Denvers resulted directly from the war against Spain, in which American success brought territorial commitments as far apart as the western Pacific and the Caribbean. Combat experience exposed the shortage of modern fighting ships, resulting in programmes for large armoured vessels, but the need to police the acquired territories required small cruisers of a type new to the US Navy.

"Cruising vessels" in the classic sense, the Denvers had no real equivalent in the British Royal Navy, although the concept was close to that of the masted-cruisers of a decade earlier still to be found on distant stations. Better described by their later categorization of "gunboats", the Denvers were usually termed "peace cruisers", an accurate description.

Never designed to fight a serious action with other ships, they were unarmoured except for a "protective deck" amidships, that had 64mm/2.5in plate only on the slopes. They were, nonetheless, well-armed, completing

with ten 127mm/5in guns. Eight of these were casemated at main deck level, with only six bearing on the broadside. None was fitted with a shield.

Where a corvette-style hull – with forecastle, poop and an open waist – might have been expected, the Denvers were flush-decked. This gave not only more spacious accommodation, necessary for duties in tropical waters, but also provided emergency troop quarters, utilized when a cruiser was summoned to quell local unrest.

They were powered for only 16.5 knots, their twin shafts giving some redundancy in the event of damage being incurred in isolated regions. Their counter sterns and lofty, but greatly

ABOVE: Usually described as "peace cruisers", the Denvers were later in their careers reclassified "gunboats". The *Cleveland* (Cruiser 19), (later CL.21) is seen here with her original ten 127mm/5in guns. After World War I, the forward two casemates were plated-in and two of their guns relocated to the upper deck. LEFT: Despite her small size, *Des Moines* (Cruiser 15) served in theatres as diverse as Canada, the Caribbean, North Russia, the Mediterranean and West Africa.

raked, funnels and masts – to say nothing of their tropical paint scheme – gave them a rather yacht-like air.

Their armament was later reduced to eight 127mm/5in guns and one 76mm/3in HA weapon. These small vessels proved to be very useful and they subsequently lasted (except for the wrecked *Tacoma*) until the 1930s.

Denver class (Cruisers 14–19)

	Built	Commissioned
Chattanooga (Cruiser 16)	Crescent Shipyard, Elizabethport, NJ	October 11, 1904
Cleveland (Cruiser 19)	Bath Iron Works, Maine	November 2, 1903
Denver (Cruiser 14)	Neafie and Levy, Philadelphia	May 17, 1904
Des Moines (Cruiser 15)	Fore River, Quincy, Massachusetts	March 5, 1904
Galveston (Cruiser 17)	Trigg, Richmond, Virginia	February 15, 1905
Tacoma (Cruiser 18)	Union Ironworks, San Francisco	January 30, 1904

Denver class (as built)

Displacement: 3,251 tonnes/3,200 tons (normal); 3,810 tonnes/3,750 tons (full load)
Length: 89m/292ft (wl); 94.1m/308ft 10in (oa)
Beam: 13.4m/44ft
Draught: 4.8m/15ft 9in (normal)
Armament: 10 x 127mm/5in (10x1) guns
Machinery: 2 steam, triple-expansion engines, 6 boilers, 2 shafts
Power: 3,730kW/5,000ihp for 16.5 knots
Endurance: 738 tonnes/725 tons (coal) for 4,075km/2,200nm at 10 knots
Protection: 64mm/2.5in (slopes in way of machinery spaces)
Complement: 330

LEFT: **A pristine** *Charleston* **(Cruiser 22) enters dry dock at Bremerton Navy Yard, Washington State. A general air of cheerful anticipation indicates that this is a homecoming. Note how the ship is being warped into the dock, the lines maintaining her alignment as she is hauled in by winch.** ABOVE: **In assisting the salvage of a submarine, stranded at Eureka, California, the** *Milwaukee* **(Cruiser 21) herself went ashore. Seen here in January 1917, she proved impossible to refloat and became a total loss. She still wears her ensign and grey, wartime livery.**

St. Louis class (Cruisers 20–22)

Authorized as 8,128-tonne/8,000-ton diminutives of the then-building Pennsylvania/Tennessee classes, the St. Louis trio only succeeded in attracting criticism as being "poor relations". Preliminary studies soon showed that the considerable size limitation would limit speed if armament and protection were to be provided to the expected standard. This would place the ships at a disadvantage compared with some foreign cruisers, and with the large armed-liners expected to be used as commerce raiders.

The first sacrifice had to be the deletion of any 203mm/8in guns in favour of an all-152mm/6in armament. A waterline belt was deemed indispensable in addition to a protective deck but, in order to confer adequate endurance, large bunkers were required, further increasing the deep displacement.

Obliged to compromise, Congress grudgingly accepted the need to increase designed displacement to 9,856 tonnes/9,700 tons. For their part, the Navy had to agree a slightly disappointing 22-knot speed and protection reduced to the point where

ABOVE: **Although having imposing looks, the three St. Louis-class ships were criticized for their light 152mm/6in armament. They were classed as "semi-armoured cruisers", yet later took "CA" (heavy cruiser) identifiers. The** *St. Louis* **(Cruiser 20), seen here, became CA.18.**

the resulting ships were described as "semi-armoured".

The 102mm/4in belt was both shallow and short, the same plate thickness also covering the eight 152mm/6in guns of the casemated main deck battery. The four weapons mounted in the superstructure at upper deck level were also protected by 102mm/4in face plates. A single unshielded centerline 152mm/6in gun was mounted both forward and aft. The lack of turrets in these positions provided a useful means of differentiating the ships from the larger armoured cruisers which, superficially, looked very similar. The protective deck

was pared down to 51mm/2in in the flat and 76mm/3in on the slopes.

The *Milwaukee* was lost by stranding in 1917 but her sisters, renumbered CA.18 (*St. Louis*) and CA.19 (*Charleston*) served until the 1930 cull of obsolete cruisers, with the entry into service of the "treaty cruisers".

St. Louis class (as built)

Displacement: 9,856 tonnes/9,700 tons (normal); 11,136 tonnes/10,960 tons (full load)
Length: 129.2m/424ft (wl); 129.9m/426ft 6in (oa)
Beam: 20.1m/66ft
Draught: 6.9m/22ft 6in (normal)
Armament: 14 x 152mm/6in (14x1) and 18 x 76mm/3in (18x1) guns
Machinery: 2 steam, triple-expansion engines, 16 boilers, 2 shafts
Power: 15,660kW/21,000ihp for 22 knots
Bunkers: 1,524 tonnes/1,500 tons (coal)
Protection: 203mm/4in (partial belt); 51–76mm/ 2–3in (protective deck)
Complement: 565

St. Louis class (Cruisers 20–22)

	Built	Commissioned
Charleston (Cruiser 22)	Newport News, Virginia	October 17, 1905
Milwaukee (Cruiser 21)	Union Ironworks, San Francisco	December 10, 1906
St. Louis (Cruiser 20)	Neafie & Levy, Philadelphia	August 18, 1906

LEFT: **Firing a festive salute (note the extra ensign at the mainmast peak), the** *Montgomery* **(Cruiser 9) is wreathed in her own smoke. Although she was named after a place, she underwent a change to release her name to a new destroyer, and was named after a person.** BELOW: **Having brought her anchor to short stay, the** *Detroit* **(Cruiser 10) is preparing to get under way. Note, from the smoke and the ensign, this activity has brought her into the wind. Her jack has already been lowered. Late in life, she was converted for merchant use.**

Montgomery class (Cruisers 9–11)

As one of the varied "ABCD Squadron" the *Dolphin* had been designed to operate against commerce but, too small to qualify as a true cruiser, she spent her life as a "peace cruiser", or gunboat.

The concept of *guerre de course* (war against commerce) remained attractive, not least through continuing French enthusiasm for it, and it was now proposed that the US Navy build three simple and inexpensive 2,000-tonne/ 1,968-ton vessels for this purpose. Congress required small hulls, in order to minimize initial cost, but proposed to use the latest technology to realize a speed of 18 knots. The two are not easily compatible, as a longer hull is more easily driven, and will reduce operational fuel costs as well as being a better sea-boat. As no builder would commit himself to an 18-knot contract speed, the requirement was reduced to 17 knots with a bonus for any improvement on this, the *Montgomery* exceeding 19 knots.

The design was very tight; plate thicknesses were defined to sixteenths of an inch (1.6mm), yet the light displacement still grew by about 10 per cent. There was no weight margin for protection, reliance being placed totally on the stopping power of coal bunkers flanking the machinery spaces. Two masts were stepped; neither was crossed but they were capable of spreading a full sail plan in order to increase cruising endurance. Nevertheless, the ships were generally regarded as gunboats.

Their designed armament – a single 152mm/6in gun forward and aft, together with eight casemated broadside 127mm/5in guns and six Howell torpedo tubes – proved to be over-ambitious, the ships being very tender. Armament was thus reduced to nine or ten 127mm/5in and only two torpedo tubes.

Obsolete, the *Detroit* was sold out in 1911. Her sisters served throughout

World War I, although *Marblehead* was renamed *Anniston* in 1918 to release the name for the new CL.12 scout cruiser.

Montgomery class (as designed)

Displacement: 2,235 tonnes/2,200 tons (normal); 2,449 tonnes/2,410 tons (full load)
Length: 78.3m/257ft (wl); 82.1m/269ft 6in (oa)
Beam: 11.3m/37ft
Draught: 4.4m/14ft 6in (normal)
Armament: 2 x 152mm/6in (2x1) and 8 x 127mm/5in (8x1); 6 x 356mm/14in torpedo tubes (6x1)
Machinery: 2 steam triple-expansion engines, 2 shafts
Power: 4,030kW/5,400ihp for 18 knots
Endurance: 5,926km/3,200nm at 10 knots
Protection: None
Complement: 275

Montgomery class (Cruisers 9–11)

	Built	Commissioned
Detroit (Cruiser 10)	Columbian Iron Works, Baltimore	July 20, 1894
Marblehead (Cruiser 11)	City Point Iron Works, Boston	April 2, 1894
Montgomery (Cruiser 9)	Columbian Iron Works, Baltimore	June 21, 1894

LEFT: **Before the advent of air reconnaissance, scout cruisers were an essential means of determining enemy disposition. This view of** *Chester,* **which took the designator CL.1, first of the new "light cruiser" sequence, clearly shows her high freeboard and small silhouette.**

Chester class (CL.1-3)

Completed in 1908, the three Chester-class scout cruisers trialled the new technologies of steam turbine propulsion and radio. They were authorized in 1904, when four pairs of experimental British scouts were fitting out. While recognizing the latter's potential, the Americans thought them too small for ocean work (they were designed primarily for North Sea operations). Their own ships were, therefore, given 16 per cent greater waterline length at a cost of 25 per cent greater displacement. The British design improved seaworthiness by using a raised forecastle and poop, linked by a lower, open waist, whereas the US approach featured a short forecastle of exceptionally high freeboard. Profile was minimized with four fairly short funnels and very little superstructure. Two very lofty masts spread the aerials for the essential radio communication. The overall appearance made little concession to grace.

The class was used to evaluate the relative merits of steam turbines and reciprocating machinery. *Birmingham* was thus conventionally powered, while *Chester* and *Salem* received Parsons and Curtis turbines, respectively. Against a contract requirement for 24 knots *Birmingham* made about 24.3 knots. *Chester* and *Salem* made about 26.5 and 26 knots respectively against an anticipated 25. The General Board, however, held endurance to be of equal value to speed.

Not intended to engage anything larger than a destroyer, the ships had only vertical (i.e. short-range) protection and a projected armament of 76mm/3in guns. These were later upgraded to 127mm/5in when foreign equivalents appeared.

Birmingham's high forecastle was utilized for Eugene Ely's historic first-ever aircraft ascent from a warship's deck in November 1910. *Chester* was renamed *York* in 1928 in order to release the name for a new "treaty cruiser". All three were discarded during 1930.

ABOVE: **An early American steam turbine warship, the** *Salem* **(CL.3) consumed enormous quantities of coal at her full speed of 24 knots. The regular and dirty task of "coaling ship" could be alleviated somewhat by mechanized facilities such as this one at Newport, Rhode Island.**

Chester class (CL.1-3)

	Built	Commissioned
Birmingham (CL.2)	Fore River, Quincy, Massachusetts	April 11, 1908
Chester (CL.1)	Bath Iron Works, Maine	April 25, 1908
Salem (CL.3)	Fore River, Quincy, Massachusetts	August 1, 1908

Chester (as built)

Displacement: 3,897 tonnes/3,835 tons (normal); 5,004 tonnes/4,925 tons (full load)
Length: 128m/420ft (wl); 128.9m/423ft 3in (oa)
Beam: 14.3m/47ft 1in
Draught: 5.1m/16ft 9in (normal)
Armament: 2 x 127mm/5in (2x1) and 6 x 76mm/3in (6x1) guns; 2 x 533mm/21in torpedo tubes (2x1)
Machinery: Direct-drive steam turbines, 12 boilers, 4 shafts
Power: 11,931kW/16,000shp for 25 knots
Endurance: 1,271 tonnes/1,250 tons (coal) for about 9,260km/5,000nm at 10 knots
Protection: 51mm/2in (belt in way of machinery spaces)
Complement: 360

LEFT: **Attending what appears to be a British Naval Review (she wears a British courtesy ensign), the *Suma* shows obvious similarities with Elswick-designed cruisers.**
BELOW: **The slightly later *Akashi* shows differences in masting and bow decoration. The dark ribband is carried at sheer strake level, giving the illusion of greater freeboard.**

Suma class

Delivered shortly before the Sino-Japanese War of 1894–95, the Elswick-built cruiser *Yoshino* created a considerable impression, underlined by the rapid acquisition of the *Esmeralda* (renamed *Izumi*) from the same yard.

The Japanese, keen to develop domestic expertise, and with these Armstrong-designed exemplars soon to be commissioned, produced a generally similar diminutive in the *Suma*. The first all-Japanese product of this type, she mounted a 152mm/6in gun forward and aft, and six 119mm/4.7in guns in slightly sponsoned openings at main deck level. She was given generous freeboard, but her builders were insufficiently vigorous in weight control, and sea trials during 1896 showed her to be tender, with inadequate stability. Modifications were required, and these were incorporated also in her sister, *Akashi*, still a year from launch.

This small modern cruiser force marked the end of piecemeal acquisition and the beginning of a coherent fighting fleet that would gain respect as the Imperial Japanese Navy.

In an era punctuated by unrest, the two ships led useful lives. In the course of the 1900 Boxer Rebellion the *Suma*, as part of a multinational force, landed Japanese marines to assist in the occupation of Tientsin. Both ships participated in the limited Japanese success of the Battle of the Yellow Sea during the Russo-Japanese War of 1904–05. Just four days later the *Akashi* received heavy mine damage at the Battle of Ulsan.

By World War I both ships were obsolete but in response to British requests for assistance in escorting Mediterranean convoys, the *Akashi* operated from Malta during 1917

as leader of two Japanese destroyer flotillas, in accordance with the terms of the Anglo-Japanese Alliance.

Both ships were demilitarized early in the 1920s, the *Suma* being scrapped in 1928 and her sister being expended as a target (ironically to air-dropped torpedoes) in 1930.

Suma class

	Built	Commissioned
Akashi	Yokosuka Navy Yard	March 30, 1899
Suma	Yokosuka Navy Yard	December 2, 1896

Suma class

Displacement: 2,753 tonnes/2,710 tons (normal)
Length: 89.9m/295ft 3in (bp); 93.4m/306ft 8in (wl)
Beam: 12.2m/40ft 1in (*Suma*); 12.7m/41ft 8in (*Akashi*)
Draught: 4.7m/15ft 5in (mean)
Armament: 2 x 152mm/6in (2x1) and
6 x 119mm/4.7in (6x1) guns; 2 x 380mm/15in torpedo tubes (2x1)
Machinery: Vertical, triple-expansion engines, 8 boilers, 2 shafts
Power: 6,263kW/8,400ihp for 20 knots
Endurance: 610 tonnes/600 tons (coal) for 22,224km/12,000nm at 10 knots
Protection: 25mm/1in (protective deck, on flats); 50mm/2in (protective deck, on slopes)
Complement: 295

ABOVE: **Compared with those of the *Suma*, the *Akashi*'s high waist bulwarks give the ship the appearance of a flush deck. In fact, she has a raised forecastle and poop.**

Asama class

Early in 1896, Armstrong laid down the armoured cruiser *O'Higgins* for Chile. The company was so confident of the design, into which it had put so much work, that it laid down two further, speculative keels. These were reserved by the Japanese, who were seeking six of the type quickly. They incorporated significant alterations at any early stage, and the final products differed considerably. Far more protection was worked into what became the Asamas, increasing displacement by some 1,626 tonnes/1,600 tons and necessitating over 1m/3ft 4in extra beam. The finer-lined Chilean vessel had no less than 30 boilers to generate the 11,931kW/16,000ihp required for 21 knots. These resulted in three very imposing funnels. The Japanese, with fewer boilers of a different type, required only two, but each handsomely exceeded the contract speed, bettering 23 knots on trials.

An unusual feature for the period was the housing of the four 203mm/8in guns in twin turrets (more correctly, gunhouses), one forward, one aft.

Fourteen 152mm/6in weapons were fitted, four in open shields in the waist, the remainder in casemates. Six casemates were located at main deck level, too low to be of much practical use.

The ships were completed in the old livery of the Imperial Japanese Navy – black hull, white upperworks, black funnels with white identification bands. A somewhat forbidding scheme, it was abandoned for all-grey paintwork in 1903, soon after the Royal Navy changed from its handsome Victorian livery.

Both ships had long lives and saw considerable action. During the Russo-Japanese War, *Asama* served at Chemulpo and the Yellow Sea, and *Tokiwa* at Port Arthur and Ulsan. Both were extensively damaged at Tsushima. During World War I, by contrast, both saw much activity but no action. With the general disarmament of the 1920s, they were downgraded to coastal defence and training, but *Tokiwa*, converted for minelaying, served actively during World War II. Both survived but were scrapped during 1947.

ABOVE LEFT: **A veteran of Tsushima, the *Asama* is pictured in an early aerial view. She is in grey livery, with her original armament and probably wears the flag of a rear admiral. Note how the light emphasizes the tumblehome amidships.**

ABOVE: **An impressive early view of *Tokiwa*, laying to anchor and dressed overall. The bulge in the stem accommodates the outboard end of a capped torpedo tube. While still serving as a training ship, *Tokiwa*, with other venerable Japanese warships, was sunk in shallow water by American aircraft in August 1945, and was scrapped in 1947.**

Asama class

	Built	Commissioned
Asama	Armstrong Whitworth, Elswick	February 8, 1899
Tokiwa	Armstrong Whitworth, Elswick	April 18, 1899

Asama (as built)

Displacement: 9,825 tonnes/9,670 tons (normal); 10,668 tonnes/10,500 tons (full load)
Length: 124.3m/408ft (bp); 134.7m/442ft (oa)
Beam: 20.4m/67ft
Draught: 7.5m/24ft 6in
Armament: 4 x 203mm/8in (2x2) and 14 x 152mm/6in (14x1) guns; 5 x 457mm/18in torpedo tubes (5x1)
Machinery: Vertical, triple-expansion engines, 12 boilers, 2 shafts
Power: 13,423kW/18,000ihp for 22 knots
Endurance: 1,422 tonnes/1,400 tons (coal) for 18,520km/10,000nm at 10 knots
Protection: 89–178mm/3.5–7in (belt); 51mm/2in (protective deck); 152mm/6in (turrets)
Complement: 700

LEFT: **Seen in an early paint scheme, the *Asama* still has her heavy fighting tops and anti-torpedo nets. Despite her battleship-like appearance, the turreted guns were only of 203mm/8in calibre with 152mm/6in ordnance in the casemates and waist. She was badly damaged on two occasions by stranding.**

LEFT: **Seen later in her career, *Iwate* has had her anti-torpedo nets removed and has only small fire-control platforms on her masts. Her secondary armament has also been reduced.** BELOW: **In obsolescence, the *Iwate* made 16 overseas cruises as a cadet training ship. Although reboilered, she retained coal firing.**

Idzumo class

The Japanese requirement for six new armoured cruisers resulted in Armstrong receiving a repeat *Asama* order. Armoured cruisers at this time had so inflated a reputation that they were held to be worthy of laying in a line of battle. The advisability of doing this depended much upon the quality of the opposition, the Japanese getting away with it against the Russians.

Not surprisingly, the new ships (*Idzumo* is sometimes rendered *Izumo*) followed the *Asama* design closely, the major difference being in the latter's dated cylindrical boilers being supplanted by Bellevilles. These large water-tube units had seen early problems but had been used successfully by Armstrong in the Chilean *O'Higgins*. More efficient, but individually of lower output, 24 Bellevilles were required. Less demanding of space, however, they enabled the Idzumos to be marginally shorter than the Asamas despite a necessary reversion to the three-funnelled *O'Higgins* arrangement.

As the new boiler outfit was also considerably lighter, a greater proportion of the ships' displacement could be devoted to protection, a weight redistribution which, in turn, led to an extra 0.5m/1ft 6in in beam. The designed displacement was the same, as was the armament, except for the deletion of the torpedo tube let into the ship's stems (in the Asamas this fitting had attracted its own 152mm/6in armour cladding).

Both ships received extensive damage at the Battle of Ulsan (1904) and again at Tsushima (1905) but proved well able to absorb it. Following a relatively uneventful World War I (although *Iwate* assisted in the capture of the German enclave and naval base of Tsingtao) both were downgraded to coastal defence ships. During the 1930s they were reboilered for reduced power, their armament also being greatly reduced. Used for training during World War II, they were sunk at Kure in shallow water in 1945.

Idzumo class

	Built	Commissioned
Idzumo	Armstrong Whitworth, Elswick	September 6, 1900
Iwate	Armstrong Whitworth, Elswick	February 22, 1901

Idzumo (as built)

Displacement: 9,906 tonnes/9,750 tons (normal); 10,435 tonnes/10,270 tons (full load)
Length: 121.9m/400ft (bp); 132.5m/434ft 10in (oa)
Beam: 20.9m/68ft 6in
Draught: 7.3m/24ft (normal)
Armament: 4 x 203mm/8in (2x2), 14 x 152mm/6in (14x1) and 12 x 76mm/3in (12x1) guns; 4 x 457mm/18in torpedo tubes (4x1)
Machinery: Vertical, triple-expansion engines, 24 boilers, 2 shafts
Power: 10,817kW/14,500ihp for 20.75 knots
Endurance: 1,575 tonnes/1,550 tons (coal) for 12,964km/7,000nm at 10knots
Protection: 76–178mm/3–7in (belt); 64mm/2.5in (protective deck); 152mm/6in (turrets)
Complement: 680

LEFT: **This impression of the *Idzumo* (often rendered *Izumo*), shows the ship with fighting tops and full armament. During the early 1920s, all the Japanese armoured cruisers landed their lower casemated 152mm/6in guns.**

Yakumo and *Azuma*

ABOVE LEFT: **Seen at about the beginning of World War I, the *Yakumo* has gained masthead fire-control platforms, but retains her anti-torpedo nets.**
ABOVE: **Aerial views of earlier ships are unusual, but valuable in giving a clear view of the mass of topside detail then common. Note the great height of the light W/T topmast extensions.**

The final pair of armoured cruisers acquired by Japan following the war with China is interesting in that one each was built in France and Germany, affording a useful comparison with their Elswick running mates.

With identical armament specifications, both ships, like the Elswicks, carried four 203mm/8in guns in twin centerline turrets. There were two fewer 152mm/6in weapons, but eight of them were located at upper deck level (four casemated and four in open shields) and only four in casemates on the main deck, where they were of limited use.

As with the second pair of Elswick vessels, both were specified with 24 Belleville boilers. In the German-built *Yakumo*, these were grouped in adjacent spaces, resulting in three symmetrically spaced funnels. The French-built *Azuma*, in contrast, enhanced survivability by separating boiler rooms with a machinery

space. This necessitated a hull some 5.5m/18ft greater in length and unevenly spaced funnels.

Both thickness of protection and endurance were also to be the same and, as displacement was not fixed, national characteristics asserted themselves. The German was the shorter, beamier and slower, reflecting the requirement for shallower-draught designs, and the philosophy that a capacity for absorbing hard knocks rated as a higher priority than providing an extra knot of speed.

The careers of each paralleled those of the four Elswick boats. Extensively and effectively employed during the Russo-Japanese War, they spent most of World War I uneventfully in the Pacific. Both were re-rated for coastal defence during the 1920s but, where the *Yakumo* was reboilered for lower power and partial oil-firing, the *Azuma* was not,

being reduced to harbour service in 1941. Rearmed virtually as an anti-aircraft cruiser, the *Yakumo* survived hostilities to be used post-war to repatriate Japanese garrisons. She, and the bomb-damaged *Azuma,* were both scrapped during 1946.

Yakumo and *Azuma*

	Built	Commissioned
Azuma	Soc. Des Ch. De la Loire, St. Nazaire	July 17, 1900
Yakumo	AG Vulcan, Stettin	June 7, 1900

Yakumo (as built)

Displacement: 9,891 tonnes/9,735 tons (normal); 10,455 tonnes/10,290 tons (full load)
Length: 124.6m/408ft 11in (bp); 132.2m/434ft (oa)
Beam: 19.5m/64ft
Draught: 7.2m/23ft 8in (normal)
Armament: 4 x 203mm/8in (2x2), 12 x 152mm/6in (12x1) and 12 x 76mm/3in (12x1) guns; 5 x 457mm/18in torpedo tubes (5x1)
Machinery: Vertical, triple-expansion engines, 24 boilers, 2 shafts
Power: 11,560kW/15,500ihp for 20 knots
Endurance: 1,320 tonnes/1,300 tons (coal) for 12,964km/7,000nm at 10 knots
Protection: 89–178mm/3.5–7in (belt), 64mm/2.5in (protective deck); 152mm/6in (turrets)
Complement: 725

ABOVE: **Although constructed to the same specification, the German-built *Yakumo* (above) and the French-built *Azuma* show clear external differences due to preferences in national style.**

LEFT: **Judging by the French pre-Dreadnought battleship in the background, this picture of *Nisshin* was taken in 1917 during her spell cooperating with Allied ships in the Mediterranean. The very symmetrical layout was typical of Italian-designed ships at about the turn of the century.**

Kasuga class

Having used armoured cruisers to good effect against the Chinese, the Japanese acquired more as friction built up, shortly afterward, with Russia. Already having built in Britain, France and Germany, they now looked to Italy.

Beginning in 1894 the Italian Navy had sought to build a new type, designed to suit its requirements. Purchasers, however, were readily available, the first four hulls going to Argentina, the fifth to Spain. The Italians then built three to their own account before Argentina ordered two more. These were laid down in 1902 as the *Mitra* and *Roca* but launched as *Rivadavia* and *Moreno* respectively. At this stage, ownership passed to the Japanese, the ships completing as *Kasuga* and *Nisshin*.

Italian fashion in major warships was to have two groups of boiler rooms separated by the machinery space. This

resulted in two funnels with exceptionally wide spacing, and with minimal superstructure set around them. Dead amidships rose a single powerful mast, creating a symmetrical, double-ended effect from which it was difficult to estimate the ship's heading.

The somewhat ad hoc nature of the acquisition was reflected in the *Kasuga* being built with a single 254mm/10in gun turret forward and a twin 203mm/8in gun turret aft, her sister having two twin 203mm/8in mountings. Both had fourteen 152mm/6in guns, of which ten were casemated at main deck level. Of limited use, these were later landed.

Delivered early in 1904, both ships were able to play significant roles against the Russian fleet at both the Yellow Sea and Tsushima. Both ships received 12 more modern boilers in 1914 and, following World War I, had their

152mm/6in secondary batteries replaced by more advanced weapons. By the 1930s both had been reduced to training duties and, in 1936, *Nisshin* was expended as a target. *Kasuga* was scrapped following World War II.

Kasuga class

	Built	Commissioned
Kasuga	Ansaldo, Sestri Ponente	December 20, 1903
Nisshin	Ansaldo, Sestri Ponente	January 17, 1904

Kasuga (as built)

Displacement: 7,783 tonnes/7,660 tons (normal), 8,621 tonnes/8,485 tons (full load)
Length: 104.8m/344ft (bp); 111.5m/366ft (wl)
Beam: 18.7m/61ft 4in
Draught: 7.4m/24ft 3in (normal)
Armament: 1 x 254mm/10in gun, 2 x 203mm/8in (1x2), 14 x 152mm/6in (14x1) and 10 x 76mm/3in (10x1) guns; 4 x 457mm/18in torpedo tubes (4x1)
Machinery: Vertical, triple-expansion engines, 8 boilers, 2 shafts
Power: 11,040kW/14,800ihp for 20 knots
Endurance: 1,209 tonnes/1,190 tons (coal) for 10,186km/5,500 miles at 10 knots
Protection: 76–150mm/3–5.9in (belt); 20–35mm/0.8–1.4in (protective deck); 120–150mm/4.5–5.9in (turrets)
Complement: 550

LEFT: **Armoured cruisers such as *Kasuga* were affected by the 1922 Washington Treaty, following which she was partially disarmed to serve out her career as a training ship, being scrapped in 1948.**

Tsukuba and Kurama classes

Determined to achieve total independence in warship production the Japanese had their first naval constructor of note, Lt (later Vice-Admiral) Kondo Motoki, qualify at the Royal Naval College, Greenwich. His first major projects were the four Tsukuba and Kuramas and the two Satsuma-class battleships, to which they bore a distinct "family resemblance".

Although ordered in 1904, the two Tsukubas were not completed until 1908, by which time the British had introduced the *Dreadnought* and the battlecruiser (still referred to as a "large armoured cruiser"). These had also exploited the advantages of steam turbine propulsion and primary oil-firing.

TOP: **The exceptionally uncluttered appearance of the *Tsukuba* contrives to give an impression of fragility. The housing of the anti-torpedo nets is particularly neat.** ABOVE: **In reality an elegant ship, the *Satsuma* had a broadside weight of about 94 per cent that of the British *Dreadnought*. Lacking the latter's steam turbine machinery, however, she was significantly slower.**

Kondo's initial enterprise was thus dated even before completion, with the problem compounded further by the *Dreadnought* being brought to builders' trials in the proverbial "year and a day", a construction time setting a benchmark against which Japan's new-found expertise would be tested.

Not surprisingly, Kondo specified an armament disposition that echoed contemporary Western practice, i.e. large-calibre weapons in centerline turrets forward and aft, with medium-calibre guns sided on two levels in casemates and open shields.

By way of comparison, at the time of the Tsukubas' laying-down the French were building the *Michelet* and *Rénan* with four 194mm/7.64in and twelve 164.7mm/6.48in guns apiece, while the British were completing the Devonshires (four 191mm/7.5in and six 152mm/6in guns). Kondo, however, decreed four 305mm/12in, twelve 152mm/6in and twelve 119mm/4.7in guns. Here, he was profiting from experience in war, choosing big guns for their penetrative power, medium calibre for shredding an opponent above his armour, and minor calibre sufficient to stop destroyers.

Battleships, he believed, should dominate from a distance and, with the Satsumas, he nearly trumped the *Dreadnought* in specifying no less than sixteen 305mm/12in guns. Only lack of finance saw the ships completed with a mixed armament of four 305mm/12in and twelve 254mm/10in guns.

ABOVE: **Completed slightly earlier than her otherwise identical sister *Kurama*, *Ibuki* was given pole masts. With optical fire-control instruments now being located in the tops, the vibration could prove unacceptable.**

As *Satsuma*'s sister, *Aki* acquired steam turbine propulsion by virtue of being laid down a year later, as did *Ibuki*, the second ship of the Tsukubas' follow-on pair. The Tsukubas' heavy main battery was paid-for in speed, which was only 20.5 knots, compared with the 22–23 knots of the aforementioned French and British ships. (To refer to the Tsukuba quartette as "battlecruisers", as they later were, was to totally misrepresent the term.)

The later *Kurama* and *Ibuki* were of rather higher power to realize 21.25 and 22.5 knots respectively. Their extra steam plant, fitted with oil sprayers in addition to coal firing, required more space, increasing overall length by 10.7m/35ft. Beam was increased by only a negligible amount, but room was found for four twin 203mm/8in turrets, which complemented the two twin 305mm/12in mountings in a "hexagonal" layout.

Japanese-designed ships of this era had a sort of fragile elegance that belied the determined manner in which they were fought. With their three funnels and lofty masts (*Kurama* had tripods) the latter pair were, perhaps marginally the more handsome, but all looked good at speed.

All, of course, were completed well after hostilities with Russia but, early in World War I, British and Australian naval forces were assisted by a Japanese squadron comprising *Tsukuba*, *Kurama* and the earlier *Asama* in the search for von Spee's fugitive force. No encounter resulted, but it would be most interesting to war-game the likely outcome of such a clash, the opposing forces being better balanced.

Shortly before, the *Ibuki* had been sharing convoy escort with the Australian cruiser *Sydney*, but it was the latter that had the good fortune to be detached, resulting in the detection and destruction of the German raider *Emden*.

Designed with insufficient experience, constructed too hastily, the four (and, indeed, the Satsumas) were not judged to be successful. *Tsukuba* blew up in 1917, while the remainder were scrapped by 1924, a consequence of Washington Treaty limitations.

ABOVE: *Ikoma*'s crew "man ship" for a fleet review at Kiel. Her five large searchlights, strategically located, indicate a continuing interest in night engagements. The lack of canvas dodgers around them give *Ikoma* a more open appearance than that of her sister. BELOW: At speed, *Ibuki* shows an elegant profile. With mixed armaments and only 20–22 knots' speed, the four were never the battlecruisers that they were labelled.

BELOW: **A fine picture of *Kurama*, with her heavy tripod masts. Note the large twin 203mm/8in turrets in the waist and the triangular day-shape hoists, probably indicating rudder angle.**

Tsukuba and Kurama classes

	Built	Commissioned
Ikoma	Kure Naval Yard	March 24, 1908
Tsukuba	Kure Naval Yard	January 14, 1907
Ibuki	Kure Naval Yard	November 1, 1909
Kurama	Yokosuka Naval Yard	February 28, 1911

Kurama (as built)

Displacement: 14,875 tonnes/14,640 tons (normal); 15,850 tonnes/15,600 tons (full load)
Length: 136.8m/449ft (bp); 147.8m/485ft (oa)
Beam: 22.9m/75ft 4in
Draught: 7.9m/26ft 1in (normal)
Armament: 4 x 305mm/12in (2x2), 8 x 203mm/8in (4x2) and 14 x 119mm/4.7in (14x1) guns; 3 x 457mm/18in torpedo tubes (3x1)
Machinery: Vertical, triple-expansion engines, 28 boilers, 2 shafts
Power: 16,778kW/22,500ihp for 21.25 knots
Bunkers: 2,032 tonnes/2,000 tons (coal) and 218 tonnes/215 tons (oil)
Protection: 152–178mm/6–7in (belt); 51mm/2in (protective deck); 152–178mm/6–7in (turrets)
Complement: 845

LEFT: The *Pisani* laying at Genoa. Note how the armoured area amidships is devoid of scuttles and how the tubular masts are stiff enough to obviate the need for standing rigging, which would inhibit upper-deck guns. ABOVE: As she appeared during World War I, *Pisani* has landed her mainmast and had the foremast considerably reduced. The lower fighting top is now a searchlight platform and a pair of canvas windsails augments the ventilation amidships.

Vettor Pisani class

Italy's first armoured cruiser (although reckoned a "Third Class battleship") was the 4,572-tonne/4,500-ton *Marco Polo*, completed in 1894. Although given a forecastle and poop, she appeared to have a flush-deck at first glance because a wide central deckhouse ran the length of the waist. Of her six 152mm/6in guns, one was carried on both forecastle and poop, with two sided at either end of the waist and able to fire to within 30 degrees of the axis. Two casemated 119mm/4.7in guns gave axial fire from either end, with six more in open shields firing broadside from the waist.

Five years later the Italian Navy returned to the same yard for the *Vettor Pisani*, one of two "Second Class battleships". Twelve 152mm/6in guns were carried but only four were sided at upper deck level, the remaining eight being casemated on the low-freeboard middle deck. There was a forecastle but no poop. Chase fire was limited to a single axial 119mm/4.7in weapon and two 152mm/6in guns sided at upper deck level but not able to bear within 15 degrees of the axis. Two 152mm/6in and one 119mm/4.7in guns could bear directly aft across the quarterdeck.

The Pisanis' profile differed from that of the *Marco Polo* largely in the widely spaced funnels. These resulted from interposing the machinery space between two pairs of boiler rooms. Stout, tubular "military masts" with fighting tops also replaced the pole masts of the *Marco Polo*.

By World War I the cruisers were obsolete and were designated for operations in support of the military. These were considerable, involving the supply and evacuation of the Serbian Army from Albania, and supporting Italian expeditionary forces in Albania and Macedonia. In 1917 both *Marco Polo* and *Carlo Alberto* were stripped for conversion to troop transports, being renamed *Cortellazzo* and *Zenson* respectively. All three were scrapped by 1922, at a time of general clear-out of obsolete and superfluous war-built tonnage.

Vettor Pisani (as built)

Displacement: 6,827 tonnes/6,720 tons (normal); 7,358 tonnes/7,242 tons (full load)
Length: 99m/325ft (bp); 105.7m/347ft (oa)
Beam: 18m/59ft 1in
Draught: 7m/23ft (normal)
Armament: 12 x 152mm/6in (12x1), 6 x 119mm/4.7in (6x1) and 2 x 75mm/2.95in guns; 5 x 450mm/17.7in torpedo tubes (5x1)
Machinery: Vertical, triple-expansion engines, 8 boilers, 2 shafts
Power: 9,694kW/13,000ihp for 19 knots
Endurance: 998 tonnes/982 tons (coal) and 120 tonnes/118 tons (oil) for 11,112km/6,000nm at 10 knots
Protection: 110–150mm/4.3–5.9in (belt); 37mm/1.5in (protective deck); 150mm/5.9in (casemates)
Complement: 504

ABOVE: Arriving for a foreign port visit, the *Alberto* has "manned ship", is lowering the accommodation ladder and has put the pinnace overside with the boat derrick.

Vettor Pisani class

	Built	Commissioned
Marco Polo	Cantiere di Castellammare di Stabia	July 21, 1894
Carlo Alberto	La Spezia Navy Yard	May 1, 1898
Vettor Pisani	Cantiere di Castellammare di Stabia	April 1, 1898

LEFT: **The sinking of the *Garibaldi* by the Austrian submarine *U-4* on July 18, 1915, was controversial; firstly because the Italian divisional commander did not cancel the operation once spotted by aircraft, and secondly because the U-boat commander did not attempt to sink the whole cruiser division, which was steaming in-line ahead.** ABOVE: **Seen pre-war, the *Garibaldi* has already adopted all-grey livery. Unusually, the forward turret housed a single 254mm/10in gun, the after turret two 203mm/8in, while the broadside armament was of 152mm/6in calibre. Because of the single mast, W/T spreaders have had to be added to the forward funnel.**

Garibaldi class

Notable for their symmetry of profile, the Garibaldis were a heavier type of armoured cruiser than the Pisanis and, built later, answered critics of the latter's light armament. They were to be capable of laying in a line of battle, yet have the flexibility necessary to conduct independent missions. This resulted in a strange assortment of weapons, with a single 254mm/10in gun turreted forward and two 203mm/8in aft. Of fourteen 152mm/6in guns, two were sided in open shields abreast each funnel, with the remaining ten casemated at main deck level, creating useful ventilation ports.

They were apparently designed to an "ideal" weight distribution, whereby 40 per cent of normal displacement was allocated to the bare hull, 25 per cent to added protection, 20 per cent to propulsion and 15 per cent to armament. The result certainly looked right, the high-freeboard, flush-decked hull looking well in the handsome black and buff livery that pre-dated the universal grey.

The 254mm/10in gun fired a 198kg/436lb projectile, compared with the 113kg/249lb shell of the 203mm/8in weapon which had a higher rate of fire. Probably the best test of this peculiar combination came with Japanese experience at Tsushima. The two Garibaldis fought in the battle line, the *Kasuga* with one 254mm/10in and two

LEFT: **At anchor on a windless day, the *Ferruccio* is shown to advantage by the hazy sun. She appears to be painted in a relatively pale livery of uniform shade. As her broadside armament is missing she is probably acting as a training ship (1924–29).**

203mm/8in guns, the *Nisshin* with two twin 203mm/8in mountings. That the Japanese subsequently retained the 254mm/10in weapon appears to indicate that fire-control complications were not insurmountable.

Having constructed five of the class to foreign account before taking on their own, the Italians found these reliable workhorses. Their involvement in the 1911 war against Turkey did not test them unduly and World War I was spent largely in the Adriatic where, in 1915, the *Garibaldi* fell victim to an Austrian

submarine. The surviving pair was relegated to training duties post-war, the *Varese* being discarded in 1923 and the newer *Ferruccio* in 1930.

Garibaldi class

	Built	Commissioned
Francesco Ferruccio Giuseppe	Venice Navy Yard	September 1, 1905
Garibaldi	Ansaldo, Genoa	January 1, 1901
Varese	Orlando, Livorno	April 5, 1901

Garibaldi (as built)

Displacement: 7,467 tonnes/7,350 tons (normal); 8,230 tonnes/8,100 tons (full load)

Length: 104.9m/344ft 2in (bp); 111.8m/366ft 10in (oa)

Beam: 18.2m/59ft 9in

Draught: 6.9m/22ft 8in (normal)

Armament: 1 x 254mm/10in; 2 x 203mm/8in (1x2), 14 x 152mm/6in (14x1) and 10 x 76mm/3in; 4 x 450mm/17.7in torpedo tubes (4x1)

Machinery: Vertical, triple-expansion engines, 24 boilers, 2 shafts

Power: 10,444kW/14,000ihp for 19.5 knots

Endurance: 1,219 tonnes/1,200 tons (coal) for 17,224km/9,300nm at 10 knots

Protection: 80–150mm/3.1–5.9in (belt); 38mm/1.5in (protective deck); 140–150mm/5.5–5.9in (turrets)

Complement: 550

Piemonte, Lombardia and *Calabria*

Being built speculatively by Armstrong, the *Piemonte* was acquired by the Italian Navy in 1888. The Elswick cruisers enjoyed a reputation for being faster and more heavily armed than Royal Navy equivalents. This was sometimes achieved through design short-cuts, such as restricted bunker space and the use of fast-running, reciprocating machinery which, while more compact, was also more prone to mechanical problems. Speed also depended upon fine hull forms, which could detract from stability. With a length-on-breadth (L/B) ratio of about 8.42, *Piemonte* was not unduly fine but still compared with 7.34 for contemporary British Apollos.

The ship was over-gunned when purchased, four of her six 152mm/6in guns being sided in large sponsons which, in so small a ship, created wetness. Both guns and sponsons were soon removed. With reduced armament, *Piemonte* was well thought of, but remained a one-off.

In 1888 the Italians also laid down the *Lombardia*, first of a domestically designed class. Four knots inferior to the Elswick ship, these had a comfortable L/B ratio of only 7.05, better able to accommodate their four 152mm/6in and six 119mm/4.7in guns. Known as "*Regioni*", the class varied considerably in detail. Deeper in the hull, they incorporated a cellular level above the protective deck, a feature lacking in *Piemonte*.

The Italian Navy had acquired the Armstrong-built *Dogali* a few years earlier and she, rather than the *Piemonte*, accounted for a distinct "family resemblance".

Calabria was a single-funnelled variant with a three-masted sailing rig. Intended for protracted colonial duties she was, like many of her British equivalents, wood-sheathed for comfort and for resistance to fouling.

Obsolete in a new century, the class found employment as submarine/seaplane tenders or as minelayers.

ABOVE: **Still lacking her armament, *Calabria* is seen here running trials in May 1897. The only single-funnelled variant of the "*Regioni*", she has her schooner-rig canvas bent and awnings furled along her length on the centreline. Note the half-cased funnel.**

Piemonte and Lombardia and Calabria classes

	Built	Commissioned
Piemonte	Armstrong, Elswick	August 8, 1889
Calabria	La Spezia Navy Yard	July 12, 1897
Elba	Cantiere di Castellammare de Stabia	December 1, 1895
Etruria	Orlando, Livorno	July 11, 1894
Liguria	Ansaldo, Genoa	December 1, 1894
Lombardia	Cantiere de Castellammare de Stabia	February 16, 1893
Puglia	Taranto Navy Yard	May 26, 1901
Umbria	Orlando, Livorno	February 16, 1894

Lombardia (as built)

Displacement: 2,428 tonnes/2,390 tons (normal); 2,844 tonnes/2,800 tons (full load)
Length: 80m/262ft 7in (bp); 84.8m/278ft 4in (oa)
Beam: 12m/39ft 4in
Draught: 4.6m/15ft 1in (normal)
Armament: 4 x 152mm/6in (4x1), 6 x 119mm/4.7in (6x1), and 8 x 57mm/2.2in (8x1) guns; 3 x 450mm/17.7in torpedo tubes (3x1)
Machinery: Horizontal, triple-expansion engines, 4 boilers, 2 shafts
Power: 5,222kW/7,000ihp for 17.5 knots
Endurance: 467 tonnes/460 tons (coal) for 7,408km/4,000nm at 10 knots
Protection: 50mm/2in (protective deck)
Complement: 257

ABOVE: **A high bulwark surrounded the extent of the armament of the *Etruria*. At either end, sided 152mm/6in guns are clearly visible, while the positions of the three starboard-side 119mm/4.7in weapons are nicely picked out by the oblique light. Note the old-fashioned tops and fidded topmasts.**

Goito class

ABOVE: The stern profile of individual ships of the class (this is the *Goito*) varied depending on whether the stern torpedo tube was located internally or on deck.

The late 1880s saw the full flowering of the French Navy's *"Jeune École"* movement, which believed that overwhelming numbers of small, torpedo-armed craft could offset the strength of the Royal Navy and also that of the Italians; the latter viewed as the "principal enemy" astride the route to and from French interests in the Levant.

Exercises showed, however, that such small craft were so slowed by a chop that they were vulnerable to larger vessels which, while not necessarily faster, could maintain speed in the conditions.

In addition to guns, these larger craft could, themselves carry torpedoes. The first British attempt, four 533-tonne/525-ton Grasshoppers of 1896, were too small, but these were immediately followed by fourteen 747-tonne/735-ton Gossamers. These, known as "torpedo gunboats", probably inspired the four Italian Goitos. Elevated to "torpedo cruisers", three were authorized in

1885 and a further one in 1887. Their designer, the great Benedetto Brin, here experimented, so that they differed very considerably.

Like their British equivalents, all carried five 356mm/14in torpedo tubes but the requirement for 18 knots resulted in differing solutions. Two were twin-screwed, the two-funnelled *Goito* making her contracted speed but the single-funnelled *Confianza* being slower by 1 knot. Both of the others were triple-screwed, the centerline shaft extending beneath and beyond the rudder blade. The *Montebello* alone had three tall, unevenly spaced funnels of exaggerated rake. She also had triple-expansion engines, against the remainder's old-fashioned double-expansion, or "compound" machinery.

Where the British ships carried one or two 119mm/4.7in guns, these were difficult to lay in poor conditions and the Italians, more realistically opted for 57mm/2.2in weapons, except in the *Confianza*.

The type proved an evolutionary dead-end in both navies as torpedo craft themselves developed into "torpedo boat destroyers". Only *Goito* and *Montebello* lasted long enough to see service during World War I.

Goito class

	Built	Commissioned
Confienza	La Spezia Navy Yard	April 11, 1890
Goito	Cantiere di Castellammare di Stabia	February 16, 1888
Montebello	La Spezia Navy Yard	January 21, 1889
Monzambano	La Spezia Navy Yard	August 11, 1889

Goito (as built)

Displacement: 856 tonnes/842 tons (normal); 1,062 tonnes/1,045 tons (full load)
Length: 70m/229ft 9in (bp); 73.4m/240ft 11in (oa)
Beam: 7.9m/25ft 11in
Draught: 3.4m/11ft 8in (normal)
Armament: 4 x 57mm/2.2in guns (4x1) and 5 x 37mm/1.46in (5x1) guns; 5 x 356mm/14in torpedo tubes (5x1)
Machinery: Three vertical compound engines, 6 boilers, 3 shafts
Power: 1,954kW/2,620ihp for 18 knots
Endurance: 180 tonnes/177 tons (coal) for 1,852km/1,000nm for 10 knots
Protection: 25–40mm/1–1.6in (protective deck)
Complement: 107

LEFT: The *Monzambano* combines a low-freeboard forward end with a torpedo-boat-style turtledeck. The extreme rake of funnels and masts gives the illusion of a list.

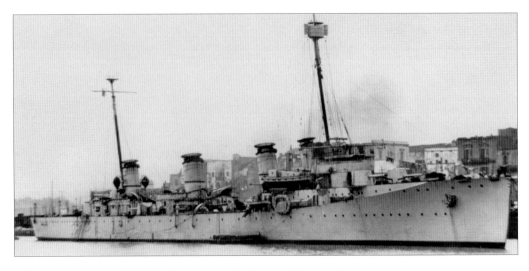

Quarto and Bixio and Aquila classes

Early scouts of the Italian Navy had struggled to reach 22 knots but, with the development of the steam turbine and oil-firing, authorization was given in 1909 for a new-style prototype in which protection and weight of armament would be subordinated to speed. The resulting *Quarto* proved to be capable of 28 knots on a displacement of some 3,271 tonnes/3,220 tons, carrying a light armament of six 119mm/4.7in guns and two torpedo tubes. This compared with the contemporary British Boadiceas (3,404 tonnes/3,350 tons, 26 knots, six or ten 102mm/4in guns, two torpedo tubes) and the German Kolbergs (4,430 tonnes/4,360 tons, 25.5 knots, twelve 10.5cm/4.1in, two torpedo tubes). With a 50mm/2in protective deck, the Kolbergs were heavier all round but the *Quarto*, with a 40mm/1.6in deck, compared very favourably with the largely unprotected Boadiceas.

ABOVE: Despite their extra funnel, the *Bixio* and *Marsala* (seen here) were of lower installed power, and slower than the *Quarto* prototype. The funnel caps were distinctive. As scout cruisers, they have high-mounted lookouts and topmasts for long-range radio communication.

The *Quarto* had four sets of direct-drive Parsons steam turbines, although only two shafts were required to transmit the full thrust via small-diameter, high-revving propellers. For years she was among the fastest ships in the Italian Navy, operating usually as a destroyer leader. She was able to carry a deck-load of 200 mines and, for a period in the late 1920s, added a small Macchi floatplane. She was discarded early in 1939.

Built in parallel with the *Quarto*, the two Bixios provided a useful comparison. Both types had a raised forecastle, but the Bixios carried their flare further aft, adopting a characteristic

ABOVE: During World War I, the *Bixio* and *Marsala* could be differentiated by the positions of their searchlights. These flanked the third funnel of the *Bixio* (seen here) and the fourth funnel of the *Marsala* (above right).

ABOVE: *Marsala*, with her searchlights in their original location above the bridge. She is approaching a berth with her starboard anchor "a'cockbill", ready for instant release in the event of a misjudgement in manoeuvring.

rising knuckle to avoid excessive width at forecastle deck level. The *Quarto*'s ten boilers required three low, evenly spaced funnels (rather reminiscent of Japanese practice) but the Bixios' 14 boilers resulted in four funnels. These were unevenly spaced as boiler and turbine spaces were alternated. The two waist guns were sided, and the superstructure was arranged capital-ship-style to allow them to fire across the deck.

The Bixios had American-designed Curtiss turbines. At full speed, these turned the propellers at 435rpm, compared with the *Quarto*'s 575rpm. This allowed a more efficient design of propeller, although three shafts were required. Nonetheless, the pair failed to reach their expected speed. Both had left the service by the end of the 1920s.

An unwritten rule of ship design is that successive classes will increase in size. The Aquilas, however, bucked this trend. Being smaller, they retained their categorization of "esploratori", being closer to a super-destroyer than to a light cruiser. Departure from the norm was due to this four-ship class having been originally ordered to Romanian account. They were already under construction in 1914 when, after some prevarication, Italy decided to enter the war in support of the Western Alliance. The ships were therefore requisitioned for the Italian Navy.

In just the three years since the laying down of the Bixios, marine engineering had advanced considerably. Steam conditions were greatly improved, while gearing reduced shaft speed, further raising the efficiency of propellers whose design was now better understood. The Aquilas, while somewhat smaller, thus disposed of over 29,840kW/40,000shp on two shafts, all being able to exceed their designed speed of 36.5 knots.

Their "cruiser" status depended largely upon their three 152mm/6in guns, but these were later reduced to four or five 119mm/4.7in weapons. As with most Italian warships, they were fitted for minelaying.

ABOVE: A wartime picture of *Aquila* at speed, her seaboat swung out for immediate use. At full speed, the endurance was poor, being limited to a little over 10 hours' steaming.

Following their service during World War I, two (*Nibbio* and *Sparviero*) were eventually purchased by the Romanians, becoming the *Marasesti* and *Marasti* respectively. As such they lasted until the 1960s. With Italy's involvement in the Spanish Civil War, the *Aquila* and *Falco* were among various warships transferred to the Spanish Nationalist Navy, many retaining their Italian crews. Acquired permanently, they served under Spanish colours until the late 1940s.

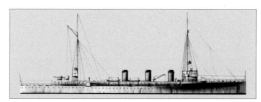

ABOVE: *Quarto*'s three regularly spaced funnels were reminiscent of those in Japanese scout cruisers. Turbine driven, she was commissioned in 1912, starting a trend to speed, allied to light construction. She is reputed to have maintained her speed until her disposal in 1938. Her relative longevity was due to an iconic status.

ABOVE: The light, fluffy smoke of the *Bixio* betrays the fact that she is still, primarily, a coal-burner. Her three superstructure blocks were configured dreadnought-style to allow the two waist guns, at least in theory, to fire across the ship.

Quarto and Bixio and Aquila classes

	Built	Commissioned
Quarto	Venice Navy Yard	May 11, 1912
Marsala	Cantiere di Castellammare di Stabia	August 4, 1914
Nino Bixio	Cantiere di Castellammare di Stabia	May 5, 1914
Aquila	Pattison, Naples	February 8, 1917
Falco	Pattison, Naples	February 20, 1920
Nibbio	Pattison, Naples	May 15, 1918
Sparviero	Pattison, Naples	July 15, 1917

Quarto (as built)

Displacement: 3,271 tonnes/3,220 tons (normal); 3,434 tonnes/3,380 tons (full load)
Length: 126m/413ft 7in (bp); 104.2m/342ft (oa)
Beam: 12.9m/42ft 4in
Draught: 4m/13ft 2in (normal)
Armament: 6 x 119mm/4.7in (6x1) and 6 x 76mm 3in (6x1) guns; 2 x 450mm/17.7in torpedo tubes (2x1)
Machinery: Direct-drive steam turbines, 10 boilers, 2 shafts
Power: 18,643kW/25,000shp for 28 knots
Endurance: 478 tonnes/470 tons (coal) and 51 tonnes/50 tons (oil) for 2,592km/1,400nm at 12 knots
Protection: 40mm/1.6in (protective deck)
Complement: 320

LEFT: Termed "Second Class battleships", the *Pisa* and *Amalfi* were completed with only a mainmast. By 1918 the *Pisa* had received a light foremast, which greatly improved her appearance, as seen here. Note the difference in size between the 254mm/10in main battery guns and the sided 191mm/7.5in weapons.

ABOVE: A third unit of this type was the Greek *Averoff*, completed by Orlando in 1910. She could be recognized by her British-style tripod masts. Less apparent was the reduction of her main battery calibre from 254mm/10in to 234mm/9.2in.

Pisa class

During 1901–03 the four Cuniberti-designed small battleships of the Regina Elena class were laid down. While not espousing Cuniberti's own ideas on the all-big-gun capital ship, they would prove to be remarkably successful on their limited, 13,005-tonne/12,800-ton displacement. Even before their launch, two similar-looking diminutives were commenced. Only some 4m/13ft 1in shorter, these were designed as armoured cruisers. Twin 254mm/10in turrets required single 305mm/12in guns at either end, and four twin 191mm/7.5in guns replaced six twin 203mm/8in weapons as secondary armament. Although the belt was thinned, horizontal protection was improved. With smaller displacement on much the same dimensions, and equipped with machinery of the same power, the Pisas were good for an additional 2 knots.

Other than to closely resemble their line-of-battle colleagues, it is not easy to explain the building of the Pisas when, over exactly the same period, the Italians built the two San Giorgios. Of almost identical size, armament power and speed, these were of entirely different layout, the boiler spaces and their three funnels being closely grouped in the Pisas but in two widely spaced blocks in the San Giorgios.

Both Pisas were completed with a single, heavy mast, stepped abaft the funnels but, by 1918, the nameship had gained a light foremast, which she retained following her 1921 reclassification as a coastal defence and training ship in which roles she served until 1937. During the late 1920s she carried a Macchi floatplane on the after superstructure but, with no catapult, its operation was cumbersome.

Her sister, *Amalfi*, was not so fortunate. On July 7, 1915, just six weeks after Italy's entry into the war, she was covering a sweep into the upper Adriatic when she was torpedoed and sunk by a German-crewed "Austrian" submarine, with the loss of 66 of her crew. Germany was not yet at war with Italy, but was operating coastal submarines from Pola.

Pisa class

	Built	Commissioned
Amalfi	Cantiere Odero, Genoa	September 1, 1909
Pisa	Cantiere Orlando, Livorno	September 1, 1909

Pisa (as built)

Displacement: 9,810 tonnes/9,655 tons (normal); 10,577 tonnes/10,410 tons (full load)
Length: 130m/426ft 9in (bp); 140.5m/461ft 2in (oa)
Beam: 21.1m/69ft 2in
Draught: 7.1m/23ft 4in (normal)
Armament: 4 x 254mm/10in (2x2), 8 x 191mm/7.5in (4x2) and 16 x 76mm/3in (16x1) guns; 3 x 450mm/17.7in torpedo tubes (3x1)
Machinery: Vertical, triple-expansion engines, 22 boilers, 2 shafts
Power: 14,914kW/20,000ihp for 23 knots
Endurance: 1,555 tonnes/1,530 tons (coal) and 71 tonnes/70 tons (oil) for 4,900nm/2,650nm at 12 knots
Protection: 76–203mm/3–8in (belt); 51mm/2in (protective deck); 38–178mm/1.5–7in (turrets)
Complement: 680

LEFT: The launch of the *Amalfi* in 1905. Ten years later she became the Italian Navy's first major loss of World War I. Supporting a destroyer sweep in the upper Adriatic, she was sunk by a locally assembled German UB submarine working from Pola.

Amiral Charner class and *Pothuau*

In 1893, a decade before Britain again began commissioning armoured cruisers, the French completed the one-off *Dupuy de Lôme*. Apparently certain of her success, they were already launching a further class of four, the smaller Amiral Charners.

Where the *Dupuy de Lôme* had a high freeboard hull, fully clad in 100mm/3.9in armour and using exaggerated tumblehome to facilitate axial fire, the Charners adopted what was effectively a shallow hull with lighter armour, the upper hull being a narrow, lightly built superstructure with side decks to accommodate six single 140mm/5.5in

turrets. Unlike the earlier ship, they carried their two 191mm/7.5in guns on the centerline, rather than sided in the waist. They retained the "fierce-face" ram bow, a feature that must have been a considerable impediment in a head sea, as the forward waterplane area decreased rapidly with its immersion.

The *Chanzy* was lost by stranding in 1907 and the *Charner* by submarine torpedo in 1916. The remaining pair were stricken following World War I.

The *Pothuau* was laid down in 1893 as a further one-off, being a closer copy of the *Dupuy de Lôme* in overall shape and depth of protection, but with her

armament disposed more in accord with that of the Charners. She carried ten 138.6mm/5.45in guns to the Charners' six and, lacking the *Dupuy de Lôme*'s marked tumblehome, depended upon sponsoned casemates.

A feature of the contemporary French cruisers was the long, continuous superstructure, which appeared to be part of the hull.

None of these armoured cruisers was ever used in the commerce raiding role for which they had been intended. *Pothuau* had light pole masts rather than the heavy "military masts" of the earlier ships. Late in World War I she lost her mainmast in favour of a kite balloon facility. She was scrapped in 1929.

ABOVE: Bows of extreme shape, such as this one, tended to make a ship bury her nose in a head sea. *Pothuau*'s bridge does, therefore, appear very well forward.

Charner class and *Pothuau*

	Built	Commissioned
Amiral Charner	Rochefort Dockyard	1895
Bruix	Rochefort Dockyard	1896
Chanzy	At. et. Ch. de la Gironde, Bordeaux	1896
Latouche-Treville	At. et Ch. de la Seine, le Havre	1895
Pothuau	At.et Ch. de la Seine, le Havre	1896

Pothuau (as built)

Displacement: 5,466 tonnes/5,380 tons (normal)
Length: 109.7m/360ft (wl); 112.9m/370ft 8in (oa)
Beam: 15m/49ft 3in
Draught: 6.5m/21ft 4in (normal)
Armament: 2 x 194mm/7.64in (2x1) and
10 x 138.6mm/5.45in (10x1) guns
Machinery: Horizontal, triple-expansion engines,
16 boilers, 2 shafts
Power: 7,758kW/10,400ihp for 19 knots
Endurance: 648 tonnes/638 tons (coal) for
8,334km/4,500nm at 10 knots
Protection: 35–60mm/1.4–2.4in (belt);
35–85mm/1.4–3.4in (protective deck);
180mm/7.1in (turrets)
Complement: 455

405

ABOVE: **Where funnels to most designers were a necessary evil, occupying valuable deck space, they were, to the French, almost a fashion statement. No elaborate trunking for the *Jeanne d'Arc* – her grouped, partly cased funnels established a very individual French style.**

Jeanne d'Arc

First to be laid down (although not the first to be completed), *Jeanne d'Arc* initiated a series of imposing, multi-funnelled French cruisers, mostly armoured, that were absolutely distinctive. All were characterized by a high-freeboard hull, a long continuous superstructure, and funnels set in two widely separated groups, the boiler spaces being likewise grouped and separated by machinery spaces. Preceding classes had been fitted with horizontal, triple-expansion engines (low in height and not extending through the protective deck) but, starting with the *Jeanne d'Arc*, the more efficient vertical type was installed.

The ship was designed by the noted constructor Émile Bertin as a prototype response to large contemporary British protected cruisers, but he failed in his attempt to achieve a significantly superior speed. Three propellers were required and it is probable that the water flow over them was less than ideal. It is reported that, despite the machinery developing about 746kW/1,000ihp more than required by contract, the ship's trial speeds did not exceed 21.75 knots against a designed 23. The proposed remedial measure of reducing the area of the bilge keels was not likely to have made a great deal of difference. Like the two British Powerfuls that preceded her, she was a prodigious eater of coal.

The *Jeanne d'Arc*'s forecastle was fully armour-clad but, from the bridge aft, the belt was two decks deep, bounded above and below by protective decks. The resulting "box" was closely subdivided and, in theory, greatly limited flooding due to action damage.

A single 194mm/7.64in turret was located at either end. On the long forecastle deck, two 138.6mm/5.45in turrets were sided forward, and two aft. Ten more 138.6mm/5.45in guns were carried at a good height in casemates and sponsons at upper deck level.

Throughout the 1920s, the ship was used for training and she was not scrapped until 1934.

Jeanne d'Arc

Built: Toulon Dockyard
Commissioned: 1903
Displacement: 11,329 tonnes/11,150 tons (normal)
Length: 145.4m/477ft 3in (oa)
Beam: 19.4m/63ft 9in
Draught: 8.1m/26ft 5in (normal)
Armament: 2 x 194mm/7.64in (2x1) and
    14 x 138.6mm/5.45in (14x1) guns;
    2 x 450mm/17.7in torpedo tubes (2x1)
Machinery: Vertical, triple-expansion engines,
    48 boilers, 3 shafts
Power: 20,880kW/28,000ihp for 21.5 knots
Endurance: 2,032 tonnes/2,000 tons (coal) for
    25,000km/13,500nm at 10 knots
Protection: 150mm/5.9in (belt); 75mm/2.95in
    (forecastle); 50mm/1.97in (protective deck);
    200mm/7.87in (turrets)
Complement: 625

LEFT: **Although of more than twice the displacement of *Pothuau*, the *Jeanne d'Arc* mounted only four more secondary guns. Her extra size and length were the cost of a further 4 knots. The considerable freeboard favoured by French designers saw their ships carry secondary weapons at a useful height.**

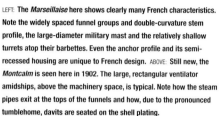

LEFT: The *Marseillaise* here shows clearly many French characteristics. Note the widely spaced funnel groups and double-curvature stem profile, the large-diameter military mast and the relatively shallow turrets atop their barbettes. Even the anchor profile and its semi-recessed housing are unique to French design. ABOVE: Still new, the *Montcalm* is seen here in 1902. The large, rectangular ventilator amidships, above the machinery space, is typical. Note how the steam pipes exit at the tops of the funnels and how, due to the pronounced tumblehome, davits are seated on the shell plating.

Kléber, Gueydon and Aube classes

Three years or more before the *Jeanne d'Arc* ran trials to prove Bertin's armoured cruiser concept, the French commenced work on two related classes, each of three ships, the 7,824-tonne/7,700-ton Klébers and the 9,662-tonne/9,510-ton Gueydons. All were powered for a realistic 21 knots but, again, their triple-shaft propulsion caused problems, not least with poor manoeuvrability and weak hull scantlings. Having fewer boilers, both classes required "only" two pairs of funnels. While their profiles were similar, the smaller Klébers could be distinguished by their two pole masts, the larger vessels having a heavier, "military" type foremast and bulkier bridge structure.

The Klébers had a homogeneous main armament of eight 164.7mm/6.48in guns in four twin turrets. Two of these were mounted centreline on the very long forecastle deck; the others were sided in the waist at upper deck level. They were designed for colonial duties and their lower hulls were wood and copper-sheathed to retard fouling. Their belt was shallow, decreasing in height from forward to aft.

More heavily protected and armed, the Gueydons copied the *Jeanne d'Arc*'s 194mm/7.6in armament at either end, but adopted the 164.7mm/6.48in gun as secondary calibre in place of 138.6mm/5.45in weapon, with only eight (rather than fourteen) being carried, in casemates. These were located on the upper deck, all but the forward pair laying above an unprotected middle deck and thus vulnerable to splinter damage from below.

The five-ship Amiral Aube class were improved Gueydons. Only slightly increased in dimensions, they nonetheless displaced a further 914 tonnes/900 tons, due mainly to a modified and better-protected layout for the secondary armament. Four of the 164.7mm/6.48in guns were now housed in single turrets at forecastle-deck level. These were fitted with armoured trunks. Two more were casemated at upper-deck level and two on the middle deck.

Kléber, Gueydon and Aube classes

	Built	Commissioned
Desaix	Penhoët, St. Nazaire	1904
Dupleix	Rochefort Dockyard	1903
Kléber	Chantiers de la Gironde, Bordeaux	1903
Dupetit-Thouars	Toulon Dockyard	1903
Gueydon	Lorient Dockyard	1902
Montcalm	Forges et Chantiers de la Méditerranée, la Seyne	1901
Amiral Aube	Penhoët, St. Nazaire	1904
Condé	Lorient Dockyard	1904
Gloire	Lorient Dockyard	1904
Marseillaise	Brest Dockyard	1903
Sully	Forges et Chantiers de la Méditerranée, la Seyne	1903

Gueydon class (as built)

Displacement: 9,662 tonnes/9,510 tons (normal)
Length: 137.9m/452ft 8in (wl); 139.8m/459ft (oa)
Beam: 19.4m/63ft 8in
Draught: 7.5m/24ft 6in (normal)
Armament: 2 x 194mm/7.6in (2x1) and
8 x 164.7mm/6.48in (8x1) guns;
2 x 450mm/17.7in torpedo tubes (2x1)
Machinery: Vertical, triple-expansion engines,
20 boilers, 3 shafts
Power: 14,914kW/20,000ihp for 21 knots
Endurance: 1,625 tonnes/1,600 tons (coal) and
51 tonnes/50 tons (oil) for 18,520km/10,000nm
at 10 knots
Protection: 60–150mm/2.4–5.9in (belt);
50mm/1.97in (protective deck); 200mm/7.87in
(turrets)
Complement: 590

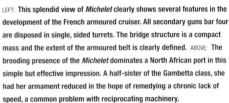

LEFT: **This splendid view of** *Michelet* **clearly shows several features in the development of the French armoured cruiser. All secondary guns bar four are disposed in single, sided turrets. The bridge structure is a compact mass and the extent of the armoured belt is clearly defined.** ABOVE: **The brooding presence of the** *Michelet* **dominates a North African port in this simple but effective impression. A half-sister of the Gambetta class, she had her armament reduced in the hope of remedying a chronic lack of speed, a common problem with reciprocating machinery.**

Gambetta and Michelet classes

The French armoured cruiser program continued apace, with the *Léon Gambetta*, first of a new and larger type, actually laid down before the last of the preceding Aubes. With an additional 8m/26ft 3in more in length and a further 2,185 tonnes/2,150 tons displacement, a Gambetta carried twice the firepower, more powerful machinery to maintain her predecessors' 22 knots, and greatly improved horizontal protection.

The greater armament was possible through the adoption of twin turrets. This approach was not universally popular as they are concentrated assets, while a pair of guns had a slower rate of fire than two separate singles. The Gambetta trio thus mounted a twin 194mm/7.64in turret on the centerline at either end, the forward one on the long forecastle deck, the after on the upper deck. Also at forecastle deck

level were three twin 164.7mm/6.48in guns per side. Again, only four secondary weapons were casemated, the forward pair at upper deck level, the after pair on the main deck, as in the Aubes. Although still bearing a strong "family likeness", their funnels were shorter, without the unusual caps.

The vertical protection scheme followed that of the Aubes, but the belt was tied to horizontal protective decks at its upper and lower edges. The space thus enclosed was closely subdivided, much of it coal-filled. This offered further protection but proved very difficult to work on those occasions when the bunkers were actually needed.

A fourth-of-class, *Jules Michelet*, carried a lighter 12-gun secondary battery. This was disposed in four single turrets along either side of the long

forecastle deck, with four casemated as before. The ship carried 20 improved boilers against the *Gambetta*'s 28. The additional 1,119kW/1,500ihp allowed her to achieve 23.2 knots on trials.

The *Gambetta* and *Hugo* carried conventional boat cranes abreast the forward funnels, and the *Ferry* and *Michelet* distinctive gooseneck cranes.

Gambetta and Michelet classes

	Built	Commissioned
Jules Ferry	Cherbourg Dockyard	1906
Léon Gambetta	Brest Dockyard	1903
Victor Hugo	Lorient Dockyard	1906
Jules Michelet	Lorient Dockyard	1908

Gambetta (as built)

Displacement: 12,751 tonnes/12,550 tons (normal)
Length: 148m/485ft 10in (bp)
Beam: 21.4m/70ft 3in
Draught: 8.2m/26ft 11in
Armament: 4 x 194mm/7.64in (2x2) and 16 x 164.7mm/6.48in (6x2/4x1) guns; 4 x 450mm/17.7in torpedo tubes (4x1)
Machinery: 4-cylinder, vertical, triple-expansion engines, 28 boilers, 3 shafts
Power: 20,507kW/27,500ihp for 22 knots
Endurance: 2,133 tonnes/2,100 tons (coal) for 22,224km/12,000nm at 10 knots
Protection: 90–170mm/3.5–6.7in (belt); 20–35mm/0.79–1.38in and 45–65mm/1.77–2.55in (protective decks); 140–200mm/5.5–7.87in (turrets)
Complement: 730

ABOVE: **Compared with the one-off** *Michelet*, **the Gambetta-class** *Jules Ferry* **is more cramped by having 12 of her 16 secondary guns mounted in sided twin turrets. There was a wide variation in funnel caps and boat cranes. The high freeboard allowed them to maintain speed.**

Renan and Rousseau class

Built over the same time span as the *Michelet*, the larger *Ernest Renan* was not so much an evolution as an alternative type. She was intended to be the first of three with an extra 9m/29ft 6in length to accommodate no less than 40 Niclausse large-tube boilers (as opposed to the 20 less reliable small-tube du Temple type in the *Michelet*). The objective was to develop the 27,600kW/37,000ihp necessary for 23 knots. (It might be noted that a British Minotaur, of the same size and displacement, could make 23 knots on 20,142kW/27,000ihp.)

Reverting to six funnels, the *Renan* was an imposing ship, armed identically with the *Michelet*, with the variation that the tertiary, anti-torpedo boat battery was increased from twenty-two 47mm/1.85in guns to a more potent

sixteen 65mm/2.6in weapons. Protection, otherwise similar, was improved with the addition of a 150mm/5.9in transverse bulkhead, closing off the after end of the armoured "box".

The further two units, *Edgar Quinet* and *Waldeck-Rousseau*, suffered the usual fate of ships that grew to a size where the armament no longer appeared to be sufficient. Primary and secondary batteries were therefore, combined into a single calibre, 194mm/7.64in, of which there were 14 guns. These were disposed in a twin turret forward and aft, three single turrets along both sides in the waist, and four in casemates. Of these, the aftermost pair was located very low, at main deck level.

Completed in 1910, this pair was the ultimate expression of French armoured

cruiser design. The type had already been abandoned elsewhere, made obsolete by the battlecruiser, to say nothing of the steam turbine and oil-fired boilers.

Despite their obsolescence, all three lasted until the 1930s, the *Rousseau* serving as Far East flagship until 1936.

Renan and Rousseau class

	Built	Commissioned
Ernest Renan	Penhoët, St. Nazaire	1908
Edgar Quinet	Brest Dockyard	1910
Waldeck-Rousseau	Lorient Dockyard	1910

Rousseau (as built)

Displacement: 14,072 tonnes/13,850 tons (full load)
Length: 156.9m/515ft (bp); 159m/521ft 11in (oa)
Beam: 21.4m/70ft 3in
Draught: 8.4m/27ft 6in (full load)
Armament: 14 x 194mm/7.64in (2x2/10x1) guns; 2 x 450mm/17.7in torpedo tubes (2x1)
Machinery: 4-cylinder, vertical, triple-expansion engines, 40 boilers, 3 shafts
Power: 27,590kW/37,000ihp for 23 knots
Endurance: 2,337 tonnes/2,300 tons (coal) for 18,520km/10,000nm at 10 knots
Complement: 840

RIGHT: The *Renan*, seen here, could be easily differentiated through her boat cranes, situated amidships. In the Rousseaus, they flanked the forward funnel group.

LEFT: **The extraordinary hull form of the *d'Entrecasteaux* is clearly visible in this picture. From the exaggerated bow to the counter, the curvature changes twice from convex to concave. The huge central casemate is virtually a battery in itself. She existed until 1938, latterly in the role of training ship.**

Friant and d'Entrecasteaux classes

Small, protected cruisers were built in considerable numbers by the late-Victorian Royal Navy for colonial duties, largely superseding sail-assisted sloops and corvettes. With fewer colonial interests, France had little requirement for such ships, and there are few examples. The five Friants are, therefore, interesting exceptions, bearing comparison with a contemporary British

Apollo or the German *Gefion* which latter type was developed much further. Like these, the three surviving Friants were obsolete by 1914 and saw active service only because of the emergency.

Even by French standards, the line of the bow was exaggerated, less a ram than an expression of national identity. The resulting very short forecastle deck saw the muzzle of the 40-calibre, 164.7mm/6.48in forward-gun almost reach to the jackstaff. Six of these guns were carried, four of them in deep sponsons. These were supported on the pronounced tumblehome and must have made for wet ships. The double row of large, rectangular ports ensured good ventilation in tropical conditions.

The contemporary *d'Entrecasteaux* doubled the Friants' displacement, and demanded a further half-set of boilers for the required 19 knots (which she never achieved). Tacked-on abaft the machinery space, these resulted in a third funnel, located well aft.

She was armed after the style of a British *Edgar*, with a centerline 240mm/9.5in gun at both end and twelve 138.6mm/5.45in secondary weapons. Two of these were carried in open mountings on either side of the waist. One level below was four casemates per side.

Extended by World War I, her life continued in a long training role, first under the Belgian flag, then the Polish. She was finally scrapped in 1938.

ABOVE: **Designed for service in tropical climates, the Friants were given a double row of large square ports, uninterrupted by a side belt as these were protected cruisers. By the end of World War I, with reduced machinery and a single funnel, she served as a submarine depot ship.**

Friant (as built)

Displacement: 3,800 tonnes/3,740 tons (normal); 4,075 tonnes/4,000 tons (full load)
Length: 94m/308ft 6in (bp); 100m/328ft 3in (oa)
Beam: 13m/42ft 8in
Draught: 6.4m/21ft (normal)
Armament: 6 x 164.7mm/6.48in (6x1) and 4 x 100mm/4in (4x1) guns; 2 x 450mm/17.7in torpedo tubes (2x1)
Machinery: Vertical, triple-expansion engines, 2 shafts
Power: 7,460kW/10,000ihp for 19 knots
Endurance: 696 tonnes/685 tons (coal) for 11,112km/6,000nm at 10 knots
Protection: 80mm/3.15in (protective deck)
Complement: 376

Friant and d'Entrecasteaux classes

	Built	Commissioned
Bugeaud	Cherbourg Dockyard	1898
Cassard	Cherbourg Dockyard	1895
Chasseloup-Laubat	Cherbourg Dockyard	1898
d'Assas	Penhoët, St. Nazaire	1895
du Chayla	Cherbourg Dockyard	1897
Friant	Brest Dockyard	1895
d'Entrecasteaux	Forges et Ch. de la Méditerranée, la Seyne	1898

LEFT: Capable of 23 knots, the *Chateaurenault* was designed as a commerce raider, a role assisted by her symmetrical, four-funnelled profile which, at a distance, resembled that of a passenger liner. Her pale paint scheme is made to look even less warlike through the addition of a narrow, dark ribband.
ABOVE: In regular warship livery the *Chateaurenault*'s armament is more apparent. During World War I she was used for trooping, and it was while acting in this capacity that she was torpedoed and and sunk off Cephalonia in December 1917.

Chateaurenault and *Jurien de la Gravière*

Like the US Navy *Columbia*, the *Chateaurenault* was designed specifically as a commerce destroyer, and given something of a mercantile appearance. That of the American was not convincing but the Frenchman adopted a straight stem and a merchant ship's counter stern. Her four plain funnels were half-cased and elegantly raked. However, like the *Columbia*, she was betrayed from a distance by the foremast being located with the bridge structure rather than on the foredeck.

Her 23-knot speed required a troublesome triple-shaft arrangement.

While she achieved contract speed, she was prone to vibration that upset gun-laying. Like the *Guichen* that followed, *Chateaurenault* was considered something of a failure and was serving as a troop transport when sunk by an Austrian submarine late in 1917.

The protected cruiser *Jurien de la Gravière* also imitated the appearance of an armoured cruiser of considerable greater capability. With her two lofty pole masts, she closely resembled the Kléber-class cruisers which were still under construction but, where she carried a similar primary battery of eight

164.7mm/6.48in guns, she had nothing else larger than a 47mm/1.85in gun.

She was also designed for war against commerce. Longer but narrower in the beam, her finer hull packed the same power as a Kléber, but her planned 23 knots was difficult to attain, although it was still of concern to the British. It was reported by the French themselves that her boilers "gave an infinity of trouble", being prone to leaks and difficult to stoke. They doubted that she could maintain 20 knots for three hours, while she consumed so much fuel that her actual range was probably only half that officially claimed. She was stricken from the active list in 1922.

ABOVE: The impressively named *Jurien de la Gravière* had the general appearance of an armoured cruiser, but lacked vertical protection. She never achieved her designed speed.

Chateaurenault and *Jurien de la Gravière*

	Built	Commissioned
Chateaurenault	Forges et Ch. de la Méditeranée, la Seyne	1900
Jurien de la Gravière	Lorient Dockyard	1901

Chateaurenault (as built)

Displacement: 8,230 tonnes/8,100 tons (normal)
Length: 134.9m/442ft 10in (bp); 140m/459ft 7in (oa)
Beam: 18m/59ft 2in
Draught: 7.5m/24ft 7in (normal)
Armament: 2 x 164.7mm/6.48in (2x1) and 6 x 138.6mm/5.45in (6x1) guns
Machinery: 4-cylinder, vertical, triple-expansion engines, 28 boilers, 3 shafts
Power: 17,900kW/24,000ihp for 23 knots
Endurance: 2,134 tonnes/2,100 tons (coal) for 13,890km/7,500nm at 12 knots
Protection: 60–100mm/2.4–3.9in (protective deck)
Complement: 605

Guichen and Descartes class

The *Guichen* and *Jurien de la Gravière* are often paired because they were both designed as commerce destroyers and resembled armoured cruisers. However, there were considerable differences between the former pair and *Guichen* whose resemblance to an armoured cruiser was far less convincing. Her hull was devoid of much of the clutter typical of larger ships, its double tier of rectangular ports emphasizing its exaggerated tumblehome.

The *Guichen* was laid down in 1895, two years before *de la Gravière*, but was completed one year after, in 1902, nearly seven years in the building. She was 4m/13ft 1in shorter but 1.7m/5ft 7in greater in the beam. Despite this extra portliness, she was still powered for 23 knots. This demanded over 40 per cent greater installed power.

Her displacement was almost half as much again, derived from no less

than 36 boilers and a heavier protective deck. Her armament, however, was lighter. No more practical than *de la Gravière,* the *Guichen* was, likewise, discarded in 1922.

Predating the *Guichen* were the Descartes, a class of four 4,115-tonne/ 4,050-ton protected cruisers. They were of a similar size but inferior to the contemporary British Astraeas. Only three out of eight of the latter class survived to see active service during World War I, but only the nameship of the French class operated in the conflict, the remaining three having been hulked pre-war. Even the less-than-onerous duties of guardship to the West Indies finally proved too much for the *Descartes* and she was disarmed in 1917.

Built in different yards, the ships' individual displacement varied somewhat. Their protective deck was overlaid with a cellular level, topped

by a light splinter deck. The four 164.7mm/6.48in guns were grouped in a casemated amidships redoubt. Located at main deck level, they fired axially along the tumblehome of the hull, a very characteristic feature.

Guichen and Descartes class

	Built	Commissioned
Guichen	Penhoët, St. Nazaire	1902
Catinat	Ch. de Granville, le Havre	1896
Descartes	Ch. de la Loire, Nantes	1896
Pascal	Toulon Dockyard	1897
Protet	At. et Ch. de la Gironde, Bordeaux	1898

Descartes class (as built)

Displacement: 4,115 tonnes/4,050 tons (normal)
Length: 99m/324ft 11in (bp); 101.1m/331ft 10in (oa)
Beam: 13m/42ft 8in
Draught: 6.5m/21ft 4in (normal)
Armament: 4 x 164.7mm/6.48in (4x1) and 10 x 100mm/3.9in (10x1) guns; 2 x 356mm/14in torpedo tubes (2x1)
Machinery: Triple-expansion engines, 16 boilers, 2 shafts
Power: 6,714kW/9,000ihp for 19 knots
Endurance: 676 tonnes/665 tons (coal) for 11,112km/6,000mm at 10 knots
Protection: 20–50mm/0.79–2in (protective deck)
Complement: 390

LEFT: Berthed in the Penfeld, under the forbidding walls of Brest's chateau, the *Guichen* is seen undergoing mechanical maintenance (note the protective covers in way of the forward funnels). Unusually, her stem was straight and vertical, while her stern (nearest the camera) was extended.

Surcouf class, *Lavoisier* and *d'Estrées*

Although classified as "Third Class cruisers", these interesting little ships were too small and of insufficient endurance to undertake protracted independent operations. They were designed to work as handmaidens to a fleet and its commander-in-chief, in a role that the French term "*avisos*" and the British "despatch vessels". Their nearest contemporary Royal Navy equivalent would be the Barracouta class, loosely termed "torpedo cruisers".

ABOVE: **High and dry, aground on a rocky shore, the** *Infernet* **is beyond redemption and is already being stripped. Note the damage to the port propeller and rudder. Although the screws protrude significantly from the hull, no above-water propeller guards are fitted.**

Stemming from several yards, the Surcoufs differed in detail and had displacements of 1,870–1,910 tonnes/ 1,840–1,880 tons. While given an armoured deck, with a splinter deck above, their hulls were not deep enough for a full cellular layer. Superstructure comprised little more than a miniscule bridge, set around the forefunnel. The funnels themselves were widely spaced and varied considerably in individual dimensions.

Four 138.6mm/5.45in guns were located in amidships casemates, sited over the tumblehome to permit something approaching axial fire. These projections again looked as if they would cause wetness.

The *d'Estrées* was of the same length but with 3m/9ft 10in or 33 per cent increase in beam. She was faster by 2 knots but only at the cost of 40 per cent greater installed power. Her larger deck space permitted four secondary 100mm/3.9in guns to be added. She differed in appearance from the Surcoufs, having two short funnels and lacking the exaggerated curvature of bow and stern.

The Lavoisier-class cruisers were of an intermediate 2,337-tonne/2,300-ton design falling between the Surcoufs and *d'Estrées*. They were fitted with only two 100mm/3.9in secondary guns, but carried a pair of 450mm/17.7in torpedo tubes.

The late introduction of the steam turbine into French shipbuilding brought

the possibility of a class of 29-knot scout cruisers. These, the proposed ten 4,572-tonne/4,500-ton Lamotte-Picquets, were never built, due to changing priorities.

Surcouf class, *Lavoisier* and *d'Estrées*

	Built	Commissioned
Coëtlogon	Penhoët, St. Nazaire	1891
Cosmao	At. et Ch. de la Gironde, Bordeaux	1891
Forbin	Rochefort Dockyard	1890
Lalande	At. et Ch. de la Gironde, Bordeaux	1890
Surcouf	Cherboug Dockyard	1890
Troude	At. et Ch. de la Gironde, Bordeaux	1890
d'Estrées	Rochefort Dockyard	1899
Galilée	Rochefort Dockyard	1897
Lavoisier	Rochefort Dockyard	1897

Surcouf (as built)

Displacement: 1,877 tonnes/1,848 tons (normal)
Length: 95m/311ft 10in (bp)
Beam: 9m/29ft 6in
Draught: 4.7m/15ft 6in (normal)
Armament: 4 x 138.6mm/5.45in (4x1) and
9 x 47mm/1.85in (9x1); 5 x 450mm/17.7in torpedo tubes (5x1)
Machinery: Vertical, triple-expansion engines, 2 shafts
Power: 4,476kW/6,000ihp for 20 knots
Endurance: 203 tonnes/200 tons (coal) for 4,444km/2,400nm at 10 knots
Protection: 40mm/1.57in (protective deck)
Complement: 190

LEFT: *Scharnhorst* and *Gneisenau* were a near-identical pair; the latter is shown here. Easily confused with the smaller Roons, they could be differentiated by their cruiser stern and the full-depth battery amidships, accommodating two 21cm/8.2in and three 15cm/5.9in guns per side. Note boats under davits as well as crane.

Scharnhorst class and *Blücher*

As with the armoured cruisers of major foreign fleets, those of the German Navy were subject to creeping escalation in size and capability. Launched in 1906, the Scharnhorsts were the last in the line of development that had begun with the *Victoria Louise*. They were the ultimate in German armoured cruisers and, as such, bear comparison with the British Minotaurs and the French *Renan*. All were powered for 23 knots but, as with capital ships, the Germans had the lowest length/breadth ratio. Both British and French opted for an armament of four main guns (234mm/9.2in and 194mm/7.64in respectively) and a relatively large number of secondaries (ten 191mm/7.5in and twelve 164.7mm/6.48in respectively). The Scharnhorsts, however, had eight main-calibre weapons of 21cm/8.2in calibre and only six intermediate 15cm/5.9in guns. Inasmuch as this permitted a heavier volume and better control of main battery fire, this was obviously an improvement. Both weapons were reliable and capable of a very respectable range.

Following previous practice, half the main armament and all of the secondary armament were casemated within a well-protected central redoubt, which also covered the machinery. The belt, as ever, was the best compromise between thickness and area to be covered.

The two sisters differed only in minor detail and, indeed, could easily be confused with the preceding Roons. The latter, however, had a pair of 15cm/5.9in single turrets in the waist at upper deck level, where the Scharnhorsts had two 21cm/8.2in guns mounted in casemates.

Excellent ships, it was the misfortune of the Scharnhorsts to be pitted in their final action against battlecruisers, ships designed specifically as the armoured cruiser's nemesis.

In April 1906 the British laid down the first battlecruiser. Referred to as a "large armoured cruiser", she was built in great secrecy. German intelligence gleaned little beyond the fact that she was to be larger and faster, carrying a homogenous battery of 234mm/9.2in guns. The last was a deliberately misleading leak by the British to conceal her true armament of eight 305mm/12in weapons.

Although Admiral Alfred von Tirpitz was reluctant to divert funds from capital ship construction to what he considered to be reconnaissance units, he nonetheless authorized a single ship in response during 1907. As the Germans considered their 21cm/8.2in gun to be at least the equal of a British 234mm/9.2in, the new ship, to be named *Blücher*, was given 12, disposed hexagon-fashion in 16 turrets.

The Germans discovered their error too late to correct it, and the *Blücher* became a one-off – larger, faster and more

LEFT: **Von Spee's flagship *Scharnhorst* urgently resupplies at Valparaiso following the Battle of Coronel (November 1914). The battle resulted in the first defeat suffered by the Royal Navy in a century, avenged shortly afterward in the Battle of the Falklands (December 1914). Note the large, single 21cm/8.2in guns amidships and the configuration of the hull.**

expensive than a Scharnhorst, but about a knot slower and completely outgunned by an Invincible-class battlecruiser.

In appearance, she resembled the true German battlecruisers that quickly followed, but was smaller and was alone in being fitted with "gooseneck" boat cranes. She was also alone in combining a single turret forward and aft with (after 1913) a British-style tripod foremast.

Too large and too valuable to be considered just another armoured cruiser, the *Blücher* was treated by the Germans as a battlecruiser but, being less capable than her peers, she was relegated to the rear of a battle line. During the long tail chase that was the Dogger Bank action of January 1915, the *Blücher* thus became the successive target of each pursuing British battlecruiser as it crept into extreme range. Having, over three hours, absorbed an estimated 70 hits, she sank with nearly 800 of her crew. Her last, great service had been to completely divert the attention of the British, allowing her three consorts to escape.

TOP: Although *Blücher* was a one-off armoured cruiser, she looked like a battlecruiser. Being employed as such would quickly prove to be her nemesis. Note the complex rigging for the deployment of her anti-torpedo nets, the large number of searchlights and the steam pinnace alongside. ABOVE: The cruelly punished *Blücher* capsizes at the Dogger Bank action in January 1915. As tail-ender of Hipper's battlecruiser line, she diverted the British sufficiently long to allow her colleagues to escape. Note the sided, amidships 21cm/8.2in guns still trained abaft the beam against her pursuers.

Scharnhorst class and *Blücher*

	Built	Commissioned
Gneisenau	AG "Weser", Bremen	March 6, 1908
Scharnhorst	Blohm & Voss, Hamburg	October 24, 1907
Blücher	Kiel Dockyard	October 1, 1909

Scharnhorst class

Displacement: 11,806 tonnes/11,620 tons (normal); 13,230 tonnes/12,990 tons (full load)
Length: 143.8m/472ft (wl); 144.6m/474ft 8in (oa)
Beam: 216m/70ft 11in
Draught: 8.1m/26ft 7in (normal)
Armament: 8 x 21cm/8.2in (2x2/4x1) and 6 x 15cm/5.9in (6x1) guns; 4 x 450mm/17.7in torpedo tubes (4x1)
Machinery: Vertical, 3-cylinder, triple-expansion engines, 18 boilers, 3 shafts
Power: 19,388kW/26,000ihp for 22.5 knots
Endurance: 2,032 tonnes/2,000 tons (coal) for 9,445km/5,100nm at 12 knots
Protection: 8–150mm/3–6in (belt); 35–60mm/1.38–2.4in (protective deck); 30–170mm/1.18–6.7in (turrets)
Complement: 765

ABOVE: The buff-and-white Far East livery of the *Scharnhorst* disguises the considerable freeboard that was a beneficial feature of German armoured cruisers. The radiussed forward sheer strake, not really a turtledeck, was a feature of their design. The voluminous coal smoke, inevitable at high speed, contrasts with the pristine paintwork.

Early light cruisers

Germany's colonial ambitions of the 1880s resulted in the building of two types of cruisers, one for "overseas" and the other for "fleet" roles. The 3,810-tonne/3,750-ton *Gefion* of 1894 was the last example of the former type prior to their being merged into a single design capable of fulfilling either purpose. Her classification of "corvette-cruiser" alluded both to her imperial duties and to her partly open waist, upon which six of her ten 10.5cm/4.1in guns were mounted. Two more were sided upon each of her raised forecastle and poop decks.

Gefion was powered for a modest 19 knots and lightly constructed, with only a 25–40mm/1–1.57in protective deck. However, her basic design was well suited for providing the basis for the Bremens of 1902 onward, themselves the beginning of a long and successful series. Confined largely to harbour

service during World War I, she was sold in 1919.

Built at the same time as the *Gefion*, the *Hela* paralleled the size and functions of the contemporary French "*avisos*". Of only half the displacement of the *Gefion*, she was also very lightly protected, carrying only four 8.8cm/3.46in guns.

She did, however, provide the basic design for a further ten "fourth rate" vessels. Of the same length as the *Hela*, but 1.2–1.4m/3ft 11in–4ft 7in greater in the beam, these were (mostly) powered for 21.5 knots, were better protected and carried a similar main battery to the *Gefion*.

Attractive little ships, they were, nonetheless, ambitious for their size. Even with an increased beam they tended to be crank.

They saw considerable action, with *Ariadne* being sunk at the Heligoland Bight action, the *Frauenlob* at Jutland,

and the *Undine* by submarine torpedo. *Niobe*, long-transferred, was sunk during World War II, a conflict which the *Arkona*, *Amazone* and *Medusa* managed to survive, serving until 1929–31.

Early light cruisers

	Built	Commissioned
Amazone	Germania, Kiel	November 15, 1901
Ariadne	AG. "Weser", Bremen	May 18, 1901
Arkona	AG "Weser", Bremen	May 12, 1903
Frauenlob	AG "Weser", Bremen	February 17, 1903
Gazelle	Germania, Kiel	June 15, 1901
Medusa	AG "Weser", Bremen	July 26, 1901
Niobe	AG "Weser", Breman	June 25, 1900
Nymphe	Germania, Kiel	September 20, 1900
Thetis	Danzig Dockyard	September 14, 1901
Undine	Howaldtswerke, Kiel	January 5, 1904
Gefion	Schichau, Danzig	June 27, 1894
Hela	AG "Weser", Bremen	May 3, 1896

Undine (as built)

Displacement: 2,743 tonnes/2,700 tons (normal); 3,160 tonnes/3,110 tons (full load)
Length: 104.4m/342ft 8in (wl); 105m/344ft 8in (oa)
Beam: 12.3m/40ft 4in
Draught: 5.6m/18ft 5in (normal)
Armament: 10 x 10.5cm/4.1in (10x1) guns; 3 x 450mm/17.7in torpedo tubes (3x1)
Machinery: Vertical, 4-cylinder, triple-expansion engines, 8 boilers, 2 shafts
Power: 4,474kW/6,000ihp for 21.5 knots
Endurance: 713 tonnes/700 tons (coal) for 8,148km/4,400nm at 12 knots
Protection: 20–80mm/0.79–3.1in (protective deck)
Complement: 255

ABOVE: **A series of ten very similar ships, the Gazelles were the German Navy's first extended light cruiser class. The bow form and general forward clutter made them wet. The *Undine*, shown here, was a further victim of submarine attack but the remainder, with modified bows, served in the post-war fleet.**

LEFT: *Hamburg* seen post-war. Bremen-class ships had three raked funnels and masts. The two Leipzigs were similar but with vertical funnels and masts, the foremast moved aft to the bridge structure. Note the Reichsmarine ensign and jack, and the Hamburg arms (*Wappen*) carried at the stem head.

Bremen class

Following an Imperial edict of 1903, all German light cruisers were named after cities. The first of these were the seven Bremens, heavily based on the *Gefion* prototype. Their design showed far better discipline in weight economy for, on a hull of basically the same dimensions, they showed 483 tonnes/475 tons (or over 12 per cent) less displacement. This in spite of carrying the same ten 10.5cm/4.1in guns in the same layout, and a thickened protective deck made the more effective by the incorporation of new Krupp-patent armour-grade steel.

At 19 knots, the *Gefion* had been too slow and a puzzling feature of the Bremens was that, while their installed power was increased by only 746kW/1,000ihp (about 11 per cent), their speed was increased by no less than 3 knots. One can only assume a very much improved underwater form.

The *Lübeck* differed in being the German Navy's first steam-turbine-propelled cruiser. The system was direct-drive and the ship was fitted with four, small-diameter propellers per shaft.

In profile, the *Gefion*'s "ploughshare" bow profile was replaced by an elongated "ram" bow. This proved to make the ships wet at higher speeds, and all were later modified. The *Gefion*'s vertical funnels and masts were given a rake in the Bremens. With a need to reduce topside weight, however, these were also modified, being reduced to half-casings.

Sometimes listed as a separate class, the *Danzig* and *Leipzig* varied in detail. In profile, they had vertical funnels and masts from the outset, while the foremast was stepped from the bridge structure rather than forward of it.

The *Leipzig* was sunk by gunfire at the Falklands in December 1914, while the *Bremen* was destroyed by mines in

the Baltic. *Hamburg* and *Berlin*, although hulked, and serving in the capacity of accommodation ships or depot ships, survived to be scrapped and scuttled (respectively) after World War II.

Bremen class

	Built	Commissioned
Berlin	Danzig Dockyard	April 4, 1905
Bremen	AG "Weser" Bremen	May 19, 1904
Danzig	Danzig Dockyard	December 1, 1907
Hamburg	AG "Vulcan", Stettin	March 8, 1904
Leipzig	AG "Weser", Bremen	April 20, 1906
Lübeck	AG "Vulcan", Stettin	April 26, 1905
München	AG "Weser", Bremen	January 10, 1905

Bremen (as built)

Displacement: 3,333 tonnes/3,280 tons (normal); 3,860 tonnes/3,800 tons (full load)

Length: 110.6m/363ft (wl); 111.1m/364ft 8in (oa)

Beam: 13.3m/43ft 8in

Draught: 5.5m/18ft 2in (normal)

Armament: 10 x 10.5cm/4.1in (10x1) guns; 2 x 450mm/17.7in torpedo tubes (2x1)

Machinery: Vertical, 3-cylinder, triple-expansion engines, 10 boilers, 2 shafts

Power: 7,460kW/10,000ihp for 22 knots

Endurance: 874 tonnes/860 tons (coal) for 7,871km/4,250nm at 12 knots

Protection: 20–80mm/0.79–3.1in (protective deck)

Complement: 295

LEFT: A pre-war picture of *München*. In the background is a Prinz Adalbert-class armoured cruiser, both of which had been lost by 1915. The *München* survived being torpedoed only to be disarmed and being reduced to an accommodation hulk before being scrapped in 1920.

LEFT: **Lead ship of a class of four, the *Königsberg* was station ship in German East Africa. Following a short raiding career conspicuously lacking in initiative, she was blockaded and finally destroyed amid the mud and jungle of the Rufiji delta. Her wreck remained until the 1960s.** ABOVE: **The *Emden* had notable success as a raider in the Indian Ocean during 1915, sinking 16 merchant ships.**

Königsberg and Dresden class

The Bremens initiated a continuous building sequence of multi-purpose light cruisers that produced, on average, two ships annually, their gradual refinement being accompanied by increasing size and displacement.

Laid down in 1905, the *Königsberg* is sometimes classified as a one-off, being the only ship with a 115.3m/378ft 6in hull. Over 4m/13ft 1in longer than a Bremen, she had reciprocating engines powered for 23 knots.

Although longer than the *Danzig*, the *Königsberg* was virtually indistinguishable except for a less protruding bow profile. Her three near-sisters had rearranged boiler and machinery spaces, resulting in asymmetrically spaced funnels. This new layout increased hull length by a further 2m/6ft 7in.

Of the three, the *Stettin* was turbine-driven and equipped with two propellers per shaft. A sister, *Stuttgart*, was

modified late in World War I to carry three seaplanes aft. Four of her ten 10.5cm/4.1in guns had to be sacrificed but she could now alternatively carry over 100 mines.

Both laid down in 1906, the *Dresden* and *Emden* readopted a three symmetrical funnel profile. The *Dresden* was also turbine-propelled, with two screws per shaft. They were also a further 1m/3ft 3in longer.

Having less cutaway on the keel profile, these classes were more directionally stable and less manoeuvrable than the Bremens, but were less tender.

Two of the class, *Emden* and *Königsberg*, became notable raiders during World War I, the former by virtue of her many successes, the latter because she holed-up in a muddy East African delta, necessitating a protracted operation to effect her destruction.

The *Nürnberg* was destroyed by gunfire at the Falklands, while her colleague, *Dresden*, escaped to spend three months as a fugitive before being run down. Cornered by British cruisers, she was scuttled in March 1915.

The final pair, *Stettin* and *Stuttgart*, were surrendered to Great Britain for demolition at the war's end.

Königsberg and Dresden class

	Built	Commissioned
Königsberg	Kiel Dockyard	April 6, 1907
Nürnberg	Kiel Dockyard	April 10, 1908
Stettin	AG "Vulcan", Stettin	October 29, 1907
Stuttgart	Danzig Dockyard	February 1, 1908
Dresden	Blohm & Voss, Hamburg	November 14, 1908
Emden	Danzig Dockyard	July 10, 1909

Emden (as built)

Displacement: 3,724 tonnes/3,665 tons (normal); 4,338 tonnes/4,270 tons (full load)
Length: 117.9m/387ft (wl); 118.3m/388ft 4in (oa)
Beam: 13.5m/44ft 4in
Draught: 5.5m/18ft 2in (normal)
Armament: 10 x 10.5cm/4.1in (10x1) guns; 2 x 450mm/17.7in torpedo tubes (2x1)
Machinery: Vertical, 3-cylinder, triple-expansion engines, 12 boilers, 2 shafts
Power: 10,066kW/13,500ihp for 23.5 knots
Endurance: 803 tonnes/790 tons (coal) for 6,945km/3,750nm at 12 knots
Protection: 20–80mm/0.79–3.1in (protective deck)
Complement: 360

LEFT: **Sole survivor of von Spee's squadron after the Falklands battle, the *Dresden* was on the run for nearly three months. Out of coal and in need of mechanical refit, she was run to ground at Mas a Tierra. Abandoned under a flag of parley, she was scuttled and already sinking as the British approached.**

LEFT: The *Augsburg* lays to a buoy in a placid Kiel Fjord. Note how the curvature of the bow profile has become less extreme. The triangular day shapes, suspended from the mainmast, are connected to the rudder chains, moving differentially as rudder angle is applied. *Augsburg*'s rudder is here amidships.

ABOVE RIGHT: Wearing a battle ensign, the *Augsburg* engages Russian forces on the Baltic, where she saw most action. She is shown with her original 10.5cm/4.1in guns but she and the *Kolberg* were later converted to carry six 15cm/5.9in weapons, together with about 120 mines.

Kolberg class

By 1907–08, when the four Kolbergs were laid down, the Germany Navy had developed a versatile strain of light cruisers, well-adapted for fleet work, although probably less so for colonial duties where coal supplies and dockyard support could be sparse.

It was important to have a speed margin over the battle fleet, and the steam turbine promised compact and lighter machinery (and lower maintenance), with the possibility of faster cruisers without a punitive growth in size. Since the turbine's introduction by Parsons, however, the Curtiss Company and several German concerns had developed their own versions. More than their British equivalents, therefore, German cruisers became "one-off" test-beds for various types of machinery. Without reduction gearing, it was also difficult to translate developed power

into thrust, the Germans experimenting with two, even four, small-diameter propellers attached to the same relatively high-revving shaft.

Each of the four Kolbergs had turbines of different origins. The *Mainz* had two shafts, the remainder four. Powered for a full 2 knots more than the preceding Dresdens, the Kolbergs were 12m/39ft 4in longer and carried an extra pair of 10.5cm/4.1in guns. Their larger hulls were much stiffer, permitting a later upgrading of armament to include six 15cm/5.9in weapons.

The latter modification became general as the British were constructing equivalent vessels, all of which carried 152mm/6in guns. Multiple German 10.5cm/4.1in guns were highly effective in producing "smothering fire", but the British 152mm/6in possessed indisputably greater stopping-power.

All such arguments were somewhat academic for the *Köln* and *Mainz*, which were overwhelmed by the 305mm/12in gun fire of British battlecruisers at the Heligoland Bight action. Following the war, the *Augsburg* was one of many comparatively new German ships scrapped, while the *Kolberg* herself, awarded to the French as reparation, served until 1929 as the *Colmar*, one of four assuming Alsatian names.

Kolberg class

	Built	Commissioned
Augsburg	Kiel Dockyard	October 1, 1910
Kolberg	Schichau, Danzig	June 21, 1910
Köln (Cöln)	Germania, Kiel	June 16, 1911
Mainz	AG "Vulcan", Stettin	October 1, 1909

Kolberg (as built)

Displacement: 4,430 tonnes/4,360 tons (normal); 4,994 tonnes/4,915 tons (full load)

Length: 130m/426ft 9in (wl); 130.5m/428ft 4in (oa)

Beam: 14m/46ft

Draught: 5.5m/18ft (normal)

Armament: 12 x 10.5cm/4.1in (12x1) guns; 2 x 450mm/17.7in torpedo tubes (2x1)

Machinery: Direct-drive steam turbines, 15 boilers, 4 shafts

Power: 14,168kW/19,000shp for 25.5 knots

Endurance: 985 tonnes/970 tons (coal) and 117 tonnes/115 tons (oil) for 6,019km/3,250nm at 14 knots

Protection: 20–80mm/0.79–3.1in (protective deck)

Complement: 365

ABOVE: One of several German cruisers to be ceded to France and Italy, the *Kolberg* became the French *Colmar*, as seen here. Note the larger 15cm/5.9in gun, modified searchlight arrangements and a Rangefinder added atop the armoured conning tower. She served the French Navy until 1929.

LEFT: **Karlsruhe** and **Rostock** were twin-screwed, higher powered versions of the four Breslau type. Stationed in Central America in 1914, the **Karlsruhe** (shown here) acted briefly as a raider but, while still being sought by Royal Navy cruisers, was destroyed by an internal explosion. BELOW: The two Graudenzes were three-funnelled versions of the Karlsruhes but, curiously, this impression of the **Regensburg** omits the "Y" gun, possibly removed to permit a full deckload of mines. The ten 10.5cm/4.1in guns were later exchanged for seven 15cm/5.9in weapons. Ceded to France, her wreck can still be seen screening Lorient U-boat pens.

Magdeburg, Karlsruhe and Graudenz classes

By the end of the first decade of the 20th century, Britain and Germany were locked into a ruinously expensive "naval race" where rivalry in cruiser construction was no less fierce than that in dreadnoughts.

In 1909, the British laid down the *Chatham*, which repeated the eight 152mm/6in gun armament of the preceding Weymouths, increased installed power to 18,643kW/25,000shp and, for the first time, put armour into a belt rather than into a protective deck. The immediate German response was the four Magdeburgs, whose similar power required 16 boilers and four funnels. Although primarily coal-fired, they could use oil sprays for mixed firing to boost acceleration and speed.

Experimentation with machinery continued. All had steam-turbine propulsion but, where the *Strassburg* had two shafts, the *Breslau* had four and the remaining pair, three.

Although the designed armament remained twelve 10.5cm/4.1in guns, all (except *Breslau*) had exchanged them for seven 15cm/5.9in weapons by 1916. Their torpedoes were now also of a harder-hitting 500mm/19.7in calibre. They were the first to add an 18–60mm/0.71–2.4in belt to a 20–60mm/0.79–2.4in protective deck.

Increased displacement was reduced by adopting longitudinal framing in place of the earlier combination of longitudinal and transverse. A new, pleasingly raked "cruiser bow" was also introduced.

Before they were completed, four Karlsruhe and Graundenz-class ships were laid down. While a further 3.5m/11ft 6in longer, they had a uniform, twin-shaft arrangement. The Karlsruhes were higher-powered repeats of the Magdeburgs, and virtually indistinguishable from them. The Graudenz pair, however, reverted to a three-funnel layout. They also introduced superimposed after guns and four torpedo tubes of heavier 500mm/19.7in calibre.

Breslau, under the Turkish flag, was sunk in the Mediterranean. Post-war, the *Strassburg* and *Graudenz* served in the Italian Navy, the *Stralsund* and *Regensburg* with the French fleet.

Magdeburg, Karlsruhe and Graudenz classes

	Built	Commissioned
Breslau	AG "Vulcan", Stettin	May 10, 1912
Magdeburg	AG "Weser", Bremen	August 20, 1912
Stralsund	AG "Weser", Bremen	December 10, 1912
Strassburg	Wilhelmshaven Dockyard	October 9, 1912
Karlsruhe	Germania, Kiel	January 15, 1914
Rostock	Howaldstwerke, Kiel	February 5, 1914
Graudenz	Kiel Dockyard	August 10, 1914
Regensburg	AG "Weser", Bremen	January 3, 1915

Graudenz (as built)

Displacement: 4,989 tonnes/4,910 tons (normal); 6,482 tonnes/6,380 tons (full load)
Length: 139m/456ft 3in (wl); 142.7m/468ft 5in (oa)
Beam: 13.8m/45ft 4in
Draught: 5.9m/19ft 3in (normal)
Armament: 12 x 10.5cm/4.1in (12x1) and 2 x 8.8cm/3.46in (2x1) guns; 4 x 500mm/19.7in torpedo tubes (4x1)
Machinery: Direct-drive steam turbines, 12 boilers, 2 shafts
Power: 19,388kW/26,000shp for 27.5 knots
Endurance: 1,301 tonnes/1,280 tons (coal) and 381 tonnes/375 tons (oil) for 10,186km/5,500nm at 12 knots
Protection: 18–60mm/0.71–2.4in (belt); 20–60mm/0.79–2.4in (protective deck)
Complement: 367

ABOVE: **The Breslau type were the first with four funnels and raked bow. The nameship appears here to be escort for the Kaiser's annual trip to Norway. Later notorious as having been transferred to Turkey in company with the battlecruiser** Goeben, **she foundered on mines early in 1918.**

LEFT: *Wiesbaden* shows off her elegant, destroyer-like lines. Note the light signal yards which, being of diagonal X-form, appear asymmetric in quarter views. The toughness of the design was demonstrated at Jutland, where she absorbed tremendous punishment before sinking, most of her crew being lost.

Wiesbaden, Königsberg (II) and Köln (II) classes

The two Wiesbadens laid down in 1913 were 2.6m/8ft 6in longer than the preceding Karlsruhe and Grundenz-class ships. Designed to carry eight 15cm/5.9in guns from the outset, they had to be superimposed aft and the remainder sided. To reduce shaft speed, both had experimental hydraulic "transformers", on either shaft, with alternative propulsion by a smaller, cruising turbine equipped with reduction gearing. Their protective scheme was similar to that in the *Graudenz* and it proved very effective at Jutland when the *Wiesbaden* withstood tremendous punishment.

The succeeding quartette of Königsbergs (II) was commenced in 1914. As was customary, all were known by "*ersatz*" titles prior to launch, by which time, in 1915–16, they were granted names of cruisers already lost in action.

Of 151.4m/496ft 9in in length, they were given protective stowage for 200 mines, a feature that probably contributed to their tendency to trim by the stern. Their appearance differed from that of the preceding Wiesbadens in that the foremost of the three half-cased funnels was slightly longer than its partners, while two single 8.8cm/3.46in

high-angle guns were located on the centreline abaft them. The *Karlsruhe* (II) was the first German cruiser with turbines driving through full reduction gearing. Since the *Graudenz*, all carried ten coal- and two oil-fired boilers. Surrendered at the armistice, the *Königsberg* (II) served until 1936 as the French cruiser *Metz*.

The Köln (II) class, commenced in 1915, was the ultimate expression of the German World War I light cruiser. These were essentially further-enlarged repeats of the Königsbergs (II) but with eight coal- and six oil-fired boilers. Slow wartime construction saw only the *Köln* (II) and *Dresden* (II) ever completed of a projected ten vessel class. Both, together with *Karlsruhe* (II) were lost by scuttling at Scapa Flow in 1919. Salvaged, the *Emden* (II) and *Nürnberg* (II) were expended by the French and British respectively in tests-to-destruction.

LEFT: This elevated view of *Köln* (II) arriving for internment at Scapa shows the sided layout of her open 15cm/5.9in gun mountings. Note that these later units had a lengthened forefunnel.

Wiesbaden, Königsberg (II) and Köln (II) classes

	Built	Commissioned
Frankfurt	Kiel Dockyard	August 20, 1915
Wiesbaden	AG "Vulcan", Stettin	August 23, 1915
Emden (II)	AG "Weser", Bremen	December 16, 1916
Karlsruhe (II)	Kiel Dockyard	November 15, 1916
Königsberg (II)	AG "Weser", Bremen	August 12, 1916
Nürnberg (II)	Howaldtswerke, Kiel	February 15, 1917
Dresden (II)	Howaldtswerke, Kiel	March 28, 1918
Frauenlob (II)	Kiel Dockyard	Scrapped, incomplete
Köln (II)	Blohm & Voss, Hamburg	January 17, 1918
Leipzig (II)	AG "Weser", Bremen	Scrapped, incomplete
Magdeburg (II)	Howaldtswerke, Kiel	Scrapped, incomplete
Rostock (II)	AG "Vulcan", Stettin	Scrapped, incomplete
Wiesbaden (II)	AG "Vulcan", Stettin	Scrapped, incomplete

Plus three un-named; never launched

Köln (II) (as designed)

Displacement: 6,726 tonnes/6,620 tons (normal); 7,605 tonnes/7,485 tons (full load)
Length: 149.8m/491ft 9in (wl); 155.5m/510ft 5in (oa)
Beam: 14.2m/46ft 7in
Draught: 6.2m/20ft 4in (normal)
Armament: 8 x 15cm/5.9in (8x1) and 3 x 8.8cm/3.46in (3x1) guns; 4 x 500mm/19.7in torpedo tubes (2x2)
Machinery: Geared steam turbines, 14 boilers, 2 shafts
Power: 23,116kW/31,000shp for 27.5 knots
Endurance: 1,118 tonnes/1,100 tons (coal) and 1,067 tonnes/1,050 tons (oil) for 10,556km/5,700nm at 12 knots
Protection: 18–60mm/0.71–2.4in (belt); 20–60mm/0.79–2.4in (protective deck)
Complement: 560

Pillau and Brummer classes

In the course of the development of the German fleet cruiser there were two further pairs of ships built that did not quite fit the mould. A pair of 4,471-tonne/4,400-ton protected cruisers was laid down by Schichau in 1913 to their own design and to the account of pre-revolutionary Russia. Named *Maraviev Amurskyi* and *Admiral Nevelskoy*, they were slightly smaller than their German counterparts, and could be distinguished by their greater freeboard and vertical stem. Their three funnels were also cased to about two-thirds their height.

The two were appropriated at the outbreak of war, and their armament changed from a planned eight 13cm/5.1in and four 63mm/2.5in Russian-pattern guns to eight 15cm/5.9in and four 5.2cm/2in guns, the latter later exchanged for two 8.8cm/3.46in weapons.

Powered for 27.5 knots and capable of carrying 120 mines apiece, they were valuable acquisitions and were

commissioned into the German Navy as the *Pillau* and *Elbing* respectively. The latter was lost at Jutland and the former taken post-war by the Italians, serving until 1944 as the *Bari*.

The second pair was the *Brummer* and *Bremse*, laid down in 1915 as fast, offensive minelayers. To facilitate their operation in British waters they were deliberately profiled to resemble Arethusa-class ships, with bows of distinctive curvature, three slender funnels of equal height and masts crossed British style. Authenticity was increased through the ability to quickly strike the mainmast. Carrying their capacity load of 400 mines they were tender but, in normal trim, they were stiffer and sea-kindly.

Their main achievement was to surprise a UK-Norway convoy in October 1917 while operating together. They sank two escorting British destroyers and ten merchantmen. Just 20 months

ABOVE: Designed to carry no less than 400 mines, the *Brummer* and *Bremse* were configured to resemble British Aurora-class cruisers. A pole mainmast could be shipped and the bow profile was more heavily curved. The pair successfully ambushed a British convoy in October 1917.

later, both were on the bottom of Scapa Flow following the grand scuttling of the interned German fleet.

Pillau and Brummer classes

	Built	Commissioned
Elbing	Schichau, Danzig	September 4, 1915
Pillau	Schichau, Danzig	December 14, 1914
Bremse	AG "Vulcan", Stettin	July 1, 1916
Brummer	AG "Vulcan" Stettin	April 2, 1916

Brummer (as built)

Displacement: 4,455 tonnes/4,385 tons (normal); 5,949 tonnes 5,855 tons (full load)
Length: 135m/443ft 2in (wl); 140.4m/460ft 10in (oa)
Beam: 13.2m/43ft 4in
Draught: 5.9m/19ft 6in (normal)
Armament: 4 x 15cm/5.9in (4x1) and 2 x 8.8cm/3.46in (2x1) guns; 2 x 500mm/19.7in torpedo tubes (2x1)
Machinery: Geared steam turbines, 6 boilers, 2 shafts
Power: 24,608kW/33,0000shp for 28 knots
Endurance: 610 tonnes/600 tons (coal) and 1,016 tonnes/1,000 tons (oil) for 10,742km/5,800nm at 12 knots
Protection: 40mm/1.57in (belt); 150mm/4.13in (protective deck)
Complement: 310

LEFT: Distinguishable from other German light cruisers by virtue of their vertical stems, *Pillau* and *Elbing* were being built to Russian account when taken over. Ceded to Italy in 1919, the *Pillau* was renamed *Bari*. As seen here, her funnels were reduced to two and, together with her masts, shortened.

FAR LEFT: **The elegant lines of the German-built *Askold* pre-date those of later German light cruisers. She also incorporated both protective deck and side belts. Guns at upper deck level are of 15cm/5.9in calibre; those on the main deck are of 76mm/3in.**

ABOVE: **Seized by the Bolsheviks in 1917, the *Askold* was taken by the British in August 1918. After two years' service as a depot ship she was offered back to the Russians, but was in so deplorable a state that she was scrapped in Germany. Of her former glory, only the Imperial eagle remains here, at the stem head.**

Askold

Hitherto weak in effective, medium-sized cruisers, the Russian Navy ordered nine in the late 1890s. Three of 6,096 tonnes/6,000-tons, (*Aurora*, *Diana* and *Pallada*) came from the Admiralty Yard at St. Petersburg but, as they were powered for only 20 knots, the design for the remaining six was put out to competition. This was won by Schichau, which was commissioned to build *Bogatyr*. The same general specification was issued to other builders for the remaining five.

Krupp's Germania Yard at Kiel only had recent experience in three of the small, 2,642-tonne/2,600-ton Gazelles, and had not built a 6,096-tonne/6,000-tonne vessel since the *Kaiserin Augusta*, completed in 1892. The *Askold*, which

they launched for the Russians in March 1900, thus contained elements of that design, but considerably refined in both form and power in order to produce a then-challenging 23-knot speed.

The *Kaiserin Augusta* could make 21 knots on 10,440kW/14,000ihp but the *Askold*, although longer and narrower, would require 17,896kW/24,000ihp. To develop this power, nine licence-built Thornycroft narrow-tube boilers were grouped in five adjacent, watertight spaces, each exhausted by a funnel. These five, quite closely spaced, earned the ship the nickname of "the packet of Woodbines", among the British, with whom she worked closely in the Indian Ocean and in the Mediterranean during World War I.

The *Kaiserin Augusta*'s flush-decked hull was retained, together with the long, narrow superstructure deck, which was profiled in plan to allow one centerline and four casemated guns to fire forward. A similar arrangement gave stern fire while two further, casemated, guns fired on the beam.

Askold's protective deck was of Krupp's patented nickel-steel plate, thickened to 100mm/3.94in on the high glacis that protected the crowns of the boilers and the three engines. On trials, the ship made a very respectable 24 knots on 17,599kW/23,600ihp.

LEFT: **Seen in Tsarist colours, the *Askold* attends a French fleet review. Although fitted for anti-torpedo nets, her stowage shelf is empty. Note that the net booms appear here, in an early picture, and above at her scrapping, but not during World War I (above left).**

Askold

Built: Germania, Kiel
Commissioned: 1901
Displacement: 6,096 tonnes/6,000 tons (normal)
Length: 129.9m/426ft 6in (bp)
Beam: 15m/49ft 3in
Draught: 6.2m/20ft 3in (normal)
Armament: 12 x 152mm/6in (12x1);
12 x 76mm/3in (12x1) guns; 6 x 381mm/15in
torpedo tubes (6x1)
Machinery: Vertical, triple-expansion engines,
9 boilers, 3 shafts
Power: 17,896kW/24,000ihp for 23 knots
Bunkers: 1,118 tonnes/1,100 tons (coal)
Protection: 76mm/3in (protective deck)
Complement: 500

Directory of Cruisers

1918 to the Present Day

Between the wars, international treaties circumscribed cruiser numbers and introduced the concept of "heavy" and "light" cruisers. Most routinely carried aircraft for spotting and reconnaissance, together with increasing numbers of lighter weapons to meet the fast-developing menace of air attack. In commerce protection, cruisers were valued particularly in the provision of convoy defence in the face of hostile air superiority. This led directly to the introduction of the specialist category of anti-aircraft cruiser.

With war, cruiser-on-cruiser actions were confined largely to fierce exchanges in the Pacific but, in all theatres, cruisers proved invaluable for gunfire support to operations ashore. Using conference-limited designs as a starting point, the United States built extended classes of standard cruiser before 1945. Mostly mothballed during the ensuing Cold War, they proved ill-suited for conversion to guided-missile status, and fell victim to block obsolescence. Bespoke guided-missile cruisers emerged, with progressive miniaturization of electronics reducing them to the scale of large destroyer-sized escorts.

LEFT: **Although hailed as a "ship of the future" on her completion in 1964, the USS *Long Beach* (CGN.9) proved to be an evolutionary dead-end, her nuclear power plant over-expensive, her solid-state 3-D radar over-complex, and her all-missile armament lacking in versatility.**

FAR LEFT: **HMS** *Kent*, probably seen here in late 1941, is considerably modified from her peacetime condition. Short tripod masts have replaced the earlier tall poles. Radars and light automatic weapons proliferate. She has not been cut down a level right aft, nor has she gained the ungainly boxy hangar, as on the *Suffolk* (right). INSET: **A battle-ready** *Suffolk* in 1942 has her main armament trained to cover each quadrant. Despite a good stability range, several of the class acquired so much extra top-weight that they were cut down aft and landed their torpedo tubes. Her original open bridge has been covered.

County classes (1926–29)

Following World War I, the British fleet was well served by large numbers of Town- and C-class cruisers, but these were not suitable for long-endurance, independent patrols in support of trade. With the wholesale disposal of large armoured and protected cruisers made obsolete by war, replacements were required. The design starting point for these was the new Hawkins class which was also held to be the reason why the Washington Treaty allowed future cruiser maxima to be 10,160 tonnes/10,000 tons displacement with a 203mm/8in main battery. As all five signatories immediately began building to these limits, the resulting ships became known as "treaty cruisers".

British designers, together with their foreign peers, found 10,160 tonnes/10,000 tons a tight stricture when tied to a 203mm/8in armament. To gain even inadequate levels of protection, the planned 74,570kW/100,000shp installed

ABOVE: **A pre-war impression, showing** *Exeter* with, incorrectly, equal-sized funnels. Neither ship was greatly modified before becoming a war casualty. Distinguished at the battle of the River Plate, the *Exeter* was lost in the Far East early in 1942. The *York* became a casualty during the 1941 battle for Crete.

ABOVE: **Bedevilled both by global tonnage restrictions and tough economies, the Royal Navy built a couple of "B"-type heavy cruisers, 2,032 tonnes/2,000 tons lighter than the Counties and with two fewer guns. The** *Exeter*, here, may be distinguished from the *York* by her vertical funnels and masts.

power for 33 knots had to be reduced to 59,656kW/80,000shp for 31.5 knots. This reduced machinery weight but, more importantly, it reduced the size of the associated spaces, allowing protection to be thickened.

The design of the twin 203mm/8in turret was novel, particularly in the available 65-degree elevation for a dubious anti-aircraft (AA) capability. Despite their spacious gunhouse, the weapons proved trouble prone. Considerable problems also attended the "for but not with" aircraft arrangements now required for independent cruiser activities.

The approved design was highly distinctive, the massive flush-decked hull featuring a continuous double line of scuttles that even flanked the machinery spaces, betraying a lack of side armour. High freeboard made for a more than usually spacious standard of accommodation but was, in itself, a subtle design feature that added depth to the hull, increasing longitudinal stiffness at little penalty in material weight.

With weight at so high a premium, the three funnels required by the spacing of the eight boilers could not have been welcome, particularly as they required subsequently to be significantly lengthened.

The first group of eight, known as the Kent class, were ordered under the 1924–25 Programme but, savaged by budgetary cuts, emerged as five British and two Australian units. Their design incorporated a partly internal anti-torpedo bulge which, too shallow to be effective, was omitted from the second group, the four Londons of 1925–26. This enabled the lines of the hull to be refined giving a theoretical extra three-quarters of a knot.

A final pair (the Dorsetshires) was added in 1926, with much the same characteristics but with heavier gun mountings and, like the Londons, lacking the Kent-type's torpedo tubes. Their protection was also redistributed and their fire-control arrangements improved.

Modernization during the 1930s saw some of what were popularly termed the Counties have their after end razed by

LEFT: Mechanics prepare *Suffolk's* Walrus amphibian for catapulting. Ideally suited for its task of spotting and reconnaissance, the aircraft greatly enhanced a cruiser's capacity for area search. First flown in 1933, the Walrus was designed by R.J. Mitchell, father of the Spitfire fighter. ABOVE: *Devonshire* as completed, arriving from the Far East with paying-off pendant streamed. Note the very generous freeboard and capital-ship style sternwalk. Her aircraft is a Hawker Osprey which, in its seaplane form, was described as a fighter/reconnaissance aircraft. As a cadet training ship, *Devonshire* survived until 1954.

one deck level, saving weight sufficient to improve protection and to add a massive box hangar for aircraft.

Alone of all the groups, the *London* received an early wartime reconstruction that saw her gain a two-funnelled profile superficially similar to that of a "Crown Colony".

Although two further-improved ships (to have been named *Northumberland* and *Surrey*) were cancelled, a pair of 8,382-tonne/8,250-ton, six-gun diminutives was built. These, *York* and *Exeter,* were the first of what were hoped would be a class of fleet cruiser of a size capable of undertaking trade protection duties. With similar machinery to their larger running mates, they were fitted with only two funnels, the fatter forward one being two trunked into a single casing.

Continuously improved, particularly in fire-control, anti-aircraft armament and, eventually, electronics, the Counties performed well under wartime conditions. *Canberra*, *Cornwall*, *Dorsetshire* and both diminutives all became war casualties. Of the various international designs of "treaty cruisers", the Counties can be fairly claimed to have been given the best-balanced design.

ABOVE: Due to the outbreak of war, *London* became the only County to undergo thorough modernization. Her new layout and appearance closely followed that of a "Crown Colony", but the high freeboard was retained.

BELOW: The British 203mm/8in gun, seen here on *London*, was introduced as a direct result of the Washington Treaty. It was a 50-calibre weapon which fired a 116kg/256lb shell. Designed for a 70-degree elevation and an optimistic rate of fire of 12 rounds per minute, the mounting was overweight.

County classes (1926–29)

	Built	Commissioned
Kent	Chatham Dockyard	June 25, 1928
Australia	Brown, Clydebank	April 24, 1928
Berwick	Fairfield, Glasgow	February 15, 1928
Canberra	Brown, Clydebank	July 10, 1928
Cornwall	Devonport Dockyard	May 8, 1928
Cumberland	Vickers, Barrow	February 23, 1928
Suffolk	Portsmouth Dockyard	May 31, 1928
London	Portsmouth Dockyard	January 31, 1929
Devonshire	Devonport Dockyard	March 18, 1929
Shropshire	Beardmore, Glasgow	September 12, 1929
Sussex	Hawthorn Leslie, Tyne	March 19, 1929
Dorsetshire	Portsmouth Dockyard	September 30, 1930
Norfolk	Fairfield, Glasgow	April 30, 1930

County classes (1926–29) (for later variants)

Displacement: 9,703 tonnes/9,550 tons (standard); 13,463 tonnes/13,250 tons (full load)
Length: 181.5m/595ft (bp); 192.7m/632ft 8in (oa)
Beam: 20.1m/66ft
Draught: 5.2m/17ft (standard)
Armament: 8 x 203mm/8in (4x2), 4 x 102mm/4in (4x1) guns and 4 x 2pdr pompom (4x1) guns; 8 x 533mm/21in torpedo tubes (2x4)
Machinery: Geared steam turbines, 8 boilers, 4 shafts
Power: 59,656kW/80,000shp for 32.25 knots
Endurance: 3,251 tonnes/3,200 tons (oil) for 23,150km/12,500nm at 12 knots
Protection: 25mm/1in (sides – amidships); 76–112mm/3–4.4in (magazines); 25mm/1in (turret)
Complement: 784

LEFT: Completed in 1936, a pristine *Hobart* is seen at Malta. The neutrality markings on "B" turret date the picture as late 1930s, during the Spanish Civil War. She also carries the twin 102mm/4in HA mountings that were added during the 1938 refit, undertaken prior to her transfer to the Royal Australian Navy.

Leander and Improved Leander classes

Throughout the 1920s the Royal Navy was well-served by the many light cruisers of the late war's emergency programmes. By the end of the decade, however, general parameters for replacements had been drawn up, designed around an eight-gun main battery of four twin 152mm/6in turrets. The desired 31.5-knot speed and 6,000 nautical mile endurance would require machinery of 47,000kW/63,000shp and a (standard) displacement of about 7,112 tonnes/7,000 tons. With facilities for two aircraft, the proposal appeared a useful compromise for both fleet and trade protection duties. Additional incentive to build was to be provided by the forthcoming 1930 London Naval Conference, which would effectively end the "treaty cruiser" race while putting a global limit on permitted light cruiser tonnage. To construct adequate numbers of these, individual displacements would need to be minimized, assisted by the new technique of welding, obviating the weight of rivets and plate overlaps.

An innovation was to group three boiler rooms together, ahead of three adjacent machinery spaces. Although the arrangement was vulnerable to a single torpedo hit, it allowed six boilers to be exhausted via a single, trunked funnel. This large and unique feature (hated by those who had to paint it) was very much the "trademark" of the five-ship Leander class of the early 1930s. Of these, *Ajax* and *Achilles* achieved fame at the River Plate, while the *Orion* survived some of the worst damage sustained by a British cruiser.

American design practice favoured alternating boiler and machinery spaces to improve survivability, and this "unit system" was incorporated in three follow-on Leanders, or Amphions, all of which

were transferred to the Royal Australian Navy. They differed externally in their two, widely spaced funnels, which resulted in cramped aircraft arrangements.

In practice, boilers could be operated at higher than designed pressures, generating power for 32.5 knots.

Leander and Improved Leander classes

	Built	Commissioned
Leander	Devonport Dockyard	March 24, 1933
Achilles	Cammell Laird, Birkenhead	October 6, 1933
Ajax	Vickers, Barrow	April 12, 1935
Neptune	Portsmouth Dockyard	February 12, 1934
Orion	Devonport Dockyard	January 18, 1934
Perth (ex-*Amphion*)	Portsmouth Dockyard	July 6, 1937
Hobart (ex-*Apollo*)	Devonport Dockyard	January 13, 1936
Sydney (ex-*Phaeton*)	Swan Hunter, Tyne	September 24, 1935

Leander class

Displacement: 7,366 tonnes/7,250 tons (standard); 9,703 tonnes/9,550 tons (full load)
Length: 159m/522ft (bp;) 168.9m/554ft 6in (oa)
Beam: 17.1m/56ft
Draught: 4.7m/15ft 6in
Armament: 8 x 152mm/6in (4x2); 4 x 102mm/4in (4x1) (later eight, 4 x 2) guns; 3 x quadruple 12.7mm/0.5in machine-guns; 8 x 533mm/21in torpedo tubes (2x4)
Machinery: Geared steam turbines, 6 boilers, 4 shafts
Power: 53,690kW/72,000shp for 32.5 knots
Endurance: 1,829 tonnes/1,800 tons (oil) for 12,964km/7,000nm at 16 knots
Protection: 25–76mm/1–3in (over machinery); 88mm/3.46in (magazines); 25mm/1in (turret roofs)
Complement: 570

ABOVE: Of the five original Leander-class ships, the nameship and *Achilles* were operated by the Royal New Zealand Navy. *Ajax*, seen here, and *Achilles* achieved fame at the River Plate action in 1939. Pictured here post-war, *Ajax* has tripod masts and four twin 102mm/4in HA mountings, and "X" turret has been removed.

LEFT: Seen post-war as a unit of the Mediterranean Fleet, the *Aurora* has wartime modifications – tripod masts, enhanced light armament, radar and extended bridge. She had a fine fighting record with Force "K", but was transferred to Nationalist China in 1945 as the *Chungking*. ABOVE: Small, agile and with good anti-aircraft armament, the four Arethusas were employed mainly in the Mediterranean. The *Penelope*, in her original condition, without ensign and making smoke, is seen here probably on contractors' sea trials. Dry-docked during the Malta blitz, she was so punctured by fragments as to be nicknamed "Pepperpot".

Arethusa class

At the same time as the Leander design development there was a requirement for a new class of small fleet cruiser – fast and handy enough to lead destroyers yet able to shadow unobtrusively, qualities well exhibited in the C- and D-classes. These, however, displaced under 4,064 tonnes/4,000 tons, considered insufficient for the new ships, which would require endurance adequate to operate in Far Eastern waters. Other desirable features included six 152mm/6in guns in twin turrets, a speed of at least 32 knots and minimum protection against destroyer gunfire.

The five proposals evolved for consideration nicely illustrate the compromises necessary in warship design, where the dominant qualities of speed, armament and protection can be improved only at the expense of each other. Of the five draft designs, the smallest could make 38 knots but was

entirely unprotected, while the largest embodied the required protection and armament but was of 6,909 tonnes/6,800 tons and could manage only 31.5 knots. An acceptable mean resulted in the 5,537-tonne/5,450-ton Arethusa design, of which the nameship was ordered under the 1931 Programme.

With machinery again disposed according to the unit system, there were two widely spaced funnels, which again constricted topside aircraft arrangements. The class was limited to only four ships, mainly because foreign fleets particularly that of the Japanese, were building large and powerful 152mm/6in cruisers which the Royal Navy needed to watch. Tonnage remaining under the London Treaty had to be devoted to these.

Much British opinion considered that the Arethusas represented "an awful lot of ship for only six guns", while the Americans thought them too small to

be of much use. The quartet nonetheless gained great credit in the Mediterranean, where the *Aurora* in particular led destroyers to considerable effect, the task for which she was intended.

The *Galatea* and *Penelope* became war losses, both to submarine torpedoes.

Arethusa class

	Built	Commissioned
Arethusa	Chatham Dockyard	May 23, 1935
Aurora	Portsmouth Dockyard	November 12, 1937
Galatea	Scotts, Greenock	August 4, 1935
Penelope	Harland & Wolff, Belfast	November 13, 1936

Arethusa class

Displacement: 5,537 tonnes/5,450 tons (standard); 7,010 tonnes/6,900 tons (full load)
Length: 146.2m/480ft (bp); 154.2m/506ft (oa)
Beam: 15.5m/51ft
Draught: 4.2m/13ft 9in
Armament: 6 x 152mm/6in (3x2), 8 x 102mm/4in (4x2) and 8 x 2pdr pompom (2x4) guns; 6 x 533mm/21in torpedo tubes (2x3)
Machinery: Geared steam turbines, 4 boilers, 4 shafts
Power: 47,724kW/64,000shp for 32.25 knots
Endurance: 1,320 tonnes/1,300 tons (oil) for 10,186km/5,500nm at 15 knots
Protection: 70mm/2.76in (over machinery); 85mm/3.35in (magazines)
Complement: 500

ABOVE: *Galatea*, seen pre-war. She has no aircraft aboard, which emphasizes the position of the after funnel, set unusually far back due to the separated boiler spaces. Like the *Penelope*, she eventually fell victim to a submarine torpedo, small cruisers proving vulnerable to hits in the machinery spaces.

Southampton and Improved Southampton classes

ABOVE LEFT: **Her back having been broken by a magnetic mine in 1939, *Belfast* was extensively rebuilt. Note the prominent bulge and funnel/mast disposition.**

ABOVE: ***Sheffield,* long a component of Force H, had the busiest war of any of the Towns. Superimposed "X" turret, seen here, was later removed.**

Japan, with some reason, felt aggrieved at what she considered inadequate tonnage quotas allocated to her at the Washington and 1930 London conferences. At the latter, global tonnage limits were agreed on for both heavy and light cruiser categories and, as few more of the former could now be built, the emphasis was now focused on ships with guns of under 155mm/6.1in calibre. British policy was to keep individual size limited in order to gain the maximum number of, what were hoped to be, inexpensive cruisers. With barely half the United Kingdom's allocation, however, Japan decided to opt for size and fighting power. To this end, she would be able to construct a dozen vessels, each of a little under 8,738 tonnes/8,600 tons displacement. In 1931, therefore, the *Mogami* was laid down, to be armed with no less than

ABOVE MIDDLE: **As designed, with four turrets, the Towns were elegant, but lacked AA defence. *Gloucester,* shown here, was destroyed by air attack in May 1941.**

ABOVE: ***Birmingham* was the only Town to lack a knuckle forward. Note, in this 1946 picture, "X" turret replaced by a quadruple 40mm/1.57in mounting, and the wartime accumulation of radars.**

five triple 155mm/6.1in turrets. Little information was released about them, but the type was also known to be fast and reasonably protected.

That the Japanese were cheating may well have been suspected but, in the absence of means of verification, both Britain and the United States were stirred to suitable response, the latter in developing the design of the 10,169-tonne/10,000-ton 15-gun Brooklyn class.

By mid-1933 the Japanese had four large light cruisers under construction and then, as treaty terms required, announced their intention of commencing a further four. The British Admiralty thus called for counter-proposals, all more modest than either the Japanese or American designs because their waterline length needed to be compatible with dry docks existing within the Commonwealth. This length realistically permitted only four turrets and would affect maximum speed.

It was required that the new ships be able to take on any other 152mm/6in-armed opponent. Vertical armour over magazines and machinery spaces was thus specified to be impervious to such calibre at any range, and horizontal protection to be good out to 14,630m/16,000yds, beyond which range 152mm/6in hits would be rare.

A first pair was ordered under the 1933 Programme and, at 9,246 tonnes/9,100 tons, were able to ship four triple 152mm/6in turrets and a realistic anti-aircraft (AA) battery of four 102mm/4in mountings. Fire control was initially limited by financial stricture rather than by space.

Three further units were added in each of the 1934 and 1935 Programmes. With the final trio, the rapidly growing aerial threat was acknowledged with thickened horizontal protection. Vertical armour was slightly thinned in order to spread it over a greater area but, even so, displacement increased by some 305 tonnes/300 tons, necessitating a small increase in both

LEFT: **En route to becoming a museum ship in 1992,** *Belfast* **shows all her post-war modifications. All surviving Towns acquired the inelegant lattice masting.** BELOW: **Completed in "Far Eastern" livery,** *Southampton* **is seen at her Tyneside fitting-out berth. The oblique lighting shows clearly the extent of her vertical protection.** BOTTOM: **Seen in 1946,** *Liverpool* **shows her wartime modifications. Her starboard anchor is catted, preparatory to the use of its cable to secure to a buoy in Malta's Grand Harbour.**

beam and installed power to maintain stability range and legend maximum speed.

With the addition of considerable wartime topweight, a major modification was the landing of "X" turret in favour of increased AA weaponry.

A final pair, commenced under the 1936 Programme, differed considerably. Restrictions on length were relaxed, enabling them to make an extra half knot on the same power. Consideration was given to fitting them with four quadruple 152mm/6in turrets, but these proved to be too complex. A major design difference was to move boilers and machinery considerably further aft, opening a considerable gap between bridge structure and fore-funnel. While this reduced smoke nuisance it did nothing for the ships' appearance. Their extra displacement allowed their after turrets to be carried one level higher, a further two twin 102mm/4in high-angle (HA) mountings to be added, and protection to be further improved.

Both types performed well under wartime conditions, with *Southampton*, *Gloucester* and *Manchester* of the original class and *Edinburgh* of the improved type becoming war casualties.

Southampton and Improved Southampton classes

	Built	Commissioned
Southampton	Brown, Clydebank	March 6, 1937
Birmingham	Devonport Dockyard	November 18, 1937
Glasgow	Scotts, Glasgow	September 9, 1937
Gloucester	Devonport Dockyard	January 17, 1939
Liverpool	Fairfield, Glasgow	November 2, 1938
Manchester	Hawthorn Leslie, Tyne	August 4, 1938
Newcastle	Vickers, Tyne	March 5, 1937
Sheffield	Vickers, Barrow	August 25, 1937
Edinburgh	Swan Hunter, Tyne	July 6, 1938
Belfast	Harland & Wolff, Belfast	August 3, 1939

Later Southampton class

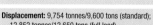

Displacement: 9,754 tonnes/9,600 tons (standard); 12,852 tonnes/12,650 tons (full load)
Length: 170m/558ft (bp); 180m/591ft (oa)
Beam: 19.8m/64ft 10in
Draught: 5.33m/17ft 6in
Armament: 12 x 152mm/6in (4x3), 8 x 102mm/4in (4x2) and 8 x 2pdr pompom (2x4) guns; 6 x 533mm/21in torpedo tubes (2x3)
Machinery: Geared steam turbines, 4 boilers, 4 shafts
Power: 61,520kW/82,500shp for 32 knots
Endurance: 2,032 tonnes/2,000 tons (oil) for 14,816km/8,000nm at 16 knots
Protection: 114mm/4.5in (over machinery and magazines); 51mm/2in (turret roofs)
Complement: 700

Improved Southampton class

Displacement: 10,516 tonnes/10,350 tons (standard); 13,466 tonnes/13,250 tons (full load)
Length: 176.4m/579ft (bp); 186.9m/613ft 6in (oa)
Beam: 19.3m/63ft 4in
Draught: 5.26m/17ft 3in
Armament: 12 x 152mm/6in (4x3), 12 x 102mm/4in (4x2) and 16 x 2pdr pompom (2x8) guns; 6 x 533mm/21in torpedo tubes (2x3)
Machinery: Geared steam turbines, 4 boilers, 4 shafts
Power: 61,520kW/82,500shp for 32.5 knots
Endurance: 2,439 tonnes/2,400 tons (oil) for 18,520km/10,000nm at 16 knots
Protection: 114mm/4.5in (over machinery and magazines); 51mm/2in (turret roofs)
Complement: 785

LEFT: **HMS** *Bermuda*, probably in the late 1950s. Her bridge has been enclosed in line with standards for nuclear warfare. Although comprehensive, her electronics are dated. The line of Carley floats in way of the forward funnel show that survival arrangements remain as poor as ever.

ABOVE: *Nigeria* was the last "Crown Colony" to retain her four triple 152mm/6in turrets, giving a more balanced profile, as originally designed. "X" turret was traditionally manned by Royal Marines, whose bandsmen may well be performing here on the turret roof.

"Crown Colony" class

With the scheduled expiry of the 1922 Washington Treaty, limitation was carried forward with the Second London Conference of 1936. This was not a success as the dictatorships were already pushing the world toward another war, and rearmament was in the air. Japan considered herself a naval power equal to Great Britain and the United States, and withdrew when her delegates failed to persuade them to agree to parity on tonnage allocations. Italy, smarting from sanctions imposed by the League of Nations following her Ethiopian adventure, refused to sign the ensuing agreement.

Although little was gained from the conference, cruiser development was affected inasmuch as the signatories agreed to continue the moratorium on heavy cruisers (subject to a let-out clause) and that 152mm/6in ships should not exceed 8,128 tonnes/8,000 tons standard displacement. No limit was imposed on numbers although these, for the British, were circumscribed by a tight fiscal policy in time of recession.

As the international climate deteriorated, British defence budgets increased. Over a dozen proposed variations on an 8,128-tonne/8,000-ton vessel were developed for Admiralty consideration, combining the functions of fleet duty and trade protection, with anti-ship or dual-purpose anti-aircraft (AA) armament. The latter was arranged around the newly adopted 133mm/5.25in weapon selected for the contemporary Dido-class cruisers. As the Admiralty had pushed unsuccessfully for a 7,112-tonne/7,000-ton upper limit, 8,128 tonnes/8,000 tons appeared generous, allowing proposed arrangements of seven, and even eight, twin 133mm/5.25in gunhouses. Their 36.4kg/80lb projectiles compared poorly, however, with the 51kg/112lb, 152mm/6in round as a ship-stopper, and the Japanese use of the latter decided the issue.

After exhaustive consideration the Admiralty, perhaps surprisingly, opted for a Southampton's scale of armament on a displacement of some 15 per cent less. Because of this

ABOVE: The blank side in way of the machinery spaces denotes the extent of the *Gambia*'s protection. Neither of those lost succumbed to gunfire, however; one was lost to bombing and the other to torpedo. *Gambia* was the last of class to serve in the Royal Navy, their material condition deteriorating rapidly.

ABOVE: Fully commissioned, *Gambia* lays in a dockyard basin as a "matey" passes with unusually purposeful stride. Elevated to the same angle, 102mm/4in and 40mm/1.57in weapons can be easily made out. *Gambia* served most of World War II under the New Zealand flag.

similarity, the new type, to be called the Fiji class (or, generically, the "Crown Colonies"), is often assumed to have been a "no-frills" diminutive. However, despite four triple 152mm/6in turrets appearing to be somewhat ambitious on the size, the design was very carefully thought out, resulting in a more spaciously laid-out hull and a smaller crew.

A major departure, from the point of view of ship design, was the adoption of a modestly proportioned transom stern. Although immediately denounced for its somewhat utilitarian appearance if offered, at minimal penalty in weight, more internal space aft and a marginal increase in speed. From the stability angle, it also offered increased buoyancy to counter a stern trim following damage. Experience also proved it to reduce propeller-induced vibration.

By the end of 1937, when the first block of five Fijis was ordered, and the provision of new cruisers was considered urgent and a further four contracts were let in the following year. All were completed after the outbreak of war and the abandonment of treaty restrictions. Additional weight, much of it located high in the ships, thus increased with each ship, eventually amounting to over 10 per cent of legend

ABOVE: In 1957, *Nigeria* was purchased by the growing Indian Navy. Before transfer, she was given a modernization to bring her up to the standard of the latest. She finally lost "X" turret and gained lattice masts which did nothing for her appearance. She is seen here as the *Mysore* in Indian dark grey livery.

displacement. Certain features, including wood deck sheathing, searchlights and one aircraft crane, were dispensed with, but the ninth hull, *Uganda*, and the final pair, had to lose "X" turret. Even this major step was largely offset by the enhancement of AA weaponry and the addition of torpedo tubes.

During 1944 there was a general move toward the removal of aircraft and their arrangements from cruisers. Always space-consuming and a considerable fire hazard, their passing caused little regret, their function being assumed by carrier-borne aircraft and the cruiser's own radars.

Of the 11 "Crown Colonies", only two, *Fiji* and *Trinidad* became war casualties, both by air attack. *Uganda*, *Gambia* and *Nigeria* served under the Canadian, New Zealand and Indian flags respectively. *Ceylon* and *Newfoundland* went to Peru after the war.

"Crown Colony" class

	Built	Commissioned
Fiji	Brown, Clydebank	May 5, 1940
Bermuda	Brown, Clydebank	August 21, 1942
Gambia	Swan Hunter, Tyne	February 21, 1942
Jamaica	Vickers, Barrow	June 29, 1942
Kenya	Stephens, Glasgow	September 27, 1940
Mauritius	Swan Hunter, Tyne	January 4, 1941
Nigeria	Vickers, Tyne	September 23, 1940
Trinidad	Devonport Dockyard	October 14, 1941
Uganda	Vickers, Tyne	January 13, 1943
Ceylon	Stephens, Glasgow	July 13, 1943
Newfound-land	Swan Hunter, Tyne	January 20, 1943

"Crown Colony" class

Displacement: 8,636 tonnes/8,500 tons (standard); 10,923 tonnes/10,750 tons (full load)
Length: 163.9m/538ft (bp); 169.2m/555ft 6in (oa)
Beam: 18.9m/62ft
Draught: 5m/16ft 6in (standard)
Armament: 12/9 x 152mm/6in (4x3/3x3), 8 x 102mm/4in (4x2) and 8/12 x 2pdr pompom (2x4/3x4) guns; 6 x 533mm/21in torpedo tubes
Machinery: Geared steam turbines, 4 boilers, 4 shafts
Power: 59,656kW/80,000shp for 32.25 knots
Endurance: 1,727 tonnes/1,700 tons (oil) for 14,816km/8,000nm at 16 knots
Protection: 82mm/3.23in (over machinery spaces); 88mm/3.46in (magazines sides); 51mm/1in (turret roofs)
Complement: 735

ABOVE: *Jamaica* was the only "Crown Colony" to ship a stump mast amidships. Offset to port, and forward of the after funnel, only its top is visible here. Note how the centre 152mm/6in gun is set in to avoid mutual interference when salvo firing.

LEFT: **Prettiest of ships, the Didos were designed for the AA defence of formations and convoys. They proved to be absolutely invaluable in the confines of the Mediterranean where, in the absence of carriers, enemy air superiority was the norm. *Sirius* is seen here leaving Malta.**

Dido and Improved Dido classes

The Royal Navy's C-in-C, Mediterranean, was more aware than most that his fleet operated in relatively confined waters which, even in the mid-1930s, were under most potential threat from land-based air power. Therefore, when the Admiralty favoured expending its treaty-limited cruiser tonnage on ships capable of both fleet and trade protection duties, he persisted with a case for a small design of fleet escort, capable of mounting barrage anti-aircraft (AA) fire in defence of the fleet or of convoys, against high-level bombing or torpedo aircraft.

At the outset, the case was weakened for lack of a suitable gun. Even in a dual-purpose (DP) mounting, a destroyer-type 119mm/4.7in lacked sufficient punch against surface targets. Trials with a proposed 130mm/5.1in were not progressed while the World War I 140mm/5.5in was not considered for development. Only toward the end of 1935 did a new 133mm/5.25in prototype become available, to be complemented by a high-angle (HA) mounting promising an 80-degree elevation.

On the strength of this the Board of Admiralty gave initial approval in June 1936 for a 5,385-tonne/5,300-ton cruiser with, unusually, five twin turrets. Three were located in superfiring, centreline positions forward, resulting in a comparatively lofty bridge structure. This, in turn, demanded tall funnels, raked to carry smoke clear of the bridge. Although the resulting large silhouette was criticized, it had a pleasing elegance, assisted by the low freeboard aft (another criticized feature).

The first five ships of what were known as the Dido class were ordered under the 1936 Programme. With the London Treaty of that year removing limitation on numbers of hulls, five more followed in the 1937 and 1938 Programmes. A final six were added in 1939 during the run-up to war. It was the misfortune of the class that the chosen 133mm/5.25in gun and mounting was also specified for the DP secondary armament of the new King George V-class battleships.

The resulting demand for 40 extra mountings greatly slowed delivery for the Didos, affecting both completion dates and final armament. Three of the first four cruisers completed with only four turrets apiece, while two later units, *Scylla* and *Charybdis*, were given an all 114mm/4.5in destroyer-scale armament.

The final five units were designated the Improved Dido class. Recast around a conventional, four-turret layout, they had a lower bridge, set further forward, together with lower

ABOVE LEFT: ***Scylla*** (seen here) and ***Charybdis*** lost their 133mm/5.25in turrets to new battleships and, in turn, each acquired four twin 114mm/4.5in mountings intended for the updating of D-class cruisers. Their armament was thus on a par with a Tribal-class destroyer. LEFT: ***Hermione*** has the full outfit of five 133mm/5.25in turrets. This was not without its problems, as the considerable weight forward of the bridge structure caused heavy pitching which resulted in structural damage. With so much topweight, stability was also a delicate issue.

ABOVE: A deck view of *Phoebe* at an unspecified date. Note the elevation of the guns in "X" mounting. Their 36.3kg/80lb shells could be fired at elevations of up to 80 degrees but the round turrets were cramped internally.

LEFT: The five Improved Didos were completed to a four-turret design, which permitted automatic AA weapons to be mounted in the old "Q" position. This in turn allowed the bridge structure to be lowered and lengthened, and the funnels to be shorter. The *Diadem's* masts appear here to have been shortened but have been doctored by the censor. MIDDLE LEFT: The lowered, vertical silhouette of the later ships lacked the elegance of the original Didos but the larger bridge structure permitted them to work efficiently as force flagships. Topweight problems continued and the *Royalist*, which landed her torpedo tubes in 1944, had not regained them in this post-war shot.

funnels. These no longer needed to be raked which, while beneficial in making their heading more difficult to determine, gave them an appearance more business-like than elegant.

In practice, the original layout proved over-ambitious, the weight of the three forward mountings causing distortion and cracking under dynamic loading in a seaway. Nor was the 133mm/5.25in gun an unqualified success. When it worked without breakdown, it worked well, but it was too heavy and lacked agility for it to be a truly efficient AA weapon.

Although several Didos were serving in the Pacific by the end of 1944, the type had limited endurance and earned its keep primarily in the Mediterranean.

Due to their limited size and questionable subdivision, the Didos were vulnerable to a single torpedo hit in a machinery space. Four of the five lost were sunk by torpedo and one by the still-new German air-launched, radio-controlled glider bomb. Four (*Bonaventure*, *Hermione*, *Naiad* and *Spartan*) were lost in the Mediterranean, the *Charybdis* in the English Channel.

Dido and Improved Dido classes

	Built	Commissioned
Dido	Cammell Laird, Birkenhead	September 30, 1940
Argonaut	Cammell Laird, Birkenhead	August 8, 1942
Bonaventure	Scotts, Greenock	May 24, 1940
Charybdis	Cammell Laird, Birkenhead	December 3, 1941
Cleopatra	Hawthorn Leslie, Tyne	December 5, 1941
Euryalus	Chatham Dockyard	June 30, 1941
Hermione	Stephen, Linthouse, Glasgow	March 25, 1941
Naiad	Hawthorn Leslie, Tyne	July 24, 1940
Phoebe	Fairfield, Glasgow	September 27, 1940
Scylla	Scotts, Greenock	June 12, 1942
Sirius	Portsmouth Dockyard	May 6, 1941
Bellona	Fairfield, Glasgow	October 29, 1943
Black Prince	Harland & Wolff, Belfast	November 20, 1943
Diadem	Hawthorn Leslie, Tyne	January 6, 1944
Royalist	Scotts, Greenock	September 10, 1943
Spartan	Vickers, Barrow	August 10, 1943

ABOVE: *Bellona* in her late World War II condition, painted in a disruptive camouflage scheme and with paravane fittings on the stem. She was used extensively in Arctic waters, where the massive accumulations of topside ice exacerbated her already tender stability.

Dido class (with intended armament)

Displacement: 5,588 tonnes/5,500 tons (standard); 7,366 tonnes/7,250 tons (full load)
Length: 147.8m/485ft (bp); 156m/512ft (oa)
Beam: 15.4m/50ft 6in
Draught: 4.3m/14ft 3in (standard)
Armament: 10 x 133mm/5.25in (5x2) and 8 x 2pdr pompom (2x4) guns; 6 x 533mm/21in torpedo tubes (2x3)
Machinery: Geared steam turbines, 4 boilers, 4 shafts
Power: 46,233kW/62,000shp for 32.25 knots
Endurance: 1,118 tonnes/1,100 tons (oil) for 10,186km/5,500nm at 16 knots
Protection: 76mm/3in (sides to machinery spaces and magazines); 50mm/2in (roofs to magazines)
Complement: 490

LEFT: **Despite their advanced armament, the Tigers were obsolete on completion.** *Tiger* and *Blake* were thus rebuilt aft to operate and support four AS helicopters for fleet support. *Blake*, here exercising with an American carrier, has lost all conventional armament except her forward 152mm/6in and 76mm/3in mountings.

Swiftsure and Tiger classes

The "Crown Colony" design was considered a success and, in interest of wartime standardization, the later, nine-gun Uganda sub-class provided the basis for two groups of near-identical follow-ons. The three Minotaurs of the 1941 Programme had their beam increased by 0.31m/1ft to compensate for additional topweight. One of them, *Bellerophon*, was completed with an extra 0.61m/2ft in the beam, effectively qualifying her to belong to the later Tiger class of the 1941 (Supplementary) and 1942 Programmes.

Minotaur was completed as the Royal Canadian Navy's *Ontario*, whereupon the first group were renamed the Swiftsure class. Of the Tigers, both the lead ship and the *Hawke* were cancelled, the earlier *Bellerophon* assuming the name *Tiger*.

For a long time, the three remaining Tigers remained incomplete. Several armament schemes were proposed for them but when, in 1954, the decision was made to proceed, it was with fully automatic, dual-purpose, 152mm/6in and 76mm/3in twin mountings. Two

152mm/6in turrets occupied "A" and "X" positions, with 76mm/3in in the "B" position and sided in the waist. Although their hulls were already upwards of ten years old and their machinery of pre-war design, the ships were extensively remodelled, with far bulkier superstructure.

The considerable increase in displacement exacted a 3-knot speed penalty.

Completed slowly in an era of severe economic stricture, the Tigers came into service too late, after the guided-missile age had already begun. Their complex new weaponry had the usual teething problems but, being already obsolescent, was never really cured of them.

With the Cold War emphasis on anti-submarine warfare (ASW) the fleet required more large specialist helicopters

and the *Tiger* and *Blake* were earmarked in 1964 for conversion to Command Helicopter Cruisers, carrying four Sea Kings apiece. Unconverted, the *Lion* was scrapped in 1972.

In their original form, the Tigers were the Royal Navy's last conventional cruisers.

Swiftsure and Tiger classes

	Built	Commissioned
Swiftsure	Vickers, Tyne	June 22, 1944
Bellerophon (renamed *Tiger*)	Brown, Clydebank	March 24, 1959
Ontario (ex-*Minotaur*)	Harland & Wolff, Belfast	May 25, 1945
Tiger (renamed *Bellerophon*)	Vickers, Tyne	Cancelled
Blake	Fairfield, Glasgow	March 18, 1961
Defence (renamed *Lion*)	Scotts, Greenock	July 20, 1960
Hawke	Portsmouth Dockyard	Cancelled
Superb	Swan Hunter, Tyne	November 16, 1945

Tiger class (before conversion)

Displacement: 9,703 tonnes/9,550 tons (standard); 11,888 tonnes/11,700 tons (full load)
Length: 163.9m/538ft (bp); 169.2m/555ft 6in (oa)
Beam: 19.5m/64ft
Draught: 7m/23ft (standard)
Armament: 4 x 152mm/6in (2x2) and 6 x 76mm/3in (3x2) guns
Machinery: Geared steam turbines, 4 boilers, 4 shafts
Power: 59,636kW/80,000shp for 29.5 knots
Endurance: 1,930 tonnes/1,900 tons (oil) for 15,742km/8,500nm at 16 knots
Protection: 82mm/3.23in (over machinery spaces); 88mm/3.46in (magazine sides); 50mm/2in (turret roofs)
Complement: 750

ABOVE: **In her original configuration, the** *Tiger* **clearly shows her "Crown Colony" ancestry. A fully automatic twin 152mm/6in turret is located at either end, with a 76mm/3in twin in "B" position and two more in the waist. Emphasis is on gunnery, with a director for each mounting, height-finding and search radars.**

LEFT: **The Omahas were considerably, and individually, modified in the course of the war. In this July 1942 picture, the *Cincinnati* (CL.6) has lost her upper casemated guns and her aircraft catapults. She was the first cruiser to be fitted with the large CXAM-1 air search radar.** BELOW: **The *Omaha* (CL.4) in her original configuration. She then had ten torpedo tubes, the portside upper deck triple mounting being just visible ahead of the mainmast. The very tall masts were for the benefit of long-range radio transmission.**

Omaha class

A first impression of the Omahas is one of an overgrown version of the "four piper" destroyers that they were intended to lead. Like them, they appeared very narrow-gutted although their length-to-breadth (L/B) ratio of 9.93 was not exceptionally high. In all, they appeared to be a good compromise of what can be achieved on a limited displacement and tight cost limit. However, their endurance was less than had been hoped for, and two, rather than four, aircraft were carried.

Earlier scout cruisers, although smaller, had high freeboard hulls that were anything but discrete, but the Omahas exhibited much of the long, easy sheerline of their destroyer charges.

A requirement for maximum end-on and broadside fire resulted in a unique gun arrangement. A narrow twin 152mm/6in turret was sited on the centreline, forward and aft. Flanking them and located at the corners of the bridge and after superstructure, were double-tiered casemates, each housing a further gun. Six barrels could therefore bear either ahead or astern and eight could be presented on either beam.

The original design dedicated the low quarterdeck to a fixed centreline catapult but design developments resulted in two trainable units being fitted one level higher, abaft the funnels.

As built, the ships had ten torpedo tubes, sided triple banks on the upper deck abaft the catapults and, below, twins at main deck level. These were closed off by shutters but, like the casemated guns, these positions proved to be very wet in adverse conditions, and the twin tubes were later removed.

By World War II standards, the Omahas lacked effective anti-aircraft fire control and their subdivision was inadequate. The low after freeboard and fine run gave very little reserve buoyancy to counter stern trim induced by action damage. Used mainly in second-line duties, however, none of their number was lost.

Omaha class

	Built	Commissioned
CL.4 *Omaha*	Seattle Construction & DD Co	February 24, 1923
CL.5 *Milwaukee*	Seattle Construction & DD Co	June 20, 1923
CL.6 *Cincinnati*	Seattle Construction & DD Co	January 1, 1924
CL.7 *Raleigh*	Bethlehem Steel, Quincy	February 6, 1924
CL.8 *Detroit*	Bethlehem Steel, Quincy	July 31, 1923
CL.9 *Richmond*	Cramp, Philadelphia	July 2, 1923
CL.10 *Concord*	Cramp, Philadelphia	November 3, 1923
CL.11 *Trenton*	Cramp, Philadelphia	April 19, 1924
CL.12 *Marblehead*	Cramp, Philadelphia	September 8, 1924
CL.13 *Memphis*	Cramp, Philadelphia	February 4, 1925

Omaha class

Displacement: 7,214 tonnes/7,100 tons (standard); 7,874 tonnes/7,750 tons (full load)
Length: 167.6m/550ft (wl); 169.2m/555ft 1in (oa)
Beam: 16.9m/55ft.4in
Draught: 4.1m/13ft 6in (standard)
Armament: 12 x 152mm/6in (2x2/8x1) and 2 (later 8) x 76mm/3in (2x1) guns; 10 (later 6) x 533mm/21in torpedo tubes
Machinery: Geared steam turbines, 12 boilers, 4 shafts
Power: 67,113kW/90,000shp for 35 knots
Endurance: 1,991 tonnes/1,960 tons (oil) for 13,149km/7,100nm at 15 knots
Protection: 76mm/3in (belt); 38mm/1.5in (protective deck)
Complement: 815

LEFT: **At Pearl Harbor, the *Raleigh* (CL.7) was hit in the machinery spaces by a torpedo, then by a bomb that passed through her. She flooded to the extent that she developed negative stability but was saved initially by lashing barges alongside. Final repairs were effected in California.**

FAR LEFT: **Oldest of the American "treaty cruisers" the two Pensacolas were unique in mounting ten 203mm/8in guns in a combination of twin and triple turrets.** *Salt Lake City* (CA.25) **here shows her distinctive bow profile and unusual "reverse bow wave" camouflage scheme.** ABOVE LEFT: **An early picture of the Northampton-class** *Augusta* (CA.31). **Although she spent the war in the Atlantic and was never fully modernized, she would gain very much more tophamper, with the tripod mainmast built around the after funnel.** BELOW: **The two Indianapolis class were an improved version of the Northamptons (***Indianapolis* **seen here). Note how the superstructure layout is dominated by the requirements of aircraft, most of which were subsequently removed as fire hazards. This late World War II picture shows her with improved directors.**

Pensacola, Northampton and Indianapolis classes

With the 1922 Washington Treaty unintentionally creating the 10,160-tonne/10,000-ton 203mm/8in cruiser the US Navy embarked on a programme of 16, whose construction was to parallel that of the Omahas.

As ever, design studies led to necessary compromise, it being decided to combine a ten-gun main battery, and protection against destroyer-calibre (i.e. 127mm/5in) gunfire with a conservative speed of 32 knots. The 203mm/8in guns would be disposed in four turrets with, unusually, triples superfiring twins to keep the maximum number of weapons "dry".

Although 32 knots necessitated only seven boilers, eight could be accommodated with little penalty, giving the ships marginally higher speed. Unlike British practice, designers saved weight with a relatively shallow, flush-decked hull, relying on pronounced flare and sheer to maintain dryness. An observation floatplane was deck-stowed on either side of the after funnel.

So carefully was weight controlled that standard displacement came out at only 9,246 tonnes/9,100 tons. Only two ships, *Pensacola* and *Salt Lake City*, were thus built to this design, which was immediately recast to become the six Northamptons (CA.26–31). These were greatly improved by having a long forecastle for dryness, with extra strength and accommodation space. One main battery gun was sacrificed in order to improve layout with three triple turrets. A hangar was built around the after funnel and compartmentalization greatly improved, primarily through subdivision of the previously large boiler spaces. For an extra 3m/10ft on waterline length and 0.31m/1ft on the beam, they could now also be protected to resist destroyer gunfire at beyond 7,315m/8,000yds.

Problems with weight distribution caused sufficient ship movement to make poor gun platforms. This was partially rectified in the following pair, *Portland* (CA.33) and *Indianapolis* (CA.35), which were again slightly longer and utilized nearly the full allowable displacement to improve protection and gunnery arrangements with improved turrets and directors.

Pensacola, Northampton and Indianapolis classes

	Built	Commissioned
CA.24 *Pensacola*	New York Navy Yard	February 6, 1930
CA.25 *Salt Lake City*	New York Shipbuilding	December 11, 1929
CA.26 *Northampton*	Bethlehem Steel, Quincy	May 17, 1930
CA.27 *Chester*	New York Shipbuilding	June 24, 1930
CA.28 *Louisville*	Puget Sound Navy Yard	January 15, 1931
CA.29 *Chicago*	Mare Island Navy Yard	March 9, 1931
CA.30 *Houston*	Newport News	June 17, 1930
CA.31 *Augusta*	Newport News	January 30, 1931
CA.33 *Portland*	Bethlehem Steel, Quincy	February 23, 1933
CA.35 *Indianapolis*	New York Shipbuilding	November 15, 1932

Pensacola/Salt Lake City (as designed)

Displacement: 9,246 tonnes/9,100 tons (standard); 10,821 tonnes/10,650 tons (full load)
Length: 173.6m/570ft (wl); 178.4m/585ft 6in (oa)
Beam: 19.9m/65ft 3in
Draught: 5m/16ft 3in
Armament: 10 x 203mm/8in (2x3/2x2) and 4 x 127mm/5in (4x1) guns; 6 x 533mm/21in torpedo tubes (2x3)
Machinery: Geared steam turbines, 8 boilers, 4 shafts
Power: 79,789kW/107,000shp for 32.5 knots
Endurance: 2,144 tonnes/2,110 tons (oil) for 12,964km/7,000nm at 15 knots
Protection: 62–100mm/2.44–3.94in (belt); 25mm/1in (protective deck); 37–62mm/1.46–2.44in (turrets)
Complement: 655

LEFT: The ill-fated *Quincy* (CA.39) seen here covering the initial landings on Guadalcanal in August 1942. Days later she was lost, together with her sisters *Astoria* (CA.34) and *Vincennes* (CA.44), in the disastrous night action off Savo Island. ABOVE: The *New Orleans* (CA.32) seen here soon after her completion, with very light masting and open bridge platforms. The Astorias had their aircraft arrangements moved aft into a bulky, full width superstructure block. Note the height of the catapults.
BELOW: *New Orleans* again. By the end of the war she had acquired two large directors, the after one atop a considerable new tower superstructure. A cowl added to the forward funnel and the port catapult was landed as weight compensation for the many new automatic weapons.

Astoria class

It will already be apparent that so-called "treaty cruisers" earned their appellation of "tinclads" through favouring armament and speed over protection. The US Navy suffered unduly in this respect through the rapidity with which it implemented its planned 16-ship programme. Designers were over-diligent in their efforts to save weight, resulting in early units being completed at nearly 914 tonnes/900 tons underweight. This could have been used to improve protection but following units were so well advanced that by the time that the situation was appreciated, little could be done.

With the final group (the Astorias), therefore, fierce debate developed over whether the extra displacement should be devoted to vertical or horizontal armour, to defeat short- or long-range fire respectively. How it was finally distributed would have a considerable "knock-on" effect on the ships overall layout.

In the event, the priority of protection was increased further at the expense of survivability. To decrease the area to be protected, machinery spaces were shortened by 4.26m/14ft. This reduced the length sufficiently to make impossible the sensible earlier unit system, whereby boiler and machinery spaces alternated. Externally, this design shift was evident in the closer-spaced funnels, which displaced the catapults and aircraft hangar further aft.

A more compact superstructure also replaced the earlier heavy tripod masts. This was made possible by improvements in radio technology, where antenna lengths were being reduced. The reduced tophamper greatly increased the unobstructed firing arcs of the ships' anti-aircraft weapons.

Three of the class were lost together in the disastrous Savo Island action of August 1942. Here, in a short nocturnal action, Japanese cruisers surprised an American-Australian force. Overwhelming short-range Japanese fire easily penetrated their armour, while uncontrollable fires were started in aircraft and boat facilities as well as in ready-use ammunition stowage areas. In two cases, a single torpedo hit put all boiler spaces out of action.

Astoria class

	Built	Commissioned
CA.32 *New Orleans*	New York Navy Yard	February 15, 1934
CA.34 *Astoria*	Puget Sound Navy Yard	April 28, 1934
CA.36 *Minneapolis*	Philadelphia Navy Yard	May 19, 1934
CA.37 *Tuscaloosa*	New York Shipbuilding	August 17, 1934
CA.38 *San Francisco*	Mare Island Navy Yard	February 10, 1934
CA.39 *Quincy*	Bethlehem Steel, Quincy	June 9, 1936
CA.44 *Vincennes*	Bethlehem Steel, Quincy	February 24, 1937

Astoria class

Displacement: 10,110 tonnes/9,950 tons (standard); 12,599 tonnes/12,400 tons (full load)
Length: 176.1m/578ft (wl); 179.1m/588ft (overall)
Beam: 18.8m/61ft 9in
Draught: 5.9m/19ft 6in (standard)
Armament: 9 x 203mm/8in (3x3) and 8 x 127mm/5in (8x1) guns; 8 x 12.7mm/0.5in MG (2x4)
Machinery: Geared steam turbines, 8 boilers, 4 shafts
Power: 79,789kW/107,000shp for 32.4 knots
Endurance: 1,935 tonnes/1,900 tons (oil) for 13,150km/7,100nm at 15 knots
Protection: 76–127mm/3–5in (belt); 57mm/2.24in (protective deck); 37–203mm/1.46–8in (turrets)
Complement: 751

Wichita and Brooklyn class

The inadequate protection of the earlier 203mm/8in "treaty cruisers" was a matter of some concern to the US Navy's designers and, when the 1930 London Naval Treaty allowed a total of 145,803 tonnes/143,500 tons of 152mm/6in cruisers, the demand from the outset was for more armour. Close behind were calls for a reckonable anti-aircraft (AA) battery and for four aircraft. Its requirements being different from those of the Royal Navy, the US Navy was ready to build 10,160-tonne/10,000-ton light cruisers in order to get what it wanted.

The rather messy aircraft arrangements in amidships locations on earlier ships had limited aircraft to two but, in the new Brooklyns, the aviation facility was banished aft. On the quarterdeck, sided catapults flanked hatch access to underdeck stowage for the required four machines. Externally, the development showed in a high freeboard and handling crane, the latter becoming a distinctive feature. The new layout was a success, greatly reducing the complexity of the earlier central structure and became the basis for later classes.

ABOVE: Last of the so-called "treaty cruisers", the *Wichita* (CA.45) was effectively a Brooklyn rearmed with three triple 203mm/8in turrets and enclosed single 127mm/5in mountings. Early in her active war she spent time in the Atlantic. A British light cruiser is visible to the left and a storeship lays on the far side of *Wichita*.

ABOVE: To a dramatic backdrop of burning oil tanks, *Phoenix* (CL.46) sorties from Pearl Harbor. The number of personnel, topside suggests that the actual raid has been completed. The ship's luck held right through until 1982 when, under the Argentinian flag as *General Belgrano*, she was torpedoed by a British submarine near the Falklands' exclusion zone.

Extra space in the waist allowed four single 127mm/5in guns to be mounted in tubs along either side. To save weight, the weapons were without shields but represented a genuine dual-purpose (DP) secondary battery. As an AA weapon the newly introduced 28mm/1.1in cannon was disliked as its projectiles had to impact the target in order to detonate. In contrast, the airbursts of a 127mm/5in gun created a distinct deterrent to a would-be attacker.

Although it was far slower-firing, the 203mm/8in gun was much preferred to the 152mm/6in by the Americans, who felt the latter lacked punch. Without sufficient heavy cruisers, the US Navy assumed, however, that they would have to work in conjunction with 152mm/6in ships and that these, therefore, should be capable of resisting 203mm/8in gunfire. For compatibility, a 32.5-knot speed was still required and, to match the new Japanese Mogamis, 15 guns were also needed. To achieve anything like the required level of protection, it was obvious that the full 10,160 tonnes/10,000 tons of displacement would be necessary.

A study was undertaken to examine whether shipping four triples rather than five twin turrets would release enough weight to make a dramatic difference to the design's immunity zone. It proved not to, so the distinctive "three turrets forward" layout was adopted, a disposition similar to that of a Mogami.

To minimize the area to be protected, the boiler spaces and engine rooms were again grouped. In the final two hulls, however, improved and smaller boilers allowed the spaces again to be divided although, as the funnels retained their spacing, this involved extra under-deck ducting.

Later modifications saw the single, 25-calibre 127mm/5in guns replaced by the new, and more effective, twin 127mm/5in 38-calibre weapon.

By treaty rules, the US Navy was still one heavy cruiser below permitted strength. Although it had only limited protection against 203mm/8in gunfire, designers modified the Brooklyn hull to accept three triple turrets with the heavier gun. The gun mountings were larger and heavier than those in the Astorias so that, for the first time, barrels could be elevated individually rather than in a common sleeve.

Only one ship, the *Wichita* (CA.45) was built to this design but she proved to be influential to the long series of war-built heavy cruisers that would shortly follow.

With fully worked-up crews, the rate of fire of a Brooklyn could be phenomenal, some being credited with ten rounds per barrel per minute. At the battle in the Surigao Strait in October 1944, for instance, individual ships were firing upwards of 1,000 rounds in the space of a quarter hour.

ABOVE: **An early wartime view of *Boise* (CL.47), the ship still painted a uniform shade of grey and lacking later electronics. The after freeboard is exceptionally generous as this was the first class of American cruiser to incorporate an aircraft hangar beneath the quarterdeck.**

ABOVE: **An interesting detail of the after end of *Philadelphia*. Note the two catapults, mounted along the deck edges and flanking the hatch access to the underdeck hangar. The aircraft crane was typical of US cruisers and has a Curtiss SOC-3 Seagull scouting and observation aircraft "on the hook".**

Wichita and Brooklyn class

	Built	Commissioned
CL.40 *Brooklyn*	New York Navy Yard	September 30, 1937
CL.41 *Philadelphia*	Philadelphia Navy Yard	September 23, 1937
CL.42 *Savannah*	New York Shipbuilding	March 10, 1938
CL.43 *Nashville*	New York Shipbuilding	June 6, 1938
CL.46 *Phoenix*	New York Shipbuilding	October 3, 1938
CL.47 *Boise*	Newport News	August 12, 1938
CL.48 *Honolulu*	New York Navy Yard	June 15, 1938
CL.49 *St. Louis*	Newport News	May 19, 1939
CL.50 *Helena*	New York Navy Yard	September 18, 1939
CA.45 *Wichita*	Philadelphia Navy Yard	February 16, 1939

ABOVE: **The career of the *Helena* (CL.50) was brief and eventful. Torpedoed at Pearl Harbor, she was repaired stateside and returned to the Western Pacific. She fought in a dozen, mainly nocturnal, actions before being struck by three torpedoes at the first battle of Kula Gulf.**

Brooklyn class (as built)

Displacement: 9,957 tonnes/9,800 tons (standard); 11,786 tonnes/11,600 tons (full load)
Length: 182.8m/600ft (wl); 185.3m/608ft 4in (oa)
Beam: 18.8m/61ft.8in
Draught: 5.9m/19ft 6in (standard)
Armament: 15 x 152mm/6in (5x3) and 8 x 127mm/5in (8x1) guns
Machinery: Geared steam turbines, 8 boilers, 4 shafts
Power: 74,600kW/100,000shp for 32.5 knots
Endurance: 2,235 tonnes/2,200 tons (oil) for 13,890km/7,500nm at 15 knots
Protection: 80–127mm/3.1–5in (belt); 50mm/2in (deck); up to 168mm/6.6in (turrets)
Complement: 870

LEFT: **Armed with the lighter and more agile 127mm/5in 38, the American Atlanta-class cruisers were more effective AA platforms than the equivalent British Didos.** *Oakland* (CL.95) **belonged to the second group, which exchanged the wing 127mm/5in turrets for six more 40mm/1.57in weapons.**

Atlanta class

Although the US Navy disliked small cruisers it found, just as the British had long before, that large ships such as the 7,112-tonne/7,000-ton Omahas were not satisfactory for fleet work, lacking the necessary agility to either support or to repulse destroyer attack. The Second London Naval Conference of 1936 created a new unit displacement limit of 8,128 tonnes/8,000 tons which resulted in a new interest in smaller hulls. In 1938, a series of design studies culminated in the choice of a 6,096-tonne/6,000-ton vessel, too small to carry aircraft, but with the ability to work with and against destroyers, while covering the fleet against air attack.

Flush decked, with a long, easy sheer incorporating a British-style knuckle forward, the Atlantas had a single-calibre

ABOVE: **Confusingly, the sunken** *Juneau* **(CL.52) was replaced by a second of the name (CL.119), one of three built to a design modified to carry twenty-four 40mm/1.57in guns. Note how the centre 127mm/5in gunhouse is carried at the same height as the farthest. There are no aircraft, the afterdeck being occupied by two twin 40mm/1.57in. A quadruple mounting superfires the 127mm/5in.**

armament of sixteen 127mm/5in 38s. Three twin mountings were located in superfiring positions forward and aft, with a further two flanking the after superstructure. Forward of these were sided quadruple torpedo tubes. Automatic weapons, as designed, were limited to four quadruples of the unloved 28mm/1.1in cannon and six of the newly introduced 20mm/0.79in Oerlikons.

Soon classified as anti-aircraft cruisers (CLAA), the class of 11 comprised three distinct groups. The first four were followed by a second, which suppressed the two 127mm/5in waist mountings for more automatic weapons.

Inadequate stability saw most boats and their crane landed and extra ballast shipped. With the final trio, the torpedoes were omitted and the two centreline mountings at either end sited at the same level. Even splinter protection was reduced to reinvest in what eventually amounted to no less than thirty-two 40mm/1.57in and sixteen 20mm/0.79in weapons.

Additional crew to man this extensive battery and the endlessly proliferating

electronics took the complement from a designed 549 to 812, with consequent overcrowding and loss of amenities.

Atlanta class

	Built	Commissioned
CL.51 *Atlanta*	Federal Shipbuilding, Kearny	December 24, 1941
CL.52 *Juneau* (I)	Federal Shipbuilding, Kearny	February 14, 1942
CL.53 *San Diego*	Bethlehem Steel, Quincy	February 10, 1942
CL.54 *San Juan*	Bethlehem Steel, Quincy	February 28, 1942
CL.95 *Oakland*	Bethlehem Steel, San Francisco	July 17, 1943
CL.96 *Reno*	Bethlehem Steel, San Francisco	December 28, 1943
CL.97 *Flint*	Bethlehem Steel, San Francisco	August 31, 1944
CL.98 *Tucson*	Bethlehem Steel, San Francisco	February 3, 1945
CL.119 *Juneau* (II)	Federal Shipbuilding, Kearny	February 15, 1946
CL.120 *Spokane*	Federal Shipbuilding, Kearny	May 17, 1946
CL.121 *Fresno*	Federal Shipbuilding, Kearny	November 27, 1946

CL.51 and 52 both lost on November 13, 1942

First Atlanta group (as designed)

Displacement: 6,604 tonnes/6,500 tons (standard); 8,474 tonnes/8,340 tons (full load)
Length: 161.5m/530ft (wl); 165m/541ft 6in (oa)
Beam: 16.2m/53ft 3in
Draught: 5m/16ft 6in
Armament: 16 x 127mm/5in (8x2) guns; 8 x 533mm/21in torpedo tubes (2x4)
Machinery: Geared steam turbines, 4 boilers, 4 shafts
Power: 55,927kW/75,000shp for 32.7 knots
Endurance: 1,473 tonnes/1,450 tons (oil) for 14,816km/8,000nm at 15 knots
Protection: 28–95mm/1.1–3.75in (belt); 32mm/1.26in (deck and gunhouses)
Complement: 549

LEFT: **Carrying no more 152mm/6in guns than, say, an 7,257-tonne/8,000-ton British "Crown Colony", the sheer size of the Worcesters appeared excessive.** *Roanoke* **is shown here. The design was no longer bound by treaty, incorporated heavy horizontal and vertical protection, and excellent subdivision. They could also maintain 32 knots.**
BELOW: **The ultimate US light cruisers of World War II design were completed too late to participate.** *Roanoke* **(CL.145) shows her twelve 152mm/6in guns, arranged in twin, fully automatic turrets. Note the fire control on its high tower, and the lack of aircraft catapults, although the crane remains.**

Worcester class

Even in wartime, some concepts can take so long in development that they are doomed to obsolescence before completion. Such was the large Worcester-class light cruiser. Well before the United States entered the war they could see at first hand the deadly result of German air attack on Royal Navy ships obliged to operate beyond air cover. The Americans' 25-calibre 127mm/5in gun was ineffective against high-level bombing while its successor, the 127mm/5in 38-calibre, had yet to be proven. It was therefore decided to develop an automatic 152mm/6in dual-purpose gun. This, it was hoped, would counter not only the high-flyer but also provide rapid, smothering fire on to a surface target. The latter role, however, enjoyed a lower priority, for it was initially proposed that most of the protection be concentrated in a thickly armoured deck.

The pattern for the standard, war-built light cruiser had already been decided. This was largely based upon a pre-war

design, and the new cruiser would need to be of an entirely new concept. The new design enjoyed little priority as the emergency programmes rightly consumed almost all the available manpower and material resources.

The size of what became the Worcester class escalated rapidly. Six twin 152mm/6in 47 gunhouses, disposed similarly to the layout of the late Atlanta class, and twelve twin 76mm/3in 50s (in place of the earlier thickets of 40mm/1.57in guns) required space; the resulting area, once armoured, increased displacement, and survivability required a unit-system machinery layout, which demanded length.

With the US Navy preferring weight of fire to volume it was proposed that the Worcester class be armed with the new automatic 203mm/8in gun, but the need to evaluate the 152mm/6in 47-calibre

(possibly against the new threat of anti-ship missiles) led to four of the class being ordered. By the time two had been completed, however, they had been superseded by carrier-borne and ship-launched missiles. The second pair were thus cancelled in August 1945.

Worcester class

	Built	Commissioned
CL.144 *Worcester*	New York Shipbuilding	June 26, 1948
CL.145 *Roanoke*	New York Shipbuilding	April 4, 1949
CL.146 *Vallejo*	New York Shipbuilding	Cancelled before launch
CL.147 *Gary*	New York Shipbuilding	Cancelled before launch

Worcester class

Displacement: 15,037 tonnes/14,800 tons (standard); 18,289 tonnes/18,000 tons (full load)
Length: 202.3m/664ft (wl); 207m/679ft 6in (oa)
Beam: 21.5m/70ft 8in
Draught: 6.5m/21ft 6in (standard)
Armament: 12 x 152mm/6in (6x2) and 24 x 76mm/3in (12x2) guns
Machinery: Geared steam turbines, 4 boilers, 4 shafts
Power: 89,484kW/120,000shp for 32 knots
Endurance: 2,438 tonnes/2,400 tons (oil) for 14,816km/8,000nm at 15 knots
Protection: 76–127mm/3–5in (belt); 88mm/3.46in (protective deck); 50–168mm/2–6.6in (turrets)
Complement: 1,560

LEFT: **Seen separately at a distance, the** *Worcester* **(CL.144) could easily be confused with a late Atlanta, a distinguishing feature being the aircraft crane. The big gun tubs amidships contain twin 76mm/3in (rather than quadruple 40mm/1.57in) to defeat the kamikazes' threat. Note the large peacetime pendant numbers.**

LEFT: **Even at completion, the Cleveland-class light cruisers (the nameship shown here) had a very crowded appearance, not least because of a heavy, dual-purpose secondary armament of six twin 127mm/5in 38s. By contrast, the masts at this stage seemed under-populated, with a surface search antenna at the foremast head and air search at the main.**

Cleveland and Fargo classes

Ship design is usually a process of evolution, with successful examples influencing their successors. The last of the treaty-limited Brooklyns was commissioned after the outbreak of war in Europe, but now, with all restrictions discarded, the problem for the US Navy was to produce light and heavy cruisers in the greatest number in uninterrupted programmes of series production. Both types were to be "no frills" workhorses and, with the Brooklyns having created a good impression, they became the starting point.

TOP: **An early overhead view of** *Cleveland* **(CL.55) emphasizes her compact superstructure, her long fine entry and generous waterplanes aft. The clear quarterdeck indicates the hangar hatch access. The starboard catapult was later removed and gun tubs added either side of the "fantail".** ABOVE: **At a little more than 10 knots,** *Providence* **(CL.82) moves clearly through a calm sea, with little disturbance. Weight accumulation was a concealed problem, however, for, when full power trials were eventually conducted, designed speed required over 8 per cent more power than that predicted.**

The final pair of Brooklyns had been redesigned, their machinery disposed on the unit system with alternate boiler and machinery spaces for enhanced survivability. They also received the new pattern 127mm/5in 38-calibre gun as a dual-purpose secondary weapon. Even before the war, however, the ships were showing signs of being cramped and of carrying too much topweight. As recast for the new Cleveland class the design was built around four, rather than five triple 152mm/6in turrets. The hull was maintained at the same length but was given extra beam. Right aft, the hull was given fuller sections and a distinct tumblehome in order to increase waterplane area and, thus, reserve stability. This was probably in response to criticism that the under-deck hangar was a large floodable space with considerable free surface.

Measures to increase stability were, however, soon offset by significant improvements in armament. In terms of footprint and weight, the twin 127mm/5in 38-calibre was superior to two singles. It was, nonetheless, not a trifling load for a light cruiser. Six were accommodated in the "hexagonal" layout that was to characterize the war-built cruisers, with one centreline gunhouse superfiring the 152mm/6in turrets at both ends, and others flanking the forward and after ends of the main superstructure.

The problem of topweight was, however, insidious. Automatic weapons first specified for the Brooklyns had been comparatively simple 12.7mm/0.5 machine-guns. These were later upgraded to the unsatisfactory 28mm/1.1in cannon. By the time that the first of the new Clevelands had been launched, shortly before the Pearl Harbor attack, the new twin 40mm/1.57in Bofors-pattern gun was being introduced. Where the twin 40mm/1.57in gun occupied much the same space and weight as a quadruple 28mm/1.1in weapon it was soon largely displaced by the quadruple 40mm/1.57in. Each of these required additional substructure and, with no available under-deck space, this meant elevating them, with a knock-on effect for the field of fire of neighbouring weapons and, of course, on ship stability. The process continued with the growing need to engage multiple aerial targets simultaneously, leading to a proliferation of directors which also needed to be located at points high in the superstructure.

With stability reserves so tight that planned improvements to radars had to be deferred, a major redesign of the ship was ordered during 1943. Externally, this showed in the massive single funnel, made possible by some rearrangement of machinery spaces. This permitted a shorter superstructure, in turn improving the "sky arcs" for AA weapons. All main and secondary gun mountings were lowered by small, but significant amounts. With the standard Cleveland-class programme in full flood, however, only two units (CL.106 and 107) were built to this revised specification.

Despite the shortcoming of an increasingly elderly and restrictive design, the Clevelands became the longest-ever cruiser series. About 35 could be considered eventually to have been completed, nine of them as fast light aircraft carriers (CVL). Thirteen more were cancelled, either outright or partially complete. Half a dozen were converted in about 1960 to interim guided-missile cruisers (CLG).

ABOVE: *Fargo* and *Huntington*, seen here, were the only two Clevelands to be completed to the revised, single-funnel configuration, which permitted a more compact superstructure with significant weight saving. Post-war, she served with the Mediterranean-based US Sixth Fleet. BELOW: Even though executing a simultaneous starboard turn, *Biloxi* (CL.80) remains remarkably vertical, thus not complicating the fire-control solution. She has fired the centre gun of No.2 turret, the barrel still recovering from recoil. This late 1943 shot shows little electronic clutter topside.

Cleveland and Fargo classes

	Commissioned		Commissioned
CL.55 *Cleveland*	June 15, 1942	CL.91 *Oklahoma City* (B)	December 22, 1944
CL.56 *Columbia*	July 24, 1942	CL.92 *Little Rock* (B)	June 17, 1945
CL.57 *Montpelier*	September 9, 1942	CL.93 *Galveston* (B)	May 28, 1958
CL.58 *Denver*	October 15, 1942	CL.94 *Youngstown*	Cancelled
CL.59 *Amsterdam* (I) (A)		CL.95 *Oakland*	July 17, 1943
CL.60 *Santa Fe*	November 24, 1942	CL.96 *Reno*	December 28, 1943
CL.61 *Tallahassee* (I) (A)		CL.97 *Flint*	August 31, 1944
CL.62 *Birmingham*	January 29, 1943	CL.98 *Tucson*	February 3, 1945
CL.63 *Mobile*	March 24, 1943	CL.99 *Buffalo* (II) (A)	
CL.64 *Vincennes*	January 21, 1944	CL.100 *Newark* (I) (A)	
CL.65 *Pasadena*	June 8, 1944	CL.101 *Amsterdam* (II)	January 8, 1945
CL.66 *Springfield* (B)	September 9, 1944	CL.102 *Portsmouth*	June 25, 1945
CL.67 *Topeka* (B)	December 23, 1944	CL.103 *Wilkes-Barre*	July 1, 1944
CL.76 *New Haven* (I) (A)		CL.104 *Atlanta*	December 3, 1944
CL.77 *Huntington* (I) (A)		CL.105 *Dayton* (II)	January 7, 1945
CL.78 *Dayton* (I) (A)		CL.106 *Fargo* (II)	December 9, 1945
CL.79 *Wilmington* (I) (A)		CL.107 *Huntington* (II)	February 23, 1946
CL.80 *Biloxi*	August 31, 1943	CL.108 *Newark* (II)	Cancelled
CL.81 *Houston*	December 20, 1943	CL.109 *New Haven* (II)	Cancelled
CL.82 *Providence* (B)	May 15, 1945	CL.110 *Buffalo* (III)	Cancelled
CL.83 *Manchester*	October 29, 1946	CL.111 *Wilmington* (II)	Cancelled
CL.84 *Buffalo* (I)	Cancelled	CL.112 *Vallejo*	Cancelled
CL.85 *Fargo* (I) (A)		CL.113 *Helena*	Cancelled
CL.86 *Vicksburg*	June 12, 1944	CL.114	Cancelled
CL.87 *Duluth*	September 18, 1944	CL.115 *Roanoke*	Cancelled
CL.88	Cancelled	CL.116 *Tallahassee* (II)	Cancelled
CL.89 *Miami*	December 28, 1943	CL.117 *Cheyenne*	Cancelled
CL.90 *Astoria*	May 17, 1944	CL.118 *Chattanooga*	Cancelled

(A) Completed as Independence-class CVLs; (B) Later converted to CLGs

Cleveland class (improved)

Displacement: 10,313 tonnes/10,150 tons (standard); 12,090 tonnes/11,900 tons (full load)
Length: 182.8m/600ft (wl); 185.3m/608ft 4in (oa)
Beam: 19.6m/64ft 4in
Draught: 5.9m/19ft 6in (standard)
Armament: 12 x 152mm/6in (4x3), 12 x 127mm/5in (6x2) and 16 x 40mm/1.57in (4x4) guns
Machinery: Geared steam turbines, 4 boilers, 4 shafts
Power: 74,570kW/100,000shp for 32.5 knots
Endurance: 1,880 tonnes/1,850 tons (oil) for 16,205km/8,750nm at 15 knots
Protection: 88–127mm/3.46–5in (belt); 50mm/2in (protective deck); 76–152mm/3–6in (turrets)
Complement: 1,250

445

FAR LEFT: **By virtue of a considerable amount of trunking, the Baltimores' four boiler rooms could be exhausted by a single funnel. The resulting Oregon City sub-class had its bridge structure further aft and the base of the funnel two levels higher. Here,** *Rochester* **(CA.124) enters the Grand Harbour, Malta.**

ABOVE: **Early units of the Baltimore class were completed with two aircraft cranes (the nameship is shown here). This was later modified to a centreline crane and gun tubs on either quarter. At this stage, all Baltimores' tertiary armament comprised 40mm/1.57in weapons, of which 48 were carried.**

Baltimore and Oregon City classes

As the war-built Clevelands sprang from the Brooklyns, so did the 203mm/8in Baltimores stem from the one-off *Wichita*, herself an adapted Brooklyn. A major difference, however, was that where the Clevelands maintained the same length with a 7.7 per cent increase in beam, the latter had waterline length increased by 10.7 per cent and beam by 15 per cent. Inevitably, this resulted in a slower ship (although this was offset by more powerful machinery) but one less plagued by chronic topweight problems.

Like the *Wichita*, the *Baltimore* carried three triple 203mm/8in turrets, with a hexagonally disposed secondary dual-purpose battery of twelve 127mm/5in 38-calibre weapons housed in six twin gunhouses. Although the US Navy preferred the 203mm/8in gun to the 152mm/6in because of its superior penetration and stopping power (a typical projectile was about twice the weight) it attracted criticism because of its relatively

slow rate of fire. At this time, the Royal Navy reckoned on experienced gun crews being able to fire about six rounds per minute per 203mm/8in barrel, and eight rounds per 152mm/6in. The US Navy, however, claimed only four rounds per minute for 203mm/8in weapons. These used similar separate ammunition, i.e. the shell was loaded before the bagged firing charge. The weight of the projectile required mechanical loading, with the guns at a fixed angle of elevation. It will be apparent that the longer the firing range, and the consequent greater difference between the required elevation and the fixed loading angle, the slower the rate of fire. A fully automatic 203mm/8in gun was under development, but would require a larger ship to accommodate it (see Des Moines class).

In 1939, when the Baltimores required statistics were being argued between the General Board and the various responsible Bureaux, it would have taken considerable prescience to

LEFT: **This post-war view of** *Toledo* **(CA.133) shows a considerable reduction in tertiary armament, now usually comprising ten twin 76mm/3in guns. Aircraft and catapults have been removed and the previously open bridge roofed over. Her welded shell plating clearly shows variations in frame spacing. Note radiussed sheer strake and forward bulwark.**

forecast the extent to which each class would be burdened by the extra manpower demanded by wartime improvements. The size selected for the Baltimores was about right, but had to be defended against criticism that it would bar the ships from using many strategically located dry docks.

Itself overburdened at this time, the newly created Bureau of Ships (BuShips) passed much of the design work to Bethlehem Steel which, not surprisingly, went on to build many of the class.

Where the Baltimores would, in service, suffer the same proliferation of automatic weapons as did the Clevelands, the weight factor was less critical. Nonetheless, they too underwent a major redesign, with superstructure rearranged around a single large funnel, reducing the tophamper that restricted both director and gun performance. Only the first eight units were thus completed in the two-funnelled configuration. Of these, only the first four had characteristic

double aircraft cranes right aft. Later ships carried only two aircraft, the smaller underdeck hangar being served by a single, centreline crane.

Other than those converted, the Clevelands were discarded quickly after the war. More useful, often as peacetime flagships, the Baltimores and the single-funnelled Oregon Citys went on to give a further decade of service. Five saw conversion to interim guided-missile cruisers while one, the *Northampton* (CA.125) was totally remodelled as a new-style command cruiser.

For those still serving as heavy cruisers, the main updated features were ten twin 76mm/3in 50-calibre guns in place of the remaining quadruple 40mm/1.57in weapons, and a remodelled bridge. The US Navy preferred enclosed bridges but, for hostilities only, adopted the British-style open bridge, from which there was a better perception of the air threat.

ABOVE: Post-war removal of catapults and aircraft gave the Baltimores a spacious quarterdeck, the crane being retained as a general-purpose utility. Space was again available for boats, most of the *Columbus*'s (CA.74) contingent here being waterborne. In 1962 the ship was recommissioned as a missile cruiser (CG.12).

ABOVE: The *Saint Paul* (CA.73) was the longest serving of the class, by virtue of having been considerably refitted to serve as a fleet flagship. Seen here on a bombardment detail off Vietnam, she has been neatly bracketed by shore batteries.

Baltimore and Oregon City classes

	Commissioned			Commissioned
CA.68 *Baltimore*	April 15, 1943	CA.126 *Cambridge*		Cancelled
CA.69 *Boston* (A)	June 30, 1943	CA.127 *Bridgeport*		Cancelled
CA.70 *Canberra* (A)	October 14, 1943	CA.128 *Kansas City*		Cancelled
CA.71 *Quincy*	December 15, 1943	CA.129 *Tulsa*		Cancelled
CA.72 *Pittsburg*	October 10, 1944	CA.130 *Bremerton*		April 29, 1945
CA.73 *Saint Paul*	February 17, 1945	CA.131 *Fall River*		July 1, 1945
CA.74 *Columbus* (B)	June 8, 1945	CA.132 *Macon*		August 26, 1945
CA.75 *Helena*	September 4, 1945	CA.133 *Toledo*		October 27, 1946
CA.122 *Oregon City*	February 16, 1946	CA.135 *Los Angeles*		July 22, 1945
CA.123 *Albany* (B)	June 15, 1946	CA.136 *Chicago* (B)		January 10, 1945
CA.124 *Rochester*	December 20, 1946	CA.137 *Norfolk*		Cancelled
CA.125 *Northampton* (C)	1953	CA.138 *Scranton*		Cancelled

(A) Completed as guided-missile cruisers (CAG); (B) Completed as guided-missile cruisers (CG);
(C) Completed as command cruiser (CLC)

Baltimore and Oregon City classes

Displacement: 13,920 tonnnes/13,700 tons (standard); 17,933 tonnes/17,650 tons (full load)
Length: 202.3m/664ft (wl); 205.2m/673ft (oa)
Beam: 21.6m/70ft 6in
Draught: 6.2m/20ft 6in (standard)
Armament: 9 x 203mm/8in (3x3), 12 x 127mm/5in (6x2) and 48 x 40mm/1.57in (12x4) guns
Machinery: Geared steam turbines, 4 boilers, 4 shafts
Power: 89,484kW/120,000shp for 33 knots
Endurance: 2,388 tonnes/2,350 tons (oil) for 18,520km/10,000nm at 15 knots
Protection: 102–155mm/4–6.1in (belt); 63mm/2.48in (protective deck); 76–203mm/3–8in (turrets)
Complement: 1,425

Des Moines class

Last and largest of the American gun-armed cruisers, the Des Moines were vehicles for the new 203mm/8in gun with an anticipated improvement in the rate of fire from three to seven rounds per minute. Design for both gun and ship began in May 1943 and the first vessels were expected to be available by mid-1945.

It was hoped that the new weapon might be installed in the existing Oregon City-class design, but the arrangements for the new gun prescribed that only two could be accommodated in a turret of the same size as the old triple. Although six of the new weapons could be expected to fire 42 rounds per minute against the 27 of nine of the old type, the General Board favoured a new-design, nine-gun vessel with proper weight margins for electronics and directors, together with improved resistance to bombs and torpedoes. Secondary and AA armament would remain as before.

Necessarily larger magazines required that the armour be extended for their protection, the increased space and weight forcing up hull dimensions and

displacement. Waterline length was thus increased by 11m/36ft (5.4 per cent), whereas beam was increased by 7.7 per cent. Despite this marginally greater portliness, however, the extra length permitted improvement of lines, so that the ships made much the same speed on the same power as the smaller Oregon Citys. The extra beam enabled torpedo protection to be improved, while greater displacement permitted much of the weather deck to be of 25mm/1in plate to initiate the detonation of bombs before deep penetration.

Limited to only three units, all completed post-war, the Des Moines could be distinguished from the Oregon Citys at a distance by their very tall main director towers. Aircraft, from this and other classes of cruiser, were being removed at about this time, although their conspicuous cranes were retained.

ABOVE LEFT: **The *Des Moines* (CA.134) is seen here refuelling from the attack carrier *F.D. Roosevelt* (CVA.42). Pre-dating the carrier's modernization with angled deck, the picture probably dates to the late 1950s. In the absence of attendant fleet oilers, it was usual to extend the range of smaller vessels through taking oil from carriers.** ABOVE: **As a flagship *Newport News* (CA.148) here carries a wide-band radio antenna right forward and on No.2 turret, their key locations emphasizing their importance. The prominent bucket-shaped device at the foremast head is a TACAN aircraft beacon.**

Des Moines class

Displacement: 17,171 tonnes/16,900 tons (standard); 21,286 tonnes/20,950 tons (full load)
Length: 213.3m/700ft (wl); 218.3m/716ft 6in (oa)
Beam: 23.3m/76ft 4in
Draught: 6.7m/22ft (standard)
Armament: 9 x 203mm/8in (3x3), 12 x 127mm/5in (6x2) and 24 x 76mm/3in (12x2) guns
Machinery: Geared steam turbines, 4 boilers, 4 shafts
Power: 89,484kW/120,000shp for 32.5 knots
Endurance: 2,718 tonnes/2,675 tons (oil) for 19,446km/10,500nm at 15 knots
Protection: 102–155mm/4–6.1in (belt); 25mm/1in and 88mm/3.46in (decks); 95–203mm/3.75–8in (turrets)
Complement: 1,800

Des Moines class

	Built	Commissioned
CA.134 *Des Moines*	Bethlehem Steel, Quincy	November 16, 1948
CA.139 *Salem*	Bethlehem Steel, Quincy	May 14, 1949
CA.140 *Dallas*		Cancelled
CA.148 *Newport News*	Newport News Drydock	January 29, 194

Guided-missile conversions

By the end of World War II the aircraft carrier embodied a fleet's offensive power to the extent that its defence was a first priority. In the early Cold War era, the threat from bomber and torpedo aircraft had been extended to include large, air-launched stand-off missiles. To provide the fleet with a layered anti-aircraft defence, capable of meeting the greatest threat at a safe distance, the Americans developed a family of ship-launched missiles with overlapping capability. These were the Talos, reportedly of 105km/65 miles slant range, the Terrier, of 32km/20 miles, and the Tartar, of about 16km/10 miles. It would prove difficult to convert existing flotilla ships to missile carriers (although several were), so remodelled cruisers formed the backbone of the first generation of fleet missile escorts.

Completed in 1955–56, the pioneer conversions were of the *Boston* (CA.69) and *Canberra* (CA.70) to "single enders", retaining cruiser characteristics forward and an after end reconfigured for two twin-arm Terrier systems and individual electronics.

Proceeding them, and almost simultaneous

with the construction of the *Long Beach* was the reconstruction of six light cruisers. Three, *Providence* (CL.82), *Springfield* (CL.66) and *Topeka* (CL.67), were Terrier-equipped and three, *Galveston* (CL.93), *Little Rock* (CL.92) and *Oklahoma City* (CL.91), mounted the Talos system. All were single-enders, the Terrier-ships having a bulkier associated tophamper.

The ultimate rebuilds in this very expensive programme were those of the *Albany* (CA.123), *Chicago* (CA.136) and *Columbus* (CA.74), completely reconfigured as "double-enders"; with Talos systems forward and aft, and Tartar systems sided in the waist.

Ungainly and looking every bit the conversions that they were, the cruisers had the advantage of relatively generous magazine capacity, surviving until the

ABOVE LEFT: **Of the six Clevelands converted to missile cruisers, the *Oklahoma City* (CLG.5) was** one of four fitted as task force command ships. The bridge structure was extended forward at the cost of No.2 triple turret and two 127mm/5in mountings. Electronic fits varied considerably between ships. ABOVE: *Albany* (CG.10) was one of three heavy cruisers converted to double-ended missile ships. Here, wreathed in her own smoke, she simultaneously launches both her heavy Talos missiles and secondary Tartars. So many weapons and guidance systems resulted in a conflict for space.

late 1970s until superseded by smaller, purpose-built "cruisers", built around later and more compact missile systems.

Guided-missile conversions

	Converted by	Recommissioned
CAG.1 *Boston*	New York Shipbuilding	November 1, 1955
CAG.2 *Canberra*	New York Shipbuilding	June 15, 1956
CLG.3 *Galveston*	Philadelphia Navy Yard	May 28, 1958
CLG.4 *Little Rock*	New York Shipbuilding	May 23, 1957
CLG.5 *Oklahoma City*	Bethlehem Steel, San Francisco	May 23, 1957
CLG.6 *Providence*	Boston Navy Yard	September 17, 1959
CLG.7 *Springfield*	Bethlehem Steel, Quincy	July 2, 1960
CLG.8 *Topeka*	New York Navy Yard	March 26, 1960
CG.10 *Albany*	Boston Navy Yard	March 11, 1962
CG.11 *Chicago*	San Francisco Navy Yard	May 2, 1964
CG.12 *Columbus*	Puget Sound Navy Yard	December 1, 1962

Albany type (as converted)

Displacement: 13,920 tonnes/13,700 tons (standard); 17,882 tonnes/17,600 tons (full load)
Length: 202.3m/664ft (wl); 205.4m/674ft 1in (oa)
Beam: 21.2m/69ft 8in
Draught: 8.2m/27ft (standard)
Armament: 4 x Talos launchers, 104 missiles (2x2) and 4 x Tartar launchers, 84 missiles (2x2); 2 x 127mm/5in guns; 1 x eight-cell ASROC AS launcher
Machinery: Geared steam turbines, 4 boilers, 4 shafts
Power: 89,484kW/120,000shp for 31.5 knots
Endurance: 14,260km/7,700nm at 20 knots (oil capacity not reported)
Protection: 102–155mm/4–6.1in (belt); 75mm/2.95in (deck); 25mm/1in (magazines)
Complement: 1,100

LEFT: **Much as originally completed, the nuclear-powered missile cruiser** *Long Beach* **(CGN.9) has two Terrier systems forward and one Talos system aft. Her only guns are two single 127mm/5in 38s about amidships. Designed-to-task, she is much more compact than an Albany conversion.**

Long Beach (CGN.9)

The successful introduction of the nuclear submarine in 1955 encouraged the US Navy's development of a family of nuclear reactors, suitable for the propulsion of a range of surface ships. The existing family of surface-to-air missiles (SAMs) was already threatened with replacement by the bulky new Typhon system and active consideration was being given to the deployment of strategic Regulus II/Polaris missiles by surface warships.

To combine these technologies, together with a minimum speed of 30 knots, required a cruiser-sized hull for which design work commenced in 1954. The bulk and weight of reactors and shielding pushed up dimensions and, although Typhon had been shelved in favour of curing faults in the existing systems, Talos was mandated.

The sheer space required for propulsion plant and missile magazines was instigating a massive shift in design philosophy, away from heavily armoured ships, designed to absorb punishment, towards larger, volume-critical ships, too large to armour, and intended to inflict pain from a range at which they, themselves, would escape it.

Completed in 1961 as something of a prestige ship, the *Long Beach* was first armed with a Talos system aft and two Terriers forward, and "for but not with" Regulus II/Polaris. She was also equipped (as an intended carrier escort) with sonar and ASROC stand-off anti-submarine missiles. Two 127mm/5in 38-calibre guns were added later when complaints were made that she was helpless against minor conventional attack, where guided missiles would be useless in response.

A major external feature was the enormous, square bulk of the bridge structure, clad on four sides by the panels of the electronically scanned SPS32/33 radars, integrated with the Naval Tactical Data System (NTDS). Later refits saw these removed, along with the Talos system. The Terrier missiles were superseded by standard SM-2 Extended Range missiles. Harpoon missiles added anti-surface ship capability and Tomahawk cruise missiles were installed for shore bombardment missions.

Long Beach (CGN.9)

Built: Bethlehem Steel, Quincy
Commissioned: September 9, 1961
Displacement: 15,342 tonnes/15,100 tons (standard); 17,374 tonnes/17,100 tons (full load)
Length: 219.7m/721ft 3in (oa)
Beam: 22.3m/73ft 3in
Draught: 9.5m/31ft (extreme)
Armament (as designed): 2 x Talos launchers, 80 missiles (1x2); 4 x Terrier launchers, 168 missiles (2x2); 1 x ASROC AS launcher; 2 x 127mm/5in 38 guns (2x1)
Machinery: Geared steam turbines, 2 pressurized, water-cooled reactors, 2 shafts
Power: 59,656kW/80,000shp for 30.5 knots
Endurance: Dependent upon stores and ordnance, not fuel
Protection: Not announced; some aluminium armour added retrospectively
Complement: 990

ABOVE: **Built to test advanced technologies, the** *Long Beach* **has been remodelled several times. Here, her Terrier systems, forward, have been replaced by Standard SM-2. Aft, her obsolete Talos has been removed, the space being taken by two Vulcan-Phalanx CIWS and two armoured Harpoon SSM launchers.**

California and Virginia classes

ABOVE LEFT: The hull of the *Mississippi* (CGN.40)
shows its clear derivation from that of the
conventionally propelled Belknaps. The MK.26
launcher on the foredeck was designed for
Standard SM-1 missiles. In this picture she lacks
the Harpoon launchers forward of the bridge and
the Tomahawk box launchers aft. ABOVE: The older
California (CGN.36) presents a more squat
appearance. Her after 127mm/5in gun is carried
one level higher and she retains basic helicopter
facilities aft. The small box forward of the bridge
is a reload facility for the ASROC launchers not
carried in the Virginias.

To complete its pioneering nuclear-propelled squadron the US Navy produced (1962–67) *Bainbridge* (CGN.25) and *Truxtun* (CGN.35), essentially modified versions of the contemporary Leahy and Belknap classes of fleet guided-missile escort.

Experience with this pair led to the slightly enlarged, flush-decked pair of Californias (completed 1974–75) and the four-ship Virginia class (1976–80). Until 1975, all were categorized as "frigates" but their size and prestigious "state" names saw them relabelled "cruisers". Neither term agrees with traditional practice but indicates the difficulty of pigeonholing newly developing types of warship.

Superficially, the two classes are very similar but the Virginias, some 4m/13ft 1in the shorter, may be distinguished by the knuckle, which was incorporated to reduce wetness on the foredeck. Both have the two-block, funnel-less profile typical of nuclear-propelled ships, and have the various elements of their all-purpose armament disposed along the centreline.

Each type has a single 127mm/5in 54-calibre gun forward and aft, their arcs limited somewhat by the twin-arm missile launchers beyond. Both launch the standard SM-1 MR surface-to-air missile (SAM) but where those on the Virginias can also launch ASROC anti-submarine (ASW) missiles, the Californias have a separate, eight-cell ASROC launcher and reload facility.

Both types have Harpoon anti-ship missiles. On the Californias these are located aft; on the Virginias, forward. A helicopter spot, without facilities, is provided right aft, but it is encumbered if armoured box launchers for Tomahawk cruise missiles are carried.

The weapons inventory is completed by AS torpedo tubes and close-in weapon systems (CIWS), mounted on the superstructure with decoy launchers and designed to destroy any incoming anti-ship missile that cannot be deflected or seduced.

It will be noted that, where nuclear propulsion has proved viable for submarines and aircraft carriers, large escorts have reverted to conventional power units.

ABOVE: In this dramatic shot, the *Arkansas* (CGN.41) is undergoing a shock test. The ship is anchored a calculated distance from a large explosive charge for the purpose of establishing the shock resistance of on-board systems.

California and Virginia classes

	Built	Commissioned
CGN.36 *California*	Newport News Shipbuilding, Virginia	February 16, 1974
CGN.37 *South Carolina*	Newport News Shipbuilding, Virginia	January 25, 1975
CGN.38 *Virginia*	Newport News Shipbuilding, Virginia	September 11, 1976
CGN.39 *Texas*	Newport News Shipbuilding, Virginia	September 10, 1977
CGN.40 *Mississippi*	Newport News Shipbuilding, Virginia	August 5, 1978
CGN.41 *Arkansas*	Newport News Shipbuilding, Virginia	October 18, 1980

Virginia class (as built)

Displacement: 10,567 tonnes/10,400 tons (light); 11,481 tonnes/11,300 tons (full load)
Length: 177.8m/583ft 8in (oa)
Beam: 19.2m/63ft (oa)
Draught: 9.6m/31ft 6in (extreme)
Armament: 8 x Tomahawks SSM (2x4); 8 x Harpoon SSM (2x4); standard SM-2 MR and ASROC ASW (68 rounds total); 2 x 127mm/5in 54 guns; 2 x CIWS; 6 x 323mm/12.7in AS torpedo tubes (2x3)
Machinery: Geared steam turbines, 2 pressurized, water-cooled reactors, 2 shafts
Power: 52,200kW/70,000shp for 30-plus knots
Endurance: Not dependent upon fuel
Protection: Not announced
Complement: 620

FAR LEFT: **Despite her scruffy appearance, the** *Ooi* **seen here in the early 1920s, was a relatively new ship. Her 140mm/5.5in gun calibre was selected as having the heaviest projectile that could be manually worked by the average Japanese seaman. Her bow profile was new in Japanese warships.** ABOVE: **Slightly clearer, this picture of** *Ooi* **shows the short well at the forward end of the long, full-width, amidships deckhouse. In 1940, this deckhouse was razed and, suitably sponsoned, each side deck was fitted with five quadruple 610mm/24in torpedo tube mountings.**

Tenryu, Kuma and Nagara classes

Intended to act as leaders for new destroyer flotillas, the two Tenryus, completed in 1919, closely paralleled the first group of British C-class cruisers. Lightly constructed, but belted, they had a raised forecastle but low freeboard aft. Four 140mm/5.5in guns were mounted singly along the centreline together with two triple banks of torpedo tubes, one of which was located, German-style, at the break of the forecastle. The 140mm/5.5in guns could elevate to no more than 20 degrees (improved to 30 degrees in later ships) but their 38kg/84lb ammunition was the heaviest that could be hand-loaded by the average Japanese sailor.

These and later derivatives could all lay mines, using temporary rails along either side deck. The mines were unusual in being intended for laying in the path of an advancing enemy squadron. They were thus laid in floating pairs, connected by a 100m/328ft cable. Any ship snagging the cable would draw the mines into it before being able to lose sufficient way.

Plans existed in the 1930s to convert the Tenryus to AA cruisers but dockyards were, at the time, fully employed with alternative naval work of higher priority.

As Japan's first modern light cruisers, the Tenryus were immediately succeeded by the five Kumas, improved and enlarged. Longer by some 20.4m/67ft, they bore much the same relationship to the Tenryus as a British D-class did to an early C-class. To decrease wetness, the raised forecastle was complemented by a long amidships deckhouse. Before and abaft of this light construction were four pairs of torpedo tubes, two on either beam. One spare torpedo was provided for each. Seven single 140mm/5.5in guns were carried disposed to give a broadside of six.

ABOVE: *Tenryu* (seen here) and *Tatsuta* were the first and smallest of this light cruiser series and make an interesting contrast with the British C-type ships that inspired them. The three funnels were based on a narrow, centreline "fiddley", bounded fore and aft by triple 533mm/21in torpedo tube mountings.

ABOVE: *Tenryu*'s appearance in the late 1930s. Note the four guns, all on the centreline. She has just raised anchor and is gathering way as her forecastle party direct a hose jet down the hawse pipe to clean mud from the anchor. The foremast was made a tripod in 1930.

The Imperial Japanese Navy (IJN) regarded the torpedo as a battle-winning weapon and, during the 1930s, developed the formidable 610mm/24in Type 93. Oxygen-propelled, it carried a warhead 50 per cent heavier than the contemporary 533mm/21in American or British torpedoes. It also enjoyed up to four times the range, and a higher speed. Doctrine emphasized night attack, using torpedo spreads in preference to gunfire, which would betray an attacker's position.

With this in mind, the heavy cruiser squadrons were to be accompanied by one or more Kumas, remodelled as "torpedo cruisers". However, only two (*Kitakami* and *Ooi*) of a planned three were so modified, their amidships section sponsored to give the deck space necessary to mount an astonishing five quadruple 610mm/24in torpedo banks per side. With changing war priorities, and the loss of the *Ooi*, the damaged *Kitakami* was again heavily modified to carry eight Kaiten midget submarines on deck. Transported on rails, these were launched over a reconfigured stern.

Of equal dimensions, six Nagara-class ships followed on from the Kumas. At 5,781 tonnes/5,690 tons, such ships were considered capable of undertaking scouting operations in support of a battle squadron. Following earlier experiment with the *Kitakami* they were equipped with an aircraft. Again following contemporary British practice, they were given a high bridge structure, in which an aircraft was accommodated, taking off from a light platform extending forward. Although this facility was soon removed in favour of a catapult, located abaft the funnels; the high bridge block remained.

The Tenryus were designed for 33 knots, the enlarged later groups for 36. Being fast and of a handy size, all were used extensively as fast transports. By 1944 American submarines infested every part of the western Pacific while carrier-based air strikes overwhelmed any ship encountered. Of the 13 units of the first three groups, just one survived the war. Of the other 11, all but two were destroyed in 1944–45.

ABOVE: **The six Nagaras were improved Kumas and designed primarily as leaders to destroyer and fleet submarine squadrons.** *Nagara* **is seen here after 1933, when her catapult and floatplane were moved aft. The curious funnel caps,**

fitted in the 1930s were probably to prevent flaming when supporting destroyers at night.

LEFT: **Probably aboard the** *Kitakami*, **whose comprehensive torpedo armament was removed in 1943, and replaced by sided tracks for up to eight Kaiten I miniature submarines. These 8.5-tonne/8.4-ton craft, launched over the stern, had a single occupant and an explosive warhead.** BELOW: *Nagara* **during the 1920s. An original similarity with British light cruisers was the elevation of the bridge structure to provide housing for a scout plane, which lifted off from the short platform extending over the forward guns.**

ABOVE: **The** *Tenryu* **shows off her destroyer-like stern and starboard-side mine rails. No aircraft arrangements are visible, so this is probably a late 1930s picture. Few of these light cruisers survived the war, the** *Tenryu* **being sunk by submarine torpedo in December 1942.**

Tenryu, Kuma and Nagara classes

	Built	Commissioned
Tatsuta	Sasebo Navy Yard	March 31, 1919
Tenryu	Yokosuka Navy Yard	November 20, 1919
Kiso	Mitsubishi, Nagasaki	May 4, 1921
Kitakami	Sasebo Navy Yard	April 15, 1921
Kuma	Sasebo Navy Yard	August 31, 1920
Ooi	Kawasaki, Kobe	October 3, 1921
Tama	Mitsubishi, Nagasaki	January 29, 1921
Abukuma	Uraga Dock Company	May 26, 1925
Isuzu	Uraga Dock Company	August 15, 1923
Kinu	Kawasaki, Kobe	November 10, 1922
Nagara	Sasebo Navy Yard	April 21, 1922
Natori	Mitsubishi, Nagasaki	September 15, 1922
Yura	Sasebo Navy Yard	March 20, 1923

Nagara class (as designed)

Displacement: 5,781 tonnes/5,690 tons (standard); 7,315 tonnes/7,200 tons (full load)
Length: 152.3m/500ft (bp); 162.1m/532ft (oa)
Beam: 14.2m/46ft 6in
Draught: 4.9m/16ft (standard)
Armament: 7 x 140mm/5.5in (7x1) and 2 x 80mm/3.1in high-angle (HA) (2x1) guns; 8 x 610mm/24in torpedo tubes (4x2); 48 mines
Machinery: Geared steam turbines, 12 boilers, 4 shafts
Power: 67,113kW/90,000shp for 36 knots
Endurance: 1,300 tonnes/1,280 tons (oil) and 345 tonnes/340 tons (coal) for 11,112km/6,000nm at 14 knots
Protection: 63mm/2.48in (partial belt); 29mm/1.14in (partial armoured deck)
Complement: 450

ABOVE LEFT: *Sendai* shows her dated gun disposion with four singles forward (two flanking the bridge) and three aft. ABOVE: Another view of the nameship. The Sendais were influenced by the preceding British "D" class, not least in the heavy and lofty tripod foremast.

Sendai class

Of the final group of six planned Tenryu class derivatives only three were built, the 1922 Washington Treaty terms diverting interest to larger "treaty cruisers". Those actually constructed retained the dimensions and main characteristics of the preceding group. These included partial mixed-firing of boilers, unusual at this late date but probably indicative of the chronic Japanese oil shortage. A rearrangement of boiler spaces brought about an anachronistic reversion to four funnels of which the foremost was rather taller to reduce the smoke nuisance on the bridge. There were three boiler rooms with four units in each. Only the forward boiler room was fitted for mixed firing.

The Sendais were equipped from the outset with 610mm/24in torpedo tubes. Perhaps coincidentally, all were laid down in 1922, the same year as the British Nelson-class battleships, the only Royal Navy vessels ever to mount 610mm/24in torpedo tubes. The Japanese Type 8, 610mm/24in torpedo had been accepted into service in 1920 and should not be confused with the oxygen-fuelled Type 94 of World War II. Sixteen were carried, again permitting one reload per tube.

As with the Nagaras, the forward flying-off arrangement was considered unsatisfactory and probably never used. Following the visit of the Sempill mission in 1921, British influence on the embryonic Japanese naval air service was strong and the Mitsubishi 1MF (Type 10) fighter designated for use aboard the light cruisers was, in fact, designed by the Sopwith team.

All the light cruisers to date had been given a distinctive "boat bow", convexly curved, but *Jintsu* of the Sendai class adopted the double-curvature, "clipper" profile that would become closely associated with Japanese warship design.

All three of the class became war casualties, two of them in battle with American ships while leading their destroyers in the fierce nocturnal engagements that were a feature of the Solomons campaign.

Sendai class

	Built	Commissioned
Jintsu	Kawasaki, Kobe	July 31, 1925
Kamo		Cancelled
Kizu		Cancelled
Naka	Mitsubishi, Yokohama	November 30, 1925
Nayoro		Cancelled
Sendai	Mitsubishi, Nagasaki	April 29, 1924

Sendai class (as designed)

Displacement: 5,995 tonnes/5,900 tons (standard); 7,732 tonnes/7,610 tons (full load)
Length: 152.3m/500ft (bp); 162.1m/532ft (oa)
Beam: 14.2m/46ft 6in
Draught: 4.9m/16ft (standard)
Armament: 7 x 140mm/5.5in (7x1) and 2 x 80mm/3.1in HA (2x1) guns; 8 x 610mm/24in torpedo tubes (4x2); 48 mines
Machinery: Geared steam turbines, 12 boilers, 4 shafts
Power: 67,113kW/90,000shp for 35-plus knots
Endurance: 1,026 tonnes/1,010 tons (oil), and 579 tonnes/570 tons (coal) for 11,112km/6,000nm at 14 knots
Protection: 63mm/2.48in (partial belt); 29mm/1.14in (partial armoured deck)
Complement: 450

LEFT: Another inherited feature of British wartime practice was the aircraft hangar in the bridge structure and flying-off platform. *Naka*, like her sisters, had them removed during the 1930s.

Yubari

Although they carried seven guns, the later 5,588-tonne/5,500-ton light cruisers could use only six of them in broadside and three (theoretically) in chase. European trends were now favouring superimposed gun positions and it was posited that, if these were adopted, along with twin mountings, the same firepower could be developed by a smaller and less expensive vessel. If construction was kept light, a similar speed might also be possible. The result was the one-off experimental "light cruiser" *Yubari*, built at the same time as the Sendais.

Six 140mm/5.5in guns were arranged with singles in the "A" and "Y" positions, superfired by twins in the "B" and "X" positions. As all were located on the centreline, six were available on the broadside and three in chase, as before. The twins were enclosed in electrically

operated gunhouses, the singles only in shields, giving a superficial impression of a mixed armament.

A new Japanese "trademark" also made its appearance in the *Yubari*'s exaggeratedly trunked funnel. All oil-fired, she had eight boilers distributed between three spaces, all being exhausted through a single large casing. This saved on the weight of separate funnels while keeping smoke well clear of the main director position, situated atop a tripod over the bridge.

By positioning two twin 610mm/24in torpedo tubes on the centreline, four were available on either broadside, similar to that of earlier ships with eight. This logical modification in armament layout permitted the hull to be shorter by some 21.9m/72ft.

Despite a shorter waterline length it was still hoped to make 35.5 knots on

TOP: **Due to her being considerably overweight, the** *Yubari*'s **lower scuttles can be seen to be very close to the waterline.** ABOVE: *Yubari* **at Shanghai shows her very destroyer-like appearance. Note how her twin 140mm/5.5in gunhouses superfire single 140mm/5.5in guns in shields.**

a three-shaft machinery arrangement. Scantlings were very light (in fact, over-light) but the hull still emerged seriously overweight. Because of the resulting deeper immersion, she failed to make 35 knots. Her designed endurance was also reduced.

Yubari

Built: Sasebo Navy Yard
Commissioned: July 31, 1923
Displacement: 3,617 tonnes/3,560 tons (standard); 4,519 tonnes/4,448 tons (full load)
Length: 132.5m/435ft (bp); 139.4m/457ft 6in (oa)
Beam: 12m/39ft 6in
Draught: 3.9m/12ft 8in (standard)
Armament: 6 x 140mm/5.5in (2x2/2x1) and 1 x 80mm/3.1in HA guns; 4 x 610mm/24in torpedo tubes; 48 mines
Machinery: Geared steam turbines, 8 boilers, 3 shafts
Power: 43,176kW/57,900shp for 34.75 knots
Endurance: 931 tonnes/916 tons (oil) for 6,111km/3,300nm at 14 knots
Protection: 57mm/2.24in (belt over machinery spaces); 25–41mm/1–1.6in (partial armoured deck)
Complement: 330

ABOVE: **Another view of** *Yubari* **laying at Shanghai. Despite a further increase in topweight, the heavily trunked funnel needed to be raised by 2m/6ft 6in.**

Katori class

When, in December 1934, Japan abrogated the Washington Treaty and commenced rapid expansion of her fleet, she required modern vessels dedicated to the sea training of the growing number of midshipmen. The construction of four new 5,893-tonne/5,800-ton vessels was therefore authorized. Spread over the building programmes of 1937, 1939 and 1941, these ran foul of higher priority construction. The final hull consequently never reached launching stage before being dismantled.

Despite a record of duplicity in declaring the true size and function of its new vessels, those of the Katoris were exactly as stated by the IJN. Imposing for their size, they were usually referred to by the Allies as "cruisers", but were so only in the sense that they undertook training cruises. Never being intended as combatants, they were built in a commercial yard and largely to mercantile standards.

For training purposes, armament, fire control, machinery, aircraft and catapults, boats, etc., all conformed to standard IJN practice, and it was the resulting external appearance that accounted for the Allies crediting them with cruiser-like qualities. The ships were, however, designed for a speed of only 18 knots, their lines being full and increasing internal space. Their high freeboard reflected accommodation spacious by contemporary IJN standards and intended to impress during foreign port visits.

Due to these unusually generous appointments, the wartime role of the Katoris was to act as flagships to second-line forces such as convoy escort and anti-submarine (ASW) groups.

From time to time, however, training of aspirant officers was still undertaken.

War saw their armament greatly supplemented by automatic weapons and by four high-angle (HA) 127mm/5in guns in twin mountings sided in the waist.

Only the *Kashima* survived hostilities. Fitted with extra topside accommodation, she was employed post-war in the repatriation of prisoners of war and garrisons of distant locations. This duty done, she was scrapped in 1947.

Katori class

	Built	Commissioned
Kashii	Mitsubishi, Yokohama	July 15, 1941
Kashima	Mitsubishi, Yokohama	July 31, 1940
Kashiwara		Cancelled
Katori	Mitsubishi, Yokohama	April 20, 1940

Katori class

Displacement: 5,985 tonnes/5,890 tons (standard); 6,858 tonnes/6,750 tons (full load)
Length: 123.5m/405ft 4in (bp); 133.5m/438ft 2in (oa)
Beam: 16.6m/54ft 6in (maximum)
Draught: 5.5m/18ft (standard)
Armament: 4 x 140mm/5.5in (2x2) and 6 x 127mm/5in (3x2) guns; 4 x 533mm/21in torpedo tubes (2x2)
Machinery: 2 sets geared steam turbines and 2 cruising diesels, 3 boilers, 2 shafts
Power: 5,965kW/8,000shp combined for 18 knots
Endurance: 611 tonnes/600 tons (oil) for 18,335km/9,900nm at 12 knots
Protection: None
Complement: 315 plus 275 trainees

ABOVE: **The training status of *Katori* is emphasized by the large freeboard hull resulting from extra accommodation. This feature defined her secondary role as station flagship.**

Oyodo and Agano class

By the 1930s the overweight 5,588-tonne/5,500-ton cruisers were proving deficient, their speed and endurance inferior to those of the new destroyers that they were expected to lead. Their broadside weight was also considered inadequate as was the reconnaissance potential of their single floatplane. As they could be replaced after 15 years of service by treaty definition, both "destroyer-and submarine-squadron flagships" were authorized during 1939.

The four destroyer leaders of the Agano class thus carried an increased main battery of six 150mm/5.9in guns in three twin turrets, two forward and one aft. Extensive trunking permitted a single, large funnel casing, with a prominent catapult abaft it. Two seaplanes (*Aichi* E13A1 "Jake") were accommodated, one on the catapult, the other on a platform over the eight torpedo tubes. Aft of the catapult, the mainmast provided a substantial post for a large aircraft handling crane.

The functions of the Japanese fleet submarine force emphasized reconnaissance as well as attack, necessitating a cruiser-flagship in addition to a depot ship, or tender. Two such flagships were authorized but only one, the *Oyodo*, was ever built.

To reconnoitre for her submarines, the *Oyodo* was designed to carry no less than six fast seaplanes of a new design. These demanded a large box hangar aft of amidships, and an after end devoted to a centreline catapult and aircraft handling facilities. The main battery was, therefore, concentrated forward in two triple 155mm/6.1in turrets. These were available following the up-rating of the Mogami-class cruisers. The aircraft never entered production and the ship was never employed as intended.

Of the Agano class and the *Oyodo*, only one ship (*Sakawa*) survived hostilities. Most capsized before sinking, possibly due to the centreline bulkheads that divided the machinery spaces.

ABOVE LEFT: **The only one of four Aganos to survive, the *Sakawa* is seen at Sasebo alongside a US naval oiler. Note the curious sheerline adopted by Japanese designers to reduce topweight. The right-hand, squarer funnel belongs to the oiler.**

ABOVE: **There was a considerable gap between the *Sakawa*'s bridge and her forward turrets, providing space for some of her 60-plus 25mm/1in AA weapons. The pole mast belongs to a ship beyond. The vertical fitting on the after side of the tripod mast, and the horns abreast the director tower were components of Japanese Mk 2 Mod 2 radar.**

Oyodo and Agano class

	Built	Commissioned
Agano	Sasebo Navy Yard	October 31, 1942
Noshiro	Yokosuka Navy Yard	June 30, 194
Sakawa	Sasebo Navy Yard	November 30, 1944
Yahagi	Sasebo Navy Yard	December 29, 1943
Oyodo	Kure Navy Yard	February 28, 1943
Niyodo		Cancelled

Agano class (as built)

Displacement: 8,027 tonnes/7,900 tons (standard); 8,667 tonnes/8,530 tons (full load)
Length: 162m/531ft 9in (bp); 174.5m/572ft 10in (oa)
Beam: 15.2m/49ft 11in
Draught: 5.7m/18ft 9in (standard)
Armament: 6 x 150mm/5.9in (3x2) and 4 x 80mm/3.1in HA (2x2) guns; 8 x 610mm/24in torpedo tubes (2x4)
Machinery: Geared steam turbines, 6 boilers, 4 shafts
Power: 74,570kW/100,000shp for 35 knots
Endurance: 1,443 tonnes/1,420 tons (oil) for 11,112km/6,000nm at 18 knots
Protection: 55–60mm/2.2–2.4in (partial side belt); 20mm/0.79in (partial armoured deck)
Complement: 800

ABOVE: **The *Oyodo* as originally completed as flagship for submarines. Her catapult is unusually long and the cranes that serve it are folded forward, against the after superstructure. Never employed as intended, the ship was later refitted with standard aircraft facilities.**

Furutaka and Aoba classes

These two very similar pairs were conceived as large scout cruisers, out-classing both the American Omaha and British Hawkins classes. Their design pre-dated the 1922 Washington Treaty, so that they were smaller and less heavily armed than so-called "treaty cruisers".

A notable new feature was the uniquely Japanese undulating sheerline. Variously interpreted as logical, a weight-saving measure or, simply, idiosyncratic, hull depth at key points was decided by adequate freeboard, either for seakeeping or for reserve stability, or for required strength. Different sections of the hull were thus governed by varying criteria, resulting in differing depths. The upper deck was connected then by a continuous sheerline that, from some angles, could appear distinctly odd. To save weight, armour was worked-in without backing plate. This design philosophy contrasts with that of the broadly contemporary British County class, who's great depth of hull conferred necessary stiffness, allowing scantlings to be significantly reduced.

As with American cruiser design, it was found that protection against 152mm/6in, rather than 203mm/8in gunfire, was only

ABOVE: *Kako* (here) and *Furutaka* were Japan's first pair of "treaty cruisers". Unusually, they displaced significantly less than the 10,160-tonne/10,000-ton limit while their 200mm/7.87in guns were of smaller calibre than the 203mm/ 8in limit. The single main-calibre turrets, shown here, were carried only until twins became available.

possible over a specific immunity band. This was compromised somewhat when, despite apparently careful control, the ships came out considerably overweight, submerging much of their belt protection. Machinery spaces were flanked by longitudinal bulkheads. The void spaces thus created, between bulkhead and shell plating were, together with a small integral bulge, intended to act as torpedo protection. In practice, it lacked sufficient depth to be effective. Again, machinery spaces were subdivided by a dubiously conceived centreline bulkhead.

The Furutakas' main battery comprised a newly developed 200mm/7.87in gun designed to out-perform the Hawkins' 191mm/7.5in guns. As completed, the ships accommodated six weapons in single centreline gunhouses, in two groups of

ABOVE:: **Three twin 200mm/7.87in turrets later took the place of six singles. The *Furutaka* here shows the resulting gap left forward of the bridge structure. Note the "beaked" bow profile and the massive trunking to the forward funnel.**
RIGHT: **Heavily retouched, this view of *Furutaka* appears to show a very obvious armoured belt, the side being slightly knuckled. Note the short funnels, later raised. The single 200mm/7.87in mountings were gunhouses rather than turrets.**

three, one forward and one aft. The centre mounting superfired its neighbours. Although the arrangement must have influenced hull length, it was only temporary, pending the entry into service of a twin turret mounting. The Aoba pair was fitted with these from the outset, the Furutakas not being retro-fitted until their late 1930s modernization. Turrets gave a higher rate of fire per gun but imposed a further 102-tonne/100-ton or more load on the ship, whose structure needed strengthening.

Following the limitations imposed on capital ships by the Washington Treaty, the IJN increased emphasis on torpedo attack by cruisers, especially at night. All four ships were consequently fitted with twelve 610mm/24in torpedo tubes. These were fixed, firing in pairs on the beam from dedicated internal compartments, two of which were abaft the funnels and one forward of the bridge. Economizing on upper deck space, the arrangement also reduced the distance the torpedoes had to drop in firing. Rearrangement during the modernization nonetheless saw the arrangement superseded by two quadruple banks, sided on the upper deck. One reload was carried for each tube.

Fitted with prominent aircraft catapults in the late 1920s, the two pairs could be separately identified through their differing arrangements. In the Furutakas the catapult was located ahead of the mainmast, resulting in a large gap between mast and after funnel. The Aobas had their catapult sited immediately ahead of the after turret, resulting in the mainmast being located farther forward.

On completion, the Furutakas received four 80mm/3.1in high-angle (HA) guns, but these were later replaced by more effective 120mm/4.7in weapons to match those in the Aobas.

All four became war losses, all but the *Aoba* being destroyed during a three-month period of vicious nocturnal battles to decide sea superiority around the Solomon Islands, late in 1942. Following action damage to the *Aoba* in 1943, there were unfulfilled plans to convert her to carry six reconnaissance float planes, located aft.

ABOVE: *Aoba* (here) and *Kinugasa* were near repeats of the Furutakas, but carried twin turrets from the outset. They differed in appearance in carrying their catapult abaft the mainmast. Note the diminishing freeboard at the after end.

LEFT: A view of the nicely uncluttered foredeck of *Aoba*. The type was well designed, *Aoba* surviving hits by no less than twenty-four 152mm/6in and 203mm/8in projectiles at the nocturnal Battle of Cape Esperance In October 1942. She was torpedoed near Manila in 1944.

LEFT: Most surviving Japanese ships, crippled by lack of oil fuel, were sunk at their anchors by US naval aircraft during July 1945. *Aoba* settled in shallow water south of Kure. Her light automatic weapons have already been removed while foliage appears to have been used in a futile attempt at camouflage.

Furutaka and Aoba classes

	Built	Commissioned
Furutaka	Mitsubishi, Nagasaki	March 31, 1926
Kako	Kawasaki, Kobe	July 20, 1926
Aoba	Mitsubishi, Nagasaki	September 20, 1927
Kinugasa	Kawasaki, Kobe	September 30, 1927

ABOVE: An early picture of *Kako* prior to her receiving twin turrets. All four of these early ships, led by the later *Chokai*, inflicted a sharp defeat on the Allies off Savo Island in August 1942. In the course of their withdrawal, *Kako* was torpedoed and sunk off Simbari.

Furutaka (as built)

Displacement: 8,076 tonnes/7,950 tons (standard); 10,414 tonnes/10,250 tons (full load)
Length: 176.7m/580ft (bp); 185.1m/607ft 6in (oa)
Beam: 16.5m/54ft 2in
Draught: 5.6m/18ft 3in
Armament: 6 x 200mm/7.87in (6x1) and 4 x 80mm/3.1in HA (4x1) guns; 12 x 610mm/24in torpedo tubes (12x1)
Machinery: Geared steam turbines, 12 boilers, 4 shafts
Power: 76,061kW/102,000shp for 34 knots
Endurance: 1,118 tonnes/1,100 tons (oil) for 11,112km/6,000nm at 14 knots
Protection: 76mm/3in (belt); 35–48mm/1.38–1.89in (partial armoured deck); 19–25mm/0.75–1in (gunhouses)
Complement: 625

Myoko and Takao classes

Having gained considerable experience with the design of the radical *Yubari* and the 7,620-tonne/7,500-ton scout cruisers, the same constructor, Hiraga, was entrusted with the first four 10,160-tonne/10,000-ton "treaty cruisers", authorized in 1923, following the Washington Conference.

As intelligence indicated (incorrectly) that treaty-limited displacement would restrict foreign equivalents to eight guns, a prime Japanese requirement was to ensure superiority with ten. However, much the same thinking led the Americans to fit ten guns in the equivalent Pensacolas and, where they combined twins and triples in a four-turret main battery, the Japanese opted for five, centreline twins. This, together with the requirement for superior speed, resulted in longer and far finer-lined hulls.

The first Myoko group was strongly influenced by the preceding classes but overall gave a more massive impression. As before, three turrets were located forward, the centre mounting superfiring the others. To avoid the necessity for

ABOVE: Unusually sharp pictures are available of *Ashigara*, which attended the British Coronation Review in 1937, following her modernization. In the course of this, she gained the prominent flat sponsons abreast the after funnel, supporting an after 127mm/5in twin mounting and a catapult pedestal.

three funnels the forward boiler space, sited directly below the bridge structure, exhausted via elaborate trunking through a heavily raked casing which, it shared with the central boilers.

Between the mainmast and after turrets was a considerable gap, directly above the machinery spaces. On the upper deck it was occupied by an off-centre rotating catapult, whose two associated aircraft were housed in a hangar immediately forward of it.

Beneath the catapult and above the machinery spaces were two under-deck compartments accommodating twelve 610mm/24in torpedo tubes. Grouped in threes, and fixed, all fired on the beam. Hiraga had opposed the arrangement on the grounds that an accidental warhead explosion could

LEFT: Taken at the British Coronation Review in 1937, this picture shows a seaplane on either catapult. The standard outfit was three Mitsubishi F1M2 Type 0 reconnaissance floatplanes but, here, the *Ashigara* appears to be equipped with the earlier Nakajima E8N2 Type 95, known to the Allies as "Dave". ABOVE: The extraordinary mass and complexity of the *Chokai's* bridge structure contrasts with the lightness of its masting. Trunking for the enormous forefunnel runs beneath the bridge structure. Note the distinctively shaped screens covering the torpedo tube mountings. Maintenance on ground tackle is being carried out forward.

LEFT: **Continuing the British connection, *Ashigara* is here seen at Malta. The reverse sheer from her after turrets is marked, the line of lower scuttles descending to the horizontal boot topping. With so many Japanese cruisers being sunk by the Americans, it is interesting that both *Ashigara* and *Haguro* were destroyed by British forces.**

catastrophically damage the ship. During the 1934–35 modernization of the class, he successfully had them removed in favour of sided quadruple banks fitted on the upper deck.

A spardeck was also fitted at this time with a catapult sponsored on both sides, and providing space for new 127mm/5in high-angle (HA) guns and directors.

Although relatively well protected, the Myokos' hull was lightly constructed, requiring later strengthening to correct weather-induced over-stressing.

Originally known as the "Improved Myoko class", the four Takaos followed on in response to numbers believed to have been authorized by the American and British navies. Virtually identical in size, they could be differentiated by much closer-spaced funnels and an even more monolithic bridge structure with a characteristically sloping forward side. Much of the internal volume of this structure was, in fact, consumed by the exhaust trunking from the forward boiler room.

From the outset, this group had two, sided catapults to serve three aircraft. Torpedo tubes were sited above the upper deck but enclosed by the spar deck above. Paired on rotating mounts, they fired through long, distinctively shaped but usually shuttered apertures in the side plating.

High power, a long hull and fine lines combined to give the classes a good turn of speed, although their designed endurance was only moderate. Protection comprised armour adequate to defeat 152mm/6in and some 203mm/8in gunfire, and longitudinal bulkheads inside a partially internal bulge ("blister") to minimize the effect of a torpedo hit.

Like the Americans, the Japanese were disappointed with their rate of fire, again governed by a fixed loading angle of 5 degrees. The main armament could be elevated to 70 degrees, but the rate of elevation or depression was only 12 degrees per second. It followed that the longer the range and the higher the elevation, the slower the rate of fire.

A further disappointment lay in the ships being overweight, their deeper-than-expected immersion detrimentally affecting both speed and endurance. As the problem of excess weight had been common to all the pre-treaty classes it suggests chronic under-estimation of weight and/or lack of building discipline rather than a deliberate flouting of agreed limits.

LEFT: **On November 5, 1944, *Nachi* was overwhelmed by US carrier aircraft in Manila Bay. Despite her rapid manoeuvring she finally sank after being struck by a claimed nine torpedoes and 20 bombs.**

Myoko and Takao classes

	Built	Commissioned
Ashigara	Kawasaki, Kobe	August 20, 1929
Haguro	Mitsubishi, Nagasaki	April 25, 1929
Myoko	Yokosuka Navy Yard	July 31, 1929
Nachi	Kure Navy Yard	April 30, 1929
Atago	Kure Navy Yard	March 30, 1932
Chokai	Mitsubishi, Nagasaki	June 30, 1932
Maya	Kawasaki, Kobe	June 30, 1932
Takao	Yokosuka Navy Yard	May 31, 1932

Myoko class (as built)

Displacement: 11,156 tonnes/10,980 tons (standard); 14,428 tonnes/14,200 tons (full load)
Length: 191.9m/630ft (bp); 203.7m/668ft 6in (oa)
Beam: 19m/62ft 4in
Draught: 5.9m/19ft 3in (standard)
Armament: 10 x 200mm/7.87in (5x2) and 6 x 120mm/4.7in HA (6x1) guns; 12 x 610mm/24in fixed torpedo tubes (4x3)
Machinery: Geared steam turbines, 12 boilers, 4 shafts
Power: 96,941kW/130,000shp for 33.5 knots
Endurance: 2,245 tonnes/2,210 tons (oil) for 13,890km/7,500nm at 14 knots
Protection: 102mm/4in (belt); 32–35mm/1.26–1.38in (armoured deck); 76mm/3in (turrets)
Complement: 765

Mogami class

The London Naval Treaty of 1930 took the heat out of the "treaty cruiser" race by capping the number of heavy cruisers (i.e. with guns of calibre exceeding 155mm/6.1in) that could be built by each signatory. Japan's allocation of 12 had already been committed but, as light cruisers could be built up to a global total of 102,062 tonnes/100,450 tons, four were ordered, two in 1931 and two in 1933. By the existing standards, they were large, their unofficial working figure of 8,636 tonnes/8,500 tons being nearer 9,652 tonnes/9,500 tons. The Naval General Staff required no less than five triple 155mm/6.1in turrets (which triggered an American response with the Brooklyns) and twelve 610mm/24in torpedo tubes. As an ambitious 37 knots was also stipulated, the resulting hull was as large as that of the preceding *Takao*. From the outset it was planned to exchange the gun mountings for twin 200mm/7.87in when required.

Hardly had the first pair launched in 1934 than a capsizing incident elsewhere brought about a general enquiry into the

ABOVE: **The four Mogamis could be recognized by their single funnel and forward turret layout. This picture shows the nameship, as built with five triple 155mm/ 6.1in guns, which were later changed for five twin 200mm/7.87in turrets.**

standards of stability acceptable to the IJN. Revised standards found the Mogamis deficient, causing them to be completed with a smaller bridge structure, no aircraft hangar and reduced deck heights. Welding, still developing as a technique, was used widely to save weight, but was responsible for many local structural failures at points of stress concentration.

The later pair, still building, had these modifications worked in, but at the expense of considerably increased displacement, due mainly to a further bulge being added outside the existing one, increasing the beam. While this measure satisfactorily raised the metacentre, it increased displacement to about 14,225 tonnes/14,000 tons. A new water-ballasting system was also added to preserve stability range in the "light" condition.

LEFT: **Still lacking some equipment, including directors and catapults, the *Mogami* is seen undergoing full-power contractor's sea trials in March 1935. Although she made a shade under 36 knots, her hull, which incorporated considerable welding, was distorted in places. Her displacement at the time was a treaty-breaking 13,170 tonnes/ 12,962 tons.**

ABOVE: **All four Mogamis were involved in the abortive attack on Midway in June 1942. Having collided with the *Mogami*, the damaged *Mikuma* (seen here) was attacked by aircraft from three US carriers. Wrecked by bombs, she was the first Japanese cruiser to be lost.** RIGHT: **More dramatic than accurate, this impression shows *Mikuma* under attack by SBD Dauntless aircraft, which also further injured the collision-damaged *Mogami*. The mainmast, seen toppling following an explosion of torpedo warheads, is noticeably absent in the photograph above.**

A single heavily trunked funnel casing served ten boilers located in four spaces in the first pair. The second pair had just eight boilers, each of higher capacity. Despite a designed output of 113,346kW/152,000shp, however, excess immersion and a fuller hull resulting from further bulging caused the operational speed and endurance to be reduced.

A light spar or shelter deck again provided space for the high-angle (HA) guns and aircraft arrangements. For the latter, two sponsoned catapults flanked an area laid out with rails for the movement of trolley-mounted seaplanes. Three aircraft were stored in the open, having lost their hangar in the quest to save topside weight. Their handling crane was stepped on a substantial tripod mainmast, located at the forward end of the handling area.

From the beginning of 1937 Japan considered herself to be no longer bound by treaties and, as part of a general fleet up-trading, the Mogamis exchanged their 155mm/6.1in triple turrets for 200mm/7.87in twins. The barrels of "B"-turret guns,

now being longer, would not tuck in behind "A" turret and needed to be elevated in order to be aligned fore-and-aft.

Badly damaged by bombing at Midway in June 1942, when her sister *Mikuma* was lost, the *Mogami* spent nearly 11 months under repair, in the course of which her after turrets were removed and a light aircraft deck added. Supported on stanchions this extended the existing deck almost to the stern. Rails and 11 seaplanes on trolleys were added, the purpose of which was to extend the reconnaissance horizon of the cruiser division.

Although the very maximum had been attempted on their displacement, the Mogamis could be counted as successful, giving very good service during the Pacific war. Other than the *Mogami*, all were lost in the Philippines following the Leyte Gulf landings of October 1944. All absorbed heavy damage before sinking; that to the *Suzuya* being caused by the progressive detonation of her own torpedo warheads, as feared by constructor Hiraga so long before.

ABOVE: **A further impression of the *Kumano* in her original, light cruiser configuration. An interesting point is that the later 200mm/7.87in guns were 50-calibre weapons, whose barrels were longer than those of the 155mm/6.1in guns that they replaced. The barrels of No.2 turret guns needed to be elevated to clear No.1 turret roof.**

Mogami class

	Built	Commissioned
Mikuma	Mitsubishi, Nagasaki	August 29, 1935
Mogami	Kure Navy Yard	July 28, 1935
Kumano	Kawasaki, Kobe	October 31, 1937
Suzuya	Yokosuka, Navy Yard	October 31, 1937

Mogami (as designed)

Displacement: 11,380 tonnes/11,200 tons (standard); 14,204 tonnes/13,980 tons (full load)
Length: 189m/620ft 5in (bp); 200.5m/658ft 6in (oa)
Beam: 20.6m/67ft 7in
Draught: 5.9m/19ft 4in (standard)
Armament: 15 x 155mm/6.1in (5x3) and 8 x 127mm/5in HA (4x2) guns; 12 x 610mm/24in torpedo tubes (4x3)
Machinery: Geared steam turbines, 10 boilers, 4 shafts
Power: 113,346kW/152,000shp for 36 knots
Endurance: 2,388 tonnes/2,350 tons (oil) for 14,168km/7,650nm at 14 knots
Protection: 25–140mm/1–5.5in (belt); 35–60mm/1.38–2.4in (armoured deck); 75–100mm/2.95–3.9in (barbettes)
Complement: 950

LEFT: **By July 1945, surviving Japanese heavy units were virtually tied to their bases, where they were systematically destroyed by rampant US carrier-based air power.** *Tone*'s **four twin 203mm/8in turrets, all forward, are clearly identifiable as she is bombed to oblivion in Kure.** ABOVE: **Struck by three heavy bombs and shocked by seven near misses,** *Tone* **began to settle. While still under attack, a tug valiantly pushed the cruiser into shallow water, where she was dismantled post-war. The mining effect of near-misses can be even more damaging than direct hits.**

Tone and Ibuki classes

As originally defined, the specification for the two Tone-class cruisers closely followed that of the Mogamis. They were laid down in 1934–35 but, before they reached launching stage, their role had been changed to that of "aircraft cruiser". Six, even eight, aircraft were to be accommodated to facilitate the ships acting as the reconnaissance element of a cruiser squadron. Their layout was changed drastically, the whole after end being devoted to the storage and operation of the aircraft. Four triple 155mm/6.1in turrets would, uniquely, be located forward, thus separating the ships' main functions.

These were major changes, and the ships were still unlaunched when, at the beginning of 1937, Japan renounced treaty obligations. This resulted in the exchange of the triple 155mm/6.1in guns for twin 203mm/8in weapons. Turret weights were almost identical but the concentration of weight forward caused design problems with trim. The first, third and fourth turrets were located at the same level, only the second being superimposed.

Twelve 610mm/24in torpedo tubes were arranged in four triples. Located on the upper deck, they flanked the catapult pedestals.

The two Tones were completed in 1938–39, but a further pair was deferred in favour of more urgent construction. Eventually laid down in the spring of 1942, they were now intended to be repeat Suzuyas, with the mainmast relocated at the after end of the aircraft deck. This was the time of Midway, however, when the loss of three fleet carriers completely changed construction priorities. Although the first-of-class, *Ibuki*, was launched in May 1943, construction was halted, only to be resumed in the December with the decision to convert the hull into that of a light carrier. This was still only 80 per cent complete when the war ended. The second hull never reached launching stage and both were scrapped.

Tone and Ibuki classes

	Built	Commisioned
Chikuma	Mitsubishi, Nagasaki	May 20, 1939
Tone	Mitsubishi, Nagasaki	November 20, 1938
Ibuki	Kure Navy Yard	
Kurama	Mitsubishi, Nagasaki	

Tone class (as built)

Displacement: 11,430 tonnes/11,250 tons (standard); 15,443 tonnes/15,200 tons (full load)
Length: 190.3m/624ft 8in (bp); 201.6m/661ft 9in (oa)
Beam: 19.4m/63ft 8in
Draught: 6.5m/21ft 6in (standard)
Armament: 8 x 203mm/8in (4x2) and 8 x 127mm/5in HA (4x2) guns; 12 x 610mm/24in torpedo tubes (4x3)
Machinery: Geared steam turbines, 8 boilers, 4 shafts
Power: 113,346kW/152,000shp for 35 knots
Endurance: 2,733 tonnes/2,690 tons (oil) for 14,816km/8,000nm at 18 knots
Protection: 55–145mm/2.17–5.71in (belt); 31–65mm/1.22–2.56in (protective deck); 70–145mm/2.76–5.71in (barbettes)
Complement: 875

LEFT: **Although unclear, this picture of** *Chikuma* **shows her four forward turrets while giving an idea of the spacious after deck, devoted to aircraft use. The centreline ramp access can be made out. She was sunk by a single air-dropped torpedo during the frantic battle off Samar in October 1944.**

San Giorgio class

Of classic Italian design, the two San Giorgios were laid down in 1905–07. They were thus roughly contemporary with the last British armoured cruisers, the Minotaurs, but were sufficiently later to allow the second unit, *San Marco*, to be equipped with steam turbines.

The layout of the armament was typical of the time, with a main-calibre turret at either end and two secondary calibre turrets on either side in the waist. The long forecastle deck was narrow in order that the wing turrets could fire while in pursuit. Other than turrets, tophamper was minimal. The bridge structure was of insignificant size, the design depending upon two widely spaced pairs of lofty funnels for its "presence". The funnel spacing was a result of the boiler rooms being widely separated about the engine rooms. As built, there was only one mast, with a heavy boat derrick, stepped well aft of amidships but during their World War I service, a light foremast was added.

Both ships were dual-fired, mainly with coal, but with oil-spray for more

rapid acceleration. By the early 1930s the pair was obsolescent. A new role was then found for the turbine-driven *San Marco* as a remotely-controlled target ship. During 1931–35 her original boilers were replaced by four oil-fired units developing 9,694kW/13,000shp for 18 knots. With all armament removed, her standard displacement was reduced to about 8,900 tonnes/8,750 tons.

In 1937–38 the *San Giorgio* was modernized for coastal defence. Reboilered with eight units, developing 13,422kW/18,000shp, she had an endurance of about 4,444km/ 2,400nm at 17 knots, sufficient for service in the Mediterranean and Red Sea. Now with just two funnels, she retained her heavy guns, these being supplemented by five twin 100mm/3.9in HA guns and six 37mm/1.46in cannon. She was sunk in the defence of Tobruk in January 1941, moored as a fixed AA and land bombardment platform.

ABOVE LEFT: **This picture of *San Giorgio* probably dates from World War I as she has been given a foremast and searchlight platforms. Her funnels have been shortened and a small navigating bridge added. Note the symmetry of the armament disposition, with four twin 190mm/7.5in turrets sided in the waist.** ABOVE: **From May 1940, the modernized *San Giorgio* acted as a floating defence for Tobruk. In January 1941, during the siege of the port by the British 8th Army, the vessel was destroyed by artillery fire.**

San Giorgio class

	Built	Commissioned
San Giorgio	Cantiere di Castellammare di Stabia	July 1, 1910
San Marco	Cantiere di Castellammare di Stabia	February 7, 1911

San Giorgio class (as built)

Displacement: 10,160 tonnes/10,000 tons (standard); 11,278 tonnes/11,100 tons (full load)
Length: 131m/430ft (bp); 140.9m/462ft 6in (oa)
Beam: 21m/68ft 11in
Draught: 7.3m/24ft
Armament: 4 x 254mm/10in (2x2), 8 x 190mm/7.5in (4x2) and 18 x 76mm/3in (18x1) guns; 3 x 450mm/17.7in torpedo tubes
Machinery: *San Giorgio* – 2 sets triple-expansion engines, 14 boilers, 2 shafts; *San Marco* – Direct-drive steam turbines, 14 boilers, 2 shafts
Power: *San Giorgio* – 13,572kW/18,200shp for 23 knots; *San Marco* – 17,150kW/23,000shp for 23.5 knots
Endurance: 1,498 tonnes/1,475 tons (coal) 50 tonnes/49 tons (oil) for 5,741km/3,100nm at 12 knots
Protection: 200mm/7.87in (belt); 45mm/1.77in (protective deck); 180mm/7.1in (turrets)
Complement: 700

ABOVE: ***San Marco* is seen entering Brindisi in December 1916, passing close to the nearly submerged wreck of the battleship *Benedetto Brin*, which had blown up at her moorings in September 1915 and upon which salvage work is still being conducted.**

Bolzano and Trento class

First of the Italian "treaty cruisers", the *Trento* and *Trieste* are considered to be sisters, with the third unit, *Bolzano*, a sub-class. The importance of the new "heavy" cruiser to the Italian Navy was underlined by their being named after cities in territories ceded to Italy following World War I.

In treaty cruiser design, the American and Japanese emphasized firepower with a ten-gun main battery. The remaining Washington signatories opted for only eight guns but with improved protection and/or speed. Ever rivals of the neighbouring French, the Italians prioritized speed by which they could accept or decline action at will or, once engaged, dictate the range. With respect to the latter the Italians, talented gun designers, developed a 203mm/8in Ansaldo-Schneider weapon capable of ranging to 28km/17.5 miles at a maximum elevation of 48 degrees. This was improved to better than 31.5km/19.6 miles in the *Bolzano* and the *Zaras*. As with capital-ship armaments, these considerably out-ranged British equivalents during 1940–43, causing considerable tactical problems.

The Trentos' hulls were flush-decked, with no forecastle. The light armour belt extended from the forward to the after magazine, its scope evidenced in photographs by the lack of

ABOVE: The near-overhead light casts the *Trento*'s hull into sharp relief. The first Italian "treaty cruisers", the pair set the pattern for the remaining inter-war heavy cruisers, with symmetrical armament layout, a heavy tripod mainmast about the after funnel and foredeck aircraft catapult.

scuttles. A light protective deck extended over the same length, with local thickening in way of barbettes.

Machinery was arranged on the unit system, with boiler spaces preceding engine rooms. Considerably the larger, the forward funnel exhausted eight boilers against the after funnel's four. Although heavily trunked, both retained symmetry, lacking the exotic architecture of their Japanese counterparts.

The bridge structure was relatively low, but an impression of massiveness was given by a substantial, wide-legged pentapod foremast supporting main and secondary gunnery directors. Ahead of the after funnel was a powerful tripod bearing further secondary directors, a searchlight platform and a boat derrick.

During World War II three floatplanes, usually Ro.43 spotter/reconnaissance aircraft, were carried. Their catapult, unusually, stretched the length of the foredeck. Eight torpedo

LEFT: *Trento*, seen in Shanghai early in 1932. Before World War II it was customary for each nation with a trading concession to station a warship here to safeguard its interests. Her flush-decked hull has little sheer, the freeboard decreasing uniformly forward to aft with no discontinuity.

tubes were paired in two athwartships compartments at maindeck level. All were fixed, firing on the beam. To operate them, a "spoon" was extended outboard to support the tube until it was clear of the ship.

The pair's lack of protection attracted adverse criticism and they were followed by the slower, but more robust, Zara class. The Bolzano was built in parallel with these, a third but considerably modified Trento.

Laid down in 1930, the Bolzano's sea-keeping was improved by the addition of a raised forecastle. The aircraft catapult was moved to a more conventional, less exposed location amidships, requiring the after funnel to be moved further aft. The bridge block was more monolithic and its designers, ever mindful of good aesthetics, blended it into the forward funnel. The same weight of armour was worked in but was rearranged for better effect in conjunction with more thorough subdivision. A handsome ship, she was the first of the big Italians to breach the Washington rules.

Torpedoed by the British submarine Unbroken in August 1942, the Bolzano was probably saved by her improved subdivision. Although put aground, her bridge and forward boiler space were gutted by fire. Salvaged, it was proposed that she be converted to a fast transport for the hazardous North Africa supply run. All main armament would be landed and magazine spaces and forward boiler room cleared for cargo. Except for sided funnels exhausting No. 2 boiler room, all the upper deck forward of the mainmast would be cleared for fighter aircraft, to be launched by a pair of catapults. The project progressed very slowly and, together with both Trentos, the Bolzano became a war loss.

ABOVE: **Completed four years after the two Trentos, their quasi-sister** Bolzano **differed significantly in being given a forecastle deck and having a trainable catapult located amidships in place of the fixed forecastle track of the earlier ships.** BELOW: **Both of** Bolzano's **funnels were capped from the outset, the forefunnel being incorporated into an enlarged bridge structure. The main director was supported by a short tetrapod. So modelled, the** Bolzano's **profile could easily be confused with that of other Italian cruiser classes.**

ABOVE: **The** Bolzano **stemmed in drydock on an unknown occasion, but prior to 1942 as the ship is not camouflage painted. The platform was not part of the hull. Detail of the after hull is, unfortunately, in deep shadow but the double curvature of the extreme stern section is unusual.**

ABOVE: **A fine-looking cruiser, the** Bolzano's **career was effectively ended when, in August 1942, she and the light cruiser** Attendolo **were torpedoed by the British submarine** Unbroken. **Gutted by fire, she was salvaged but was never again to see active service.**

Bolzano and Trento class

	Built	Commissioned
Trento	Orlando, Livorno (Leghorn)	April 3, 1929
Trieste	Stab. Tecnico Triestino, Trieste	December 21, 1928
Bolzano	Ansaldo, Genoa	August 19, 1933

Trento (as built)

Displacement: 10,485 tonnes/10,320 tons (standard); 13,513 tonnes/13,300 tons (full load)
Length: 193.9m/636ft 6in (bp); 197m/646ft 6in (oa)
Beam: 20.6m/67ft 8in
Draught: 6.6m/21ft 8in (standard)
Armament: 8 x 203mm/8in (4x2) and 16 x 100mm/3.9in (8x2) guns; 8 x 533mm/21in torpedo tubes (4x2)
Machinery: Geared steam turbines, 12 boilers, 4 shafts
Power: 111,855kW/150,000shp for 35 knots
Endurance: 2,245 tonnes/2,210 tons (oil) for 7,685km/4,150nm at 16 knots
Protection: 70mm/2.76in (belt); 50mm/2in (protective deck); 100mm/3.9in (turrets)
Complement: 720

467

LEFT: **The generous forward freeboard of the *Zara* is emphasized here as she lays, "Mediterranean moored", stern-on to the dockside. With war, the lowest line of scuttles, aft as well as forward, were blanked-off as a damage control measure.** BELOW: **Mussolini showed immense pride in his armed forces, not least the navy, which staged regular reviews. Here he takes passage in the *Zara* for an official visit to Libya. Note that the after turrets, each with its own rangefinder, have followed their director on to a near-maximum bearing forward of the beam.**

Zara class

Like the Trentos, the Zaras had a foredeck catapult but, having a greatly revised machinery layout, had a more compact appearance with closer-spaced funnels. Similar to the *Bolzano*, they had a forecastle deck.

Decisions regarding the over-light construction of the Trentos must have been taken without any experience with the class for the first of the Zaras, *Fiume*, was laid down less than four months after the completion of the *Trieste*. From the outset with the heavier new class, the Washington displacement of 10,160 tonnes/10,000 tons would be treated as a guide rather than a limit.

The same eight-gun battery was required, but on a hull with heavier scantlings and considerably more protection. To gain a proposed 200mm/7.87in belt, the Ministero della Marina was prepared to accept a sustained sea speed of 32 knots, slow by Italian standards.

British suspicions that the class did not conform to agreed limits was confirmed when, during the Spanish Civil War, the *Gorizia* suffered an incapacitating aviation fuel explosion and had to be towed to Gibraltar for emergency docking. Surreptitious but "careful" measurements of her underwater form indicated a normal displacement of "about 10 per cent"

greater than that declared. There was considerable variation between the four ships of the class but *Gorizia*, the heavier, was in fact some 17 per cent over limit.

Even with generous interpretation of limits, the desired 200mm/7.87in belt had proved impossible, the Zaras having 150mm/5.9in, tapering to 100mm/3.9in below the normal waterline. Extending from forward to after magazines, the belts were closed at either end by 120mm/4.7in transverse bulkheads. The same area was overlaid by a 70mm/2.76in maindeck and a 20mm/0.79in upper deck, thick enough to initiate the detonation of a bomb or projectile prior to deep penetration. Barbette protection, compared with that of the

ABOVE: **The Italian Navy invested in battleships rather than aircraft carriers, a decision that proved severely limiting. Here, in March 1941, the *Pola* is wreathed in her own gun smoke as she tries, unsuccessfully, to avoid being torpedoed by British carrier aircraft.**

ABOVE: **Despite their size, the Zaras had an almost destroyer-like elegance, seen to good effect in this *contre-jour* study of the *Pola*. Last of the four, she differed from the rest in having the forefunnel casing merged, *Bolzano*-like, into the bridge structure.**

ABOVE: The Zaras operated as a coherent cruiser squadron and here the *Gorizia* lays in Taranto, with the *Fiume* in the foreground. Their funnels were trunked and carefully styled to enhance the ships' appearance. Note the unusual access arrangements to the bridge structure.

ABOVE: Seen in 1940, "Mediterranean-moored", stern-on to her berth, the *Gorizia* had two floatplanes on her forecastle catapult. Originally, these were Piaggio P.6 bis, changed for Ro.43 in 1938. The ship still retains a fourth twin 100mm/3.9in mounting, later removed, at the break of the forecastle.

Trentos, was greatly increased. The Zaras were effectively proof against 152mm/6in and some 203mm/8in fire, and certainly do not deserve to be included in the general mythology that all Italian cruisers were "tinclads".

The major design concession was the reduction of installed power to 70,841kW/95,000shp and a waterline shorter than that of the Trentos by some 15m/49ft 3in. Careful hull design, including a bow bulb, nonetheless realized 32–33 knots, the *Fiume* and *Pola* being the slowest.

Their weakness lay in their unusual machinery layout. For the power, only two shafts were required. The eight boilers were arranged in an unorthodox fashion, with only three transverse pairs. The engine room for the longer starboard shaft lay to starboard with a seventh boiler on its port side. There was a reverse arrangement for the much-shorter port shaft. All the spaces were divided by a centreline bulkhead, a feature which, not for the first time, would prove disastrous.

On March 28, 1941, the *Pola* was hit by a single 457mm/18in torpedo from a British carrier aircraft. The starboard boiler space flooded and the starboard shaft that passed through them was damaged. The dangerous resulting list had to be corrected by counter-flooding the port spaces which, in turn, immobilized the port-side engines. All propulsive power was lost but, believing the pursuing British fleet to be at a safe distance, the Italian admiral ordered the *Fiume* and *Zara* to stand by her. With only a pair of destroyers in support the trio was surprised by the battleships of the British Mediterranean Fleet, being blasted at close range by 381mm/15in salvoes that no cruiser could withstand. In what became known as the night battle of Matapan, all the Italian vessels were lost, virtually without reply.

Zara class

	Built	Commissioned
Fiume	Stab. Tecnico Triestino, Trieste	November 23, 1931
Gorizia	Odero Terni Orlando, Livorno	December 23, 1931
Pola	Odero Terni Orlando, Livorno	December 21, 1932
Zara	Odero Terni Orlando, la Spezia	October 20, 1931

Zara (as completed)

Displacement: 11,847 tonnes/11,660 tons (standard); 14,498 tonnes/14,270 tons (full load)
Length: 180m/590ft 10in (bp); 182.8m/600ft (oa)
Beam: 20.6m/67ft 8in
Draught: 6.2m/20ft 3in (standard)
Armament: 8 x 203mm/8in (4x2) and 16 x 100mm/3.9in (8x2)
Machinery: Geared steam turbines, 8 boilers, 2 shafts
Power: 70,841kW/95,000shp for 33 knots
Endurance: 2,398 tonnes/2,360 tons (oil) for 9,908km/5,350nm at 16 knots
Protection: 150mm/5.9in (belt); 70+20mm/2.76+0.79in (protective decks); 150mm/5.9in (turrets)
Complement: 840

ABOVE: Working up to maximum speed, the *Fiume* makes a fine sight. The picture shows clearly how the four legs of the tetrapod span the bridge structure proper, and support the platforms and main battery director above. Having considerable flare, the forecastle is sculpted to avoid excessive width at its after end.

LEFT: Although the light cruiser designers were not those of the heavy cruisers, there was much similarity in their approach, not least in the masting. The *Cadorna* was one of the second pair, which moved the mainmast ahead of the after funnel. This created a gap for angled aircraft catapults.

da Barbiano and Cadorna classes

During the 1920s the French began constructiing considerable numbers of what popularly became known as "super-destroyers". Mostly exceeding 2,743 tonnes/2,700 tons, several made 40 knots on trials and, carrying a respectable armament of five 138mm/5.43in guns and six torpedo tubes, constituted a threat not only to destroyers but, in an enclosed Mediterranean context, to trade. In response the Italian Navy laid down a quartet of small, but very fast, light

cruisers in 1928. With their usual sense of history, the Italians named the ships after the Condottieri, the "soldiers of fortune". At about 5,283 tonnes/5,200 tons at what was "Washington standard displacement", they carried an adequate eight 152mm/6in guns and four torpedo tubes in paired mountings.

To match the speed of the French, about 44 per cent of waterline length was devoted to boilers and machinery (compared with about 39 per cent in the big 10,160-tonne/10,000-ton treaty

cruisers (the "diecimille"). Run in the routinely ultra-light Italian trials condition, the lead ship notched up over 42 knots, but sustained sea speed was nearer 37.

Construction had to be very light, so light that even their crews referred to them as "*cartoni animate*". Too narrow for centreline bulkheads, machinery spaces were bounded by double light longitudinal bulkheads to limit flooding from light-calibre fire.

Two seaplanes, Cant 25s or, later, Ro.43s, were accommodated in the forward superstructure and transferred by rail to the foredeck catapult. On most, a mine cargo could be shipped.

The two Cadornas, effectively a sub-group, followed immediately. On the same dimensions, their slightly improved arrangements increased displacement and immersion, in turn reducing speed. Externally, they differed, mainly in having the catapult relocated aft, so that the tripod mainmast was moved ahead of the after funnel.

All except the *Cadorna* became war losses, three in surface action, and two to submarines.

ABOVE: Like her 203mm/8in counterparts, *da Barbiano* had a catapult track laid into the foredeck. Just visible immediately abaft "B" turret is the door of one of two sided hangars for floatplanes. The pole mainmast, later considerably heightened, is abaft the after funnel.

da Barbiano and Cadorna classes

	Built	Commissioned
Alberico da Barbiano	Ansaldo, Genoa	June 9, 1931
Alberto di Giussano	Ansaldo, Genoa	February 5, 1931
Bartolomeo Colleoni	Ansaldo, Genoa	February 10, 1932
Giovanni della Bande Nere	Cant. Castellammare di Stabia	April 17, 1931
Luigi Cadorna	CRDA, Trieste	August 11, 1933
Armando Diaz	Odeo Terni Orlando (OTO), la Spezia	April 29, 1933

da Barbiano (as built)

Displacement: 5,232 tonnes/5,150 tons (standard), 6,934 tonnes/6,825 tons (full load)
Length: 160m/525ft 2in (bp); 169.3m/555ft 9in (oa)
Beam: 15.5m/50ft 10in
Draught: 5.1m/16ft 9in (standard)
Armament: 8 x 152mm/6in (4x2) and 6 x 100mm/3.9in (3x2) guns; 4 x 533mm/21in torpedo tubes (2x2)
Machinery: Geared steam turbines, 6 boilers, 2 shafts
Power: 70,841kW/95,000shp for 37 knots
Endurance: 1,270 tonnes/1,250 tons (oil) for 7,037km/3,800nm at 18 knots
Protection: 18–25mm/0.71–1in (vertical); 20mm/0.79in (horizontal); up to 23mm/0.91in (turrets)
Complement: 505

Montecuccoli and d'Aosta classes

The two Montecuccolis, laid down in 1931–33, comprised the "third group" of Condottieri. Their construction paralleled that of the French La Galissonniere class, to which their dimensions and displacement were very similar. Where the French opted for a greater beam and an extra gun, the Italians again chose speed, the lead ship making 38.7 knots on trials with machinery at about 19 per cent overload.

The third group were some 16m/52ft 6in longer than the second with only 1m/3ft 4in increase in beam. Armament remained the same and the extra displacement was due to improved protection. A 60mm/2.4in belt stretched from the forward to after magazines and was paralleled by an inboard longitudinal bulkhead of 25mm/1in. Over the length of the machinery spaces a third light bulkhead was interposed. A 20–30mm/ 0.79–1.18in protective deck overlaid the belted area. The ship's immunity zone

against 152mm/6in gunfire was calculated at 13,500–22,000m/ 14,764–24,059yds.

Great effort went into the ship's external appearance. The bridge block was reduced to a lower bridge surmounted by a two-decked conical structure which supported the main director. There was no foremast, a lofty tripod mainmast being tightly grouped with the after funnel. Secondary directors flanked either funnel, while aircraft and catapult were accommodated amidships. Up to 96 mines could be carried.

The two "fourth group" Condottieri, the d'Aostas, were, oddly enough, built at the same time as the Montecuccolis. Slightly beamier, slightly heavier and slightly better protected, they differed externally in having an upper bridge

below the level of the main director, and funnels of equal size. In the third-group ships the forward funnel exhausted four of the six boilers; in the fourth, each funnel exhausted three boilers.

Only the *Attendolo* became a war loss and this was to heavy bombers. Under peace treaty terms the *d'Aosta* was ceded to Soviet Russia and the *Savoia* to Greece.

Montecuccoli and d'Aosta classes

	Built	Commissioned
Muzio Attendolo	CRDA, Trieste	August 7, 1935
Raimondo Montecuccoli	Ansaldo, Genoa	June 30, 1935
Emanuele Filiberto Duca d'Aosta	OTO, Livorno	July 13, 1935
Eugenio di Savoia	Ansaldo, Genoa	January 16, 1936

Montecuccoli (as built)

Displacement: 7,508 tonnes/7,390 tons (standard); 8,977 tonnes/8.835 tons (full load)
Length: 166.7m/547ft 2in (bp); 182.2m/598ft 1in (oa)
Beam: 16.6m/54ft 6in
Draught: 5.6m/18ft 4in (standard)
Armament: 8 x 152mm/6in (4x2) and 6 x 100mm/3.9in (3x2) guns; 4 x 533mm/21in torpedo tubes
Machinery: Geared steam turbines, 6 boilers, 2 shafts
Power: 79,044kW/106,000shp for 37 knots.
Endurance: 1,676 tonnes/1,650 tons, (oil) for 7,222km/3,900nm at 14 knots
Protection: 70+35mm/2.76+1.38in (vertical); 30–35mm/1.18–1.38in (horizontal); 70–90mm/2.76–3.54in (turrets)
Complement: 578

ABOVE: **Visually, the pair of d'Aostas differed from the Montecuccolis in the upper bridge structure, now a stump conical section surmounted by a command bridge below the director. The clipper stem and clean lines gave an impression of grace and power. This picture shows *Eugenio di Savoia*.**

Abruzzi class

The final pair of Condottieri, the "fifth group", comprised the *Abruzzi* and *Garibaldi*. Of a size with the preceding d'Aostas, they were, nonetheless, far removed from the original concept governing the early groups.

Their authorization in 1933 coincided with the Italian Navy embarking on the extensive rebuilding of the Cavour-class battleships and the ordering of the two new Littorios, cornerstones to the Italian claim of "*Mare Nostrum*". Modern cruisers were required to complement the battle squadrons and robustness was more important than speed, for which the requirement was a sufficient margin over that of the capital ships.

Eight boilers, five large and three small, generated 74,600kW/100,000shp, a reduction on earlier cruisers. Although boiler spaces still alternated with engine rooms, extensive trunking enabled the two funnels to be closely spaced. Two catapults were fitted, flanking the after funnel and up to four aircraft could be accommodated.

Armour was arranged according to a new scheme with a 30mm/1.18in side belt backed by an arcing 100mm/3.95in bulkhead, which left a lenticular void space of a maximum 1m/3ft 4in depth. A further light longitudinal bulkhead ran inboard of this combination. The protective deck above was thickened to 40mm/1.57in.

TOP: This pre-war picture of *Abruzzi* emphasizes the inherent simplicity of warships prior to the missile age. The heavy derrick, stepped on the mainmast, served both catapults and boats. The curved object on the ship's side, right aft, is a propeller guard, which was lowered when alongside.

ABOVE: The final pair of Condottieri reverted from the unit system of machinery layout employed earlier. By more closely grouping the boiler spaces, the funnels were closer together and flanked by the two catapults. "A" and "Y" turrets were triples, superfired by twins in "B" and "X" positions. *Giuseppe Garibaldi* is shown here.

The Abruzzis were the only pair to mount ten 152mm/6in guns. These were distributed symmetrically forward and aft, with twin turrets superfiring triples. The guns themselves were of a new 55-calibre model, superseding the earlier ships' 53-calibre weapons. Improved muzzle velocity gave their 50kg/110lb projectiles a range of 24,900m/27,231yds, an increase of about 2,249m/2,460yds.

Longer than the Zara-class heavy cruisers, the Abruzzis' size was emphasized by their substantial forward freeboard, which was carried back to the forward funnel. Bridge structure was again kept low with, originally, no foremast other than a simple antenna pole. They were the only cruisers in the series to have a pole, rather than tripod, mainmast.

LEFT: Scarcely recognizable following her rebuilding, the *Garibaldi* is seen here in the mid-1960s. Her after end is dominated by the search and guidance radar systems for a single Terrier SAM. Her funnels have been trunked into a single casing and, forward, she has two twin 135mm/5.3in mountings.

LEFT: **Although the *Abruzzi* served in the post-war fleet until 1961, she was not converted to a missile cruiser. She was, however, thoroughly modernized, with considerably changed superstructure, masting and added electronics. She kept her original main-calibre armament.**

By early 1944 the Italian Navy was co-operating with those of the Allies and, with radars and improved communications being made available, the *Abruzzi* gained a light lattice foremast. Earlier dazzle painting gave way to a variation of Measure 12, a dark-grey hull with lighter grey upperworks, although the dark funnel caps were retained.

Both cruisers survived into Italy's full NATO membership, and electronics now proliferated. By the early 1950s the *Garibaldi* had joined a light foremast, crossed with a conventional yard, and a mainmast crowned with the outsized dish of an American SK series air search radar, an addition that did nothing for her appearance.

Although the nameship was scrapped in 1961, the *Garibaldi* underwent a near five-year rebuilding, emerging in 1962 as a guided-missile cruiser. Of the original ship, only the hull remained recognizable. A larger and more complex bridge structure was surmounted by one of two substantial lattice masts bearing a full range of American electronics. Aft were twin Terrier directors and launcher. Surprisingly, there were also four vertical-launch tubes for Polaris ICBMs.

(Dummy missiles were certainly fired but the policy on these remains unclear.)

A replacement set of boilers was trunked into a single, large, capped funnel and developed power for a reduced speed of 30 knots. All original guns were removed. The forward turrets were replaced by twin mountings for a new-pattern 135mm/5.3in dual-purpose (DP) gun, while eight single 76mm/3in weapons were distributed along either side of the waist.

This was a classic case of new wine in old bottles and, by the time that she went for disposal in 1978, the *Garibaldi* had seen 41 years of service. Her rebuilding had proved to be complex but had provided the necessary experience to progress to the next generation of purpose-built missile ships.

Abruzzi class

	Built	Commissioned
Luigi di Savoia duca degli Abruzzi	OTO, la Spezia	December 1, 1937
Giuseppe Garibaldi	CRDA, Trieste	December 20, 1937

ABOVE: **Very imposing in her original form, the *Garibaldi* lost much of her "presence" when she was extensively rebuilt in 1960–61. She is shown here laying to buoys.**

Abruzzi (as built)

Displacement: 9,581 tonnes/9,430 tons (standard); 11,725 tonnes/11,540 tons (full load)
Length: 171.8m/564ft (bp); 187m/613ft 10in (oa)
Beam: 18.9m/62ft
Draught: 6.1m/20ft (standard)
Armament: 10 x 152mm/6in (2x3/2x2) and 8 x 100mm/3.9in (4x2); 6x 533mm/21in torpedo tubes (2x3)
Machinery: Geared steam turbines, 8 boilers, 2 shafts
Power: 74,570kW/100,000shp for 33 knots
Endurance: 1,725 tonnes/1,695 tons (oil) for 7,408km/4,000nm at 13 knots
Protection: 100+30mm/3.94+1.18in (vertical); 40mm/1.57in (horizontal); up to 135mm/5.3in (turrets)
Complement: 640

Etna class

Together with destroyers, this pair of small cruisers was ordered to Siamese (Thai) account in 1938. With Italy's involvement in the war, work progressed slowly until, in December 1941 and shortly after Pearl Harbor, they were requisitioned.

As designed, they were diminutives of the later Condottieri, but with a single funnel and only one forward turret. However, just after being launched, they underwent considerable remodelling.

Responsibilities for the endless resupply of the Axis armies in North Africa were haemorrhaging the Italian merchant fleet. Fast warship/transports such as those used by the British to supply Tobruk and Malta were an attractive proposition, able either to make a high-speed solo overnight run, or to supplement and cover a convoy.

In place of the planned 152mm/6in battery, the pair was now fitted with three twin 135mm/5.3in dual-purpose mountings, ten new-style 65mm/2.56in weapons in single mountings and six twin 20mm/0.79in guns.

Cargo spaces totalling about 525 cubic metres/687 cubic yards were arranged forward and aft, each served by a small crane. Short-term troop accommodation was also provided forward and in the after superstructure. Deck cargoes, typically cased petrol, could be stowed in the open space abaft the funnel, intended originally for aircraft and catapult.

Work progressed at a very leisurely pace for, although the ships had obvious utility, they overlapped with the programme for a dozen Capitani Romani which, capable of 40 knots and mounting a similar scale of armament on little over half the displacement, were considered more valuable. Both were competing for increasingly scarce resources as Italy's

ABOVE: **This picture is a digital rendition showing how the Etna class would have looked. As designed, the Etnas resembled reduced Montecuccolis, with one funnel and no superimposed forward turret. Note the torpedo tube aperture.** BELOW LEFT: **Conceived together, destroyed together. Neither ship survived to serve in either the Thai or Italian Navy.**

war effort stuttered to a halt. When Italy agreed an armistice in September 1943, the still-incomplete pair was taken by the Germans. Never progressed above the weather deck, both hulls were eventually found scuttled in shallow water off Trieste.

Etna class

	Built
Etna (ex-*Taksin*)	CRDA, Trieste
Vesuvio (ex-*Naresman*)	CRDA, Trieste

Etna class (as proposed for Italian AA cruisers)

Displacement: 5,985 tonnes/5,890 tons (standard); 6,512 tonnes/6,410 tons (full load)
Length: 141m/462ft 10in (bp); 153.8m/504ft 10in (oa)
Beam: 14.5m/47ft 8in
Draught: 5.9m/19ft 3in (projected)
Armament: 6 x 135mm/5.3in (3x2), 10 x 65mm/2.56in (10x1) and 12 x 20mm/0.79in (6x2) guns
Machinery: Geared steam turbines, 3 boilers, 2 shafts
Power: 29,828kW/40,000shp for 28 knots
Protection: 60+20mm/2.4+0.79in (vertical); 20–35mm/0.79–1.38in (horizontal); none (turrets)
Complement: 580 (projected)

Capitani Romani class

It will be recalled that French super-destroyers of the early 1920s begat the early Condottieri as an Italian response. Just five years later, however, the Condottieri had evolved into a quite different type of cruiser, but the French *contre torpilleur* had continued an uninterrupted line of development. Faced in 1938 with the new Mogadors (2,997 tonnes/2,950 tons, eight 138mm/5.43in guns, 40+ knots), the Italian Navy again sought a counter.

The Capitani Romani, with their resonant Roman names, were less than 6m/19ft 8in longer than the Mogadors but had machinery developing 20 per cent more power. Their main battery of eight 135mm/5.3in was similar and they were unprotected except for the use of toughened alloys in vital areas. An aircraft, without catapult, was planned but never adopted. Portable tracks along the side decks enabled up to 70 mines to be carried.

At only 3,805 tonnes/3,745 tons standard displacement they were classed officially as "*esploratori oceanici*" but were always known as light cruisers. Twelve were ordered during 1939, all from commercial yards. These suffered badly from lack of resources, from bombing and from fluctuating priorities. As a result only three of the class were ever commissioned into the Italian Navy during the war. Several hulls remained incomplete due to sabotage or to bomb damage. Of those taken by the Germans at the armistice in September 1943 none was ever finished, with the near exceptions of *Caio Mario* and *Cornelio Silla*.

In 1948 the *Attilio Regolo* and *Scipione Africano* were ceded to France as war reparation, being renamed *Chateaurenault* and *Guichen* respectively. The *Pompeo Magno* and the salvaged *Giulio Germanico* went on to give the Italian Navy useful post-war service. Rearmed and re-equipped to NATO standards in the early 1950s, they served until 1975 as the *San Marco* and *San Giorgio* respectively.

Capitani Romani class

	Built	Commissioned
Attilio Regolo	OTO, Livorno	May 14, 1942
Caio Mario	OTO, Livorno	
Claudio Druso	Cantieri del Tirreno, Riva Trigoso	
Claudio Tiberio	OTO, Livorno	
Cornelio Silla	Ansaldo, Genoa	
Giulio Germanico	Cant. di Castellammare di Stabia	January 19, 1956
Ottaviano Augusto	Cant. Navali Riuniti, Ancona	
Paolo Emilio	Ansaldo, Genoa	
Pompeo Magno	Cant. Navali Riuniti, Ancona	June 4, 1943
Scipione Africano	OTO, Livorno	April 23, 1943
Ulpio Traiano	Cant. Navali Riuniti, Palermo	
Vipsanio Agrippa	Cantieri del Tirreno, Riva Trigoso	

LEFT: ***Attilio Regolo* and her sister *Scipione Africano* were ceded to France in 1948, being renamed *Chateaurenault* (here) and *Guichen* respectively. Rearmed with a mix of ex-German 10.5cm/4.1in and Bofors 57mm/2.24in guns, 12 AS torpedo tubes and new electronics, they served as Command Ships/Flotilla leaders until the 1960s.**

Capitani Romani class (as projected)

Displacement: 3,733 tonnes/3,675 tons (standard); 5,415 tonnes/5,330 tons (full load)
Length: 138.7m/455ft 3inn (bp); 142.9m/469ft 1in (oa)
Beam: 14.4m/47ft 3in
Draught: 4.1m/13ft 6in (standard)
Armament: 8 x 135mm/5.3in (4x2) and 8 x 37mm/1.46in (8x1) guns; 8 x 533mm/21in torpedo tubes (2x4)
Machinery: Geared steam turbines, 4 boilers, 2 shafts
Power: 82,027kW/110,000shp for 40+ knots
Endurance: 1,400 tonnes/1,375 tons (oil) for 7,871km/4,250nm at 18 knots
Protection: None
Complement: 420

LEFT: With the two Dorias, Italian designers produced a stylish solution to the difficult combination of single-ended missile cruiser and facilities for four anti-submarine warfare (ASW) helicopters. Later in her career, *Duilio* is seen with her after four 76mm/3in guns removed. BELOW: *Duilio*'s usual helicopter flight comprised the relatively small Agusta-Bell AB 204B. Greater capacity and versatility inevitably leads to larger aircraft, but the Wessex-type Sikorsky being accepted here is not an AS helicopter. The thimble-shaped antenna atop the mainmast is a TACAN air control antenna.

Andrea Doria class

The conversions of the *Garibaldi* into an interim missile cruiser gave the Italian Navy operational experience in this new form of air defence while it was constructing purpose-designed ships. These, the Andrea Dorias, marked the transition from the traditional cruiser, essentially a surface-warfare ship with dual-purpose secondary artillery, to a multi-purpose task force component armed primarily for area air defence and the protection of a group against submarine attack. In that the Dorias were also a commitment to NATO multi-national forces they also marked the end of a long line of individual Italian cruisers, designed to work independently in purely national interests.

The Dorias, therefore, marked the transition from fast, protected, weight-critical warships to volume-critical vessels with considerable bulk but virtually no protection – the subtle objective being to avoid being hit rather than to trade direct blows with an opponent. However, despite these differences in philosophy the ships retained their Italian individuality.

As built, each deployed a Terrier surface-to-air missile (SAM) system forward but, during the late 1970s these were modified for the standard SM-1 ER (extended range) weapon. This was supported by eight single 76mm/3in guns located along either side of the superstructure.

For the anti-submarine (AS) role the ships had hull-mounted sonar, supported by mobile sets deployed by any of three small helicopters accommodated in the after superstructure. These could also deliver AS torpedoes, in addition to those from the ships' six 324mm/12.75in tubes.

Because of the general stand-off nature of modern naval warfare, speed is no longer a major design priority. Two, well-separated, combined boiler and machinery spaces were installed that developed power sufficient for 30 knots.

The two ships were discarded in the early 1990s, *Caio Duilio* in 1990 and *Andrea Doria* in 1992.

Andrea Doria class

	Built	Commissioned
Andrea Doria (C553)	Cantieri del Tirreno, Riva Trigoso	February 23, 1964
Caio Duilio (C554)	Cant, della Navalmeccanica, Castellammare di Stabia	November 30, 1964

Andrea Doria class

Displacement: 6,620 tonnes/6,500 tons (standard); 7,430 tonnes/7,300 tons (full load)
Length: 144m/472ft 8in (bp); 149.3m/490ft (oa)
Beam: 17.3m/56ft 9in
Draught: 5m/16ft 4in (standard)
Armament: 1 x twin standard SM-1 ER launcher (40 missiles); 8 x 76mm/3in (8x1) guns; 6 x 324mm/12.75in AS torpedo tubes (2x3)
Machinery: Geared steam turbines, 4 boilers, 2 shafts
Power: 44,742kW/60,000shp for 30 knots
Endurance: 1,117 tonnes/1,100 tons (oil) for 11,112km/6,000nm at 15 knots
Protection: None
Complement: 485

LEFT: This amidships detail of the *Doria* shows her full outfit of 76mm/3in guns. The two after weapons have been located on pedestals which, with liferafts, have constricted the side deck to the extent that it has been widened. The boats, stacked vertically, are handled neatly by a small crane.

Vittorio Veneto

Originally intended to have had a sister (reportedly to have been named *Italia*), the *Vittorio Veneto* remains a one-off larger version of the Andrea Dorias. Like them, she is termed a "cruiser" by virtue of size and capability.

Up to nine helicopters can be carried, hangared below the four-spot flight deck, forward of which are the interconnecting elevators. Because of the required hangar headroom, the after end has a greater freeboard than the forecastle deck, giving a hull form best described as a "raised quarterdecker".

As with the Dorias, the ship was designed around the Terrier surface-to-air missile (SAM) system. This was subsequently updated to the so-called Aster system, whose launcher can handle either standard SM-1 ER SAMs or ASROC anti-submarine (AS) missiles. For anti-submarine warfare (ASW) the ship has a triple-layered capability, consisting of helicopters, ASROC and ship-launched torpedoes. In anti-aircraft

warfare (AAW) the same applies, with SAMs, 76mm/3in and 40mm/1.57in guns, all with their own directors.

Where the smaller Dorias had little defence against surface ships, the *Veneto* has four canister-launched Otomat Mk2 "Teseo" Surface-to-surface missiles (SSMs), whose active homing head gives a theoretical capability out to 150km/93 miles. Her small AB-212 helicopters are also able to deploy air-to-surface missiles (ASM) such as the French AS-12.

To facilitate access to the two machinery spaces, to improve "sky arcs" and to minimize interaction between electronic systems, funnels and masts are combined in rather unlovely "macks".

Over the years, much of the ship's original American-sourced fire control radars have been replaced by indigenous equipment. With a 40x18.5m/131x61ft flight deck, the ship is far from the classic cruiser, whose handsome appearance has been lost in the high and spiky profile

inseparable from a multiplicity of modern systems. Long a favourite as a flagship by virtue of her size, she was decommissioned to the reserve in 2003.

Vittorio Veneto (C550)

Built: Cantieri Riuniti, Castellammare di Stabia
Commissioned: July 12, 1969
Displacement: 8,280 tonnes/8,150 tons (standard); 9,652 tonnes/9,500 tons (full load)
Length: 170.6m/560ft (bp); 179.6m/589ft 6in (oa)
Beam: 19.4m/63ft 8in
Draught: 5.5m/18ft (standard)
Armament: 1 x twin Aster launcher for standard SM-1 ER or ASROC missiles (60 missiles carried); 4 x Otomat Mk2 Teseo SSM; 8 x 76mm/3in (8x1) and 6 x 40mm/1.57in (3x2) guns; 6 x 324mm/12.75in AS torpedo tubes
Machinery: Geared steam turbines, 4 boilers, 2 shafts
Power: 54,436kW/73,000shp for 30.5 knots
Endurance: 1,219 tonnes/1,200 tons (oil) for 11,112km/6,000nm at 20 knots
Protection: None
Complement: 557

RIGHT: **During 1981–83, the *Veneto* was extensively modernized, exchanging the Terrier system for Aster, capable of launching either Standard SM-1 ER or ASROC missiles. Four Otomat SSM launchers were sided in the waist and three, fully automatic, Dardo twin 40mm/1.57in mountings added.**

ABOVE LEFT: **Although fighting under Free French colours alongside the Allies, the *Gloire* contrived for a period to sport what was probably the most extreme disruptive paint scheme of the war. This style of "dazzle painting" made a ship's heading difficult to estimate.** ABOVE: **Something of a puzzle. Along with her sisters, *Gloire* landed her mainmast to improve anti-aircraft (AA) defences. Here, however, equipped with radar and in post-war livery, she again caries her heavy mainmast with the distinctive crosstree, designed for spreading floatplane derricks.**

La Galissonnière class

Judged to be very successful for their size, the six La Galissonnières were laid down between 1931 and 1933, exactly paralleling the six Italian Condottieri of the last three groups. These increased displacement successively from about 7,671–10,110 tonnes/7,550–9,950 tons but the French ships maintained 7,824 tonnes/7,700 tons and a standard design.

The *Emile Bertin* was also built over the same period, and there was a distinct commonality of design, but with the installed power reduced in order to release displacement for improved protection, notably a shallow side belt extending from forward to after magazines. The altered weight distribution necessitated a small increase in beam, with an overall speed penalty of about 3 knots maintained speed.

Contemporary Italian cruisers favoured two-shaft propulsion with each shaft delivering up to 41,000kW/55,000shp. Only with the La Galissonnières did the French adopt this lighter and less complex arrangement, albeit with lower loading per propeller.

The new and effective 152mm/6in main-calibre gun was retained in three triple turrets. As built, the after superstructure terminated in a bulky box hangar accommodating up to four small aircraft, although two large Loire 130 flying boats were more usual. A prominent pole mainmast supported two derrick-cranes, one each for boats and aircraft. The catapult was located atop the after turret, by which it could be trained. Mast and aircraft facilities were removed on the three of the class that served with Allied forces.

The other three, *La Galissonnière*, *Jean de Vienne* and the *Marseillaise*, were scuttled at Toulon in November 1942. The first two were salvaged by the Italians, who commenced their refurbishment. This was still incomplete when the Italians capitulated in September 1943, Taken by the Germans, the two, still unfit for sea, were destroyed by Allied bombing.

The three survivors continued in service until the 1950s.

La Galissonnière class

	Built	Commissioned
Georges Leygues	Penhoët, St. Nazaire	December 4, 1937
Gloire	Forges et Chantiers de la Girone	December 4, 1937
Jean de Vienne	Arsenal de Lorient	April 15, 1937
La Galissonnière	Arsenal de Brest	December 31, 1935
Marseillaise	Ateliers et Chantiers de la Loire	October 25, 1937
Montcalm	Forges et Chantiers de la Mediterranée	December 4, 1937

La Galissonnière class (as designed)

Displacement: 7,702 tonnes/7,580 tons (standard); 9,084 tonnes/8,940 tons (full load)
Length: 172m/564ft 7in (bp); 179.5m/589ft 2in (oa)
Beam: 17.5m/57ft 5in
Draught: 5m/16ft 5in (standard)
Armament: 9 x 152mm/6in (3x3) and 8 x 90mm/3.54in HA (4x2) guns; 4 x 550mm/21.65in torpedo tubes (2x2)
Machinery: Geared steam turbines, 4 boilers, 2 shafts
Power: 62,638kW/84,000shp for 31 knots
Endurance: 1,544 tonnes/1,520 tons (oil) for 10,186km/5,500nm at 15 knots
Protection: 75–120mm/3–4.7in (vertical); 38mm/1.5in (protective deck); 75–100mm/3–3.94in (turrets)
Complement: 540

LEFT: **Every inch a cruiser, *La Galissonnière* looks splendid as built and carrying neutrality colours painted-up on "B" turret. The Loire 130 flying boat is mounted on its catapult atop the after turret. A double hangar was housed in the after superstructure.**

LEFT: **Pre-war, the *Duquesne*
was equipped with an aircraft
catapult abaft the funnels and
served by a derrick stepped on
the mainmast. The circular disc
halfway up the foremast was a
"range clock", informing other
ships in a squadron of the range
at which she was firing.**

Duquesne class

Lacking battlecruisers or fast
battleships, the French Naval Staff
required that the two Duquesnes, first
of the French "treaty cruisers", act as
scouts ahead of the battle fleet. To gain
and maintain contact with the enemy
would require speed, good seakeeping
and endurance. A secondary
requirement, that of preventing enemy
ships interdicting essential lines of
communication, required substantial
armament. Probably the greatest
influence on the design process,
however, was the intelligence that
the Italian Trentos would ship eight
203mm/8in guns and be capable of 34
knots. These were the lowest figures that
the French could accept, but the weight
required for armament and machinery
left less than 5 per cent of the total
displacement available for protection.
The resulting hull, although very sea-
kindly with its raised forecastle and
generous freeboard, had thin protection
only in way of magazines, turrets and
conning tower. Subdivision, however,
was thorough, and a stiffened
longitudinal bulkhead paralleled the
shell plating in way of the machinery
spaces. The ships, nonetheless, were
not proof against even destroyer gunfire.

Weight was saved by putting the
design and supply of machinery out to
commercial competition, but margins

RIGHT: **Between the wars,
floatplanes were the obvious
means of increasing the scouting
radius of a cruiser. During
World War II they were largely
abandoned as a fire hazard
and because a proliferation of
aircraft carriers rendered them
redundant. The torpedo-like
object on the *Duquesne*'s
bulkhead is a towed paravane.**

remained so tight that the specified
100mm/3.9in secondary weapons
had to be downgraded to 75mm/
3in guns.

An aircraft catapult was located
between the after funnel and the pole
mainmast. One aircraft was stowed on
the catapult, a second sharing the boat
deck between the funnels.

As with the Italians and the Americans,
the French Navy had sufficient reservations
about this, their first treaty cruiser,
to authorize only two, with an eye to
subsequent modification.

With war, the ships lay demilitarized
and deteriorating at Alexandria until 1943.
Reactivation for Free French service came
too late for them to contribute significantly.
Mainmast and aircraft arrangements
were removed in 1945, but, by 1949,
both ships had been reduced to static
harbour training duties.

Duquesne class

	Built	Commissioned
Duquesne	Arsenal de Brest	January 25, 1929
Tourville	Arsenal de Lorient	March 12, 1929

Duquesne class (as built)

Displacement: 10,160 tonnes/10,000 tons
(standard), 12,599 tonnes/12,400 tons (full load)
Length: 185m/607ft 3in (bp); 191m/627ft (oa)
Beam: 19.1m/62ft 8in
Draught: 5.9m/19ft 3in
Armament: 8 x 203mm/8in (4x2) and
8 x 75mm/3in HA (8x1) guns;
6 x 550mm/21.65in torpedo tubes (2x3)
Machinery: Geared steam turbines, 8 boilers, 4 shafts
Power: 89,484kW/120,000shp for 33 knots
Endurance: 1,869 tonnes/1,840 tons for
9,260km/5,000nm at 15 knots
Protection: 20–30mm/0.79–1.18in (in way of
magazines); up to 30mm/1.18in (turrets)
Complement: 605

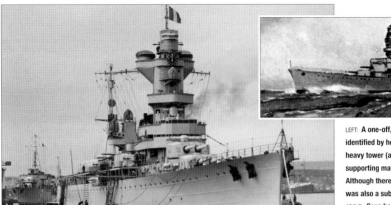

LEFT: A one-off, the *Algérie* could easily be identified by her lack of forecastle deck and heavy tower (as opposed to a tripod foremast) supporting main and secondary directors. Although there was a single funnel, there was also a substantial after superstructure.

ABOVE: Seen here as built, the *Algérie* was modified during internment. The heavy mainmast and aircraft catapults were removed and a light pole mast erected on the after superstructure.

Suffren class and *Algérie*

The Duquesnes had the speed and seakeeping necessary to reconnoitre ahead of a slow battlefleet, but were vulnerable to the fire of even the large destroyers being built by Italy. With the rumoured speed of the planned new 152mm/6in Condottieri, the French Naval Staff looked for better protection, if not immunity, in the next group of French cruisers.

As the Duquesnes' new 203mm/8in twin turrets had proved to be effective, four were again specified, leaving a question of balance between protection and speed while remaining within the 10,160-tonne/10,000-ton limit.

Laid down in 1926–27 the first pair, *Suffren* and *Colbert*, while strongly resembling the Duquesnes, differed in having a much reduced power of 73,100kW/98,000shp, transmitted via three shafts. For a resulting penalty of about 1.5 knots it was possible to incorporate side belts of 50mm/2in and internal bulges.

Following on in 1928–29, the *Foch* and *Dupleix* were improved further with deep internal longitudinal bulkheads of 54mm/2.1in and 60mm/2.36in respectively, roofed by a protective deck of up to 20mm/0.79in and 30mm/1.18in respectively. Even this did not give the required 152mm/6in immunity zone and a major redesign was undertaken.

The resulting one-off, *Algérie*, saved weight at the expense of seakeeping through the elimination of the forecastle deck. Installed power was further reduced to 62,638kW/84,000shp. This was generated by six boilers of advanced design, but survivability was compromised somewhat by grouping them together in order that they could be exhausted through a weight-saving single funnel. This reduction in weight was slightly offset by a conservative reversion to four-shaft propulsion. Weight-saving permitted both 110mm/4.3in belts and a protective deck that was 80mm/3.1in thick over the axial half,

with 30mm/1.18in over the wing spaces. Longitudinal wing bulkheads were 20–40mm/0.79–1.57in thick. A full secondary armament of twelve 100mm/3.9in guns could also be included inside the mandated displacement limit.

Suffren class and *Algérie*

	Built	Commissioned
Colbert	Arsenal de Brest	1931
Dupleix	Arsenal de Brest	1932
Foch	Arsenal de Brest	1931
Suffren	Arsenal de Brest	1930
Algérie	Arsenal de Brest	October 19, 1934

Algérie (as built)

Displacement: 10,160 tonnes/10,000 tons (standard); 13,894 tonnes/13,675 tons (full load)
Length: 180m/590ft 10in (bp); 186.2m/611ft 3in (oa)
Beam: 20m/65ft 8in
Draught: 6.2m/20ft 4in (standard)
Armament: 8 x 203mm/8in (4x2) and 12 x 100mm/3.9in (6x2) guns; 6 x 550mm/21.7in torpedo tubes (2x3)
Machinery: Geared steam turbines, 6 boilers, 4 shafts
Power: 62,638kW/84,000shp for 31 knots
Endurance: 2,946 tonnes/2,900 tons (oil) for 14,816km/8,000nm at 15 knots
Protection: 110+20–40mm/4.3+0.79–1.57in (vertical); 30–80mm/1.18–3.1in (deck); 70–100mm/2.76–3.9in (turrets)
Complement: 620

LEFT: Of the four Suffrens, only the nameship, which fought with the Allies, survived; all three of her sisters were scuttled at Toulon in 1942. With her mainmast removed, the *Suffren* is seen at the end of World War II. She has Measure 22 paintwork, with mid-grey hull and haze-grey upperworks.

de Grasse and *Colbert*

Laid down at Lorient in November 1938 as a single-funnelled light cruiser, conforming to the new treaty limit of 8,128 tonnes/8,000 tons, the *de Grasse* was designed to carry three triple 152mm/6in turrets. Her construction was halted by war and she was finally launched in 1946. Towed to Brest, in 1951 the hull was taken in hand for completion as a large anti-aircraft cruiser, joined in 1953 by a near sister, *Colbert*.

Colbert's funnel was located further aft, and she lacked *de Grasse*'s forecastle deck. To reduce wetness, she had a knuckle, forward. By virtue of her transom stern, she was shorter, but she was also beamier. The *de Grasse* had more powerful machinery, developing 78,300kW/105,000shp for a maximum speed of 33.5 knots.

Both differed radically from earlier French cruisers in having a "pyramoidal" profile, rising from either end to a maximum amidships. Fitted out as a command cruiser and task force flagship, the *de Grasse* had a pole mainmast in contrast to the *Colbert*'s two lattice masts.

The ships' armament layout was identical and comparable only with that of the smaller American Atlantas in their original form. Sixteen 127mm/5in guns in twin mountings were arranged symmetrically, four forward, four aft, with two of each sided. Twenty Bofors-pattern, 57mm/2.24in guns, mainly sided, were also carried in twin mountings.

The prematurely aged *de Grasse* finished her

career as a nuclear task force flagship in the Pacific but during 1970–72 the newer *Colbert* was thoroughly reconstructed as a missile cruiser. All 127mm/5in guns were landed in favour of just two new-style 100mm/3.9in mountings forward. Six twin 57mm/2.24in mountings were retained. Located aft was a French Masurca SAM system with a range of 48km/30 miles, while four canister-launched MM38 Exocet SSMs were sited to flank the forward bridge structure.

She served as Mediterranean flagship until finally discarded in 1997.

de Grasse and *Colbert*

	Built	Commissioned
de Grasse (C610)	Arsenaux de Brest et de Lorient	September 3, 1956
Colbert (C611)	Arsenal de Brest	May 5, 1959

ABOVE: **Although completed in much the same configuration as *de Grasse*, the post-war *Colbert* was heavily remodelled in 1970–72. She was given a French-built Masurca SAM system and helicopter pad aft and two single 100mm/3.9in guns forward. Six twin 57mm/2.24in mountings were grouped amidships.**

Colbert (as built)

Displacement: 8,636 tonnes/8,500 tons (standard); 11,176 tonnes/11,000 tons (full load)
Length: 174.9m/574ft 2in (bp); 181.9m/597ft 2in (oa)
Beam: 19.3m/63ft 6in
Draught: 5.7m/18ft 9in (standard)
Armament: 16 x 127mm/5in DP (8x2) and 20 x 57mm/2.24in HA (10x2) guns
Machinery: Geared steam turbines, 4 boilers, 2 shafts
Power: 64,130kW/86,000shp for 32 knots
Endurance: 7,408km/4,000nm at 25 knots
Protection: 50–80mm/2–3.1in (vertical); 50mm/2in (protective deck)
Complement: 975

Emden (III)

Inheriting a famous name, the *Emden* (III) was the first major warship built for the renascent German Navy. This, still lacking its design facilities following World War I, used the hull form of the *Köln* (II) of 1918. Topside, the ship differed in adopting two more heavily trunked funnels in place of the earlier three. A new-style, heavy tubular "battlemast" was stepped through the bridge structure, topped-off with the main director, incorporating a long-base rangefinder. Prone to vibration, this had to be shortened as were, subsequently, the funnels for weight reduction.

As planned, the armament was to include eight 15cm/5.9in guns in new-pattern twin turrets, and eight torpedo tubes in paired mountings. The still-active Allied disarmament commission, however, objected to further gun design, the ship having to take eight single mountings, four of which had to be sided. Four torpedo tubes also had to be suppressed. Protection and subdivision were on a scale similar to the *Köln*, and much weight was saved through an early use of welding. Endurance was much improved, significant to her role as training cruiser for up to 160 officer cadets, who were accommodated in an enlarged after superstructure. As the command of the then-Captain Karl Dönitz, the *Emden* (III) made several world cruises.

During the 1930s the mainmast was suppressed in favour of a light pole, braced to the after funnel, in order to improve the firing arcs of the anti-aircraft (AA) armament. A plan to retro-fit the originally proposed armament of four twin 15cm/5.9in mountings and to improve the AA battery came to nothing with the onset of war in 1939.

As a one-off design, that of the *Emden* (III) was interesting in bridging those of the two world wars. Having spent the war in Baltic and Norwegian waters, she was scuttled near Kiel in May 1945.

LEFT: **Seen leaving Kiel in the early 1930s,** *Emden* (III) **shows her handsome profile. Both the forward "battlemast" and mainmast have been shortened, and a foretopmast added. During 1934, her funnels were lowered by 2m/6ft 7in. Note the torpedo tubes, sided at the break of the forecastle.**

Emden (III) (as built)

Built: Wilhelmshaven Naval Dockyard
Commissioned: October 15, 1925
Displacement: 5,388 tonnes/5,300 tons (standard); 7,102 tonnes/6,990 tons (full load)
Length: 150.5m/494ft (wl); 155.1m/509ft 1in (oa)
Beam: 14.2m/46ft 7in
Draught: 5.2m/16ft 10in (standard)
Armament: 8 x 15cm/5.9in (8x1) and 3 x 8.8cm/3.46in HA (3x1) guns; 4 x 50cm/19.7in torpedo tubes (2x2)
Machinery: Geared steam turbines, 10 boilers, 2 shafts
Power: 34,228kW/45,900shp for 29 knots
Endurance: 889 tonnes/875 tons (coal) and 1,219 tonnes/1,200 tons (oil) for 12,038km/6,500nm at 15 knots
Protection: 75–100mm/3–3.9in (belt); 20–40mm/0.79–1.57in (protective deck); 50mm/2in (gun mountings)
Complement: 475 plus 160 cadets

K-class, *Leipzig* and *Nürnberg*

Laid down in 1926, the three K-class were an extrapolation of the *Emden*. Some 18.5m/60ft 8in longer on the waterline, they carried nine 15cm/5.9in guns in three triple mountings, one forward, two aft. The two latter were staggered either side of the centreline to simplify ammunition handling.

The hull layout resembled that of the *Emden* (III) in that the short forecastle was continued well aft as a long centreline deckhouse. Four triple 53.3cm/21in torpedo tube banks were located on the side decks thus formed. A conspicuous crane served the floatplane catapult between the funnels. Three twin 8.8cm/3.46in HA mountings were grouped around the after superstructure.

Long endurance was important for trade warfare and the gearboxes driving the shafts could be powered by diesel engines as a more economical alternative to the steam turbines.

Although not particularly fast, the Ks were crank, despite efforts at weight-saving. The *Leipzig*, laid down two years later, therefore, had an extra 1m/3ft 4in on the beam for much the same length. Both boiler rooms exhausted through a single, heavily trunked funnel. All her main-calibre mountings were on the centreline. A further pair of 8.8cm/3.46in guns was added but 25mm/1in had to be shaved off the protection to the main gunhouses.

Five years later a fifth unit, the *Nürnberg*, was laid down. She was essentially a repeat, but some 4m/13ft 1in longer. Externally she differed in having a large bridge structure. Her catapult was abaft the funnel, the *Leipzig*'s before.

Both later cruisers had three shafts, with steam turbines on the outside and a cruising diesel in the centre.

All three of the K-class became war casualties, two by bombing, one by torpedo. The *Leipzig* was scuttled, laden with gas shells, by the British in 1946. The *Nürnberg* became the training cruiser *Admiral Makarov* in the Soviet fleet, more a trophy than a useful asset.

K-class, *Leipzig* and *Nürnberg*

	Built	Commissioned
Karlsruhe (III)	Deutsche Werke, Kiel	November 6, 1929
Köln (III)	Wilhelmshaven Naval Dockyard	January 15, 1930
Königsberg (III)	Wilhelmshaven Naval Dockyard	April 17, 1929
Leipzig (IV)	Wilhelmshaven Naval Dockyard	October 8, 1931
Nürnberg (III)	Deutsche Werke Kiel	November 2, 1935

K-class (as built)

Displacement: 6,096 tonnes/6,000 tons (standard); 7,823 tonnes/7,700 tons (full load)
Length: 169m/554ft 9in (wl); 174m/571ft 2in (oa)
Beam: 15.2m/49ft 11in
Draught: 5.6m/18ft 4in (standard)
Armament: 9 x 15cm/5.9in (3x3) and 6 x 8.8cm/3.46in HA (3x2) guns; 12 x 53.3cm/21in torpedo tubes (4x3)
Machinery: Geared steam turbines and cruising diesels, 6 boilers, 2 shafts
Power: 48,470kW/65,000shp (steam); 1,350kW/1,800bhp (diesel) for 32 knots maximum
Endurance: 1,372 tonnes/1,350 tons (oil) for 13,519km/7,300nm at 17 knots
Protection: 75–100mm/3–3.9in (belt); 75mm/3in (turrets)
Complement: 515

LEFT: An impression of *Nürnberg* at about 1936. She has a more built-up bridge structure than the earlier *Leipzig*, and no aircraft crane. Ceded to the Soviet Union post-war, she served the Russians as a training ship until the early 1960s.

Blücher class

LEFT: The *Hipper* was completed with a near-vertical stem that did nothing for her appearance. At her stem head she carries the crest of Admiral Franz Hipper, commander of the High Seas Fleet's battlecruiser squadron during World War I. Note the pronounced anti-torpedo bulge. ABOVE: In April 1940, the German Navy put troops ashore at six points in invading Norway. *Hipper* is seen here at Trondheim whence, together with four destroyers and four auxiliaries, she transported 700 military personnel with their equipment.

With no real design starting point, the designers of the Blüchers reportedly used the French *Algérie* as a yardstick although, in practice, there was little similarity. The Anglo-German Naval Agreement of June 1935 provided for the Germans to build up to 35 per cent of British tonnage in the major categories of surface ship. It was to be binding for six years, commencing January 1, 1937. Over this period the tabled German construction programme included no less than 18 cruisers, modern ships which would, qualitatively, pose real problems for the Royal Navy. British requests to slow the programme were ignored, with the first pair of heavy cruisers, *Blücher* and *Admiral Hipper*, being quickly laid down. The German action was completely legal in that the pair were permitted replacements for the (admittedly far smaller) *Berlin* and *Hamburg* of the rump fleet left to Germany by the Versailles Treaty. Before they were in the water, three further slightly enlarged units had been commenced.

Similarities with the *Algérie* included the flush-decked hull, of which the original bow design had quickly to be changed to one with increased sheer and freeboard, to reduce wetness and to improve overall seakeeping.

ABOVE: *Hipper* survived World War II only to come to this sorry end. Festooned with camouflage netting to safeguard against air attack, she was scuttled in a flooded dry dock in Kiel. Refloated, she was grounded nearby and scrapped.

In line with existing treaty requirements (to which Germany had not been a signatory), standard displacement was declared at 10,160 tonnes/10,000 tons, although the fact that this was exceeded (by over 40 per cent) was an open secret.

Earlier German armoured cruisers had employed an effective 21cm/8.2in gun, and the one concession made was to fit a new and untried 20.3cm/8in weapon to conform to Washington

LEFT: Following early forays into the Atlantic, *Hipper* spent most of her war in Norwegian waters. This view, from the signal bridge, looks over the lower rangefinder and forward turrets to the prominent air recognition insignia on the forecastle. The original design provided for triple 15cm/5.9in turrets. ABOVE: Too few to make any impact in ocean warfare, Germany's heavy warships were gradually confined to the Baltic and Norwegian waters, where *Hipper* is seen here, probably in company with the *Lützow* or *Scheer*. The threat posed by their presence prevented British units being sent to assist in the Pacific War.

standards. Like the Japanese, the Germans designed the ship to carry triple 15.5cm/6.1in guns but with the interchangeable option of twin 20.3cm/8in. The "light cruiser" version was never built.

Aesthetically, the ships were pleasing, business-like but graceful, their profile resembling that of the Bismarck-class battleship at a distance. The low navigating bridge was topped by a tower which replaced the earlier "battlemast". At its head was the main battery director, with back-up located lower down on both forward and after superstructures. Six twin 10.5cm/4.1in secondary mountings were carried, associated with four of the spherical-topped, stabilized "Wackeltopf" directors. Twelve torpedo tubes were fitted in four triple upper-deck mountings.

Although of a size that suggested commerce warfare, the Blüchers were not fitted with economical cruising diesels. Indeed, the advanced steam condition adopted for their machinery not only gave repeated problems but also resulted in a less than hoped for endurance.

A rotating catapult was located abaft the funnel. It was served by a pair of cranes, which handled both boats and the three hangared Arado 196 floatplanes.

Both *Admiral Hipper* and *Blücher* were completed in 1939. The former made a couple of raiding cruises but spent most of the war inactively in Norwegian waters. Barely six months after being commissioned, her sister was destroyed by Norwegian shore batteries while attempting to run German army units into Oslo during the invasion of April 1940.

The slightly enlarged *Prinz Eugen* was completed in July 1940 but, besides being involved in the high-profile episodes of the *Bismarck* pursuit (May 1941) and the up-channel dash of the *Scharnhorst* and *Gneisenau* (February 1942), she achieved little of note. As an American post-war prize, she was expended as a target ship in the course of the trials at Bikini Atoll.

ABOVE: **Following her cession to the United States in 1945, the *Prinz Eugen* was sailed there and much photographed. In contrast with the earlier *Hipper* (see opposite) she has the so-called "Atlantic" bow, with greater sheer and flare, and no external bulges. Note the complete radar outfit.**

Almost complete in 1942, the *Seydlitz* was dismantled for conversion to a light aircraft carrier, the project never being completed. Also never completed, the *Lützow* was transferred to the Soviet Navy in 1940 under the terms of the "non-aggression" pact.

ABOVE: **Following technical assessment and a publicity tour of American ports, the *Prinz Eugen* was expended by the US Navy in the 1946 Bikini A-bomb tests. Seen here on arrival, she is still complete with her Arado floatplane. Note the American ensign.**

Blücher class

	Built	Commissioned
Admiral Hipper	Blohm n. Voss, Hamburg	April 29, 1939
Blücher	Deutsche Werke, Kiel	September 20, 1939
Lützow	Deschimag, Bremen	
Prinz Eugen	Germania, Kiel	August 1, 1940
Seydlitz	Deschimag, Bremen	

Admiral Hipper

Displacement: 14,275 tonnes/14,050 tons (standard); 18,492 tonnes/18,200 tons (full load)
Length: 195.5m/641ft 9in (wl); 205m/672ft 10in (oa)
Beam: 21.3m/69ft 10in
Draught: 5.8m/19ft (standard)
Armament: 8 x 20.3cm/8in (4x2) and 12 x 10.5cm/4.1in (6x2) guns; 12 x 53.3cm/21in torpedo tubes (4x3)
Machinery: Geared steam turbines, 12 boilers, 3 shafts
Power: 98,432kW/132,000shp for 32 knots
Endurance: 3,688 tonnes/3,630 tons (oil) for 8,148km/4,400nm at 19 knots
Protection: 80mm/3.1in (vertical belt); 30–50mm/1.18–2in (protective decks); 70–105mm/2.76–4.1in (turrets)
Complement: 1,390

Kirov, Chapaev and Sverdlov classes

Following the 1917 revolution the Soviet Navy was neglected, its design and construction base eroded as the state wrestled with reorganizing its vast population, infrastructure and resources. Five-year plans were eventually instigated to modernize the fleet and, in the absence of indigenous expertise, design and construction supervision for a new class of cruiser, the *Kirov* was entrusted to the Italian firm of Ansaldo. The Soviet Union was not bound by the limitations of the Washington Treaty but the usually quoted figure of 8,941 tonnes/8,800 tons standard displacement was probably deliberately understated. The Kirov class was slightly longer, narrower and finer than the newly completed Italian Zara class. They were more lightly protected and carried three triple 180mm/7.1in guns, against the four twin 203mm/8in mountings of the Italians. The former were up to 19 percent heavier than officially stated and it is probable that the Kirov class were actually closer to 10,160 tonnes/10,000 tons.

ABOVE: Ansaldo at Genoa are believed to be the source of the original design of the Kirov class. Dating from the late 1930s, it certainly echoes Italian style of the period, particularly in the heavy tetrapod structure above the bridge. This unit, unusually, has the tripod mainmast abaft the after funnel.

Considerably disrupted by World War II, the programme saw only five (*Kalinin*, *Kirov*, *Maksim Gorki*, *Molotov* and *Voroshilov)* completed, with a further two (*Kaganovitch* and *Zhelezniakov)* destroyed before launch.

At the same time a class of 152mm/6in "light" cruisers, the Chapaev class was laid down. At 187m/613ft 6in by 17.5m/57ft 5in they were of a similar size with, but finer than, the Kirov class. In profile, they were very similar to the Italian Trento class but with four triple 152mm/6in turrets in place of the latter's four twin 203mm/8in. Powered for a respectable 34 knots, all could carry up to 120 mines on deck. All four of the class (*Chapaev*, *Chkalov*, *Kuibyshev* and *Zhelezniakov* [II]) were completed post-war, between 1948 and 1950.

LEFT: Cleaning gun barrels aboard a Kirov. Unusually for so late a date, the guns can be seen to have been designed into a common sleeve and, therefore, not capable of being elevated or depressed independently.

ABOVE: An unidentified "Improved Kirov", which differs from the example above in having a prominent director tower located on the bridge structure ahead of a tripod foremast, and the mainmast moved ahead of the after funnel. Torpedo tubes have been landed in favour of large motor launches.

At about 11,481 tonnes/11,300 tons, the Chapaev class offered a useful and balanced design that, suitably "stretched" by Soviet designers, begat the 13,716-tonne/13,500-ton Sverdlov class of the early 1950s. Handsome ships, these retained the old Italian features of a tower-type bridge structure and substantial tripod mainmast close ahead of the after funnel. The funnels themselves were more closely spaced, however, and the forecastle deck was extended well aft.

Larger even than the American Worcester class, the Sverdlov class was anachronistic, conventional, gun-armed cruisers born into the missile age. Of the 24 believed to have been planned, only 14 were actually completed. Their Cold War role was as commerce destroyers, a purpose for which they were endowed with considerable range.

From the outset, individual ships varied in details, particularly with respect to their electronic instrumentation. All appear to have had permanent mine rails let into the after deck.

As such large ships, they attracted some criticism for the choice of a 152mm/6in main battery. This was to overlook that Soviet ships were expected to operate in heavy northern and oceanic conditions. Size is of obvious benefit, contributing to dryness, steadiness and ability to maintain speed. The designers had been able to resist the common navy blandishments to arm the ship to the limit that it can accommodate, thus negating the size advantage.

During the early 1970s the Admiral Senyavin and Zhdanov were converted to command cruisers. Major topside modifications included the suppression of two and one after turret respectively to create helicopter facilities and accommodation for a short range SA-N-4 SAM system.

One unit (Dzerzhinski) was converted to deploy a medium-range SA-N-2 SAM system, the installation of which displaced the "X" turret. No others were similarly modified, the Russians repeating the American experience of finding that volume-critical systems do not fit satisfactorily into weight-critical hulls.

Totally obsolete by the 1980s, the Sverdlov class was, nonetheless, retired only slowly, being valuable as gun-armed fire-support ships and as impressive platforms for "showing the flag" in the Third World. They were among the last conventional cruisers in service.

ABOVE: **In many respects, the Sverdlovs were enlarged Kirovs with a fourth triple turret. The last significant class of conventional cruisers, they were obsolete even when new. Note the size of the fully stabilized twin 100mm/3.94in mountings and German World War II pattern directors on the Aleksandr Suvorov.**

Sverdlov class

	Built	Commissioned
Admiral Lazerev	Baltic Shipyard, Leningrad	November 1952
Admiral Nakhimov	Severodvinsk, Shipyard	1952
Admiral Senyavin	Severodvinsk Shipyard	July 1954
Admiral Ushakov	Baltic Shipyard, Leningrad	August 1953
Aleksandr Nevski	Marti Shipyard, Nikolaev	1952
Aleksandr Suvorov	Marti Shipyard, Nikolaev	1953
Dmitri Pozharski	Baltic Shipyard, Leningrad	1953
Dzerzhinski	Amur Shipyard, Komsomolsk	1954
Mikhail Kutuzov	Marti Shipyard, Nilolaev	1955
Molotovsk	Severodvinsk Shipyard	September 1954
Murmansk	Severodvinsk Shipyard	1955
Ordzhonikidze	Amur Shipyard, Komsomolsk	1952
Sverdlov	Baltic Shipyard, Leningrad	1951
Zhdanov	Baltic Shipyard, Leningrad	January 1952

ABOVE: **This 1957 picture of Sverdlov clearly shows her Italian lineage. The class was built with an eye to commerce raiding but, as conventionally armed cruisers in a missile-controlled environment, they would have been vulnerable. Like their foreign peers, they were difficult to modernize.**

Sverdlov class (as built)

Displacement: 13,716 tonnes/13,500 tons (standard); 18,594 tonnes/18,300 tons (full load)
Length: 200m/656ft 6in (bp); 210m/689ft 4in (oa)
Beam: 21.5m/70ft 7in
Draught: 7.2m/23ft 8in
Armament: 12 x 152mm/6in (4x3) and 12 x 100mm/3.9in (6x2) guns; 140 mines
Machinery: Geared steam turbines, 6 boilers, 2 shafts
Power: 82,027kW/110,000shp for 32 knots
Endurance: 3,860 tonnes/3,800 tons (oil) for 18,520km/10,000nm at 13 knots
Protection: 25–50mm/1–2in and 50–75mm/2–3in (protective decks); 75–100mm/3–3.9in (turrets)
Complement: About 1,000

FAR LEFT: **Old wine in new bottles.** *Mendez Nuñez* **was modernized and rearmed as an AA cruiser during 1944–47. Her 120mm/4.7in gun mountings were redesigned for higher elevation although there is little evidence that they were effectively radar-laid. Note two funnels and new bow form.**

ABOVE LEFT: **As built, the** *Mendez Nuñez* **shows her close relationship with British cruiser design of late World War I. The lack of forward sheer resulted in wet ships but, instead of a "trawler bow", the Spanish opted for the design at left.**

Mendez Nuñez class

Heavily influenced by the pre-World War I British Birmingham-class design, the one-off *Reina Victoria Eugenia* was completed by Ferrol Dockyard in 1922 as Spain's first "modern" cruiser. Her nine single 152mm/6in guns were necessarily disposed, however, so as to give only five in broadside. During the Spanish Civil War (1936–39), she was extensively rebuilt, her royal name being changed to *Republica*, and then again to *Navarra*. Funnels were reduced from three to two and an unlovely tower bridge structure added. By virtually eliminating masts, cutting down the after deck by one level and suppressing three mountings, it was possible to put six single guns on the centreline, permitting an improved six-gun broadside.

Building in parallel at Ferrol were the near-sisters *Don Blas Lezo* and *Mendez Nuñez*, of the same length as the earlier ship but a full 1.2m/4ft less in the beam. This combined with an 80 per cent increase in shaft horsepower and a six-gun armament (supplemented by two twin torpedo tube mountings) permitted a 3.5-knot increase in speed. There was also a considerable decrease in the thickness of the belt armour. As completed, the pair was roughly equivalent to the British D-class of 1918. All three were seven to eight years under construction.

Following her sister's loss by stranding in 1932, the *Mendez Nuñez* was modernized during 1944–47. Rearmed as an anti-aircraft (AA) cruiser, she was given eight 120mm/4.7in guns on high-angle single mountings, unusually, three being superimposed at either end. The torpedo armament was increased to two triple tubes. The hull was reduced by one level from the new blockhouse bridge, aft, while two capped and trunked funnels replaced the original three. A new, curved bow profile and increased forward sheer completed a distinctive and rakish new look. With the commissioning of new tonnage, the ship was stricken for disposal in the late 1950s.

Mendez Nuñez class

	Built	Commissioned
Don Blas Lezo	Ferrol Dockyard	November 4, 1924
Mendez Nuñez	Ferrol Dockyard	March 3, 1923

Mendez Nuñez (as rebuilt)

Displacement: 4,755 tonnes/4,680 tons (standard); 6,147 tonnes/6,050 tons (full load)
Length: 134m/440ft (bp); 140.7m/462ft (oa)
Beam: 14m/46ft
Draught: 4.4m/14ft 4in (standard)
Armament: 8 x 120mm/4.7in (8x1) guns; 6 x 533mm/21in torpedo tubes (2x3)
Machinery: Geared steam turbines, 12 boilers, 4 shafts
Power: 33,556kW/45,000shp for 29 knots
Endurance: 737 tonnes/725 tons (oil) and 812 tonnes/800 tons (coal) for 9,260nm/5,000nm at 13 knots
Protection: 12–25mm/0.47–1in (belt); 25mm/1in (protective deck)
Complement: 370

ABOVE: **Never modernized, the** *Don Blas Lezo* **(or** *Blas de Lezo***) retained her original appearance until her disposal after 1945. Her World War I features included the prominent armoured conning tower before the bridge structure and the sided 15cm/5.9in guns flanking the forward funnel.**

Galicia class

Continuing the modernization of the Spanish fleet, the Ferrol Dockyard produced the three, more ambitious Galicia class in an overlapping programme with the Mendez Nuñez class, which were British-designed and effectively remodelled versions of the Royal Navy E-class. The nameship was built as the *Principe Alfonso*, becoming the *Libertad*, then *Galicia* during the Civil War. The *Cervantes*, last-built, had slight differences in armament.

As designed, the class had its eight 152mm/6in guns disposed messily, with twin mountings superfiring singles at either end and with a third twin mounting located amidships. Protection and propulsive power were on a similar scale to those of the E-class, although the machinery layout was more concentrated. For their day, the Galicia class was considered fast, being powered at 33 knots for the specific function of out-running enemy commerce raiders. Only *Cervantes* took 12 torpedo tubes, the others six.

Original bridge structures were small, with fire control exercised from a short tripod foremast but, during the course of the 1940–46 reconstruction, this changed to a heavy, compact bridge with director tower and the light masting then typical of Spanish warships. The funnels gained prominent caps and the main battery was reorganized with four twin 152mm/6in mountings disposed in orthodox symmetry. This freed space in the after waist for an aircraft, and associated crane and catapult. By now somewhat anachronistic, these were only retained for any length of time by the *Cervantes*.

For secondary armament, *Galicia* and *Cervantes* had four twin 88mm/3.46in mountings, the *Cervera* two twin 105mm/4.1in guns. Both calibres suggest that the weapons may have been German sourced.

ABOVE: **The *Cervera*'s eight 152mm/6in guns were arranged unusually, with "A" and "Y" mountings (hidden by awnings) being singles, while "B", "Q" (amidships) and "X" were twins. This post-war picture shows her with her pendants painted up NATO-style and with new electronics.**

Although the *Cervantes* was heavily damaged by torpedo (from an Italian submarine) while serving as the Republican flagship during the Civil War, the class proved to be durable, giving good service until being stricken in 1966.

Galicia class

	Built	Commissioned
Almirante Cervera	Ferrol Dockyard	October 16, 1925
Galicia	Ferrol Dockyard	January 3, 1925
Miguel de Cervantes	Ferrol Dockyard	May 19, 1928

Galicia (as modernized)

Displacement: 8,382 tonnes/8,250 tons (standard); 10,059 tonnes/9,900 tons (full load)
Length: 175.2m/575ft (bp); 176.5m/579ft 6in (oa)
Beam: 16.5m/54ft
Draught: 5m/16ft 6in (standard)
Armament: 8 x 152mm/6in (4x2) and 8 x 88mm/3.46in (4x2) guns; 6 x 533mm/21in torpedo tubes (2x3)
Machinery: Geared steam turbines, 8 boilers, 4 shafts
Power: 59,656kW/80,000shp for 33 knots
Endurance: 1,727 tonnes/1,700 tons (oil) for 9,260km/5,000nm at 15 knots
Protection: 35–75mm/1.38–3in (belt); 25mm/1in (protective deck)
Complement: 565

ABOVE: **Built somewhat later, the *Cervantes* had her armament arranged conventionally, forward and aft. This allowed space abaft the funnels for a catapult and floatplane. The rather unusually configured handling crane jib was lowered to deck level when not in use.**

LEFT: The *Canarias* as rebuilt in the 1950s to the original two-funnelled design. She is probably laying in the eponymous islands, for the merchantman to the left is a Fred Olsen "tomato boat" that traded there regularly. ABOVE: The stump foremast, visible here, was an original fitting, but had been removed by the end of World War II. The original design trunked the funnels of a British County into two, but the Spanish took it a stage further with a single, arched casing that also incorporated searchlights.

Canarias class

The final British cruiser design acquired by the Spanish at this time was based on that of the County class. Two units were built, their construction taxing the nascent Spanish shipbuilding industry to the utmost. Laid down in 1928, they were not completed until 1936. The original British-built County class, with their gently raked funnels and masts had considerable dignity. The Spanish ships had near-identical hulls and main batteries, but were finished with bridge and funnel casing of extraordinary bulk and surpassing ugliness – "Odeon" architecture at its worst. Of proportions that would have graced an aircraft carrier, the funnel was heavily trunked to exhaust all boilers, while incorporating searchlight platforms. The huge block of bridgework appeared truncated in the absence of a foremast, all flag-signalling being conducted from a yard on the light mainmast.

Unlike the British, the Spanish were not tightly constrained by Washington Treaty limitations on displacement. They therefore added twelve fixed torpedo tubes, grouped in threes and firing on the beam from main deck level, to the secondary battery of eight 119mm/ 4.7in guns in open HA mountings. Considerably more protection was also worked in. However, although a catapult and aircraft facilities were originally specified, they appear to have never been fitted.

While still a comparatively new ship, the *Baleares* was torpedoed and sunk during March 1938 in the only event approaching a fleet encounter of the Civil War. She was serving as Nationalist flagship, while the Republicans were effectively under Soviet Russian command.

The lone *Canarias* underwent a major refit in the early 1950s, losing her torpedo tubes, and acquiring a light tripod foremast and the two vertical funnels with which she was first designed. Greatly improved in appearance, she served until 1975. Representing considerable investment, the pair were a disappointment in never being able to realize their potential.

Canarias class

	Built	Commissioned
Baleares	Soc. Español de Construccion Navale, Ferrol	1936
Canarias	Soc. Español de Construccion Navale, Ferrol	September 10, 1936

ABOVE: The ill-starred *Baleares*, torpedoed and sunk during the Civil War. For some reason, "Y" turret has been landed, although this may be because the twin 203mm/8in mounting, originally developed for the Counties, was known for its mechanical shortcomings.

Canarias (as built)

Displacement: 10,841 tonnes/10,670 tons (standard); 12,446 tonnes/12,250 tons (full load)
Length: 181.6m/596ft (bp); 192,8m/636ft (oa)
Beam: 19.5m/64ft
Draught: 5.3m/17ft 4in (standard)
Armament: 8 x 203mm/8in (4x2) and 8 x 119mm/4.7in HA (8x1) guns; 12 x 533mm/21in torpedo tubes (4x3)
Machinery: Geared steam turbines, 8 boilers, 4 shafts
Power: 67,113kW/90,000shp for 33 knots
Endurance: 2,844 tonnes/2,800 tons (oil) for 14,816km/8,000nm at 15 knots
Protection: 36–50mm/1.4–2in (belt); 25mm/1in (turrets)
Complement: 765

Gotland

Traditionally neutral in modern times, Sweden has a long and relatively deserted coastline. Shallow and fringed with skerries, it is not easy to police by conventional naval craft, consequently aircraft are generally more effective.

Because the Swedish fleet is necessarily small, its ships need to fulfil more than a single function, and the *Gotland*, laid down in 1930, was configured as a small cruiser forward and aviation ship aft. Her concept pre-dated those of the Japanese Tone and Ise classes, and modern hybrids such as the Russian Moskva class, French *Jeanne d'Arc* and Italian *Vittorio Veneto*.

On an ice-strengthened, flush-decked hull, the *Gotland* had an unusual

disposition for her six 152mm/6in guns. One twin turret fired forward, flanked by single weapons located in casemates, in the latter's last-recorded use. A second twin turret fired aft, across the flight deck.

The flight deck was a lightly constructed spar deck, which covered the after third of the ship's length. It was laid with three fore-and-aft tracks bearing eight self-propelled trolleys, each of which carried a Hawker Osprey floatplane with wings folded. Three more knocked-down aircraft could be stowed below. Forward of the tracks was a turntable-mounted, compressed air catapult which could be aligned with any of the tracks. Aircraft were recovered by a crane located right aft. The tracks had the alternative use, typical on Swedish ships, of accommodating up to 100 mines, which were laid over the stern.

Obsolete by 1943, the *Gotland* lost her aircraft-related equipment, which was replaced on the spar deck by modern anti-aircraft (AA) weapons. The ship served in the dual role of AA and training cruiser until 1955, when she was taken in hand for modernization. The two casemated 152mm/6in and all four

LEFT: **This late-1930s photograph shows the attractive lines of the *Gotland*'s ice-strengthened hull. The starboard 152mm/6in casemate and the strange "pillar-box" director tower are also evident. Soon afterward, the aviation fittings would be removed in favour of further AA guns.**

TOP: **Seen here in her original condition, the *Gotland* has one of her Osprey floatplanes right aft. Note how the bridge is flanked by single 152mm/6in guns in casemates. The after twin turret, not very evident, is flanked by triple torpedo tube mountings.**
ABOVE: **This outboard profile shows rather more clearly the arrangement of this hybrid cruiser/ aviation ship. The inherent weakness, of course, is that aviation ships are complex, fragile things that have no business pretending that they can absorb damage while acting as cruisers.**

75mm/2.95in guns were landed in favour of additional 40mm/1.57in weapons, together with modern fire-control equipment. The *Gotland* was sent for scrap in 1962.

Gotland (as built)

Built: AB Götaverken, Göteborg
Commissioned: December 16, 1934
Displacement: 4,826 tonnes/4,750 tons (standard); 5,639 tonnes/5,550 tons (full load)
Length: 130.2m/426ft 6in (wl); 133.4m/437ft 6in (oa)
Beam: 15.4m/50ft 7in
Draught: 5m/16ft 6in (standard)
Armament: 6 x 152mm/6in (2x2/2x1) and 4 x 75mm/2.95in (4x1) guns; 6 x 533mm/21in torpedo tubes (2x3)
Machinery: Geared steam turbines, 4 boilers, 2 shafts
Power: 24,600kW/33,000shp for 27.5 knots
Endurance: 853 tonnes/840 tons (oil) for 7,400km/4,000nm at 12 knots
Protection: 28–50mm/1.1–2in (protective deck); 28–50mm/1.1–2in (turrets)
Complement: 450

Tre Kronor class

Unique in appearance, the *Tre Kronor* (Three Crowns) and *Gota Lejon* (Gothic Lion) were laid down in 1943 to underline Sweden's intention to keep her water neutral. Neither, however, could be completed before 1947.

Due to their heavy, ice-class plating, the hulls looked beautifully faired, the belt being almost invisible. However, the two rows of scuttles that flanked the machinery spaces showed it to be quite shallow. The hull was of a long-forecastle type, with tripled torpedo tubes located at the break.

Unusually the main battery was of seven guns, disposed as a triple 152mm/6in turret forward and two superfiring twins located aft. All were of semi-automatic Bofors design and capable of a 70-degree elevation.

The ships were designed without masts, having only spreaders for W/T aerials. However, raked tripods were fitted prior to their entry into service. The funnels were also most distinctive. Being streamlined and with pronounced rake, they echoed mercantile conventions of the time, Sweden being a major shipbuilder.

As built, the bridge structure was also streamlined and with numerous platforms. Sweden's fear of a neighbouring nuclear exchange, however, resulted in the general enclosure and "cleaning-up" of a ship's structures. As a result, both ships acquired squared-off, blockhouse-style bridges in 1951–52. The secondary 40mm/1.57in armament was also considerably enhanced. Like most Swedish ships, they were equipped with permanent minelaying rails.

Tre Kronor had a comparatively short life, being paid off in 1964. Soon afterwards, Sweden adopted the policy that, as large fighting ships would not survive a nuclear exchange in the confined Baltic Sea, the future fleet would comprise only small combatants and submarines, housed in nuclear-bomb-proof shelters. All warships of destroyer size and above accordingly went for disposal. As part of this procedure, the *Gota Lejon* was purchased by Chile in 1971. As the *Latorre*, she served until the early 1980s.

Tre Kronor class

	Built	Commissioned
Gota Lejon	Erikoberg Mek. Verstad, Göteborg	December 15, 1947
Tre Kronor	Götaverken, Göteborg	October 18, 1947

Tre Kronor class (after 1951–52 refit)

Displacement: 8,128 tonnes/8,000 tons (standard); 10,160 tonnes/10,000 tons (full load)
Length: 180m/590ft 6in (wl); 181.9m/597ft (oa)
Beam: 16.5m/54ft 2in
Draught: 5.9m/19ft 6in (standard)
Armament: 7 x 152mm/6in (1x3/2x2) and 27 x 40mm/1.57in (1x4/10x2/3x1) guns; 6 x 813mm/32in torpedo tubes (2x3)
Machinery: Geared steam turbines, 4 boilers, 2 shafts
Power: 7,460kW/100,000shp for 33 knots
Protection: 75–125mm/2.95–4.92in (vertical belt)
Complement: 455

ABOVE: *Tre Kronor*'s Bofors-designed 152mm/6in guns were credited with an exceptional 70-degree elevation, making them suitable for long-range AA barrage. On her mainmast is British-pattern air-search and height-finding radar of 1945 vintage. The surface search radar is Dutch-sourced.

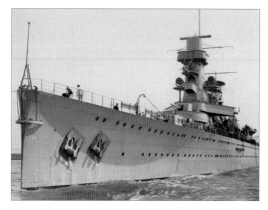

LEFT: **The complexity of large combatants taxed the resources of the small Dutch constructive design department to the limit and German influence is plain to see. Although much smaller and more lightly armed, the *de Ruyter* has more than a passing resemblance to the German "pocket battleships", then coming into service.** ABOVE: **Weight distribution was apparently a problem for the *de Ruyter* for, although she has two twin 15cm/5.9in aft, the forward twin is superfired by a single at O1 level. The unique funnel was designed to keep smoke clear of the bridge structure.**

Java class and *de Ruyter*

Neutral during World War I, the Netherlands nonetheless felt the need to update their naval presence in their extensive East Indies Empire. Two new ships, *Java* and *Sumatra*, were thus laid down in 1916. At 6,757 tonnes/6,650 tons and armed with ten 15cm/5.9in guns, they were rather larger and better armed, but slower, than contemporary British and German fleet cruisers.

Armament, machinery and considerable know-how stemmed from German sources and so it was not surprising that the delivery date of April 1918 was not achieved. By the time that the pair was completed in 1925–26,

cruiser design had moved on under the impetus of the 1921–22 Washington Treaty, and the ships were obsolescent. A third unit, the marginally larger *Celebes*, was approved in 1917 but, little advanced, was cancelled in 1919.

Alterations during the 1930s included the suppression of the tall signal masts in favour of a German-style "battlemast" forward and a stump mainmast. A gantry was added between the funnels to support lifting gear for two float planes.

During the early 1930s the Netherlands Navy again secured approval for a third cruiser. She, the *de Ruyter*, was criticized for being

under-armed but her fewer guns were much more efficiently arranged. In profile, she was strongly reminiscent of a German "pocket battleship", although with superimposed gun mountings. As built, her single vertical stack had a "parasol" cap, which was soon removed. The tower-like bridge structure was topped-off with a long-base optical rangefinder, and masting was confined to light poles and W/T spreaders. Finer-lined, the *de Ruyter* was 2 knots faster than the Javas.

Both *de Ruyter* and *Java* were lost in the Far East early in 1942 but the *Sumatra*, little used, was expended as part of the Gooseberry breakwater off Normandy in June 1944.

ABOVE: **A 1930s modernization saw the *Java*'s tall pole masts reduced, as shown here. The *Java*'s reduced armament reflects her training status.**

de Ruyter

Displacement: 6,553 tonnes/6,450 tons (standard); 7,951 tonnes/7,825 tons (full load)
Length: 170.8m/560ft 8in (oa)
Beam: 15.7m/51ft 5in
Draught: 5m/16ft 4in (standard)
Armament: 7 x 15cm/5.9in (3x2/1x1) and 10 x 40mm/1.57in guns
Machinery: Geared steam turbines, 6 boilers, 2 shafts
Power: 49,216kW/66,000shp for 32 knots
Endurance: 1,320 tonnes/1,300 tons (oil) for 12,594km/6,800nm at 12 knots
Protection: 30–50mm/1.18–2in (belt); 30mm/1.18in (protective deck); 30mm/1.18in (gunhouses)
Complement: 437

Java class and *de Ruyter*

	Built	Commissioned
Java	de Schelde, Vlissingen	May 1, 1925
Sumatra	Nederlandsche Sch. Maats, Amsterdam	May 26, 1926
de Ruyter	Wilton-Fijenoord, Rotterdam	September 16, 1936

Tromp class

Authorized in 1935, this interesting little pair equated roughly to the British D-class in terms of size and armament. Although more modern, they shared an auxiliary function as leaders of destroyer flotillas, also common to the Imperial Japanese Navy, which both were destined to meet. Their displacement was probably the smallest that could comfortably combine six 15cm/5.9in guns with a 32.5-knot speed

and light protection. Even so, their machinery was very concentrated and vulnerable to a single hit.

Fate decreed that the two, instead of being identical sisters, were completed very differently. The reason for this was that they were ordered from the same yard, which had only one suitable slipway. First-of-class *Tromp* was launched in May 1937. *Heemskerck* was commenced immediately but launched in mid-September 1939. With the German invasion of May 1940 (by which time the *Tromp* was already in the Far East), the incomplete *Heemskerck* was taken to Britain for completion. Portsmouth Dockyard armed her with five twin 102mm/4in high-angle (HA) guns, standard in the Royal Navy.

Significantly the Dutch contributed the advanced Hazemeyer stabilized fire-control system, later to be further developed by the British. The *Heemskerck* made an excellent anti-aircraft (AA) escort but, with the entry of Japan into the war in December 1941, she was sent east.

Both ships were fortunate. *Tromp*, the only one to carry the floatplane for which they were designed, was damaged in February 1942 and sent to Australia for

ABOVE LEFT: **The concept of an inexpensive light cruiser/destroyer leader was given a new interpretation in the two Tromps, probably the smallest ships that could carry three twin 15cm/5.9in mountings. Their destroyer-like appearance is belied by the long-base rangefinder atop the bridge structure.** ABOVE: **Late in her career,** *Tromp* **is seen at the 1953 British Coronation Review. She has been fitted with new, Bofors-pattern 15cm/5.9in mountings and a modern range of electronics. Aircraft fittings have long been removed but the modified funnel still appears to have an eddy problem.**

repairs. She thus missed the subsequent virtual annihilation of the ABDA (Australian, British, Dutch and American) forces. *Heemskerck* likewise missed this fate simply through arriving too late. Although prematurely aged by over-use both survived the war, served until the mid-1950s.

ABOVE: **Towed to Britain for completion in 1940,** *Heemskerck* **was given standard 102mm/4in twins and British electronics.**

Tromp

Displacement: 4,216 tonnes/4,150 tons (standard); 4,927 tonnes/4,850 tons (full load)
Length: 130m/425ft 6in (bp); 131.9m/433ft (oa)
Beam: 12.4m/40ft 9in
Draught: 4.6m/15ft (maximum)
Armament: 6 x 15cm/5.9in (3x2) and 4 x 40mm/1.57in (2x2) guns
Machinery: Geared steam turbines, 4 boilers, 2 shafts
Power: 41,759kW/56,000shp for 32.5 knots
Endurance: 874 tonnes/860 tons (oil) for 7,778km/4,200nm at 15 knots
Protection: 50–65mm/2–2.56in (belt); 36mm/1.42in (protective deck)
Complement: 380

Tromp class

	Built	Commissioned
Tromp	Nederlandsche Sch. Maats, Amsterdam	1939
Jacob van Heemskerck	Nederlandsche Sch. Maats, Amsterdam	1941

LEFT: **Much altered over the years, the two Zeven Provinciën class were laid down prior to World War II but completed post-war as orthodox 152mm/6in cruisers. *De Ruyter* remained in this configuration but the lead ship, seen here, was converted 1962–64 as a single-ended Terrier SAM guided-missile cruiser.**

de Zeven Provinciën class

Intended as replacements for the Javas, this pair first resembled an extrapolation of the de Ruyter of 1936, but with ten 152mm/6in guns, disposed in two twin and two triple turrets. Barely commenced when the Netherlands were overrun in 1940, the two hulls were advanced slowly under German supervision. It was their influence that gave the de Ruyter the "Atlantic bow" which made her slightly longer than her sister.

By 1945, de Zeven Provinciën had been launched but the Eendracht (late Kijkduin) was still on the stocks. Long since ordered from Bofors, their gun mountings had been incorporated into the Swedish Tre Kronors.

It was decided to complete the two ships to a revised design that incorporated the advances made during the war. Again, an all Bofors outfit was specified – four twin 152mm/6in, four stabilized twin 57mm/2.24in and six twin 40mm/1.57in guns.

Machinery was rearranged on the unit system, requiring two funnels against the de Ruyter's one. Soon after completion, the tripod mainmast was relocated from its position abaft the after funnel to a position immediately before it. The forward funnel was incorporated into the foremast.

Before completion, the Eendracht was renamed to commemorate the de Ruyter, lost in 1942. The ships also exchanged names.

During the early 1960s, both were slated for conversion to the American-sourced Terrier surface-to-air missile (SAM) system but cost considerations saw only the nameship so modified. In the process, she lost her after turrets and had the after deck raised by one level, making the hull flush-decked.

In 1937 the unconverted de Ruyter was sold to Peru, being renamed Almirante Grau. Three years later she was joined by her sister, which, herself assumed the name Grau, the earlier ship being renamed Aguirre, Before transfer, de Zeven Provinciën was stripped of her Terrier system, her after end being modified for the accommodation and operation of helicopters.

de Zeven Provinciën class

	Built	Commissioned
de Ruyter	Wilton-Fijenoord, Rotterdam	November 18, 1953
de Zeven Provinciën	Rotterdam Drydock Company	December 17, 1953

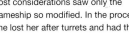

de Zeven Provinciën (as built)

Displacement: 9,906 tonnes/9,750 tons (standard); 12,116 tonnes/11,925 tons (full load)
Length: 180m/590ft 6in (bp); 185.5m/609ft (oa)
Beam: 17.3m/56ft 8in
Draught: 5.6m/18ft 6in (standard)
Armament: 8 x 152mm/6in (4x2), 8 x 57mm/2.24in and 8 x 40mm/1.57in guns
Machinery: Geared steam turbines, 4 boilers, 2 shafts
Power: 63,384kW/85,000shp for 32 knots
Endurance: 12,778km/6,900m at 12 knots
Protection: 75–100mm/2.95–3.94in (belt); 25+25mm/1+1in (protective decks)
Complement: 965

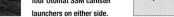

LEFT: *De Zeven Provinciën* in her original configuration. Following sale to Peru her after end, stripped of Terrier, was converted for flight pad and hangar space for three large helicopters. *De Ruyter* kept her full main battery but had two elevated platforms added amidships, supporting four Otomat SSM canister launchers on either side.

LEFT: Built in Italy in the late 1920s, the two Browns bear comparison with contemporary Italian cruisers. The choice of 190mm/7.5in guns was unusual. A new calibre for the Argentinians, it had been a popular size in the British Royal Navy and was at that time fitted in the Improved Birminghams. ABOVE: The size of the *Veinticinco de Mayo*'s (*25 de Mayo*'s) guns is clearly visible. Although only three twin mountings were carried they, together with protection, made the pair considerably overweight and tender. As a weight-saving measure, the Italian-pattern director is supported on a tripod, rather than a more rigid tetrapod.

Almirante Brown class

Included in the Argentine Navy's ten-year expansion and modernization programme of 1926 was a class of three heavy cruisers. This category of ship was much in vogue at the time because of the "cruiser race" developing between the signatories of the Washington Treaty. In the event, fiscal restraints reduced the class to only two ships.

At the same time Italy was constructing her first pair of "treaty cruisers", the Trento class. They were of strikingly attractive and modern design and the Argentine Navy, already operating ships of Italian origin, ordered what was effectively a pair of diminutives. The *Veinticinco de Mayo* (*25 de Mayo*) was laid down in the same yard as the *Trento*, just a month after the latter's launch in October 1927. She inherited a very similar arrangement of forward superstructure – funnel, heavy tripod foremast, bridge and superimposed turrets. In place of the

Trento's flush-decked hull, however, that of the Brown class was of the long forecastle deck type, with the break just forward of the after turret.

In British terms, the Brown class equated in size to the yet-to-be-built Leander class, to which there was also a passing resemblance, emphasized by the single, dominant funnel which, in both cases, exhausted adjacent boiler spaces. A major difference lay in the heavier 190mm/7.5in calibre of the Brown class main battery, an unusual size that may have had its origins in the Elswick-manufactured guns mounted uniquely in the earlier British Hawkins class. Because of their size and weight, only three twin turrets were mounted. A useful dual-purposes (DP) secondary battery of six twin 100mm/3.9in guns was also carried.

Other than the tripod for supporting the fire control arrangement, masting was very light. A catapult and floatplane (typically a Vought OZU Corsair) were located between funnel and mainmast.

Of well-balanced design, the Brown class served until 1961.

Almirante Brown class

	Built	Commissioned
Almirante Brown	Orlando, Sestri Ponente	September 16, 1931
Veinticinco de Mayo (*25 de Mayo*)	Orlando, Livorno	September 16, 1931

Almirante Brown class

Displacement: 6,909 tonnes/6,800 tons (standard); 8,941 tonnes/8,800 tons (full load)
Length: 163.1m/535ft 5in (bp); 166.2m/545ft 9in (oa)
Beam: 17.9m/58ft 7in
Draught: 5m/16ft 3in (standard)
Armament: 6 x 190mm/7.5in (3x2); 12 x 100mm/3.9in (6x2) guns; 6 x 533mm/21in torpedo tubes (2x3)
Machinery: Geared steam turbines, 6 boilers, 2 shafts
Power: 63,384kW/85,000shp for 32 knots
Endurance: 2,336 tonnes/2,300 tons (oil) for 14,816km/8,000nm at 14 knots
Protection: 36–70mm/1.18–2.76in (belt); 25mm/1in (protective deck); 50mm/2in (turrets)
Complement: 600

LEFT: The *25 de Mayo* towards the end of her career in the 1950s. She has landed her catapult and pole masts, gaining an Italian-style tripod mainmast.

La Argentina

Following the worst of the 1930s recession, the Argentine Navy was able to order a third cruiser to complement the Brown class. Following considerable diplomatic pressure, British yards secured the order for not only the cruiser but also a flotilla of destroyers.

Bearing the proud name of *La Argentina*, the cruiser was laid down in January 1936. Although intended to be completed as part of a trio with the Brown class, the ship's design complicated logistics by introducing a new range of gun calibres.

Fitted as a training cruiser, the ship resembled the British Arethusa class, "stretched" by some 10m/32ft 10in. On a moderate 6,705 tonnes/6,600 tons displacement she carried three triple 152mm/6in mountings, (of the same pattern as those then being fitted to the British Southampton class) in place of the three twins of the 5,334-tonne/ 5,250-ton Arethusa class. Where the latter had a secondary armament of four twin 102mm/4in high-angle (HA) guns, *La Argentina* carried only singles. The British ships had a short forecastle deck but, in order to provide extra accommodation for her training role, the Argentinian had her forecastle extended to the after turret similar to the Brown class. This meant that the sided triple torpedo tubes, located amidships at upper deck level, had to be mounted behind screens.

A prominent feature was the enormous glazed wheelhouse area, for the purpose of navigation instruction. Widely spaced boiler spaces and, hence, funnels, provided topside space for a catapult and two aircraft. As delivered, these were standard Walrus amphibians, but these were later replaced by Curtiss SOC-1 Seagulls, the last type of floatplane to be produced for the US Navy.

Following World War II (in which a neutral Argentina played no active part) the ship exchanged her 102mm/4in guns for 40mm/1.57in weapons, and acquired a mixture of radars. Her systems out-dated, she was discarded in 1974.

La Argentina

Built: Vickers-Armstrong, Barrow
Commissioned: January 31, 1939
Displacement: 6,705 tonnes/6,600 tons (standard);
  7,747 tonnes/7,625 tons (full load)
Length: 155.4m/510ft (bp); 164.6m/540ft 2in (oa)
Beam: 17.2m/56ft 6in
Draught: 5m/16ft 3in
Armament: 9 x 152mm/6in (3x3); 4 x 102mm/4in
  (4x1) guns; 6 x 533mm/21in torpedo tubes (2x3)
Machinery: Geared steam turbines,
  4 boilers, 4 shafts
Power: 44,742kW/60,000shp for 31 knots
Endurance: 1,504 tonnes/1,480 tons (oil) for
  18,520km/10,000nm at 12 knots
Protection: 75mm/2.95in (belt); 50mm/2in (deck);
  50mm/2in (gunhouses)
Complement: 560 plus 60 cadets

ABOVE: **Although replete with details from contemporary British cruisers, *La Argentina* is very different
overall. The extended forecastle deck and two-level accommodation below the bridge structure betray
her training status. The very large navigating bridge, for the purpose of instruction, is also evident.**

Glossary

AS Anti-submarine.

Aft At or towards the rear or stern.

Anglo-German Naval Agreement (1935) Agreement for German fleet to be built up to fixed proportion of Royal Navy strength. This permitted 51,000 tons of heavy cruisers and 67,000 tons of light cruisers for Germany.

Armourclad *see* Ironclad.

Armoured cruiser Generally, a cruiser fitted with belt (i.e. vertical) armour in addition to protective deck (horizontal).

bhp Brake Horse Power. The power developed at the engine, i.e. before deductions are made for mechanical losses.

BL Breech-loading (gun).

Ballast Permanent or temporary weight carried by a ship to improve stability or trim.

Barbette Originally, the open-topped armoured enclosure from which a gun was fired; later, the standing or fixed part of the gun mounting, protecting the hoists and connecting the turret to the magazines.

Barque (rigged) Vessel with three or more masts, all of which are square-rigged except the aftermost (mizen), which is fore-and-aft rigged.

Barquentine (rigged) Uusally a three-masted vessel, square-rigged on only the foremast, fore-and-aft rigged on mainmast and mizen

Battle cruiser Ship armed with battleship-sized guns, but in which armour has been dispensed with for speed and manoeuvrability.

Beam The maximum width/breadth of a ship at the waterline.

Belt Vertical side armour, usually about the waterline.

Belted cruiser Early style with thick side armour, of limited area, but little other protection.

Bilge The lowest part of the hull of a ship, where the side turns into the bottom.

Bilge keel Fins or narrow wings at the turn of the bilge, designed to improve stability

Blister (or Bulge) Outer layer of hull compartmentation, added usually to improve a ship's resistance to torpedo damage.

Block ship A battleship converted into a floating battery intended to defend habours.

Boiler, cylindrical Similar to locomotive boiler, in which water surrounds hot flue with steam drawn from the top. Heavy, due to weight of water.

Boiler, water tube Water passes through lengths of large/small bore tube supported within combustion chamber. Lighter; less water in boiler.

Bow The forward end of a ship.

Bowsprit Spar which extends forward from the bows. Its length is extended by the associated jib boom.

Breastwork Raised armoured bulkhead to protect a gun and its moving parts

Brig Two-masted vessel, square-rigged on both masts.

Brigantine (rigged) Usually, a two-masted rig, with square sails on the foremast and fore-and-aft on the mainmast.

Bulkhead The internal vertical structures within a ship.

Bulwark Solid planking or plating along the edge of the deck to afford protection.

Bunkers Embarked fuel. A bunker is a fuel storage compartment or tank.

C-in-C Commander-in-Chief.

CIWS Close-in Weapon System.

Calibre Bore or diameter of a gun barrel, e.g. 5in. The length of the barrel is expressed in "calibres", e.g. a 54-calibre barrel is 270in in length.

Cantilever To support a structure or member at one end only.

Capital ship A generic name given to the largest and most powerful ships in a navy.

Casemate Gun position, usually armoured, built into the hull or superstructure of a warship. The gun may often be run in and its aperture closed-off by shutters.

Casing, funnel The casing forms the outer funnel, enclosing the hot smoke pipe(s). Some cruisers, especially German, had half-cased funnels to save topweight.

Catapult Aboard a cruiser, the means to directly launch an aircraft. Usually powered by cordite charge or compressed air.

Cellular (layer) Level immediately above a protective deck, closely subdivided to limit flooding in the event of damage.

Chariot A two-manned torpedo used to attack enemy shipping when in harbour.

Cofferdam Watertight bulkhead separating and protecting magazines and engine rooms.

Compound armour Composite plate of tough iron substrate with welded-on hard steel facing.

Compound engine Double-expansion engines. Having expanded partially in the high-pressure cylinder, steam is transferred to expand further in a larger-diameter, low-pressure cylinder before being exhausted to a condenser.

Copenhagen Reference to the British attack on the Danish capital and fleet in 1807.

Coppered Having underwater hull surfaces covered in thin copper plates in order to reduce fouling and to maintain speed.

Corvette Three-masted, ship-rigged, flush-decked warship, with a single gundeck and no forecastle or poop. Classified as a Sixth Rate.

Counter stern Style of stern where the above-water hull, supported on cant frames, projects well abaft the rudder.

Cruiser stern Style of stern where the hull abaft the rudder is fully plated, increasing waterplane area and buoyancy.

Derrick Spar, pivoted at lower end and rigged for lifting and transferring cargo or boats.

Displacement, full load or "deep" Weight of ship (expressed in

tons of 2,240lb) when fully equipped, stored and fuelled.

Displacement, standard Weight of ship less fuel and other deductions allowed by treaty.

Draught (or Draft) Mean depth of water in which a ship may float freely.

Dressed overall A ship dressed *en fête*, flying lines of flags between her masts, when not underway.

Dwarf bulkhead Low bulkhead intended to stop the free flood of water.

Fighting top Platform, usually circular, located on lower mast for the mounting of light, anti-personnel weapons.

Flare Curved overhang of hull at bows and stern, designed to throw water clear and to dampen pitch amplitude.

Floatplane (or Seaplane) Aircraft with external floats intended, usually, to be launched by catapult and to be recovered from the water.

Flotilla A squadron in the Royal Navy before NATO standardization.

Flying deck A deck suspended between two parts of the superstructure so that the deck below can be kept clear for mounting guns

Fore-and-aft Parallel to the major axis of the ship.

Forecastle Forward part of a ship.

Freeboard Usually, the vertical distance from waterline to weather deck. Effectively, it is the vertical height between the waterline and the lowest aperture through which the ship can flood.

Gunhouse Revolving, covered gun mounting that is not based on a barbette.

Grand Fleet Usually, the wartime title of the British battle fleet.

Great White Fleet USN fleet that circumnavigated the globe to demonstrate the coming-of-age of the USA as a sea power.

Gross registered tons (grt) Measure of volumetric capacity of a merchant ship. One gross ton equals 100 cubic feet (2.83cu m) of reckonable space.

Guerre de Course Sustained campaign against commercial shipping.

Gunport Aperture, usually square, cut in side of ship to permit broadside fire. Closed by portlid when not in use.

Gunwales Upper edge of the side of a vessel.

Harvey Nickel steel armour plate introduced in early 1890s. Homogenous composition but with hardened face and tough annealed back.

Heel Lean or tilt of a ship.

High Sea(s) Fleet The primary German battle fleet of World War I.

Horsepower Unit of power equal to 746 Watts.

ihp Indicated horsepower. Specifically, the power delivered by the pistons of a reciprocating steam engine.

Ironclad A ship protected by vertical iron plating.

Kite balloon Aerostat deployed by ships for observation purposes.

Knuckle Line of discontinuity in curvature of side plating, usually to avoid excessive flare at weather deck level.

Krupp An improvement on Harvey armour, introduced about 1896. A nickel-chromium-manganese steel was used, selectively heated and water-chilled.

Laid down Reference to when a new ship was first placed on the construction slip.

Length (bp) Length, between perpendiculars. Usually the distance between the forward extremity of the waterline at standard displacement and the forward edge of the rudder post. For American warships, lengths on "designed waterline" and "between perpendiculars" are synonymous.

Length (oa) Length, overall.

Length (wl) Length, waterline. Measured at standard displacement.

Line ahead When ships form up in a line.

Line-of-battle ship A ship large enough to be in the line.

London Treaty First of 1929–30, Second of 1935–36. Treaties reaffirming and modifying the Washington Treaty of 1921–22.

MLR Muzzle-loading Rifle.

Main deck In British practice, the level below the upper deck.

Metacentre Roll and return to upright slowly.

Metacentric height Relationship between a ship's centres of gravity (fixed) and buoyancy (variable). Essential component of stability.

Monitor Low freeboard coast defence vessel.

NATO North Atlantic Treaty Organization.

nm Nautical mile. One nautical mile per hour equals one knot.

Naval Defence Act Usually, that of 1889, which provided for the Royal Navy to be built up to the "Two Power Standard", maintaining it at the strength of the next two largest navies combined.

Ordnance Armament and ammunition of a ship.

Pocket battleship Small German battleship designed in the interwar years to circumvent restrictions on total tonnage and size.

Pole mast A stick-like mast to carry aerials or flags.

Pom pom The name for a type of 1- or 2-pounder gun derived from the sound of its firing.

Port Left side.

Plan "Orange" American war plan, periodically updated, for use against Japan.

Protected cruiser One whose protection comprises an armoured deck, usually vaulted, overlaid with a "cellular" layer, closely subdivided.

Quarter Between the beam and the stern.

Quick-firing (QF) Guns, up to 152mm/6in calibre, which accepted "fixed" ammunition, i.e., charge and projectile combined. In American parlance, Rapid Fire.

Ram Underwater beak or spur on the bow for striking the enemy.

RFA Royal Fleet Auxiliary.

Running rigging That part of a ship's rigging used for setting and trimming the sails.

Screw Propellor.

shp Shaft horsepower. Power is transmitted by a shaft at a point ahead of the stern gland. It does not, therefore, include mechanical losses in stern gland and A-bracket, if fitted.

Seaplane *See* **Floatplane**.

Schooner (rigged) Vessel with two or more masts, fore-and-aft rigged on both, or all.

Scuttle Correct term for what is popularly termed a "porthole".

Sheer Curvature of deckline in fore-and-aft direction, usually upward toward either end.

Sheathed Simply "coppered" or, less frequently, a metal hull, timbered below water, then coppered.

Sheer strake Run, or strake, of plating along ship's side adjacent to the upper deck and following sheer line. May be highly stressed, so fashioned from heavier plate.

Shell plating General term for all plating that forms the outer skin of a vessel.

Ship (rigged) A three-masted vessel that is square-rigged on all three masts.

Sided Situated toward the side(s), as opposed to the centreline, of a ship.

Sloop In context of this book, a small unrated warship with two or three masts, square-rigged throughout. These were termed Brig Sloops and Ship Sloops respectively.

Spar deck A deck of light construction, one level above the uppermost strength deck.

Splinter deck A thin armoured deck, situated beneath a thicker one and designed to stop any fragments being projected downward.

Stability range Total angle through which, from a position of equilibrium, a ship is statically stable.

Starboard Right side.

Stern Rear of a ship.

Sponson In warships, platforms projecting beyond the line of the hull, usually supporting guns which can thus be trained closer to the ship's main axis.

Standing Rigging That part of a ship's rigging supporting masts and spars.

Theatre The area in which a ship or fleet operates or a naval campaign takes place.

Triple-expansion Three or four-cylinder engine in which the steam expands progressively through high, intermediate and low pressure stages.

Tripod mast A mast having extra legs to carry the weight of direction-finding and gunnery control positions

Tumblehome Much the reverse of Flare. Higher decks are made progressively narrower to reduce topweight and to facilitate sponsoning of guns.

Turbine, steam Multi-stage, bladed rotor which revolves under the action of steam passing through the blades. Virtually vibration-free.

Turret Revolving armoured gun house.

Two Power Standard *See* **Naval Defence Act**.

USN United States Navy.

Upper deck The uppermost continuous deck of a ship.

Uptake Conduit conducting products of combustion to the funnel.

Van The front of a formation of ships.

W/T Wireless Transmission, i.e. radio.

Waist That part of the upper deck between forecastle and quarterdeck.

Warsaw Pact Eastern military bloc. Essentially a counter to NATO.

Washington Treaty Arms limitation agreement of 1921–22 that had a profound effect on the development of the cruiser.

Key to flags

For the specification boxes, the national flag that was current at the time of the ship's use is shown.

 Argentina

 Austria-Hungary

 Brazil

 Britain

 Chile

 France

 Germany

 Germany: World War I

 Germany: World War II

 Greece

 Italy: civil ensign

 Italy: 1848–1946

 Japan

 Netherlands

 Russia

 Spain

 Sweden

 Turkey

 USA

 USSR

Acknowledgements

The publisher would like to thank the following individuals and picture libraries for the use of their pictures in the book. Every effort has been made to acknowledge the pictures properly, however we apologize if there are any unintentional omissions, which will be corrected in future editions.

l=left, r=right, t=top, b=bottom, m=middle, lm= lower middle

Alinari Archives-Florence:
118m (Touring Club Italiano); 118b; 119m (De Pinto Donazione); 119bl; 119br Malandrini Ferruccio); 180t (De Pinto Donazione); 180m; 180t (De Pinto Donazione); 181b (De Pinto Donazione); 182t (De Pinto Donazione); 182m (De Pinto Donazione); 250t (De Pinto Donazione); 251m Instituto Luce); 251b (De Pinto Donazione); 253mr (De Pinto Donazione).

Australian War Memorial:
41mr (H12319);
48 tr (P00433.001);
57ml (P02018.327);
57mr (P02018.345);
57b (P005999.014);
75tl (P00952.003;
140t (300238);
140b (ART09749).

Cody Images: 8t; 8m; 9tr; 9mr; 9bl; 14–15; 16t; 16bl; 17m; 18bl; 18br; 19br; 20t; 20mr; 21tr; 21b; 22t; 22m; 23t; 23ml; 23mr; 31b; 32t; 32bl; 33tr; 33mr; 33br; 34; 35t; 35ml; 35mr; 36b; 37t; 37mr; 37br; 38t; 39tl; 39tr; 40t; 41bl; 43ml; 46t; 47tr; 47b; 48tl; 48br; 49tl; 49tr; 49m; 50tl; 50tr; 51t; 51mr; 51br; 56t; 59tr; 63tl; 63tr; 68b; 69t; 69mr; 70t; 71t; 71mr; 71br; 74; 75m; 76br; 77bl; 77br; 78mr; 78b; 79t; 79m; 80tl; 80br; 81; 82tl; 88tl; 88bl; 90t; 90b; 91t; 91b; 92t; 94t; 94m; 94mr; 95tl; 95tr; 95mr; 96mr; 97m; 97bl; 97br; 98tl; 98tr; 98mr; 99m; 99bl; 100mr; 102t; 102b; 103t; 104t; 104b; 105t; 105b; 107t; 107m; 107b; 112t; 112m; 113t; 113m; 113b; 114t; 114b; 115ml; 115mr; 115b; 116tr; 117t; 118t; 120t; 121m; 121b; 125t; 126t; 127t; 128t; 128b; 134t; 134m; 134b; 135b; 136; 138tl; 138tr; 138mr; 143mr; 146b; 147ml; 148mr; 149tl; 149tr; 150mr; 151br; 153t; 154t; 155tl; 155tr; 155mr; 158tl; 159t; 159b; 160b; 161t; 164b; 165tl; 165m; 167t; 167m; 168t; 168m; 168mr; 169mr; 169b; 170tl; 170tr; 170m; 171t; 171m; 172tl; 172tr; 172mr; 172b; 173mr; 173b; 174t; 174mr; 175t; 175m; 176–7t; 176br; 177m; 181mr; 183t; 185b; 190t; 190mr; 191mr; 191bl; 192m; 192b; 193t; 194t; 194mr; 199tr; 199ml; 199mr; 199m; 200bl; 200br; 201tl; 201ml; 201mr; 202t; 202m; 203t; 203ml; 203mr; 204tl; 204tr; 205tl; 205tr; 205ml; 205lm; 207mr; 207b; 210t; 211tl; 211tr; 211ml; 211lm; 212t; 213t; 213mr; 215t; 215ml; 216t; 216m; 216tl; 216tr; 216ml; 218bl; 219br; 220tl; 220tr; 221t; 221ml; 221mr; 223mr; 225mr; 226tl; 226tr; 227t; 227mr; 228t; 229t; 229b; 230t; 231t; 231ml; 231mr; 232; 233t; 233ml; 233mr; 234; 235t; 235ml; 235mr; 236b; 237m; 237b; 238t; 238bl; 239tr; 239m; 239b; 240tr; 240b; 241tr; 241mr; 241b; 242t; 242mr; 243tl; 243tr; 243m; 244t; 245t; 245mr; 245lm; 247tl; 247tr; 247mr; 248tl; 248tr; 249tl; 249mr; 252t; 252bl; 253t; 253ml; 254–5; 255tr; 256tr; 256bl; 257; 258tr; 258b.

Mary Evans Picture Library:
33ml; 41ml; 66; 164t.

Syd Goodman: 53ml; 53tr; 141ml; 141mr; 141bl; 148t; 150t; 151m; 156b; 157t; 178t; 198t; 206b; 207ml; 208t; 209tl; 209tr; 209mr; 220tl; 220tr; 221t; 221ml; 221mr; 223ml.

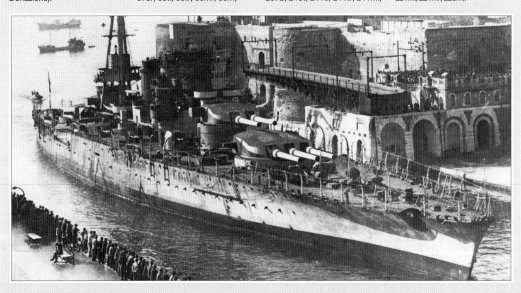

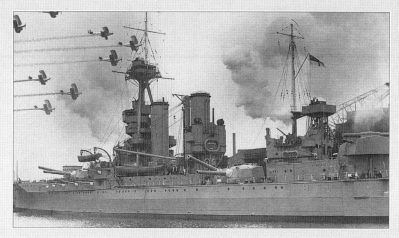

67mr; 69b; 92bl; 93mr; 93b; 96tl; 97br; 99br; 100t; 106mr; 157ml; 157mr; 158tr; 158mr; 160t; 161tr; 161ml; 161mr; 162tl; 162ml; 166t; 167mr; 196–7; 213ml; 214t; 215tr; 219tr; 219ml; 219mr; 219bl; 222; 223t; 223mr; 225mr; 227ml; 228ml; 246b.

Walker Archive: 28; 110tr; 110mr; 110bl; 111t; 111b; 178mr.

Research for the images used to illustrate the cruisers section of this book was carried out by Ted Nevill of Cody Images, who supplied the majority of the images.

The publisher and Ted Nevill would like to thank all those who contributed to this research and to the supply of additional pictures: Anova Images; ArtTech; Richard Cox; Jim Culbertson; Photographic Section, Naval Historical Center, Washington, DC, USA; Still Pictures, National Archives and Records Administration, College Park, Maryland, USA; US Merchant Marine Academy, Kings Point, NY, USA; US Navy.

Imperial War Museum Photograph Archive: 17b (Q22212); 19t (Q40607); 26 (Q68264); 27m (MH24467); 29t (Q13942); 29m (Q13941A); 30bl (Q55499); 30br (Q22156); 31tr (Q22155); 36tr (Q38938); 39tr (Q22687); 43t (Q20613); 52m (HU87084); 60br (A8953); 61tl (Q20352); 61lm (A21164); 76t (Q41317); 80tr (Q22284); 106t (Q22357); 108t (Q22258); 108bl (Q41314); 109t (Q22279); 109mr (Q13412); 116tl (Q41298); 116mr (Q41285); 117b (Q19930); 124 (Q22446); 126b (Q41361); 129t (Q70143); 129b (Q70145); 163t (Q22411); 166b (MH6158); 184m (Q20283); 184b (Q20287); 186 (Q22227).

Institute for Maritime History: 188tl; 188tr; 188mr; 189ml; 189b.
Library of Congress: 25tl; 27tr; 44m; 45t.

Maritime Prints and Originals: 38b (Courtesy of Michael French Esq.); 40m (Courtesy of Captain R. A. de S. Cosby LVO RN); 133t (Courtesy of Paul Winter Esq.); 135mr (Courtesy of Captain R. A. de S. Cosby LVO RN); 137t (Courtesy of Commander W. A. E. Hall RN); 147t (Courtesy of Simon Keeble Esq.).

National Archive of Scotland: 103m (UCS 1/116/4).

North Sands Picture Library: 130; 143lm; 145m; 194bl; 195t; 195m.

Novosti: 123; 85t.

Curt Ohlsson: 75tr; 188tl; 188tr; 188mr.

Royal Naval Museum: 53tr; 53ml; 53mr; 82br; 83m; 83b; 84mr; 84bl; 85t; 85mr; 86tl; 86tr; 86m; 87t; 87mr; 88tr; 89tl; 89tr; 89m; 137m; 139t; 142t; 142mr; 143b; 144m; 144b; 145t; 147mr; 152t; 153mr.

Erwin Sieche: 21m; 187t; 187b.

Topfoto: 103mr; 163ml.

US *Missouri* Museum: 224t; 224b; 225tl; 225ml; 259b.

US Naval Historical Center: 24tr; 25mr; 42t; 42mr; 43mr; 44t; 45mr; 52tl; 52–3t; 54tl; 54b; 55mr; 55lm; 55br; 56bl; 58t; 59tl; 59mr; 59br; 60t; 61tr; 61ml; 62t; 62m; 63br; 67t;

Index

Tsukuba class

Hercules

Nürnberg

Marco Polo

Jeanne d'Arc

Yavuz Sultan Selim

Furutaka

Mogami class